MIRROR OF THE SOUL

To Janet and George

with very best wishes

John Dewey

16 July 2011

JOHN DEWEY was born in London in 1942. He studied languages at Cambridge, and also has a Master's degree from Nottingham University for his dissertation on Hermann Hesse and Dosto-yevsky. For many years he taught German and Russian in schools and further education. Several of his translations have appeared in the series *Glas New Russian Writing*, among them Boris Yampolsky's novel *The Old Arbat* (nominated in 2006 for the Translation Award of the American Association for the Advancement of Slavonic and East European Literatures), and *The Nomadic Soul*, a collection of stories by Irina Muravyova. His published verse translations include a substantial selection for the 15-volume *Complete Works of Pushkin in English* (2001-2003), and a version of Pushkin's narrative poem *The Bronze Horseman* which was shortlisted for the 1996/1997 John Dryden Translation Prize. He was twice winner of the *Journal of Russian Studies* Poetry Translation Prize. Articles by him on Tyutchev and the poet Annensky have also appeared in academic publications. *Mirror of the Soul* grew from a longstanding love of Tyutchev's poetry, which he first encountered and came to admire as a student.

MIRROR OF THE SOUL

A Life of the Poet Fyodor Tyutchev

JOHN DEWEY

BRIMSTONE PRESS

First published in 2010
Copyright © John Dewey

The right of John Dewey to be identified as the author of
this work has been asserted by him in accordance with the
Copyright, Designs and Patents Act 1988.

ISBN 978-1-906385-23-1

Published by Brimstone Press
PO Box 114
Shaftesbury
SP7 8XN

Printed and bound in Great Britain by
CPI Antony Rowe, Chippenham and Eastbourne

To the memory of

Nikolay Yefremovich Andreyev

Contents

Acknowledgements

My first and by far greatest debt of gratitude is to Dr Ronald Lane, Britain's leading authority in the field of Tyutchev studies. It is my good fortune to have enjoyed his enthusiastic and active support for the project from start to finish, not least in the form of a steady flow of books, articles and unpublished material generously supplied from his own collection. Dr Lane subjected my work in progress and the completed text to meticulous scrutiny, making many stimulating comments and useful suggestions for improvement (any remaining defects are my own). Without his unfailing help, advice and encouragement this book would have been much the poorer.

Warmest thanks are due to two other Tyutchev scholars of note: Dr Arkady Polonsky in Munich, and Dr Gennady Chagin in Moscow. They too freely provided books and articles, and our many fascinating discussions by correspondence over the years have helped to shape and test a number of the ideas and hypotheses developed in the book. When I visited Munich, Dr Polonsky was kind enough to take me around the various places connected with Tyutchev in that city, a subject on which his knowledge is second to none.

I should like to pay tribute to the unsung custodians of our cultural and historical heritage employed in archives, libraries and institutes of every description. Nearly all of those with whom I came into contact, whether in person or by correspondence, handled my often obscure queries with patience and professionalism. Especial thanks go to Herr Fritsch and his staff at the Staatsarchiv in Amberg for helping me to find my way through the uncatalogued family archive of the Counts von Lerchenfeld; Dr Richter of the Stadtarchiv at Fürth; and Dr Jürgen König and Herr Oelschläger of the Archive of the Evangelical-Lutheran Church in Bavaria (Landeskirchliches Archiv der Evangelisch-Lutherischen Kirche in Bayern), Nuremberg.

I am most grateful to Count Philipp von Lerchenfeld for granting permission to work in his family archive and publish material from it, also for the hospitality shown by him and his wife during a memorable visit to their home at Schloss Köfering. My special thanks too to Yelena Ustinova, Editor-in-chief of Klassika Publishers in Moscow, who came to the rescue at a crucial stage of book production by generously agreeing to our use of illustrations from Klassika's splendid six-volume edition of Tyutchev and even arranging the supply of digital copies.

Much appreciated was the kindness of Frau Henriette von Bothmer, for many years custodian of her family's private archive, who supplied me with information and gave permission to quote from unpublished material. I also thank Dr Karl Köckenberger for allowing me to make use of letters to his great-grandfather from Tyutchev's first love Amélie. A present-day descendant of Amélie in Finland, Mr Magnus Linder, was good enough to send details of her family background from the Thurn und Taxis archive at Regensburg. Madame Véronique Muller of the Cercle Généalogique d'Alsace in Strasbourg went to the trouble of locating documents relating to Hortense Lapp in the local archives. To all of these my thanks, as to the following who helped in a variety of ways: James Dingley, Josef Fendl, Natasha Perova, Ulrich von Prittwitz und Gaffron, Konstantin Pavlovich Sidorenko, Aleksandr Timofeyevich Suslov, Nicola Vidamour and Albrecht Widmaier.

I am grateful to the Editors of *The Slavonic and East European Review* for permission to make use of material from my article 'Tiutchev and Amalie von Lerchenfeld: Some Unpublished Documents', published in Vol.79, No.1 of that journal (January 2001, pp.15-30). I also thank Raduga Publishers, Moscow, for allowing me to reproduce Peter Tempest's translation of the poem 'Tears of humanity, tears of humanity...' from the anthology *Russian 19th-Century Verse. Selected Poems by Pushkin, Baratynsky, Tyutchev, Koltsov, Lermontov, Fet, Nekrasov* (Raduga Publishers, Moscow, 1983, p.199).

I am greatly indebted to my son Chris, without whose expert assistance and advice on all matters relating to computers I should have been lost. And finally I thank my wife Wilma, not only for help with sorting through and deciphering documents in the old German script, but for her continuing patience, understanding and encouragement. That she never once complained at finding herself decoyed into Tyutchev's footsteps on holidays abroad was particularly appreciated.

List of Illustrations

1. The reconstructed manor house at Ovstug, now a museum devoted to Tyutchev.
2. 12 Herzogspitalgasse, Munich, the first floor of which housed the Russian Embassy from 1808 to 1825. (Author's photograph.)
3. Schloss Köfering, seat of the Counts von Lerchenfeld. (Author's photograph.)
4. Tyutchev, 1825. Pencil, unknown artist.
5. Amalie (Amélie) von Krüdener, 1827. Oil by Joseph Stieler.
6. Donaustauf. Lithograph by unknown artist, mid-19th Century.
7. View of the Danube from the ruins of Donaustauf castle. (Author's photograph.)
8. Eleonore Tyutcheva, mid-1820s. Oil, unknown artist.
9. Clotilde von Bothmer, early 1830s. Oil, unknown artist. (Private collection. Photograph by Henriette von Bothmer.)
10. Ernestine von Dörnberg, 1833. Lithograph by G. Bodmer from the original oil portrait by Joseph Stieler.
11. Tyutchev, March 1838. Watercolour by Hippolite von Rechberg.
12. Yelena Denisyeva, late 1850s. Daguerrotype.
13. Tyutchev, 1850-1851. Photograph by K. Dauthendy.
14. Ernestine Tyutcheva, 1862. Photograph by I. Robillard.
15. Nikolay Tyutchev, brother of the poet, 1856. Photograph by S.L. Levitsky.
16. Anna Aksakova, Tyutchev's eldest daughter, 1864. Photograph by H. Denier.
17. Tyutchev, 1867. Photograph by S.L. Levitsky.

(No. 11 is also used for the cover illustration.)

Picture credits:

Tyutchev Museum, Muranovo: Nos. 4, 8, 10-11, 13-17.
Autotravel.org.ru: No. 1.
Bayerische Verwaltung der staatlichen Schlösser, Gärten und Seen, Schloss Nymphenburg, Munich: No. 5.
Staatliche Graphische Sammlung, Munich: No. 6.
Institute of Russian Literature (Pushkin House) of the Russian Academy of Sciences, St Petersburg: No. 12.

Nos. 4, 8, and 10-16 are reproduced from: F.I. Tyutchev, *Polnoye sobraniye sochineniy i pis'ma*, Moscow (Klassika), 6 vols., 2002-2004, by kind permission of the publishers and with their technical assistance.

Every effort has been made to contact all copyright holders. The author will be happy to rectify in future editions any errors or omissions brought to his attention.

Notes on Transliteration, Names, Dates and Currency

For the transliteration of personal names, quotations and publication titles in Cyrillic I have used the BGN/PCGN romanisation system in the slightly modified form adopted by many publishers. This replaces *ë* with the more phonetic *o* or *yo* (thus *Gorbachov*, *Pigaryov* rather than *Gorbachëv*, *Pigarëv*). Endings in *-iy* after *g, zh, k, kh, ch, sh* and *shch* (i.e. where there can be no room for doubt) are simplified to *-y* (*Boratynsky*, *sypuchy* rather than *Boratynskiy*, *sypuchiy*); the same ending in names is also simplified as, e.g., *Dmitry, Arkady* (rather than *Dmitriy, Arkadiy*). The soft sign, usually rendered as an apostrophe, has been generally omitted in names, but is retained in references as an aid to catalogue searches (thus *Muravyov* in the text, *Murav'yov* in references). Established English spellings for members of the imperial family and certain other well-known Russians have also been used in the main text, for example: *Nicholas I* (not *Nikolay*); *Leo* (not *Lev*) *Tolstoy*; *Tchaikovsky* (not *Chaykovsky*). Conversion of references to other conventions such as the Library of Congress system should be straightforward.

Russian surnames exist in masculine and feminine form. The feminine is usually formed by adding —a to the masculine (Tyutchev, Tyutcheva); however, adjectival surnames take the feminine ending —aya (Tolstoy, Tolstaya). In addition, all Russians have a patronymic as middle name, formed from the given name of their father, e.g. Pyotr Ivanovich (= son of Ivan), Aleksandra Mikhaylovna (= daughter of Mikhail).

Until the 1917 Revolution Russia adhered to the Julian (Old Style) calendar, which in the 19th century was twelve days behind the Gregorian (New Style) calendar in use in the rest of Europe. Except where otherwise stated, dates in the chapters covering periods when Tyutchev was resident in Russia (1, 12-15) are Old Style (OS), and those in chapters covering the years spent abroad (2-11) are New Style (NS). In cases where confusion could arise (for example, letters or travel between time zones) both dates are given in the format OS/NS, e.g.: 12/24 June 1836; 31 March/12 April 1821; 23 December 1856/ 4 January 1857.

During Tyutchev's lifetime two forms of official currency co-existed in effect in Russia: the 'hard' silver rouble, and 'soft' paper money ('assignats', later treasury notes). For most of this period paper notes were not convertible into silver, although the Treasury periodically determined an official parity, fluctuating in practice between about three and four paper roubles to one silver. Throughout the book the term 'roubles' on its own should be taken to mean paper roubles; silver roubles are specified as such. As a rough-and-ready guide to the purchasing power of sums quoted in terms of present-day (2010) pounds sterling, paper roubles may be multiplied by a factor of three, silver roubles by twelve.

Preface

Why a biography of Tyutchev in English? It is a fair enough question, given that few outside Russia and the enclosed world of Slavic studies will have heard of him, let alone read his verse. Settings of his poems by composers including Tchaikovsky and Rakhmaninov, or the occasional quotation in books (invariably in prose translation) of his poetic dictum that 'Russia cannot be understood with the intellect', are unlikely to have left any lasting impression of the name.

In the case of some minor versifier this would be neither here nor there. Yet in Russia Tyutchev has long been revered as one of that country's greatest poets. First published in any quantity by Pushkin, his verse was later acclaimed in glowing terms by Turgenev, Tolstoy and Dostoyevsky. Other poets have been particularly lavish in their praise, Afanasy Fet calling him for instance 'one of the greatest lyric poets ever to have existed on this earth'. This is no exaggeration. What Tyutchev's output may lack in quantity (some 200 short lyric poems in all, discounting translations and the political and occasional verse) it makes up for in the sheer quality of its artistic genius, allowing comparisons with the best of Goethe, Pushkin, Keats or Verlaine.

Why this major figure should for so long have escaped attention in the wider world is no great mystery. Unlike his better-known contemporaries Pushkin and Lermontov, who also wrote prose works and dramas, Tyutchev produced only lyric verse, a notoriously delicate growth always most at home in its own native soil. Not for nothing did Robert Frost famously define poetry as that which gets lost in translation. This above all has prevented Tyutchev's reputation from crossing borders.

I first came under the spell of his verse long ago, as a student. Years later I began to translate the poems in the hope of introducing them to the English-speaking world. All the translations used in this book are my own, with one exception: Peter Tempest's brilliant and unsurpassable version of 'Tears of humanity, tears of humanity...'. (Tyutchev's relatively few poems in French have been left in the original, with prose translations in the Notes.) My versions observe in general (though not pedantically so) the metre and rhyme schemes of the originals, as it seemed to me that to abandon these completely would be to rob the poems of an essential part of their artistic appeal. The overall aim was to end up with something Tyutchev might have written himself, were he still alive and his native language English. That is of course a wildly over-ambitious goal, although one which I am sure most translators of poetry would admit to if pressed. Where it has proved unattainable, one hopes the versions arrived at may be appreciated in much the same way as piano reductions of great symphonies: pale substitutes for the real thing no doubt, yet affording reflected glimpses of an original creative vision.

The biography can be said to have had its origins in the translations. Tyutchev presents us with an example of lyric genius in its purest form, able through the alchemy of poetry to transmute the stuff of everyday reality into visions of the sublime. Like Blake he shows us 'a world in a grain of sand'. In his case the grains of sand were the fleeting impressions and impulses of day-to-day existence, his poems the pages of an intimate diary — 'the mirror of his soul', as one contemporary put it. Like all poems they must in the end speak for themselves, without any need for biographical or critical exegesis. At least, the originals must; for translations, which require the reader to take so much on trust as regards artistic merit, the position is not so clear-cut. All translation is already in part explication: of a culture and milieu, of modes of thought and expression unfamiliar to the reader. Anything which can bring greater understanding, a deeper penetration to the elusive text behind the translated word, is surely to be welcomed.

In a sense, then, the biography started life as an extended footnote to and commentary on the translated poems. Inevitably, it soon became much more. Writers, composers and painters are never exclusively that: all have parallel lives in the 'real' world which interact with and — often if not always — enrich their artistic creation. Tyutchev's loves, his political enthusiasms, his wit, the complexities and contradictions of his character, the broad sweep of events in Russia and Europe which he observed and commented on so avidly — all these demanded their part in the story too.

The first full-length biography of Tyutchev, published just a year after his death, was by his son-in-law, the Slavophile writer Ivan Aksakov. Although it is certainly well written, with some particularly fine passages on the lyric verse, one is always aware of the author's concern to present his subject as a leading light of the nationalist movement. Especially valuable for later biographers is Aksakov's recording of family memories, still fresh at the time of writing, relating to Tyutchev's earlier years.

It was to be the best part of century before the next biography appeared: Kirill Pigaryov's *Zhizn' i tvorchestvo Tyutcheva* (*The Life and Work of Tyutchev*), published in 1962. As the poet's great-grandson, Pigaryov continued the tradition of family chronicler begun by Aksakov. Although fairly concise (the purely biographical section of the book runs to just over 170 pages) and shown by later research to contain the odd factual error, Pigaryov's account remains a classic. For it and his many other publications on the poet he is still rightly regarded as the doyen of Tyutchev scholars.

Vadim Kozhinov's 1988 biography, published in the series *Zhizn' zamechatel'nykh lyudey* (*The Lives of Remarkable People*), is an engagingly written and highly readable account. At just under 500 pages and with a print-run of 150,000 it is the longest and probably most widely read life of Tyutchev in Russian. Although it can be criticised in certain respects (some of Kozhinov's interpretations of events are open to dispute; like Aksakov, he tends to overstate Tyutchev's political importance; there are no source references), it is nevertheless arguably one of the best to date.

Gennady Chagin's outstanding work of 2003, *Tyutchevy* (*The Tyutchevs*), extends to a history of the entire family, while concentrating in the main on its most famous son. Chagin's research throws much valuable new light on the poet's life and family background. Semyon Ekshtut's *Tyutchev, tayny sovetnik i kamerger* (*Tyutchev, Privy Councillor and Chamberlain*), published the same year, limits itself to an account of Tyutchev's service career, political activities and family life, with practically no reference to his poetic achievements.

The closest approach to a biography in English so far is Richard Gregg's brilliant monograph of 1965, *Fedor Tiutchev: The Evolution of a Poet*. The opening chapter gives a brief (22-page) survey of Tyutchev's life, after which Gregg proceeds to analyse poems written at various periods from what he terms 'the biographical and psychological points of view'. Whether or not I have always agreed with his interpretations, they have proved consistently thought-provoking and productive of further debate.

Much the same could be said to a greater or lesser extent of all the biographies mentioned. However, for the factual basis of my own account I have gone back to the available primary sources, both published and unpublished. Two fairly recent monuments of Tyutchev scholarship proved particularly useful in this respect: the substantial collection of materials devoted to Tyutchev in the series *Literaturnoye nasledstvo* (*Literary Heritage*, 2 parts, 1988-1989); and *Letopis' zhizni i tvorchestva F.I. Tyutcheva* (*Chronicle of the Life and Work of F.I. Tyutchev*), an ongoing project of the Tyutchev Museum at Muranovo, which under the editorship of Tatyana Dinesman has at the time of writing reached the year 1860 in the poet's life. Of work published outside Russia, Ronald Lane's many articles have provided a wealth of invaluable new material, in particular for the years spent by Tyutchev in western Europe. Arkady Polonsky's publications also contain useful information on the Munich years. Full details of these and all the works mentioned can be found in the 'Sources' section at the back of the book.

I hope that Tyutchev scholars will find much to engage their interest in my book; even more so, that it will help to generate a long overdue appreciation of Tyutchev's poetry in the wider world.

1 Childhood and Youth
(Moscow, 1803 - 1822)

i Prologue

One Sunday in the early summer of 1822 a large ornate carriage was to be seen negotiating the ruts and potholes of Armyansky Pereulok, or Armenian Lane, a quiet back street in one of the more select quarters of Moscow. The date was 11 June by the old Julian calendar, under which Russia was obliged to tag along behind the rest of Europe by those 'fateful twelve days'[1] seen by many as emblematic of a more deep-seated laggardliness.

Turning into the courtyard of one of the street's sizeable mansions, the carriage drew to a halt, and from it stepped a tall man of lean build in his early fifties, followed by an elegantly attired lady some ten years his junior whose pale, drawn appearance suggested delicate health. With his strong aquiline features and military bearing the man cut an impressive, some would say for his age even dashing figure. An empty sleeve pinned back to the breast of his jacket added to the air of bravura. Count Aleksandr Osterman-Tolstoy, General of Infantry in the Imperial Russian army, had distinguished himself in many a campaign of the Napoleonic Wars. At the battle of Kulm in August 1813 his left arm had been torn to shreds by a French cannonball and had to be amputated on the field of conflict. Before the surgeon set about his work, Osterman-Tolstoy had ordered fifes and drums to be played at full pitch so that his soldiers should not hear their commanding officer's involuntary cries of pain.[2] Now retired, he spent much of his time abroad, and at the present moment he and his wife were about to leave Russia for a protracted stay in western Europe.

He had come to the imposing three-storey house of Ivan and Yekaterina Tyutchev at 11 Armenian Lane to collect their son Fyodor. Yekaterina was a distant cousin of his, and he had offered to take her son with him as far as Munich. After Fyodor's graduation from Moscow University the previous autumn, Osterman-Tolstoy had used his considerable influence to get his young relative into the Foreign Service, arranging a posting for him as trainee diplomat at the Russian Embassy in Bavaria. The slightly-built, fresh-faced eighteen-year-old was waiting, his bags packed. Ready to leave with him was a long-standing family servant, Nikolay Khlopov. Formerly employed as Fyodor's governor, he had willingly agreed to accompany his young master to Munich as manservant, with strict instructions from Ivan and Yekaterina Tyutchev to watch over their son and report back regularly by letter on his welfare and progress.

Earlier that day the family had as usual attended Sunday mass at the nearby church of St Nicholas at the Pillars before driving to the Iverskaya Chapel, built into a gateway guarding the entrance to Red Square and containing one of the most revered icons in all Moscow. This image of the Mother of God, the exact copy of an original on Mount Athos, was held to work miracles, offering especial protection to those about to undertake a journey. At home now his mother led him to her own icon of the Blessed Virgin, before which they bowed down three times;[3] then, pressing into his hands a cherished volume of church canticles which had once belonged to her aunt, she enjoined him not to neglect his Orthodox faith in foreign parts.[4] Amidst final tearful embraces and farewells from his parents and younger sister Darya, Fyodor joined the General and his wife in their carriage. The servants had already loaded his trunk and valises, and Khlopov was sitting on the box next to the coachman, who stirred the horses into motion with a flick of his whip. Fyodor continued waving to the little group standing outside until the carriage turned into Maroseyka Street. Ahead of them lay a journey of three to four weeks, allowing for stops on the way.

Soon Osterman-Tolstoy's carriage was clattering over the cobblestones of Red Square, past the extravagantly florid domes of St Basil's Cathedral and skirting the embattled red-brick walls and towers of the Kremlin. Next they headed along the Arbat with its many patrician mansions to join the Mozhaysk highway. As they left the city for open country the coachman gave the horses their head, and before long Moscow had shrunk to a distant vista of spires and gilded domes shimmering through the dust and haze of the road behind them like so many candles lit in devotion to heaven above. Moscow the city of white stone, ancient heart of Russia, with her countless churches and venerable monasteries. Moscow the Third Rome, as she had been proclaimed in times past: divinely anointed heir to the mantle of universal empire after first Rome and then its successor Constantinople had fallen to the barbarians. 'Two Romes have fallen, but a third remains standing, and a fourth there shall not be...'[5] Could it be that Russia would one day reclaim its Muscovite inheritance and revive such ancient dreams? The question would preoccupy Tyutchev greatly in years to come; for the present he was more intent on his journey and where it was taking him. He can hardly have guessed at the time what a momentous turning-point in his life it would prove to be. Apart from infrequent visits on leave he would spend the next twenty-two years abroad, absorbing western ways and western ideas. And even after settling in Russia again he would continue to strike many as being, in the words of one who knew him well, 'a thoroughbred offspring of Europeanism', and 'almost a foreigner' in his own country.[6]

ii Antecedents

It may have occurred to young Fyodor that in embarking on a diplomatic career he was following in the footsteps of his earliest recorded ancestor. On the eve of the battle of Kulikovo in 1380 Grand Duke Dmitry of Moscow sent a certain Zakhary Tyutchev — a 'man of cunning' according to the chronicles — as emissary to the Golden Horde. Zakhary's outspoken demand for a reduction in the tribute exacted from Moscow by its Tatar overlords was rejected out of hand by Khan Mamay, some of whose lieutenants threatened his life, yet he managed to extricate himself and return to Moscow with useful military and political intelligence on the Golden Horde. Shortly afterwards the Grand Duke was able to win an important victory over the Tatars at the battle of Kulikovo near the river Don, for which he was known thereafter as Dmitry Donskoy.[7]

There must have been other Tyutchevs before Zakhary, although no record of them appears to have survived. According to family legend the clan was founded in the late thirteenth century by a Venetian merchant named Dudgi who is said to have settled in Russia after accompanying Marco Polo on his voyages.[8] There is no hard evidence for this tradition, which the distinguished Tyutchev scholar (and great-grandson of the poet) Kirill Pigaryov believed to be no more than another instance of 'the characteristic penchant of Russian landowners for linking their origins to this or that foreign immigrant'.[9] More recent research derives the surname from the word for shepherd or goatherd in Ugyur, a Turco-Tataric language, suggesting that the Tyutchevs were in fact one of the many aristocratic families (including for instance the Turgenevs, Gogols, Chaadayevs, Kireyevskys and Rimsky-Korsakovs) who owed their origins to intermarriage during the two and a half centuries of Tatar rule following the Mongol invasion of 1237-1240.[10] Whatever the truth of the matter, Tyutchev appears to have embraced the version current in his family, providing as it did a ready-made poetic myth of himself as a displaced soul forever banished from some ancestral paradise in the sunlit south.[11]

Over the centuries Zakhary Tyutchev's descendants served the Grand Dukes of Moscow and later Tsars of Russia in various military and civil capacities, receiving honours and land in return. Towards the end of the seventeenth century one Daniil Tyutchev acquired the estate of Znamenskoye near Uglich in Yaroslavl province, 120 miles to the north of Moscow, and made this the seat of his branch of the family.[12] Here at the end of the 1730s was born Daniil's grandson Nikolay Andreyevich Tyutchev, the grandfather of our poet.[13] Nikolay's colourful life would fill the pages of a book in itself. Having trained as an army officer, he was sent in the early 1760s in charge of a detachment of military mapmakers to carry out a survey near the main Kaluga road to the south of Moscow. He and his men were billeted on the estate of Troitskoye, some ten miles from the city centre and belonging to a thirty-year-old widow, Darya Saltykova.[14] This was the notorious 'Saltychikha', who has gained a dubious footnote in history for the sadistic cruelty with which she tortured and murdered her serfs. Whether or not she seduced the young Nikolay is not clear, but when he began to court and then proposed to an eligible young lady in Moscow at the beginning of 1762 Saltykova's fury knew no bounds. She ordered two of her serfs to blow up the house of Nikolay's fiancée with gunpowder, and punished them severely when the attempt failed. Next she sent more serfs with orders to waylay and club to death the young couple as they travelled along the Kaluga road. Fortunately Nikolay was tipped off; he reported Saltykova to the authorities, and a long process of investigations and trials was set in motion at the instigation of the Empress Catherine herself, during which the full extent of Darya's crimes came to light. She was eventually found guilty, stripped of her nobility and property and sentenced to life imprisonment in a convent cell.[15]

Nikolay married his young bride, Pelageya Panyutina, in April 1762, and they settled on the country estate of Ovstug in Bryansk district, about 220 miles south-west of Moscow, which she had inherited from her parents. Until the Emancipation Decree of 1861 the wealth of a Russian aristocrat was measured in serfs rather than acreage, and by those standards Nikolay and Pelageya can be said to have started life together in decidedly modest circumstances. He owned only some 160 adult male serfs (women and children were not counted), while she brought a further 20 to the marriage. Yet 26 years later they had — 'by our own efforts, helping each other', as they themselves put it — increased their holdings fifteenfold to the impressive figure of 2,715, having in the meantime inherited Znamenskoye and acquired various other lands including Saltykova's former estate of Troitskoye.[16]

The charge of 'debauchery and wilfulness verging on frenzy' levelled against Nikolay by his grandson's first biographer, the somewhat unworldly Ivan Aksakov, can probably be discounted, based as it seems to be partly on the alleged youthful fling with Saltykova, and partly on one eyewitness account of a particularly drunken party at Ovstug at which the host had to be carried out unconscious.[17] It is unlikely that a total reprobate of the kind implied by Aksakov would have been elected District Marshal of Nobility by his peers, as Nikolay was in 1782.[18] More pertinent perhaps is the question of how he came by his wealth. Even the most enterprising and diligent of landowners could hardly have earned enough from his estates to finance gains on such a scale. Nor were there rewards from service to the state, for Nikolay had retired from the army at a fairly early age with the rank of Captain.[19] It could be, as suggested by one writer,[20] that like so many others at the time Nikolay contrived to acquire land and serfs through a series of dubious law suits, exploiting chaotic property laws and his own expertise as a land-surveyor to achieve his ends. However, there is no firm evidence for this, and it may be that he was simply lucky or shrewd enough to make his fortune through speculation. Whatever the origins of their prosperity, he and Pelageya made good use of it to renovate and improve their estates of Znamenskoye and Ovstug, including the construction of a handsome stone church for each.[21] Pelageya bore her husband three sons and four daughters, all of whom survived into adulthood.[22] Their eldest son, Dmitry, was disinherited by them at the age of 23 for eloping with a cousin against their wishes, a misdemeanour followed by a number of discreditable brushes with the law.[23] As a result the main family estate at Znamenskoye passed to the second son, Nikolay, while the youngest, Ivan, inherited Ovstug and Troitskoye.[24]

Born at Ovstug in 1768,[25] Ivan Nikolayevich Tyutchev received a private education at home before being sent to study at the Greek Academy (*Grechesky korpus*) in St Petersburg. Founded by Catherine the Great as part of her ambitious 'Greek project' to liberate Constantinople from the Turks and place her grandson (pointedly christened Constantine) on the throne of a restored Byzantium, the academy was intended to train the sons of noblemen as civilian and military cadres for the envisaged state. As an article of Russian foreign policy the project died together with Catherine, although its ethos lived on in the hearts and minds of those educated at her foundation. After graduating, Ivan was commissioned into the guards, enabled by his parents' relative wealth to afford the expensive lifestyle expected of a young subaltern in the capital. However, he appears to have found military life not to his taste and after a time retired with the modest rank of Lieutenant. Settling in Moscow, he met and fell in love with Yekaterina Tolstaya, a young woman of aristocratic birth and some beauty. In 1798 they were married.[26]

Since losing her mother at the age of twelve, Yekaterina had been living with her aunt Anna Osterman. Left to cope with eleven children, Yekaterina's father had asked his sister Anna, married to the wealthy Count Fyodor Osterman, to take Yekaterina into their care, and with no children of their own she and her husband had been happy to do so.[27] The Count was the son of Heinrich Ostermann, a German of humble origins from Westphalia who had enlisted for military service with the Tsar in 1704, subsequently converting to the Orthodox faith and Russifying his name to Andrey

Osterman. An able soldier and administrator, he enjoyed a meteoric rise, first under Peter the Great and then the Empresses Catherine I and Anne, culminating in appointments as Chief Minister to the Crown and from 1725 to 1740 *de facto* Minister of Foreign Affairs. For his outstanding services he was showered with land and honours, including elevation to the title of Count.[28] Apart from inheriting his fortune and title, his two sons Ivan and Fyodor pursued distinguished careers of their own, including in Fyodor's case a spell as Governor-General of Moscow.[29]

After their marriage Ivan and Yekaterina Tyutchev retired to the family estate at Ovstug, where in Aksakov's words 'they settled into the well-known life of freedom and ease led at that time by almost all Russia's prosperous and leisured landowning class not belonging to the upper ranks of officialdom or burdened with government service'.[30] It was a life well suited to Ivan, who according to Aksakov displayed 'an unusual placidity and gentleness' and was in general 'a sensible man with a calm and commonsense view of things', much liked for his qualities as a 'congenial and generous host', yet apparently endowed with 'neither exceptional intellect nor talent'.[31] Another contemporary has drawn attention to Ivan's philanthropic efforts on behalf of famine victims,[32] a side of his father's nature also stressed by the ten-year-old Tyutchev in a poem addressed to him on his birthday:

> A loving spouse and father, to be sure,
> True friend of good and patron to the poor.[33]

Yekaterina may have shared her husband's commitment to helping the needy, but appears to have differed from him sharply in other respects. Contrasting her 'remarkable intellect' with that of the stolid, easygoing Ivan, Aksakov tells us she was 'slightly-built and of nervous disposition, inclined to hypochondria and possessed of a morbidly developed imagination'.[34] It was a union of opposites, but one that appears to have worked, for by all accounts they enjoyed a loving and harmonious married life.

iii A Moscow Childhood

It was at Ovstug that Ivan and Yekaterina's first children were born: Nikolay on 9 June 1801; and, towards eight o'clock on the morning of 23 November 1803, a second son, Fyodor (the name no doubt chosen in deference to Yekaterina's uncle and former guardian Fyodor Osterman).[35] From early on it became apparent that whereas Nikolay had inherited his father's looks together with his equable and practical nature, little Fyodor 'both in external appearance (he was very thin and of small stature) and inner psychological makeup [...] resembled his mother to an extraordinary degree'.[36] Finding, like their parents, that their disparate characters complemented each other perfectly, the two brothers became very close and were on the whole to remain so throughout their lives.

A fortnight before Tyutchev's first birthday his great-uncle Fyodor Osterman died, and soon afterwards the family moved from Ovstug to live with Yekaterina's widowed aunt Anna in Moscow.[37] With no immediate family of her own, Anna was glad to have her beloved niece back at her side and to hear the rooms of her house echo with the cries and laughter of children, who allowed themselves to be cosseted and indulged by their doting 'Grandmama Osterman'.[38] Over the next six years in Moscow Yekaterina gave birth to a further three sons, all of whom died in infancy or early childhood. The survival of an only daughter, Darya, born on 5 June 1806, was felt to be a particular blessing.[39]

It was thus in Moscow that little Fyodor (affectionately known as 'Fedya' or 'Fedinka') spent his formative years, apart from summer visits with the family to their estates at Ovstug and Troitskoye; and to the end of his days he would think of himself as a true Muscovite.[40] A century after ceding its status as capital to St Petersburg, Moscow had long since had to come to terms with the role of second city of the Empire. There was a provincial, almost rural feel to the place compared with the contrived urbane elegance and European polish of Peter the Great's 'window on the West'. The tone was set by nobles who for the most part, unlike their St Petersburg counterparts, either showed little ambition for government service or had retired from it. Moscow was said in common parlance to be the nation's heart, St Petersburg its head.[41] Yet the old capital was no intellectual backwater; on the contrary, a freer and more critical spirit flourished there than in the more regimented atmosphere of St Petersburg. As observed by a Western visitor to the city some years later, 'almost all the men of liberal opinions, and those whose politics do not suit those of the day, retire hither, where they may find fault with the Court, the Government, &c. as much as they please, without much fear of interruption'.[42] Although westernised in manners and education, the Moscow nobility retained a familiarity with peasant ways through long summers spent on their out-of-town estates, and in general the pulse of traditional Russian life continued to beat more freely here than amidst the enforced Europeanism of Peter's artificial creation to the north. Not surprisingly, it was in Moscow that the great debate between Slavophiles and Westernisers over Russia's cultural identity and future would arise in years to come. In the late eighteenth and early nineteenth century, however, Moscow's nobles were still for the most part intent on enjoying the privileges of wealth, including the construction of palatial mansions outside the walls of the old city centre that in style and conception seemed more like country estates.

The Ostermans' house, in Tryokhsvyatitelsky Pereulok, or Three Saints' Lane, was typical of these. The main building, a substantial two-storey structure with a ground plan measuring 114 by 57 feet, was for the exclusive use of the owners and their guests, with servants housed in separate accommodation in the grounds. Other outbuildings included a coach-house, stables and storehouses for provisions. Behind the house was a kitchen garden and orchard with a sizeable greenhouse. All in all the plot covered some four acres.[43] It was common to see cows, poultry and other livestock roaming the grounds of such households, while less perishable foodstuffs would be supplied from the landowners' out-of-town estates. Self-sufficiency was, wherever feasible, considered a worthy aim. There seemed after all little point in paying a tailor, pastrycook or musician when one could train up a household serf to do the same job for nothing. On the other hand there was no scrimping when it came to imported luxury goods such as silk and other expensive fabrics, wine, coffee, cigars, and foreign delicacies of every kind. Lavish entertainment and generous hospitality were expected of a Moscow noble, who would often have a number of impoverished hangers-on living more or less permanently under his roof. Relatives, no matter how distant, were made especially welcome.

Such was the patriarchal, comfortable world of extended and interlocking aristocratic families, familiar from the pages of *War and Peace*, in which Tyutchev grew up. Life conformed to a reassuring pattern of tradition and routine: dinner at three or four, evening tea around the candlelit samovar, balls, soirées, theatre visits, summers on the country estate, winter skating on the frozen river Moskva... Above all there were the rites and festivals of the Orthodox Church: for those such as Tyutchev's mother a matter of deep and genuine faith; for others, including the poet himself in years to come, little more than a token of what it meant to be Russian. As a grown man who found himself unable to believe, he would later write with a certain nostalgia of that changeless 'Russo-Byzantine world in which life and religious observance are but one'.[44] Next to 'Grandmama' Osterman's house stood the seventeenth-century church of Three Saints in the Haymeadows (Tryokh Svyatiteley v Kulishkakh) after which the street took its name, and in whose registers for these years the names of Osterman, Tolstoy and Tyutchev figure prominently — including that of little Fedya himself, twice enrolled at the tender age of three and five respectively as godparent to children born in his great-aunt's house.[45]

It was by all accounts a happy childhood. Tyutchev later called it 'the best time of my life',[46] and remained ever grateful to his mother and father for the 'rare parental affection' shown towards him and the other children, for 'all their love and affectionate care'.[47] Outsiders too were struck by the harmonious and loving atmosphere of their household. 'Looking at the Tyutchevs, I thought about family happiness,' one of the young poet's university friends would later note in his diary. 'If only everyone could live as simply as they do!'[48] Portraits of Tyutchev as a young child show him bright-eyed and mentally alert,[49] and Aksakov confirms that from his earliest years 'he stood clearly apart from the rest of [the family], displaying all the signs of exceptional gifts'. It was because of these precocious talents, Aksakov believes, that little Fedya 'straight away became the darling and pet of his grandmama Osterman, his mother and all around him'.[50] Among the latter were two no doubt equally doting great-aunts, Anna Osterman's sisters Marfa and Varvara.[51] There was also his paternal grandmother Pelageya Tyutcheva, whom he is known to have visited at her Znamenskoye estate on at least one occasion with his father and brother. 'Fedinka is more affectionate towards me than I can describe,' she enthused, writing of their stay with her towards the end of 1810. 'He says many people loved him in Moscow, but "nobody loves me as much as my grandmama!" And he says he couldn't love anyone more [than me]'.[52]

It was Aksakov's considered view that all this female affection had been overdone to the point of indulgence, and that together with his cosseted upbringing as a child of the serf-owning landed gentry it explained much in his later development. In particular, 'from childhood on he had an aversion to any discipline, to any exertion of will or hard work'.[53] It was an assessment shared by others close to Tyutchev. Complaining on one occasion of his total inability to face up to painful decisions, his second wife commented that this was not surprising, given that throughout his life 'all his inclinations and whims have been constantly satisfied'.[54] Nor can it be denied that these early experiences coloured his later love relationships, causing him (as one critic has observed) to prize in women above all else 'the assurance that he was adored'.[55]

A peasant wet-nurse and nanny were at that time the norm for children of the Russian nobility; a boy would also have assigned to him a peasant 'uncle' (*'dyad'ka'*) who would serve his charge, often into adult life, in the combined roles of governor, mentor and valet. Tyutchev's *dyad'ka*, Nikolay Afanasyevich Khlopov, was a former serf who had been granted his freedom by his previous master. He was employed to look after the four-year-old Fedya in 1808, when he himself was in his late thirties, and stayed with the family until his death in 1826.[56] Aksakov characterises him as 'literate' and 'pious', and says he was 'held in high esteem by his masters'.[57] Tyutchev developed a close bond with his *dyad'ka*, and even in old age still fondly recalled his 'passionate attachment — in times gone by — to the long-departed Nikolay Afanasyevich'.[58]

Much has been written of the role played by such peasant nannies and 'uncles' in reconnecting the children of the Europeanised Russian nobility with the language, traditions and customs of their own people. Pushkin for one remained ever grateful to his nanny Arina Rodionovna, who had fired his youthful imagination with her folk tales, songs and proverbs. Tatyana's nanny in *Eugene Onegin* is clearly based on her; while in Savelich, Pyotr Grinyov's devoted and long-suffering manservant in *The Captain's Daughter*, Pushkin gives us an affectionate portrait of the archetypal peasant 'uncle'. Khlopov's influence on the young Tyutchev will have been comparable. It must for instance have been largely with Nikolay Afanasyevich that little Fedya gained any confidence in speaking Russian, since the members of his family communicated with each other almost exclusively in French.[59] In this they merely followed the accepted convention of the day (as reflected in the opening chapters of *War and Peace*). And as a result, to the end of his days Tyutchev would in most circumstances find it easier to express himself in French than in Russian.[60] The one important exception was his poetry.

In common with other boys of their class, Tyutchev and his brother Nikolay received a private education at home. Little is known about Fedya's early encounters with formal tuition beyond Aksakov's general statement that 'thanks to his remarkable abilities he was able to make exceptionally good progress in his studies', and that 'even then [...] studying was for him not hard work, but the satisfaction of a natural desire for knowledge'.[61] Although he had probably even before this learnt to read and write both in French and Russian, Aksakov flatly asserts that the family milieu in which Tyutchev grew up 'was completely devoid of any literary interests, in particular as regards Russian literature'.[62] This has been disputed by a more recent biographer, who points to later evidence, including the family's association with the poet Zhukovsky, that Tyutchev's parents took a keener interest in the literary and intellectual developments of the day than Aksakov's remark would suggest.[63]

Among the many visitors to Anna Osterman's house was her great-nephew Aleksandr Osterman-Tolstoy.[64] As neither Count Fyodor's marriage to her nor that of his brother Ivan had been blessed with issue, the two Ostermans had looked elsewhere for an heir. Their sister Sofya had married a Tolstoy, and it was upon her grandson Aleksandr that their choice eventually fell. Born in 1770 to parents with little wealth of their own, he had impressed Catherine the Great as a young guards officer, and under her and Alexander I (whose outwardly liberal and humane political ideals he admired) had proved himself in military campaigns, rising in rank and distinction to become an influential figure at court. Marriage to a wealthy heiress, Princess Yelizaveta Golitsyna, had ensured his financial security. From his great-uncles Osterman he inherited not only the title of Count but their considerable fortune, the only condition being that he change his name to Osterman-Tolstoy; his and his wife's combined income was subsequently estimated at half a million roubles per annum.[65]

In a world where a judiciously dropped word at court could make or break a career Osterman-Tolstoy was clearly a useful person to know. Moreover, he and Tyutchev's mother had more in common than their tenuous bond as distant cousins might suggest. Both had in a sense been adopted by the Ostermans, and both had been assigned an inheritance (hers admittedly much more modest than his). Already in December 1805 Anna Osterman had made over to Yekaterina lands and some 500 serfs in Vladimir province;[66] and when her aunt died in May 1809, Yekaterina found she had also been left the house in Three Saints' Lane. However, she and her husband decided against staying there; the following January the house was sold, and the search began for a new home in Moscow.[67] After some time in rented accommodation they found what they wanted: a handsome gentleman's residence which had belonged to the wealthy Prince Ivan Gagarin, recently deceased.[68] On purchasing the old house in 1790 Gagarin had commissioned a complete reconstruction in the neoclassical style by Matvey Kazakov, a prolific architect responsible for much public and private building in Moscow before and after 1800. Situated at what is now 11 Armenian Lane, it was less than half a mile to the north of Three Saints' Lane, on the other side of busy Maroseyka Street. With its three storeys and a frontage of some 140 feet it was considerably larger than the Ostermans' house, although standing in a smaller plot. A contemporary print shows an elegantly proportioned building of fifteen bays, the long sweep of the facade broken up near either end by slightly projecting sections housing the two main entrances and linked by a first-floor balcony supported by Corinthian columns. Large glazed doors opened out onto the balcony from a spacious dining room which doubled as ballroom.[69]

For this palatial residence (which still survives, much altered) Yekaterina agreed to pay the sum of 55,000 roubles; and at the end of 1810, just in time for Christmas, the family moved into their new home.[70] They themselves occupied the best rooms on the first floor, which were laid with parquet flooring and in general more luxuriously appointed. Some of the more modest second-floor rooms were let out, while others were reserved for visitors and guests, including a few widowed or impoverished relatives kept on out of charity. As at Three Saints' Lane, the servants were accommodated in outbuildings.[71]

The Tyutchevs' splendid new residence was an adequate reflection of their financial standing. At this time Ivan Nikolayevich and Yekaterina Lvovna owned between them (including the estates Yekaterina had received from her aunt Anna) well in excess of 1,700 serfs.[72] While this by no means put them among the super-rich, it did mean they belonged to the top three per cent or so of landowners in terms of wealth.[73] The 'anarchist prince' Pyotr Kropotkin recalled that his father, who in the 1840s owned about the same number of 'souls' (1,200) as Ivan Nikolayevich, was accounted a rich man. Kropotkin gives a fascinating glimpse into the privileged life accorded by such wealth:

We were a family of eight, occasionally of ten or twelve; but fifty servants at Moscow, and half as many more in the country, were considered not one too many. Four coachmen to attend a dozen horses, three cooks for the masters and two more for the servants, a dozen men to wait upon us at dinner-time (one man, plate in hand, standing behind each person seated at the table), and girls innumerable in the maid-servants' room, — how could anyone do with less than this?[74]

Although the Tyutchevs' household may not have been run on quite such a lavish scale (one estimate puts the number of their servants in Moscow at between thirty and forty),[75] the lifestyle they enjoyed will have been more or less comparable.

The area into which they had moved was one favoured by the well-to-do aristocracy, as exemplified by their immediate neighbours. To the right of them lived Senator and Privy Councillor Fyodor Ivanovich Levashov; to the left the Lazarevs, an Armenian family who were among the wealthiest landowners in Russia. More or less opposite, on the corner of Maroseyka Street, stood a magnificent three-storey mansion purchased in 1793 and completely renovated before his death three years later by Field-Marshal Count Pyotr Rumyantsev, one of Catherine the Great's most distinguished generals.[76] The Tyutchevs soon established cordial relations with their neighbours, especially Ioakim (or Yekim) Lazarev, a wealthy Armenian whose father had settled in Moscow in the middle of the eighteenth century and made his fortune dealing in precious stones, silks and other fabrics. His family had built an Armenian church opposite their house, to be followed by a school which would later evolve into the renowned Lazarev Institute of Oriental Languages. It was in recognition of the Lazarevs that around 1800 the street was renamed Armenian Lane.[77]

Inhabited by the educated nobility, the quarter of the city in which the Tyutchevs lived (roughly that bounded by Myasnitskaya and Novaya Basmannaya Streets to the north and Maroseyka, Pokrovka and Staraya Basmannaya Streets to the south) had by the end of the eighteenth century become an important centre of cultural activity. One writer has described it as being in this respect something of a focal point for developments in the country at large.[78] It was certainly home to several prominent figures in Russian culture in the late eighteenth and early nineteenth centuries. At the north-eastern end of the district, in Yelokhovskaya Street, lived for instance the bibliophile Count Aleksey Musin-Pushkin, whose collection of rare books and manuscripts was used by the historian Karamzin. Musin-Pushkin is best remembered for having discovered the manuscript of the twelfth-century Russian epic poem *The Tale of Igor's Campaign*.[79] Count Nikolay Rumyantsev, whose father had built the mansion opposite the Tyutchevs, had his own house not far from them on Maroseyka Street. Foreign Minister of Russia from 1807 to 1814, Rumyantsev was another passionate collector whose holdings would later form the nucleus of the Russian State Library.[80] Around the corner from the Tyutchevs in Krivokolenny Lane lived with his parents the young Dmitry Venevitinov, two years younger than Tyutchev and like him destined to become a poet.[81] Aleksandr Pushkin was born just outside the area, in Baumanskaya Street, but from 1801 to 1803 his parents rented accommodation in the grounds of Prince Yusupov's palace in Bolshoy Kharitonevsky Lane, halfway between Myasnitskaya and Pokrovka Streets.[82] His uncle Vasily Pushkin (also a poet) lived not far away in Staraya Basmannaya Street.[83] Before leaving Moscow at the age of twelve to enter the imperial *lycée* at Tsarskoye Selo near St Petersburg, Pushkin was befriended by the older Aleksandr Turgenev, whose father was Rector of Moscow University (and whom

Tyutchev too would come to know much later, as an adult). The Turgenevs lived in Petroverigsky Lane, just to the south of Maroseyka Street, and among frequent visitors to their house at the beginning of the nineteenth century were Karamzin and the poets Zhukovsky and Dmitriev.[84]

The area was rich in other cultural associations too. Within a few minutes' walk of the Tyutchevs' house were several buildings of architectural and historical interest. Coming out of their courtyard, one saw more or less opposite, on the corner of Chrysostom Lane (Zlatoustinsky Pereulok), the finely decorated mid-seventeenth-century parish church of St Nicholas at the Pillars (Nikolaya v stolpakh), a handsome example of the five-domed neo-Byzantine style favoured by the Graecophile Patriarch Nikon. Sadly, this no longer stands, having fallen victim to Stalin's reconstruction plans in the 1930s. Among those buried in its graveyard was Artamon Matveyev, prominent as a government minister in the seventeenth century, whose house stood nearby on the site subsequently occupied by the Lazarevs. It was in this house that Matveyev brought up his young ward Natalya Naryshkina, later to become the second wife of Tsar Alexis and mother of Peter the Great.[85]

Turning into Chrysostom Lane, one came to the ancient monastery which had given that street its name. In 1479 Grand Duke Ivan (Ioann) III had replaced its wooden main church of St John Chrysostom with one built of stone in honour of his name-saint; this and other parts of the monastery (including a further three churches) were in turn largely rebuilt during the seventeenth and eighteenth centuries. Among those interred within its walls were Peter the Great's trusted lieutenant Admiral Count Fyodor Apraksin, and Count Aleksandr Rumyantsev, father of the aforementioned Field-Marshal.[86] From here it was a short walk into Maroseyka Street and, turning east, to the junction with the southern end of Armenian Lane, where the elegant church of Saints Cosmas and Damian was situated, one of several built or rebuilt by Kazakov in the neoclassical rotunda style around the turn of the century.[87] A little further east in Pokrovka Street (the continuation of Maroseyka Street) stood an even more impressive church: that of the Assumption of the Blessed Virgin (Uspeniya Bozhiey Materi, chto na Pokrovke). Built at the very end of the seventeenth century by Pyotr Potapov in a 'Moscow baroque' style influenced by Ukrainian and western models, with its three main towers, bell-tower and thirteen domes it gave the initial impression of a whole cluster of separate churches. Closer examination revealed these individual features to be subordinated to an overall conception of great harmony and spiritual beauty: an ethereal heavenward striving reminiscent of the gothic. Potapov's masterpiece was a source of wonder to all, and of inspiration to later architects such as Bazhenov and Rastrelli.[88] Seeing it for the first time as a young man, the distinguished Soviet scholar of medieval Russian literature Dmitry Likhachov was immediately spellbound by what seemed to him 'the embodiment of some mysterious idea, the vision of something unimaginably beautiful', and later recalled this as the moment when his abiding passion for the culture of old Russia had been born.[89] Even Napoleon was so impressed that he ordered a special guard to be placed on the church during the great fire of 1812. Stalin was altogether less inclined to such sentiment; in the 1930s this jewel of Russian architecture too was demolished at the stroke of a pen.[90]

Tyutchev's childhood was by no means confined to these Moscow streets, for in the summer the family would usually decamp to their country seat at Ovstug. Travelling there via Tula and Oryol by horse-drawn carriage, on inferior and poorly maintained dirt roads, with overnight stops and changes of horses at post-houses, took anything up to four days.[91] They were always glad to reach the sleepy provincial town of Bryansk, which marked the final stage of their journey. From here they headed north-west along the Roslavl road, and after some twenty miles took a right turn from the highway into Ovstug, a sizeable village set amidst gently rolling hills and birch forests. Driving past peasants' traditional wooden cottages on either side of the road, they reached the stone church built by Ivan Nikolayevich's father and turned into their estate. Ovstug manor overlooked the village and the elegant baroque dome and spire of the church from elevated ground in a fairly modest landscaped park of avenues and groves falling away to a lake below. The house has long since disappeared, replaced with a larger structure by Tyutchev's father in the late 1820s.[92] This in turn eventually fell into disuse and was finally demolished just before the First World War. The house now open to the public is a faithful reconstruction, completed in 1985, of that built by Ivan Nikolayevich.[93]

For the children Ovstug provided a freedom for play and imaginative development denied them in the city. Returning there in his mid-forties for the first time in over a quarter of a century, Tyutchev was painfully moved by this encounter with the 'enchanted world' of his childhood, seen now as unvarnished reality stripped of the illusions of youth: 'the old garden; four great lime-trees, well-known in the area; a rather insignificant avenue of trees some hundred paces in length which had seemed immeasurable to me: all that magnificent universe of my childhood, so populated and varied, all contained within the confines of a few square yards...'.[94] For all his later ambiguous feelings towards Ovstug, he could never forget that it was where he had been born and spent the first year of his life, before the move to Moscow. Here it was after all that (as he writes in one of his poems) 'thought and feeling first within me dawned'.[95]

iv 1812

It was a matter of some regret to Ivan Aksakov that he never heard any personal reminiscences of the year 1812 from Tyutchev.[96] In the letters too all we find is one laconic reference to Moscow having been in that year 'the theatre of Napoleon's tribulations and of mine'.[97] Yet Aksakov is surely right in supposing that the War of the Fatherland left as indelible a mark on the young Tyutchev as on the rest of his generation.[98] Four decades on he would recall in verse Napoleon's fateful invasion of Russia on 12/24 June 1812, and the spectacular initial advances made by his forces:

> Triumphantly his troops marched on
> With standards cheerfully aflutter,
> Fixed bayonets glinting in the sun,
> While bridges groaned with cannon-clatter —
> And like some god enthroned on high
> He seemed to soar above the action,
> With watchful and imperious eye
> Subjecting all to his direction...[99]

Against Napoleon's Grand Army of over half a million men — the largest the world had ever seen, drawn from the length and breadth of Europe — stood three Russian armies numbering in all no more than 200,000. In these circumstances Alexander I and his generals had no option but to adopt a strategy of withdrawal and scorched earth, pinning their faith on those most formidable of allies, the geography and climate of Russia. Occupying first Vilna (to the jubilation of the Polish population) and then Smolensk, Napoleon advanced on Moscow. On 26 August a set-piece stand at Borodino some 75 miles west of the city resulted in horrific casualties on both sides, but failed to stop the invader in his tracks. Among the fallen that day were Tyutchev's young cousin Aleksandr Bezobrazov and the fiancé of another cousin, Nastasya Meshcherskaya.[100] The Russian Commander-in-Chief General Kutuzov now decided to abandon Moscow to the enemy without further engagement, and its inhabitants were advised to leave.

The Tyutchevs loaded as many of their possessions as they could onto waggons and — like the Rostovs in *War and Peace* — headed for Yaroslavl.[101] Although Tyutchev himself has left no account of these events, reminiscences of others who were about the same age at the time give some idea of how they must have appeared to a boy still only eight years old. Mikhail Pogodin, three years older than Tyutchev and later a friend of his at university, left the city for Vladimir with his family and neighbours. Food was in short supply: he remembered a kindly landowner's wife near Vladimir providing bread and cheesecake for the children. When Pogodin heard that the French had occupied Moscow on 2 September, 'it was as if my eyes had been opened, and my heart was torn with grief'. He and his family eventually found somewhere to stay in Suzdal.[102] A more detailed account is given by Aleksandr Koshelyov, who was only six at the time. He and his family left their country estate at Bronnitsy near Moscow for Kolomna on the very day that Napoleon's troops entered the city. 'The main road from Bronnitsy to Kolomna was jam-packed with carriages, carts and people on foot, all in a slowly moving column that stretched all the way from Moscow. There was sadness on everyone's face; hardly anyone was heard to speak; a deathly silence hung over this sad procession. Young men and those of mature age were all in the army or militia; only old men, women and children were to be seen in the carriages, on the carts and among the throngs of those making their way on foot. The memory of this strange, sad migration (I cannot call it a journey) has remained with me vividly, leaving a dismal impression.' They found Kolomna overrun with refugees, and Koshelyov's father decided to take the family on to Tambov, where his brother lived. 'Again at Kolomna nearly everyone left at the same time, and at the ferry crossing over the Oka there was a terrible jam and crush and the most frightful chaos. Throughout our journey to Tambov there was no end of rumour and gossip; it seemed as if Napoleon was hard on our heels. In Tambov we finally found proper permanent accommodation [...]'.[103]

No doubt the Tyutchevs had equally chaotic conditions to contend with during the long trek to Yaroslavl. To add to their difficulties, Ivan Nikolayevich and Yekaterina Lvovna had five young children to care for, ranging in age from Nikolay, who was eleven, through Fyodor, Darya and the three-and-a-half-year-old Dmitry to the youngest, Vasily, born just after the move to Armenian Lane and now barely eighteen months old.[104] Dmitry was to die in April 1815, as recorded together with other family births, marriages and deaths in the registers of the Tyutchevs' parish church of St Nicholas.[105] However, there is no such entry for little Vasily, who simply disappears from the record. He appears to be the 'brother who expired in infancy' referred to by Tyutchev in a later poem,[106] and two of the poet's biographers have suggested that this tragic event occurred far from Moscow during the upheavals of 1812.[107]

There is some reason to doubt Aksakov's claim that the Tyutchevs spent the whole period of evacuation in Yaroslavl, a popular destination for those fleeing Moscow and presumably subject to the same severe shortage of accommodation as that encountered by the Pogodins and Koshelyovs in Vladimir and Kolomna. Ivan Nikolayevich's ailing seventy-three-year old mother was living on the family estate of Znamenskoye near Uglich, no more than 60 miles away, and (as pointed out by the Tyutchev scholar Gennady Chagin) it is difficult to believe that he did not take his wife and children to stay there.[108] Indeed, it is highly likely that other members of the Tyutchev clan also took refuge in the ancestral nest at this time of crisis, including Ivan Nikolayevich's brother Nikolay, who had inherited the estate, and (as suggested below) their sister Nadezhda Sheremeteva.

Napoleon had expected his occupation of Moscow would force the Russians to sue for peace. Instead he soon found himself surrounded by fires started apparently on the orders of the city's Governor-General, Count Rostopchin. Within a few days the whole inner city and much of the outlying suburbs had been reduced to smouldering ruins. On 7 October, just over a month after taking up residence in the Kremlin, Napoleon withdrew from Moscow, and his much depleted Grand Army began the long march west. A mere 10,000 of the once seemingly invincible force of half a million were destined to survive the disastrous campaign.[109] The last ragged and demoralised remnants recrossed the Neman on 2/14 December without their leader, who had left for Paris days before, his dreams of conquest shattered.

For the Tyutchevs the general rejoicing at Russia's deliverance was overshadowed by the death at Znamenskoye on 3 December of Ivan Nikolayevich's mother. Following her burial next to her husband in the graveyard of the village church, the family no doubt stayed on for a while to sort out her affairs and celebrate the customary requiem mass forty days after her death.[110] Their first sight of Moscow again after the occupation was, as for other returning refugees, a sobering experience. 'Dead horses lay everywhere along the road,' Pogodin recalled. 'Birds of prey flew around in flocks. Whole streets had burnt down. Smoke-blackened walls, chimney-stacks left protruding; people in rags and tatters; practically no carriages.'[111] The six-year-old Koshelyov too was traumatised by what he saw, to judge from what he still remembered in old age: 'The charred walls of stone-built houses; solitary chimneys where wooden buildings had once stood; tracts of waste ground with people wandering across them — all this shocked me to such an extent that the memory has remained with me vividly to this day.'[112] It may be that over these dramatic months the young Tyutchev witnessed similar horrors, which he was reluctant to speak of in later years. Certainly there is every reason to agree with previous biographers that the events of 1812 coloured his view of the world for life, inspiring in particular, as in so many of his young contemporaries, a fervent and abiding sense of patriotism.[113]

The Tyutchevs were greatly relieved to find their house one of the few to have survived the conflagration. During the occupation a French general had commandeered the Lazarevs' house for his own use, and both he and an Armenian in Napoleon's retinue had persuaded their Emperor to ensure that the area surrounding the

Armenian church was effectively guarded against incipient fires.[114] By contrast the Tyutchevs' out-of-town estate at Troitskoye had suffered badly, pillaged by the Grand Army on its way through in October during the doomed attempt to reach Kaluga. In the circumstances it was decided to move on to Ovstug and stay there until some semblance of normality had returned.[115]

v Raich

It was at about this time that a twenty-year-old would-be university student, Semyon Raich, was welcomed into the Tyutchev household as tutor to young Fedya. While others seem to have been employed on an ad hoc basis, it was now apparently felt that the boy needed a permanent mentor to oversee his studies and give them a more purposeful direction, especially in view of the disruption caused by the war. Of slight build and dark complexion, Raich (the *nom de plume* under which he became known: his real name was Amfiteatrov) seemed to some almost monk-like in his ascetic lifestyle and single-minded devotion to the muses.[116] Aksakov remembers him as 'original in the highest degree, unselfish, pure, eternally in the realm of idyllic reveries'.[117] Born the son of a village priest near Kromy in Oryol province, he too was originally destined for the priesthood, but during his training developed a passion for poetry, in particular that of Derzhavin, and on graduating decided his vocation was to the pen rather than to the cloth.[118] It would be 1821 before he saw his first work in print, after which (as he later recalled) 'I devoted myself completely to Poetry, and no seductive prospects — neither financial gain, nor a career in government service with promotions, honours and the guarantee of a fortune — could divert me from it'.[119] In the meantime, on leaving the seminary he resolved to make himself financially independent as a first step towards his dream of studying at Moscow University. At the end of 1810, after six months as tutor to a landowner's family in Oryol province, he was recommended to Ivan Nikolayevich's sister Nadezhda Sheremeteva and moved to her estate at Pokrovskoye in Moscow province to teach her children.[120] As Napoleon approached Moscow in 1812 Raich volunteered for military service, but on reporting at the appointed time found his regiment had left the city two weeks before. Instead he headed for Uglich and Yaroslavl (presumably following his employer to the family refuge at Znamenskoye), and then to 'N.N. Sheremeteva's Bryansk village'.[121] From this we may deduce that Nadezhda and her children accompanied her brother Ivan Nikolayevich and his family to Ovstug to escape the devastation in and around Moscow. And it was probably after they had settled in there that the hopeful young poet agreed to become tutor to the ten-year-old Fedya (an appointment which incidentally seems further to contradict the family's alleged lack of literary interests).

For the first eighteen months or so Raich's tutorial duties were discharged at Ovstug, the Tyutchevs having let their house in Armenian Lane and installed themselves in the country.[122] Raich was to remember this as a time when, like Napoleon in exile, he 'languished [...] in the Bryansk forests, far from the burnt-out University of Moscow'.[123] Yet such misgivings were soon outweighed by the attractions of his new job. 'I was amazed and gratified by my congenial young charge's uncommon gifts and passion for learning,' he wrote later; 'after three years or so he was no longer my pupil but my comrade, — so quickly did his inquisitive and receptive mind develop!'[124]

It seems to have been at Ovstug that Tyutchev, guided and encouraged by Raich, took his first poetic steps. One day while walking together in woods near the churchyard, he and his tutor (a keen advocate of teaching out of doors)[125] came across a dead turtle-dove lying in the grass. It was decided to give the creature a proper burial, with an epitaph in verse composed for the occasion by young Fedya himself.[126] Although this has not survived, another poem of the same period — a birthday ode to his father written in 1813 or 1814 — shows Tyutchev to have been (no doubt with help from Raich) already adept in the art of versification.[127] The incident with the turtle-dove was recalled by Tyutchev many years later as he walked in the same woods with his daughter Darya. He also told her how as a boy he had loved to come to this quiet spot on spring evenings to pick violets, which as darkness fell seemed to grow ever more fragrant. Such moments had, he said, produced in him 'an indefinite feeling of mystery and veneration'. 'These woods, this garden, these avenues were a whole world for Papa, a world complete in itself,' commented Darya, writing of this to her sister Yekaterina.[128] Already, it seems, Tyutchev's youthful imagination had fixed on themes central to his later verse: the mysterious allure of nature and the world of the senses; a fascination with states of transition (in this case dusk); and — even at this tender age — intimations of the finite nature of all earthly existence.

By the autumn of 1814 conditions had improved sufficiently for the family to leave Ovstug and return to Moscow.[129] Before the war Ivan Nikolayevich had briefly entered government service, only to retire again at the end of 1810.[130] Fired perhaps by a patriotic desire to help in his country's reconstruction, he now re-entered service as an official in the Kremlin department of building works with the civil rank of Court Councillor (equivalent to Lieutenant-Colonel).[131] In the autumn of the following year Raich at last realised his dream of enrolling as a student at Moscow University. He left the Tyutchev household for a while, but returned in 1816 to prepare young Fedya for university entrance while continuing his own studies in the Faculty of Moral and Political Studies.[132] Nikolay had no doubt also received the benefit of Raich's tuition; but he seemed more cut out to be a soldier, and in March 1816 he and his cousin Aleksey Sheremetev were admitted to the prestigious Military Academy recently founded in Moscow by the cultured and reform-minded General Nikolay Muravyov. Situated in Muravyov's own house in Bolshaya Dmitrovka Street, the academy trained young men of noble birth for positions as officers on the general staff.[133]

At about the same time Nadezhda Sheremeteva moved to Moscow to be with her cadet son, taking rooms for herself, Aleksey and her young daughters Pelageya and Anastasiya in the house of her brother Ivan Nikolayevich in Armenian Lane.[134] A cultivated woman of progressive views, she maintained on her estate at Pokrovskoye a choir, orchestra and theatrical troupe, all staffed from the ranks of her serfs.[135] She took an active interest in the literary and intellectual scene, gaining the friendship and respect of such figures as the poet Vasily Zhukovsky and the political thinker Pyotr Chaadayev. In later years she would become a close friend and confidante of Gogol. Her independence of mind and forthright character set her apart from her contemporaries, many of whom were shocked by such 'unladylike' behaviour on her part as wearing her hair short, dressing simply and driving around town in an open drozhky rather than an enclosed carriage.[136]

Meanwhile Tyutchev's education entered upon a new phase. To help him prepare for entrance to Moscow University, in the autumn of 1816 he successfully applied for permission to attend lectures there on an unofficial basis as a so-called 'voluntary auditor' ('vol'noslushatel' '). Over the next three years he took regular advantage of this, always accompanied by Raich.[137] His tutor also took him to private seminars on literature given by one of the university's foremost teachers, Professor Aleksey Merzlyakov, himself a published poet.[138] These sessions were open to all, including on occasion literary figures of some renown, and Merzlyakov would encourage younger participants to read out and discuss their own poetic attempts.[139]

During these years summers would usually be spent (perhaps in view of the relatively short university vacation) at the now restored Troitskoye rather than in distant Ovstug. Raich later remembered this as one of the happiest periods of his life, devoted to encouraging the further development of his 'uncommonly talented' pupil and friend: 'With what pleasure I recall those delightful hours when — staying at the family's estate outside Moscow — Fyodor Ivanovich and I would leave the house equipped with Horace, Virgil or one of our Russian writers and, finding somewhere to sit in the woods or on a hillock, would lose ourselves in reading, delighting in pure enjoyment of the beauty to be found in poetic works of genius!'[140]

Already in 1815 Raich had embarked on a translation of Virgil's *Georgics*, determined to prove that Russian could compete with French as a vehicle for rendering Latin verse. According to Raich, for about a year he showed his work in progress only to the twelve-year-old Tyutchev, who was himself 'already initiated into the mysteries of Poetry and [...] composing *con amore*', and in whose literary judgement he had complete faith. It seems the pupil was encouraged to emulate his teacher, for Raich tells us that Tyutchev's compositions at this time included translations, executed 'with remarkable success', of Horace's odes [141] While none of these has come to light, an ode written just after Tyutchev's twelfth birthday to mark the New Year of 1816 reflects themes found both in Horace and in Raich's revered model, Derzhavin. It opens with a meditation on the illusory nature of time ('Eternity's unsteady, flickering mirror') and the frailty of human existence:

> Where mighty Memphis stood, wild beasts now roam contented;
> Through Babylon's remains the desert winds make moan;
> While Troy's proud ramparts lie fragmented,
> With thorns and brambles overgrown!..

Death and nemesis must come to all, including the rich and powerful. At the crucial hour neither gold, nor rank, nor fawning sycophants will be of any avail to the grandee; indeed, if during his lifetime he had 'dared with avaricious hand/ To snatch the daily bread of widows and of orphans' or 'banish far from home the grieving family', he can expect to suffer the fires of eternal damnation, tormented by the shades of his victims:

> Behold a fearful throng: thy long-dead victims waken!
> With hideous grin on thee advance their bloodied ranks!..
> Through barbarous abuse their lives were rudely taken:
> Now see how they repay barbarity with thanks![142]

From its innocuous beginning as a celebration of the New Year the poem has turned into an indictment of social injustice in general, and perhaps the excesses of serfdom in particular. Even taking into account what it must owe to the guiding hand of Raich, there is ample evidence of the talent claimed by the latter for his young pupil in this, the most substantial and impressive of the half-dozen surviving poems known to have been written by Tyutchev before his fifteenth birthday.[143]

On 3 July 1817 Professor Merzlyakov wrote to a correspondent that his 'little academy' had dispersed for the summer. Although he may have meant the boarding school he and a fellow-academic had been running since 1813,[144] the reference is more likely to the informal group of young poets he had gathered around him. The same letter informs us that one of these, Tyutchev, had before leaving for Troitskoye given the Professor some of his poems, which at the time of writing Merzlyakov had not yet managed to look at.[145] When he did, he was sufficiently impressed to read one out at a meeting of the Society of Lovers of Russian Literature on 22 February 1818. This learned society, of which Merzlyakov was a founder member, was attached to the university and consisted of 35 full members, including such established poets as Zhukovsky, Ivan Dmitriev and Vasily Pushkin, together with a larger number of young associate members elected for their perceived potential as writers or critics. In the protocols of the Society the poem by Tyutchev read out on that date is named as 'The Grandee. An Imitation of Horace'.[146] Although no text with this title has survived, it is now generally assumed (as first suggested by the critic Georgy Chulkov) to have been in fact the ode originally written for the New Year of 1816, suitably revised and re-titled.[147] At the next meeting of the Society on 30 March, both Tyutchev and Raich were — no doubt on Merzlyakov's initiative — elected associate members.[148] In February 1819 a further poem by Tyutchev was read out to the Society. Entitled 'Missive from Horace to Maecenas, in Which he Invites him to Dinner in the Country', it is a loose translation, much longer than the original, of one of Horace's odes (*Odes*, III, 29).[149] It has been pointed out how one passage on the theme of time becomes particularly extended and elaborated in Tyutchev's version (lines 52-63).[150] This topic, which had already occupied him in his earlier 'imitation', would provide the subject matter for much of his mature verse. The poem was published in the *Transactions* of the Society later that year, becoming the first of his compositions to appear in print, and was followed by further submissions and publications.[151] According to Aksakov, these early literary successes were celebrated as a 'great triumph' by the young poet and his family.[152]

Among those to witness Tyutchev's début at the Society of Lovers of Russian Literature was the poet Zhukovsky.[153] He had come to Moscow with the imperial family in October 1817, when the Tsar had inaugurated ten months of celebrations to mark the fifth anniversary of the city's liberation by laying the foundation stone of a new national monument, the church of Christ the Saviour.[154] Russia's foremost living poet (Derzhavin had died in 1816, while the seventeen-year-old Pushkin's fame still lay in the future), Zhukovsky had recently been appointed teacher of Russian to the new wife (a daughter of the King of Prussia) of Grand Duke Nicholas (later Nicholas I), brother of the Tsar. In years to come he would remain in the employ of Nicholas and his wife Alexandra as tutor to their children.[155]

On his arrival in Moscow on 9 October,[156] Zhukovsky was allocated rooms at the Chudov monastery inside the Kremlin, and soon began to make the rounds of friends and acquaintances in Moscow. It may have been through one of these, Nadezhda Sheremeteva, that he came to know the Tyutchevs, who invited him to dine with them at Armenian Lane already on 28 October.[157] After this Ivan Nikolayevich's work at the Kremlin must have afforded further opportunities to keep in touch. Early on the morning of 17 April 1818, not long after Tyutchev's first successes at the Society of Lovers of Russian Literature, his father took him to visit Zhukovsky at the Chudov monastery.[158] The golden domes of the Kremlin churches gleamed against a clear blue sky: it was, as Tyutchev still vividly remembered over half a century later, the first bright spring-like day of the year. While waiting for the 'unforgettable' Zhukovsky in his 'quiet, unassuming cell', they were startled to hear all the bells of the Kremlin ring out, followed by the roar of a cannon salute. Eventually their host appeared with a glass of champagne in his hand to announce the happy news that Grand Duchess Alexandra Fyodorovna had given birth to a son (the future Tsar Alexander II).[159]

Whether or not during his stay in Moscow Zhukovsky was shown examples of Tyutchev's verse by his proud parents, he certainly heard Tyutchev's 'Imitation of Horace' read out to the Society of Lovers of Russian Literature on 22 February 1818. Given the generous recognition and encouragement he had already accorded Pushkin in St Petersburg, it seems likely he would have reacted similarly to a promising young poet in Moscow. Certainly some years hence he would play an important part in furthering Tyutchev's public career as a poet. 'No falsehood dwelt in him, no contradiction — / He reconciled, encompassed all within', Tyutchev wrote of Zhukovsky after his death. 'In spirit he was truly, like a dove, / Pure and intact'.[160]

vi Moscow University

By the following year (1819) it was apparent to all that at fifteen Tyutchev was already quite capable of studying for a degree, and appropriate preparations were set in hand. Raich, his work in the Tyutchev household now done after nearly seven years there, moved on to that of the Muravyovs on Bolshaya Dmitrovka, where he was employed as tutor to the General's thirteen-year-old son Andrey.[161] Since Nikolay Tyutchev and his cousin Aleksey Sheremetev had graduated from Muravyov's Military Academy two years previously (both going on to serve as junior officers in St Petersburg), relations between their families had remained close. During Aleksey's time at the academy his mother had invited the widower General's only daughter, Sofya, to come and live with her in Armenian Lane as a companion to her own daughters Anastasiya and Pelageya. Some time later romance blossomed between Pelageya and one of Sofya's brothers, Mikhail Muravyov, and in August 1818 they were married.[162] It was a common enough pattern in this society of extended noble families, where patriarchal virtues of hospitality and matriarchal efforts at match-making conspired to weave an intricate network of interlocking relationships.

In the summer of 1819 the family took the opportunity to make a now rare visit to Ovstug, aware no doubt that their son's academic plans would rule this out for the next year or so.[163] After their return Tyutchev submitted his formal application to Moscow University, and following an entrance examination was enrolled as a full student of the

Philological Faculty at the beginning of November, a couple of weeks short of his sixteenth birthday.[164] He began attending lectures in the newly opened magnificent university building on Mokhovaya Street, overlooking Manège Square in the shadow of the Kremlin. Designed by Domenico Gilliardi, it stood on the site of Kazakov's earlier building destroyed in the fire of 1812.[165] Although of later foundation than its counterpart in St Petersburg, Moscow University had long since overtaken its rival in size to become by far the largest institute of higher education in Russia, with 800 or so students divided between the four faculties: Philology; Moral and Political Studies; Physics and Mathematics; and Medicine.[166] In common with other students of the Philological Faculty Tyutchev was expected to attend lectures covering the core syllabus of Russian, Old Slavonic and Latin language and literature, and the history and theory of fine arts; there were also obligatory courses, provided by lecturers from other faculties, in ecclesiastical history, physics, and statistics as applied to the study of political economy.[167] The teaching staff were by and large of humble social origin: for a noble to become a professor was almost unheard of.[168] Salaries were far from generous, and only those professors with a steady second income from private tuition or running boarding schools managed to make a good living. These were the select few who (as one student of the time recalled) 'in their carriages pulled by teams of four and with liveried flunkeys on the footboards [...] appeared to us as important dignitaries'. By contrast, the academic rank and file, 'wearing frieze overcoats, went about on foot or took cheap cabs' and 'had the appearance of pariahs pursued by fate'.[169] Evidently little had changed in the sixty years since Sumarokov's wry observation:

> O dancer! You are rich. Professor! You are poor.
> Brains may command respect; but legs, it seems, much more.[170]

Not surprisingly, such 'pariahs' often found it difficult to maintain an air of authority before undergraduates who were in the main their social superiors. 'What on earth am I to do with you, gentlemen?' Nikifor Cherepanov, Professor of History, was once heard to ask his students. 'You are all wealthy and prominent people; you'll end up as generals, and then you'll come to me and say: "You're a fool, Cherepanov!"'.[171] Quite a few of these young aristocrats thought it beneath them to enrol as full students, attending lectures instead as 'voluntary auditors', which entitled them to take a lower examination for entry into government service.[172] One sensitive soul later claimed to have abandoned the idea of university altogether after his very first lecture, so shocked had he been by the 'unseemly behaviour and rudeness' of some of these unenrolled students before the Professor's arrival.[173] Another witness recalls student life at this time being 'free-and-easy', with only those guilty of gross drunkenness or brawling finding themselves hauled before the Rector.[174]

The absence of heavy-handed discipline encouraged young minds to develop a sense of critical awareness and pursue intellectual interests of their own (a state of affairs which would change radically after the accession of Nicholas I). Tyutchev certainly took advantage of this, reading widely and attending lectures not on the syllabus, for instance those on political economy and on natural and civil law given by Professor Christian Schlözer (son of the eminent historian August Ludwig Schlözer) in the Faculty of Moral and Political Studies.[175] University records for his first year show good attendance in compulsory subjects that interested him (Russian literature, the history of fine arts), but a marked falling-off in others such as physics and statistics as the year wore on.[176] The overall impression is of a gifted student who chafed at the restrictions of the official syllabus, preferring to follow his own bent and (as we shall see) relying heavily on last-minute cramming to pass exams.

The most influential and respected of Tyutchev's lecturers was undoubtedly Professor Merzlyakov, who as we have seen had for some time already counted the promising young poet among his protégés. 'Squat, broad-shouldered, with a fresh, open face, smoothed-down hair and a kindly smile, this son of cold Siberia was possessed of an ardent soul and a meek heart,' one of his students later wrote, pointing out that he was 'at heart a poet', having published translations of Virgil and other classical authors into 'beautiful, sonorous, forceful verse', as well as original works of his own including popular romances, some of which became widely known in musical settings.[177] Although schooled in the precepts of classicism, he was catholic in his tastes, and his lectures would embrace such varied topics as the medieval *Tale of Igor's Campaign* and Russian folk poetry.[178] He preferred on the whole to discuss individual works, rejecting any systematic theory of literature as an impediment to creativity. 'Here is your system,' he would tell his listeners, pointing to his heart.[179] According to another student, he would mount the lectern with a volume of poetry by Lomonosov, Derzhavin or some other writer, open it at random and launch into a brilliant extempore disquisition on the poem chanced upon. 'In the critic and professor could be discerned the poet by vocation,' recalls this witness. 'These improvisations would on occasion send his listeners into raptures, becoming etched in their memory. The whole audience would be electrified by some lucid thought or spark of feeling.'[180] On off days Merzlyakov could be less impressive: one student remembered him as 'sometimes magnificent', but 'often lazy' and immoderately partial to strong drink, which 'not infrequently [...] so tied his tongue and confused his thoughts that he was incapable of teaching'.[181] Tyutchev was clearly influenced, and on occasion even inspired, by his literary mentor's somewhat mercurial talent, but was by no means uncritical of him, complaining once to a fellow-student that he found Merzlyakov's approach too unsystematic, and that he ought instead to 'show us the history of Russian literature, [..] what influence each of our writers has had on its progress, how exactly each has fostered the improvement of the language, how one differs from the other, and so on'.[182]

Although none of Tyutchev's other lecturers could approach Merzlyakov in charisma, they were competent enough teachers who undoubtedly played some smaller part in his intellectual development. The hapless Cherepanov for instance apparently took pains to make his lectures interesting and relevant, incorporating into them material from Karamzin's recently published *History of the Russian State* and even taking his account of events as far as the war of 1812.[183] Schlözer was remembered as 'a very intelligent person, very learned and most affable'.[184] A complete contrast to Merzlyakov was Professor Mikhail Kachenovsky, who lectured in the Philological Faculty on the history and theory of fine arts. Arcane academic disputes alone had the power to excite this dry intellectual: whenever he touched on them in his lectures, 'his cheeks, habitually pale, would become flushed with a fiery scarlet and his eyes glint from behind his spectacles [...]. In his mind's eye he would see his learned opponents before him, and would strike them down with the shafts of his inexorable analysis.'[185]

By the end of his first year both Tyutchev and his parents evidently felt there was little to be gained from further study, for in June 1820 he and another student applied to be awarded a pass degree, asking for their previous years as 'voluntary auditors' to be taken into account. Although supported by the faculty board, their unusual request was turned down by the university's governing council, which agreed instead to grant them each a consolatory certificate of merit, to be awarded at the grand end-of-year ceremony on 6 July.[186] On that date students and staff gathered in the great hall of the university in the presence of various secular and ecclesiastical dignitaries, including the Governor-General of Moscow, together with wives and other invited guests. The students were smartly turned out in the dark-blue dress uniform with crimson collar, complete with ceremonial sword, worn only on such formal occasions.[187] There was singing by the choir, speeches in Russian and Latin, and the presentation of medals and certificates of merit to students. At one stage of the proceedings an ode composed by Tyutchev for the occasion was declaimed to the assembled gathering by a university orator.[188] A lengthy piece of just under 200 lines entitled 'Urania', with its obligatory neoclassical form and archaic poetic diction it is typical of the public ode as practised by Derzhavin, Merzlyakov (who probably commissioned it) and other poets of the period. Even so, there is an unmistakably romantic flavour to the opening lines:

> A new world! Can it be? O wondrous revelation!
> New strength, like flame, engulfs my fervent soul outright!
> Who grants to me, a youth, the eagle's soaring flight?
> They are the muses' gift, these wings of inspiration!
> The earthly vale surpassed, I hasten on my way —
>> Fled is that world so mired and rooted
>> In vain pursuits and pale excitements of the day —
>> And, bathing all as if with solar ray,
>> The ether from my lids polluted
>>> Sweeps earthly dust away...

In his state of exaltation the poet is transported over the 'boundless sea' to the island home of Urania, one of the nine muses. Taking his cue from Schiller's poem 'Die Künstler' ('The Artists'), Tyutchev portrays Urania as the ideal of heavenly truth, revealed to us in earthly terms as beauty. At one point he even paraphrases Schiller:

> What captured us once on earth as *illusion*,
> As *Truth* now before us stands plainly revealed![189]

There follows a roll-call of great poets of the past who were inspired by ideals of beauty and truth: Homer, Virgil, Tasso, Camoëns, Milton, Klopstock, Lomonosov (the 'Russian Pindar') and Derzhavin (significantly, no French poets are named). The ode concludes with the obligatory eulogy to Alexander I, the 'Hero-Tsar' and 'Tsar of hearts', whose foreign policy is lauded by way of an allusion to the ancient Roman practice of closing the gates to the temple of Janus only in peacetime:

Thy hand of all-compelling power
The gates of Janus has made tight!
Through *thee* peace reigneth at this hour;
Thou art our glory, our delight![190]

Within a few days of its public presentation 'Urania' was issued as an offprint by the Moscow University Press: a further 'triumph' for the young poet.[191]

Among those who gathered round to congratulate Tyutchev after the ceremony was one young man of thoughtful expression whose general demeanour and bearing set him apart from the students of aristocratic birth. Three years older than Tyutchev, and in the year above him at university, Mikhail Pogodin had been born a serf, but at the age of six he and his whole family had been granted their freedom as reward for their father's faithful service to his master as household steward.[192] Like other non-noble *raznochintsy* (literally, 'those of different rank'), Pogodin was obliged to supplement his meagre state scholarship grant with earnings from private tuition, and since 1819 had been employed as resident tutor to the children of Prince Ivan Trubetskoy.[193] Now in conversation with Tyutchev he mentioned that he would be accompanying the Trubetskoys for the summer to their estate at Znamenskoye, some ten miles to the south of Moscow. Tyutchev replied that he would be staying with his own family at Troitskoye, only five miles away, and insisted that Pogodin come to visit them. After further urging in letters from Tyutchev, on 9 August Pogodin left Znamenskoye to trudge the dusty road to Troitskoye on foot.[194] Years later the encounter with Tyutchev was still fresh in his memory: 'a slip of a boy, red-cheeked and dressed in a small green jacket, he was lying propped on one elbow on the sofa, reading a book'.[195] This turned out to be the novel *Agathodämon* by Wieland, prompting lively discussion of the German author's doubts as to the divinity of Jesus, in the course of which other writers (Lessing, Schiller, Addison, Pascal, Rousseau) were cited as witnesses for or against. The debate then widened out to include foreign literature and learning in general, and the 'obstacles to enlightenment in Russia' (perhaps a reference to the censorship regime). Pogodin was evidently impressed: 'Tyutchev is a fine young man', reads the comment in his diary for that day.[196]

Further visits by Pogodin to Troitskoye cemented their friendship, and with the start of the new academic year in September they began attending lectures together and meeting on a regular basis to exchange views. Pogodin's diary and Tyutchev's surviving letters to him from this period give some idea of the range of their reading and interests. Apart from the classics (Virgil, Horace, Lucretius) they studied more recent writers such as Pascal, Rousseau (his *Confessions* and *Julie, ou la Nouvelle Héloïse*) and Chateaubriand. Pride of place, however, went to German literature, then still a relatively new arrival on the European cultural scene; both were persuaded of its 'richness', 'universality' and 'superiority over French literature', seeing it as the model for a similar cultural renaissance in Russia.[197] The names of Goethe, Schiller, Herder, Wieland and Lessing appear frequently in their discussions; the great critic and theorist of romanticism August Wilhelm Schlegel and the historians August Schlözer and Johann Müller are also mentioned. In the writing of their own country they sought eagerly for the green shoots of an independent and national literary movement which might emulate that of Germany. The twelfth-century epic poem *The Tale of Igor's*

Campaign, rediscovered only in 1795, seemed evidence of a lost native tradition comparable in excellence to that of the *Nibelungenlied* or the *Chanson de Roland*; on one occasion Tyutchev even suggested that Pogodin translate this masterpiece of medieval literature into Latin, presumably to make it more accessible to western scholars.[198] Among contemporary writers it was Karamzin, Zhukovsky and — as we shall see — the up-and-coming Pushkin who claimed their particular attention.

Despite these shared intellectual interests they were in some ways an oddly assorted pair. Pogodin's struggle for self-improvement had made him not only single-minded in the desire to succeed, but often unrealistic in his ambitions (he dreamed for instance of winning a fortune on the lottery and founding a school on the proceeds).[199] Something of a rough diamond, forthright to a degree, he wore his faults and virtues alike openly on his sleeve.[200] Tyutchev by contrast was very much the urbane young aristocrat, assured of effortless success through his privileged background and influential contacts. As a fee-paying student he was in a better position to follow his own interests at the expense of the prescribed syllabus. For the poor scholarship boy Pogodin, obliged to work his way through university and prove himself over the academic hurdles, this was not so easy. This could leave him at a disadvantage in conversation with Tyutchev, causing him on at least one occasion to claim knowledge of books he had never read.[201] He was also put off by what he felt to be a certain air of intellectual arrogance surrounding his precocious young friend. Despite his 'rare, brilliant gifts', he confided to his diary, Tyutchev 'sometimes takes much upon himself and makes judgements which are unfounded and partial in the extreme'.[202] Even many years later the young Tyutchev's 'judgements from on high concerning Wieland and Schiller, Herder and Goethe, whom he gave the impression of receiving in his ante-chamber' still seemed to rankle with Pogodin. All this, he recalled, had nevertheless 'aroused a desire to compete with his erudition'.[203]

They differed subtly, too, in their general attitude and view of the world. The serious-minded Pogodin seems for instance to have baulked somewhat at Tyutchev's religious scepticism. He was clearly shocked by their conversation at Troitskoye on writers denying the divinity of Christ: 'I do not understand,' he commented in his diary afterwards, 'how such intelligent, learned people — people who desired the happiness of those similar to themselves — as Rousseau, Wieland, etc. could have decided to publish and disseminate their doubts on this score'.[204] Early in 1821 Tyutchev gently mocked his friend's observance of the customary religious rites during Lent: 'I grant you remission of all the sins you intend to tell the priest of at confession,' he wrote to him; 'do the same for me'.[205] In the same flippant vein is a little epigram written possibly at about the same time, the first line of which quotes a well-known Orthodox Lenten prayer:

> 'Help us forswear all empty chatter'!
> Henceforth, then, in conformity
> With our agreement in this matter,
> Expect to hear no prayers from me.[206]

This too (if he ever saw it) may have offended Pogodin's religious sensibilities. However, even he had to share his friend's amusement at the parish priest of St

Nicholas's use of numerology in one of his sermons to 'prove' that the names of Voltaire, d'Alembert and Diderot add up to 666.[207]

In politics Tyutchev and Pogodin seem at this formative age to have been broadly in tune with what most of their generation perceived to be the spirit of the times. Alexander I's espousal of enlightened liberal ideals earlier in his reign had encouraged expectations of constitutional reform, while the Napoleonic wars had provided an object lesson on the fragility and impermanence of apparently entrenched political systems. Many of the young officers who served in those campaigns had returned to Russia enthused by new ideas picked up in the West and intent on applying them at home. When the Emperor moved with his court to Moscow in the autumn of 1817 he was accompanied by the Imperial Guard, in which were to be found nearly all the members of the recently formed Union of Salvation. This small secret society of some twenty conspirators, dedicated to the abolition of autocracy, was the first manifestation of what later became known as the Decembrist movement. During the court's ten-month sojourn in Moscow the society reconstituted itself as the Union of Welfare, a still secret but much larger organisation of overtly humanitarian cast intended to recruit a wider range of sympathisers. The true aims of the society, and the radical measures envisaged to achieve them, were known only to the inner leadership, ordinary members being required to pass through various degrees of initiation on the masonic pattern.[208] Two of these leaders from the original Union of Salvation were Aleksandr and Mikhail Muravyov, and it was no doubt largely thanks to them that their father's Military Academy in Moscow became a particularly fertile recruiting ground, providing in all some twenty members.[209] On becoming tutor to the Muravyov family Raich too was persuaded to join, although in common with most of the rank-and-file recruits he appears to have been unaware of the organisation's hidden agenda.[210]

Tyutchev and Pogodin could not fail to be caught up in the general sense of excitement, and in conversation with each other hailed 'the free, noble spirit of thought which has appeared in our country in recent times'.[211] Pogodin writes of his employers the Trubetskoys discussing such questions as whether monarchs 'must be no more than executors of the popular will',[212] and one can imagine that the Tyutchevs' house in Armenian Lane witnessed similar debates, instigated perhaps by Nadezhda Sheremeteva or her son-in-law Mikhail Muravyov. From the evidence of his diary, Pogodin himself held fairly radical views at this time, on one occasion even expressing his admiration for that 'great happening' the French Revolution.[213] Yet on the whole he appears to have believed tyranny and social injustice would best be abolished by a revolution from above rather than below, and dreamt of a utopian future when a new Peter the Great would relinquish his throne and the landowners their serfs, ushering in a golden age of equality and justice.[214] From somewhat later evidence it is clear that Tyutchev fully shared his friend's opposition to serfdom, censorship and the abuse of power, although there is some room for doubt as to whether he would have been quite as thorough-going in his egalitarianism as Pogodin.

News of the Greek uprising against Turkish rule at the beginning of March 1821 was received with enthusiasm both by freedom-lovers and those (Tyutchev's father and the Graecophile Osterman-Tolstoy no doubt among them) who still cherished Catherine the Great's dream of liberating Greece from Ottoman rule and bringing it under the Russian imperial wing. Both groups were dismayed by Tsar Alexander's refusal, in strict adherence to the principles of the Holy Alliance, to support the freedom-fighters. Discussing all this on 16 March, Tyutchev and Pogodin hoped the insurgents led by Alexander Ypsilanti might still drive out the Turks unaided, and evidently shared the widespread feeling of discontent at Russia's policy of non-intervention. 'Commonplace monarchs in our age, commonplace ministers and military leaders — and such great events', is how Pogodin sums up the tenor of their debate that day.[215] The liberation of Greece and the Balkans was the necessary prerequisite for an even grander project first adumbrated by August Ludwig Schlözer, one of the German historians admired by Tyutchev and Pogodin, namely a political union embracing all the Slavs.[216] It seems Pogodin at least had already taken this idea to heart, for elsewhere in his diary he again indulges his fantasies of a new Peter the Great, capable of achieving in this instance 'the unification of all the Slav peoples into one whole, one state'.[217] And although Pogodin's laconic diary entries give no indication of what exactly was covered in his discussions of Schlözer with Tyutchev, it would seem quite possible that in the latter, too, the seeds of Panslavism were sown already at this early stage.

On 1 November 1820 Tyutchev and Pogodin discussed Pushkin's ode 'Liberty' as an example of the 'free, noble spirit of thought' they had detected at large in their country.[218] In May Pushkin had been exiled to the south of Russia for this and other poems distributed in manuscript, as well as for various outspoken public utterances against the government. The central message of 'Liberty' (a copy of which Tyutchev had made and passed on to Pogodin)[219] is that monarchs should respect the law and renounce the tyranny of arbitrary rule:

> Oh, kings, you owe your crown and writ
> To Law, not nature's dispensation;
> While you stand high above the nation,
> The changeless Law stands higher yet.[220]

There was nothing particularly exceptionable in this, nor in Pushkin's even-handed condemnation of both despotism and revolutionary lawlessness. The problem lay in his choice of examples: Louis XVI of France and Paul I, the father of the current Tsar. In 1801 a group of plotters had (almost certainly with Alexander's passive acquiescence if not collusion) strangled the increasingly despotic and arbitrary Paul in what was to prove the last of imperial Russia's palace revolutions. Although the facts of the case became widely known (prompting Madame de Staël's famous characterisation of Russia as 'a despotism mitigated by strangulation'), the official version insisted that Paul had died of a fit of apoplexy. Pushkin's vivid description of the assassination in his poem, and his condemnation of both Paul and his murderers, were clearly a provocation aimed directly at Alexander I. Tyutchev responded with a poem of his own entitled: 'To Pushkin's Ode on Liberty'. It begins by drawing a parallel between Pushkin and an earlier scourge of tyrants, the Greek poet Alcaeus:

> Aflame with freedom's sacred fire,
> To drown the dismal sound of chains

Alcaeus' shade has seized the lyre,
Now cleansed of slavery's vile stains.

Happy are those like Pushkin ('the muses' favoured son') to whom it has fallen to proclaim 'sacred truths' to 'unyielding tyrants' without respect to rank or throne. Yet Tyutchev concludes his poem on a cautionary note:

Sing praises fit for each occasion —
Let your sweet harmonies ignite
In despots hardened to persuasion
A love of beauty, truth and light!
But sing no song that stirs sedition,
Defames the crown or brings it harm —
To inspire in kings a disposition
To kindness be your poet's mission:
To foster goodwill, not alarm![221]

These lines show the young Tyutchev to be a supporter of enlightened absolutism. While fully endorsing Pushkin's ideals of freedom and the rule of law, he evidently believed these were best achieved through reasoned argument and persuasion, not the confrontational and provocative stance adopted by the older poet. Under the rules of the censorship Tyutchev's reference to a banned work meant that his poem in turn could not be published, and indeed it was not printed in full during his lifetime. For this reason alone there can be no suspicion that it was written to ingratiate himself with the authorities. On the contrary it appears, like the poem which had occasioned it, to have circulated in clandestine copies, one of which was obtained by Vladimir Gorchakov, a close friend of Pushkin in his southern exile. During a visit to Moscow early in 1821 Gorchakov often came to the house at 11 Armenian Lane to see Aleksey Sheremetev, an old friend from their days together at the Military Academy, and was introduced to Tyutchev, whose precocious talent — especially as revealed in his reply to Pushkin's 'Liberty' — impressed him greatly.[222] He took a copy of Tyutchev's poem back to Kishinyov, where he and Pushkin were then stationed, and almost certainly showed it to his friend.[223] Of Pushkin's reaction nothing is known for certain, although it has been suggested that a dismissive comment on young poets in general made later that year in conversation with Gorchakov and others ('the majority of them write verse only because their hands itch') may have been aimed at least in part at Tyutchev.[224] However, there is no evidence that Pushkin went on to harbour any sort of lasting grudge.[225]

Tyutchev for his part certainly seems to have welcomed Pushkin's early poetic achievements. On the same day that they discussed the ode 'Liberty' (1 November 1820), he and Pogodin talked about Pushkin's recently published folk-tale in verse, *Ruslan and Lyudmila*. With its informal narrative tone, colloquial language and witty digressions this work threw down a challenge to the neoclassical school and introduced full-blown romanticism into Russian literature for the first time. It found a ready echo among the younger generation, but more conservative critics were perplexed and outraged by its daring innovations. Merzlyakov for one had criticised the poem in his lectures; and complaints about 'our stupid professors' recorded by Pogodin in his conversation with Tyutchev that day may have been partly directed at him. If so, they are more likely to have come from Tyutchev, for Pogodin appears to have been initially reluctant to ignore the verdict of his revered mentor. 'I expressed my admiration for certain descriptions in Pushkin's *Ruslan and Lyudmila*,' he writes, but adds as an afterthought: 'in general, however, it contains such incongruities and absurdities that I don't understand how they could have occurred to him'.[226] (Later he would recall how he and his contemporaries 'began secretly to admire *Ruslan and Lyudmila*, despite ourselves and despite Merzlyakov'.)[227] Another harsh critic at the university was Professor Kachenovsky, who used his publication *Vestnik Yevropy* (*Herald of Europe*) to attack the poem. Pogodin and Tyutchev attended one of his lectures on the same day as their discussion of Pushkin,[228] and it may have been on this very occasion that — as later recalled by Pogodin — Tyutchev sat oblivious to Kachenovsky's words, engrossed in dashing off epigrams against him.[229] An incomplete version of one of these has survived among Pogodin's papers (significantly enough on a sheet also containing a partial copy of Pushkin's 'Liberty' in Tyutchev's hand):

Charon and Kachenovsky

Charon: You say you're from the living? By your looks —
So thin and dry — I'd say without equivocation
For some time your black soul had suffered hell's damnation.

Kachenovsky: I'm thin and dry, my friend, from reading books...
And then (what use prevarication?)
I've always been irate, vindictive, full of bile,
And all my life thin as a pencil...[230]

Kirill Pigaryov has suggested that this was a riposte to the Professor's attacks on *Ruslan and Lyudmila*.[231] If so, Tyutchev was following the example of Pushkin, who as a master of the brief epigram himself composed several lampooning Kachenovsky.[232] Indeed, much of Tyutchev's verse written in the early 1820s bears the imprint of Pushkin's poetic revolution. There is for instance a predilection for chatty, often humorous verse epistles addressed to close friends,[233] and in general a move away from the studied archaism of 'Urania' towards the more natural rhythms and vocabulary of contemporary speech. Later, in Germany, he would discover his own poetic voice; but at this period it is certainly no exaggeration to describe him as — in the words of one critic — 'seduced [...] by the genius of Pushkin'.[234]

Tyutchev had not lost touch with Raich after the latter's move to the Muravyov household in the autumn of 1819. His former tutor was now studying for a master's degree in the Philological Faculty, so there were opportunities to meet and attend lectures together.[235] Raich also very soon founded a literary circle to further his new charge Andrey's interest in the subject. This met every Thursday evening at the Muravyovs' house to read and discuss new works of Russian authors, together with original pieces and translations composed by the members themselves.[236] In the summer of 1822, soon after Tyutchev had left Russia, the group was formally constituted with a chairman (Raich), a secretary who kept minutes, an archive, and all the other trappings of a fully-fledged society; but in these early years its gatherings appear to have been held on a much more informal basis.[237] Memoirs by those who belonged to the group during the five years or so of its existence provide us with the names of some 20 individuals who are known at one time or another to have attended its meetings.[238] At first they seem to have been drawn largely from the university (Tyutchev, Pogodin, Mikhail Maksimovich, Raich himself) or from General Muravyov's Military Academy (Prince Valentin Shakhovskoy, who had graduated in the same year as Tyutchev's brother and then stayed on as an instructor,[239] and cadets such as Nikolay Putyata and Sergey Poltoratsky). After Tyutchev's departure for Germany there was an influx of new members who had recently graduated from the Moscow University Boarding School for Sons of the Nobility (*blagorodny pansion*), including Vladimir Odoyevsky, Stepan Shevyryov and Vladimir Titov. At school these young men had been introduced to German philosophy, including that of Schelling, by two of their teachers, Professors Mikhail Pavlov and Ivan Davydov.[240] By the time he left the school in the summer of 1822 Odoyevsky in particular was already a fervent disciple of Schelling;[241] and the following year, as well as joining Raich's circle, he and other like-minded youths calling themselves the 'Lovers of Wisdom' ('*lyubomudry*') began meeting separately to share their enthusiasm for the German philosopher.[242]

Tyutchev later came to know most of these 'Lovers of Wisdom', many of whom went on to achieve distinction in their chosen fields: Odoyevsky as a writer and thinker, the tragically short-lived Dmitry Venevitinov as a poet, Stepan Shevyryov as an academic and poet, and the brothers Ivan and Pyotr Kireyevsky as leading lights of the Slavophile movement. Given his own later interest in Schelling, it might be thought important to know if Tyutchev came into contact with any of these young men before his departure for Germany. He would not have encountered them at meetings of Raich's circle, for those who joined appear to have done so after he had left for Germany; nor has any evidence survived that he knew one or more of them in some other context. Even if he did, they were all younger than himself (aged between thirteen and seventeen at the time he left Moscow for St Petersburg to join the Foreign Service), and with the possible exception of Odoyevsky are unlikely as yet to have commanded any great authority on the subject of philosophy.[243] Whether he came to know anything of Schelling's teachings independently of them at this time is another matter. At university he attended lectures on Latin language and literature given by the same Professor Ivan Davydov who is said to have been instrumental in awakening Odoyevsky's interest in German philosophy.[244] While these will have afforded little opportunity for discussion of Schelling, there were no doubt meetings in other, less formal settings (gatherings of the Society of Lovers of Russian Literature, for instance, of which Davydov was an active member). Clear evidence that Tyutchev took note of what the Professor had to say on philosophical matters comes in a letter to Pogodin of June 1821 requesting the loan of two of Davydov's publications: a speech on Greek and Roman philosophy, and (as far as can be judged from the incomplete title) either his manual on the history of philosophy or an elementary introduction to logic.[245] Yet there is no specific reference to Schelling. In the final analysis it is Tyutchev's letters to Pogodin, and the latter's diary records of their conversations, which provide us with the most persuasive evidence on this question. If Tyutchev had been seriously interested in Schelling at this time, one would expect the philosopher's name to crop up somewhere among the host of writers and thinkers discussed by him with Pogodin; but there is nothing (nor, indeed, any reference to other German idealist philosophers such as Kant or Fichte).[246] Tyutchev may well have heard of Schelling before leaving Russia; he may even have had some vague idea of what he stood for; but it seems to have been in Germany that he finally came to grips with his teachings.

The diaries and letters also give an insight into Tyutchev's second year at university. As the end-of-year examinations approached in the summer of 1821, he began to ply Pogodin (who was preparing for his finals) with requests for helpful textbooks, model answers and the like, referring to himself in one letter as the 'constant suppliant' and Pogodin as his 'benefactor'.[247] Pogodin later recalled with some amusement priming his friend ('who would soon already be thinking about Canning and Metternich') with pass notes on ancient history extracted from the standard university textbook.[248] Such last-minute cramming was necessary after a year in which Tyutchev had, to put it mildly, rested on his laurels, missing more than one in three of Kachenovsky's lectures on the history and theory of fine arts and even one in five of Merzlyakov's on Russian literature (in his report Merzlyakov cites 'illnessses' as the reason, although no other evidence can be found for these).[249]

In the event all seems to have gone well. By now Tyutchev's sights were in any case set beyond the confines of student life. For some time his parents had felt — no doubt with Osterman-Tolstoy's encouragement — that he would do well in the Foreign Service, and were eager for him to start as soon as possible.[250] Already in May 1821 he had once more requested permission to take his finals early, on this occasion by-passing the university authorities altogether by sending his application direct to Prince Andrey Obolensky, Director of Education for the Moscow district.[251] Obolensky appears to have known the Osterman-Tolstoys, and as an honorary member of the Society of Lovers of Russian Literature[252] was probably acquainted with Tyutchev too. Lacking the authority to rule on the application himself, Obolensky forwarded it to the Minister of Religious Affairs and Education in St Petersburg, Prince Aleksandr Nikolayevich Golitsyn.[253] He knew of course that Golitsyn, a lifelong friend and confidant of Alexander I, was one of the most powerful figures at court.[254] That Obolensky should have promptly submitted such an unusual request to his distinguished superior, together with a recommendation that it be given favourable consideration, strongly suggests he knew it already enjoyed influential support in high places. Such support can only have come from Osterman-Tolstoy. He was certainly well placed to provide it, for his sister Natalya was married to the Minister's brother Mikhail Golitsyn, and he himself was close to their sons Aleksandr, Valerian and Leonid (his and the Minister's nephews), who for a time even came to live in his St Petersburg house.[255] What is more, Osterman-Tolstoy's wife Yelizaveta Alekseyevna was herself a Golitsyn by birth, albeit apparently more distantly related to the Minister.[256] All of which suggests that Golitsyn allowed himself to be swayed by Osterman-Tolstoy, who like him enjoyed a position of influence at court, and to whom he was bound by ties of family loyalty. How else, indeed, are we to explain Obolensky's visit to Osterman-Tolstoy's wife in Moscow at the beginning of August to report unofficially that the matter was in the bag, with formal confirmation to follow shortly from St Petersburg?[257] The document in question, signed by Golitsyn on 20 August, gave exceptional permission for Tyutchev to take his final examinations a year early in consideration of his previous academic achievements and time as a 'voluntary auditor'. It was also made clear that Tyutchev's case was to be considered unique, and that in future no further permission of this kind would be granted.[258]

Tyutchev could now approach his finals with equanimity. Certainly this time round there appear to have been no appeals for help to Pogodin (who would have been in a good position to provide it, having graduated himself that summer).[259] It was after all scarcely conceivable that any of the all-powerful Minister's underlings would dare to fail his favoured protégé. On the appointed date — 8 October — Tyutchev presented himself to a panel of six professors chaired by Merzlyakov for the viva voce examination then in current practice. Each of the professors posed questions relating to his own specialism, to which, according to the written report, the examinee replied 'very thoroughly, lucidly and satisfactorily'. We can be sure that his easy eloquence enabled him to put on an impressive performance. The panel voted unanimously to recommend Tyutchev for the 'kandidat' degree (equivalent to honours), which would qualify him to enter government service at grade twelve in the Table of Ranks.[260]

vii Diplomatic Manoeuvres

The road was now open for a career in the Foreign Service, a prospect which Tyutchev himself seems to have regarded with indifference. If we are to believe Aksakov, 'the ambitious plans of his father and mother were of scant concern to the happy-go-lucky graduate. Leaving it to his elders to decide his future fate, he devoted himself entirely to living for the present'.[261] There may have been an element of passivity and even helplessness in this, a feeling that he could achieve little by his own unaided efforts. After confirmation of his degree by Obolensky on 23 November (his eighteenth birthday) and receipt of his diploma the following month, it was time to travel to St Petersburg to apply for admission to the Foreign Service. On or about 1 February 1822 he left Moscow, accompanied by his father and his former dyad'ka Khlopov, now promoted to manservant. Arriving in St Petersburg on the 5th, they were put up for the duration of their stay by the ever hospitable Osterman-Tolstoy in his sumptuous mansion overlooking the river Neva on the English Embankment (now No. 10). From here it was but a short stroll to the Foreign Ministry at No. 32, where already on 21 February Tyutchev was admitted to the Foreign Service with the civil rank of Provincial Secretary (equivalent to an army Lieutenant), but as yet without any specific posting.[262]

With Osterman-Tolstoy working behind the scenes to procure a suitable post for him, he made the most of his first visit to the northern capital. His brother Nikolay had arrived home in Moscow at the beginning of January on three months' leave from his duties on the General Staff,[263] and probably rejoined him in St Petersburg only later; even so, there was no shortage of companions from his own age-group to help him find his feet in the city. Lacking children of his own, Osterman-Tolstoy liked to surround himself with young people he thought of as nephews and nieces, however distantly related in fact. At this time he had living in his house, apart from Tyutchev, the latter's cousin Dmitry Zavalishin, and the brothers Aleksandr, Leonid and Valerian Golitsyn whose uncle the Minister had recently proved so accommodating.[264] Tyutchev will probably have remembered Zavalishin, who was slightly younger than himself, from his cousin's childhood visits to Moscow;[265] now he had grown into a gifted and highly principled if somewhat vain young man, who two years previously — aged only sixteen — had been appointed instructor in mathematics and astronomy at the St Petersburg Naval Academy after graduating there with flying colours. Later in 1822 he would set off on a two-year circumnavigation of the globe as naval officer attached to a scientific expedition.[266]

Osterman-Tolstoy encouraged his 'nephews' to make free use of the various theatre boxes and stalls to which he subscribed,[267] and was no doubt able to provide them with an entrée into other society gatherings. Tyutchev was of course particularly drawn to the literary life of the capital. He is known for instance to have made the acquaintance at this time of Yakov Tolstoy, a guards officer, minor poet and friend of Pushkin.[268] There were also meetings with the writer Aleksandr Kornilovich, whom he may have known already from Moscow (Kornilovich had passed out from Muravyov's Military Academy in 1816, a year before Nikolay Tyutchev and Aleksey Sheremetev, and had stayed on in Moscow until 1820, taking some part in the literary life of the city).[269] Tyutchev showed Kornilovich a verse translation he had completed in Moscow of Lamartine's poem 'L'Isolement', and was encouraged by him to revise this for presentation to the St Petersburg Free Society of Lovers of Russian Literature, of which Kornilovich was a member. On 20 March Kornilovich read it out at a meeting of the society attended by such well-known poets from Pushkin's circle as Aleksandr Bestuzhev, Fyodor Glinka (cousin of the composer), Kondraty Ryleyev and Anton Delvig (Tyutchev was not present). The members voted by twelve to one to publish the translation in the society's journal.[270] (By a coincidence the earlier version had been presented to the Moscow Society of Lovers of Russian Literature just two days previously; this too was subsequently printed in that society's *Proceedings*.)[271]

No further evidence has survived of Tyutchev's contacts during the three and a half months he spent in St Petersburg. Yet if we take the young men he is known to have associated with there (Zavalishin, the Golitsyn brothers, Yakov Tolstoy, Kornilovich) as a representative sample of the many more he must have met, an interesting picture emerges. Most notably, all with the exception of Leonid Golitsyn (who at nineteen was probably too young) would subsequently be implicated in the Decembrist revolt of 1825. At this stage, however — idealistic and deeply concerned for the future of their country as they undoubtedly were — most had not even joined a secret society, let alone been initiated into the inner leadership's conspiratorial plans for a coup d'état. So far their activities were limited to discussing such matters as the pros and cons of a constitutional monarchy or republic, and whether the use of force was justified in order to achieve them. Zavalishin informs us that heated debates of this kind took place in the house of Osterman-Tolstoy, who would sit in on them himself, encouraging his young relatives to speak freely on 'affairs of state and politics'.[272] In Tyutchev's case little encouragement will have been required.

Some evenings as a distraction from such weighty matters these young men would no doubt all pile into a horse-drawn sleigh and glide through icebound streets, past the overpoweringly elegant facades of palaces, mansions and ministries, to arrive at their patron's box in a packed, overheated theatre and sit through some French play, a

Russian comedy by Fonvizin or perhaps the ballet. Then it would be on to a ball or soirée, in avid search not of social kudos, but of news, ideas, argument, intellectual sustenance. It was a time of high seriousness, when instead of handing in swords as required before dancing, young guards officers would enter the ballroom still wearing them in a show of disdain for such empty pursuits.[273] One — the poet and future Decembrist Fyodor Glinka — would even arrive mentally prepared with a list of topics to tick off as he made the ballroom his public tribune, excoriating in turn administrative corruption and incompetence, serfdom, Arakcheyev's military colonies, and other abuses.[274]

Tyutchev's associates in St Petersburg seem to have been cast in much the same mould. Zavalishin for instance thought of himself as 'serious' and decried the 'constant card games and emptiness of society life'.[275] Yakov Tolstoy's earnest approach to life even found itself the butt of Pushkin's gentle humour:

> Rare-ripe philosopher, you shun
> All joys of life, all celebration:
> The games of youth have always won
> Your cold and silent condemnation.
>
> You flee all social merry-making
> For dull ennui and mood depressed,
> For Epictetus' lamp forsaking
> The golden goblet Horace blessed.[276]

While yielding to none of his companions in the seriousness and depth of his intellectual interests, Tyutchev did differ from Zavalishin, Tolstoy and others in his attitude towards the *beau monde*. Unlike them, he would throughout his life find himself inexorably drawn to ballroom, banqueting hall or salon: partly, it is true, by their superficial glitter and glamour, but even more by the prospect of mingling with the great and the good, in the hope perhaps of influencing their views or at least receiving from them some titbit of inside information on matters political or diplomatic. The presence of beautiful women was a further undoubted attraction. Drawing on what he had evidently been told by 'those who knew him at the time', Aksakov informs us that on leaving university, Tyutchev — already 'a fervent devotee of feminine beauty' — threw himself into the social whirl and 'enjoyed success'.[277] While claiming that throughout his life Tyutchev remained essentially untouched by the vanities and pretensions of high society,[278] Aksakov was forced to admit that his subject's hankering for the bright lights might be at least in part attributable to a massive imbalance between intellect and will. Endowed with a 'powerful and resolute mind' that was 'constantly hungry, inquisitive, serious, intent on elucidating all questions of history, philosophy and knowledge in general', he was nevertheless according to Aksakov cursed with 'pusillanimity', 'weakness of will verging on the pathological' and 'a soul with an insatiable craving for pleasure, excitement and entertainment, passionately devoted to the impressions of the current day'.[279]

What can be inferred of the romantic attachments hinted at by Aksakov? He is predictably vague on this score, merely quoting his informants to the effect that in

Tyutchev's conduct at this time there had been 'nothing resembling riotousness and debauchery', and commenting from his own, much later, personal knowledge of his subject that 'riotousness and debauchery were not in his nature: for him only those pleasures were of value which afforded scope for heartfelt emotion or passionate poetic love'.[280] Given what Aksakov knew (but declined to reveal) of Tyutchev's later amatory exploits, we might feel justified in regarding his claim with a certain degree of scepticism. Yet it is only fair to point out that it receives unexpected support from a memoirist otherwise critical of Aksakov's reticence in such matters (and certainly more forthcoming in his own treatment of the subject). Writing in 1903, Tyutchev's son Fyodor (himself the result of an extramarital liaison) insisted that, for all his affairs, his father had never been 'what we would call a libertine, Don Juan or Lovelace [...]. To his relationships with women he brought such a wealth of poetry, such a refined delicacy of feeling, such gentleness, that [...] he was more like a pagan priest worshipping his idol than someone who takes pleasure in the act of possession'.[281]

Whatever may be made of all this, as far as any teenage romances are concerned we can only resort to speculation. Subject as he surely was to the usual stirrings of adolescent love, Tyutchev will have had no problems in finding an object for his affections, if only among the many young females, including cousins and more distant relatives, constantly visiting or staying in his parents' Moscow house. Crushes of this kind, usually innocent and short-lasting, were of course not uncommon in such close-knit extended families. We know that Tyutchev's sister Darya and his cousin Aleksey Sheremetev formed an attachment while Aleksey was living in the house (in their case this deepened with the years into a mutual love so strong that they eventually resolved on marriage, only to find their hopes dashed by the combined opposition of Church and parents to a union between cousins).[282] Towards the end of his teens Tyutchev too would certainly have been capable of falling seriously in love (even the delicate Aksakov concedes that by then he had developed 'a heart susceptible to passionate, reckless infatuations').[283] All that is certain is that any such blossoming romance would have been cut short by his departure for St Petersburg not long after his eighteenth birthday, and for Munich a few months after that.[284]

By May Osterman-Tolstoy had managed to obtain a suitable posting for his young relative: on the thirteenth of that month came official confirmation from the Foreign Ministry of Tyutchev's appointment as a supernumerary junior Attaché at the Russian Embassy in Munich.[285] A trainee post carrying no pay, it was the traditional entry route into the service for young men of independent means, offering excellent prospects for anyone with the ability and will to succeed. There would be no financial problems for Tyutchev, whose parents had already agreed to pay him an annual allowance. Even the travel arrangements had been taken care of, for Osterman-Tolstoy would himself soon be leaving for western Europe and was prepared to offer Tyutchev a place in his carriage as far as Munich. For all his admiration of Alexander I, the Count had been alienated by the government's ever more conservative policies. An ardent Philhellene, he had some years previously surrounded himself with Greeks and even learnt their language in the confident hope of being appointed Commander-in-Chief of a Russian expeditionary force to aid their fellow-countrymen in the struggle against Turkish rule. Alexander's abandonment of the Greek insurgents to their fate in 1821 and dismissal the following year of Count Kapodistrias, a Greek patriot from Corfu who since 1815 had shared the functions of Russian Foreign Minister with the pro-Metternich Karl von Nesselrode, provoked widespread dismay that Russia's historic ambitions in the so-called 'Eastern question' should have been sacrificed so readily to the principles of the Holy Alliance.[286] Disgruntled, Osterman-Tolstoy decided to turn his back on his country for a while. In fact he would spend most of the remaining 35 years of his life in self-imposed exile, returning to his native land only for short infrequent visits (the death of his revered patron Alexander and accession of Nicholas I in 1825 appears to have been the final deciding factor).[287]

It may have been with Osterman-Tolstoy that Tyutchev returned to Moscow at the end of May, for the Count also needed to go there before heading west (possibly in order to collect his wife).[288] These last three weeks at home in Armenian Lane must have been a time of mixed emotions for Tyutchev. Of course, he looked forward with eager anticipation to immersing himself in the world of European civilisation and absorbing its intellectual atmosphere at first hand. Yet as the prospect drew closer he was no doubt also troubled by a sense of powerlessness, an awareness that his destiny was being shaped by others. Soon, whether he wanted or not, he would be torn away from family and friends, uprooted from the comfortable and familiar world of Moscow in which he had grown up. 'It's an odd thing, the fate of a human being,' he mused in a letter to his parents years later. 'Mine had to make use of Osterman-Tolstoy's remaining arm to fling me so far from you.'[289] As the critic Richard Gregg has observed, 'this juxtaposition of fate, amputation and forceful removal from one's family in a single sentence has a psychological significance that goes beyond the exigencies of wit'.[290] And to underline the point Gregg quotes several other passages from Tyutchev's letters in which separation, whether in space or time, is likened to an amputation.[291]

A related image of separation and bereavement frequently found in Tyutchev's poetry is that of the orphan. Again Gregg cites many examples, pointing out that it makes its first and perhaps most striking appearance in Tyutchev's translation of Lamartine's 'L'Isolement', completed apparently at about the time he was being pointed in the direction of a career in the Foreign Service.[292] Striking, because Lamartine himself nowhere uses the image, whereas Tyutchev introduces it into his version no less than three times.[293] 'L'Isolement' expresses feelings of loneliness and alienation from the world evoked by the absence of a loved-one (whether through separation or death is not made clear): the poet feels there is nothing left for him in this 'land of exile' and longs to join the dead leaves he sees being borne away by autumnal gales. As would so often be the case, Tyutchev seems to have chosen a poem to translate not just on artistic merit but because its content reflected current feelings and concerns of his own. Indeed, the only other translation he is known to have made at this time, of 'Hektors Abschied' ('Hector's Farewell') by Schiller (itself a version of the Greek hero's leavetaking from his wife and infant son as described in Book 6 of *The Iliad*), is on a similar theme.[294]

On 27 May Tyutchev attended a routine meeting of the Society of Lovers of Russian Literature. One or more of those present will no doubt have pointed out to him (if he had not been aware of it already) a contribution by one of the Society's members, the Moscow University assistant lecturer Ivan Snegiryov, to that month's edition of the St Petersburg journal *Otechestvennye zapiski* (*Notes of the Fatherland*). In his article, a survey of works presented at the Society's meeting in Moscow on 18 March, Snegiryov describes Tyutchev's Lamartine translation as 'very good verses [...] by Mr Tyutchev, a promising young poet'.[295] It was a pleasing enough first review to speed him on his way to Germany.

Also present at the meeting on 27 May was Pogodin; although in a hurry to join the Trubetskoys at Znamenskoye, he lingered afterwards for a chat with Tyutchev about literary developments in Moscow and St Petersburg. 'He is going to the Munich Embassy as Attaché,' Pogodin noted in his diary. 'A marvellous posting.' Before they parted, Tyutchev assured his friend he would keep in touch by post (a promise he appears not to have kept).[296] Two weeks later he was already on his way to Germany in Osterman-Tolstoy's carriage.

2 A Golden Time
(Munich, 1822-1825)

i Years of Apprenticeship

The first section of Tyutchev's journey west as far as Smolensk traced the route of Napoleon's advance on and retreat from Moscow in 1812. Osterman-Tolstoy had played a leading role in those events, both in Kutuzov's councils of war and as a commander leading his men into the thick of battle. Now his first-hand accounts of the campaign no doubt helped to while away the hours in the jolting carriage. Day after day they travelled over the monotonous, seemingly unending plain, via Brest-Litovsk and Warsaw (since 1815 the kingdom of Poland had been part of the Russian Empire), with overnight stops in post-houses and inns so vermin-ridden that the prudent traveller took his own camp bed with him. At last they crossed the frontier into Prussia and then into Austria, and there was a tangible sense of drawing closer to that civilisation to which most educated Russians then aspired. Even the landscape changed, the severe northern plain giving way to the rolling foothills of the Carpathians.

A few years later the Marquis de Custine recorded his own impressions on entering Prussia after four months spent in Russia: 'I hear the language of freedom, and feel as if in a vortex of pleasure, a world carried away by new ideas towards inordinate liberty. And yet I am only in Prussia [...] I see a lively country freely cultivated [...] and the change warms and gladdens my heart.' He was struck by the contrast in practically every aspect of life: 'Good roads throughout the distance, good inns, beds on which one may lie, the order of houses managed by women [...] the varied architecture of the buildings, the air of freedom in the peasants, and the gaiety of the female sex among them.'[1]

As a Frenchman Custine may be thought to be biased; yet elsewhere he quotes the observations of a Lübeck innkeeper on the many Russians passing through that port on their way to and from the West: 'When they arrive in Europe they have a gay, easy, contented air, like horses set free, or birds let loose from their cages [...]. The same persons when they return have long faces and gloomy looks; their words are few and abrupt; their countenances full of care.'[2] In Tyutchev's own later poems and letters references to returning to Russia with a heavy heart and expressions of nostalgia for the West run as a constant countertheme to his proclaimed patriotism. It seems unlikely that this first encounter with western Europe will have been anything other than a liberating experience for him.

Years later Tyutchev recalled arriving in Germany that summer 'to the sounds of *Der Freischütz*.'[3] After its premiere in Berlin the previous year, Weber's opera had gone on to take the German-speaking world by storm. In the spring of 1822 Heinrich Heine wrote from Berlin of its continuing phenomenal success there, with tickets hard to obtain even after some thirty performances, a picture repeated in Vienna, Dresden and Hamburg. He also reported being 'hounded from early morning until late at night' by 'always the same melody, the song of all songs,' namely the bridesmaids' chorus from Act III, 'Wir winden dir den Jungfernkranz'. Children trilled it outside his window on their way to school, his landlady's daughter sang it in the house, organ-grinders and fiddlers churned it out in the street, carousing students took up the refrain by night, until it seemed to Heine that even the dogs were barking it out.[4]

Apart from a brief transit through Prussian Silesia, Tyutchev's first real encounter with what was then thought of as Germany would have been in the city of Vienna.[5] (At a time when Germany was little more than a conglomeration of independent states with a common language it was still quite natural for German-speaking Austria to be considered part of it.)[6] Here *Der Freischütz* had received its first performance in February of that year to the same popular acclaim as elsewhere.[7] It can be imagined that the musical Viennese took up its melodies with no less gusto than the Berliners, and that on his arrival Tyutchev experienced something similar to the melodic assault humorously described by Heine. So he found himself at once immersed in the tide of German Romanticism: not in this case the inward and intense poetic vision of a Novalis or Hölderlin, but a more popular manifestation deriving its inspiration from the culture and traditions of the *Volk*. It was a heady experience which thanks to the evocative power of music he would never forget.

From Vienna it is likely that they took the favoured route to Munich via Salzburg, which had the best roads and most picturesque views.[8] Tyutchev will have been impressed by his first sight of the Alps, which feature in several poems inspired by later visits.[9] At last, a month after leaving Moscow, they glimpsed the spires and towers of Munich rising from the plain. With something over 60,000 inhabitants at that time the Bavarian capital was about a quarter of the size of Moscow,[10] and no doubt this disparity will have struck Tyutchev as it did another Russian visitor, Pyotr Kireyevsky, seven years later. To give his parents some idea of its size, Kireyevsky describes Munich in a letter to them as being hardly more extensive than Myasnitskaya Street (near where both they and Tyutchev's parents lived.)[11] It is, he continues, 'quite attractive, and would be beautiful if it did not lie on a vast plain, which is completely flat and covered for the most part with marshes and half-withered bushes. The streets here are not so narrow and smoke-blackened as in other German cities; the buildings are mostly new and handsomely constructed; there is much greenery [...].' While impressed by the Gothic cathedrals, he complains that there are only two or three in the whole city, and misses the plethora of domes and belltowers so typical of Moscow and other old Russian cities.[12]

'Mr Fyodor Tyutchev, the new Attaché assigned to my Mission, has just arrived. Notwithstanding the small amount of work this official will have to do during the initial stages of his stay here, I shall endeavour to ensure that he does not waste his time, which is so precious for one of his age.'[13] Thus the Russian Ambassador in Munich, Count Ivan Illarionovich Vorontsov-Dashkov, reported Tyutchev's arrival to the Foreign Ministry in St Petersburg. In a despatch written nearly three years later he was to sum up Tyutchev's contribution to the work of the Embassy over that period as being of no great significance.[14] The young Attaché's *Lehrjahre*, or years of apprenticeship (the phrase is that of his friend Karl Pfeffel),[15] seem to have involved nothing more demanding than copying documents or writing to dictation. Many of these papers survive, executed in a neat copperplate far removed from the scrawl of his later years. Although his duties were fairly light, from the evidence of dated documents in his hand he does appear to have stayed in Munich for most of the time in the first year or so,[16] working at acquiring the varied social accomplishments required of a diplomat. The staff of the Embassy, situated then on the first floor of No. 12 Herzog-spitalgasse,[17] was relatively small: in February 1823 the list of full-time officials consisted of the Ambassador, First Secretary Mikhail Tormasov and Second Secretary Alexander von Krüdener, with Tyutchev and Count Henryk Rzewuski listed as super-numerary Attachés.[18] Henryk came from a family of 'several attractive and brilliantly clever brothers and sisters', children of the Polish Count Adam Rzewuski.[19] Henryk's sister Karolina Sobanska was the object of one of Pushkin's more serious infatuations; another sister, Ewa Hanska, later married Balzac.[20] Although Tyutchev and Rzewuski would serve together as Attachés in Munich for several years,[21] our only evidence for their relations at this time comes from Tyutchev's report of a chance meeting with him in Warsaw many years later. 'Henri' Rzewuski, he wrote, 'seemed delighted to see me, and at once recalled to me all my former impressions of him'.[22]

Wedged between Prussia and Austria, Bavaria had been viewed by Russia as a vital piece on the European chessboard at least since 1779, when Catherine the Great offered it Russia's protection against Austrian expansion.[23] In the post-Napoleonic era it was fear of revolution, rather than of Prussian or Austrian hegemony, which tended to determine Russian policy towards the German states. As far as Bavaria was concerned, that policy was defined by Foreign Minister Nesselrode in a directive of 1833 to his Ambassador in Munich as being to maintain and support Russia's alliance with Austria and Prussia, which in Nesselrode's words represented 'the sole guarantee of public order' in Europe.[24] In practice this involved monitoring, and if necessary applying diplomatic pressure to ensure, Bavaria's adherence to anti-revolutionary measures orchestrated by the Austrian Foreign Minister von Metternich and implemented through the framework of the German Confederation. In particular a rigorous system of censorship was applied to nip all critical thought in the bud. Metternich's aims were supported by Tsar Alexander I, who had abandoned earlier liberal dreams of reform, by his successor Nicholas I, and by Nicholas's brother-in-law King Friedrich Wilhelm III of Prussia. Yet despite dynastic links binding Bavaria to Russia (the wives of King Maximilian I and of Tsar Alexander I were sisters), at the time of Tyutchev's arrival in Munich Maximilian was managing to tread a moderately independent path. In 1818, in common with other South German rulers, he had granted his kingdom a limited constitution, including a consultative assembly. His ministers were fairly lax in implementing Metternich's repressive policies, and in general there was a greater sense of freedom than in Austria or Prussia.

Maximilian's son Ludwig was a patron of the arts, and after his accession in 1825 he made it his ambition to transform Munich into the 'Athens of the North'. Yet even in his reign the Bavarian capital never really acquired the same cultural significance as, say, Dresden or Weimar, not to mention the cosmopolitan allure of Paris, Berlin or Vienna. Ivan Gagarin, who joined the Russian Embassy as Attaché in 1833 and went on to serve in both Paris and Vienna, later dismissed Munich as 'not one of those major centres which act as a focus for outstanding individuals and first-rate intellects.'[25] Heine too complained of the atmosphere of 'petty-mindedness' ('*Kleingeisterei*') prevailing during his fairly brief stay there, when he found himself the target of conservative and clerical attacks.[26]

On the positive side, Munich society offered the young Tyutchev scope for elegant conversation in the company of urbane men and beautiful women. It was, as he indicated to his friend Pogodin on his first leave back in Moscow, a small and self-enclosed world comprised largely of courtiers.[27] Apart from the King and Queen themselves, the heir apparent Crown Prince Ludwig and other members of the royal family also held court, surrounded by the prominent aristocratic families von Giech, von Yrsch, d'Arco-Valley, von Cetto, von Zweibrücken and others, who in their turn, together with the diplomatic corps, ensured a continuous social round. The winter season began on 12 October, a date initiated by King Maximilian in double celebration of his own name-day and the wedding anniversary of Crown Prince Ludwig and Princess Therese (and still marked today by the Munich Oktoberfest).[28] Celebrations continued through New Year and the Carnival season, ending on Ash Wednesday. In the summer, accompanied by much of the diplomatic corps and fashionable Munich society, the court would remove to Tegernsee, a lakeside resort in the foothills of the Alps where in 1817 King Maximilian had acquired a former Benedictine abbey as the royal family's summer residence.

Tyutchev seems to have adapted readily to his new environment. Ivan Gagarin (who admittedly observed him in action only a decade later) recalled that he was by then 'completely at home' in this world of courtiers, diplomats and aristocrats, that he was valued by them for his 'brilliant witticisms' and considered 'original, witty, amusing.'[29] Even after three years in Munich the apparent change in Tyutchev was enough for his old friend Pogodin to note with evident distaste: 'he smells of the court.'[30] Yet it was a purely external adaptation: inwardly he remained unseduced by courtly values. 'It is difficult to imagine a courtier with less of the courtier about him than Tyutchev,' wrote Ivan Aksakov, who knew him much later in Russia. According to Aksakov, he valued his position as a key affording entry to gatherings of the great and powerful and allowing him to indulge his consuming interest as an observer of and commentator on the political scene.[31]

While thus engaged in polishing his social skills, he no doubt found the general intellectual level of conversation left much to be desired compared with the debates of his university friends in Moscow. Typical is is the exchange in a Munich salon between Tyutchev and an unnamed society beauty recalled by Gagarin: ' "I am reading a history of Russia." "Madam, you surprise me." "It is the history of Catherine II..." "That surprises me less." "...by Madame d'Abrantès." "That surprises me not at all." '[32] (Laure d'Abrantès's book on the reign of Catherine II, published in 1834, achieved its great popularity more as a compendium of entertaining gossip than for any historical accuracy.)

According to Karl Pfeffel, who first met him in 1830, Tyutchev found his intellectual equals in Munich only in two much older men: the philosopher Friedrich Schelling and the statesman Count Maximilian de Montgelas.[33] (Had Pfeffel known Tyutchev earlier, he would surely have added the name of Heine.) Tyutchev first got to know Schelling after the philosopher was appointed to a professorship at the new

Munich University in 1827, but it is likely that he knew Montgelas much earlier. Maximilian von Lerchenfeld records various meetings with both Montgelas and Tyutchev in his diary for 1823 (of which more below), and although they are never mentioned together, it would be strange if their paths had not crossed already then in the small world of Munich society. Montgelas (1759-1838) had presided over the fortunes of Bavaria as First Minister of the Elector, later King, Maximilian from 1799 to 1817. A supporter of enlightened absolutism, he had introduced liberal reforms during the period of Napoleon's supremacy. Under his administration Bavaria became a kingdom and almost doubled its territorial size. Although in 1813 he took Bavaria out of its alliance with France and into the anti-Napoleonic coalition, his continuing pro-French sympathies led to his dismissal from office in 1817. Aleksandr Turgenev testified to Montgelas's 'unusual erudition and memory' after a meeting with the retired statesman in 1834, when their conversation ranged over English, French and German writers and historians. 'There can be few authoritative writers of history who know their subject as well as this minister,' wrote Turgenev.[34] Tyutchev too must have sought conversation with this man over forty years his senior as a welcome oasis amidst the arid chit-chat of Munich salons.

We do not know where Tyutchev lived during these early years in Munich. As an unpaid Attaché he had to make do on an allowance of 6,000 roubles a year from his father,[35] and his finances probably stretched to no more than a couple of modest upper-storey rooms not too far from the Embassy. Returning home from his duties or from some grand ball or soirée, he would be greeted by the homely Russian discourse of his manservant Khlopov who, the poet's first biographer tells us, 'remained faithful to all Russian customs, and made for himself in Tyutchev's German apartment a cosy little Russian corner with icons and icon-lamps... He took on the young diplomat's housekeeping and cooked his meals for him, treating him, and on occasion foreign friends of his, to Russian dishes.'[36] He also diligently reported back to his master and mistress in Moscow on the activities of their son, who tended to be somewhat slapdash about writing. (Unfortunately, neither Khlopov's letters nor any from Tyutchev to his parents from this period have survived). All in all Khlopov took care of the material aspects of living for his notoriously unpractical young master.[37] Evidently their relationship was more one of mutual friendship and respect than that of master and servant. Khlopov later bequeathed an icon to his young charge, with the inscription: 'In memory of my sincere love and concern for my friend Fyodor Ivanovich Tyutchev;'[38] while nearly fifty years on Tyutchev could still write of his tender feelings for his old dyad'ka.[39]

Although no letters of Tyutchev's as such have survived from his first year or so in Munich, a couple of epistles in verse show that he kept in contact with at least some of his Moscow friends. The first, written in the same light conversational style affected by Pushkin in his epistles and not intended for publication, was addressed in January 1823 to his cousin Aleksey Sheremetev. After some years in the Horse Guards in St Petersburg, Sheremetev had been appointed Adjutant to Count Pyotr Tolstoy in Moscow, a posting which he appears to have found less than exciting after the life of an officer in the northern capital. Commiserating, Tyutchev advises him to find diversion in looking for a suitable bride (preferably the heiress to some large estate):

> You'll find with ease among the crowd
> Of Moscow's fair enchantresses
> Some beauty aged fifteen who is
> With mind and soul (and souls) endowed.[40]

He also stayed in touch with Raich, who by now had transformed his literary circle into a formal society with plans for its own publications. These were first realised at the beginning of 1823 with the almanach *Novye Aonidy* (*New Æonides*), a selection of what was claimed to be the best of the previous year's published work, including (among reprints of poetry and prose by such established writers as Pushkin, Vyazemsky and Zhukovsky) Tyutchev's translation of Lamartine's 'L'Isolement'.[41] Then in the spring of 1823 a proposal was mooted for the society's own regular journal, serious discussion of which continued throughout the year.[42] Almost immediately Raich appears to have invited his former pupil in Munich to become in effect a corresponding member and submit material for the projected periodical. Over the next couple of years Tyutchev provided several poems and translations which (although the journal itself never materialised) Raich was eventually to publish together with other accumulated works of his literary circle in the almanach *Severnaya lira* (*The Northern Lyre*) in 1827.[43] One of the earliest of these was a translation of Schiller's 'An die Freude' ('Ode to Joy') dated February 1823.[44] With it Tyutchev enclosed a missive in verse, 'To my Friends, on Sending Schiller's "Ode to Joy" ', in which he ponders on the irony of presenting those absent friends (Raich and his young collaborators) with this particular translation:

> How can I voice such gladsome phrases,
> So far from those for whom I care,
> With none to feel for my despair —
> How can this muted lyre now sing Joy's praises?[45]

The reference to the poet's 'muted lyre' is perhaps somewhat misleading. It may be that the sudden transplantation to Munich did affect Tyutchev's poetic output for a while; yet as far as we can tell from the surviving poems, he produced no less in his first three years there than he had in the three years before leaving Russia. Over both periods he managed on average about a line of original verse a week, matched by an equivalent amount of translation. And notwithstanding the occasional hint of riches to come, both the quantity and quality of his output remained little more than that of a talented young amateur.

Heine's collection of verse *Tragödien nebst einem lyrischen Intermezzo* (*Tragedies Together With a Lyrical Intermezzo*), which appeared in April 1823, appears to have made a particular impression on him, for he translated two love poems from it.[46] In one, 'Ein Fichtenbaum steht einsam...' ('A spruce tree stands secluded...'), the said tree dreams in its snowy northern wastes of a solitary young palm tree on a sunbaked rock face in some distant eastern land. When Tyutchev sent the poem to Raich (it was among those published in *Severnaya lira*), he added the title 'From Foreign Parts', absent in the original. He often translated poems with which he felt some personal affinity; here the theme of loneliness and separation had clearly struck a chord.

Two visits by Russians in 1823 helped to relieve any sense of isolation he may have felt. In March the former diplomat Prince Pyotr Kozlovsky arrived in Munich, and Tyutchev appears to have come to know him quite well during his stay.[47] Kozlovsky had been Russian Ambassador to the courts of Sardinia, Baden and Württemberg, but his outspoken liberal views and open republican sympathies had put him increasingly out of step with official policy during the second half of Alexander's reign. The measure of the man is given by an incident towards the end of his life. Approaching the now ailing Kozlovsky one day at a ball, the Emperor Nicholas I told him he need not stand up. 'I could not even if I wanted to, your Majesty,' came the reply. 'There are sixty million hands holding me back.'[48] In 1820 his advocacy of parliamentary democracy and support for Italian insurgents against Austrian rule had led to his dismissal from government service. He spent the following thirteen years travelling Europe in a private capacity, frequenting literary and political salons and gaining the friendship of many influential figures. The Marquis de Custine met Kozlovsky on his way to Russia in 1839 and recorded his conversation at some length.[49] The Prince's erudite and astute analysis of matters historical and political, as evidenced by Custine's account, would in itself have fascinated Tyutchev whether he agreed with it or not. Throughout his life he relished debating such topics, especially if it meant sparring with someone his intellectual equal who held opposing views (Chaadayev, for instance). Yet in this case there may have been little disagreement.

A letter written to Kozlovsky nearly two years after their meeting recalls the Prince's visit to Munich as being 'the Golden Age of my stay in this city,' and declares: 'it is enough for me that you should know that there is somewhere in this world a being devoted to you heart and soul, a *faithful follower* who loves you and serves you, *in spirit and in truth*, and who as recompense for all his trials and tribulations does not even have any reasonable hope of seeing his much-loved master again.'[50] In the same letter Tyutchev writes: 'There are indeed very few people in whose feelings one could have such faith as to believe after a separation of two years, and in spite of all the changes necessarily wrought by time, that one stands with them in the same degree of affection as on parting from them [...] It is the faith owed to God alone, and to those fine spirits who are (with all due respect to the doctrine of divine right) His sole acknowledged representatives on our poor earth.'[51] Although we should be wary of reading too much into the extended religious imagery of master and disciple (the only point of the letter seems to have been to recall the writer to Kozlovsky's attention, and much of it is clearly an attempt to impress through wit and irony), there is behind all the stylistic pirouetting an unmistakable hint that Tyutchev seriously shared his 'master's' liberal views at this time.

Firmer evidence of this comes from the second Russian visitor to Munich in 1823. At the end of August Dmitry Sverbeyev, an acquaintance from university days in Moscow, arrived on his way to a diplomatic posting in Switzerland. The two friends spent three or four days visiting museums and theatres together before going on to Tyutchev's rooms for late-night convivial conversation.[52] Sverbeyev was an outspoken critic of autocracy. Asked once at a gathering of St Petersburg dignitaries how many classes there were in Russia, he replied without hesitation, 'Two: despots and slaves.'[53] One evening at Tyutchev's he rather predictably crossed swords with a member of the Bavarian state assembly of staunchly conservative and Catholic convictions. As

Sverbeyev later recalled, he was fully supported in this by his host: 'My and Tyutchev's religious views and political beliefs infuriated him, while the political belief that the whole people, and not just its educated portion, has the right to participate in government seemed to this feudal-Catholic baron tantamount to the doctrines of the French terror; he argued against us in favour of serfdom.'[54]

From this it would seem undeniable that at the time Tyutchev professed what could be loosely termed 'western' liberal views. However, some qualifications need to be made. For a start, it is worth bearing in mind the generally observed tendency (noted for instance by Russia-watchers as far apart in time, background and outlook as the Marquis de Custine and George Orwell) for western political concepts to take on a life of their own when transplanted to Russian soil. Consequently 'liberalism' in a Russian context may often denote something only superficially resembling its western counterpart. We should also remember Tyutchev's age at the time. It is not unusual for a young man of nineteen or twenty to voice the ideals espoused by most of his peers, nor for both him and them later to modify their views in the light of experience. Tyutchev in particular, who had in him more than something of the 'chameleon poet', seems to have engaged at this stage of his life in trying out and discarding different ideas and attitudes almost as a kind of intellectual game. Ivan Gagarin, who knew him some ten years later, vividly likened him to a prism refracting all the colours of the rainbow, rather than an independent source of light; according to Gagarin, at that time Tyutchev was 'inclined to think that all opinions contain the truth, and that any opinion could be defended by sufficiently convincing arguments'.[55] Finally it is important to note that the two great issues which were to divide Tyutchev's generation still lay in the future. The first addressed the question of how their shared ideals of constitutional government, freedom of speech, abolition of serfdom and so forth could best be achieved. Was a violent overthrow of the existing order required, as the Decembrists believed, or could one still hope for reform from above, as promised by the earlier part of Alexander's reign? The second question arose much later, and asked in effect whether the desired new political, legal and social framework should be modelled on tried and tested western institutions, or developed in accordance with Russia's quite different historical experience and traditions. How Tyutchev responded to these issues will become apparent in due course.

ii Amélie

Among those invited to sample Khlopov's *borshch*, *kulebyaka* or *bliny* may have been the young Count Maximilian von Lerchenfeld. Four years older than Tyutchev, the Bavarian aristocrat was, like his Russian counterpart, a university graduate training in Munich for a diplomatic career.[56] The two probably met not long after Tyutchev's arrival in Bavaria. Maximilian came from a family of diplomats, which over an unbroken span of five generations would continue to serve Bavaria and then Germany with great distinction. His father had died not long before his tenth birthday, leaving him the only child of the widowed Countess Maria Anna. Soon afterwards he came to know of a half-sister, the result of his father's liaison with Princess (*Fürstin*) Therese von Thurn und Taxis in Regensburg, some five or six miles from the Lerchenfelds' country seat at Köfering. Therese is known to have given birth to five illegitimate children,[57] although it is not at all clear whether all were fathered by the Count. According to the version of events handed down in the Lerchenfeld family, as Maximilian's father lay dying he asked his wife to look after his illegitimate daughter Amalie, then just over a year old and in the care of foster-parents. Whether from a sense of Christian duty, or out of respect for her dying husband's wishes, or to provide her only child with a companion, the Countess magnanimously agreed to raise Amalie as her foster-daughter. First registered as Amalie Stargard, on 1 August 1823 she was granted the title von Sternfeld by the Grand Duchy of Hessen.[58] This was no doubt through the good offices of Princess Therese, who continued to take an interest in her unacknowledged daughter's fate from a distance. Through her mother Amalie was connected to royalty, being *de facto* niece to Queen Louise, consort of the King of Prussia, and cousin to Alexandra Fyodorovna, wife of the future Russian Emperor Nicholas I.[59]

Tyutchev would have met Amalie (or Amélie, as she was usually known) through Maximilian. He later recalled that she was fourteen at the time.[60] As Amélie is known to have been born in the spring of 1808 (the exact date has never been established),[61] it seems most likely that she and the Countess Maria spent the winter season 1822/1823 in Munich and that Tyutchev was introduced to them both then, at some time before Amélie's fifteenth birthday.

As his unpublished diaries and letters from this period show,[62] Max (as he preferred to be called) moved easily in Munich society circles, which included members of the diplomatic corps. He seems to have enjoyed a particularly close relationship with the Russian Embassy staff. Diary entries for the period 1822-1824 make it clear that he cultivated the acquaintanceship of Vorontsov-Dashkov, visiting and dining with him regularly at times when the Ambassador was in Munich. In the summer of 1823 visits by Tormasov, von Krüdener and Tyutchev to the von Lerchenfelds' estate at Köfering are recorded in Max's diary. Krüdener appears to have been the most frequent visitor, staying there on three occasions between June and August. Max also records his own visit to Tegernsee from 27 to 29 June. The royal family and court had evidently already arrived for the summer; Vorontsov-Dashkov too had just taken up residence. Max notes that he met the Ambassador there and (on 29 June) went for a walk with Krüdener followed by a boat trip on the lake.[63] Before this, on 10 June, Max had organised a day trip from Munich to Starnberg and its lake, this time taking Amélie along too. From Starnberg they all headed for Possenhofen, a village on the western shore of the lake: 'Drive to Possenhofen, arrival of the others, good; jolly dinner; rain, a pity; trip back by water.'[64] One wonders if 'the others' may have included any of his friends from the Russian Embassy, perhaps even Tyutchev himself.

During one of Max's stays at Köfering that summer his diary records for the evening of Saturday 12 July: 'Arrival of Tyutchev, great joy, good news.' Max and Krüdener, who had been at Köfering since 4 July, were clearly pleased to see the young Attaché. As the diary tells us, it had been a very hot day, and after an eleven-hour journey by post-chaise from Munich Tyutchev too was no doubt glad to reach the Lerchenfelds' stately country home with its cool moat and spacious gardens, and to enjoy the convivial company of friends. The following day Max showed the young diplomat round the estate and surrounding area: 'Morning, working and about with Tyutchev, good; afternoon, walk to Egglfing, good; evening talking, good.' (Typical of

Max's laconic diary notes is a tendency to grade his experiences, usually on a three-point scale of good, middling or bad: '*gut*', '*so*', '*schl[echt]*'). Apart from conversation, in which Tyutchev would have participated with enthusiasm, activities mentioned over the next few days are gaming with dice ('bad and boring' on one occasion, 'heated' on another); hunting ('not good'); a visit to the von Cettos' estate at nearby Eglofsheim; and, in the evenings, singing ('good').[65] Perhaps there were also the games of skittles mentioned elsewhere in the diaries; if so, Max forgot to record them here. Amélie would certainly have taken a leading part in the singing. Ten years later in St Petersburg the poet Vyazemsky (who found her 'a very attractive and sweet young wench, quite unpretentious, and completely German in nature') heard her perform 'German romances with Tyrolean yodelling, so that you almost expected her to go round curtseying to the audience afterwards with a collection plate'.[66] And even when nearly seventy she could still captivate the audience of a charity concert with her voice.[67]

Max's tantalisingly elliptical diary jottings can of course tell us nothing of the atmosphere of those days at Köfering, not to mention the emotional response of those involved. Somewhat more revealing in this respect is a charming letter sent by Max to Amélie some three years later, by which time she was married and living in Munich. The letter, dated 8 June 1826 and written in English (which Max hopes 'shall encourage you to be very diligent in your lessons,' while for his part 'I need practice just as much') includes a description of summer days at Köfering:

> If only you could be at Koef[ering] at this moment, all is so fine, so green, the days are so very long! The parties of ninepins could now last till nine a clock! What a delightfull thing that would be, to play three hours every day! — But there is no play, no song this year! Amélie the soul of all is not here! (Please read these last two lines as verse!) And really that is very true, there is no play and no song! The Piano is shut for all the time! Poor Mama is beginning to weap as often as she tries to open it, and I had all pains to persuade her to play thrice a weak with the skoolmaster and I did not sing a single time. There is no pleasure to bark quite alone.[68]

Now a more focused picture presents itself: *Hausmusik* on a summer evening in an elegant drawing room of the castle; the young Count and his slenderly-built half-sister are singing a duet, with the old Countess at the piano; among the guests, a short, plump-faced youth with rosy cheeks listens intently, moved perhaps by the music, perhaps by feelings of his own, his eyes never straying from the young girl's delicate face; sitting next to him is an older man, taller and more solidly built; he too seems preoccupied with the girl...

The following Friday, 18 July, Tyutchev returned to Munich with Max and Krüdener. The day before Max had noted in his diary the preparations for their departure, adding: 'little one almost sad.' Had Tyutchev's attentions found some response with Amélie (to whom this surely refers)?[69] Back in Munich three days later Max noted: 'Tyutchev major *confidence*, very good [...]'. Max uses the French word '*confidence*', for which there is no neat German equivalent, in the sense that Tyutchev had confided something important to him. Whether this concerned his growing feelings for Amélie must remain a subject for conjecture. What is fairly certain is that his visit to Köfering had affected him deeply in some way, for apparently on the same day that he unburdened himself to Max (21 July) he wrote the poem 'Tears', arguably his first original (though still immature) attempt at the Romantic lyric form. It culminates in a pæan to weeping as emotional release ('sacred spring of tears,/ Divine Aurora's morning dew'), after first celebrating the sensual delights of nature and (in verse three) of feminine beauty (possibly a stylised vignette of Amélie herself):

> I love it when the vernal breezes
> Flush a young maiden's face and seek
> To ruffle through her silken tresses
> Or kiss the dimples on her cheek.[70]

It must have been later that year that Tyutchev and Amélie first declared their love for each other. Our evidence is a poem of 1830, apparently written as a reminiscence of their youthful romance:

> That day remains in memory
> The dawning of life's day to me:
> She stood unspeaking, like the swelling
> Of waves her bosom rising, falling;
> Her cheeks, flushed with Aurora's light,
> Now kindling fast and burning bright —
> Till, like the youthful sun ascendant,
> A golden pledge of love, resplendent,
> Burst from her lips... and I beheld
> A whole new undiscovered world![71]

Kirill Pigaryov suggested that this poem refers to an adolescent attachment in Russia before Tyutchev's departure for Germany in 1822, and that the immediate inspiration was a meeting with the girl in question (now a woman) in the summer or autumn of 1830 in St Petersburg, where Tyutchev was staying on leave.[72] Although by its very nature Pigaryov's hypothesis can never be definitely disproved, there is nothing to back it up in what is known of Tyutchev's social contacts in St Petersburg that year. Indeed, the poem appears to have been written not in St Petersburg at all, but either during the overland journey back or (more likely) soon after Tyutchev's arrival in Munich at the end of October (NS).[73] It may well have been inspired by meeting Amélie again after an absence of five months. She was after all, as Tyutchev later acknowledged, his first serious love. Writing to his parents after meeting her in 1840, he commented: 'You know the affection I feel for [her] and may easily imagine the pleasure I had in seeing her again. *She is, after Russia, my most long-standing love.*'[74] And it is of course to the intensity and transforming power of first love that the varied images of dawn and sunrise in the poem refer. The same imagery is also found in a poem written at the time of his romance with Amélie, where he describes her burgeoning feelings for him as the 'golden dawn' of love.'[75] 'That day remains in memory...' may belong to the category of poems written (as Ronald Lane has shown)[76] to mark anniversaries of memorable dates in Tyutchev's life. If so, it would be possible to date the beginning of the courtship tentatively to the late autumn of 1823.

The young lovers' attachment cannot have gone unnoticed for long. Years later the story was still told in Tyutchev's family of how he and Amélie had exchanged watches as tokens of their love; apparently this was reported to the poet's mother in one of his letters by Khlopov, who complained angrily that in return for his watch with a gold chain his master had received only one with a plain silk band.[77]

Max's diary for the rest of 1823 gives no real insight into how the relationship developed. An entry towards the end of the year implies that Amélie was attending the Max-Josef-Stift (also known as the Royal Institute) in Munich. This boarding school for girls had strict rules allowing pupils to leave the premises during term time only in exceptional circumstances,[78] which would have made meetings difficult. The entry in question, for Sunday 30 November, reads in full: 'Morning some work then church and with Amélie Institute Tutu [*indecipherable*] oh what a pity evening at home then Cetto not bad.'[79] (As he got to know Tyutchev better, Max often used the nicknames 'Tutu' and 'Tuterle', as we shall see from his letters.) The missing punctuation of the original, reproduced here in translation, makes it difficult to interpret what is meant. Do the indicipherable word or abbreviation (appearing to consist of a single 's') and Max's expression of regret refer to Amélie and Tyutchev, or just Tyutchev, or do they perhaps form a completely separate item of information? All we can say is that the two names are linked here in a context now beyond our reach, while pointing to indirect evidence quoted below that Max was perhaps not too unsympathetic towards their courtship.

As summer returned, Amélie and her foster-mother would have spent more time at Köfering, joined by Max when he could get away. Unfortunately his diary for 1824 has entries only up to 6 April, and these contain no references to Tyutchev. We can be fairly sure, however, that Amélie's presence at the Lerchenfelds' country estate will have drawn the young enamoured poet there whenever his duties permitted. One such visit, apparently in May 1824, is testified by a poem written nearly a decade later. In it Tyutchev recalls a trip he and Amélie had made to the romantic ruins of Donaustauf Castle, a medieval fortress overlooking the Danube.[80] A prominent feature of the landscape around Regensburg, it is situated a mile or so beyond the present eastern outskirts of that city, and some five or six miles to the north of Köfering. Serious damage from the Thirty Years' War was never repaired, and much later the ruin passed into the possession of the von Thurn und Taxis family.[81] At the time in question Amélie's mother and her husband the Prince were thus master and mistress of Donaustauf.

In the poem Tyutchev recalls, caught as in a snapshot, one idyllic moment of their visit, which is given added poignancy by the narrator's implicit awareness of subsequent events. Amélie (the 'fairy princess' of line 7) gazes without a care into the distance, and by implication into the future (for throughout the poem the distinction between images of space and time is deliberately blurred),[82] blissfully unaware of the gathering shadows of 'fleeting life' (line 24).

> A golden time still haunts my senses,
> A promised land from long ago:
> We two, alone as shadows lengthened;
> The Danube, murmuring below.

And on that hill where, palely gleaming,
A castle watches over all,
You stood, a fairy princess, leaning
Against a moss-grown granite wall —

With girlish foot so lightly touching
Those ruins of times past — to view
The sun's long, lingering valediction
From hill, from castle, and from you.

A gentle breeze in passing ruffled
Your clothing and caressed your hair,
And from wild apple branches sprinkled
White blossoms on your shoulders fair.

Carefree, you gazed into the distance...
Last rays flashed through the glowing red;
The river sang with added brilliance
From shrouded banks as daylight fled.

And still you watched with joy unclouded
Till all that blissful day be gone,
While overhead the cool dark shadow
Of fleeting life sped gently on.[83]

It is not difficult to locate the spot where Amélie and Tyutchev must have stood, behind a low wall bounding what was once the outer bailey of the castle and over-looking a steep slope which falls away sharply to the village below. From here extensive views open out, with the broad Danube dominating the immediate foreground, while beyond that to the south a flat plain stretches into the distance. The whole castle mound, including the fortress itself, is heavily wooded; yet there is today no sign of Tyutchev's wild apple trees. Were they never anything more than poetic convention? Were they perhaps displaced by more vigorous species over the years? Or (and this would seem the most likely explanation, given the other accurate details in the poem) is Tyutchev's description, some ten years after the event, correct apart from his naming of the actual variety of tree? In this case it seems he could have had in mind the false-acacias which still grow in profusion on the site, and which every May shed their fragrant white blossom.

As the poem recalls, dark shadows were about to fall upon the idyllic scene. Amélie had now turned sixteen and was of marriageable age. A strikingly beautiful girl of aristocratic upbringing and with royal connections, she would not want for suitors. As for the final choice of husband, that decision would rest, certainly not with Amélie herself, nor with her foster-mother or Max, but with Princess Therese von Thurn und Taxis, who in this matter at least still seems to have felt entitled to exercise her rights as mother. Apart from the fact that he and Amélie were in love, Tyutchev had little to offer in the marriage stakes. Still not even legally of age, with no means and uncertain prospects, unambitious and generally unpractical in his attitude to life, he must have seemed out of the running to more hard-headed observers.

A serious rival made his play soon enough. Throughout the summer of 1824 Alexander von Krüdener stayed at Köfering, pressing his suit with Amélie. On 21 September Max wrote to his mother from Munich that society circles there were awash with malicious gossip about these goings-on: 'the relationship of Krüdener and Amélie occupies me greatly and, I cannot deny it, causes me much worry. You have no idea, dear Mother, of all the things people are saying here: everyone is asking me when the wedding is, and the like [...]; those of a hostile disposition express shock at Krüdener's protracted stay, while the sympathetically inclined say at best how sorry they are for Amélie, since all are united in their opinion of his character.' Quite apart from this Krüdener was in trouble at the Embassy for his protracted absence from duty. 'Let him damn well stay where he wants,' Vorontsov-Dashkov had fumed, 'we don't need him any more.' Tormasov too was resentful of the heavy workload caused by his junior's absence. Max then discloses to his mother that his informant at the Embassy was Tyutchev: 'Tutu told me most of this, and says he wrote to you in such terms that if you were to read the letter out, Krüdener must immediately realise that the others desired him to return.'

No doubt alerted as a result of Max's letter and that of Tyutchev (which has not survived) to the scandalised gossip in high society and the displeasure of his superiors, Krüdener was back in Munich by 24 September. That evening Max had a man-to-man talk with him about his intentions towards Amélie. By now her compromised reputation could probably be saved only by a proposal of marriage (which may well of course have been part of Krüdener's calculation). The following day (25 September) Max reported to his mother that he was satisfied with Krüdener's response, adding: 'nor do I now doubt for an instant that I shall manage to set it all right and be able to vouchsafe you a really happy future, if only you and Amélie are prepared to follow my advice for the time being'. Max goes on to say that he advised Krüdener to accept Vorontsov-Dashkov's rebuke calmly and without protest, in which case he is sure there will be no further trouble for him at the Embassy. All in all, he concludes, 'I [...] shall be so happy when everything ends well; all I want indeed is your and Amélie's happiness!'[84]

The fact that marriage negotiations were not concluded until four months later may have had more to do with Amélie's reluctance than with any obstacles put up by Princess Therese. At thirty-eight Krüdener was old enough to be his prospective fiancée's father; and although society at that time may have considered this un-exceptional or even desirable, Amélie seems to have had views of her own on the subject (as hinted at in one of Max's letters, quoted below). In fact the memoirs of Grand Duchess Olga Nikolayevna, who came to know Amélie well at the Russian court some years later, state quite unequivocally that she was married to Krüdener without her consent.[85] As for Tyutchev, it is not too difficult to imagine his initial anger and disappointment, tempered perhaps by a hope that love would somehow find a way. A poem written some two months after these events tells us much about his state of mind:

To N.

Your dear gaze, innocently charged with passion —
The golden dawn of feelings heaven-sent —
Could not, alas, persuade them to relent...
But shames them with its silent admonition.

Those false hearts in which truth can find no place
Flee, O my friend, as if from condemnation
That childlike gaze of love: an evocation
Of childhood past they cannot bear to face.

But I see only heaven's benefaction
In your sweet gaze; a well-spring pure and still,
It lives within my soul and ever will,
Sustaining me with visions of perfection...

So too above: the realm where spirits dwell
Is radiant with their astral luminescence;
Below, in sin's dark night, that same pure essence
Of fire consumes all like the flames of hell.[86]

The view of Georgy Chulkov and later critics that this was addressed to Amélie seems indisputable, given the date of composition.[87] Gennady Chagin has suggested on the basis of the poem that at the end of 1824 Tyutchev himself decided formally to request Amélie's hand in marriage, and that although she was willing, her relatives turned him down in favour of Krüdener.[88] Although there is no other direct evidence for this, it does seem a credible interpretation of the poem. The strength of the young girl's love is not enough to win over her hard-hearted elders, the deeper psychological motivation for whose opposition is laid bare in verse 2. And the poet's own involvement, hinted at by his 'alas' in line 3, becomes clear enough in verse 3. On its first publication in Russia the poem had the date '23 November 1824' printed beneath it, which lends further support to Chagin's supposition. This was after all Tyutchev's twenty-first birthday, when he came of age and would have been able to make a proposal in his own right.[89] Whether he did in fact or not, what is fairly clear from the poem is that Amélie was still resisting the plan to marry her off to Krüdener, on the not unreasonable grounds that she loved not him, but Tyutchev. Yet such considerations cut no ice with Princess Therese and her circle. In their eyes this still immature, somewhat irresponsible young Russian with neither means nor position to his name was — though doubtless charming, and certainly clever — simply not a suitable match for Amélie compared with the solid, mature Baltic-German Baron, whose prospects for advancement seemed by contrast tangible enough.

Just before Christmas 1824 Max left to take up his first diplomatic post as Attaché at the Bavarian Embassy in Paris, and from there wrote frequently (now in French) to his mother. A few letters to Amélie have also survived. These reveal Max's genuine affection and concern for *'la belle Amélie'* as he calls her in one letter (12 January

1825), with their references to gifts of gloves, shoes and hats to be sent from Paris, and advice on such matters as writing letters, improving her French, attending balls during the Carnival season, and even the need for a healthy regime of long walks, washing in cold water and taking a glass of beer before retiring. It is as if he felt the need to supply the paternal role missing in her life. 'I suppose, dear Amélie, you don't take too kindly to all these sermons worthy of an old Papa?' he actually jokes after one of his disquisitions (4 April 1825).

Negotiations for the marriage went ahead in his absence, between Max's mother and Krüdener on the one hand, and Princess Therese on the other. A further complication was that members of the Russian diplomatic service had to obtain the Emperor's permission to marry. Alexander I would almost certainly have taken a particular interest in this application from a kinsman, however distant, of his recently deceased former spiritual adviser Juliane Krüdener — even more so as the proposal was for marriage to a cousin of Grand Duchess Alexandra Fyodorovna (born Princess Charlotte of Prussia), the wife of his brother Nicholas.

On 2 February Max tells his mother he has been worrying about the possibility of bad news from St Petersburg, while a letter written two days later suggests that he hoped Princess Therese might be able to use her influence with her royal relations if necessary. At about this time, however, the marriage arrangements appear to have been finally agreed, for on 12 February Max writes:

I have just received, dear Mother, your letter No. 10 with the account of your successful negotiations with the Pr[incess]; what perfect news you give me! I am absolutely pleased and delighted! So the fate of our dear little girl [*notre bonne petite*] is decided, all our wishes are granted! Ah, how I should like to be near you to share in your happiness, and to see the joy of a certain Baron; how all this will add to his impatience!

Am[élie] will never be able to thank you enough for all that you have done for her! That last interview must have been terrible for you, and I am sure that if Am[élie] knew it, she would indeed acknowledge the full extent of your devotion.

Do we detect in these last words perhaps a hint at Amélie's less than wholehearted enthusiasm? After suggesting the following autumn as a suitable time for the wedding, and assuring his mother that he will be in Köfering for the happy event, Max continues:

I cannot tell you what pleasure this news gives me, and I cannot understand the calmness which runs through your whole letter! It really seems as if the second business you tell me of, that concerning Tuterle, has made your blood run so cold with fright that it has prevented you from expressing your joy at the first. What antics you all get up to in your dear old Munich, always these tragic affairs![90]

For enlightenment as to the 'second business' concerning 'Tuterle' we must turn to an unlikely source: an icon later commissioned by Khlopov as a bequest to his young master, and now preserved in the Tyutchev Museum at Muranovo. It depicts the Virgin and Child, surrounded at each corner by images of saints whose days in the Orthodox calendar correspond to memorable dates in Tyutchev's life in Munich. Glued to the back are notes in Khlopov's hand explaining the significance of these dates. One reads: '19 January 1825, Fyodor Ivanovich must remember what happened in Munich as a result of his impropriety, and what danger there was.' Another directly below it states: '20 January, that is on the very next day, it ended well.' According to Kirill Pigaryov, oral tradition in the family related these inscriptions to a duel in which Tyutchev was nearly embroiled because of his love for Amélie.[91]

It is undoubtedly the scandal surrounding this incident to which Max refers. Bearing in mind that all the dates in Khlopov's notes follow the Orthodox church calendar, Tyutchev was presumably challenged to a duel on 31 January NS. Unfortunately Max's letter throws no further light on the nature of the 'impropriety,' or more literally 'immodesty' (*'neskromnost'*), on Tyutchev's part which according to Khlopov sparked the duel. The fact that Max's mother reported the incident at the same time as the engagement of Amélie and Krüdener suggests that the two events are not unconnected. Perhaps it was Tyutchev's continuing attentions to Amélie which provoked the challenge; perhaps, irascible as he could be, he was goaded into making an insulting remark to Krüdener or one of the other parties involved. Nor is it clear whether the challenge came from Krüdener himself or someone else (one of Princess Therese's sons, for instance). Whatever the circumstances, some form of conciliation the following day almost certainly saved Tyutchev (who as far as we know never handled a gun in his life) from sharing the fate of Pushkin and Lermontov. Unlike them, of course, he would have died before achieving anything of real poetic note.

On 13 February, less than two weeks after the closely averted duel, Vorontsov-Dashkov officially requested four months' leave for Tyutchev on the grounds that 'personal affairs' required his return to Russia.[92] This was granted, but Tyutchev took advantage of it only at the beginning of June, when he left Munich for Russia.[93] Although the record states that he reported back on time, he was actually away for over eight months, returning in February 1826.[94] No doubt Vorontsov-Dashkov had in the circumstances considered it best for Krüdener's young rival to take protracted leave and was then quite prepared to turn a blind eye to his failure to return on time.

'Say goodbye to dear Tuterle for me,' Max wrote to his mother on 27 March after learning of his planned departure. 'Tell him it's too bad of him to leave us, that Munich is one of those charmed cities where one doesn't feel at home as long as one is there, but which one cannot leave without many regrets. Tell him not to forget me, that I am most genuinely fond of him, and that I hope to see him with us once again.' And again on 10 April: 'my fond farewells to Tyutchev!'[95]

These sentiments go far beyond the routine courtesies, and together with Max's reaction to the duel scandal tell us much about his attitude to his friend. We might suppose that he had always shown more sympathy than his elders for Tyutchev's courtship of Amélie, and may even have encouraged it, at least in the early stages. Another interesting feature of these passages is their note of finality, suggesting that Tyutchev may originally have intended not to return to Munich, but apply for a new posting while in Russia. Vorontsov-Dashkov's request for leave on his behalf speaks indeed of Tyutchev's wish to spend the spring in St Petersburg,[96] where he would have been ideally placed to do so. However, if this was the plan, nothing came of it.

It is not clear why he postponed taking his leave until the beginning of June. Amélie left to spend the summer in Köfering at the beginning of April,[97] so from that point of view there was nothing to keep him in Munich. Perhaps he stayed on to press his case for appointment to a court rank, which apparently his father was keen for him to obtain, supported in Munich by Countess Osterman-Tolstaya, who had several times petitioned Vorontsov-Dashkov on his behalf. On 22 May the Ambassador wrote to Foreign Minister Nesselrode recommending Tyutchev for this honour not as a reward for his services to date — for as Vorontsov-Dashkov admits, although Tyutchev had 'carried out his duties completely successfully' during his three years at the Embassy, the work he had done was in fact 'of no great significance' — but rather in recognition of his future potential.[98]

Tyutchev appears never to have kept a diary, and the only letter of his from this period to survive (to Prince Kozlovsky) gives no real insight into his state of mind at the time. We do of course have the poems. 'To N.' has already been discussed. Another, 'A Gleam,' has been dated between 1824 and the summer of 1825, and so is roughly contemporaneous.[99] Its central image is that of the Aeolian harp, previously used by his mentor Raich to symbolise poetry in its role of mediator between heaven and earth.[100] In Tyutchev's version, although there is no reference to poetry, an Aeolian harp sounding its mournful notes at dead of night also represents the intersection of the spiritual and material worlds:

> Each breath of zephyrs intertwining
> Draws from its strings a cry of woe...
> You'd say an angel's harp were pining
> For heaven in the dust below!
>
> O, how our soul then soars, rejoicing,
> From earth to the immortal sphere!
> The past we would enfold, embracing
> It like the wraith of one still dear.
>
> How we believe with faith unceasing,
> How with bright joy our hearts are filled!
> While in our veins ethereally coursing
> The dews of heaven are distilled!

However, Tyutchev continues, we soon awake from this 'magic dream,' aware that 'To worthless dust it is not granted/ To breathe the sacred fire of gods.' We raise ourselves to scan the sky outside 'with anxious and bewildered gaze' —

> And then sink back, weighed down and listless,
> Bedazzled by a single ray,
> To find not sweet repose, but restless,
> Tormented dreams till break of day.[101]

The 'single ray' could be interpreted here literally as the first light of the sun, but it also clearly refers back metaphorically to the earlier brief vision of a higher spiritual dimension (the 'gleam' of the title).

The first of a number of Tyutchev's poems on the Romantic theme of night, in which mundane, 'real' day is opposed to immanent and mysterious night, 'A Gleam' has been seen by critics from Tolstoy on as the earliest true example of his poetic genius.[102] While this is undoubtedly so, its close kinship with 'To N.' has been generally overlooked. Both poems express a stoic awareness of the ultimate incompatibility of the real and the ideal, of the earthly and the heavenly; and both employ essentially the same image ('sacred fire' in 'A Gleam', 'pure fire' in 'To N.') for that transcendental realm to which fallen man may attain, if at all, only with difficulty and at great potential danger to himself. And while Tyutchev's abiding interest in philosophical questions is apparent in the *ideas* expressed in these poems (as Aleksandr Nikolayev has pointed out, the rather laboured final verse of 'To N.' bears close similarity to a passage in Schelling's *Philosophical Inquiries into the Nature of Human Freedom*),[103] the overall pessimistic *tone* pervading them can certainly be related to the facts of Tyutchev's life at the time.

Tyutchev finally left Munich on 1 June.[104] Three months later, on 31 August, Amélie and Krüdener were married at Köfering. (As she was Catholic and he Protestant, there would normally have been two ceremonies, although in this case only details of the Protestant one have survived.)[105] Far away in Moscow Tyutchev was no doubt prepared for the inevitable. We have no record of his immediate reaction to the marriage; yet clearly detectable in some of his later references to Amélie is a note of retrospective sadness and regret, of sympathy for (as he perhaps saw it) a young life denied the chance to blossom naturally. As Baroness von Krüdener, Amélie was to enjoy great success at court and in high society, first in Munich and later in St Petersburg, where she and her husband took up residence in 1836. Soon after their move there Tyutchev wrote from Munich to his parents in Moscow: 'Do you see Madame de Krüdener sometimes? I have certain reasons to suppose that she is not as happy in her glittering position as I should wish. Poor dear, splendid woman. She will never be as happy as she deserves to be.'[106] Something of the same feeling informs the poem 'A golden time still haunts my senses...'.

The idea of marriage being motivated by anything other than mutual love was repugnant to Tyutchev, even more so that anyone should be forced or cajoled into such a union by others. Many years later his eldest daughter Anna wrote of him: 'In marriage he sees and acknowledges nothing apart from passion, and considers marriage acceptable only for as long as there is passion.'[107] For him this was no mere affirmation of Romantic faith, but a deeply held conviction born of bitter experience. Nothing illustrates this better than an incident from later in his life. In the spring of 1847 Anna herself received a proposal of marriage from a certain Konstantin Tolbukhin, a wealthy landowning cousin of her father from Yaroslavl, whose feelings however she did not reciprocate. The mismatch in their ages — she was eighteen, he thirty-seven — was practically the same as between Amélie and Krüdener at the time of their marriage. The poignant echoes of his own youth will have been too strong for Tyutchev to miss. Sadly he told his cousin that as Anna was not willing, the proposal could not be accepted, and then — 'deeply moved' according to Anna — came to inform her of what he had said to Tolbukhin. 'So, you are always free to choose,' he added (as she recorded in her diary that evening). 'Not many fathers would have acted as I did. It was a very advantageous match. Any other father would have used his influence to urge this marriage on you, whereas I let you follow your own inclination. Many will condemn me; perhaps you yourself will say one day: I was eighteen, Papa should have taken the decision himself and forced me to comply.' To which in her diary Anna makes the simple but eloquent comment: 'No, dear Papa, I shall always be infinitely grateful to you for not selling me for thirty thousand a year.'[108]

3 A Time of Destiny
(Russia, 1825-1826)

i Home Leave in Moscow

On 11/23 June 1825, three years to the day after they had left for Munich, Tyutchev and Khlopov arrived back in Moscow.[1] Travelling by the same route in reverse, they had been able to meet up in Warsaw with Tyutchev's elder brother Nikolay, who was now stationed there.[2] In Moscow his parents' joy at being reunited with their younger son was soon augmented by the news that his appointment to the court rank of Gentleman of the Chamber (*Kammerjunker*) had been confirmed.[3] A week or so later the family circle was completed when Nikolay arrived home on four months' leave.[4] Not knowing when they might all be together again, their parents seized the opportunity to commission — as on previous occasions — matching portraits of the two brothers, this time in pencil.[5] Fyodor's in particular is one of the more accomplished portraits we have of him. The unknown artist has caught the slight veneer of gravitas and social finesse acquired by the young diplomat during his first years abroad, while the fresh, open features and unruly hair reveal something of the poet and thinker. He seems ill at ease in the formal starched collar worn for the sitting; from the absorbed, abstracted expression of his eyes and pensive set of his lips it is evident that his thoughts are elsewhere.

At about the same time Nikolay Khlopov too arranged for a painting to be done. No doubt already aware that failing health would prevent him from accompanying Tyutchev abroad again, he set about commissioning the icon commemorating their life in Munich together which he was later to bequeath to his master.[6]

Although Raich was no longer in Moscow, having left earlier that year to work as tutor to a family in the Ukraine,[7] some of his group of protégés were around, and Tyutchev was able to renew contact with former fellow-students. Pogodin immediately noticed the veneer of Western sophistication acquired by his friend, and was none too impressed. 'Saw Tyutchev, who has arrived from foreign parts,' he noted in his diary after their first meeting. 'He talks volubly, although it's clear he didn't do too much work there; he smells of the court.'[8] Pogodin's first impression was confirmed by Tyutchev's cousin Dmitry Zavalishin, who met him that year and subsequently described him as 'a completely German courtier, a lover of etiquette, and an aristocrat in the full sense of the word.'[9]

Pogodin and Tyutchev met on various occasions during the summer and autumn, usually at Znamenskoye, where Pogodin was still employed as tutor to the Trubetskoys, or at the Tyutchevs' Troitskoye estate. No doubt both were glad of the company of an intellectual equal, although the difference in class which had meant so little during their university days now seems to have been felt more acutely by the scholar born as a serf. Especially galling for Pogodin must have been what he saw as the 'little flirtation' with Tyutchev at Znamenskoye of the married Princess Aleksandra Golitsyna (once the object of his own adoration),[10] who continuously engaged him in conversation even though she claimed not to find him attractive. 'O, grandees!' Pogodin confided to his diary. 'I think, and am now convinced, that there is something in their blood inimical to other classes. It must be so, in accordance with physical laws.'[11] The following day he notes: 'Has Tyutchev aroused resentment in me with his triumphs, or what?'[12] And several weeks later: 'Talked to Tyutchev, conversation with whom I find difficult. He wittily compared our scholars to savages eagerly seizing upon objects washed up from a shipwreck.'[13] Wittily perhaps; yet to the ambitious young Pogodin (himself only recently elected to the Society of Russian History and Antiquities)[14] the jibe must have smacked of westernised arrogance and condescension.

Despite these difficulties the two friends managed to continue the discussions of literature, philosophy and politics broken off three years before. Tyutchev lent Pogodin the latest volumes of poetry by Hugo and Lamartine he had brought from Munich, as well as a book on Byron, whose death had caused such a stir the previous year.[15] Pogodin was gathering material for his literary almanach *Uraniya*, published at the beginning of 1826, which as well as containing poetry and prose by members of the 'Lovers of Wisdom' group (Venevitinov, Shevyryov, Oznobishin, Odoyevsky and Pogodin himself) and their mentors Raich and Merzlyakov, was also supported with contributions from Pushkin, Vyazemsky and Boratynsky.[16] Tyutchev gave Pogodin 'A Gleam' and two other poems for inclusion in the almanach.[17]

Merzlyakov was in Moscow at the time, and it is likely that Tyutchev took the opportunity to look up his old Professor.[18] It was also to be expected that, like Pogodin, other members of the 'Lovers of Wisdom' group associated with Merzlyakov would seek out this envoy with fresh first-hand news of Germany, the country whose philosophy and literature they held in such high esteem. There is indeed some evidence of such meetings. In November Tyutchev's cousin, naval Lieutenant Dmitry Zavalishin, came to stay for a while at his relatives' house in Armenian Lane while on his way from St Petersburg to spend leave in Kazan. With him he brought Griboyedov's satirical comedy *Woe from Wit*, which, rejected by the censors as politically subversive, was now circulating in manuscript copies. As Zavalishin later recalled, Tyutchev, his brother Nikolay and cousin Aleksey Sheremetev immediately seized upon his copy and, aware that it was more accurate than others circulating in Moscow, gave public readings of it 'in various places, including the house of Princess Zinaida Volkonskaya.'[19]

No doubt present at some of these readings were such former students of Moscow University as Stepan Shevyryov, Dmitry Oznobishin, Vladimir Odoyevsky, Dmitry Venevitinov and others, who all knew each other well, many of them being employed together in the archive department of the Foreign Ministry (the so-called 'archive youths'), and who were united by a love of philosophy and literature. These young intellectuals would meet informally for discussion at each other's houses and at various literary and musical salons such as that of Avdotya Yelagina, the mother of Ivan and Pyotr Kireyevsky, held at her house at Krasnye Vorota. Pre-eminent among these was the salon of Princess Zinaida Volkonskaya at her sumptuous mansion in Tverskaya Street. A talented writer, singer and composer, and famed for her beauty and intellect, Princess Zinaida cultivated the friendship of Pushkin, Vyazemsky, Mickiewicz,

Chaadayev, Venevitinov and other leading lights of the cultural scene. 'At Volkon-skaya's house,' Vyazemsky later recalled, 'were united representatives of high society, dignitaries and beautiful women, the young and those of mature years, people employed in intellectual work, professors, writers, journalists, poets, artists. Everything in this house bore the stamp of service to art and the realm of thought...'[20]

One of Princess Volkonskaya's protégés was the acknowledged leader of the 'Lovers of Wisdom' group, Dmitry Venevitinov. Two years younger than Tyutchev, he was already expected by those who knew him to achieve greatness as a poet and thinker. It was apart from anything else this enormous sense of potential that would all too soon make his early death at the age of just 21 so hard for his friends to bear. In 1825 he was still living at the parental home in Krivokolenny Lane (*Pereulok*), where his mother held an artistic salon of her own and his friends would often gather.[21] The following year Pushkin would read scenes from his play *Boris Godunov* at the Venevitinovs' on returning to Moscow from exile.[22] Tyutchev's parents lived just a few minutes' walk away, and it is quite possible that he had known Venevitinov before going to Munich; now the likelihood of seeing him at social and literary gatherings was high, especially at Princess Volkonskaya's where Venevitinov was a favoured guest. Indeed, Tyutchev apparently recalled such encounters in a later poem:

> At glittering soirées you saw him mainly:
> Now waywardly amused, now sad or stern,
> Aloof, or lost in secret thought in turn —
> How could you miss the poet marked so plainly!
>
> Observe the moon: by day hard put to muster
> Its strength, it hangs, a vapid wisp of cloud;
> But when night falls, a god resplendent-browed
> Casts over sleeping woods his potent lustre![23]

The grammatical forms of the Russian original make it clear that the 'you' addressed is a male, and we may assume that Tyutchev is actually reproaching himself for failing to recognise a fellow-poet. According to Pigaryov the poem was written at the very end of 1829 or the beginning of 1830.[24] In a lucid and persuasive commentary Ivan Gribushin suggested it was inspired by the publication in 1829 of a posthumous edition of Venevitinov's poetry, which could have been sent to Tyutchev by one of his friends in Russia (Raich?), or brought to Munich by Pyotr Kireyevsky in September of that year.[25] Gribushin gives various reasons for his identification, including some clearly deliberate references in the poem to Venevitinov's own 'The Poet', and the close similarity of the person depicted in verse 1 to him as described by his contemporaries.[26] Tall and strikingly handsome, with chiselled features, large light-blue eyes and an ample brow encompassing a powerful intellect, he seems to have felt ill at ease in society, although he came from a wealthy aristocratic family himself. According to the Decembrist and poet Aleksandr Odoyevsky, 'His general demeanour betrayed a recent entry into high society; yet his look of complete refinement [...] and smile filled with sadness, the inappropriateness of which he attempted to conceal beneath a slight veneer of irony, all made me feel that he was somewhere far away, not only from this ball, but from this world.'[27] Or as recalled by Venevitinov's friends in their introduction to the posthumous edition of his poetry: 'despite the gaiety, even utter abandon with which he would often yield to a passing mood, his character was completely *melancholy*.'[28]

In these few lines Tyutchev delivers both a tribute to a fellow-poet and a general comment on poetic reputation. Gribushin claims that 'day' and 'night' in the poem stand for life and death, and accordingly interprets verse 2 as Tyutchev's way of saying that Venevitinov found recognition as a poet only after his death.[29] However, this is too simplistic a reading, based on a highly selective analysis of Tyutchev's use of day/night imagery in other poems which ignores most of that motif's complex ramifications (as, to take just one example, in 'Amidst the throng, in uncouth din of day...', written apparently as a companion piece to 'At glittering soirées you saw him mainly...' on the same manuscript sheet and using the same image of the moon by day and by night, yet manifestly *not* referring to life and death).[30] It would be nearer the mark to say that in Tyutchev's poetry in general 'day' denotes the finite world of appearances in which the material aspect of our lives is played out, while 'night' stands for the limitless, largely unknowable and disturbingly mysterious realm of the soul. If life and death are contained within these categories, then only as part of the wider picture. What the poem really tells us is that the impact of great works of art is hardly ever immediate, in either sense of the word. And this is as true of Tyutchev's own poetry as of Venevitinov's.

That Tyutchev should have overlooked the poetic gifts of Venevitinov in 1825 is understandable: not only had none of the latter's poetry yet been published, but the attention of their whole generation had in any case been diverted from matters of high art and philosophy to more burning topics of the day. Tyutchev arrived home in the summer of that year to find Moscow awash with intellectual ferment and speculation on the subject of political reform, while behind the scenes the Decembrists were already plotting to overthrow the Tsar. Something of the infectious atmosphere of those days is conveyed in the memoirs of Aleksandr Koshelyov, a member of the 'Lovers of Wisdom' group. One evening in February or March of 1825 the eighteen-year-old Koshelyov attended a gathering at the Moscow house of a second cousin, the Decembrist Mikhail Naryshkin. 'At this gathering,' he recalled, 'were Ryleyev, Prince Obolensky, Pushchin and several others who were subsequently sent to Siberia. Ryleyev read out his patriotic reflections; and everyone agreed on the necessity to have done with the present government. This evening made the strongest impression on me; the following morning I recounted all I had heard to Ivan Kireyevsky, and together we set off to the house of Dmitry Venevitinov, where Rozhalin, who had just graduated from university, was also living at the time. We talked much that day of politics and of the need to bring about a change in the system of government in Russia. As a result of this we applied ourselves with particular zeal to the works of Benjamin Constant, Royer-Collard and other French political writers, and for a time German philosophy slipped from the forefront of our attention.'[31]

The house of Tyutchev's parents had for some time been a gathering-place for those plotting the overthrow of autocracy. Ippolit Zavalishin (brother of Dmitry) later informed the authorities that when he stayed there in the spring of 1823 Aleksey Sheremetev and Ivan Yakushkin were also living in the house. (Tyutchev's cousin

Sheremetev was on the very periphery of the Decembrist movement, but Yakushkin, who had recently married Sheremetev's sister, was one of the leading plotters). According to Ippolit Zavalishin, a frequent visitor to the house at that time was another Decembrist, Pavel Koloshin, and 'here they spoke quite freely about the government, religion, and so on.' He also mentions one particular meeting there at which the foregoing were joined by Raich (who had been a member of the Moscow branch of the Union of Welfare before 1821) and one of the leading Decembrists, Aleksandr Bestuzhev.[32]

In fact it is most unlikely that Tyutchev's parents knew the true purpose of the meetings taking place under their roof, although like so many others they sympathised with the general aim of reform. In 1821 Tyutchev's father and a friend, Nikolay Levashov, had helped to organise famine relief for peasants in central Russia hit by the disastrous harvest of the year before. 'Neither Levashov nor Tyutchev was a member of the Secret Society,' Ivan Yakushkin later wrote of this, 'yet they acted completely in its spirit. [...] At that time there were many people in Russia like the Levashovs and Tyutchev who acted in the spirit of the Secret Society *without even suspecting it themselves.*'[33]

Like his father, Tyutchev shared the Decembrists' wider aims of freedom of expression, abolition of serfdom and general political reform. His advocacy of these in Munich has already been noted; now in Moscow he vigorously attacked the status quo in discussions with friends. 'Russia is a country of barracks and bureaucracy,' he told Pogodin. 'Everything revolves around the *knout* and rank. We have known proclamations, but not action.' According to Pogodin these were but a few of the barbed aphorisms which he heard his friend scatter in conversation.[34] Yet had Tyutchev known at that stage of the Decembrists' plans for overthrow of the government by force, he would not have condoned them. Essentially his position never changed from that of the seventeen-year-old who had enjoined Pushkin in verse not to 'stir sedition' or 'defame the crown'.

On the evening of 26 November/8 December Tyutchev, his brother and sister and their cousins Aleksey Sheremetyev and Dmitry Zavalishin attended a ball at the house of Prince Dmitry Golitsyn, the Governor-General of Moscow. Zavalishin, who had joined the secret society the previous year, later recalled that he left the ball early, as he had urgent letters to write to his co-conspirators in St Petersburg before leaving for Kazan. At three in the morning he was still writing in his study on the second floor of the Tyutchevs' house when he heard carriages draw up in the street outside, followed by the sound of voices in the entrance hall. 'I thought,' Zavalishin later recalled, 'that this was my cousin Darya and her brothers back home again, and that they wanted to tell me something about the ball. But I soon realised from the rattling of several sabres and sound of footsteps that a whole crowd was coming. [...] Instantly the thought flashed into my mind: had they come to arrest me? My hand instinctively snatched the important letter I had just written; I set light to it and threw it in the fireplace, then ran towards the approaching company to prevent them from entering the study and seeing the burning letter; yet scarcely had I lifted the door-curtain when Aleksey Sheremetev, who was walking ahead of the others, caught sight of me and called out: "The Tsar is dead; tell us what we should do!" ' His visitors were a group of Decembrists and sympathisers who had just heard the electrifying news at the ball.[35]

The death of Alexander I on 19 November/1 December in Taganrog on the Sea of Azov did indeed take the Decembrist movement unawares. Although the secret society had two years earlier split into two separate groups — the Northern Society based in St Petersburg and led by Kondraty Ryleyev, Nikita Muravyov, Nikolay Turgenev, Prince Yevgeny Obolensky and Prince Sergey Trubetskoy, and the Southern Society led by the more radical Pavel Pestel, who commanded a regiment stationed in the Ukraine — by November 1825 both groups were in agreement that the time was ripe for a military insurrection, and had provisionally set the date for the summer of 1826.[36] The sudden death of Alexander I put a line through these plans, but also presented the Decembrists with a golden opportunity. It was naturally assumed that Constantine, the oldest of Alexander's surviving brothers and official heir apparent, would ascend to the throne. However, having morganatically married a Polish commoner, Constantine was unable to provide a legal heir, whereas his younger brother Nicholas already had a son (the future Alexander II) who could assure the continuity of the dynasty. To get round this problem Constantine agreed in 1823 to renounce the throne in favour of Nicholas in the event of Alexander I's death. Inexplicably, this agreement was kept secret (even from Nicholas himself), and Constantine continued to be referred to officially as the heir apparent. Alexander could not have done more to create a power vacuum after his reign if he had tried; it was a situation the Decembrists now sought to exploit to the full. At the time of Alexander's death Constantine was in Warsaw as Commander-in-Chief of the army in Poland; Nicholas in St Petersburg, still in the dark as to the succession, and fearing military unrest if there were an interregnum, himself immediately took the oath of allegiance to his older brother and ordered it to be administered throughout the Empire. Soon it became known that Constantine had apparently declined to accede to the throne, yet he failed to come to St Petersburg or to issue a clear statement on the subject. In this confusion the Decembrist plotters, most of whom were serving officers, were able to stir up unrest in their regiments, portraying Constantine as a liberal who had the interests of the common soldier at heart (which was far from the truth) and Nicholas as an autocrat bent on seizing power from the rightful successor (which was only half-true).

The uncertainty continued for three weeks. The general mood of the young intellectuals in Moscow at this time is captured well by Koshelyov in his memoirs: 'During this period [...] we frequently, almost daily, gathered at the house of M.M. Naryshkin, who was a central source for all the rumours and news reaching Moscow from St Petersburg. There was no end of discussion. I shall never forget one conversation which took place at that time about what should be done in Moscow in the event of good news being received from St Petersburg. One of those present at the discussion, Prince Nikolay Ivanovich Trubetskoy [...], adjutant to Count P.A. Tolstoy who then commanded a corps stationed in and around Moscow, undertook to deliver his commanding officer bound hand and foot. There was no end to the proposals and debates; to a youth such as myself it seemed that Russia was on the brink of its own great 1789 revolution [...] We German philosophers forgot Schelling & Co. and went every day to the riding school and fencing hall to learn to ride and fence, thus preparing for the action we envisaged for ourselves.'[37]

Very soon after the news of Alexander I's death reached Moscow, Tyutchev prepared to leave for St Petersburg. Understandably for a member of the Northern

Society, Zavalishin also wanted to return to the capital, but later claimed that Osterman-Tolstoy, then staying in Moscow, forbade him to do so in view of the dangerous situation. According to Zavalishin, Osterman-Tolstoy told him: 'I shall only allow Fyodor [i.e. Tyutchev] to go to St Petersburg; he is harmless, although even in his case I have ordered him to get away to his post in Munich as soon as he can [...].[38] Deferring to Osterman-Tolstoy, Zavalishin travelled on to Kazan and missed the subsequent events in the capital.

Tyutchev left Moscow by 3/15 December at the latest; his brother Nikolay may have set out even a few days earlier.[39] Their reasons for going to St Petersburg are not wholly clear. Any hope Tyutchev may have had of applying for a new posting must by now have seemed decidedly forlorn, given the turmoil of events and the inevitable sudden decline in Osterman-Tolstoy's influence following the death of his august patron. Why then did he and Nikolay head for the capital at this crucial moment? Certainly both had already overstayed their official leave; there may also have been some requirement to report to their superiors before returning to duty; Tyutchev could in any case argue that the journey to Munich via St Petersburg and Berlin took no longer than via Minsk and Warsaw, and was on better roads. Even so the conclusion seems inescapable that these factors served only as excuses, and that what really drew them was the exciting prospect of witnessing great events at first hand. Although they would not have known of the planned insurrection, it was clear that momentous changes were in the air, and they wanted to be where the action was. Nor were they alone in this. 'Just imagine,' Prince Dmitry Golitsyn, Governor-General of Moscow, reportedly told Osterman-Tolstoy at this time, 'all the ensigns are up in arms and have taken it into their heads to go galloping off to St Petersburg.'[40]

Yet if these junior officers were impatient to change history, Tyutchev desired rather to watch it unfold. Ivan Gagarin, who later came to know him well, wrote: 'They say there are people so passionately devoted to the theatre that they will suffer any hardship and even go without meals in order to attend. Tyutchev was to some extent of this kind. [...] His most profound, most heartfelt enjoyment was to witness the spectacle presented by the world, to follow its changing events with unflagging curiosity, and to share his impressions with those around him.'[41] Karl Pfeffel agreed: 'Tutchef [...] a besoin de tout voir et de tout connaître.'[42] ('Tyutchev [...] needs to see everything and be acquainted with everything.') It was a fascination that was to stay with him always: whether during the Crimean War, when at Peterhof he was to stand gazing out towards the mighty British and French fleets massed in the Gulf of Finland, feeling 'that everything around me was taking part, as I was myself, in one of the most solemn moments in the history of the world;'[43] or towards the end of his life when, having recently passed through Berlin at the outbreak of the Franco-Prussian War, he would write of that conflict: 'What is taking place before our eyes [...] is like a production of some great drama conceived and composed according to all the principles of art.'[44] His most vivid poetic expression of this feeling comes in a piece on Cicero's lamentation of the bloody end of the Roman republic. Probably inspired by a visit to Rome in the summer of 1829,[45] the poem is, as Lev Pumpyansky has indicated,[46] steeped in Hegel's view of history as a rational and ultimately beneficial process at work beneath the surface appearance of catastrophe and upheaval. (Pumpyansky quotes the German philosopher's dictum that happy times are empty pages of history; Russians of a later epoch singularly lacking in such pages have taken lines 9-10 of the poem as a proverbial dictum invested not so much with Tyutchev's Beethovenian pathos as with the bitter irony of the Chinese curse: 'May you live in interesting times.')

Cicero

Midst storms of civil strife and woe
The orator was heard to say:
'Too late I set out on life's way
And now through Rome's dark night must go!'
Yet, taking leave of Rome's past grandeur,
From on the Capitolian Hill
Her setting star, majestic still,
You saw in all its sanguine splendour!..

Thrice-blessed he who has visited
This world at times of destiny!
As guest at their high table he
With gods has sat and broken bread —
On their bright pomp his eyes has feasted,
Of their high councils known the truth,
And though but mortal yet has tasted
Their chalice of eternal youth![47]

Among those in Armenian Lane from whom Tyutchev had to take a sad farewell was Nikolay Afanasyevich Khlopov, who had served him for nearly two decades as governor and manservant. Now in his mid-fifties, Khlopov was too unwell to accompany his master back to Germany. His health continued to deteriorate after Tyutchev's departure. On 5/17 March 1826, knowing that the end was near, he wrote on the back of the icon specially commissioned by him: 'In memory of my sincere love and concern for my friend Fyodor Ivanovich Tyutchev this icon is to become his property on my death. Signed 5 March 1826, Nikolay Khlopov.'[48] This brief dedication to the man he saw more as friend than master speaks for itself. Khlopov died at the Tyutchevs' house in Moscow on 16/28 May 1826, from what the official record describes as 'a weakening of the stomach.' He was 56 years old.[49]

ii The Decembrist Revolt

By 6/18 December at the very latest both Tyutchev and his brother were in the capital.[50] If they had hoped for excitement they were not to be disappointed. Although officially proclaimed Emperor, Constantine remained stubbornly in Warsaw, refusing either to come to St Petersburg or to issue a statement making it clear that he had renounced the throne. Rumours abounded that both he and his younger brother Michael, who was close to him, had been placed under arrest. On 12/24 December Nicholas received intelligence reports of an impending insurrection, and this seems to have finally persuaded him to take decisive action. On his orders a manifesto was drawn up declaring him Emperor, to be publicly proclaimed on 14/26 December, when the new oath of allegiance to him would also be administered. Learning of these preparations, the conspirators hastily agreed their own plan of action. On the morning of 14/26 December they would occupy Senate Square with rebel troops, prevent members of the Senate from taking the oath of allegiance, and force that body to issue a manifesto in favour of a constitutional form of government.

At this stage most in St Petersburg, including the Tyutchev brothers, would have been aware only of something momentous in the air. The general atmosphere in the days before the insurrection is recalled by one of the plotters, Vladimir Steingel: 'A kind of sombre foreboding hung over the capital. All were alarmed by the very mysteriousness of the assiduous activity clearly taking place on both sides. Instead of a greeting, people meeting each other in the street would say: "Well, what's tomorrow going to bring?" '51

They had their answer on the morning of 14/26 December. As recalled by an eyewitness, 'at about ten o'clock the beat of drums and repeated shouts of "Hurrah!" rang out on Gorokhovy Prospekt. A column of the Moskovsky Regiment with colours flying, led by Captain Shchepin-Rostovsky and the two Bestuzhevs, marched into Admiralty Square and turned towards the Senate, where they formed a square.'52 Other rebel forces converged to join them, and eventually some 3,000 men and 30 officers were assembled. As word spread among the citizens of the capital, spectators gathered in large numbers around Admiralty Square (the eastern continuation of Senate Square). A contemporary water-colour of the scene shows noblemen in western-style overcoats and top hats and ordinary folk in their traditional fur coats, including a scattering of women and children. Many are hotly debating the events unfolding before them, while some have climbed onto trees, walls or rooftops for a better view. Was Tyutchev among them? Although we have no certain proof, everything we know about him suggests that he was.

The rebel troops arrived too late to prevent the Senate from taking the oath of allegiance to Nicholas, for its members had already assembled at seven o'clock for that purpose and then dispersed. Meanwhile the majority of the St Petersburg garrison was proceeding to take the oath. At this stage decisive action such as an attempt to seize the Winter Palace might have won the day for the insurgents; however, Prince Trubetskoy, appointed 'dictator' by his co-conspirators, failed to appear and take command, having apparently judged the numbers present insufficient to ensure success. Without overall leadership the rebel soldiers could do little but wait for reinforcements, shivering without overcoats in subzero temperatures. There was freshly fallen snow, and a raw wind from the east.53

The stand-off continued. Count Miloradovich, Governor-General of St Petersburg, rode up on a borrowed horse and attempted to persuade the insurgents to return to barracks. 'Suddenly,' recalls Steingel, 'a shot rang out; the Count spun round, his hat went flying, and he slumped down on the pommel of his saddle; and in this position the horse carried him back to the apartment of the officer to whom it belonged.'54 He had been shot by Pyotr Kakhovsky, one of the rebel leaders, and died later that day.

Nicholas now left the Winter Palace and, mounting a white horse, led troops loyal to himself to the scene of the insurrection. 'All were struck [...] by his majestic if somewhat melancholy composure,' concedes Steingel.[55] There were further unsuccessful attempts at mediation by military commanders, a Metropolitan in episcopal robes and even Grand Duke Michael, who was threatened with a pistol by Wilhelm Küchelbecker for his pains. By now Prince Yevgeny Obolensky had assumed command of the rebels, but the initiative had clearly been lost, and his only hope was for more troops to defect.

All attempts at peaceful resolution having failed, Nicholas was urged by his senior commanders to use force. Several cavalry charges were ordered, but the unshod horses slipped on the icy ground, and rifle fire from the insurgents managed to repel them. It was now three o'clock in the afternoon, and already the short December day was giving way to dusk. Reluctantly Nicholas agreed to clear the square with canister shot, and three heavy ordnance pieces were drawn up. General Sukhozanet ordered a warning volley with blanks, but this had no effect. 'Then,' reports Steingel, 'came the whistling of canister shot; immediately everyone broke rank and scattered in different directions, except for those who had fallen. It would have been possible to leave it at that, but Sukhozanet ordered more firing along the narrow Galerny Lane and across the Neva towards the Academy of Arts, where most of the crowd of spectators had fled!'[56] In the panic soldiers and spectators alike were crushed to death, while others retreating across the frozen river were drowned when cannon balls cracked the ice.[57]

As night fell Nicholas was anxious to remove all visible traces of the rebellion. An armed cordon was thrown around the whole area of Senate Square. 'Many fires were lit,' writes Steingel, 'by the light of which throughout the night the dead and injured were removed and the blood which had been shed was washed from the Square. [...] It was all done in secret, and the true number of those who lost their lives or were wounded remained unknown.'[58] In fact the number of dead was officially set at 80, although eyewitnesses testify to at least 200.[59] However, even the latter is an underestimate, based apparently only on the number of corpses left lying in the Square. A list compiled by an official of the Ministry of Justice has survived which details 1,271 dead, including 903 'common people.'[60] Ordered by Nicholas to dispose of the bodies by morning, the St Petersburg chief of police resorted to desperate measures, according to an account left by an official of the Third Section (secret police): 'During the night a large number of holes were cut through the ice covering the Neva, into which were lowered not only corpses, but also allegedly many wounded who had no chance of avoiding the fate which awaited them. [...] When the ice melted on the Neva, the corpses of the unfortunate victims of the Decembrist revolt were swept out to sea.'[61]

The rebellion had been crushed, more brutally perhaps than even Nicholas would have wished. 'Voilà un joli commencement de règne! ' ('A fine way to start one's reign!') he had bitterly remarked as the cannon were trained on the insurgents in the Square.[62] A subsequent armed revolt in the south by the Chernigov Regiment was also defeated. In the following days and weeks hundreds of arrests were made. Several of those arrested or investigated were known personally to Tyutchev, as he himself told Ivan Gagarin a few years later.[63] Of course, he was never as close to the Decembrists as Pushkin, who famously declared them to be his 'friends, brothers, comrades.'[64] Even so it is clear from the facts reviewed earlier that he knew at least a dozen, and there may have been more for whom the evidence is missing. Some were related to him, either by blood (Aleksey Sheremetev, who in any case was only on the fringes of the movement, and Vasily Ivashov), or by marriage (Dmitry Zavalishin and Ivan Yakushkin). Yakushkin had earlier played a leading role in the movement, yet at the end of 1825 had been living for some time in seclusion on his estate near Smolensk. He learned of Alexander's death while travelling with his family to Moscow, where they arrived on 8/20 December (missing Tyutchev, who had left for St Petersburg about a week earlier).[65] Here Yakushkin made contact with his brother-in-law Aleksey Sheremetev, who was living in the Tyutchevs' house, as well as with other local members of the secret society. When news broke of the insurrection in St Petersburg, Yakushkin tried to organise an armed uprising in Moscow in support of it (as adjutant to General Pyotr Tolstoy, Sheremetev was in a key position). These attempts bore no fruit, however, and he knew there was nothing more to do but await the inevitable. On 10/22 January 1826 he was arrested in his house in Moscow and taken to St Petersburg to be interrogated.[66] Twelve days later his wife Anastasiya gave birth to a son; Anastasiya's mother Nadezhda Nikolayevna Sheremeteva was a godparent, together with Aleksey Sheremetev and Tyutchev's father.[67] Dmitry Zavalishin had already been arrested in Simbirsk on 30 December/ 11 January; on 11/23 January it was the turn of Mikhail Muravyov, another son-in-law of Nadezhda Sheremeteva.[68] These shock-waves from the Decembrist revolt rocked the Tyutchevs' house in Armenian Lane, where the Sheremetevs also lived. Fearing for her son Aleksey (and clearly in the know as far as her family's underground activities were concerned), Nadezhda Nikolayevna now sent her steward on an urgent mission to the family estate at Pokrovskoye, with precise instructions to lift the floorboards at a particular spot in one of the rooms. There he would find secret correspondence and other papers, which he was to burn immediately.[69]

The effect of all this on Tyutchev's parents, particularly his mother, can be imagined, knowing as they did that both their sons had been in St Petersburg since before the insurrection. Nor, as subsequently became apparent, were their anxieties unfounded. On 26 April/ 8 May 1826, in the course of the exhaustive investigation of the revolt directed personally by Nicholas, a denunciation of Dmitry Zavalishin written by his younger brother Ippolit was submitted to the Emperor. Two months later Ippolit was apparently asked for details of individuals who may have known of his brother's seditious plans, and in a second document dated 25 June/7 July he reported on several, including Fyodor and Nikolay Tyutchev and their cousin Aleksey Sheremetev. Here he writes for instance that in St Petersburg not long after the revolt[70] he heard Tyutchev say to his brother Nikolay: 'Zavalishin [i.e. Dmitry] was very careless; he revealed various crazy ideas [*bredni*] to anyone prepared to listen to him.' (In the document 'crazy ideas' has been underlined by Tsar Nicholas.)[71] As for Nikolay, he points out that he was a very close friend of the brothers Pyotr and Pavel Koloshin (both active Decembrists), and in particular during the winter of 1823 saw Pavel Koloshin daily. He concedes that this was probably in connection with Koloshin's proposed marriage to Countess Aleksandra Saltykova, which was being arranged in the Tyutchevs' household in Armenian Lane, yet adds: 'But it would be desirable to know whether Koloshin revealed to Tyutchev [i.e. Nikolay] any plans or at least the existence of the Moscow secret society. Tyutchev is of a phlegmatic nature, however, and would in my opinion not have been inclined to become a member of it.'[72]

Turning to Aleksey Sheremetev, he reports on the latter's participation in the outspoken political discussions in the Tyutchevs' house in 1823 referred to previously (Ippolit was staying there himself between February and June of that year), singling out for special mention one meeting attended not only by the known Decembrists Ivan Yakushkin and Pavel Koloshin, but also Aleksandr Bestuzhev, 'who had at that time come to Moscow for reasons unknown to me.' (As we now know, Bestuzhev had been sent by the Northern Society to liaise with the Moscow branch.) According to Ippolit, 'Sheremetev is of a fiery, ambitious temperament and could easily have had his head turned by the plotters' fantasies.'[73]

On the report is a note in Tsar Nicholas's hand: 'Very interesting; all this must be taken into fresh consideration.'[74] The officials investigating the conspiracy will have taken this as a clear instruction to interrogate not only Dmitry Zavalishin but also if necessary those mentioned in the report on the issues raised. Zavalishin was already under detention in the St Peter and Paul Fortress, awaiting sentence together with his fellow-plotters, and the others (even Tyutchev, who was back in Munich) could if necessary be summoned to the capital for questioning. Unlike Aleksey Sheremetev, Tyutchev probably had little to fear from investigation. His reported reference to the Decembrists' 'crazy ideas' makes his attitude clear, and Osterman-Tolstoy's (or Zavalishin's) description of him as politically harmless is probably not far off the mark. At most he would have to explain why he had not reported anything he may have heard. Nikolay on the other hand would have rather more awkward questions to answer. Had Pavel Koloshin told him anything about the secret organisation in 1823? What did he know about the meeting in his parents' house that same year attended by Bestuzhev, Yakushkin and other Decembrists? And possibly the most searching question: why had he resigned his commission so soon after the Decembrist revolt? According to his service record he took this step on 5/17 March 1826 'for family reasons.'[75] It may be that Nikolay had to hand some plausible explanation of these reasons (although none is evident). In fact the timing of his resignation suggests it may have been his form of protest against the treatment of friends and comrades implicated in the uprising. It has been calculated that General Muravyov's Military Academy in Moscow produced in all some twenty known Decembrists.[76] Four of these were cadets in the same year as Nikolay and Sheremetev.[77]

On 5/17 July, just ten days after Ippolit Zavalishin had written his report, the special tribunal set up to try the Decembrists announced its verdicts. Many were to be broken on the wheel or decapitated, the rest received penal servitude in Siberia for life or lesser periods. Five days later Nicholas exercised his prerogative of clemency to commute all but five of the death sentences and reduce most of the others. Ivan Yakushkin and Dmitry Zavalishin both received twenty years instead of life. On 13/25 July the sentence of death by hanging ordained by Nicholas was carried out on the five leading Decembrists, who included Ryleyev and Pestel. The ropes of three of the condemned broke at the first attempt; they fell to the ground and had to be hanged a second time. This was not enough to dampen the defiant spirit of Sergey Muravyov-Apostol, whose legs had been broken in the fall. 'My God, they can't even hang people properly in Russia!' he commented bitterly.[78] The whole gruesome scene was witnessed by Yakushkin and Zavalishin, lined up with the other prisoners to watch their comrades die.

In the following days and weeks parties of convicted Decembrists set out under guard on their long journey into penal servitude in the mines of Siberia. Before Zavalishin left, he had to endure further interrogation over two days on the allegations in his brother's report. Questioned about his relationship with the Tyutchev brothers and Aleksey Sheremetev and what he knew of their political beliefs and connections, he was able to deflect suspicion from them. Of Sheremetev (who probably had most to fear from investigation) he said: 'I considered him completely incapable even of political discussions, let alone actions,' going on to characterise him as altogether too lazy and disorganised to have been thought suitable revolutionary material.[79] Of Tyutchev he testified: 'Concerning Russia I had no political discussions with him, and listened more to his accounts of Germany [...]. One thing I can flatly assert, namely that Fyodor Tyutchev was very attached to the late Emperor.'[80] At this late stage Zavalishin's replies appear to have satisfied his interrogators, for no action was taken against Tyutchev, his brother or his cousin. Whether they and their families ever discovered how close a brush they had had with the secret police we do not know. Even so Tyutchev's mother was so shocked and distressed by the arrests in her family that four decades later she was still plagued by the fear that her son Fyodor, by then a high-ranking and respected courtier and official under the liberal Tsar Alexander II, might yet be sent to Siberia.[81]

In the immediate aftermath of the revolt Tyutchev had met with a familiar face from home. As yet unaware of events, Mikhail Pogodin had left Moscow for meetings with writers in St Petersburg, learning of the revolt only in the course of his journey. Delayed by a ban on movements in and out of the capital, he finally arrived on 24 December/5 January, and met Tyutchev, who was staying in the same hotel.[82] By now Pogodin was anxious about his own position. Before he left Moscow his friend Pyotr Mukhanov (another graduate of General Muravyov's academy) had asked him to deliver a letter to Ryleyev; now Pogodin thanked his lucky stars that he had departed before such an incriminating document could be brought to him. Soon afterwards he was shocked to receive news of Mukhanov's arrest in Moscow.[83] Worst of all, his almanach *Uraniya*, due for publication in January, contained various literary works of a free-thinking tendency, among them his own short story 'The Beggar' portraying the evils of serfdom, and he began to imagine that he too could be arrested as an intellectual accomplice of the Decembrists. In the general atmosphere of fear and suspicion he considered suppressing the almanach, but was reassured by Tyutchev, who persuaded him to go ahead with publication. In the event there were no unpleasant repercussions.[84]

In other respects Pogodin's visit was most rewarding. He was received by the revered historian and writer Nikolay Karamzin, with whom he discussed history and politics (the conservative Karamzin was predictably scathing about the Decembrists). The shy young scholar made a favourable impression on this doyen of Russian historians, and was given his blessing on parting. He also met Zhukovsky, not to mention such minor writers as Count Khvostov and Faddey Bulgarin.[85] This was all in the space of about three weeks. Tyutchev, ignoring Osterman-Tolstoy's imprecations, stayed over seven weeks in the capital. Did he too meet Karamzin, Zhukovsky (whom he had known as a teenager) and other writers? In the absence of hard evidence we can only speculate that this would have been likely (the one certainty being that there could have been no meeting with Pushkin, who spent this whole period isolated on his estate at Mikhaylovskoye).

Shortly before he was due to return to Munich Tyutchev was no doubt as surprised and delighted as his father (who threw his hat in the air when the news reached Moscow)[86] to see his cousin Dmitry Zavalishin free again, and to hear his account of how this had come about. While interrogating Zavalishin in person, Tsar Nicholas had apparently expressed sympathy for his reforming zeal, castigating only his misguided adherence to revolutionary methods. 'What do you want a revolution for?' Zavalishin claimed the Tsar told him. 'I myself am your revolution: I myself will do everything you seek to achieve through revolution.'[87] In his defence Zavalishin replied that the previous year he had submitted suggestions for reform in the navy, but they had been ignored. Nicholas ordered a search for his memorandum, and when it was found, declared himself in agreement with it. On 16/28 January he ordered Zavalishin to be set free and announced the formation of a committee to look into inadequacies in the navy.[88]

After his release Zavalishin returned to the house of Osterman-Tolstoy, who had in the meantime returned to the capital.[89] Here over the next few days Tyutchev no doubt had ample opportunity to hear his cousin's account of events. Both, it seems, were taken in by the Tsar's tactics. An astute judge of human frailties, Nicholas sensed which Decembrists would respond best to kid gloves and which to an iron fist in yielding information; his pose as a new Peter the Great who would impose reform from above was all part of this cat-and-mouse game. On 2/14 March Zavalishin would be re-arrested,[90] and as we have seen he was eventually sentenced first to death and then to penal servitude and lifelong exile. However, it was with feelings of relief and optimism about the new regime that on 20 January/ 1 February Tyutchev left for Germany.

He travelled with Prince Konstantin von Löwenstein-Wertheim, a Bavarian diplomat bearing despatches to his monarch from Nicholas I. They arrived in Munich in the early hours of 5/17 February.[91] News of the insurrection had so far been limited to rumours and bland official communiqués, and members of the diplomatic corps seized on these two colleagues with up-to-date first-hand news. In the following days Württemberg's Ambassador in Munich sent his King two despatches based on accounts he had heard from Löwenstein-Wertheim 'and above all Embassy Attaché Tyutchev' which reveal something of the latter's views on the revolt and its aftermath. According to these accounts emanating in the main from Tyutchev, the leaders of the coup in St Petersburg had acted independently of 'the general movement of educated circles of the nation,' in particular of the main secret society, said to be based in Moscow, which 'had hoped to receive the most necessary reforms from the hands of the Emperor, i.e. from Alexander himself, who knew about this and was already prepared to change the whole system.' However, Trubetskoy and the other plotters in St Petersburg — who are said not even to have belonged to the main society — 'wanted to play the leading role and claim all the glory for themselves. The plans for murders connected with this were completely alien to the main society.'

Even allowing for some distortion in this version of Tyutchev's views, it is clear that he saw the revolt in Senate Square as an abortive escapade stirred up by a few hotheads out of touch with the vast consensus of progressive opinion, which favoured peaceful reform. This misinterpretation of events (together with his apparent belief in a 'main society,' non-violent in its methods, based in Moscow) shows if nothing else that he had never been privy to the secret plans of his Decembrist acquaintances. It also confirms that for all his desire for reform he was implacably opposed to revolutionary methods. While condemning the leaders of the revolt, the analysis reported in these despatches refers to the existence of 'crying inadequacies' in Russia, and concludes: 'Fruitful reforms are expected, which will be carried out after the funeral of the Emperor Alexander and the coronation of Emperor Nicholas in Moscow.' Moreover, the despatches speak of Nicholas showing 'amazing restraint and unprecedented energy' in his conduct of the investigations, and report that 'many the Emperor set free immediately.' There follows an account of Zavalishin's experiences (he is mentioned not by name, but as 'a certain outstanding naval officer,' a description of which he would no doubt have approved).[92]

Tyutchev had clearly been impressed by the Tsar's apparent mercy to his cousin; if his overall evaluation of Nicholas I seems naively euphoric in hindsight, it is worth recalling that many others, among them Pushkin, were also taken in for a time. Even three years later such an astute observer of the political scene as Heine could hail Nicholas as 'the standard-bearer of freedom' for his support of the Greek independence movement.[93] And to begin with there were indeed some hopeful signs: the sacking of the hated Arakcheyev, who had presided over the reactionary policies of the second half of Alexander's reign; the personal audience granted by the Tsar to Pushkin, when he lifted the exile imposed on the poet by his predecessor; in foreign policy, a shift away from slavish observance of the terms of the Holy Alliance to a more pragmatic emphasis on Russia's national interests (soon to be manifested in Nicholas's support for the Greek insurgents against Turkish domination). Yet eventually it became apparent that these were little more than cosmetic features, and that far from being a new Peter the Great, Nicholas was at heart a much stauncher reactionary than his brother Alexander.

In the late summer of 1826 official news reached the Russian Embassy in Munich of the sentences passed on the Decembrists. In common with all other servants of the crown Tyutchev had to sign an undertaking never to belong to a secret society.[94] These have usually been assumed to be the circumstances in which the following was written:

14th December 1825

> By Tyranny you were corrupted,
> And at its sword you met defeat:
> Which stern, impartial Law accepted
> As sentence justified and meet.
> The common people have not tarried
> In spurning you for oaths betrayed —
> And, for posterity now buried,
> Your memory will quickly fade.
>
> O victims of a headstrong notion!
> What did you dream of as your goal —

That your scant blood, shed in libation,
Could melt the immemorial pole?
Scarce, reeking, had it flashed like garnet
In that primordial icy waste,
Than iron winter breathed upon it
And each last crimson blot effaced.[95]

In fact it seems more likely, as suggested by Aleksandr Ospovat, that the poem was written the following year. As he points out, news that in some cases indignant peasants had hurled mud and abuse at Decembrists on their way to exile (lines 5-6) and that the burial place of those executed had been kept secret (lines 7-8) would by then have had time to reach Tyutchev in letters from family or friends. A book on Russia by the French dramatist and poet Jacques-François Ancelot published in April 1827, in which the Decembrist revolt is portrayed in essence as no more than an attempted aristocratic coup, and a brochure attacking Ancelot's thesis by Tyutchev's acquaintance Yakov Tolstoy, published in Paris in the summer of that year, may according to Ospovat have provided the immediate occasion for Tyutchev (who was in Paris himself in July 1827) to write his poem.[96]

More important than the exact date of composition is Tyutchev's overall verdict on the Decembrists. His prediction that they would be forgotten by posterity has of course proved wildly inaccurate. Certainly it smacks more of wishful thinking than of reasoned prognosis, suggesting that he saw their enterprise as a shameful or at best foolish episode best consigned to oblivion. His condemnation of them is indeed made clear enough. The charge is partly one of formal illegality in breaking their oath of allegiance to the crown (the 'oaths betrayed' of line 6); here, says Tyutchev, the Law has taken its impartial course and found them guilty. (The summary procedures of the specially convened tribunal, which tried the defendants *in camera* and to all intents and purposes *in absentia*, became known only much later.) More seriously, the Decembrists are accused in line 1 of having been corrupted in a moral sense by the very tyranny they claimed to oppose: in other words of having descended to the level of tyranny in resorting to its violent methods.

Tyutchev's attack on the Decembrists might be suspected of being nothing more than a self-serving attempt to curry favour with the new regime. Yet this is clearly not the case. Apart from anything else, he knew there was absolutely no prospect of his poem being published in the foreseeable future. The official line enforced by the censors was (in a foretaste of Soviet practice) to treat the Decembrists simply as non-persons, expunging all mention of them from the record. In other words this was a poem written 'for the drawer', which appeared in print for the first time in fact only some years after Tyutchev's death,[97] proof enough that the views expressed are his alone. Nor are those views at all flattering to the existing regime. In verse 1 Tyutchev deliberately chooses for it the term 'tyranny' ('*samovlast'ye*') in preference to the more neutral 'autocracy' ('*samoderzhaviye*'), while the images in verse 2 ('immemorial pole', 'primordial icy waste', 'iron winter') evoke a harsh and invincible power inimical to all growth and development.

If Tyutchev's attitude to the Decembrists is essentially not much different from that reported in the Württemberg Ambassador's despatches, what has changed in the interim is his perception of the Tsar's willingness or ability to reform the system. After the executions and life sentences visited on the Decembrists the sanguine picture of an energetic and merciful new Tsar, prepared to initiate the same 'fruitful reforms' demanded by them, prepared even to incorporate the very 'revolution' they had wanted, has given way to a bleak and profoundly pessimistic view of the prospects for change.

One critic, Georgy Chulkov, has detected in this poem the seeds of Tyutchev's later political and historico-philosophical views. He points in particular to the chilling soul-lessness stressed in the imagery of verse 2 as the overriding quality of the autocracy, which leads it to rely on brute force and repression as an instrument of power. The revolutionaries having allowed themselves to be corrupted by this same way of thinking, the resultant clash is witnessed by the poet as a 'historical tragedy.'[98] Implicit in Tyutchev's critique of both sides, according to Chulkov, is his later search for a less formalistic and legalistic, more organic political theory, in which positive spiritual, cultural and religious values would take precedence over negative force.[99]

This is to look far ahead, however. For the moment there were present realities to come to terms with. Nicholas's 'iron winter' had begun. It would continue for nearly thirty years.

4 Great Festival of Wondrous Youth (Munich, 1826-1829)

i Nelly

Already on 23 January 1826 Max von Lerchenfeld in Paris knew of his young Russian acquaintance's plans. 'So dear Tyutchev is returning to us,' he wrote to his mother on that day — 'I'm very pleased at that, as long as he doesn't freeze on the way — promise to embrace him for my part, and tell him it is very good of him to return to us.'[1] Much had changed in Munich during the eight months of Tyutchev's absence. Although he knew his beloved Amélie was now Baroness von Krüdener, it must have been an added blow to find her already four months pregnant. (Her son Nikolaus Arthur was born on 20 July).[2] At the Embassy, which had recently moved from Herzogspitalgasse to new premises on the Karolinenplatz,[3] there were also changes afoot, for Tormasov had died on 25 January, leaving a vacancy for the post of First Secretary.[4] 'Let us hope Krüdener will be able to turn it to his advantage,' was Max von Lerchenfeld's first response to the news,[5] and in fact Krüdener was duly promoted on Vorontsov-Dashkov's recommendation. In the normal course of events Tyutchev might have hoped to step into Krüdener's shoes as Second Secretary, but his prolonged absence went against him, and for the time being the post was left vacant.[6] Over the next couple of years Krüdener was to take over the running of the Embassy as Chargé d'Affaires for months at a time, while Tyutchev continued to languish in his unsalaried supernumerary post.[7] The sudden rise of his rival in love must have been especially galling.

The dramatic events in Russia following the death of Alexander I had overshadowed a more ordered transition of power in Bavaria. Crown Prince Ludwig had succeeded to the throne on the death of his father Maximilian on 13 October 1825. Something of a poet himself, the new King was an enthusiastic patron of the arts and learning. Studies at Göttingen, then the most free-thinking of the German universities, had been followed by an art education in Italy, where Ludwig became close to German artists of the medievalist Nazarene group led by Peter Cornelius. Back in Munich while still Crown Prince he had commissioned his first major artistic project, a museum to house the many pieces of classical sculpture acquired during his stay in Italy. Designed by Leo von Klenze, who as Ludwig's court architect was later to transform the face of Munich (he was also employed by Nicholas I to rebuild the New Hermitage in St Petersburg), the Glyptothek was built in a neoclassical style more reminiscent of Rome than Greece. Cornelius was chosen to decorate the interior. After his accession Ludwig embarked on an ambitious programme of building and patronage designed to transform his capital into a 'new Athens', no less. Work on a further temple to the arts, the Pinakothek, began in April 1826; this was to be home to an extensive collection of paintings. The same year Ludwig moved the university from Landshut to Munich, attracting leading scholars to the new seat of learning. Foremost among them was the philosopher Friedrich Schelling, whose inaugural lecture on 26 November 1827 was heard by a packed audience.

Heine no doubt spoke for some when he in effect dismissed the whole idea of Munich the new Athens as a laughable oxymoron.[8] Yet visitors to the Bavarian capital seem on the whole to have been favourably impressed by Ludwig's grand project, including such western-leaning Russians as Pyotr Vyazemsky and Aleksandr Turgenev.[9] The contrast with the intellectual climate in their own country was striking enough. An enlightened and cultured monarch, liberal in inclination, prepared to rule within a constitutional framework, generously supportive of the arts and learning — here was a model they could have wished for Russia.

It is likely that Tyutchev would have shared his compatriots' views in this respect. Whether the new general atmosphere of optimism abroad in Munich helped to compensate in some way for the setbacks in his personal and professional life is another matter. More immediate and tangible consolation was in any case afforded in the person of a young widow whom he came to know well soon after returning from Russia. Eleonore Peterson had come to Munich to be with her mother following the death of her husband the previous autumn. Alexander Peterson had been, like Krüdener, a Baltic German employed in the Russian diplomatic service, and it was only natural that Eleonore should turn to the Russian Embassy in Munich for help in sorting out her late husband's affairs.[10] Left with four sons aged between six months and seven years,[11] and with no means of her own, she was also in need of financial support. For this she had a strong case. Peterson's father before him had been a diplomat, serving indeed for a time as Ambassador in Munich.[12] Peterson himself had risen in the service to the substantial rank of Active State Councillor, equivalent to that of a Major-General in the army.[13] This was a typical rank for an Ambassador, held for instance by both Vorontsov-Dashkov and his successor,[14] and yet Peterson appears to have had no official post as such in Germany. His mission was in fact a secret one, as recently published details of a letter sent to him in 1817 by the Foreign Minister, Count Nesselrode, make clear. His instructions were to travel between the capitals of the various German states and, posing as a private individual, to cultivate contacts in government and society circles with the aim of gathering information of use to Russian diplomacy.[15] In short, Peterson was an intelligence agent.

The widow and orphans of such a high-ranking official engaged in matters of state security will have been treated generously. Writing to Nesselrode five years later, Eleonore referred to the 'favour' in which her late husband had stood with the Foreign Minister, and to the latter's personal assurance, given to her at the time of his death, that her four sons (all Russian subjects) would be taken care of.[16] We may be sure that at the time Eleonore was granted a pension for their upkeep. Later Nesselrode personally intervened to ensure that three of them gained entrance to the St Petersburg Naval Academy.[17]

There was certainly no prospect of financial support from Eleonore's family. Her father, Karl von Bothmer, was a Count and former Ambassador; yet by the time of Peterson's death circumstances had brought him to the brink of destitution.[18] Born in 1770 to a well-established Hanoverian family, Karl had embarked on a career as courtier, and in 1799 married Antoinette von Hanstein, daughter of the Governor of Kassel. Their first child, Eleonore (or Nelly as she was known in the family), was born in Hanover on 19 October 1800.[19] Altogether Antoinette bore her husband twelve children, two of whom died in infancy.[20] In 1804 Karl was appointed Ambassador of the Kingdom of Württemberg to the Bavarian court and moved with his family to Munich. After a further spell as Ambassador in Dresden he inherited from a benefactress, and in 1814 returned to Munich with his wife and children in a private capacity. Although he contrived to have the title of Count 'confirmed' there (having inherited through his branch of the family only that of Baron), his attempts to obtain a post at the Bavarian court were unsuccessful. This in no way deterred Karl, who confessed to a 'propensity to extravagance,'[21] from living well beyond his means. At their newly acquired town house and country estate the Bothmers entertained the cream of Munich society, hosting lavish balls, banquets and other junketings. The inevitable crunch came in 1820, when rising debts forced Karl to sell both their properties while his wife was away undergoing medical treatment in Switzerland. Various attempts at recovering something of his fortune through speculative investments failed in turn, culminating in the bankruptcy of a venture in Bessarabia in 1825. By now unable to show his face in Munich, whose fickle society had turned its back on him, he had moved first to Bayreuth and then finally been forced to accept the hospitality of charitable relatives. Although he appears to have been genuinely devoted to his wife, she had separated from him and at the time of his final ruin was living with the younger children and her unmarried sister Karoline von Hanstein in Munich. Here, unlike Karl, she enjoyed the sympathy of society, and as a result of her petitions to King Maximilian was even granted financial support for her children.[22]

Nelly had married at the end of 1817,[23] and was thus to some extent insulated from direct involvement in her family's plight, although it must have affected her emotionally. Peterson, described by his father-in-law as 'honourable, highly educated and affectionate,'[24] seems to have made her happy; according to Karl, despite some unspecified 'dark clouds' on the horizon to begin with, they eventually enjoyed a 'blessed and happy' union.[25] Their first son, Karl, was born in 1819, followed by Otto, Alexander and Alfred.[26] We have practically no information on the places to which Peterson's roving commission took him in these years, apart from indications that in the last year or so of his life he and Nelly may have been settled in Nuremberg.[27] Wherever they lived, they will have come to Munich from time to time to visit Nelly's mother and younger brothers and sisters. Karl makes it clear in his account that after his move to Bayreuth in the summer of 1823 his wife was living in Munich again, having returned from Switzerland; also, it was Peterson who negotiated the separation agreement between them.[28] Thus it is quite possible that Tyutchev met Nelly already during his first three years in Munich. It would be natural enough for Peterson on such visits to have sought the company of his colleagues and fellow-countrymen at the Russian Embassy, and to have introduced his wife to them. In any case Tyutchev will have known all about Nelly's family, whose dramatic reversal of fortune was the talk of the town. Apart from anything else, his superior Mikhail Tormasov, First Secretary at the Embassy, seems to have taken a personal interest in the case. This is apparent from Max von Lerchenfeld's letter to his mother of 5 February, quoted from earlier. Here he comments on the news of Tormasov's death: 'I regret the latter with respect to the

Bothm[er] family, of whom he was the sole support [*l'unique soutien*], and who are certainly to be pitied. What terrible blows Providence has dealt this family one after the other; it is a grave lesson to all who spend their lives in complete insouciance, putting their faith only in worldly goods! What on earth will that poor woman do now, and how will she [endure] this last blow of fortune?'[29] Exactly how Tormasov helped Nelly's mother and her family is not known: perhaps by supporting the petitions for financial aid which Karl mentions her making to King Maximilian.

Whether or not Tyutchev and Eleonore had met earlier, it was after his return from Russia early in 1826 that these two unhappy individuals were drawn together in a common need for solace. Nelly's innate kindness, her loving and sensitive nature, were long remembered in the Tyutchev family.[30] Contemporaries such as Heinrich Heine and Darya Ficquelmont also testified to her considerable charm and wit.[31] 'She understands the human heart so well; whichever of its strings you may touch, it will find an echo in her,' the young Ivan Gagarin later confided to his diary of a certain 'Madame T.' in Munich who is almost certainly Eleonore.[32] All these qualities shine through in her surviving letters. Although in appearance she could not lay claim to the cool classical perfection typified by Amélie, her portraits suggest great feminine charm, warmth and compassion. There is also more than a hint of frailty and vulnerability to which Tyutchev — sensitive to her bereavement after his own loss of Amélie — was no doubt drawn. As she responded, attracted in part by his legendary wit and eloquence, mutual sympathy developed into a more compelling bond. By the time spring had turned to summer they both knew that anything less than a lasting commitment was unthinkable.

It was in some respects an unusual relationship. The widowed mother of four young sons, three years older than Tyutchev and of delicate constitution, Nelly had in time to assume a protective role, providing a fixed anchorage in the life of her brilliant but unpractical, emotionally erratic and still in many ways immature partner. Years later he would write of her that 'this poor woman is endowed with a strength of spirit comparable only with the tenderness of her heart. [...] never has one human being been loved by another as I have by her.'[33] And to their daughter Anna he confessed that for him Nelly had been 'life itself' and 'so necessary to my existence that to live without her seemed to me as impossible as living without a head on one's shoulders,' to which he added with further hyperbole that at any time during their years together she would have been prepared to die for him without the slightest hesitation.[34] Noteworthy in these comments is the emphasis on her love for him, rather than vice versa. This was to be typical of other, later relationships too (in the perceptive words of one critic, 'what he prized above everything else in a woman [was] the assurance that he was adored'),[35] and may be attributed at least in part perhaps to the pampered early upbringing by doting females indicated by Aksakov.[36] In Eleonore's case there is indeed more than a hint of her having taken on something of the role and function of mother towards him. She could even make light of the fact in letters to Tyutchev's more practical brother, at various times referring to her husband as 'our little child,' talking of assuming a 'right of protection or guardianship' over him, or complaining that she would rather travel with three babes in arms than with him on his own.[37] Yet in spite of all this the undoubted depth of their feelings for each other held out the prospects of a happy enough marriage.

Once Tyutchev's proposal had been accepted (probably in the late spring or early summer),[38] there were serious practical difficulties to be overcome. The difference in religion (she was Lutheran, he Russian Orthodox) was not a bar to marriage in either Bavarian or (more crucially) Russian law, although it did require two separate ceremonies to be held. However, for the Orthodox ceremony (the only one recognised in Russian law) Tyutchev as a serving diplomat would first have to seek official permission to marry from St Petersburg, and in view of his still unsalaried status it is quite possible that this would not have been granted. The bureaucratic process involved in authorising and arranging a ceremony was in any case long and complicated, and the nearest Russian Orthodox church was in Weimar. But it may have been financial considerations that presented the most formidable stumbling-block. Once it became known in official circles that Eleonore had remarried, she would stand to forfeit any pension or financial support received from the Russian government in respect of her children by Peterson. The burden of support would pass to her new husband; yet Tyutchev could scarcely get by himself on the allowance from his parents, let alone feed another five mouths.

Faced with such obstacles, Tyutchev would no doubt have been prepared for them simply to live together, yet for a woman of Eleonore's social position and religious beliefs this was not an option. The solution they appear to have hit on was a single ceremony in a Lutheran church, after which they kept their marital state secret as far as possible. Although to date it has not proved possible to trace the records of such a ceremony, that they did marry in 1826 seems indisputable: not only does Aksakov give this as the year, but more importantly Tyutchev himself in letters twice by implication dates their marriage from then.[39] Tatyana Dinesman has convincingly narrowed the time down to August 1826 on the basis of recently discovered diplomatic documents showing that Tyutchev was given permission by Vorontsov-Dashkov to leave Munich 'on necessary business' ('*po nadobnosti*') at the end of July 1826 and was away until the end of August.[40]

On the face of it, Munich itself would have seemed the most obvious choice as wedding venue. Eleonore and her family belonged to an active local Protestant community of some 6,000 souls (nearly 8% of the city's population), who under laws introduced earlier in the century by Maximilian and his First Minister Montgelas enjoyed freedom of worship and full equality before the law with Catholics. Maximilian's second wife Karoline, formerly Princess of Baden, had stipulated on marriage in 1799 that she and her large retinue be allowed to practise their Lutheran faith, and had brought her own chaplain with her to Munich for that purpose. Ludwig Friedrich Schmidt was a charismatic preacher whose ecumenical outlook and concil-iatory nature disarmed much of the initial distrust and hostility of Catholics towards the newcomers. Services for Karoline, her ladies-in-waiting, court officials and servants were held at first in a room at Schloss Nymphenburg, later in the court chapel of the *Residenz*, the main royal palace in Munich. The first church in the city dedicated to Lutheran worship was completed only in 1833; until then services in the royal chapel were open to all Protestants in Munich — and indeed to Catholics, many of whom were drawn by Schmidt's qualities as preacher. In 1818 he relinquished his parish duties to take up an administrative post at the Ministry of the Interior with overall responsibility for Protestant church affairs in Bavaria, while continuing to be the Queen's chaplain.[41]

Before 1833 Lutheran marriages in Munich were consecrated either in the sacristy of the royal chapel or in private houses and duly recorded in the official church registers.[42] However, searches by various scholars have found no record of a marriage between Tyutchev and Eleonore in the city.[43] Clearly the need to maintain secrecy prompted them to go elsewhere, which would explain Tyutchev's absence from the capital on unspecified 'necessary business' during August. Where exactly the wedding took place remains unknown. The little Lutheran church at Burgfarrnbach Castle near Nuremberg, where Eleonore's sister Louise had married Count Ludwig von Pückler Limpurg two years previously, would have provided a suitably discreet location; yet there is no record of a marriage there either.[44] One possible clue may lie in Schmidt's move earlier in the year to Würzburg, where the recently widowed Queen Karoline had made her new residence. She had naturally wanted to keep her chaplain, and he had loyally resigned from his government post in order to follow her there. One is tempted to speculate that Tyutchev and Eleonore used their court connections to arrange for Schmidt to marry them in Würzburg. Unfortunately, the relevant documentary evidence is no longer available, all church registers for the Protestant congregation in that city having been destroyed during the Second World War.[45]

Not long after the wedding fate dealt the Bothmers a further harsh blow. Nelly's mother had been in poor health for some time, and worries over the family's financial plight can only have made things worse. She died on 13 October.[46] This left three under-age sons to be taken care of,[47] whom their father (now destitute and living with relatives away from Munich) could do nothing to support. With four boys of her own, Nelly could not take them on, but was happy for her seventeen-year-old sister Clotilde to move in and assist with child care. Their unmarried aunt Karoline von Hanstein, who had lived with the Bothmers since Nelly was born, helping to look after her and her younger brothers and sisters, also joined the household at this time. In fact it may have been the other way round. Some years later Aunt Karoline is known to have been running a *pension* or guest house in Munich (at 4 Briennerstrasse).[48] Renting a house and sub-letting rooms or apartments was a not unusual way for a woman without means to generate a modest income, and it could well be that Karoline was forced into this when the Bothmer family first ran into financial trouble. A guest house would certainly have provided ideal cover for Tyutchev and Nelly during their early years together, enabling them to live together as man and wife while maintaining an outward pretence of being no more than residents in the same building.

Even nearly two years later Heine, a frequent guest at their house, still referred to Tyutchev and Nelly as being 'secretly married.'[49] Yet by then their marriage must have been a fairly open secret in Munich society, which fed on gossip and scandal. Apart from family and close friends, it seems likely that from the outset Tyutchev's colleagues too were in the know. Required in August 1826 by the Russian government to obtain from all Embassy officials a sworn undertaking never to belong to secret societies, Krüdener (acting as Chargé d'Affaires) had found himself in the position of having to explain Tyutchev's absence. His communiqué to St Petersburg, which fails to say where Tyutchev had gone, or why, stating merely that he had been given permission by the Ambassador to leave Munich 'on necessary business,' smacks of cautious evasion to say the least. (The fact that Vorontsov-Dashkov had been away on protracted leave since April also raises questions. Had his permission been obtained with some difficulty and inevitable delay by letter? Or was Krüdener perhaps being less than generous with the truth on this occasion?)[50] It was in fact probably only the St Petersburg authorities who had to be kept in the dark, to ensure that Eleonore kept her pension. While not openly advertising their marriage in Munich, she and Tyutchev were clearly not too concerned about revealing all to such as Heine (who was not slow in passing the news on).[51] Even a relative stranger from Russia entertained by the Tyutchevs as he passed through Munich in the summer of 1828 (Grigory Olenin) had Eleonore introduced to him as Tyutchev's wife.[52] In Bavaria, where their Lutheran marriage was legally valid, there was after all little reason for conspiratorial secrecy. And if word did reach the ears of the St Petersburg authorities, it could always be denied as a product of the Munich rumour mill.

A more pressing concern was the need for Eleonore to avoid becoming pregnant. Until they were married according to Orthodox rites any offspring would be considered illegitimate under Russian law, and would consequently forfeit the privileges of nobility. Yet given their financial situation, regularising their position in this way was out of the question until Tyutchev had a salaried post, of which for some time there seemed no prospect. On 29 April 1828 he was however at last appointed to the post of Second Secretary which had remained vacant since the death of Tormasov.[53] After nearly six years of service he could look forward to his first salary, and he and Nelly could throw caution to the wind. By the beginning of August she was pregnant. Tyutchev, who must have long since made plans for such a contingency, immediately submitted his application for official permission to marry.[54] This had to go through Foreign Minister Nesselrode, whose absence from Russia caused a delay of three months, so that Tsar Nicholas's assent was obtained only on 17/29 November. It was time they could ill afford to lose in the circumstances. After this the bureaucratic wheels continued to grind slowly as the matter was passed to the church authorities in St Petersburg to make arrangements for a ceremony at Weimar, the nearest Russian Orthodox church to Munich. By January 1829 Tyutchev was still waiting for news, and growing decidedly anxious. Apart from the real danger of their child being born illegitimate under Russian law, the long journey to Weimar in winter was looking increasingly inadvisable for Nelly.

At this point matters were taken in hand by Ivan Potyomkin, recently appointed to replace Vorontsov-Dashkov as Russian Ambassador. In September 1828 the medieval Salvatorkirche in Munich had been converted to use by the Greek Orthodox Church. Intended by King Ludwig as a place of worship for the growing number of students and other subjects of the new Greek state expected in his capital, it came as a godsend for Tyutchev and Nelly. Thanks to Potyomkin's intervention it was in the dark, rather sparse interior of this little church in the Altstadt that on 8 February 1829 their marriage was finally solemnised in the eyes of the Orthodox Church. It was a simple ceremony in unassuming surroundings (years later, describing the opulent splendour of a baptism attended by the Tsar and his family in one of the imperial chapels of Tsarskoye Selo, Tyutchev would recall by contrast 'the humility of our poor Greek chapel in Munich');[55] yet no doubt both he and Nelly were relieved when the officiating priest, Father Kalaganis, exchanged the rings on their hands and proclaimed them man and wife. For the now visibly pregnant bride the whole affair must have been something of an embarrassing ordeal, even though the congregation accepted that she and her groom were already respectably married, and that this Greek solemnisation was little more than a formality to satisfy Russian legal requirements. It seems unlikely that any member of Tyutchev's family was present. As recently as December his uncle Nikolay (his father's brother) had been in Munich, from where he had gone on to visit the Rhine.[56] However, there is nothing to suggest that he might have returned to Munich and stayed on for the ceremony.

At about the time of the wedding Tyutchev and Nelly moved into an apartment in a newly-built house at 248 Ottostrasse, just a few minutes' walk from the Embassy (the house, later renumbered 4, no longer stands).[57] Their previous address is unknown; wherever it was, they clearly needed more spacious accommodation. And it was in their Ottostrasse apartment that on 3 May 1829 Nelly gave birth to their daughter Anna.[58]

These early years of their marriage were later recalled by Tyutchev as a time of great happiness. At the beginning of 1828 they had been visited by Nikolay, and together with him and Clotilde had travelled to the Tyrol to experience the Alps in winter. Years later Tyutchev still had fond memories of the trip: 'How young everything was then, how fresh and beautiful!' he reminisced to his daughter Anna.[59] Nikolay may also have taken the opportunity to travel in western Europe on his own (there is no evidence that he returned to Russia to fight in the war against Turkey).[60] In any case by May 1829 he was back in Munich as a godparent at Anna's christening,[61] after which he appears to have stayed on for a year. There will also have been trips into the countryside around Munich: perhaps to the lakeside resort of Tegernsee, to Köfering with the Krüdeners, or to stay with Nelly's sister Louise and her husband at Burgfarrnbach, their palatial country residence outside Nuremberg (all places they are known to have visited in later years). The boys could be left at home in the care of their nurse, supervised perhaps by Aunt Karoline, leaving the parents free to travel unencumbered.

In 1827 and 1828 Tyutchev and Eleonore are known to have paid fairly lengthy visits to Paris, prompted in the words of one contemporary by 'the desire to see and get to know one of the great centres of modern civilisation'.[62] French political and cultural affairs had continued to occupy Tyutchev in Munich. His enthusiasm for the verse of Lamartine and Hugo, from which he made translations, has already been mentioned. While happy enough to accept honours and rewards from the Restoration government of King Charles X, these two leading figures of the French Romantic movement were close to the liberal opposition in their political views. Tyutchev himself subscribed regularly to the liberal journal *Le Globe* following its appearance in 1824, and if we are to believe Ivan Gagarin 'fully supported its position'.[63]

Their first visit to the French capital took place in the summer of 1827. Tyutchev had visiting cards with their Paris address printed specially for the occasion, one of which has survived. It reads: 'Monsieur de Tuttchef, Gentilhomme de la Chambre de S[a] M[ajesté] l'Empereur de Russie. Rue d'Artois No. 21', and has a handwritten note in Russian by Tyutchev on the back: 'Begs permission to pay his respects to Vasily Andreyevich', to which someone else has added the date '1827'. 'Vasily Andreyevich' is Zhukovsky, who is known to have been in Paris that year from 23 May to 10 July.[64] The card appears to have been returned (it is preserved in the Tyutchev family archive), suggesting that Zhukovsky was not at home on that particular occasion. That they did meet in Paris is confirmed by Zhukovsky's diary, which notes that on 7 July he attended a (presumably, Orthodox) mass with one of the Russian diplomats in Paris, a certain Dolgoruky, and there met Tyutchev and another diplomat, Divov. Later that day Zhukovsky was invited to a 'magnificent dinner' given by the Russian Ambassador Charles-André Pozzo di Borgo, whose other guests included the Papal Nuncio, such luminaries of French political life as Talleyrand and Villèle, and 'the whole Russian diplomatic corps', among whom Tyutchev is also named.[65]

There is no direct evidence as to when Tyutchev and Eleonore might have arrived in Paris or how long they stayed (diplomatic documents in Tyutchev's hand placing him in Munich on specific dates are completely lacking for 1827).[66] However, certain deductions can reasonably be made from the known facts. Zhukovsky's copious diary entries for his stay in Paris, in which the names of those he met are listed in scrupulous detail, contain no reference to Tyutchev until 7 July, three days before his own departure. Indeed, we may assume that attempting to visit Zhukovsky (who apart from anything else could provide him with an *entrée* into Parisian society) would have been one of Tyutchev's first priorities on arrival. All this makes it unlikely that he and Eleonore will have reached the French capital much before the end of June. That they moved into what were evidently rented rooms rather than a hotel and even had visiting cards printed for that address suggests that they planned a fairly lengthy stay, at least into August and perhaps beyond. Their lodgings in the rue d'Artois, just north of the Champs Élysées, were well situated for the kind of social networking implied by the visiting cards.[67] This will no doubt have centred on the Russian Embassy, perhaps also on the well-known salon in the rue du Bac of Henriette, divorced wife of the mineral-ogist Count Razumovsky. A friend of François Guizot and other leaders of the liberal opposition, the Countess also kept an open welcome for any Russians happening to be in Paris. Among the latter was Zhukovsky, who visited her frequently during his stay; she also befriended and patronised the political refugee Nikolay Turgenev and his brother, the scholar and writer Aleksandr.[68] Tyutchev would later get to know Aleksandr well in Munich, but as he was also in Paris at this time,[69] it may well have been there that they first met.

After a few weeks Tyutchev and Eleonore will have found their social activities severely curtailed by the annual summer migration of court and society to the country. Tyutchev was evidently speaking from experience when three years later he dissuaded a compatriot from going to Paris in high summer on the grounds that there was 'nothing to do' there then.[70] Rather than kick their heels in the deserted capital, it is easy enough to imagine him and Eleonore following some of the leading lights of Parisian society to where the action was. That they did precisely that is suggested by one of his poems:

Summer Evening

The sun's oppressive blazing orb
Has long been shaken from earth's head;
Now sea-waves languidly absorb
The dying glow of lambent red.

Bright stars already from the deep
Have risen, and with heads still wet
Prise up in their majestic sweep
Heaven's vault, that weighs upon us yet.

The air is stirred into a breeze:
A quickening torrent, fresh and fleet;
And lungs restored draw breath with ease,
Disburdened of day's stifling heat.

And all at once a tremor sweet
Thrills Nature to the very core,
As if she'd dipped her burning feet
In waters sprung from crag and tor.[71]

This vivid seashore sketch can be reliably dated to no later than the summer of 1828[72] and was clearly drawn from nature. But where? By that time the only place within easy reach of the sea Tyutchev is known to have been at the height of summer was Paris in 1827. (He and Eleonore did, it is true, return there in 1828, but perhaps as a result of their experience the previous year timed their visit for late spring, rather too early for the conditions described.) As to the actual location, for the Parisian *beau monde* of that period the only seaside resort worthy of consideration was Dieppe. A Princess of the royal household, Charles X's young widowed daughter-in-law Madame de Berry, had been paying the Normandy port regular visits for sea-bathing since 1824, making it through her patronage one of the most elegant resorts of its kind in Europe. By 1827 it boasted its own *établissement des bains*, promenade and casino, and was attracting visitors who included royalty and aristocrats. The previous summer a theatre had been opened by the Princess, herself a great patroness of the arts, and plays and operas were regularly performed.[73] A daily express coach service ensured easy access from the capital.[74]

On 6 August 1827 Madame de Berry was greeted by cheering crowds as she entered Dieppe for what had become an annual visit. Her six-week stay was marked by banquets, balls (one attended by 1,200 people), soirées and various musical and dramatic offerings. Performers included Rossini, who sang duets with his wife to piano accompaniment, and the young Irish baritone Michael Balfe, the Figaro in that year's Paris production of *The Barber of Seville*. The highlight of the whole visit was a grand fête at the ruined castle of Arques near Dieppe on 6 September, where the Princess, her daughter and a large crowd were treated to a mock battle re-enacting Henri IV's victory there in 1589. On 19 September Madame de Berry left Dieppe along a route lined with double ranks of troops and National Guards.[75] It is not difficult to imagine Tyutchev being drawn to all this spectacle and activity from a deserted metropolis where there was 'nothing to do'. And although it is impossible to say exactly when he and Eleonore might have come to Dieppe and for how long,[76] a visit coinciding at least in part with that of Madame de Berry would seem the most likely explanation of how the poem 'Summer Evening' came to be written.

ii Clandestine Joys

All in all the early years of marriage were for Tyutchev, as he later reminisced to his daughter Anna, 'filled with the most ardent emotions. [...] Those days were so beautiful, we were so happy! We thought they would never end.'[77] In rose-tinted retrospect it was no doubt easier to recall more of the ups than the downs of his marriage. Yet for those first years at least there are independent witnesses to their happiness. After Aleksey Sheremetev had stayed with them for six weeks at the end of 1829, a mutual aunt reported to Tyutchev's sister Darya: 'Aleksey writes praising Fyodor Ivanovich's wife! Thank God he's happy with her, I'm sincerely glad for him [...].'[78] Darya herself met Eleonore for the first time the following year. Much later she remembered being struck at the time by her brother's 'passion [which was] so mutually felt', and commented: 'looking at them, one would have thought they would love each other for ever — in this world and the next [...].'[79]

It is during this relatively carefree period in the second half of the 1820s (the 'great festival' of 'wondrous youth' commemorated in a later poem)[80] that Tyutchev's mastery of the lyric form first becomes fully apparent. And not surprisingly, the poems of this period are, as Richard Gregg has pointed out, generally far more optimistic and positive than his later ouput.[81] Despite the occasional darker note, the dominant theme is, as in the following examples, a celebration of *joie de vivre* and delight in the beauties of nature.

Thunderstorm in Spring

I love those storms so unexpected
In early May — the first of spring —
When thunder playfully projected
Sets all the blue sky echoing!

Peal follows peal with youthful clatter;
Then dust flies as a rainburst sheds
Its glistening drops, to fall and scatter
Like pearls, while sunlight gilds their threads.

From mountain heights a torrent surges,
Song fills the woods from countless throats;
And sound of stream and birdsong merges,
All chorusing the thunder's notes.

You'd say that Hebe — prone to blunder —
While letting Zeus's eagle sup
Had, laughing, spilled the foaming thunder
And shed it earthwards from her cup.[82]

Evening

Above the valley floats a ringing
Of distant bells: their muted sound,
Like cranes in close formation winging,
Soon dies, by rustling foliage drowned...

And, like a sea in spring, flood-swollen,
Day spreads before us bright and still —
While shadows that have gently stolen
Along the vale sweep on at will...[83]

Spring Waters

Although the fields are white with snow,
Fast-flowing waters speak of spring:
Rousing the meadows as they go,
They run on, sparkling, clamouring...

To all the valley they proclaim:
'Rejoice, for spring is on the way!
We come as heralds in spring's name,
Sent on, these tidings to convey!'

Rejoice, for spring is on the way!
And on its heels the merry round
Of Maytime, day by tranquil day,
When warmth and light and life abound...[84]

The same hedonistic sense of revelling in the joys of life permeates the only two love lyrics to survive from this period. In 'Hide-and-seek' ('*Cache-cache*' as Tyutchev titles it in French), the poet has arranged a tryst with his beloved at midday, but on arriving at her sunlit room at the appointed hour can see no sign of her. He knows she must be hiding somewhere: 'Her magical closeness I feel all around,/ Its rapturous essence imbuing the air.' Where can she be? Her presence is felt everywhere: in the fragrant blushing roses and pinks on the window sill, which seem to gaze at him with a knowing expression; in the strings of her harp, which he imagines still vibrating from her touch; in specks of dust sparkling in a beam of sunlight with the same fire he has seen burning in her eyes; even in a butterfly that has found its way into the room, fluttering from one flower to the next.[85]

Quite apart from its interest as a fairly extreme example of pathetic fallacy, the poem raises awkward biographical questions. Was it written at the time of Tyutchev's courtship of Nelly in 1826, and is she the harp-playing tease, as one critic claimed some forty years after the poet's death?[86] It is possible (even if the critic in question has been shown to be unreliable in other respects, and in this instance produces no supporting evidence). If anything, more of a case could be made for the 'mischievous girl' ('*shalun'ya*') and 'sylph' ('*sil'fida*') addressed here being Amélie (a young mother still in her teens, still no doubt the carefree 'fairy princess' she had appeared a couple of years before), rather than the more mature Nelly. However, she could be anyone.

The second of the two poems is quite patently not addressed to Nelly, and reveals an undeniable dark side to their supposedly happy marriage.

> *To N.N.*
>
> You love, and can dissemble to perfection:
> When unobserved in crowded company
> My foot encounters yours, you give reply —
> And do not blush beneath that fair complexion!
>
> Unchanged your mask of unconcerned abstraction,
> Unchanged the movement of your lips, your smile...
> Your husband — hateful guardian — meanwhile
> Admires your pliant charms with satisfaction.
>
> The hand of fate and deeds of men conspire
> To make clandestine joys the ones you treasure;
> You know the world... that it would rate our pleasure
> As treachery adds but to your desire.
>
> The bloom of innocence has long since faded
> From youthful cheeks, of modesty now bled,
> As all too soon Aurora's rays have fled
> From roses with young fragrances pervaded.
>
> So be it! More alluring to the mind,
> More pleasing to the senses is the image
> Of grapes cool-shaded from the sun's fierce homage,
> Their blood agleam through verdant trails of vine.[87]

This has the distinction of being the only original poem by Tyutchev to have been rejected for publication by both Raich and then Pushkin.[88] Did they (even the broad-minded Pushkin) sense that the flaunting of infidelity in this clearly autobiographical piece could lead to scandal if made public? Or did they simply acknowledge that the censors were unlikely to pass it anyway? In the event the poem remained unpublished in Tyutchev's lifetime.[89] Even from our own permissive age it has elicited the stern but just comment: 'This is a truly immoral poem, for the poet seems to be not so much committing adultery for the sake of love as indulging in love for the sake of adultery.'[90]

So much then (as the same critic, Richard Gregg, points out with further examples)[91] for Ivan Aksakov's claim, the substance of which has been repeated *ad nauseam* almost to the present day, that there is a 'total absence of coarse erotic content' in Tyutchev's poetry, that in comparison with other poets of his time 'his muse

104

can be called not only modest, but somehow demure.'⁹² Of a piece with this is
Aksakov's reticence (understandable enough given the restraints of the time and the
need to protect those still living) about his subject's private life, which apart from other
considerations he appears to have dismissed as largely irrelevant to the main purpose
of his book. He confines himself to telling us that before leaving Russia Tyutchev was
'an ardent devotee of feminine beauty', that he arrived in Munich in 1822 with 'a heart
susceptible to passionate, reckless infatuations', and that there 'his private life was not
lacking in personal romantic dramas, *which however can be of no interest whatsoever
to our readers*'.⁹³ In private Aksakov more forthcoming, writing to one of Tyutchev's
daughters with regard to his projected book: '[Tyutchev's] biography is a difficult
matter; it is rich not so much in outward as in its inner content, yet in this content a
central place is taken up by that side of his life which can least of all be revealed to the
public. "*L'abus des affections humaines*" [over-indulgence in affairs of the heart] —
that expression or rather self-definition so often repeated by him in his letters — that
characteristic trait of his life and moral make-up which explains so much in his poetry
and his being — all this must be kept quiet.'⁹⁴

Yet Tyutchev himself was the first to admit his own fallibility, as the remark just
quoted by Aksakov (evidently from letters now lost) demonstrates. In one letter to his
daughter Darya, Tyutchev confessed to being burdened with what he describes as 'this
terrible quality which has no name and which destroys all equilibrium in life, this thirst
for love [...].'⁹⁵ 'Over-indulgence', 'thirst for love': the phrases are eloquent, and suggest
that he was aware of being in thrall to something that can only be classed as an
addiction.

Together with the rest of Tyutchev's family, Aksakov decided for reasons which no
doubt seemed good at the time that it was appropriate to keep what he calls 'that side'
of the poet's life hidden from public view. The veil was lifted somewhat only thirty
years after Tyutchev's death by his illegitimate son Fyodor, offspring of a late
extramarital liaison. In a brief memoir of his father published to mark the centenary of
his birth, Fyodor criticised Aksakov's biography for skirting around what he calls 'a
trait running like a red thread through [Tyutchev's] life, which paralysed his actions,
pushed all other interests into the background, and allowed him no satisfaction in any
other sphere.' This was, as might be guessed, 'his somehow quite extraordinary
adoration and veneration of women, which is rarely encountered in such a degree.'⁹⁶
More specifically, Tyutchev 'throughout his life, until his very last days, was attracted
to women and enjoyed almost legendary success with them [...].'⁹⁷

Fyodor's uncle Aleksandr Georgievsky, who knew Tyutchev in the last decade of his
life, was even more explicit in a memoir published only fairly recently. Here he writes:
'Devotion to feminine beauty and the charms of feminine nature was Fyodor
Ivanovich's constant weakness from his earliest youth — a devotion which was
accompanied by very serious but usually short-term and even fleeting passions for this
or that individual.'⁹⁸ From another witness we learn that Tyutchev was wont to refer to
his brief flings as '*des bluettes*' ('sparkles' or 'twinklings' — a term which so appealed to
Nicholas I that he adopted it for his own amatory adventures).⁹⁹ As for the 'legendary'
success with women, Georgievsky explains that 'with his intellect and wit, with his
education and refined manners he was indeed a captivating personality and could
charm anyone he wanted to with ease, especially if they were ladies [...].'¹⁰⁰

Fyodor and Georgievsky knew Tyutchev only towards the end of his life, yet both agree that his addiction to the pleasures of the flesh dated from his youth (a fact curiously enough corroborated by Aksakov in his own coy phraseology). Karl Pfeffel, who was close to Tyutchev in Munich in the 1830s, later recalled the 'cult of beauty' to which his friend was then devoted.[101] Another intimate from those years, Ivan Gagarin, has even preserved some of his comments on the subject. 'There is an infinite number of desirable women, each with a charm of her own,' Tyutchev once told him. 'Imagine a man capable of discerning and appreciating that which is charming in each of them, endow him with strength in proportion, and you will have Don Juan.'[102]

All this enables us to see the two surviving love poems written by Tyutchev in his mid-twenties in a new and yet still puzzling light. Clearly they (and especially 'To N.N.') are not the fruits of some isolated extramarital fling, but reflect a deep-seated pattern of serial infidelity. The puzzle lies in reconciling this with Tyutchev's memories of an apparently happy marriage to Nelly in these years, which was also the impression gained by others at the time. One is driven to the conclusion that Nelly — 'meekness personified' as her daughter Anna later remembered her —[103] was prepared to overlook his philandering as long as her own position was not seriously threatened. In Georgievsky's opinion, only a woman capable of 'a love that is completely self-sacrificing, unselfish, unbounded, unending, undivided and prepared for anything' could ever hope to tie down in a lasting relationship 'such an easily enamoured and inconstant poet, flitting from one blossom to the next, as Tyutchev was.'[104] Although Georgievsky was writing of his sister-in-law Yelena Denisyeva, his words apply equally to any of Tyutchev's long-term relationships, the success or otherwise of which seems to have depended heavily on the attitude of the female partner. In the case of Yelena, Georgievsky was certain that her liaison with Tyutchev (which lasted fourteen years and resulted in three children) was accompanied on his part by a series of 'fleeting affairs, leaving no trace'.[105] For Nelly too this must have been an unpleasant fact of married life, to which she responded with selfless, unconditional, almost maternal love, providing her husband's vacillating and restless nature with much-needed if largely undeserved comfort and support

On the evidence of the poem 'To N.N.' some of Tyutchev's affairs may in fact have been more serious than the one-night stands implied by Georgievsky. The poet and his secret lover have clearly known each other for some time, for he can remember when she was still an innocent, blushing girl. Now she has become hardened and cynical through her marriage to a man who in the poet's eyes treats her as little more than his property, the object of his gratification, to be jealously guarded from the attentions of others (lines 7-8). Verse 3 hints that the marriage was contracted against the girl's better instincts, that through the workings of fate and the influence of those around her she has been forced into a false position in which true fulfilment can be found only at the expense of resorting to duplicity.

All of this applies to Amélie's situation as Tyutchev would have seen it after her marriage to Krüdener. As for Amélie's own attitude, the known facts of her subsequent life provide evidence enough that she regarded her forced union as at best a marriage of convenience, entailing few if any obligations of fidelity on her part. In a letter to Tyutchev from Florence in October 1828 Heine asked to be remembered to 'Madame déchargeuse d'affaires Amalie von Krüdener' (of whom he had just been reminded by seeing the Venus de Medici).[106] He could rely on Tyutchev getting the point of his joke title for Amélie: a snide reference not so much to her husband's diplomatic position as to affairs of a more scandalous kind.

On a visit to the Russian capital with her husband in the summer of 1833 Amélie was introduced to the court and St Petersburg society by Max von Lerchenfeld, who had been appointed Bavarian Ambassador the previous year. She made a great impression. Darya Ficquelmont, the Austrian Ambassador's Russian wife, described Amélie in her diary as 'first of all a great ornament for any social gathering, as well as genuine, *natural* (something beyond value in this country) and without pretension.'[107] Men on the other hand seem to have sensed (as Heine had) a more predatory quality. 'We have the Munich beauty Madame Krüdener here,' the poet Pyotr Vyazemsky wrote to Aleksandr Turgenev from St Petersburg on 15/27 June. 'She's very sweet, vivacious and attractive, but hasn't managed to get her claws into me yet.'[108] The following year Turgenev himself met Amélie in Munich. On 29 March he noted in his diary that at a dinner at the Russian Ambassador's he had sat next to 'the beautiful Madame Krüdener,' and (an echo perhaps of Tyutchev's 'hateful guardian'?) that 'her husband kept looking.'[109] Among Amélie's many admirers during her visit to St Petersburg was Pushkin: Vyazemsky describes him at a party given by the Ficquelmonts, 'palpitating with his interest of the moment, blushing, when he gazed at the Krüdener woman, and constantly hanging around her'.[110]

Pleased at the success of his half-sister's foray into Russian high society, Max von Lerchenfeld clearly nursed ambitions to make the arrangement more permanent and worked behind the scenes to facilitate Krüdener's transfer to St Petersburg. This was officially confirmed in October 1835.[111] Not long afterwards Max wrote to Amélie with practical advice on moving to the Russian capital and an assurance that he would help in setting up home, adding that 'the Emperor is looking forward most sincerely to your being here'.[112] She and Krüdener left Munich for St Petersburg the following May.[113] Amélie was soon able to consolidate her position in Russian society and to enjoy the particular attention of Tsar Nicholas himself. In one of her few surviving letters she refers to receiving a personal annual stipend from the Emperor from 1836 to 1844 as compensation for moving to Russia, which she claims she had been reluctant to do.[114] She was also given her own residence in St Petersburg, next to that of the Tsar's daughter, Grand Duchess Maria Nikolayevna.[115] A glimpse of her life at court is given in the diary of another society lady, Aleksandra Smirnova:

That winter [1838-1839] was one of the most splendid. [...] There was dancing every week at the Anichkov Palace, in the white drawing-room: no more than a hundred persons would be invited. The Emperor devoted his particular attention to Baroness Krüdener, but flirted like a young wench with everyone, and relished the rivalry between Buturlina and Krüdener. [...] Once at the end of the ball [...] Baroness Krüdener and I sat down together in a corner by the fireplace. She was wearing a white dress, with green leaves entwined in her blonde curls; she looked stunningly beautiful, but was not very happy. Across the room at an angle from us the Tsar was standing in the doorway with Ye. M. Buturlina, whom everyone found attractive more for her carefree gaiety than for her beauty, and he appeared to be engaged in lively conversation with her. [...] I said to Madame Krüdener: 'You had supper with him, but today the final honours go to her.' 'He's a strange man,' she said. 'These matters need after all to have a result, yet with him there is never a conclusion, he does not have the heart for it; he attaches a curious significance to fidelity. All these stratagems with her prove nothing.'[116]

From this it seems fair to conclude that Amélie did not share the Tsar's scruples about marital fidelity, and that if she never actually became his mistress it was not for want of trying. In due course, however, Amélie's star at court began to wane. Nicholas's daughter Olga Nikolayevna later recalled that to begin with her parents had both been enchanted by Amélie, the Emperor in particular believing that they had found in her 'a sincere friend', but that things eventually changed when the Empress 'saw through her'. 'A strange woman!' comments Olga Nikolayevna (who like her mother clearly resented Amélie as a potential threat to her parents' marriage). 'Concealed beneath her amiable exterior and charming, often amusing nature was cunning of the highest order.'[117] Amélie then turned her attentions to Count Alexander von Benckendorff, the elderly and ailing chief of Nicholas's notorious Third Section, or secret police. (As Nicholas himself put it, he 'relinquished his place' to Benckendorff.)[118] In Olga Nikolayevna's judgement the day-to-day running of the Third Section suffered badly as a result of Amélie's influence on its chief. 'She made use of him coldly, disposing in a calculating fashion of his person, his money and his connections wherever and in whatever way she considered advantageous; yet he did not even notice this.'[119]

Whatever the substance of Olga Nikolayevna's accusations, coloured as they may have been by personal resentment and jealousy, it is clear that Amélie had managed to make enemies at court. By March 1845 Aleksandra Smirnova is describing her in her diary as 'an unpleasant German' with 'an inordinate greed for money', and claiming that the Tsar had recently spoken of her with displeasure and accused her of ingratitude and hostility towards Russia.[120] The previous year Nicholas had given Krüdener the post of Ambassador to Sweden. According to Olga Nikolayevna this was done in order to remove Amélie discreetly from the scene. Amélie's response was to claim an attack of measles as an excuse for not accompanying her husband.[121] From then on she seems to have been a rare visitor in Stockholm, dividing her time mainly between St Petersburg in the winter and Köfering in the summer. As Olga Nikolayevna tartly observes in her account, the final outcome of Amélie's diplomatic indisposition was the birth in 1848 of a son fathered by her latest lover, Count Nikolay Adlerberg.[122] In January 1852, while wintering in St Petersburg, she learned of Krüdener's death in Stockholm. She sent her older son Nikolay to the funeral but did not attend herself, contenting herself in letters to the family's steward Georg Köckenberger with conventional expressions of grief, at the same time giving detailed instructions concerning her late husband's estate and effects.[123] Soon she was involved in unseemly haggling with the Emperor and Empress over the level of her pension.[124] Three years later, still attractive and youthful-looking at 47, she married Adlerberg, who was eleven years her junior.[125] A favourite of Tsar Alexander II, he was later appointed Governor-General of Finland, and Amélie found a new role in Helsingfors society.[126] By all accounts her second marriage was much happier than the first.

It was only natural that Tyutchev should have kept himself informed about

Amélie's progress at court (there is evidence that they corresponded with each other, although any letters are now lost). 'I have certain reasons to suppose that she is not as happy in her glittering position as I would wish,' he wrote to his parents in 1837. 'Poor, dear, excellent woman. She will never be as happy as she deserves.'[127] And indeed, her subsequent life (at least until she met Adlerberg) would appear to prove Tyutchev right. Her restless search for power, wealth and sexual adventure, undertaken as compensation for a loveless forced marriage, could never bring lasting fulfilment.

News of the Krüdeners after their arrival in St Petersburg in 1836 reached Tyutchev in a letter from his friend and former colleague Ivan Gagarin. Gagarin's letter has not survived, but some idea of its contents is given by Tyutchev's reply dated 7/19 July. 'Your details concerning our fair Esther and her Mordecai gave me great pleasure,' he writes.[128] At first glance the reference is puzzling, for in the biblical account Mordecai is not Esther's husband but an older relative who adopted her when she was orphaned. This could be a derisive allusion to Krüdener's age; yet the main thrust of Tyutchev's wit becomes apparent from the rest of the story as told in the Book of Esther. The Jew Mordecai serves at the court of the Persian King Ahasuerus, who is so captivated by Esther's beauty that he takes her as one of his concubines and eventually makes her his Queen. The implied King Ahasuerus of Tyutchev's biblical allusion can only be Tsar Nicholas.

So revealing are some of the references to Amélie in this and other letters that Gagarin felt obliged to omit them when, after the poet's death, he sent copies to Ivan Aksakov as material for the latter's biography (Amélie was still alive).[129] A later request by the owner of Gagarin's archive to publish the letters was refused by Tyutchev's widow on the grounds that they were 'doubtless too intimate.'[130] However, the originals have in the main survived, and we can now read those passages considered so delicate at the time. Thus in the letter of 7/19 July already quoted Tyutchev is sarcastic about Krüdener's abilities as a diplomat, but adds that in his new job 'the adorable nature of his wife' will protect him from any consequences of his incompetence, and suggests that the Baron's friends ('if he has any') would do well to reassure him as to the inherent security of his position.[131] As for Amélie herself:

> I am dying to write to her [...] but am prevented by a stupid reason. I asked a favour of her, and now my letter might appear an attempt to remind her of this. Ah, what misfortune! What need must one be in to ruin one's friendship in such a way! It's as if one had no means of covering one's nakedness other than by making a pair of breeches from a canvas by Raphael... And yet of all the people I know in the world she is without contradiction the one to whom I should be the least averse to feeling myself obliged...[132]

Writing to Gagarin three days later, he encloses a letter to Amélie from her Munich friend Jeanette Paumgarten, which the latter has asked to be 'smuggled' to her in the diplomatic post:

> Attempt to acquit yourself honorably of this little act of treason. There are after all cases where the objective justifies the means, and since in the present case it is undeniably Madame [Krüdener] who is the objective of the letter, this is one

which could justify far greater enormities... I suppose the moments are now less rare when one can speak to our beautiful friend other than with a third person present. How I should love to see her again at one of these moments... Jeanette and I often speak of her, but that is all vague and does not satisfy me. Indeed, it is only with her that I like to speak of her, for she is, after me, the one who knows herself best... Tell her not to forget me: my person, of course, only my person, she can forget the rest... Tell her that if she were to forget me, some misfortune would befall her... She would be visited by a little wrinkle on her forehead or cheek, or by a little strand of grey hair, for it would be an apostasy from the memories of her youth. My God, why have they made a constellation of her... She was so lovely on this earth.[133]

Tyutchev's abiding attachment to Amélie, a decade after they had gone their separate marital ways, could hardly be more clearly or more frankly expressed. Even those other 'acts of treason' and 'enormities' committed for Amélie's sake at which he hints leave little to the imagination. Nor can the identity of the irksome 'third person' be in much doubt. (Whether, as Tyutchev appears to suggest, Krüdener really had relaxed his guard now that a certain claimant to his wife's favours was over a thousand miles away is another question.) Yet perhaps one of the most striking features of this passage is the way in which it echoes the content and imagery of 'To N.N.' The poem too dwells on and justifies treachery, while the resented third person appears in the guise of 'hateful guardian'. And in both letter and poem outward signs of maturing or ageing in the woman are seen as tokens of an inner falling away from innocence and integrity.

Tyutchev and Amélie remained lifelong friends; on more than one occasion she was to use her influence in high places to further his career. Although we cannot be absolutely certain that their relationship ever went beyond friendship or amorous attachment, it seems highly likely: the evidence is circumstantial but strong. From all that we know of both of them, it would be surprising indeed if they had not become lovers at some time in the mid- to late 1820s. And if Amélie could point to the sham of her marriage to Krüdener in justification, for Tyutchev there was no such excuse. Eleonore would have to continue suffering her husband's infidelities; he for his part was laying up a store of guilt for the future.

iii Heine

Among the artists and intellectuals attracted to Ludwig's new Athens was the thirty-year-old Heinrich Heine. The liberal publisher Johann Friedrich von Cotta needed a co-editor for his projected journal *Neue allgemeine politische Annalen* (*New Universal Political Annals*), to be published in Munich, and Heine (then still better known as a witty and trenchant commentator on the current scene than as a poet) seemed the ideal candidate. His fame rested largely on two best-selling volumes of *Reisebilder* (*Travel Sketches*), in which he had expressed libertarian political views close to Cotta's own. Heine accepted the post on generous terms, cautiously stipulating a six-month contract to begin with. He arrived in Munich on 26 November 1827,[134] but was very soon beginning to doubt the wisdom of his move. Work on the journal brought little fulfilment, and throughout the winter he was plagued with illness. In conservative and clerical circles his radical political and religious views, combined with his Jewish background, met with open hostility. The intellectual climate of Munich he found 'insipid and wretched,' 'trivial,' and dominated by 'small-mindedness' ('*Kleingeist-erei*').[135] Already he was dreaming of escape to Italy.

His only consolation came from a small circle of close friends who included his co-editor on the journal Friedrich Lindner, the dramatists Eduard von Schenk and Michael Beer, and Tyutchev. Beer, brother of the composer Meyerbeer and an old acquaintance of Heine's from his Berlin days, had been drawn to Munich by King Ludwig's artistic patronage and become friendly with Schenk, one of Ludwig's ministers, who had been entrusted with moving the university from Landshut.[136] Apart from writing plays, Schenk was widely held to be responsible for tidying up, if not re-writing, the King's poetic efforts (a rumour eventually borne out after Schenk's death, when a marked deterioration was observed in the standard of his royal patron's verse). Although Tyutchev is known to have associated with members of this group in 1828,[137] he may have known some if not all of them earlier, before Heine arrived on the scene. Certainly he would have sought acquaintance with the celebrated young German poet, whose work he already admired. They probably first met in February or March 1828, not long after Tyutchev had returned from his trip to the Tyrol with Eleonore, Clotilde and Nikolay.[138]

Soon Heine, with his finely-chiselled features and ironic smile, self-assured yet quick to bridle, was a constant guest in the Tyutchevs' house. No doubt the maternally inclined Eleonore was happy to offer domestic sanctuary to this restless free spirit who seemed to find it so hard to settle anywhere. (To a contemporary who found him still living out of a suitcase after several months in Hamburg he 'had the appearance of a traveller who has alighted from a stage-coach only the day before and spent a rather restless night in a hotel.')[139] Heine's own account of his life in Munich at this time is given in a letter to his friend Karl Varnhagen von Ense dated 1 April 1828:

> Some delightful female acquaintanceships — which are, however, conducive neither to my health nor my enthusiasm for work. [...] À propos! Do you know the daughters of Count Bodmer [*sic*] [...]? One of them, already no longer in the first bloom of youth, but infinitely charming and secretly married to my dearest friend here, a young Russian diplomat named Tutscheff, and her still very young and beautiful sister, are the two ladies with whom I keep the most pleasant and amiable company. At midday these two, my friend Tutscheff and I often make up a foursome for lunch, and in the evenings, when I find a few more beauties there, I chatter away to my heart's content, mostly ghost stories. I know how to find some pleasant oasis anywhere in the great desert of life.[140]

Heine obviously relished the wit and erudition of his 'dearest friend' in Munich, deriving from his conversation perhaps as much refreshment as he did from the charming company of Eleonore and Clotilde. Both were adept conversationalists, Tyutchev specialising in the extended pyrotechnic tirade, Heine in the brief but deadly ironic interpolation or invocation of the absurd. Their common language was French, which both spoke fluently. In intellectual matters too they had much in common. Both had a deep interest in philosophy; both were engrossed with political issues of the day, tending to see these in their wider historical context; both were inclined to take a critical scalpel to the status quo. Above all they shared a passion for literature. Among the topics discussed appears to have been Goethe's position as revered patriarch of German literature. We know that Heine greatly admired Goethe's poetry, but was critical of what he saw as the way in which both the poet and his works had been appropriated for its own use by the political establishment. Perhaps he told Tyutchev of his pilgrimage to see Goethe some four years before, when he had been alienated by the cool reception given him and shocked at the old man's physical condition ('his face yellow, like that of a mummy; his toothless mouth working anxiously; his overall appearance a picture of human frailty').[141] Tyutchev, like Heine, held Goethe in the highest esteem as a poet; yet although he himself never met the great man,[142] he clearly also had views on the more contingent aspects of his celebrity. In an article written in Munich and published in the *Neue allgemeine politische Annalen* Heine quotes 'a certain witty foreigner' as comparing the ageing Goethe to a former bandit leader who, having seen the error of his ways and settled down to life as a staid and respectable burgher, 'attempts to observe all the philistine virtues in every smallest detail, and experiences the most painful embarrassment if one of his colleagues from the Calabrian forests should happen to bump into him and wish to renew their former friendship.'[143] *Ex ungue leonem*: the style of the *mot* is, as first pointed out by Yury Tynyanov, unmistakably that of Tyutchev, the only 'witty foreigner' known to have associated with Heine in Munich.[144] It affords us a brief glimpse of lively discussions the two poets must have had at the Tyutchevs' apartment or while strolling through the streets and parks of the city; perhaps too in Heine's rented rooms at the Rechberg-palais, the stately town house of the Counts von Rechberg,[145] or just around the corner in the congenial atmosphere of the snug little Hundskugel Inn (the oldest in Munich and, like the Rechbergpalais, still standing today).

In the course of their talks Heine does appear to have learned something of his companion's poetic activities and ambitions. In his one surviving letter to Tyutchev he observes that poets are typically remiss about writing to their friends, and adds: 'This remark applies to you as well.'[146] It is likely that Tyutchev will have shown Heine some of his verse published in various rather obscure Russian journals and almanachs. Of particular interest was his translation of Heine's 'Ein Fichtenbaum steht einsam...' ('A spruce tree stands alone...') in Raich's *Severnaya Lira* of 1827, which has the distinction of being the first published translation of a Heine poem into Russian.[147] Heine was no doubt flattered that his new friend had even noticed this piece, let alone translated it, given that only 270 copies of the collection in which it first appeared had been sold.[148] Knowing no Russian, Heine would have been unable to form any judgement as to Tyutchev's verse, although the small amount published, including several translations, may have led him to suspect that the young Russian diplomat was little more than a talented amateur. Tyutchev will have done nothing to persuade him otherwise. He was inspired to produce a further half-dozen translations of Heine's poems at about this time. One of these, 'Das Herz ist mir bedrückt, und sehnlich...' ('My heart is sick, and yearningly...'), is an interesting choice, with its Nietzschean vision of a world in which both the old God and Satan are dead.[149] There was never any chance of Tyutchev's version being approved by the censors, and in fact it remained unpublished until after the Bolshevik revolution.[150] Did he choose it for its atheist message? This seems likely, given the religious scepticism expressed, albeit more cautiously, in some of his own poems of the 1830s.[151] And we are reminded of how his religious and political views had outraged a conservative Bavarian aristocrat a few years before.

That he shared some of Heine's political views too is suggested by 'Napoleon's Grave', an original poem composed in 1827 or 1828.[152] The figure of Napoleon had become something of a touchstone for radical thinkers. He was admired by Heine, even more so by Lindner.[153] As published in Raich's journal *Galateya* in 1829, Tyutchev's poem is a fairly innocuous description of the grave on St Helena (probably based on that given in Sir Walter Scott's biography of Napoleon, which appeared in 1827),[154] together with a meditation on how the mighty are fallen. Yet two missing lines marked by rows of dots suggest that the censors had come across something they considered too complimentary to the former Emperor. A similar fate befell another poem dating from 1832 which paraphrases Heine's description of Napoleon (in *Französische Zustände*) as a genius who combined the 'eagles of inspiration' in his head with the 'snakes of calculation' in his heart.[155] Submitted for publication in Pushkin's journal *Sovremmenik* in 1836, it was rejected *in toto* by the censors.[156] (After the 1848 revolution Tyutchev's attitude towards Napoleon changed: he added eight lines to the piece to give it a clearly negative slant, attributing the French leader's fall, interestingly enough, to his lack of religious faith.)[157]

The literary fall-out of the friendship between Heine and Tyutchev was by no means all in one direction, for in Heine's work too echoes have been detected of their conversations in the spring and summer of 1828. On 10 May news reached Munich that Russia had declared war on Turkey.[158] For most of May and June Tyutchev and Eleonore were in Paris,[159] but after their return we may be fairly sure as to the main topic of discussion between the two poets. The war promised to settle once and for all the question of Greek independence from Ottoman rule, a cause espoused by liberals throughout Europe, Heine included. For Tyutchev there was the added prospect of seeing Catherine the Great's 'Greek project,' of which Osterman-Tolstoy had so often spoken, rise again from the ashes. His poem 'Oleg's Shield,' published in *Galateya* the following year, invokes a fabled Russian campaign of the 10th century in which Prince Oleg of Kiev is said to have hung his shield on the gates of Constantinople as a token of victory.[160] And after the successful conclusion of the war in September 1829 he produced a Russian verse translation of King Ludwig's poem hailing Tsar Nicholas's victory, which the Ambassador enclosed with a copy of the original in an official despatch to St Petersburg.[161]

In Italy later in the summer of 1828 Heine one day found himself discussing the progress of the Russo-Tukish War with a Baltic-German subject of the Tsar on the battlefield of Marengo, scene of one of Napoleon's most decisive victories. The irony of the situation was not lost on him. Autocratic Russia, which had proved to be Napoleon's nemesis, was now in the position of championing the cause of Greek liberty more energetically than any other nation. For liberals everywhere, Heine concluded, Tsar Nicholas had become 'the standard-bearer of freedom.'[162] 'A strange transformation!' (he continues in his *Reisebilder*, or *Travel Sketches*, from Italy). Lovers of freedom had been forced to realise 'who is our friend, or rather the bogeyman of our enemies.'¹⁶³ These comments are in themselves perhaps not particularly surprising; Heine would after all not be the first to marvel at the unexpected shifts in allegiance brought about by *Realpolitik*. What does come as a shock is the passage immediately following, in which without a trace of irony Heine holds up Nicholas's Russia as a shining model of democracy. Russia, he argues, is free of the evils of feudalism and clericalism, for in that country nobility is granted in return for service to the state, while the power of the church has been effectively curbed. As for the absolutism of tsarist rule, it is in fact no more than a benevolent dictatorship concerned to put into practice those 'liberal ideas of the contemporary age' with which he claims the current Russian administration to be 'imbued.' What is more, with its Empire of many peoples and races covering a sixth of the globe, Russia is said to provide an example of 'Christian' cosmopolitanism, free of the 'heathen' sin of nationalism. England, which despite Magna Carta Heine sees as irredeemably in thrall to feudal institutions, comes off badly by comparison: 'In England freedom arose from historical circumstances, in Russia from principles.' That 'Russia is a democratic state' seems to him beyond dispute.¹⁶⁴

On what did Heine base these startling conclusions? The idea of tsarist autocracy as a 'democratic' institution, with direct links to the people bypassing vested interests, was one later developed by the Slavophiles. On the other hand the concept of a wise ruler in the mould of Peter the Great or Catherine, wielding absolute power in the cause of reform, seems to owe more to the Age of Enlightenment. Both views have affinities with those known to have been held by Tyutchev after his eventual return to Russia, when, although in many respects close to the Slavophiles, he shied away from their wholesale anti-Westernism, and in particular their negative assessment of Peter the Great. Not surprisingly, several scholars have detected his influence in Heine's panegyric to Russian autocracy.¹⁶⁵ It is certainly not hard to imagine the German poet being won over in Munich by the eloquence of this erudite, urbane and thoroughly westernised Russian who was clearly very much his own man. As one of these scholars has concluded, 'To enlist Heine's pen on the side of Russia was a major, albeit perhaps unconscious, success of Russian diplomacy.'¹⁶⁶

If it was a success, it was a partial and temporary one. Tsar Nicholas's threatening opposition to the July Revolution of 1830 in Paris, and his subsequent brutal suppression of the Polish insurrection of 1830-1831, finally opened Heine's eyes. Although still prepared to acknowledge 'the anti-feudalist principle of the equality of all citizens' in Russia, he now reviled the erstwhile 'standard-bearer of freedom' for having made himself the henchman of the European aristocracy. As for the absolutism so recently hailed as an instrument of progressive reform, it was now dismissed as incompatible with constitutional freedom.¹⁶⁷

Tyutchev appears to have noted with approval Heine's originally favourable comments on Russia soon after their publication in Part III of *Reisebilder* in January 1830 (some extracts from the book had previously appeared in a newspaper, but not Chapters 30 and 31, which deal with the visit to Marengo).¹⁶⁸ This is apparent from his appropriately poetic reaction to that whole section: a translation into Russian verse of the concluding passage of Chapter 31, in which the new day dawning over the battlefield becomes for Heine a portent of the coming dawn of freedom for mankind:

As if beneath a triumphal arch of massive cloud the sun now rose —
victoriously, radiantly, confidently, heralding a splendid day. Yet I felt like the
poor moon, which still hung in the sky, growing ever fainter. It had trudged its
solitary path across the firmament in desolate night, when happiness slumbered
and only ghosts, owls and sinners were abroad; and now — as the young day
broke forth with jubilant rays and the flickering red of dawn — after one last
mournful glance at the great light of the world it must take its leave, to vanish
like ethereal mist.

'It will be a splendid day!' my travelling companion called out to me from
the carriage. Yes, it will be a splendid day, softly repeated my praying heart, and
trembled with melancholy and joy. Yes, it will be a splendid day: the sun of
freedom will warm the earth more gladly than the aristocracy of all the stars; a
new race of men will blossom forth and grow, conceived in the free embrace of
volition, not on a couch of duress and under the watchful eyes of ecclesiastical
tax-gatherers; and with this freedom of birth in men too free thoughts and
feelings will be begotten, of which we who are born as slaves can have no
inkling — ah! just as they will have no inkling of how dreadful was that night in
whose darkness we had to live, of how desperately we had to fight, with foul
ghosts, dull-witted owls and whited sepulchres of sinners! [...] I have never set
great store by literary fame, and whether my songs are praised or censured is of
little interest to me. But be sure to place a sword on my coffin; for I was a
valiant soldier in the war to liberate mankind.[169]

For his translation[170] Tyutchev uses blank verse, skilfully capturing the stately
rhythms of Heine's prose passage (roughly the second half of which is quoted above).
And while rendering the meaning of individual sentences fairly closely, he rearranges
the order of paragraphs to make the text read as a self-contained piece rather than an
extract. These added features make his translation a poetic statement in its own right.
But a statement to whom? Certainly not Heine, who knew no Russian. Nor to a wider
reading public: the poem's political content ruled out any prospect of publication in
tsarist Russia (it first saw print only in 1926). One might be tempted to see it as no
more than a routine exercise in translation. But then why the significant choice of text,
why the careful editing? And how to explain the spilling-over of imagery from it (the
moon by day) into other poems of his at this time?[171] As so often with Tyutchev's poetry
we suspect that for him the question of readership was in a sense quite irrelevant. For
him true poetry — whose spirit 'Descends to us, the sons of earth/ A vision, of celestial,
birth'[172] — was quite literally not of this world. Even to say that he wrote for posterity
would be to suppose too palpable a target audience. Perhaps in some way difficult to
put into words he felt his poetry was addressed to a timeless Platonic realm, a
community of like-minded souls dead and unborn: that 'Elysium of shades' within the
soul which he invokes in one of his poems.[173] And in this context his translation of
Heine may indeed be seen as a statement: as a cryptic acknowledgment, perhaps, of his
own contribution to the section on Marengo; no doubt also as a declaration of
sympathy with Heine's ecstatic vision of freedom; but above all, and particularly in the
closing section, as a tribute from one poet of genius to another.

Heine's letter to Varnhagen von Ense leaves little doubt that it was as much the prospect of charming female company (in particular that of Clotilde) as the need for intellectual stimulation which drew him to the Tyutchevs' household. Of his general state of mind during those first winter months in Munich he later wrote:

> It was winter then in my soul as well; my thoughts and feelings were as if snowed in, I felt so dead and withered [...]. At last the day came when everything changed completely. The sun broke through in the sky and gave the earth, its ancient child, the milk of its rays to drink [...], the whole of nature smiled, and this smile was called spring. Then in me too a new spring began [...]. Was it a brown-haired or a blonde sun which awakened spring in my heart again?[174]

Eleven love poems written by him in Munich in 1828, later included in his collection *Neuer Frühling* (*New Spring*), are thought to be addressed to Clotilde.[175] Still only nineteen when Heine first met her,[176] she was indeed, as he found her, 'very young and beautiful'. Her portrait, painted only a couple of years later, shows her as a graceful, aristocratic young woman, her attractive oval face framed by brown hair swept up in an elaborate fashionable coiffure. Large hazel eyes gaze out with a pensive, almost dreamy expression, and there is something enigmatic about the unaffected smile flickering on her delicate rounded lips. All this will have struck a chord with the poet in Heine; others too were taken with 'the graceful and charming Clotilde Bothmer' (as Ivan Gagarin remembered her from this period).[177] She was certainly no languid hothouse lily: forced by her family's difficulties to cope with the practicalities of life from an early age, she now earned her keep by helping to look after Eleonore's four young sons, a task to which (to judge from later reports) she took with enthusiasm.

In May and June, with Tyutchev and Eleonore away in Paris, there were more opportunities for Heine and Clotilde to be alone together. The *Neuer Frühling* poems written in Munich chronicle their blossoming romance. The very first in the cycle parallels Heine's own prose account of the coming of spring. Sitting beneath a white tree, the poet feels that his heart, like the whole of nature, is in the grip of winter. Suddenly he notices white flakes falling on him from above, and assumes it is snow, before realising 'with a joyous shock' that the tree is scattering fragrant spring blossoms down on him:

> How it thrills, this sweet enchantment!
> Winter into May is turning:
> Snow transfigured into blossom,
> Love anew within you burning.[178]

Another poem expresses the joy felt when he sees his beloved walk past. Rejoicing, his heart is spontaneously drawn to follow 'in her lovely wake'. However,

> Then you turn around, and gaze at
> Me with eyes so wide and true
> That, unnerved, my heart can hardly
> Bring itself to follow you.[179]

On another occasion he roams the most frequented avenues in the city's parks, 'Under each straw hat impatient / To espy my lovely's features.' But he does not find her, 'And the birds in all the bushes / Make mock of the lovelorn fool.'[180] However, a further poem records that they are at last united (the political metaphor here seeming to hint playfully at Clotilde's family links with Russia):

> To conclude the Holy Alliance
> Our two hearts did agree;
> They lay so close together
> In perfect harmony.
>
> But, oh! that rose so youthful
> Upon your breast deployed
> (Poor party to our treaty)
> Was crushed and near destroyed.[181]

Towards the end of his life Heine fondly reminisced to a friend about this time in Munich. He remembered one day visiting a picture gallery with a young lady who was particularly keen on his poem 'Ein Fichtenbaum steht einsam...'. Here they were both enchanted by a humorous genre painting of a girl dozing with a book open on her knees, while a youth playfully tickles her nose with an ear of corn to wake her up. 'I commissioned a young painter to make a copy of the painting for my lady friend,' Heine recalled, 'and to tease her for her overblown enthusiasm, I inscribed that poem about the spruce tree in very fine handwriting on the open page of the book'[182] The lady friend in question has been reliably identified as Clotilde.[183] That Tyutchev's translation of the poem had appeared in print the previous year was by now probably known within the family, as well as to Heine, and this might at least partly explain both Clotilde's impressionable enthusiasm for it and Heine's ironic teasing. And, as Yury Tynyanov has pointed out, it is surely no coincidence that Heine subsequently chose to preface the whole *Neuer Frühling* cycle with lines from 'Ein Fichtenbaum steht einsam...' as epigraph .[184]

In July 1828 Heine's six-month contract as co-editor of *Neue allgemeine politische Annalen* came to an end; the future of the journal seemed in any case to be in doubt. For Heine this came as a welcome release. Whenever the distant Alps had been visible from the city, he had gazed longingly at them, dreaming like Goethe before him of 'the land where citrons bloom' that lay beyond. More prosaically, a journey to Italy promised material for a further volume of the *Reisebilder*, which with any luck would sell as well as the first two. Yet he still intended if possible to return to Munich. For some time he had been angling for a professorship at the university (even, it was suspected, toning down the radical content of his articles in the *Annalen* in order to curry favour with the King). The prospects for this now seemed excellent: Schenk had already interceded with Ludwig on his behalf, and gained even more say in the matter when appointed Minister of the Interior on 1 September. It was with high hopes that Heine left for Italy at the beginning of August.

But he had made powerful enemies in Munich, and they did all in their power to block his appointment. They were encouraged by August von Platen, a minor poet whose inflated view of his own importance had been injured by satirical remarks about him in Part II of the *Reisebilder* ('typically Jewish behaviour', Platen fumed in one of his letters.)[185] Soon after Heine's departure for Italy a vitriolic article attacking him appeared in the journal *Eos*, organ of the reactionary Catholic right in Munich. Written by the theologian and Church historian Ignaz Döllinger, the article was openly anti-Semitic.[186]

In the face of such opposition Schenk was unable to secure the King's approval for a professorship. Having asked the Minister to write to him *poste restante* at Florence with confirmation of the appointment, Heine was dismayed to find no letter waiting when he arrived there on 1 October. It was to his 'dearest friend in Munich' that he instinctively turned for help, writing the same day to Tyutchev with a request to forward an enclosed letter to Schenk and then call on him a few days later; for 'as you are a diplomat, it will be easy for you to find out how things stand with my affair without Schenk suspecting that I have asked you to keep me informed about it or believing himself absolved of any obligation to write to me himself.'[187] Heine's letter concludes with greetings to various acquaintances in Munich, in particular 'to Madame Tyutchev; she is a splendid woman. I love her very much — and will leave it at that! If I were not as tired as I am, I should no doubt find a less trivial phrase.' He also sends his regards to 'your charming sister' (evidently meaning Clotilde).[188]

We do not know how Tyutchev responded to his friend's request (no further correspondence between them has survived). Presumably the die was already cast, and there was nothing more he could usefully do. Nor can we be certain that Heine saw Tyutchev, Eleonore or Clotilde during the two weeks he spent in Munich in December 1828 on his return from Italy (although it would be surprising if he had not). On or about Christmas Day he left Munich for good, heading for Hamburg.[189] One of the poems in the *Neuer Frühling* cycle seems to mark this departure:

> Once more have I been torn away
> From one I gave my heart entire,
> Once more have I been torn away —
> And yet to stay my one desire!

There follows the image of the poet's carriage rumbling across a bridge as it carries him once more away from happiness, from the one he 'gave [his] heart entire', while down below the muddied waters of the river flow past. The poem concludes:

> Farewell, my love! Though far away,
> For you my heart will always blossom.[190]

It was a year and a half before the two poets would meet again. In June 1830 Tyutchev, Eleonore and Clotilde left Munich to spend four months' leave in Russia. On their way to Lübeck to board the steamer to St Petersburg they took the opportunity to call on Heine, then living in isolation in the village of Wandsbek near Hamburg.[191] Since they had last met, Heine's sparring with Platen had developed into a bitter polemical war which attracted public attention throughout Germany. Platen had published a satirical play attacking Heine and his associates which included snide references to Heine's Jewish origins; in the third volume of his *Reisebilder* Heine responded in kind, lampooning Platen, and in particular his homosexuality. Most of the critics ignored Platen's anti-Semitism and took Heine to task, not so much for homophobia as for a gross breach of decorum. Although we have no direct evidence of Tyutchev's attitude to all this, the very fact of his visit to Heine in the immediate aftermath of the affair speaks volumes. And he would almost certainly have deplored the crude anti-Semitism which underlay much of the hostility to his friend.[192]

'Tyutchev with his wife and sister-in-law did me the touching kindness of visiting me here on their way to Petersburg,' Heine wrote to Varnhagen von Ense a few days later. In the same letter he regretted having subjected his unexpected visitors to his bad mood at the time, brought on by political disappointments and unspecified personal frustrations. 'So a dear lady friend — a lady friend whom indeed I love as if she were my own soul — had to endure a great deal of unpleasantness from me for no other reason than that she is a Hanoverian Countess and belongs to a lineage of the most aristocratically irksome kind. This is an illness, and one of which I have to be ashamed. For [...] this lady friend consoled me in my distress, for which I have to thank the most plebeian of scoundrels (I am beset by much domestic trouble) [...].'[193]

We cannot be absolutely sure that the lady friend Heine claims to love so dearly is Clotilde rather than Eleonore, both of whom bore the title of Countess. Yury Tynyanov has even suggested that either or both could have been the object of Heine's affections during his stay in Munich. As evidence he cites one of the poems translated by Tyutchev, 'In welche soll ich mich verlieben...' ('With which one should I fall in love...'), a light-hearted piece in which the poet, unable to choose between two attractive women, compares himself to Buridan's ass between its two bundles of hay.[194] However, it is now known that Heine's poem was probably written in England in 1827, before he had met either Eleonore or Clotilde;[195] also, the two women in it are not sisters, but a mother and daughter;[196] as for Tyutchev's translation, it was written much later, between 1834 and 1836.[197] We also now know that for most of the 'new spring' of 1828 Eleonore was away in Paris with Tyutchev, making it most unlikely that she rather than Clotilde was the addressee of the love poems written at that time. There is admittedly, as we have seen, Heine's declaration that he loved Eleonore 'very much'; but this was in a letter to Tyutchev, who will consequently have understood it as referring to little more than a friendly attachment to which he could hardly take exception.

Just a month after this inauspicious meeting Heine's black mood was transformed to rejoicing by news of the July Revolution in Paris, which swept the restored Bourbon dynasty from power. Alarmed, the rulers of the German states imposed strict anti-revolutionary measures, and any hopes Heine had of contagious democratic impulses spreading across the Rhine were soon dashed. The following year he finally turned his back on Germany and moved to Paris, where he lived in self-imposed exile for the rest of his life, continuing to participate in German literary and political life from afar.

Tyutchev evidently took more than a passing interest in his fellow-poet's new life abroad. Writing from Munich in June 1831, Michael Beer told Heine that he and Tyutchev frequently met and often talked about him; in particular, they agreed that being in Paris was advantageous both for him and his public.[198] For some time Heine too remembered the new friends he had made in Munich. In 1832 he asked an acquaintance travelling there to find out from Friedrich Lindner 'if the Tyutchevs are still living in Munich, and what they are doing';[199] two years later he again asked for news of them in a letter to Lindner himself.[200] Although by this time any direct communication between them had clearly ceased, on Tyutchev's part at least a kind of poetic dialogue was maintained. He continued to take an interest in Heine's work and to develop his own poetic response to it, increasingly (as with his version of the Marengo passage) in the form of adaptation and variation rather than 'straight' translation. Some time after its first publication in 1834, for instance, he produced a version of Heine's short poem 'Es treibt dich fort von Ort zu Ort...' ('You are driven on from place to place...') which is in no way a translation, more the literary equivalent of musical variations on a theme.[201] Starting off fairly close to the original, it very soon develops into areas more relevant to Tyutchev's own concerns at the time, resulting in a piece more than twice as long as Heine's poem. At the end the opening stanza is repeated in the manner of a musical restatement of the theme. His last version, again free, of a Heine poem ('Der Tod, das ist die kühle Nacht...': 'Death is cool night...') dates from 1868. In this case a musical analogy may have been intended, for Tyutchev gives his poem the title 'A Motif of Heine'.[202] In all Tyutchev produced some twelve translations or versions of Heine poems, more than from any other poet except Goethe. Even his translations of Goethe (including, apparently, the whole first act of *Faust*, Part Two, which was later destroyed)[203] may have been prompted by Heine, whose enthusiasm for the originals has already been mentioned. Certainly the great majority of them appear to have be been written within a couple of years of their first meeting.[204] More importantly, their friendship was followed by a remarkable flowering of Tyutchev's own verse, both in terms of quality and quantity.

Critics have detected the influence of Heine on various poems by Tyutchev,[205] and in general it does seem to be the case that he was encouraged to experiment with certain characteristic features of Heine's verse, in particular a predilection for the lyric fragment as form, the use of 'unpoetic' language and subject matter, and irony. Yet this was never slavish imitation. A striking illustration of this is a poem whose biographical background has already been discussed in full: 'To N.N.', written indeed at about the time Heine was in Munich.[206] The potentially prosaic subject of two adulterous lovers playing footsie, with its ironic deflation of both the Romantic ethos and conventional morality, can justly be seen as in the manner of Heine. Yet the evocative final image of ripened grapes glistening through rank vines in the oppressive summer heat is pure Tyutchev: with all its connotations of forbidden fruit and sensual beauty it imbues the whole poem with that remarkable intensity and seriousness of purpose to be found in the best of his mature work. Friendship with Heine may well have inspired him to create; but already he was too much the German poet's equal to play the role of mere pupil.

5 Philosophical Intermezzo

i Schelling

Of the fairly distinguished company of scholars assembled by King Ludwig for his new seat of learning, the most outstanding by far was Friedrich Schelling. Revered throughout Europe as the leading philosopher of the Romantic movement, in his time friend and confidant of Goethe, Schiller, Hölderlin, Novalis, Tieck and the Schlegel brothers, he was now in his fifties and had published nothing of note for nearly twenty years. Yet he continued to labour at a vast philosophical project which he was confident of being able one day to present to the world as the summation of his life's work. Many were won over by his formidable intellect and charismatic personality. Contemporaries reported being 'charmed' and 'elevated' in his presence, and remarked on 'a spiritually commanding power' from his large bright eyes.[1] 'You cannot imagine what a strange feeling one has when one *sees* at last that grizzled head, which is perhaps the *first* of its age', the awe-struck Pyotr Kireyevsky wrote to his brother Ivan after first meeting Schelling face to face.[2]

On 26 November 1827 his inaugural lecture in Munich was received with a standing ovation from the packed audience.[3] He was by no means new to the city, having spent several years there as a member of the Munich Academy of Sciences. Now he returned after seven years as a professor at Erlangen. In his wake came other scholars sympathetic to his philosophical approach and keen to join him at the new university. The philosopher Franz Xaver von Baader, a devout Catholic with a particular interest in mysticism and the occult, had known Schelling since the turn of the century, and had quite early introduced him to the works of the sixteenth-century mystic and philosopher of nature Jakob Böhme. Baader was a controversial figure, viewed by some as little more than a charlatan, while others — notably Schelling and Hegel — apparently held his thought in high esteem.[4] Although no direct evidence has survived that Tyutchev and Baader knew each other, it would seem likely that they did, if only as mutual acqaintances of Schelling. Tyutchev later translated a short poem by Jakob Böhme into Russian, and expressed his great admiration for what he called 'one of the greatest minds ever to have passed through this world';[5] but he could as easily have been introduced to Böhme's ideas by Schelling as by Baader.

Other Russians who met Baader noted that his fervently held Catholicism in no way prevented him from questioning the authority of the Pope and taking up a position sympathetic to the doctrines of the Orthodox Church.[6] He could even be considered a forerunner of the ecumenical movement, for he saw the Russian Church as a key to reconciling Catholicism and Protestantism, and even dreamed of founding an Academy of Religious Studies in St Petersburg as a means of promoting this goal.[7] Alerted to his intentions, the Russian secular and spiritual authorities predictably viewed him with the deepest suspicion. His one attempt to travel to St Petersburg, in 1822, was doomed to ignominious failure: arrested in Russia's Baltic provinces and handed over to the Prussian police as a dangerous agitator, he was eventually released only after the intervention of the Bavarian Ambassador in Berlin.[8]

Much later Tyutchev himself was to propose a reunification of the eastern and western Churches, and towards the end of his life welcomed as a possible first step towards this the breakaway movement of Old Catholics (*Altkatholiken*) in Germany, who rejected the newly proclaimed doctrine of papal infallibility.[9] The movement was led by the theologian Ignaz Döllinger, who had earlier been a close associate of Baader in Munich. They had for instance both collaborated on *Eos*, the journal in which Döllinger's vitriolic attack on Heine was printed. At the time this connection alone, quite apart from Baader's tarnished reputation in official Russian circles, may have dissuaded Tyutchev from seeking closer contact with him.

Better known than Baader was the Professor of Natural Sciences Gotthilf Heinrich von Schubert. Like Baader he had known Schelling for many years, having first met him while studying at the University of Jena. Strongly influenced by Schelling's philosophy of nature, Schubert rejected a purely materialist and mechanistic approach to science. His seminal works *Ansichten von der Nachtseite der Naturwissenschaften* (*Views of the Night Side of the Sciences*, 1808), *Die Symbolik des Traumes* (*The Symbolism of the Dream*, 1814) and *Geschichte der Seele* (*History of the Soul*, 1830) foreshadow much of later psychoanalytical theory in their investigation of the hidden world of the subconscious, particularly as revealed in dreams. These ideas were of obvious appeal to writers, painters and composers of the Romantic period, apparently including Tyutchev, in whose poetry some parallels with passages in Schubert's works have been detected.[10] Although it seems most unlikely that Tyutchev would have gone out of his way to avoid someone whose ideas were so congenial, we have again, as with Baader, no documentary evidence that they ever met. We know for instance that Aleksandr Turgenev sought out Schubert's company and attended his lectures during his relatively short stays in Munich in 1832 and 1834, and that they appear to have struck up a cordial relationship. Yet although Turgenev's diary shows that he sometimes went straight from meeting Tyutchev to see Schubert, or vice versa, suggesting that they belonged to the same social network, tantalisingly he never records them as being together.[11]

Another outstanding disciple of Schelling was Lorenz Oken, who lectured on medicine. Pyotr Kireyevsky was particularly impressed with him during his year in Munich (September 1829 to October 1830), and spent much time with him.[12] When his brother Ivan arrived in April 1830, Pyotr introduced him too to Oken.[13] Yet again, as with Schubert in Turgenev's diary, there is no mention in the Kireyevskys' letters of Tyutchev and Oken ever being in the same place at the same time. And while this is not to say that they never met, it does seem fair to conclude that for Tyutchev it was Schelling himself, rather than his circle of followers and associates, who represented the main interest.

As we have seen, it is likely that Tyutchev gained some superficial knowledge of Schelling's philosophy already as a student in Moscow. However, it seems to have been after arriving in Munich that he embarked on a more serious study of it. He will soon have learned of the new-found enthusiasm of his Moscow acquaintances for Schelling, whether through letters or from his university friend Dmitry Sverbeyev during the latter's visit in the late summer of 1823. Indirect evidence of Tyutchev's own interest is found in the last two lines of his poem 'To N.', written at the end of 1824.[14] These, it will be recalled, turn out to be a paraphrase of a passage in Schelling's *Philosophical Inquiries into the Nature of Human Freedom*, an indication that he was familiar with the work at this time.[15]

Personal acquaintance with Schelling after the latter's arrival in Munich in 1827 will have given a further impetus. As to when the two first met, all we can say with any certainty is that it was during the philosopher's first year there. While staying in Paris in May and June of 1828, Tyutchev attended lectures given at the Sorbonne by the historian François Guizot, the philosopher Victor Cousin and the literary historian Abel Villemain.[16] These were all members of the so-called 'Doctrinaires', a liberal grouping founded by Pierre Royer-Collard which opposed the reactionary Restoration regime of Charles X and favoured a constitutional monarchy on British lines. Their recent reinstatement to university posts after years of official persecution had been an event of great political significance. Tyutchev took a particular interest in the group from a distance in Munich, subscribing to their journal *Le Globe* and (if we are to believe Ivan Gagarin, to whom he later lent copies) sympathising with many of their ideas.[17] It is not surprising to learn from another source that while in Paris he not only attended lectures given by the 'Doctrinaires' but frequently met and associated with them in person.[18] Of particular interest to Tyutchev was Cousin, an admirer of German idealist philosophy, especially that of Schelling. His lectures on the history of philosophy given at the Sorbonne from April to July 1828 were published later that year;[19] and on 27 November Schelling wrote to him: 'I have had the pleasure of seeing your first lectures, printed as pamphlets. Mr Tyutchev passed them on to me.'[20] (Tyutchev clearly had a high opinion of Cousin's lectures, as well as those of Guizot, for he later gave the published texts of both to the young Pyotr Kireyevsky to study.)[21]

Less than a year after this first mention of Tyutchev by Schelling, the two of them were said by Friedrich Thiersch, the Rector of Munich University, to be 'very closely acquainted'.[22] At about the same time Schelling spoke in glowing terms of Tyutchev to Pyotr Kireyevsky, calling him 'an excellent person, a most knowledgeable person, with whom one is always glad to converse'.[23] Some idea of what these conversations may have touched on is given in the same letter, in which Kireyevsky reports on his first meeting with the philosopher:

[Schelling] questioned me on the state of our literature, and said he had heard it was making rapid progress [...]. He spoke of the difficulties of the Russian language for foreigners, and of how important its study was nevertheless; he praised its sonority; he said that he had heard a great deal about our Zhukovsky, and that by all accounts he must be an outstanding person.[24]

Who was Schelling's informant as to the state of Russian literature? Several members of the Moscow 'Lovers of Wisdom' group were later to make the pilgrimage to Munich to sit at the feet of their revered guru, but Kireyevsky was the first. Some information on Zhukovsky and other Russian writers could have come from Aleksandr Turgenev or the philosopher Pyotr Chaadayev, both of whom Schelling had met in Karlsbad in August 1825.[25] However, more than four years had passed since then, during which time he had not met or been in correspondence with either of them.[26] A much more likely source was Tyutchev, his close acquaintance at the time, whom he singles out for praise immediately after the passage just quoted. Revealing too in the same letter are Schelling's reported comments on the Russo-Turkish War (news of Russia's victory, which ensured Greek independence, had reached Munich only two weeks before):[27]

> Russia [...] has been vouchsafed a great destiny, and never before has she given expression to her power so fully as she has now. Now for the first time the whole of Europe, or at least all right-thinking individuals, look to her with sympathy and wishes for success, and regret only that in the present situation her demands are, perhaps, too moderate.[28]

Might these sentiments too not reflect discussions with that congenial and knowledgeable young man from the Russian Embassy, with whom it was always such a pleasure to converse? From quite early on Tyutchev seems to have seen it as his unofficial role to win friends for Russia's cause in the West. Already in the case of Heine we have seen some indications of this, and there is plenty of evidence for it from later years. Given his wit and charm, his incisive mind and rhetorical skills, it was a role into which he slipped easily, always retaining the freedom to say what he thought, and never allowing himself to be used as an unthinking mouthpiece for official policies. The same integrity and independence of thought can be found in his attitude to Schelling's philosophy, as was to become evident in the next stage of their relationship.

Schelling had published nothing new since his *Philosophische Untersuchungen über das Wesen der menschlichen Freiheit* (*Philosophical Inquiries into the Nature of Human Freedom*) of 1808. After returning to Munich in 1827 he came increasingly to consider that much of his earlier work, as well as that of Hegel, although necessary in its day, represented what he now termed a 'negative' philosophy. The way forward must be to develop a new, 'positive' philosophy whose aim would be no less than to interpret the whole course of history as a process of God's self-revelation and indeed self-realisation in the world of appearances. It was with this in mind that in May 1830 he began a new course of lectures entitled 'The Philosophy of Revelation'. They were attended by Ivan Kireyevsky, whose pithy comment in a letter home indicates the new direction taken: 'Schelling's system has so matured in his head since he ceased publishing, that like a ripe fruit it has completely detached itself from the branch on which it began to form, and fallen down as a plump little apple between History and Religion.'[29]

Two years later Schelling's ambitious work in progress was taking clearer shape. On the evening of 29 July 1832 Aleksandr Turgenev arrived in Munich for a short stay. The whole of the following day was spent attending lectures at the university, including one given by Schelling (who recognised Turgenev from Karlsbad in 1825 and afterwards invited him to his house). Turgenev noted in his diary: 'Heard Schelling lecture, and regretted that Chaadayev wasn't there with me. How he would have appreciated this Christian genius, who has returned to the path of truth and is now preaching Christ in higher philosophy.'[30] That evening Turgenev met Tyutchev for the first time at a soirée given by the Russian Ambassador; the following day (31 July) they met again and talked 'about Schelling, etc.' No doubt the philosopher's new intellectual quest came under discussion, although Turgenev's laconic diary entry mentions neither this nor Tyutchev's views on the subject, restricting itself to first impressions of the young diplomat ('an educated Russian, has read a lot and speaks well').[31]

Turgenev subsequently informed Chaadayev of his encounters with their old Karlsbad acquaintance, which prompted Chaadayev to write to Schelling:

> At the present time I have learnt from one of my friends who recently spent a few days in your area that you are lecturing on the *Philosophy of Revelation*. [...] I confess that when reading your works I often had a premonition that your system would at some stage inevitably give rise to a religious philosophy; yet I cannot find the words to tell you how happy I was to learn that the most profound thinker of our age has conceived this momentous idea of the fusion of philosophy with religion.[32]

Whether or not he attended Schelling's lectures himself, Tyutchev was evidently well aware of his new line of philosophical inquiry. Returning to Munich for a second visit in 1834, Turgenev noted in his diary for 2 April that at a supper given by the Dowager Queen at the Palais Maximilian he 'chatted with the clever Tyutchev about diplomats, about the philosophy of Cousin and Schelling, etc.'[33] As suggested by the Tyutchev scholars Konstantin Azadovsky and Aleksandr Ospovat, their discussion that evening probably centred on the introduction Schelling was preparing to the German translation of a book by Cousin on French and German philosophy.[34] Cousin's work was published in Germany later that year, although a preliminary version of Schelling's introduction (dated 2 May 1834 in the book) had already appeared in a Munich journal the previous November.[35] Schelling attached great importance to this, his first publication for several years, using it to outline the tenets of his new philosophical system, and in particular to attack Hegel for the first time in print. Its appearance caused quite some stir at the time; and in view of Tyutchev's personal interest in both Cousin and Schelling it is inconceivable that he would have been unaware of it. In fact just nine days after the supper at the Palais Maximilian, he and Turgenev had an opportunity to discuss matters philosophical with Schelling in person as the three of them strolled together through the Arcades, a fashionable passageway of shops and coffee-houses between Ludwigstrasse and the Hofgarten. According to Turgenev, for two hours that afternoon they talked among other things 'of Hegel's atheism; of his posthumous works; of the immortality of the soul (his public lecture on which I had heard in Berlin); of his anti-Christianity, to which he, just like his followers, would not admit'. Turgenev went on to speak of his own meetings with Hegel and some of his followers in the summer of 1827.[36]

Any contribution Tyutchev may have made to the philosophical debate on this occasion is not recorded by Turgenev. However, there were other opportunities. Karl Pfeffel — who first got to know Tyutchev in 1830, becoming more closely acquainted three years later —[37] recalled being present at some 'very interesting conversations' between him and Schelling at this time.[38] On one occasion, for instance, Tyutchev told Schelling exactly what he thought of his grand project to reconcile philosophy with religion:

You are attempting an impossible task. A philosophy which rejects the supernatural and wants to prove everything by reason must inevitably drift towards materialism before sinking in atheism. The only philosophy compatible with Christianity is contained in its entirety in the catechism. One must either believe what St Paul believed, and after him Pascal, and kneel before *the Folly of the Cross*, or deny everything. The supernatural is in the final analysis that which is most natural in man. It has its roots in a human consciousness vastly superior to what we call reason: that poor reason which acknowledges only what it comprehends, which is to say *nothing*![39]

We are not told how Schelling replied to this. Although he is known to have reacted sharply to attacks on him in print, there is no evidence that he took the cut and thrust of private philosophical debate personally. Indeed, despite their differences he and Tyutchev apparently continued to value each other's company. The writer and translator Nikolay Melgunov, who met Tyutchev in September 1836, described him in a subsequent article on Schelling as one of the latter's Munich friends.[40] And before Melgunov left Munich for Augsburg, where Schelling was staying, Tyutchev made a point of asking him to convey his greetings to the philosopher.[41] In a letter from Munich at the time Melgunov indicates that Tyutchev was not the only one of Schelling's circle to express reservations about his current philosophical approach: 'It is disappointing that Schelling is not here,' Melgunov writes. 'As to what even his friends are saying about him, that is disappointing in the extreme: from all accounts it is apparent that he has had his day and will produce nothing new.'[42]

Yet Schelling still had influential admirers. Among them was King Friedrich Wilhelm IV of Prussia, who in 1840 offered him a chair at the University of Berlin, hoping that he would (as the King put it) help to eradicate 'the dragon's seed of Hegelian pantheism'.[43] Schelling accepted. Although Hegel had been dead for ten years, the influence of his followers was still paramount in the Prussian capital, and Schelling's appointment was seen as highly provocative. His inaugural lecture on 15 November 1841 was a major event. Among those attending were Bakunin, Engels and Kierkegaard.[44]

With Schelling's move to Berlin Tyutchev's personal contacts with him of necessity ceased. Karl Pfeffel goes so far as to mention the philosopher's departure as one of the factors which persuaded Tyutchev eventually to leave Munich and return to Russia for good.[45] While this claim is probably exaggerated, it does help to dispel one persistent myth. The impression has sometimes been given that Tyutchev's philosophical disagreements with Schelling led to a serious personal rift between the two.[46] Yet if that were so, Pfeffel (who knew Tyutchev well and witnessed his discussions with Schelling) would surely not have felt able to imply that they were so close in 1841.

From afar Tyutchev followed Schelling's exploits in the Hegelian dragon's lair with some interest. Karl Varnhagen von Ense met Tyutchev in Bad Kissingen in July 1842 and reported in his diary that he 'knows [Schelling] very well, is conversant with his present situation there, and is surprised that that he continues to make a dazzling impression in Berlin'.[47] The surprise was not misplaced. Once the whiff of controversy had dispersed, numbers attending Schelling's impenetrable lectures on the Philosophy of Revelation and the Philosophy of Mythology began to dwindle, and after 1846 he ceased lecturing at the university altogether.[48] The *magnum opus* intended as a summation of his mature philosophy, with which he had struggled for decades, remained unfinished at his death in 1854. Perhaps after all it had been, as sensed by Tyutchev, an impossible task.

Tyutchev's reservations concerning Schelling's late philosophy are clear enough, but they tell us nothing of his attitude towards the earlier and much more influential philosophy of nature. His letters and other prose writings are silent on the matter, the only indication to have come to light so far being the previously mentioned textual parallel in the poem 'To N.' A much later poem, hitherto unremarked in this context, appears to offer more conclusive evidence. In September 1844 Tyutchev returned to Russia (for good, as it transpired), and that autumn in St Petersburg he can hardly have remained unaware of one of the publishing sensations of the year. Vladimir Odoyevsky's *Russian Nights*, a collection of stories linked by the imagined dialogues of a group of friends, caused much heated debate and controversy for its airing of ideas close to those of the Slavophiles. At one point in the book, recalling the time some twenty years before when he and his contemporaries had fallen under the spell of Schelling, the character known as 'Faust' (who is clearly Odoyevsky's *alter ego*) famously compares the philosopher to Columbus: 'At the beginning of the nineteenth century Schelling was what Christopher Columbus had been in the fifteenth: he discovered a part of man's world about which there had been only shadowy legends — *his soul!*'[49] A poem written in 1844 would appear to be Tyutchev's response to this passage.[50] If so, his judgement on Schelling's philosophy of nature can be in no doubt:

Columbus

Columbus, genius supreme! —
Who, having mapped the world in all its splendour,
To accomplish the unfinished scheme
Of world creation tore the veiling screen asunder,
And with divine hand from mist-wreathed infinity
Plucked forth a treasure none had yet detected —
A new world, unknown, unexpected —
Revealing it at last for all to see.

So human genius has ever
Been linked in close affinity
Through ties of blood that naught can sever
With nature's vital energy.
What genius pledges, nature hastens
In concrete form to realise:
Roused by a kindred voice, she listens —
And soon a new world greets our eyes.[51]

Apart from this our best hope must be to examine Tyutchev's poetry as a whole for more general echoes of Schelling's philosophical teachings. This is difficult ground, already well-trodden by scholars and critics, on the more clear-sighted of whom we shall rely to find a way through. But first we need to gain some idea of the teachings themselves.

ii The Philosophy of Nature

In common with the other major German idealist philosophers of his age (Fichte, Hegel, Schopenhauer), Schelling took as his starting point the ground-breaking work of Immanuel Kant. Kant's great achievement a generation before them had been to establish beyond all doubt that there were clearly defined and insurmountable limits to human understanding. This dealt a crushing blow to the comfortable Enlightenment consensus that through a continuing process of rational thought and scientific discovery mankind could eventually discover all there was to know about the universe. Kant's rigorous analysis of the ways in which the human mind perceives, and reaches conclusions about, the world demonstrated in particular that the concepts of time, space and causation cannot be proved to have any objective existence outside of us, but seem rather to be a structure or organising principle imposed by the mind upon the world in order to make sense of it. This is by no means to say, as some philosophers had argued, that it is 'all in the mind', that nothing exists outside individual consciousness. According to Kant there certainly is an objective reality 'out there' (he calls it the *noumenon*, or 'thing in itself'), but it remains unknowable to us as such, mediated to us as it is through the distorting lens of our built-in perceptual and interpretative mental faculties. As St Paul put it more simply, 'we see through a glass darkly'.

Kant's findings struck equally at the more dogmatic manifestations of both science and religion. If the concepts of space, time and causation have no objectively verifiable reality, natural science may well use them to construct an empirically adequate map of the world as it appears to us, but is hardly entitled to present that as a revelation of ultimate truth. As for religion, if God exists, then by definition outside the world of phenomena or things-as-we-perceive-them, and thus beyond our rational comprehension. There is nothing to stop us believing in God as an act of faith, but any attempt to construct logical or rational proofs of His existence will be a waste of time.

The consequences of this intellectual earthquake were felt for years to come. As Schopenhauer put it, 'Kant had destroyed the old dogmatism, and the world stood in shock before the smoking ruins'.[52] For Heine he was 'that great destroyer in the realm of thought' who 'far exceeded Maximilian Robespierre in his terrorism'.[53] And commenting on the revolutions of 1848, Tyutchev wrote in similar vein that 'sixty years of destructive philosophy [in Germany] had completely dissolved all Christian beliefs and developed, in this absence of all faith, the supreme revolutionary sentiment: intellectual arrogance'.[54] This suggests he saw Kant's *Critique of Pure Reason* (1781) and *Critique of Practical Reason* (1786) as the beginning of that process. (The remarks occur in a political article prompted by alarm at the spread of revolution throughout Europe in 1848; whether by then he had come to see Schelling's *Naturphilosophie* too as 'destructive' is not clear.)

In his Philosophy of Nature Schelling develops Kant's critique of purely mechanistic views of reality. Far from being no more than an accumulation of dead matter driven by impersonal forces, for Schelling the whole universe is a single living organism embodying a unity of matter and mind, which are but two aspects of the one underlying reality or 'world soul': 'Nature is designed to be visible mind, and mind to be invisible nature'.[55] Schelling called this concept the 'philosophy of identity' (*Identitätsphilosophie*). Humankind is part of the overall unity, its particular function being to provide the organ through which nature achieves consciousness. The whole is a manifestation of the divine: all things are contained in God (Schelling uses the term 'panentheism', distinguishing this from pantheism which simply equates the world of phenomena with God). Nature (and by this Schelling means the whole of creation, the universe) evolves through a never-ending dynamic process in which opposing principles are resolved in a higher synthesis, this in its turn becoming part of a new antithesis, and so on, taking nature to ever higher levels of development. Far from simply creating the universe and leaving it to run according to some preordained plan, God is at each and every stage intimately involved in an ongoing process of creation through the dialectic of becoming. The world we perceive around us — Kant's world of phenomena — is thus the result of a noumenal will, of what Schelling calls the 'infinite self-volition' ('The imprint of this eternal and infinite self-volition is the world').[56]

This identification of a noumenal will as the ultimate reality behind the world of appearances bears more than a passing resemblance to Schopenhauer's later theory in *The World as Will and Representation*. In fact, despite being generally dismissive of Schelling (as he was also of Fichte and Hegel), Schopenhauer did grudgingly concede that there was much of value in the *Naturphilosophie* and was probably more influenced by it than he cared to admit.[57] Yet there are important differences. The will referred to by Schelling is of divine origin and works to achieve goodness and harmony, while in Schopenhauer's system it is a blind amoral force with no apparent purpose other than to realise itself in the phenomenal world. Where they are agreed is in seeing all natural forces such as gravity or magnetism as expressions of the underlying will. Here as elsewhere Schelling opposes what he calls the 'empty formalism' of the mechanistic approach — the conceit that our investigation of the universe need go no further than deriving mathematical descriptions of how it appears to behave. It would be about as illuminating, he suggests, to 'explain' a work of literature by cataloguing the various letters which appear in it and describing the process by which it was printed.[58]

iii The World-View of Tyutchev's Munich Poetry

> Belief in fabled myth has perished:
> Cold reason has laid waste to all...

So Tyutchev had lamented already before leaving Russia in 1822, going on to express — in an echo of Schiller's poem 'Die Götter Griechenlands' ('The Gods of Greece') — his yearning for an age which could still regard the universe as a living entity endowed with soul: 'Where are you now, O ancient peoples!/ Your world was temple to the gods'.[59] Clearly this was fertile ground for Schelling's teachings to take root in. Yet before turning to that important influence we need to examine the broader artistic and intellectual climate which helped to shape Tyutchev's verse in Germany.

In very general terms, much of the poetry of his Munich years can be seen as an attempt — comparable to that undertaken by Goethe, Hölderlin and others — to recover for the modern age something of the lost mythopoetic vision of the world evoked in the poem just quoted. A certain spiritual affinity with ancient Greece in particular has been remarked on by several commentators. For the Symbolist Andrey Bely, Tyutchev was quite simply an 'archaic Hellene',[60] while in the poem 'Two Voices' Aleksandr Blok discerned 'an Hellenic, pre-Christian, tragic sense of Fate'.[61] One of Tyutchev's most perceptive critics, Boris Kozyrev, found his poetry to contain strong parallels with teachings of the early pre-Socratic philosophers Thales and Anaximander.[62] Thales' intellectually bold reduction of the bewildering variety of natural phenomena to one underlying indestructible element, namely water, is related by Kozyrev to the myriad images in Tyutchev's verse of water and moisture as symbols of a universal force or 'world soul', life-giving and spirit-enhancing, from which all individual forms arise and to which all eventually revert. Kozyrev shows how Anaximander put Thales' idea on a more metaphysical footing, replacing water as the basic substance with an abstract concept referred to as '*apeiron*', or the infinite, which appears also to share certain characteristics with Hesiod's idea of the original chaos from which all in the world has sprung. Anaximander characterises *apeiron* only in negative terms: it is imperishable and ultimately immutable, and has no origin and no ending in time. According to him, all individual phenomena represent a transgression against the unity of *apeiron*, and by a universal law of justice (or natural equilibrium) are doomed to revert to the underlying all-encompassing essence or principle.[63] Kozyrev goes on to quote an impressive array of poems by Tyutchev reflecting the ideas of Thales and Anaximander.[64] He concludes that Tyutchev will almost certainly have been acquainted with the work of these philosophers, at the same time stressing that the various parallels observed in his verse are more likely to have resulted from an 'inner affinity' with their teachings than from any 'conscious borrowing' on his part.[65]

Another link to the thought of ancient Greece may have come through reading Hölderlin. (Together with Schelling and Hegel — fellow-students at Tübingen University, with whom he even shared a room — Hölderlin had early developed an enthusiasm for the pre-Socratic philosophers which was to leave a lasting imprint on his work.) In an article identifying undoubted parallels between Tyutchev's poem 'Two Voices' and Hölderlin's 'Hyperions Schicksallied' ('Hyperion's Song of Fate'), the critic Aleksandr Neuslykhin points out that although 'Two Voices' was written much later, Tyutchev may have first come across Hölderlin's poem soon after arriving in Germany (a second edition of the novel *Hyperion*, in which it appears, was published in 1822).[66] This view is supported by a reading of the novel itself, on whose pages we encounter a poetic world remarkably similar in many respects to that of Tyutchev's verse from his Munich years. Some examples may help to illustrate this.

The eponymous hero of *Hyperion* (and Hölderlin's *alter ego*) is a young Greek who at the time of the Russo-Turkish war of 1770 dreams of restoring ancient Hellas not just in name but in spirit too. In letters to a German friend and to his beloved, Diotima, he gives voice to his faith in a reborn religion of nature:

To be one with All that lives, to return in exultant oblivion of self into the All of nature: there is the culmination of thoughts and joys, there is the sacred summit, the place of eternal rest where noonday is robbed of its heat and thunder its voice, and the raging sea is as a rippling cornfield.[67]

As in Tyutchev's poems and the teaching of Thales, water — the sea — becomes an image of the underlying oneness of nature. Here Hyperion is describing a sea voyage:

In vain does the brooding mind resist the sway of sea and air. I gave myself up to them, asking nothing of myself and others, seeking nothing, thinking of nothing, and let the boat rock me half-asleep, imagining myself to be lying in Charon's barque. O, it is sweet to drink thus from the chalice of oblivion.[68]

Yet too often his desire to be at one with nature is frustrated. He feels that mankind is cursed to remain separate, a jarring note in the harmonious whole:

What is man? [...] How does something like that come to be in the world: chaotically fermenting, or rotting, like a dead tree, and never coming to maturity? How does nature tolerate this never-ripening fruit among her sweet vines?[69]

What ultimately sets man apart, Hyperion realises, is not so much his conscious awareness of the world, but rather the over-developed faculties of reason and analysis through which he is driven to view it. Echoing Faust's well-known monologue, Hyperion tells his German friend that he regrets years spent in dry academic study:

I became so very clever in your country, painstakingly learning to differentiate myself from my surroundings; and now I stand alone in this beautiful world, cast out from the garden of nature where I grew and flourished, withering in the noonday sun.
O, man is a god when he dreams, a beggar when he reflects [...].[70]

The resolution of this debilitating war of opposites (and here Hölderlin gives us his view of the poet's mission in the modern world) must be sought in a higher synthesis in which all branches of knowledge — science, philosophy and religion included — are accorded equal rights and acknowledged to derive from one unifying creative impulse: in a word, from poetry. In discussions with his companions Hyperion at one point puzzles them by asserting that the achievements of ancient Athens in philosophy can be directly attributed to its pre-eminence in poetry and literature. But what, one of them asks, can the 'cold sublimity' of philosophy possibly have to do with poetry? Hyperion replies that poetry is quite literally the 'beginning and end' of philosophy: 'Like Minerva from Jupiter's brow, [philosophy] springs from the poetry of infinite divine Being. And so finally that which is irreconcilable in it merges once again in the mysterious wellspring of poetry.'[71] This was Schelling's position too.[72] Nor would he have disagreed with Hölderlin's conviction that there are certain sacred mysteries about which the poet-philosopher must remain silent. As Hyperion writes to Diotima:

Believe me, and know that I tell you this from the depths of my soul: language is a great excess. The best after all remains ever elusive, sequestered in its fathomless reaches like a pearl on the seabed.[73]

It would be wrong to claim that Hölderlin exercised any kind of exclusive influence on Tyutchev at this time. The examples quoted are intended merely to show how the latter's verse reflected or refracted (like the prism of Gagarin's analogy) certain elements of the general intellectual atmosphere in Germany with which he felt an affinity. Hölderlin's 'antique' world-view would have been such an element — as, indeed, was Goethe's, as already indicated in the section on Heine. We shall return to Goethe in due course. Now we must consider the question of how Schelling may have influenced Tyutchev as a poet.

iv Philosopher and Poet

Schelling's philosophy of nature had an obvious appeal for creative artists of the Romantic period. Yet the very ease with which certain aspects of it can be found in their works should put us on our guard. Can we really speak in such cases of Schelling's influence, or is it not rather a matter of his having systematically formulated and developed in his writings ideas more generally subscribed to at the time? The question is particularly relevant to the *Identitätsphilosophie* principle of the unity of mind and matter, man and nature, examples of which certainly seem to abound in Tyutchev's poetry. Snowy Alpine peaks gilded by the rising sun appear like some fabled clan of golden-crowned rulers fallen in battle, now at long last roused from their age-old sleep;[74] autumn leaves call on the wind to blow them from their 'tiresome' branches so that like the migrating birds they too can fly far away;[75] an autumn evening has about it a 'gentle smile of transience and waning' that suggests saintly suffering;[76] as the oppressive heat of a summer's day gives way to the chill of evening, a shiver seems to run through the very veins of Nature, as if she had plunged her burning feet into icy spring water;[77] a willow bends over a stream, its leaves striving like thirsting lips to catch the elusive waters, yet the stream runs on regardless, revelling in the sunshine and mocking the willow's unrequited yearning.[78]

Clearly, none of this is specific enough to be taken as evidence of Schelling's influence. To find that we must turn to a programmatic poem written at some time in the first half of the 1830s:

> Nature is not what you would have it:
> No lifeless cast, no mask of death —
> In nature there is love, and freedom,
> A soul, a tongue, a living breath...
>
> . . . .
> . . . .
> . . . .
> . . . .

You see a tree, its leaves and blossom:
The gardener stuck them there, no doubt?
The growing foetus — is it moulded
By alien forces from without?

. . . .
. . . .
. . . .
. . . .

They live, unseeing and unhearing,
In this world as if plunged in gloom;
From distant suns they sense no breathing,
No life within the waves' white spume.

In their dead heart no spring has blossomed,
Their soul sees not the heavenly light;
For them the forests have not spoken,
And mute is all the star-filled night!

And, agitating streams and forests,
In tongues that owe no earthly source,
With them the thunderstorm has never
By night held friendly intercourse!

Yet who will blame them? Can a deaf-mute
Conceive the organ's depth and reach?
Alas, no sound his soul will quicken:
Not even his own mother's speech![79]

Verses 2 and 4 were deleted by the censors when the text was first published. This has made it even more difficult to ascertain what exactly impelled Tyutchev to write the poem, and against whom it is directed (the manuscript is lost). The most plausible and well-founded suggestion is that made by Hans Rothe. He argues that it was written in the spring of 1833 in response to an article by Heine which championed Schiller's view of nature as more 'progressive' than that of Goethe. Heine was writing as spokesman of the radical 'Young Germany' group of writers, and in Rothe's view the 'you' addressed in the poem refers to this group, including Heine. (Tyutchev uses the form '*vy*', equivalent to French '*vous*', which in the context is almost certainly plural.) In this interpretation 'Nature is not what you would have it...' is a fervent apologia for the Goethean concept of nature.[80] As Rothe points out, it echoes in certain details a poem Tyutchev had written the previous year to mark the death of Goethe. In this the great poet is said to have 'prophet-like, with thunderstorms conversed' — the very ability denied in the later poem to those who see nature merely as a conglomeration of inert matter. He is portrayed in essentially Schellingian terms as the supreme creative artist, organically and harmoniously at one with the spirit of nature. In an extended metaphor Tyutchev describes him as 'the finest leaf' to grow on 'mankind's lofty tree', nourished by its 'purest sap' and by the 'purest rays of the sun'. Now, as if from a wreath, the leaf has fallen from the tree, yet not at the bidding of external forces such as wind or rain, but entirely of its own accord.[81] The same image of the leaf, associated with the idea of organic growth in accordance with internal laws and free of all imperatives from without, is of course found in verse 3 of 'Nature is not what you would have it...'. In defending Goethe's concept of nature, that poem by implication defends something in many respects indistinguishable from Schelling's; for Goethe admired Schelling's philosophy,[82] seeing him as an ally in the struggle against Newtonian science, and assimilated many of his ideas into his own works.[83] For this reason alone it would be just as accurate to call the poem an apologia for Schelling's *Naturphilosophie* as mediated by Goethe.

The missing verses evidently fell victim to religious, rather than political, censorship. As Dmitry Blagoy points out, the first (heavily censored) half of the poem appears to be directed against the traditional doctrine of an omnipotent deity controlling every aspect of the universe, while the second (uncensored) half turns its attack on 'crude mechanistic concepts of nature as a bare mechanism, a soulless machine'.[84] If we accept this interpretation (which is compatible with Rothe's), it becomes possible to imagine something of what the missing verses may have contained, at least in very broad outline. The following is offered as no more than an informed guess:

> (Verse 2): [Nor is your God the God of nature:
> No inward-dwelling vital force,
> He merely sets the worlds in motion
> And keeps them to their charted course.]

> (Verse 4): [Your distant God is soon forgotten;
> What's then left over will suffice
> For those dull souls who see creation
> As one vast meaningless device.]

Dogmatic consistency is the last thing one should expect of a poet, especially one whose mode of thought at this time (it will be recalled) was likened by his friend Ivan Gagarin to the action of a prism. Or as Gagarin put it in another of his letters: 'He was possessed of a Goethean indifferentism and a poetic nature which took in and reflected everything around him'.[85] So it should come as no surprise to find Tyutchev taking on occasion an apparently more detached and even ironic stance towards the Goethean-Schellingian view of things than that adopted in 'Nature is not what you would have it...'. This would on the face of it seem to be the case with an enigmatic poem written at least three years earlier, in other words at about the time of his early personal contacts with Schelling:

Where sky and scorched earth intermingle
Like livid smoke, now as of old
Untouched by care, forever cheerful,
Lives Madness, piteous to behold...

He delves into the burning desert
Beneath the sun's tormenting rays,
Glazed eyes cast upwards, as if searching
For something in the cloud and haze...

Then with a sudden start he crouches,
One keen ear to the cracked earth bent,
And listens, avidly attentive,
His face a mask of pure content...

He thinks he hears the joyous music
Of water coursing underground:
Now murmuring lullabies so gently,
Now bursting forth with mighty sound!..[86]

A helpful gloss on this is provided by Tyutchev himself in a poem which he dedicated to Afanasy Fet over thirty years later. Here he tells his friend and fellow-poet that whereas nature has endowed certain individuals with a 'blind, prophetic instinct' enabling them to sense the presence of water in the 'earth's dark depths', he — Fet — has been favoured by the 'Great Mother' with the far more enviable gift of being able on occasion to glimpse nature herself 'beneath the visible exterior'.[87] Kirill Pigaryov concluded reasonably enough that both here and in the earlier 'Madness' Tyutchev was referring to water-diviners.[88] It seems clear that in both poems their intuitive if rudimentary sensitivity to natural forces is presented as emblematic of that far higher rapport with nature enjoyed by the archetypal poet-seer-philosopher as envisaged by Schelling or Hölderlin. The only puzzle is why in the earlier poem this exalted figure should be depicted as a madman.

Acknowledging Pigaryov's commentary on the poem, and citing actual examples of dowsers or water-diviners held in high esteem by Schelling and his followers, Naum Berkovsky has claimed 'Madness' to be a direct attack on the philosopher. For him it is a polemical tract in which Tyutchev 'resolutely and angrily declares his opposition to any ideas of a Schellingian nature'.[89] A different source for the poem's central image is suggested by Vera Milchina. She quotes a discussion of Goethe's ballad 'Der Fischer' ('The Fisherman') in Madame de Staël's widely-read *De l'Allemagne* in which the German poet's rapport with nature is explicitly likened to that of a water-diviner. Although Tyutchev is likely to have known de Staël's influential book anyway, Milchina points out that he could have come across the relevant passage from it in 1821, when it was quoted in full in a Russian critical review of Zhukovsky's translation of 'Der Fischer'. In support of this she is able to demonstrate an obvious textual borrowing from that translation in 'Madness'.[90] (It is worth adding that at some time before 1830 Tyutchev also appears to have made a translation, now lost, of 'Der Fischer'.)[91]

Berkovsky's and Milchina's suggestions are both convincing, and may indeed be accepted as equally valid if we see the mad water-diviner as representing a whole school of thought rather than any single figure associated with it. (A further dash of allusion is suggested by the fate of Hölderlin, who in 1806, after just a few years of intense — perhaps too intense — poetic creation, became mentally ill and had to be taken into care for the remaining four decades of his life. Tyutchev is likely to have known of this.) More open to dispute is the claim made by these critics that Tyutchev's attitude towards the subject of his poem is polemical (Berkovsky) or 'sceptical' (Milchina).[92] This fails to take into account the link often made by the Romantics between genius and madness. It also ignores another important literary source for the poem. As François Cornillot has pointed out, at much the same time as writing 'Madness' Tyutchev translated two extracts from *A Midsummer Night's Dream*, including part of a speech by Theseus at the beginning of Act V.[93] Here with gentle irony Shakespeare has the down-to-earth Duke of Athens describe as a form of madness the enslavement of lovers and poets to the illusory world of their imagination ('The lunatic, the lover and the poet/ Are of imagination all compact'). The lover for instance can discern 'Helen's beauty' in the most unremarkable of faces. As for the poet, his 'eye, in a fine frenzy rolling,/ Doth glance from heaven to earth, from earth to heaven' (an image, as Cornillot reminds us, that resurfaces in verse two of Tyutchev's poem), and his pen turns 'things unknown' into 'shapes', giving 'to airy nothing/ A local habitation and a name'.

Seen in this light, the self-irony of 'Madness' is really no harsher than Shakespeare's. To the commonsensical world at large the water-diviner must of course seem the very embodiment of wretched or 'piteous' ('*zhalkoye*') madness; yet Tyutchev's portrayal of him does much to undermine this judgement. There is always something curiously attractive about cheerful perseverance in the midst of adversity, however deluded or misplaced it might be; we are forced to acknowledge at least the man's integrity of purpose in his search for a higher and better reality, and may even begin to see in him something of the prophet in the wilderness. Cornillot concludes that he represents poetry, surviving against all the odds in the scorched desert of modern rationalism.[94] For another commentator, Anatoly Liberman, he is 'Tyutchev's double, pitted against indifferent mankind and unyielding nature'.[95] What finally justifies the 'madman' is his striking vision or hallucination (purely auditory in nature, for he seems to be the archetypal blind poet) of water issuing from the desert. This far surpasses in beauty and authenticity anything in the 'real' world of arid emptiness around him. Here in fact we see this scorned outsider engaged in something that has been a central concern of human beings since earliest times: the creation of myth, art and belief as talismans against the enigmatic and often terrifying reality into which they find themselves so inexplicably thrust. If that is madness, it has much to commend it. And if Tyutchev had Schelling at least partly in mind, it was certainly not with any intention of pillorying him.

Other comments on Tyutchev's engagement (or lack of it) with Schelling can be dealt with more briefly. One critic has for instance argued that Tyutchev saw the latter's philosophy as little more than a rag-bag to be plundered for suitable poetic imagery, or more precisely 'a kind of metaphysical map on which he could chart his emotions'.[96] This is surely an over-simplification: if the two poems just discussed show anything, it is that he could become passionately engaged with the philosophy as such. Then there is the related charge that Tyutchev is not really a philosophical poet at all, or at least not one of any originality.[97] This is of course true in the strict sense that he never composed the kind of philosophical treatise in verse that we associate with, say, Lucretius or Pope. But that would be to deny poetry any relationship to philosophy other than the purely formal and functional one of providing a framework for the expression of ideas external to itself. In fact the affinity between them clearly goes much deeper than that. Poetry and philosophy can after all be said to pursue a common goal in that both seek to present the world around us in a fresh light or from an unexpected perspective in order to give new insight into our being in it. What distinguishes them is how they go about achieving this. As Gerhard Dudek argues in an illuminating article on Tyutchev,[98] the poet and philosopher may be vouchsafed the same basic philosophical experience or insight, but deal with it in different ways. The philosopher reduces it to abstract concepts, which he or she then develops in a reasoned argument underpinned by logic. The poet on the other hand aims to convey the raw primal experience itself in all its immediacy, in particular through the use of metaphor, which for Dudek provides the vital link from poetry to philosophy. For it is above all through metaphor that the poet is enabled 'to transpose his completely subjective, personal, once-seen experience into the realm of generality and abstract thought, without in so doing being obliged to give up anything of its vividness or intensity of feeling, and without having to resort to the philosopher's abstract mode of expression'.[99] Dudek cites a range of poems to illustrate his general thesis and support his particular contention that Tyutchev has every right to be considered 'one of the original philosophers among poets'.[100] Among them is the following striking example:

The Fountain

See how the fountain's sparkling jet
Cascades in spray that drifts and dances,
Fragmenting sunlight into glances
Of flame and lambent violet.
To heaven the dazzling beam would soar:
It reaches, touches heights transcendent,
But then is doomed to sink, resplendent
In mists of fire, to earth once more.

O never-failing fountain-head
Of human thought and speculation!
What enigmatic dispensation
Keeps your unflagging waters fed?
How eager is your heavenward thrust!
Yet your insistent beam, deflected
By some unseen hand, is directed
Back down, to splash into the dust.[101]

It would be easy enough to say that Tyutchev saw a particular fountain as a parable for the limitations of human thought. Yet the poem inspired by this insight is more than purely allegorical in intent. The image of the fountain is no mere illustration of the underlying idea, but part and parcel of it: we sense that it is the *same* inexhaustible vital force which impels both the spurting jet of water and human thought in its continual searching and probing. It is here perhaps that Tyutchev comes closest to illustrating Schelling's *Identitätsphilosophie* through metaphor. Like any effective metaphor, the image of the fountain asserts its right to independence, to indicate and illuminate in its vividly perceived 'thereness' completely new aspects of the poem's basic idea. The fountain itself is an artefact, stressing perhaps the idea of human thought as artifice or construction (taking us back to the world of 'Madness'). The swirling mist of droplets refracting the sun's rays could be seen as an image for the way in which our thought and perception can do no more than reflect the undivided light of ultimate reality in a plethora of brilliant but momentary and unconnected intimations of truth. We also find that productive element of ambiguity so typical of rich metaphor. What exactly is the 'unseen hand' preventing human thought from reaching 'transcendent' heights: God, impersonal Fate, inexorable laws of nature, our limitations as human beings? It could be any or all of these; the interpretation is left open for us. 'All that is transient is but a metaphor', wrote Goethe:[102] through contemplation of the world of phenomena in which we have our being we may perhaps gain some inkling of the underlying noumenal reality. So too with the poem: we are left to interpret its imagery as best we can, just as we are left to interpret the metaphor of the world itself.

A similar pattern — an image from the natural world followed by exploration of its metaphorical significance — is found in many of Tyutchev's poems. Here for instance are two short lyrics dwelling on the sense of alienation from the rest of nature brought about by conscious reflection in man:

> What a wild place this mountain gorge is!
> Towards me darts a stream: it seeks
> New haunts below, and onward forges...
> My path leads on to lonely peaks.
>
> The summit reached eventually,
> I sit at peace. . . You, stream, have hurled
> Yourself on down into the valley —
> See how you like it in man's world![103]

* * * * * * * * *

> Here where the forest thins, a kite
> Strikes upwards, seeking space and height —
> Soars up in swerving flight and on
> Towards the skyline — and is gone.

So Nature bids her offspring fly
On wings of vibrant power, while I
Must sample dust and sweat and gall:
Lord of the earth, yet in its thrall![104]

In these little poems, as in many of Caspar David Friedrich's paintings, the observing eye is included in the landscape, yet set apart from it. Friedrich typically places his human figures in the foreground, with their back turned to us (to the world of man, of civilisation, of consciousness even), gazing out at the sublime, mysterious and ultimately unattainable world of nature. Here too the poet has resolutely set his back upon a corrupt and imperfect human realm and yearns to be part of nature, at one with its healing life force. Yet he knows that this is impossible, that the very fact of being conscious prevents it. Having eaten of the tree of knowledge, we are forever banished from the Garden of Eden. It is the Romantic dilemma in a nutshell, and the germ of much existential despair.

All this undoubtedly demonstrates a keen interest in general philosophical questions. However, it is to Tyutchev's metaphorical treatment of the themes of night and day that most critical attention has been directed in the search for evidence of Schelling's specific influence. By itself the presence of these themes in his work proves very little. The 'night theme' so pervades the whole of pre-Romantic and Romantic literature, music, painting and thought, from Edward Young through to Caspar David Friedrich and beyond, that it can hardly be attributed to the influence of any one individual. In fact critics have discovered interesting textual parallels between some of Tyutchev's 'night' poems and passages in the works of several German Romantic poets including Novalis, Eichendorff and Tieck, as well as of the philosopher Schubert.[105] The following, for instance, can be read as an elaboration on general Romantic themes:

How tranquilly the darkly verdant garden
Is sleeping, cradled in the blue of night!
Through branches white with apple-blossom's burden
How tranquil glows the moon's pale-golden light!

Whole hosts of stars, as at the world's beginning,
Shine forth, mysterious in the boundless sky;
And strains of distant music faintly dinning
Sound softer than the spring that speaks nearby.

A veil now hides the world of day completely;
All labour rests, all movement flags and dies...
Above the sleeping town awake, as nightly,
The strangest murmurings, like forest sighs...

Whence could this ghostly chorus have arisen:
From mortals' disembodied thoughts in flight,
Heard though unseen, by sleep freed from their prison
To swarm amidst the chaos of the night?[106]

139

Although Tyutchev shared the widespread fascination of Romantic writers with the night theme, his treatment of it has been held by critics to be more 'objective' and 'classical',[107] and to show 'a greater degree of metaphysical abstraction and richness of meaning'.[108] This is apparent in the following example:

Day and Night

That mystic realm where spirits crowd —
A nameless dark abyss — lies hidden
(For so the gods on high have bidden)
Beneath a gold-embroidered shroud.
Day is that golden-glittering veil:
Day, that the soul of mortals quickens
And offers healing when it sickens —
That men and gods as comrade hail!

But all too soon day yields to night,
Which tears aside the veil concealing
That fateful world beneath, revealing
All that lay hidden from our sight:
The fearful dark abyss, outspread,
Laid bare with all its dismal spectres
And naught between that might protect us —
That's why night fills us with such dread![109]

Sarah Pratt takes this poem as the starting-point for one of the most illuminating analyses to date of Schellingian ideas in Tyutchev's poetry, which it will be fruitful to examine in some detail.[110] Central to her argument is the image of the metaphysical abyss used by both Schelling and Tyutchev. As she points out, Schelling derived his concept of the abyss (*Abgrund*) at least in part from his study of Jakob Böhme, in whose work the *Abgrund* (or *Ungrund*, as he also terms it) refers to the primeval chaos in which all is still undifferentiated potentiality, contained and united in 'the not yet revealed God'.[111] (Schelling held Böhme in high esteem, describing him once as 'a miracle in the history of humanity and especially in the history of the human mind'[112] — a judgement echoed by Tyutchev's own previously quoted assessment of the early seventeenth-century philosopher and mystic.).

Pratt points out that Tyutchev's poem rests on a double metaphor: 'On one level we find the images of night and day; on the next level these are transformed into the golden shroud and the abyss, respectively; and on the ultimate level, the whole complex comes to represent two opposing metaphysical principles, one apparently positive and one apparently negative.'[113] The golden shroud of day is only apparently a positive image, because it is 'but a cover that can be torn off at any moment, a superficial amenity that has nothing to do with the ultimate reality of metaphysical existence'.[114] The abyss too would appear to be a negative image, 'but it elicits respect and awe in addition to terror, for it carries the weight of metaphysical reality'.[115]

In a later poem Tyutchev takes this ambiguous complex of night and day imagery further:

> Now holy night has claimed the heavenly sphere
> And rolled back, like a golden awning
> Above the void, congenial day: its cheer
> And solace banished until morning.
> Like spectral mist the outward world has fled...
> And man in naked helplessness, resembling
> An orphan with no place to lay his head,
> Confronts the dark abyss in fear and trembling.
>
> Thrown back upon the self with all its shifts,
> Thought dispossessed and mind denied existence,
> Lost in the vastness of his soul, he drifts,
> Finding without no purchase, no resistance.
> Like some lost dream he struggles to recall
> The world of light and life, the world external...
> And must accept his birthright to be all
> That is elusive, alien and nocturnal.[116]

The image of day as a veil concealing the terrible abyss from human sight replicates that in 'Day and Night', yet here positive aspects of the abyss only hinted at in the earlier poem become more apparent. Night is 'holy' (that the holy can be terrifying is an insight common to most religions), and although face to face with this ultimate reality man feels abandoned and disorientated, in Pratt's words he nevertheless 'sinks into the abyss, no longer simply the "dark abyss," but now a symbol of man's own soul in its relation to the holy night'[117] ('Lost in the vastness of his soul, he drifts'). And 'having taken the spiritual plunge into the abyss, man receives the mystical revelation of his native heritage'[118] ('And must accept his birthright to be all / That is elusive, alien and nocturnal').

Pratt relates this again to Schelling's concept of the abyss, quoting in particular his discussion in the philosophical dialogue *Bruno* of the identity of things in eternity, defined by him as '[that supreme unity] which we regard as the holy abyss from which everything proceeds and to which everything returns'.[119] As to man discovering his true spiritual roots — his 'birthright' or 'native heritage' ('*nasled'ye rodovoye*' in the original) — in the dark irrational abyss of what would come to be known as the unconscious, Pratt points to another passage from Schelling, this time from his *Philosophical Inquiries into the Nature of Human Freedom*.[120] In this he expresses his view of the development of the universe from inorganic matter to organic, and then to consciousness in man, as resulting from a necessary cosmic struggle between light and darkness, harmony and chaos:

> [...] the world as we now behold it is all rule, order and form; but the unruly lies ever in the depths as if it might again break through, and order and form nowhere appear to have been original, but it seems as if what had initially been

unruly had been brought to order. This is the incomprehensible basis of reality in things [...]. Without this preceding gloom, creation would have no reality; darkness is its necessary heritage.[121]

Quite apart from the general similarities between this and Tyutchev's image of the abyss, Pratt points to the more specific terminological parallels (Schelling's 'holy abyss' and 'necessary heritage', Tyutchev's 'holy night' and 'native inheritance') as possible evidence of a more direct link. However, she is prepared to concede that these similarities (in particular the way in which both Schelling and Tyutchev 'utilize two images of the abyss, one with predominantly negative overtones and one with predominantly positive overtones') could still be construed as coincidental. It is, she argues, 'the manner in which the two images finally merge in the concept of *Indifferenz*, the force of undifferentiation that can terrify with its ability to destroy the individual ego or bless with its revelation of the sublime nature of art, that establishes the strongest link between the poet and the philosopher.'[122] To illustrate this she quotes one of Tyutchev's most remarkable poems:

> See on the trackless river, riding
> Through waters quick once more and free:
> A cavalcade of ice-floes gliding
> Down to the all-engulfing sea.
>
> By night they loom impenetrably,
> Shoot rainbow-glances in the sun;
> Yet as they melt inexorably
> Their journey's end can be but one.
>
> All, great and small, must soon — foregoing
> What shape or form they had — in this
> One fateful elemental flowing
> Merge with the fathomless abyss!..
>
> You, phantom of the mind's invention,
> The self — that 'I' we all proclaim:
> What is your meaning, your intention,
> Your destiny, if not the same?[123]

Written after the poet's return to his homeland, and inspired by the dramatic sight of the ice breaking up on the Neva, this is a perfect example of Dudek's 'basic philosophical experience' transmuted into poetry. Pratt relates its elaboration of the abyss image to the Schellingian notion that (as she puts it) '*Indifferenz* is both the native source and the point of return for all phenomena of the metaphysical universe'.[124] Indeed, as she points out, Tyutchev even seems to quote the term in line 11 of the poem, where (in the original) he speaks of the former ice-floes intermingling at sea *'bezrazlichny, kak stikhiya'* ('undifferentiated, as [one] element', i.e. as water).[125]

Some have detected elements of Schopenhauer's philosophy in this poem in particular, as well as in others by Tyutchev.[126] Yet on balance it seems unlikely that he was among the select few to read *The World as Will and Representation* during the years of almost total neglect between its publication in 1818 and the first stirrings of wider recognition in the early 1850s. He may well have come to know it later, when it became the talk of intellectual circles throughout Europe (the novelists Turgenev and Tolstoy, and the poet Afanasy Fet, with all of whom Tyutchev was on friendly terms, were among its Russian admirers; indeed it was Fet who, with Tolstoy's active encouragement, first translated it into Russian).[127] However, any direct influence of Schopenhauer's thought on his poetry during his years in Munich seems highly improbable. What would appear to be evidence for this in the poems is more likely explicable, as previously suggested, in terms of Schopenhauer's assimilation of certain aspects of Schelling's philosophy. An important distinction to recall here is that, as we have seen, for Schelling the noumenal will producing and driving the world of phenomena is ultimately of divine origin, and is working towards the realisation of ever greater harmony and goodness, whereas for Schopenhauer it is blind, unconscious and undirected. (That such a purposeless will should bring about a universe that appears to be ordered rather than chaotic can strike even a self-declared admirer of Schopenhauer's philosophy as one of its inconsistencies.)[128] In his engagement with Schelling's philosophy of nature Tyutchev seems quite independently to have reached a position close to that of Schopenhauer. Critical of Schelling for attempting to combine religious belief with philosophy, he would probably have preferred Schopenhauer's system in so far as it functions without any recourse to a divine being as guiding principle.

Common to both Schelling and Schopenhauer is the idea that the highest purpose of existence lies in renunciation of the world of phenomena and reunion with the one undifferentiated ultimate reality, whether that is thought of as the noumenal will, the world soul, God, or whatever. This can be achieved through religious meditation and practice or philosophical contemplation, but also through art. It is in this context (to return to Sarah Pratt's analysis) that the concept of the individual self absorbed into the *Abgrund* becomes a positive one in Schelling's philosophy. To complete her argument that Tyutchev's portrayal of the metaphysical abyss is essentially Schelling-ian, evoking both terror and yearning, Pratt is able to point to some of of his poems in which this generally so fearsome image is seen to be attractive and desirable.[129] Else-where too Tyutchev can express the same metaphysical longing for union with the absolute without any reference to the abyss:

> Shadows fall, dove-grey, and mingle;
> Colours drain, all sound falls dumb;
> Life and movement melt to fickle
> Dusk and to a distant hum...
> On the air a moth in motion
> Unseen scribes its whirring scrawl...
> Hour of yearning past expression!..
> All within me, I in all!..

143

Tranquil dusk, flood all my being
With a draught of potent sleep;
In your soothing, tranquil-flowing,
Fragrant balm my senses steep —
Let oblivion's clouded potion
All my feelings overrun...
Let me taste annihilation,
With the sleeping world made one![130]

Leo Tolstoy loved this poem, which always moved him to tears, particularly the line 'All within me, I in all'.[131] Perhaps, as Richard Gregg has suggested, he had it in mind in *War and Peace*, where Pierre Bezukhov is granted a similar epiphany while contemplating the moonlit Russian landscape as a captive of the French: the awareness that 'all this is mine, and all this is in me, and all this is me!'.[132]

That Tyutchev could sometimes (as here) be attracted to the abyss, and sometimes be terrified by it has puzzled some critics as an apparent inconsistency. Chronology undoubtedly provides part of the answer, for later events in his life would conspire to shake youthful optimism and induce an altogether bleaker view of the world. Yet this is by no means the whole story. As he confesses in one of his poems, his 'prophetic soul' and 'heart/ In thrall to anguish' were doomed to a kind of dual existence 'on the shifting border/ Between two worlds lived out apart'.[133] 'Day' — life in the world of phenomena — led him to fear and avoid the absolute; yet the 'prophetic soul' of the poet was also in touch with and drawn to the mysterious realm of night, of the abyss and extinction. It was just this ability of the creative artist to open a door onto the absolute, to make the infinite visible in the finite, that Schelling valued so highly. 'For the philosopher,' he wrote, 'art is supreme precisely because it reveals to him as it were the holy of holies, where in eternal and original union that which is divided in nature and history, and which in life and action just as in thought must be eternally unreconcilable, burns as if with one flame.'[134]

Like so many of his contemporaries, Tyutchev came to share this exalted vision of the artist. In his verse from about 1830 on poets take on the mantle of seerlike figures entrusted with sacred mysteries. Pushkin is 'a sounding-board' for the gods[135] Goethe, 'prophet-like, with thunderstorms conversed';[136] Fet has on occasion been vouchsafed glimpses of 'Great Mother' nature as she really is.[137] And in one poem he writes revealingly that the poet is endowed with 'powers elemental' which 'to all things but himself extend'.[138]

In the light of this it might at first glance seem paradoxical that for most of his life Tyutchev cultivated a curious public façade of self-deprecation and denial with regard to his own position and role as poet. He was happy to dismiss his poetic manuscripts as 'scribblings' (*paperasses*), and the poems themselves as mere 'rhymes'.[139] Collections of his poems were published during his lifetime only thanks to the efforts of others, usually with no collaboration or even apparent interest on his part. Individual poems submitted by him to journals frequently appeared anonymously or with just the initials 'F.T.'. Many of his poems, including some of his very best, he did not even attempt to publish; they came to light only after his death. Even among friends and acquaintances the subject was taboo. His fellow-poet Fet recalls that he 'painstakingly avoided not only conversations about his poetic activity, but even allusions to it'.[140] More specifically, he 'would flinch painfully at the slightest allusion to his poetic gift', so that 'no-one dared to broach the subject with him'.[141]

Various theories, some more plausible than others, have been advanced for this eccentric behaviour, which undoubtedly had complex roots (we shall return to the subject in due course). Yet it was Fet who seems to have come closest to unpicking the main strand of Tyutchev's motivation. 'Not for nothing did you so assiduously hide your flame,' he wrote after the poet's death; 'you will forever remain the favourite of a select few. The many will never be able to understand you!'[142] It does indeed seem to be the case that the carefully cultivated façade was a protective shell designed to shield the poetic shrine within against desecration from without, and that in his heart of hearts Tyutchev knew himself to be one of the select brotherhood of poet-seers. All this is hinted at in what has become one of his best-known poems, written apparently during the first year or so of his acquaintanceship with Schelling:

> *Silentium!*
>
> Be silent, guard your tongue, and keep
> All inmost thoughts and feelings deep
> Within your heart concealed. There let
> Them in their courses rise and set,
> Like stars in jewelled night, unheard:
> Admire them, and say not a word.
>
> How can the soul its flame impart?
> How can another know your heart,
> The truths by which you live and die?
> A thought, once uttered, is a lie,
> The limpid spring defiled, once stirred:
> Drink of it, and say not a word.
>
> Make but the inward life your goal —
> Seek out that world within your soul:
> Mysterious, magic thoughts are there,
> Which, if the outer din and glare
> Intrude, will fade and be not heard:
> Drink in their song — and not a word![143]

One is led to wonder whether this reflection on the limitations of language might not have been written in response to one of Schelling's lectures. (The Latin injunction of the title — then still used to call students to order at German and Russian universities — could be seen as an ironic pointer in that direction).[144] 'Silentium!' was another favourite of Tolstoy's, and he was fond of reciting it to others. 'What a remarkable piece!' he once exclaimed. 'I know of no better poem.'[145] For him it was quite simply 'the very model of a poem in which every word is in the right place'.[146] The qualities admired by Tolstoy speak for themselves: by his mid-twenties Tyutchev had reached the summit of his creative powers. From now on his poetry becomes more intense, more passionate, more inward. As if enthused by Schelling's grand vision of the supreme role of art, he produces lyrics of true genius. It was perhaps the finest and most lasting gift the philosopher could have bestowed on the poet.

6 Anni Mirabilis
(Munich, 1829-1830)

i A Change of Fortune

At seven o'clock on the morning of 3 May 1829 (the first fine sunny day that year, as Tyutchev later recalled)[1] the cries of a new-born child burst upon the sedate Sunday peace of Ottostrasse. When the father was ushered in to see his wife and baby daughter, he found things much quieter. 'You were so calm and collected,' he later told his eldest daughter, 'that your mother herself had to point out to me the special significance of the little rolled-up bundle of linen placed at her feet.'[2] Three weeks later in a private ceremony at the Tyutchevs' house the child was christened Anna by the Greek Orthodox priest from the Salvatorkirche. The godparents were Tyutchev's brother Nikolay and (represented in her absence by Clotilde) his mother.[3]

Tyutchev's failure even to notice the new arrival was indicative. Untouched by the great Romantic fascination with childhood, he was to take little interest in his offspring during their formative years, leaving their upbringing to his wife and other female carers. Paternal concern was, he once conceded, 'a virtue which I am far from possessing'.[4] Indeed, he was quite open about having only 'very moderate feelings of parental affection',[5] even attempting to justify this logically. Was parental instinct not after all a form of egotism, of pride in one's possessions, and therefore hardly to be admired? As soon as they were old enough to follow this line of reasoning (perhaps even before) his children not surprisingly found it puzzling and hurtful. 'It is all extremely paradoxical,' the eighteen-year-old Anna wrote in her diary one day after a particularly heated discussion on the subject with her father. 'Every day he craves society, feels the need to see people who are nothing to him, and yet his children hold no attraction for him.'[6] During their argument she had spoken of her own affection for her one-year-old brother Ivan and of the need she felt to see him and play with him. 'With me it's just the opposite,' Tyutchev had replied: 'I feel the need not to see him.'[7]

This lack of bonding with his children did have its redeeming features. He was never tempted to slip into the role of possessive, autocratic paterfamilias, never fearful he might lose face by revealing his own shortcomings. As a result his children found themselves respected as individuals and confided to as equals, which helped to compensate for his emotional distance. As another of his daughters remembered, he 'never made anyone feel that he was their superior; that is why he was so much loved, above all by his children and his subordinates'.[8]

If Tyutchev was not exactly overwhelmed with joy at becoming a father for the first time, he still had many reasons to be thankful that spring. The loving and devoted woman who had borne his child could now at last be openly acknowledged as his lawful wife. They had settled into their new apartment; and although Tyutchev's salary as Second Secretary of 800 silver roubles per annum was not enough to support a family, it was a useful supplement to the allowance paid out of revenue from the family estate.[9] Moreover, he now had his foot on the first rung of the diplomatic career ladder and could expect further advancement. Not the least of his blessings was a congenial and sympathetic chief in the person of the new Ambassador, Ivan Potyomkin. Since the latter's arrival in Munich the previous October he and Tyutchev had developed a close and cordial relationship. Tyutchev later commented warmly on Potyomkin's friendship in letters to his parents.[10] 'Dear, splendid fellow!' he writes on one occasion, adding with a dash of hyperbole that he and the Ambassador were quite simply 'two hearts just made for one another'.[11] Potyomkin for his part was impressed by his Second Secretary's 'rare talents' and 'outstanding ability',[12] and was not slow to recommend him for promotion. He also assigned him a more active role in the work of the Embassy. From about this time despatches in Tyutchev's hand show increasing signs of having been composed by him (or at least with his collaboration), rather than merely copied or written to dictation.[13]

The war between Russia and Turkey, which had hastened the announcement of both Potyomkin's and Tyutchev's appointments the previous spring, dominated the early months of the new Ambassador's tenure. Articles critical of Russia's conduct of the war (and by implication of King Ludwig's support for it) began to appear in Cotta's influential *Allgemeine Zeitung* (*Universal Gazette*); while rumours that one of these articles had originated with the Austrian government caused a certain amount of fluttering in the diplomatic dovecotes. Tyutchev's role in all this is signalled by several despatches in his hand, with appended translations by him from German into French of one of the offending articles and of Ludwig's decree on measures to be taken against the newspaper.[14] One of these despatches, dated 5/17 February 1829, suggested enlisting the services of an accomplished journalist sympathetic to the Russian cause to counteract such attacks in the Western press; enclosed was a letter to Foreign Minister Nesselrode from the journalist Friedrich Lindner volunteering to undertake just such a task.[15] Lindner, a Baltic-German subject of the Tsar living in Munich, was a friend of Cotta and in 1828 had been Heine's co-editor on the *Neue Allgemeine Politische Annalen*.[16] Tyutchev had known him since before Potyomkin's arrival in Munich, and it was probably he who recommended him to the Ambassador as a potential ally in the war of words. Indeed, the whole idea of attempting to influence Western public opinion in this way may have originated with Tyutchev: it is of a piece with his own efforts vis-à-vis Heine and Schelling, and foreshadows his later activity in courting Western spokesmen for Russia. Not that the idea itself was in any way original; at any given time governments throughout Europe were bankrolling a small army of willing hacks. (Lindner, it must be said, appears to have volunteered his services from a sense of patriotic duty rather than for monetary reward.) Nesselrode agreed to the proposal, stipulating that Lindner should not be given any specific instructions but be allowed to write independently, thus retaining his authority as a political commentator.[17] In the event Potyomkin was able to report six months later that Lindner's articles in the *Allgemeine Zeitung* had succeeded in pushing that distinguished and authoritative organ of the press towards 'a more equitable appreciation' of Russian policy towards Turkey.

The same despatch also mentions that Lindner had encouraged other contributors to the newspaper, in particular Friedrich Thiersch, the Rector of Munich University and a leading supporter of the cause of Greek independence, to take a similar line.[18] In fact it sems that Thiersch (who knew Tyutchev well at this time, and was highly appreciative of his intellectual and diplomatic abilities)[19] was persuaded as much by Tyutchev as by Lindner to defend Russia in print. Confirmation is provided by events just a few months later, in February 1830, when on the eve of the crucial London Conference to decide the future of Greece the *Allgemeine Zeitung* reprinted over several days an anonymous article from the Turkish newspaper *Courrier de Smyrne* (*Smyrna Chronicle*). The article accused Russia of plotting to turn Greece into its vassal province, and appealed to the other protecting powers, Britain and France, to defend the newly-independent state against its 'enemy'. Once again the hand of Austria was suspected (Metternich deeply resented Tsar Nicholas's apostasy from the Holy Alliance in supporting Greek independence, and by threatening to ban the *Allgemeine Zeitung* in Austria was in a position to exert considerable financial pressure on Cotta). Tyutchev immediately rushed off an impassioned and eloquent letter to Thiersch calling on the prominent Philhellene to rebut in print the calumnies of this 'incredible article', which he describes as 'the crudest insult ever made to the common sense of the public': 'it is for you, Sir, who have nobly linked your name to the destiny of Greece, to take up once more the interests of a cause which are being so shamefully violated through misrepresentation'.[20] It is not known if or where Thiersch might have published such a rebuttal, but he evidently continued to defend Russian policy in the press. A year later he and Lindner were each rewarded for their journalistic services with the gift of a ring from the Tsar.[21] Tyutchev's initiative (for his it undoubtedly was) had clearly produced results.

His literary prospects had also taken a turn for the better (although, character-istically, not through any effort on his part to promote his work). In 1828 marriage plans had forced his unworldly former mentor Semyon Raich to seek ways of supplementing his meagre income as private tutor. He rather reluctantly settled on the idea of publishing a literary journal (seeing this as 'a temporary apostasy, a deviation from my self-imposed rule of serving Literature without thought of personal gain'.)[22] Initial omens for the journal, to be titled *Galateya*, were good, with such prominent figures as Pushkin and Vyazemsky offering encouragement and practical support. Raich contacted Shevyryov and other former protégés for contributions, including Tyutchev, some twenty of whose poems and translations were published during the two years of the journal's existence. Among these are such early lyric masterpieces as 'Thunderstorm in Spring', 'Insomnia', 'Summer Evening' and 'Evening', and the political meditations 'Napoleon's Grave' and 'Oleg's Shield'. There were a further dozen or so which Raich did not manage to publish before the journal's demise, as attested by autograph manuscripts still in his possession some years later.[23] None of the corres-pondence accompanying all these poems sent by Tyutchev between 1828 and 1830 has survived, apart from a brief yet revealing extract quoted by Raich in his 'Letter to a Friend Abroad', published in the first issue of *Galateya* in January 1829.[24] This shows Tyutchev buoyed up with patriotic sentiment at his country's military and diplomatic successes in the conflict with Turkey, and eager to learn from Raich of any stirrings of comparable renewal in the cultural sphere (the passages from his letter as quoted by Raich are given here in italics):

'...*What is happening, or rather, is* <u>*anything*</u> *happening in the Russian literary world?*' you ask me in one of your letters. I should like to reply to your ironic question in the first instance with a brief letter. For a long time I have been wanting to write to you about a subject close to both our hearts. You evidently have a somewhat vague and ill-defined conception of Russian literature, and of intellectual developments in Russia in general. And not surprisingly, for more than six years have passed since you left your native land, and moreover you judge the products of our literature on the basis of foreign translations of a few Russian books. '*A few days ago*' — these are your words — '*a few days ago I came across the translation of a book by B[ulgari]n; I read it with something akin to an overflowing heart. The infant-like description of an infant society! A strange business! As a state, Russia is a giant; yet as a society, a mere infant. Yet I hope and believe that this infant is destined to grow to manhood, and that one ninth of the earth's surface will come to occupy a corresponding space in the intellectual sphere. Until then let us console ourselves by applying to Russia the lines of Virgil:*

> *Tu regere imperio populos, Romane, memento;*
> *Hae tibi erunt artes; pacisque imponere morem;*
> *Parcere subjectis, et debellare superbos.*
> [Be it your task, Roman, to hold imperial sway over the nations;
> These shall be your arts: to establish the order of peace,
> Spare the vanquished and subdue the arrogant.]'[25]

 I too, dear friend, share with you this comforting faith, this sweet hope [...].Oh, if only you knew how many changes have taken place just in literature since you left your native land, the direction that literature has taken, and with what haste, if not speed, it hurries forward [...].[26]

Here we find clearly formulated by Tyutchev for the first time that prophetic vision of Russia's future destiny which impressed many of his Western listeners, and which was to be such a determining factor in his own political credo.

ii Travels in Italy

Around the middle of May 1829 the little Russian community in Munich welcomed Princess Zinaida Volkonskaya, passing through on her way from Russia to Italy.[27] Accompanying the charming and cultured Princess on her travels were her son Aleksandr and foster-son Vladimir, then seventeen and fifteen years old respectively, together with a whole retinue of servants and attendants. Among the latter was the young poet and literary critic Stepan Shevyryov, employed as tutor to Aleksandr.[28] As one of the 'Lovers of Wisdom' group he may well have met Tyutchev at Princess Zinaida's Moscow salon in 1825. He certainly did so now in Munich, as his diary confirms.[29] Here were two young poets, both protégés of Raich, both with a penchant for philosophical themes, who had seen their work published in the same journals and almanachs. A critic would soon be naming them, together with Aleksey Khomyakov, as leading members of the 'German School'.[30] Clearly they had much to talk about. For Shevyryov this will have included his recent travels with the Princess and her entourage. Just a few days before in Dresden they had met Nikolay Rozhalin, a young critic and translator also close to the 'Lovers of Wisdom' circle, who was employed at the Russian Embassy there but keen to move to Munich.[31] Shevyryov and Rozhalin had accompanied Princess Zinaida on a visit to Goethe in Weimar, and had sat in awed silence while she chatted easily with the great man, whom she knew from a previous occasion.[32] A year before Goethe had commented favourably in print on a review of *Faust* published by Shevyryov; yet any hopes the latter may have had of being recognised were sorely disappointed: it seems that Goethe mistook Rozhalin for the Polish poet Mickiewicz and Shevyryov for one of his retinue.[33]

Perhaps the most remarkable aspect of the two Russian poets' conversation is that it was conducted almost entirely in French. Writing to Pogodin not long afterwards, Shevyryov commented on the compatriots he had come across abroad: 'All the Russians we have met here have become Frenchified and taken on diplomatic airs. I started a conversation with Tyutchev in Russian; he was unable to continue. However, he can certainly rattle on eloquently in French, and has a good head on his shoulders. His application is evident enough, for all his diplomatic swaggering.'[34] This must have struck a chord with Pogodin, whose own nascent Slavophilism had found Tyutchev's westernised ways similarly distasteful in the summer of 1825.

After a few days the Princess and her party left Munich on their way to Rome, where she was to settle permanently. Some sort of seed must have been sown in Tyutchev's mind, for only a month later he too left Munich to rendezvous with them in Italy. Princess Zinaida loved to have bright young minds about her, especially if they were artistically inclined, and the most likely explanation is that she invited Tyutchev and his family to visit her in the south. And while the demands of a newborn baby ruled this out for Eleonore, they would, to say the very least, have presented no obstacle to Tyutchev. Ambassador Potyomkin agreed (perhaps at Princess Zinaida's persuasion) to let him take unofficial leave over the dead summer months.[35] So it was that soon after 20 June he left Munich and headed for the Alps with his brother Nikolay, who had also met the Princess and her retinue during her stay.[36]

They would be retracing the steps of Goethe as described in his *Italian Journey* (*Italienische Reise*), and more recently Heine, extracts from whose Italian *Travel Sketches* (*Reisebilder*) had appeared in print the previous December.[37] According to Karl Pfeffel, in years to come Tyutchev would often speak of the pull of the south, quoting Mignon's song from Goethe's *Wilhelm Meister* with its invocation of 'the land where citrons bloom' and yearning cry: 'Dahin! Dahin!' ('There would I go!')[38] The brothers knew they would be visiting what had long been held to be the Tyutchevs' ancestral homeland. This family tradition, with its connotations of loss and exile, was to become a fertile poetic myth for Tyutchev. A later poem full of nostalgic longing for Italy refers to it fairly clearly:

> And another land — that cherished
> Homeland — rises into view:
> Paradise, which guilt ancestral
> Means its sons must now eschew...[39]

Known facts concerning the brothers' itinerary are sparse.[40] We might assume a brief visit to Florence, which lay on their path south; however, they cannot have stayed long, for by 1 July or thereabouts they had already reached Princess Zinaida and her party in Rome.[41] On 5 July the Princess together with Shevyryov, her son Aleksandr and the rest left for the island of Ischia, where she was to take the waters.[42] Although Tyutchev and Nikolay joined them there later, they probably decided to stay on in Rome first. This, Tyutchev's only visit to the Eternal City, left a deep and lasting impression on him. In a short poem written twenty years later he could still conjure up Rome, 'deserted and majestic' by night, her 'eternal remains' seeming in the moonlight to belong to some magical vanished world.[43] Here, at what he was to call the very 'root of the Western world',[44] where the stones themselves spoke of violent past upheavals and world-shaping events, his fascination with the elemental forces of history was allowed full play. It found expression in the poem 'Cicero', written either during his stay in Italy or shortly thereafter.[45] Another poem, dating from the following year, also seems to reflect experiences in Rome:

Mal'aria

How sweet is this divine wrath! — this mysterious essence
Of Evil spread abroad, concealed in everything —
In wayside flowers, the crystal waters of a spring,
The very sky of Rome, the sunlight's iridescence...
Unclouded still is heaven's lofty edifice,
Unchanged the gentle rhythm of your breast's dilation,
Still treetops stir at the warm breeze's inspiration,
Still fragrant is the rose — and all is Death, all this!

Who knows, perhaps indeed all nature is invested
With colours, odours, sounds and voices that foretell
Our final hour, while easing with their genial spell
The final agony with which all shall be tested.
If so, that envoy whom the Fates have deputised
May use them as an airy cloak to mask his features
When he arrives to summon forth us earthbound creatures,
Ensuring that his fearsome coming is disguised![46]

The immediate stimulus for this poem has been shown to be a passage in Madame de Staël's novel *Corinne, ou l'Italie*[47] (a significant choice, perhaps, given that Princess Zinaida was nicknamed 'la Corinne du Nord').[48] In this the author also contrasts the visible beauty of nature around Rome with the invisible but deadly danger of the pestilential air, concluding that 'all this is death'. Then the words of Oswald (a friend of the heroine visiting the Rome area with her) are quoted:

'I love,' Oswald said to Corinne, 'this mysterious, invisible danger, this danger lurking beneath an outward appearance of most agreeable impressions. If death is, as I believe, no more than the call to a happier existence, why should the perfume of flowers, the shade of beautiful trees, the refreshing evening breeze not be entrusted with bringing us the news? Without doubt the government must in every way show vigilance in the preservation of human life, but nature has secrets which the imagination alone can penetrate [...].'[49]

Although this clearly provided a matrix for Tyutchev, his poem completely transforms the underlying sense of the original, as Richard Gregg has shown.[50] Oswald's view of death is traditionally Christian: for him the fear of suffering and extinction is negated by the assurance of divine mercy and a blessed afterlife. Tyutchev on the other hand turns Oswald's invisible 'danger' of death into an invisible 'Evil' or 'divine wrath' permeating the whole of nature. 'Not unlike the Manicheans,' (writes Gregg), 'who believed the entire world to be the work of Satan, and then resignedly went ahead and enjoyed its beauties to the full, Tiutchev sees death-breeding Evil in the loveliest sensual experiences, a circumstance which, however, does not prevent him from declaring and celebrating his love for them.'[51] In this context the 'divine wrath' ('bozhy gnev') of line 1 can hardly be equated with the Biblical concept; similarly, the messenger of the Fates in verse two is more a figure from pagan mythology than the grim reaper of Christian iconography.

Gregg detects 'inner inconsistency' in Tyutchev's reworking of Madame de Staël.[52] He is right to do so; but wrong to criticise the poem too severely for it. Most of the inconsistencies noted can be justified in terms of that duality of appearance and reality, of the phenomenal and the noumenal, which forms the philosophical basis of so much of Tyutchev's poetry. The veil of charming appearances used here by the fateful messenger to conceal the terrors of death has its counterpart in the veil of day flung over the awful void of night at the bidding of the gods in 'Day and Night'.[53] In both cases the veil hides a reality from which we shrink: the existence of an impersonal, morally indifferent life-force providing the motive power for all nature. It is the will in Schopenhauer's philosophy, Tennyson's 'nature red in tooth and claw'; Vladimir Solovyov calls it in his essay on Tyutchev 'the dark root of universal being'.[54] In so far as it is instinctual, non-rational and undifferentiated in character, the conscious individual may perceive it equally (and often simultaneously, as here) as evil, suffering and death, or as a healing transcendent force. If these are inconsistencies, they are ones incapable of resolution, arising from our very being in the world. Although intended as a criticism, Gregg's statement that in 'Mal'aria' nature appears as 'a quick-change artist'[55] is in this sense quite illuminating. Nature may indeed appear, as in an optical illusion, now as natura naturans, now as natura naturata, now beneficial, now threatening, or in a variety of other contradictory guises. Tyutchev's own response to such ambivalence seems to have been an increasing sense of existential despair, culminating near the end of his life in a bleak little four-line poem comparing nature to a sphinx, in which he wonders whether, behind all the tantalising air of mystery, there is actually any riddle to be solved at all.[56]

There are other ways too in which 'Mal'aria' diverges from its literary source. For instance, the scene depicted in the first verse is clearly distinct from that in the novel. This suggests that, quite apart from changing the whole philosophical slant of Madame de Staël's account, Tyutchev has grafted on to it recollected experiences of his own. In particular the woman in line 6 (it seems unlikely to be a man), whom we assume to be lying peacefully asleep next to the poet, has no counterpart in the original. Is she no more than the product of poetic imagination, or a real person, the object of some romantic dalliance in Italy? Although the latter would be quite in character, we have no real way of telling. In either case we are reminded that for Tyutchev the sexual impulse was an integral part of the 'dark root of universal being', that chaotic principle constantly threatening to break through the flimsy veil of consciousness and disrupt the fancied harmony and order of our waking lives. In this sense the Evil permeating sensual beauty in 'Mal'aria' finds its parallel in later, more overt love poems, which speak of 'that evil life, with its unruly passion' flowing through lovers in their most intimate moments,[57] and of the lethally destructive power of 'passion's blind intoxication'.[58]

Leaving Rome, Tyutchev and Nikolay headed south for Naples and then Ischia, where Princess Volkonskaya and her entourage were already installed. She is known to have stayed on the island from 12 July to 12 August; beyond that there is no indication of when exactly the two brothers arrived, or how long they remained there.[59] The Bay of Naples and Ischia left an imprint on Tyutchev's poetic imagination to rival that of Rome. First impressions as he and Nikolay approached Naples by mail coach will have been of green slopes rich with orange and olive groves, with glimpses down to the curving bay and its sapphire waters below. After arriving in the city and finding lodgings somewhere in its bustling, noisy streets, they may have refreshed themselves after the journey with an evening stroll along the shore, admiring the views of Vesuvius to the east, its smoking summit inflamed by the setting sun, and of Ischia to the west, guarding the mouth of the bay. To reach Ischia Tyutchev had to make his first real journey by sea: at least ten miles, even if the shorter route was taken from Pozzuoli to the west. He was not a particularly good sailor, as we know from later evidence, and sudden squalls are not uncommon in the Bay of Naples. It may have been this crossing which inspired the poem 'Dream at Sea', written during his stay on Ischia.[60] It begins with a vivid description of just such a storm at sea:

> Our craft tossed by tempest and buffeting seas,
> I drowsed, letting wind and waves rage as they please.
> In me I felt two infinities play:
> They held me enslaved in their unbridled sway.
> All around me, like cymbals, the cliffs clashed and rang,
> To each other the winds called, the waves roared and sang.

The 'chaos of sounds' lulls the poet into a strange waking dream ('unhealthily vivid, uncannily mute') which seems to hover above the roaring darkness. In this dream — reminiscent of Prospero's vision of 'cloud-capped towers, the gorgeous palaces,/ The solemn temples, the great globe itself'[61] —

> Towers, palaces, labyrinth-gardens showed fair,
> And teeming crowds silently swarmed everywhere.
> I came to know faces not met with before,
> Mysterious beasts, birds fantastical saw...

Intoxicated by the power of his own poetic imagination, for a moment he imagines himself possessed of a divine omnipotence:

> Like a god, on the heights of creation I strode,
> While, unmoving beneath me, the world brightly glowed.

But at this very moment it becomes apparent that, like Prospero's 'insubstantial pageant', the vision cannot be sustained. The roaring deep, 'like the howl of a sorceror', shakes the poet from his trance-like state,

> And into that still realm of visions and dreams
> Burst in foaming breakers with wild roars and screams.[62]

In line 3 Tyutchev undoubtedly makes a verbal nod to Pascal, as pointed out by Gregg.[63] Yet it can be no more than a nod: the 'two infinities' at whose mercy the poet finds himself are patently not those discussed in the famous opening passage of the *Pensées* (the infinitely large and the infinitely small), but rather, as Ralph Matlaw puts it, 'the dream and the sea',[64] or in more general terms the poetic imagination and the life of nature. Underlying the poem is, as both Matlaw and Sarah Pratt argue,[65] a Schellingian view of the creative artist — and above all the poet — as one uniquely able to tap into that spirit or life force which is the eternal reality behind the shifting, fragile world of appearances. Yet Gregg is also right to suggest an analogy with Prometheus:[66] The poet's encroachment on the divine is at the same time an act of hubris, punished with his abrupt return to sober reality as the roaring of the sea, 'like the howl of a sorceror', intrudes on his consciousness. In this sense the poem can be read as 'among other things, a parable of the romantic apotheosis of man and of its dangerous consequences'.[67] Gregg's attempts to identify the sorceror as Schelling fail to convince, however;[68] more likely is his suggestion of a reference to the sorceror in Goethe's famous ballad, enraged that 'his magic has been abused and the floodgates opened'.[69] On the other hand Tyutchev could be referring again to that most celebrated conjuror of tempests, Prospero. Pascal, Schelling, Goethe, Shakespeare... the list of possible sources for the poem is by no means exhaustive.[70] Nor is this an unusual case: scholars have unearthed scores of literary echoes in Tyutchev's verse, sometimes (as here) several together in the same poem.[71] Yet such is Tyutchev's skill in transmuting and combining these sources for his own purposes that the result never appears derivative or even obvious. What we are left with is rather a subtle sense of the individual poem being embedded in a much wider intellectual tradition. The existence of a number of strangely allusive poems which (in the words of one critic who has reviewed the evidence) 'enigmatically point to their source in some reading matter [...] yet to be established'[72] only helps to reinforce this general observation. Tyutchev felt himself part of a timeless realm of the spirit, an 'Elysium of shades'[73] inhabited by the great creative minds of every epoch; his poetry must at least in part be seen as a dialogue with that realm.

During his stay on Ischia Tyutchev may have taken the opportunity to explore its rocky coastline (hinted at in 'Dream at Sea') with Shevyryov and the young Aleksandr Volkonsky, or they may have hired mules to ascend Mount Epomeo for the panoramic view of the Bay of Naples from its summit. Their conversation will inevitably have centred on poetry. Having to some extent filled the gap left in the 'Lovers of Wisdom' group by Venevitinov's death, Shevyryov was very much the up-and-coming young poet and critic. In 1827 and 1828 he had published a series of articles in the group's journal, *Vestnik Yevropy* (*Herald of Europe*), expounding Schellingian ideas on art, in particular that of poetry as the original and highest art form.[74] His own poems (including some on the night theme beloved of Tyutchev)[75] had already attracted critical praise; even Pushkin would soon be writing of his 'genuine talent'.[76] Not the easiest of men to get on with (his friend Pogodin had to admit to his 'strict and demanding attitude, his quick temper and uncontrolled tongue'),[77] Shevyryov held trenchant views on the current state of Russian poetry and did not hesitate to assert them vigorously. He felt that contemporary poets (including Pushkin, to whom he addressed an epistle in verse outlining his theories)[78] had submitted too easily to the influence of French models, allowing their verse to become smooth, elegant and superficial at the expense of of vitality, passion and profundity. 'My verses are too discordant, often harsh and crude. But there are reasons for this,' he later wrote in the introduction to his translation of part of Tasso's *Gerusalemme liberata*. 'I left for Italy with the last sounds of our monotonous muse echoing in my ears... I turned to our first masters, and found strength in them... and was ashamed of the effeminacy, weakness and poverty of our contemporary Russian language...'[79] Unfortunately, although Shevyryov may have been right to rebel against the sing-song metrical regularity of so much Russian verse at the time, he himself as a poet never proved equal to the task of reform. The attempted introduction of Italian syllabic verse into Russian in his translation from Tasso was singularly unsuccessful; as for his original poems, even the best showed few signs of the metrical experimentation he had demanded as a critic.

No doubt all this was talked about on Ischia. For Tyutchev it was a rare opportunity to discuss his own work with a fellow-poet — almost certainly in French, if Shevyryov's experience in Munich is anything to go by.[80] Nor was their association limited to purely theoretical discussion. Shevyryov for his part produced two patriotic odes during his stay on the island. The first, 'To my Uncomely Mother', contrasts Italy — a striking beauty, but in thrall to her 'importunate lover' Austria — with the 'uncomely' yet dearly beloved Mother Russia, who has produced so many glorious children.[81] The second, 'Petrograd', in some respects foreshadows Pushkin's later (and incomparably greater) 'Bronze Horseman': here Shevyryov portrays Peter the Great first subduing the unruly elements to build his new capital by the sea, and then keeping guard over the city in the shape of Falconet's famous equestrian statue.[82] That something in the nature of a poetic workshop took place on Ischia is suggested by the existence of copies made by Shevyryov and Aleksandr Volkonsky of three of Tyutchev's poems written at the time.[83] One, 'Dream at Sea', is clearly an exercise in the kind of metrical irregularity (reproduced in the translation given above) that Shevyryov was calling for.[84] Another, 'Sea Stallion' — similarly inspired, it seems, by stormy weather in the Bay of Naples — brilliantly encapsulates in its single extended metaphor the Schellingian concept of nature as the visible multiple expression of one underlying life force:

Sea Stallion

Hot-blooded stallion of the sea
With mane of lucent green —
Now wild, capricious, running free,
Now placidly serene!
Raised by a tempest far from here
Amidst unending seas,
You learnt from it to shy, to rear,
To canter as you please!

I love to see you charge, unchecked
In your imperious force,
When — steaming, tousle-maned and flecked
With foam — you set your course
For land, careering headlong o'er
The brine with joyful neigh,
To dash hooves on the sounding shore
And — vanish into spray![85]

'There is perhaps no other poem in world literature in which inanimate and animate nature have been perceived and depicted as a unity in such complete measure,' writes Gerhard Dudek of this (adding that only Wordsworth's 'I wandered lonely as a cloud...' and Shelley's 'Ode to the West Wind' and 'The Cloud' can approach it in this respect).[86] The third of the poems written on Ischia, 'My soul aspires to be a star...'[87] has been shown to display close parallels with Aleksey Khomyakov's 'Wish' ('Zhelaniye'), written two years earlier.[88] It may be that Shevyryov had the text of this with him in Italy, and that Tyutchev's variation on it was composed as some kind of poetic exercise. Certainly in the copy made at the time by Aleksandr Volkonsky Tyutchev's poem bears exactly the same title as Khomyakov's.[89]

The whole experience of Italy had borne him up on a tide of poetic inspiration which was to sweep on into the following year. About two dozen of his best poems were written in these two years, most between the summer of 1829 and the autumn of 1830;[90] there were also many translations. And this was from a man who over his long creative life was to manage on average some four original poems of quality a year. Nothing evokes this state of creative intensity better than the line in 'Dream at Sea' which depicts him striding, godlike, 'on the heights of creation'; yet as the poem implies, it was a height from which one could fall to earth with a crash.

Leaving Ischia on 12 August, Princess Zinaida and her party spent about three weeks on the shores of the Tyrrhenian Sea before returning to Rome on 11 September.[91] Whether the Tyutchev brothers left Ischia with them is not known; in any case they travelled on to northern Italy on their own, arriving in Milan by 6 September.[92] After that we lose track of them again until their return to Munich on or around 24 September after an absence of some three months.[93] Tyutchev and Shevyryov apparently kept in touch through correspondence for a while, for writing to

Pogodin on 27 October from Rome, Shevyryov passed on greetings from Tyutchev, which he can have received only by letter.[94] Nothing of their correspondence has survived, which in view of Tyutchev's general unreliability as a letter-writer is in any case unlikely to have been voluminous.

iii Clotilde

Nikolay stayed on in Munich until the following spring, returning to Russia with Tyutchev and family when they travelled there on leave. There was always a close attachment between the two brothers, despite the striking differences in character. Next to his urbane and polished younger brother Nikolay might appear socially clumsy, even if his heart was in the right place. Or as Tyutchev's second wife put it, he was 'full of consideration, notwithstanding his somewhat coarse familiarity and inelegant manners'.[95] Where Tyutchev was disorganised and impractical, his brother was, according to Ivan Aksakov, 'notable for his extreme meticulousness and precision'.[96] Tyutchev's daughter Darya found that her uncle easily surpassed her father in the sphere of 'practical qualities, order and logic in everyday affairs'.[97] Yet Nikolay remained proud of and deeply attached to his brilliant but wayward brother, and was always ready to spring to his aid in whatever trouble he might land himself. Tyutchev appreciated what he saw as Nikolay's 'firm friendship' and 'affection, which will never change in a thousand years'[98], and was equally fond of him. 'You know how much he [Tyutchev] loves you, and what influence you can have on this mind which you know so well [...]', Eleonore wrote to Nikolay at one particularly difficult time, '— you, his brother, his *only* friend!'[99]

Apart from fraternal affection, was there perhaps some other attraction to keep Nikolay in Munich for so long? The previous year he and Clotilde, Eleonore's younger sister, had accompanied the Tyutchevs on their trip to the Tyrol. Now twenty, the beautiful Clotilde was a desirable match for any bachelor. She continued to live in the Tyutchev household, helping to care for her sister's four sons and the newly-arrived Anna, circumstances which would have provided fertile ground for any latent romantic sentiments to blossom. If they did, the Russian Orthodox Church's ban on marriage between in-laws would have presented a serious obstacle. And for whatever reason, Nikolay never did marry.[100]

While all this must remain speculation, we are on somewhat firmer ground as regards Tyutchev's feelings towards Clotilde. These were revealed in a poem addressed to her towards the end of his life, after they had met for the first time in many years. In it he looks back nostalgically to the 'golden time' of his youth and evokes 'heartfelt feelings' reawakened on seeing her again, ending with the declaration:

> You have not lost that old enchantment,
> And still I love you as before!..[101]

For further evidence we must turn to a much earlier poem dating from the 'golden time' itself:

> Encountering you both together,
> I saw in her yourself new-made:
> That same sweet voice; that look so winning;
> The freshness, as of day's beginning,
> That once your countenance displayed.
>
> And all, as in a magic mirror,
> Took on substantial shape once more:
> The pain and joy of past endeavour;
> Your erstwhile youth, now lost forever;
> The love for you that once I bore![102]

The sisters have been identified as Eleonore and Clotilde,[103] and Tyutchev most likely wrote the poem soon after his return from Italy. Perhaps he had imagined that absence would make the heart grow fonder. If so, his first sight of Nelly — now approaching thirty, and inevitably worn by the rigours of bearing and rearing five children — was clearly a disappointment when contrasted with the youth and fresh beauty of her younger sister. Suddenly, 'as in a magic mirror', the cooling of his ardour towards his wife had been put into brutally sharp focus. As Richard Gregg emphasises, in the poem 'Clotilde's beauty provokes no amorous advances or passionate avowals'.[104] Indeed, all we can justifiably deduce from this and the preceding piece is that Clotilde's 'enchantment' and 'freshness, as of day's beginning' aroused the poet's love; whether things were taken any further it is impossible to judge. Not surprisingly, letters written by Clotilde to Tyutchev's daughters in later years are silent on the subject; indeed (and this could be open to more than one interpretation) they make no reference to Tyutchev at all.[105] His only recorded comment, apart from the poems, is the previously quoted one made to his daughter Anna when she was seventeen: 'The first years of your life [...] were for me filled with the most ardent emotions. I spent them with your mother and Clotilde. Those days were so beautiful, we were so happy! We thought they would never end.'[106]

That, it would seem, is all we have to go on. Unless, that is, the enigmatic 'maiden' ('*deva*') addressed in a couple of poems in the 1830s is also Clotilde. It would be a not unreasonable assumption, given that Eleonore, Amélie and other married or widowed women of Tyutchev's circle are by definition ruled out (Clotilde did not marry until 1839). Yet the truth of the matter is that we cannot really be sure. With that very important reservation in mind, let us turn to the first of the two poems (the other will be discussed in due course):

> In the air's oppressive silence,
> Presaging a storm to come,
> Sultry is the scent of roses,
> Harsh the dragonfly's shrill hum.

Hark! From that white hazy storm-cloud
Echoes now the thunder's crash;
And the darkening sky is girded
Round by lightning's darting flash...

Life in supercharged abundance
Fills the fevered air entire,
Spilling like some godly nectar
Through our veins its sensuous fire!

Maid, what stirs the milk-white veil of
Gauze upon your youthful breast?
What has made those eyes once lustrous
Cloud o'er with a look oppressed —

Made the vestal flame of blushes
Fade, grow pallid, and expire? —
Made each breath you draw more painful,
Touched your lips with searing fire?

Seeping through your silken lashes,
Two tears on your pale cheeks lie...
Or could they be scattered raindrops
From the gathering storm on high?..[107]

This is as much a philosophical poem as a love lyric. Once again the natural and human realms are presented in turn and shown to be as one, with the gathering thunderstorm of the first two verses mirroring and mirrored by the girl's emotional outburst in verses 4 to 6. So complete is the identification that by the end we cannot be sure whether it is tears or raindrops we see on the girl's cheeks. The transitional link is made in verse 3, where we are told that it is the same urgent life-force filling the world of nature and pulsing through the veins of poet and girl. As the simile in that verse indicates, it is a divine or noumenal force originating from beyond the visible world: it is indeed that 'dark root of universal being' identified by Solovyov as central to Tyutchev's world-view.

Could it be the poet's philosophical perspective that allows him to view the girl in such a curiously detached way? After all, he is apparently able to feel at one with the whole of nature, yet at the same time is (or pretends to be) unaware of what is causing the girl to suffer such strong emotion. But as Richard Gregg has shown, there is more at work here than mere philosophical detachment. Gregg uses this poem among others to illustrate what he identifies as 'an *erotic attachment to the spectacle of feminine suffering*'[108] in some of Tyutchev's verse. The theme recurs in allegorical form in another poem written at about the same time (and not mentioned by Gregg in this context):

Why, O willow, to the river
Do you bend your head so low?..
And with leaves that lips resemble
(Lips with burning thirst a-tremble)
Try to catch its racing flow?

Though with every leaf you quiver,
Yearning for the wayward stream,
Still it dashes onward — dancing,
Gaily in the sunlight glancing,
Laughing at your futile dream.[109]

This is clearly about unrequited love, but presumably not the poet's. He seems rather once more the detached observer, questioning (as in the previous poem) a passion which verges on obsession. Do his sympathies lie with the willow's lovesick yearning, or with the stream's mocking hedonism? It is impossible to tell: the poem's romantic irony accords equal validity to either perspective. And returning to 'In the air's oppressive silence...', do we not sense the same ironic detachment, the same ambivalent attitude towards love as suffering? More than that: there is, as perceived by Gregg in this poem with its 'essentially decadent theme',[110] as in others, a restrained and yet clearly detectable note of gloating *Schadenfreude*. Here Tyutchev's poetry undoubtedly reveals some of the darker corners of his psyche; whether it also reflects aspects of his relationship with Clotilde must remain an open question.

iv The Kireyevsky Brothers

On 26 September 1829, just a day or so after Fyodor and Nikolay had returned from Italy, a shy young Russian student presented himself at the Tyutchevs' Ottostrasse apartment. Introducing himself as Pyotr Kireyevsky from Moscow, he explained that he was newly arrived in Munich and had come for letters sent by his mother and brother for him to collect at that address.[111] His visit was not unexpected. Earlier that year Kireyevsky's mother Avdotya Yelagina had made arrangements for him to study in Munich, confident that Tyutchev — 'a young married man of very good character', whose parents she knew well in Moscow — would help the socially awkward twenty-one-year-old Pyotr to find his feet there.[112] Avdotya Yelagina was a woman of cultured interests; the salon held at her house on Krasnye Vorota Square was outshone in Moscow only by that of Princess Volkonskaya.[113] Her second husband Aleksey Yelagin was one of the first Russians to study the works of Kant and Schelling, an enthusiasm he had passed on to his stepsons Ivan and Pyotr Kireyevsky before they became active members of the 'Lovers of Wisdom' group.[114]

Now in Munich Pyotr was looking forward with eager anticipation to meeting the great Schelling in person for the first time. ('You cannot imagine,' he wrote to Ivan afterwards, 'what a strange feeling it is to see at long last that grizzled head containing perhaps the leading mind of its age: to sit face to face with Schelling!')[115] Soon after arriving he had learned during a courtesy visit to Friedrich Thiersch, the Rector of Munich University, that both the latter and Schelling were on friendly terms with

Tyutchev, whose intellect and erudition Thiersch had gone on to praise.[116] Later Kireyevsky was to hear Thiersch's commendation of Tyutchev echoed in even more glowing terms by Schelling himself.[117] All this reflected glory must have coloured the young man's initial attitude towards Tyutchev with a sense of awe, mingled with a certain wariness, the result of having heard unfavourable comments about him back in Moscow[118] (possibly from Pogodin, who had found his old friend's courtly airs so insufferable on his last visit).[119] These apprehensions proved unfounded, however, for according to his brother he was 'at once completely disarmed by Tyutchev's behaviour towards him'.[120] 'I visit Tyutchev a couple of times a week without fail,' Pyotr wrote to his mother and stepfather some time later, 'and love him and all his family for their intelligence, erudition and extraordinary kindness. They receive me and treat me in the kindest and most attentive way imaginable'.[121]

Kireyevsky had found lodgings in the house of the sculptor Joseph Heinrich Kirchmayer at No. 1 Karolinenplatz, almost next door to the Russian Embassy at No. 3 and no more than two or three minutes' walk from the Tyutchevs in Ottostrasse.[122] He was helped in his studies by Tyutchev, who lent him books on history and philosophy.[123] Eleonore too took him under her wing, sympathetic to the shyness, stuttering and lack of confidence in speaking French of which he himself was painfully aware.[124] He was invited to spend New Year and the Orthodox Christmas festival with them, and noted their German custom of decorating a tree for the children.[125] Not long afterwards Eleonore asked him to teach her Russian, which prompted his mother to compare him teasingly in one of her letters to Saint-Preux, the tutor and lover of Julie in Rousseau's La nouvelle Héloïse. The force of his protestations to the contrary suggests that he may indeed have harboured a secret admiration for the motherly Eleonore, who in the event soon abandoned the lessons, claiming she could not spare the time.[126]

In mid-October a more familiar face from Moscow was welcomed in Tyutchev's household. His cousin Aleksey Sheremetev was visiting Germany, and stayed in Munich as a guest of the family for some six weeks.[127] Like Nikolay, his old comrade from the Military Academy, Aleksey had resigned his commission in the aftermath of the Decembrist revolt. For him too this had been a matter of honour, a token act of solidarity with brother-officers whose fate he, Aleksey, had so nearly shared.[128] Among more mundane news and gossip exchanged by the cousins, Aleksey had a sombre tale to tell of how their family were still suffering the aftershocks of December 1825. Tyutchev knew that his cousin Anastasiya, Aleksey's younger sister, was married to the leading Decembrist Ivan Yakushkin, who had been sentenced to twenty years' penal servitude in Siberia. Now he learned that in 1827 she and her mother Nadezhda Sheremeteva had made three journeys to Yaroslavl, staying there several months in the hope of a brief reunion with Ivan as he was transported in chains to Siberia. Their efforts were finally rewarded on 15/27 October, when his convoy passed through the town and they were able to make what proved to be their final farewells.[129] Like so many of the wives and fiancées of the 'state criminals', who showed true heroism in abandoning the cosseted aristocratic life they knew for the harsh rigours of Siberia, Anastasiya was determined to join her husband in exile. She petitioned the Tsar, who at first prevaricated and finally agreed only on condition that she leave her two young sons behind. Still she was prepared to go, her mother having agreed to care for the boys in Moscow; but now Yakushkin himself forbade it, declaring that their sons' need for their mother must take precedence over his and Anastasiya's personal happiness.[130] Tyutchev probably now heard for the first time these heart-rending details, which were too sensitive to be confided in letters routinely intercepted and read by Third Section agents. It may even be that his own inevitably reawakened memories of the Decembrist revolt combined at this point with more recent ones of Rome to inspire the poem 'Cicero' ('Thrice-blessed he who has visited/ This earth at times of destiny').

Aleksey left Munich at the end of November, spending some time in Vienna before returning to Russia.[131] At about this time Tyutchev seems to have seen a chance for further promotion. Max von Lerchenfeld, now Bavarian Chargé d'Affaires in St Petersburg, was back in Munich on leave (his diary records a visit to the Tyutchevs on the evening of 6 October),[132] and may well have brought inside information on possible openings for his brother-in-law Krüdener. This would have left the field clear for Tyutchev to step into the latter's shoes as First Secretary, as he was to hope to do on later occasions. Whatever the exact prospects were, his aunt Nadezhda Sheremeteva in Moscow was evidently informed of them, for she volunteered to go to St Petersburg and plead his cause with the powers-that-be. However, by the end of December it was clear that nothing would come of it, and Tyutchev wrote to his aunt thanking her for her offer of help, which 'in the changed circumstances' would no longer be required.[133] In the same letter he reflects on the visit of her son Aleksey, whose 'rare qualities of spirit' and 'very fine character' he commends: 'Quite apart from myself, he has left here in Munich friends who are sincerely devoted to him. A day does not pass but that he is mentioned in conversation, and for the first few days after his departure he did indeed leave such a gap in our household as if he had been living with us for several years.'[134]

Enthused by his younger brother's letters, Ivan Kireyevsky had by now decided to join him in Munich. In March 1830 he travelled to Berlin, where he was received by Hegel and wrote home of his elation at being 'surrounded by the leading minds of Europe'.[135] From there he journeyed on to Dresden and met up with Rozhalin, who had decided to leave his post at the Embassy and study in Munich. They set out for the Bavarian capital together, arriving on 10 April, the day before Easter Sunday.[136] Ivan was pleased to find his brother more self-assured and confident in his new surroundings.[137] He moved into Pyotr's cramped lodgings, and to begin with they were joined by Rozhalin, all three sleeping in one room.[138]

Orthodox Easter that year fell on Sunday 18 April, a week later than in the Western calendar. Hoping for some reflection of the great festival as celebrated in Russia, the Kireyevskys and Rozhalin attended mass at the Salvatorkirche; but the Greek service in this little Gothic church did nothing to assuage their feelings of homesickness. They were also surprised to find that the only other Russians present were Tyutchev and his brother Nikolay, who invited them back for dinner. 'The two brothers and Fyodor Ivanovich's wife are very nice people, and I hope to see them often while I am here', Ivan wrote, recounting the day's events.[139] There were plenty of opportunities for this: three weeks later Rozhalin grumbled in a letter to the Kireyevskys' mother that Pyotr 'is constantly dragging us to the Tyutchevs, whom I have visited four times without ever managing to say a single word to the lady of the house, and whom I am in consequence unlikely to visit again'.[140] Three years previously in Pogodin's journal

Moskovsky vestnik (*Moscow Herald*) Rozhalin had favourably reviewed some of Tyutchev's poems.[141] Now he was clearly ill at ease in his presence. The son of a fairly humble official in Moscow, he seems like Pogodin before him to have felt alienated by the aura of social confidence radiated by the aristocratic Tyutchev and his family.[142]

Ivan had up-to-date news on literary developments in Moscow, including one in which both he and Tyutchev were involved. Raich's journal *Galateya*, which had looked so promising at its launch, was running into stormy waters. Readers had turned away from it, unimpressed by the generally poor standard of its contents and irritated by unedifying polemical attacks on a rival journal, *Moskovsky telegraf*. 'I think Raich must have taken to drink — it would be impossible for anyone sober to plumb such depths of bad taste, and in such a short time,' wrote Vyazemsky, who had been so supportive at the outset.[143] His sentiments were echoed by Pushkin, who viewed with particular disdain Raich's attempts to bolster falling circulation with illustrations of the latest Paris fashions.[144] All this Ivan (who had seen his friend Pushkin in St Petersburg before leaving for Berlin)[145] will have passed on to Tyutchev. Only at the beginning of March Tyutchev had sent Raich a packet containing more poems for *Galateya*, including a few to be included in Mikhail Maksimovich's almanach *Dennitsa* (*Dawn*) for 1831 (published the following January),[146] but after this his correspondence with Raich appears to have ceased.[147] No doubt he was persuaded by what he heard from Ivan Kireyevsky to wash his hands of *Galateya*, remembering it some years later only as a 'rather fatuous journal'.[148] By the end of 1830 Raich had in any case been forced to close it down.

Ivan may also have shown Tyutchev his own article surveying the previous year's achievements in Russian literature, published in January in Maksimovich's *Dennitsa* for 1830. Quite apart from its importance as one of the first serious critical analyses of Pushkin's work, it is of interest for containing a brief and inaccurate reference to Tyutchev. Kireyevsky mentions Shevyryov, Khomyakov and Tyutchev as outstanding proponents of the 'German school' of Russian poetry, while conceding that in 1829 Tyutchev had published only one poem.[149] What Kireyevsky appears to have had in mind was a fairly run-of-the-mill tribute in verse to Raich in the journal *Ateney* (*Athæneum*).[150] That such an acute critic should have overlooked eight for the most part far more accomplished pieces by Tyutchev published in *Galateya* in 1829 is perhaps indicative of how easily the occasional spark of excellence could go unnoticed amidst the surrounding mediocrity of Raich's journal. Whether Tyutchev pointed out this omission to Kireyevsky is a matter of conjecture; certainly none of the critics who commented on his article did so.

v Summer in St Petersburg

'It's a pity for my brother that they are travelling to Russia', wrote Ivan soon after meeting the Tyutchevs.[151] After five years abroad Tyutchev was due another home leave. Apart from the prospect of a family reunion (his parents were understandably eager to see their daughter-in-law and granddaughter for the first time), there was also a practical reason for the visit. Eleonore's two eldest sons from her first marriage, Otto and Karl Peterson, were now of an age (ten and eleven respectively) when it was necessary to think of their education. At the time of Peterson's death the Russian

Foreign Minister Count Nesselrode had given her an assurance that he would look after the interests of her sons, who were Russian subjects, and had recently reaffirmed this to her brother Felix Bothmer, currently employed in the Customs Department at St Petersburg.[152]

On 28 or 29 May Tyutchev and Eleonore left Munich on four months' leave, heading for St Petersburg where they planned to petition the Foreign Minister. Should Tyutchev be granted an audience with Nesselrode, so much the better: he could also press his case for advancement in the diplomatic service. They took the one-year-old Anna with them as well as Karl and Otto, and were accompanied by Nikolay (returning home after more than a year abroad) and Clotilde.[153]

Informing his mother and stepfather of the Tyutchevs' departure, Ivan Kireyevsky added: 'If you see their father, thank him warmly for his son: no-one could have been kinder than he has been towards our Pyotr [...]. I wish Tyutchev would stay in Russia for good. He could be of use through his mere presence, for the number of such European people in our country can be counted on one's fingers.'[154]

It is worth emphasising that for Kireyevsky at this stage in his life 'European' was a term of the highest praise, implying culture, learning and philosophical awareness of the highest order. *Yevropeyets* (*The European*) was the title given to the journal he founded two years later, which was closed by the censorship after two issues for its supposedly revolutionary and free-thinking tendencies.[155] It was only thanks to Zhukovsky's intercession with the Tsar that Kireyevsky escaped being sent into exile.[156] The authorities had taken particular exception to his article 'The Nineteenth Century', which speaks of a 'Chinese wall' dividing Russia from Europe and only partially breached by the efforts of Peter the Great and Catherine II to let in 'the air of the enlightened West'.[157] In a survey of Russia's past the article concludes that the country's continuing 'profound stagnation' and 'paralysis of intellectual activity'[158] compared with Europe are due to historical factors, in particular the apparent absence of any tradition linking Russia to the culture of classical antiquity.[159] These may seem unexpected sentiments from one who a decade later would be a leading light of the Slavophile movement, preaching Russia's higher spiritual qualities and distinct path of development; yet Kireyevsky's case was by no means unique.

From Munich the Tyutchevs travelled north to Hamburg and Wandsbek (where they paid their visit to Heine), then on to Lübeck and the nearby port of Travemünde to embark on the steam packet for Kronstadt and St Petersburg.[160] Max von Lerchenfeld had used this newly instituted paddle-steamer service the previous September,[161] and may well have recommended it to them while in Munich. Although offering little saving in total journey time from southern Germany to St Petersburg, it was somewhat cheaper and certainly more relaxing than the purely overland route. In reasonably fair weather the sea voyage took 78 hours, and the internationally mixed company of passengers could pass the time pleasantly enough in conversation in the main saloon or taking the air on deck. The approach to St Petersburg through the Gulf of Finland was described by the Marquis de Custine, who took the same route to Russia a few years later:

As one advances up the Gulf, the flat marshes of Ingria terminate in a little wavering line drawn between the sky and the sea; this line is Russia. It presents the appearance of a wet lowland, with here and there a few birch trees thinly scattered. The landscape is void of objects, and colours; has no bounds, and yet no sublimity. [...] To reach St Petersburg, you must pass a desert of water framed in a desert of peat earth: sea, shore and sky, are all blended into one mirror, but so dull, so tarnished, that it reflects nothing.[162]

At Kronstadt, a grim naval fortress on a flat island in the Gulf, passengers had to transfer with hand luggage to a smaller steamer ('dirty and ill-constructed' according to Custine),[163] the Travemünde packet drawing too much water to proceed any further. First, however, there were lengthy customs and passport controls of a confused and paranoid intricacy to be endured ('In Russian administration, minuteness does not exclude disorder', commented Custine on these procedures, which were enough to convince him that he was entering 'the Empire of Fear').[164] At last, after steaming up the Neva to St Petersburg and mooring at the English Quay near Falconet's equestrian statue of Peter the Great, they were free to disembark.[165]

Tyutchev's parents had agreed to come to St Petersburg with his sister Darya so that the whole family could spend the summer there together.[166] Eleonore and Clotilde were accorded a warm welcome which did much to dispel their dispiriting first experience of the country at Kronstadt. Years later Clotilde still recalled 'the kind solicitude' shown towards her by Tyutchev's mother in particular.[167] And when Tyutchev was obliged to leave Nelly in his parents' care on a subsequent visit to St Petersburg, he was reassured to know she could rely on their 'support and love under any circumstances'.[168]

Settling the future of the Peterson boys was a first priority, but to their dismay they learned on arrival that Nesselrode had gone abroad for the summer, leaving no definite date for his return.[169] Now all they could do was wait for him to show up again, in the meantime making the most of their stay in St Petersburg. There was certainly much to see. For Eleonore and her sister it was all new, while for Tyutchev too there were ongoing improvements to Peter the Great's showcase European capital to be admired. 'With every year St Petersburg gains in elegance and beauty,' observed another visitor to the city that summer. 'Magnificent columns are now in place at St Isaac's Cathedral, each fashioned from a single piece of granite. Work has begun on erecting a memorial column to the late Emperor, the only one in the world hewn from a single piece of stone. [...] all the arts are flourishing'.[170] They had arrived in time for the magical 'white nights' of midsummer, those 'pensive nights of moonless light/ And lambent dusk' celebrated by Pushkin, when

> Dusk directly (as if plotting
> To keep the golden skies alight)
> Hands on the torch to Dawn, allotting
> A brief half-hour to cheated Night.[171]

Nocturnal boat trips on the Neva, strolls along empty streets, past immense sleeping palaces, with the gilded spire of the Admiralty still gleaming in the sun like a beacon... All this was there to enchant — and perhaps divert them from the often less than salubrious conditions behind the splendid façades: that 'squalor, so full of promise for the future, of our dear native land' sarcastically referred to by Tyutchev on a later occasion.[172] Custine was to marvel at the contrast between 'the almost fabulous magnificence' of the Admiralty spire and 'the revolting dirtiness' of his room at the Hotel de Coulon,[173] supposedly the best in the city, which he described as 'a palace without, and an ornamented stable within'.[174] For the Tyutchevs, constrained by financial considerations to seek more modest accommodation, things can hardly have been much better.

Only a few snapshots have survived of their participation in the social life of the capital that summer. It was the time of year when the *beau monde* of St Petersburg migrated to the leafy dacha district of the Islands, a delta of low-lying land in the mouth of the Neva too marshy for habitation during the rest of the year. On 10/22 July Eleonore is recorded as a guest at the dacha (in truth a sumptuous summer residence, complete with grounds and hothouse plants) of *Oberhofmeister* Dmitry Durnovo, one of the Tsar's most prominent courtiers. Also there was the fifty-year-old blind poet Ivan Kozlov, a friend of Pushkin, Zhukovsky and Vyazemsky; it was he who noted her presence (together with the infant Anna) in diary notes dictated to his daughter.[175] Just over a week later Darya Ficquelmont, the Russian wife of the Austrian Ambassador (better-known to family and friends as Dolly), recorded in her diary that she had met the Tyutchevs (perhaps at one of the fashionable soirées held at her residence in the Austrian Embassy, a splendid mansion designed by Quarenghi overlooking the Neva). Eleonore, 'a pretty woman', she describes as 'still young, but so pale, so delicate and of such languorous appearance that one might take her for a charming apparition; she is witty, and seems to me to have some pretensions to quickness of mind, something which sits uneasily with her generally vaporous air'. She was not particularly taken with Tyutchev, 'a little man who wears glasses and is very ugly, but who speaks well'.[176] It was also natural that Tyutchev should seek out Max von Lerchenfeld, now Chargé d'Affaires at the Bavarian Embassy. 'Tutu came to see me yesterday,' Max wrote to his mother on 26 July/ 7 August: 'he is extremely annoyed at not finding Count Nesselrode here, and regards his voyage as having been undertaken so to speak without object, and probably without result.'[177]

We may assume that Tyutchev — whose desire to be informed and to persuade always drew him unerringly to centres of power — cultivated these and other contacts in St Petersburg high society. He and Eleonore seem for instance to have gone on to develop a reasonably close relationship with Durnovo and his family, for soon after arriving on their next visit to St Petersburg in 1837 they are known to have been paid a visit by the latter's son.[178] Links were also maintained with the poet Kozlov, whose diary records visits from 'the interesting and most amiable Tyutchev' on 12/24 August, 16/28 August and 25 August/6 September. On the second occasion the sisters Helena and Celina, daughters of the famous Polish pianist Maria Szymanowska, were also present.[179] No doubt Kozlov passed on the latest literary news and gossip to Tyutchev, while both here and elsewhere there would have been opportunities to catch up with the literary journals. Tyutchev may have been gratified to read in a back number of Delvig's *Literaturnaya gazeta* (5/17 February) a review of the Moscow journals by Vyazemsky, who, while generally scathing in his comments on Raich's publication, nevertheless concedes (with playful reference to the Greek legend providing the journal's title) that 'Tyutchev and Oznobishin, who appear in *Galateya* from time to time, may be thought of as momentary Pygmalions who attempt to breathe life into this dead lump of stone'.[180] Vyazemsky appears to have been the only critic discerning enough to have noticed and appreciated Tyutchev's poems in *Galateya*. Aleksandr Ospovat points out that they could easily have met at this time.[181] They certainly moved in the same circles, for Vyazemsky also associated with Kozlov and the Szymanowska sisters, and frequented Darya Ficquelmont's salon. Ospovat even proposes a possible venue for their first meeting: the traditional lavish outdoor celebrations for the Empress's birthday on 1/13 July at Peterhof, also attended that year by Zhukovsky, an old friend of the Tyutchev family.[182]

Even more intriguing is the question of whether Tyutchev could have met Pushkin, who was in St Petersburg from 19/31 July to 10/22 August.[183] Apart from childhood years in Moscow, when they might have glimpsed each other at children's balls, these three weeks are the the only period in the lives of the two poets when they were in the same place at the same time. Yet disappointingly it seems almost certain that no meeting took place. If it had, Tyutchev would surely have mentioned it at some point — to Ivan Gagarin, for instance, with whom he frequently discussed Pushkin's poetry in the mid-1830s.[184] Yet neither in Gagarin's lengthy reminiscences of Tyutchev, nor in those of other contemporaries who knew him, is there any reference to such a meeting; Tyutchev's own letters and recorded utterances are equally silent. While in St Petersburg Pushkin was preoccupied with his forthcoming marriage and connected financial worries, and kept himself largely aloof from the social round, spending most of the time with his friend the poet Delvig. Even so Tyutchev could easily have asked Pushkin's friends Kozlov or the Ficquelmonts for an introduction, had he been determined enough to meet him. It may have been feelings of diffidence or even inadequacy that dissuaded him. In the issue of *Literaturnaya gazeta* containing Vyazemsky's favourable reference to him Tyutchev would also have come across an appreciative review by Pushkin of Ivan Kireyevsky's survey of Russian literature in 1829, published not long before in the almanach *Dennitsa*. 'Of the young poets of the German school,' Pushkin writes, 'Mr Kireyevsky mentions Shevyryov, Khomyakov and Tyutchev. The genuine talent of the first two is indisputable.'[185] While the wording of this is perhaps unfortunate, all it really tells us is that, acquainted neither with Tyutchev personally nor with his poetry, Pushkin felt unable to comment on him.[186] It is almost certain, for instance, that — like most of the critics, including Kireyevsky — Pushkin had failed to register the poems by Tyutchev scattered through various issues of the reviled *Galateya*. Shevyryov and Khomyakov, on the other hand, he knew well from meetings with them and the rest of the 'Lovers of Wisdom' circle in Moscow in the autumn and winter of 1826-1827, since when he had followed their poetic and critical output with interest and approval. Even so, assuming that the ever-sensitive Tyutchev read Pushkin's comment (which is likely, if ultimately unverifiable), he would surely have been downcast at this further and most striking example of critical neglect. He may have felt it more appropriate to avoid what could have proved to be an awkward meeting until his poetic talent had gained wider recognition. Perhaps by the time of his next visit to Russia they would be able to meet on more equal terms. What he could not know was that by then Pushkin would be dead.

While Pushkin was still in St Petersburg the city's ruling circles were alarmed by dramatic news from Paris. In what amounted to a royalist *coup d'état* against the constitutional settlement which had restored the Bourbon dynasty, the autocratic French monarch Charles X had issued ordinances dissolving the elected chambers and limiting the freedom of the press. The response was three days of fighting in Paris from 27 to 29 July (NS) which drove Charles from his throne and ushered in a constitutional monarchy with the liberal Louis Philippe, head of the house of Orléans, as King. Less than a month later the spark of revolution spread to Brussels, where Walloon nationalists rose up against Dutch rule and secured the birth of Belgium as an independent state. Fearing further threats to the doctrine of legitimacy and the very fabric of Congress Europe, Tsar Nicholas made plans for military intervention in the West. Strict censorship ensured that no details of these revolutionary events appeared in the Russian press; Pushkin was obliged to visit highly-placed acquaintances to find out what was going on,[187] and we may assume that Tyutchev tapped his sources in the diplomatic community and at court in the same way.

Heine, whom the Tyutchevs had found so depressed on their recent visit, was elated at the news — and eventually emigrated to Paris, where he felt 'like a fish in water' in the France of Louis Philippe.[188] Tyutchev was no doubt gratified to see Guizot, whom he knew and respected, become Prime Minister and take on the role of reforming scholar-statesman, while the equally admired Victor Cousin was also given important official positions. As late as 1844 he was still prepared publicly to express his qualified approval of the bourgeois monarchy ('I certainly acknowledge all that is due to the King of France, I admire his skill, I wish a long life to him and his system').[189] Yet his response to the events of July 1830 could never be as straightforward as Heine's. In public, and in his capacity as a diplomat, he had of course to be careful what he said on such a sensitive issue.

Karl Pfeffel later recalled him soon after the July Revolution defending the 'wisdom and necessity' of Charles X's ordinances;[190] but at the time Pfeffel was not closely acquainted with him,[191] and may well have heard him say this on some public or semi-public occasion requiring an exposition of official Russian policy. As that policy hardened in response to the revolutionary events of 1830-1831, Tyutchev was in fact to find himself in an increasingly difficult situation. After meeting him in Karlsbad in the summer of 1834, Friedrich Lindner reported in a letter to Heine that Tyutchev 'no longer dares to express any opinion other than that of the Holy Alliance'.[192] And Ivan Gagarin, who knew him at that time, recalled that in his public utterances he 'avoided saying anything which might do him harm in high places, preferring to develop ideas which were of a nature to please'.[193]

Only in private conversation with friends could he afford to be frank, and Gagarin's accounts of such cosy chats à deux can therefore be taken as a fairly reliable guide to what he really thought. His attitude to the Paris journal Le Globe, the organ of the liberal 'Doctrinaire' opposition in the last years of the Restoration, has already been mentioned. According to Gagarin, he 'used to read [Le Globe] with particular enthusiasm' and was 'in complete agreement with the line taken by [it]'; he also encouraged his younger friend to borrow from his collection of back numbers.[194] As for the July Revolution, Gagarin recalls:

He acknowledged the presence of a revolutionary principle, the violation of law and order, but at the same time remained a supporter of liberal ideas; there is no contradiction in this. Charles X had taken it upon himself to violate the basic law; this was responded to with another violation. People of a one-sided persuasion accept one violation and reject the other. Impartial people have to accept that there was a violation on both sides.[195]

This has the ring of truth. Tyutchev was temperamentally and intellectually unsuited for the role of dogmatist (he once confessed that he was 'by nature condemned to impartiality'),[196] and his even-handed rejection here of both tyranny and revolution can be seen as a continuation of the stance taken in his poem on the Decembrist revolt.

As the summer dragged on, the possibility was explored of enrolling Karl and Otto at the St Petersburg Naval Academy; but until Nesselrode returned no final decisions could be made. There were also other family affairs to deal with. That summer Vera Ivashova, a cousin of Tyutchev's mother, was staying in the capital with her husband Pyotr and eighteen-year-old daughter Yekaterina. The two families had enjoyed a close relationship in Moscow until 1817, when Pyotr had retired from the army with the rank of General and the Ivashovs had moved to Simbirsk. Now they were reunited. The Ivashovs' son Vasily was one of the Decembrists sentenced to penal servitude in Siberia, and they had come to St Petersburg in the hope of obtaining permission to visit him.[197] One day they told the Tyutchevs of an unexpected development. They had just received a letter from Madame le Dantu, the family's former French governess, now living in Moscow. It appeared that her daughter Camille had been much taken with the dashing young officer Vasily on his visits home to Simbirsk, although she had kept her feelings to herself. After his arrest and sentence she had begun to pine, imagining the object of her affections languishing in chains in Siberia, and had even fallen ill. Eventually she confessed her feelings to her mother, begging her to be allowed to travel to Siberia and marry Vasily. All this Madame le Dantu now explained in her letter to Vasily's parents in St Petersburg. They in turn wrote to Vasily, who remembered Camille with affection and after some initial hesitation declared himself willing to marry her.[198] All that remained now was the delicate task of petitioning the Tsar for his consent to the marriage.

Years later Tyutchev mentioned Vasily Ivashov in a letter as 'one of those unfortunates exiled to Siberia, who entered into a romantic marriage with a young Frenchwoman, a matter in which I had some part'.[199] As suggested recently by Gennady Chagin, Tyutchev's assistance almost certainly consisted in drafting the letter in French which Camille submitted to the Emperor.[200] She would have had no experience in such matters, and Tyutchev with his diplomatic and linguistic skills was the obvious person to turn to within the family. His efforts bore fruit on 23 September/5 October, when Count Benckendorff informed the Ivashovs that His Imperial Majesty had no objection to the union. Camille and Vasily were married in Siberia the following year, and had several children. They died in exile, aged thirty-one and forty-three respectively, in the same year, 1839.[201]

Meanwhile Karl and Otto had been placed in a boarding house run by one of the instructors at the Naval Academy, who had started coaching them for the entrance exam, and Felix Bothmer had been appointed their guardian in St Petersburg.[202] It was now three months since the Tyutchevs had arrived, yet there was still no sign of

Nesselrode. Tyutchev's leave would soon be running out, but another even more urgent problem is revealed in a letter from Max von Lerchenfeld to his mother on 5/17 September:

> For some days I have been looking for a piece of malachite that I should like to send to Amélie via the Tyutchevs; they are awaiting only the return of Count Nesselrode before setting off, and if the Count delays any longer will be forced to leave without having seen him. For Madame is pregnant again, and has no more than the time required to return to Munich. I hardly ever see her, because she is unwell and cannot sleep, and because they are staying in such modest accommodation that they have never wanted to invite me there. It must be a pretty spartan establishment. As for him, he comes nearly every day to see me, and to sigh for the moment when he will once again set eyes on the bell-towers of the Frauenkirche.[203]

This would seem to suggest that Eleonore's pregnancy was already advanced. However, this is the first time it receives any mention in a series of seven letters written by Max to his mother over the course of the preceding five weeks, during which period he had by his own account seen Tyutchev frequently, and Eleonore on the odd occasion. Nor, apparently, had Dolly Ficquelmont noticed anything obvious back in July. A more likely interpretation is that Eleonore had discovered she was pregnant only in St Petersburg, and was now anxious to return to Munich before worsening weather conditions, and in particular the end of the navigation season, left her stranded in Russia for the winter.

Tyutchev too was keen to leave his native land, but for quite different reasons, as Max's account makes clear. Here we see him in what would become the familiar guise of exile in his own country, yearning for his spiritual home in the West.

Fortunately it was just a few days later that Nesselrode finally returned from abroad.[204] On 11/23 September Eleonore was able to send her letter (no doubt prepared well in advance with guidance from Tyutchev) requesting Nesselrode's intercession in the matter of her sons and subtly reminding him of his promises of financial support.[205] As a result Tyutchev was summoned to an interview with the Foreign Minister, where he received favourable assurances concerning his stepsons (and perhaps took the opportunity to hint at an improvement in his own career prospects as well).[206] Final arrangements were made for Karl and Otto to start their course at the Naval Academy in January, and at last Tyutchev, Eleonore and Clotilde could prepare to depart.

On Saturday 20 September/ 2 October Max von Lerchenfeld informed his mother that they would be leaving the following Wednesday, i.e. 24 September/ 6 October.[207] These last few days together with their son and his family were savoured to the full by Tyutchev's parents, who stayed on in St Petersburg with Darya for some considerable time after their departure,[208] presumably because by September the cholera epidemic sweeping through southern and central Russia had reached the Moscow area.[209]

For reasons which are not absolutely clear Tyutchev, Eleonore and Clotilde took the overland route back to Munich. The most likely explanation is that so late in the navigation season all the remaining sailings were fully booked. The long and exhausting journey by stagecoach must have been an ordeal for the frail and delicate Eleonore, preoccupied with one infant and anxious for another, as yet unborn. The impractical and often moody Tyutchev was of little help to her. As she was to write when contemplating their next journey to Russia, 'his presence does nothing to ease the rigours of travel; I should just as soon have three young children to cope with on a journey, as Théodore'.[210] For his part, Tyutchev quite often found the experience of travelling in itself conducive to poetic creation, as testified by manuscript notes such as 'on the way to' a certain place, or 'on the journey' appended to many of his poems. Quite apart from the stimulus of new sights and sounds, any journey was after all a human re-enactment of those states of transition and becoming (dusk, dawn, spring, autumn, rainbows, storms) which so exercised his poetic imagination in the world of nature.[211] On a purely physiological level, the rhythmic motion of a coach or (later) railway carriage — like the rocking of the boat in 'Dream at Sea' — could induce that dreamlike state between sleeping and waking in which he was able to divine and tap into hidden wellsprings of inspiration.[212] Now too in the bleakness of Russia's nothwestern border provinces, near the Western Dvina River of Livonia, or present-day Latvia, a poem took shape in his head:

> Across Livonia's fields I journeyed on my way;
> Around me all was gloom and desolation...
> The sparse soil underfoot, the sky of washed-out grey —
> All bred a mood of pensive meditation...

Pondering on the region's troubled past, in particular those centuries when its inhabitants were subjugated by the Order of Teutonic Knights, he realises that the 'deserted river' before him and the oak forests lining its banks would have been spectators to the events of 'that dark and bloodstained page of history'. The piece concludes with a characteristic reflection on nature's sphinx-like indifference to human concerns:

> Indeed! — for you alone survive
> As witnesses from that long-vanished era.
> Could I but question you, your answers might contrive
> To bring that lost world one step nearer!..
> But nature with a smile impenetrably blank
> About the past remains forever silent [...][213]

This is the first in a cycle of seven poems composed during and just after the journey. They represent a remarkable resurgence of creativity after the barren months in St Petersburg, when (*pace* Pigaryov) there is no evidence of his having written anything.[214] Another poetic description of the same borderlands vividly captures the rigours of the journey:

> Knee-deep in sand our horses flounder...
> We journey onwards — daylight fades —
> The shadows of dark pines engender

One sea of intermingled shades.
What dismal parts! A chill appalling —
Dense woods, now black, on every side —
And from each bush, morose, unsmiling,
Stares night, a monster hundred-eyed...[215]

Later the spectacle of dawn rising over the Austrian Alps (their route evidently took them via Warsaw and Vienna)[216] inspired a further poetic travel sketch. Here the snow-covered mountains appear before sunrise to be gazing out into the darkness, their 'eyes so deathly-frozen' seeming to 'chill the heart with icy fear'. They slumber, 'awe-inspiring, mist-enveloped', like some mythical race of kings fallen in battle, spellbound until recalled to life. But then the east grows light, the senior monarch's crown glistens, golden, in the first rays of dawn, and the spell is broken:

Soon the spreading light suffuses
Heads of younger brothers too,
And the crowns of all this reborn
Family now glow anew!...[217]

Some commentators have read this as an allegory in which the Alps represent the Slav family of nations, presently dormant but about to stir into life, led by their 'elder brother' to the East.[218] If the perceived parallels are more than coincidental, this would indeed be the earliest documented expression of Tyutchev's later Panslavist views.

Autumnal landscapes provide the theme for a further two poems in the group. In the first, as in 'Nature is not what you would have it...', the forests have quite literally 'spoken', and we sense something of the same animistic vigour as in 'Sea Stallion':

Leaves

Let fir-trees and pine-trees
Lie idle, and sleep
All winter through, mantled
In snow fresh and deep —
Like quills of a hedgehog
Their needles protrude,
And though never fading,
Are never renewed.

Yet we playful creatures
Burst forth bright and gay,
And but for a brief time
On branches we stay.
Throughout all the summer
In beauty we grew —
We frolicked with sunbeams
And bathed in the dew...

173

But now birds fall silent,
And flowers lie dead —
The sunbeams grow paler,
The breezes have fled.
So why should we linger,
To fade and grow sere?
O let's hasten after
And fly far from here!

Come, winds wildly raging,
O do not delay
From these tiresome branches
To tear us away!
Come quickly now, tear us
Away to join you!
And as you fly, bear us:
We'll fly with you too!..[219]

The second depicts autumn in the more reflective and elegiac tones to be found in some of Tyutchev's later nature poetry:

Autumn Evening

These radiant autumnal evenings hold
A poignant and mysterious fascination:
The sighing of sere leaves all crimson-gold;
Trees hectic-flushed with motley coloration;
And tranquil, mist-enveloped azure skies
Above an earth forsaken in its sorrow;
While now and then chill gusts of wind arise
As harbingers of storms upon the morrow;
Decay, exhaustion — and on all impressed
That gentle smile of transience and waning,
Which in a sentient being would suggest
A saintliness that suffers uncomplaining.[220]

Gregg points to the 'runaway personification' in the last four lines,[221] and suggests that 'in the poet's impressionable mind the abandoned, aging and meekly smiling face of autumn has, for a moment, become the aging and meekly smiling face of his own abandoned Nelly'.[222] To this illuminating insight we would add that Eleonore's suffering may have resulted at least as much from what is now known of her condition during and after the arduous journey home, as from her feelings of abandonment.

They reached Munich on 13/25 October, having spent nineteen days on the road.[223] Soon afterwards written confirmation arrived from Count Nesselrode that Karl and Otto had been admitted to the Naval Academy.[224] This reassuring news, and their sense of relief at being home again, were somewhat offset by the departure of their new friends Ivan and Pyotr Kireyevsky, who left Munich to return to Russia on 28 October and 9 November (NS) respectively.[225] Then, in December, came disturbing news of a serious uprising in Poland. Tsar Nicholas's plans to use the Polish army as part of his proposed expeditionary force against the 'illegitimate' regimes established by revolution in France and Belgium had met with strong resistance from the Poles, who for the most part sympathised with these countries and their new governments. By the middle of December (NS) the insurrection had become so widespread that the Viceroy, Nicholas's brother Constantine, was forced to withdraw from Poland together with all Russian troops. For the moment the country had achieved independence; but Nicholas was already preparing an overwhelming military intervention to crush the rebellion. Throughout Europe there were manifestations of popular support for the Poles. Determined to maintain a pro-Russian stance, and alarmed at the possible spread of revolutionary activity, King Ludwig of Bavaria sent in sabre-wielding cuirassiers to disperse student demonstrations in Munich and issued a decree ordering all foreign students to leave the capital.[226]

On 30 December Rozhalin, still studying in Munich, was obliged to swallow his pride and pay Tyutchev 'a forced visit' for the first time since May to find out if he was affected by the decree. Tyutchev was able to inform him that the King had revoked the order, and invited him to dinner on New Year's Day. This was not a success. Whether deliberately or not, Rozhalin was once again made to feel his social inferiority vis-à-vis Tyutchev and family. 'Here he was very much the Russian diplomat and nobleman, and I the poor Russian beggar,' Rozhalin wrote to the Kireyevskys' mother on 2 January, 'and this day filled me with such despondency that I am still affected by it today: I cannot occupy myself with anything, and feel as if unwell.'[227]

As we have seen, it is difficult to be precise about when Eleonore's child would have been due. What is fairly certain is that (there being no record of any issue) the pregnancy must have ended in a miscarriage or stillbirth. Several years later, while expecting Tyutchev's third child, Eleonore confided to a distant relative of his who was in Munich at the time that she had experienced two unsuccessful pregnancies.[228] One was evidently in 1830; of the other, which could equally have occurred during her first marriage, nothing further is known. It was for both parents a distressing conclusion to what had been on the whole a happy — and for Tyutchev as poet, highly productive — two years.

7 A Chaos of the Mind
(Munich, 1831-1833)

i Political Commentaries

During most of 1831 Tyutchev's work at the Embassy centred on political developments in Bavaria. The largely advisory *Landtag* or parliament provided for under the 1818 constitution assembled for a new session on 1 March and soon became the scene of heated debates in which the King and his ministers were subjected to strong criticism on such matters as electoral law, censorship and the budget.[1] In June the deputies even managed to force the dismissal of the Minister of the Interior, Tyutchev's acquaintance Eduard von Schenk, after he had failed to gain parliamentary assent for a tightening of censorship. The new restrictions on the press sought by King Ludwig were enacted in any case by royal decree the following March.[2] Outside parliament too there was a groundswell of popular unrest and opposition, culminating in riots in southern Bavaria and Nuremberg in 1832, together with the Hambach Festival in May of that year when some 30,000 members of student corporations (*Burschenschaften*) gathered in the Bavarian Palatinate to voice their support for a united democratic Germany.[3] The clash between crown and parliament was particularly ominous, with its echoes of events leading to the July Revolution in France. Metternich and Tsar Nicholas alike were alarmed at what they perceived to be pernicious revolutionary ideas spilling across the Rhine. Through the German Confederation they exerted pressure on King Ludwig and other German rulers to stifle freedom of expression.

So much had Potyomkin by now come to rely on his young protégé's abilities as a political analyst that of the eight despatches on Bavarian parliamentary debates sent by the Russian Embassy in 1831 all but one are not only in Tyutchev's hand but also evidently composed by him.[4] The last in particular, dated 21 December/ 2 January, has been described as 'more like an article on current affairs than a diplomatic despatch'.[5] In this, a retrospective summary and analysis of the year's debates, we see Tyutchev cutting his teeth as a writer on politics. He singles out the dispute over censorship as the root cause of the stand-off between parliament and government, and true to form is critical of each side's position on the matter. On the one hand he deplores the weakening in Bavaria and elsewhere over recent years of 'the feeling of respect for authority: that spontaneous confidence in its wisdom, all those habits of order and obedience, which constitute the sinews of younger societies' (he means Russia). This has led to a form of anarchy in which warring parties and individuals jostle to manipulate the levers of power. On the other hand, in Bavaria in particular 'these anarchic pretensions are singularly encouraged by the inconsistent course of the government, which is an unavoidable consequence of the personal character of the King. In the absence of any settled system, each party seeks the honour of influencing government policy, and as the censorship is nothing more or less than the expression of that policy, it must necessarily participate in these perpetual fluctuations and so increase the intellectual anarchy which it should be its mission to contain.' What is required in Tyutchev's view is legislation to 'organise' the press 'according to more ordered principles': a 'strong, intelligent, homogenous censorship', capable equally of 'revising bad doctrines and inseminating good ones'.[6]

Interesting here is the implied conservative view of societies and nation states as living, growing organisms with an instinctive ('spontaneous') awareness that their various parts must remain subservient to the whole, yet at the same time subject to a 'weakening' of these 'sinews' through disease or ageing. This differs radically from the rationally-based contractual groupings of individuals posited by classical liberal theory. From here it is but a short step to Tyutchev's later ideas on the the disintegrative force of the revolutionary principle, or to the 'decadent West' of Slavophile theory (a concept he himself was always to have some difficulty squaring with his own experience).

Yet if this is conservatism, it is conservatism of a highly individual and outspoken kind. In what is after all an official document Tyutchev manages not only to level personal criticism against Russia's loyal ally King Ludwig, but also to outline his own views on censorship, a subject normally taboo during the reign of Nicholas. And although on the face of it his advocacy of a system capable of 'revising bad doctrines and inseminating good ones' seems far from liberal, in the context of Nicholas's 'iron winter' it can only be read as a veiled plea for greater freedom of expression. In a much later memorandum, written during the political thaw following the death of Nicholas I, he was to argue passionately against the suppression of dissident views by brute force, calling on the government instead to win the debate in conditions of a free press and free speech.[7] As recently pointed out by Tatyana Dinesman, the ideas and even some of the actual terminology of this memorandum are foreshadowed in the despatch of 1831.[8]

One of Tyutchev's few letters to survive from the early 1830s provides further evidence of his independent and outspoken attitude towards official policy at that time. 'At the risk of appearing indiscreet to the post office official who will open this letter,' he writes to his brother Nikolay at the end of 1832, 'I cannot refrain from saying a few words to you on the subject of politics.' He goes on to discuss King William of Holland's threats, backed by Russia, to reoccupy the newly-independent state of Belgium, and in describing William as 'headstrong' ('mauvaise tête') makes his own attitude to all this clear enough.[9]

Such routine office work as the writing of despatches was for Tyutchev the least appealing aspect of his work as a diplomat. He much preferred to get out and about, taking the temperature of the political, social and intellectual life around him, and influencing opinion where possible. Keeping himself informed of developments through extensive reading of the European press was another important part of this process. His meetings with the playwright Michael Beer in the summer of 1831, at which among other things they discussed their mutual friend Heinrich Heine, have already been mentioned.[10] The following January Heine began to contribute to Cotta's *Allgemeine Zeitung* a series of articles from Paris on the post-revolutionary situation there under the general heading *Französische Zustände* (*French Conditions*).[11] These expressed the hope that France's revolution of 1830 would be emulated in Germany and other European countries: in one he writes for instance of his conviction that 'not only is the specific French revolution not yet completed, but that the far more comprehensive universal revolution has only just begun'.[12] Not surprisingly, he greeted the Hambach Festival and other signs of opposition in Germany as welcome forebodings of this.[13] Under pressure from Metternich, Cotta was increasingly forced to edit out offending passages, and Heine eventually refused to supply further articles, publishing instead in December 1832 an uncensored version of *Französische Zustände* in France, with a specially written introduction in which he warns the German rulers that one day their people will rise as one to 'shake off your soldiers and from pure high spirits crush your own heads with their little finger, so that your brains spurt up to the very stars'.[14]

We do not know if Tyutchev read this particular blood-curdling prophecy, but he was evidently familiar with the original articles in the *Allgemeine Zeitung*, as shown by his appropriation of Heine's characterisation of Napoleon in one of them for his own poem on the subject.[15] And while he will certainly have appreciated Heine's passionately argued and historically informed analyses of current affairs, there can be no question of his having been swayed by the call to revolution. On that issue he and his fellow-poet now found themselves on opposite sides of the barricades. Nowhere is this more apparent than in their differing responses to the Polish uprising. For Heine this was another battle in the ongoing campaign for freedom, on a par with the Greek struggle for independence and the July Revolution. Tsar Nicholas finally succeeded in crushing the rebellion on 8 September 1831 (NS), when after six months of fighting Russian troops occupied Warsaw. In the process he had forfeited all the credit gained with Heine and Western liberal opinion in general for his support of Greek independence. To his superiors in St Petersburg Potyomkin reported widespread condemnation by public opinion in Bavaria of what he called this 'brilliant victory of devotion to duty over subordination', and at the same time made a formal protest to King Ludwig about anti-Russian articles in the Bavarian press.[16]

'Nothing annoyed Tyutchev as much as threats and abuse directed at Russia by foreigners', Ivan Aksakov was later to write,[17] and we may assume that on this occasion too his patriotic feelings were offended by Western reaction. Yet his poetic response to the taking of Warsaw, 'As Agamemnon gave his daughter...', is actually more moderate in tone than Pushkin's verses on the same subject, 'To the Slanderers of Russia'. Not intended for immediate publication, Tyutchev's poem can be taken to reflect his personal view of the conflict. He compares the taking of 'unhappy Warsaw' by Russian forces to Agamemnon's readiness to sacrifice his daughter Iphigenie: it is a 'fateful blow', the 'price paid in blood' to secure Russia's 'unity and peace'. Yet any triumphalism is rejected, in particular any attempt to laud the crushing of the rebellion as a victory for the principle of autocracy:

> But spare us those inglorious laurels
> Prepared by hands in thraldom tied!
> Autocracy's Koran was never
> The cause for which we fought and died!

Here Tyutchev distances himself from fulsome official encomia of the kind Potyomkin felt obliged to include in the despatch quoted earlier. Whether or not the phrase 'autocracy's Koran' can be interpreted as a veiled criticism of Tsar Nicholas's attempted rapprochement with Turkey after the Treaty of Adrianople, it is clear that for Tyutchev the motivation of ordinary Russian soldiers ('our valiant people') fighting in Poland is of a quite different order from that slavish submission to authority seen as characteristic of the Ottoman Empire ('The janissary's pliant bloodlust,/ The axeman's blind obedience'). Rather they are inspired by a deeply held faith in the mission of the Russian people:

> To gather beneath Russia's banner
> The Slavs, by common kinship blessed,
> And lead them on to new awareness
> As allies in a noble quest.

This is no purely human enterprise: the Russian people are following 'a star', hastening to 'the mysterious goal' in the 'enactment of a higher plan'. As for Poland, Tyutchev indicates her part in the grand design through a play on heraldic imagery. For the time being she, 'our kindred eagle', has fallen into 'the purifying flames', pierced by 'a fraternal arrow' —

> But be assured: the Russian people
> Your ashes will preserve and prize,
> And from their dust our common freedom
> Shall one day, like the phoenix, rise.[18]

Again, as in 'Cicero', we sense the same fascination with brutal and bloody events which are if not exactly justified then at least glamorised as the workings of some grand cosmic plan. The poem is also remarkable for its demonstration that the Panslavist credo informing so much of Tyutchev's later political writing was already fully formed in all its essentials at the beginning of the 1830s. Like the movement for German unity which may have inspired it, Tyutchev's Panslavism presented a radical and for the time being utopian alternative to the status quo. Tsar Nicholas's policies of adherence to the Holy Alliance and preservation of the Ottoman Empire ruled out any possibility of liberation for the Slav peoples, most of whom lived under Austrian, Prussian or Turkish rule. And Tyutchev's stated belief in 'our common freedom' was exactly the kind of pernicious free-thinking the Tsar was determined to stamp out at any cost. As a diplomat Tyutchev must have chafed under the constraints of having publicly to represent policies with which in private he profoundly disagreed.

ii A Sea of Troubles

In the spring of 1832 the Tyutchevs moved to a new apartment at No. 1 Karolinen-platz.[19] Although no more than a few hundred yards from their old home in Ottostrasse, it was definitely a move upwards in terms of social prestige. Named after the second wife of King Maximilian I, the Karolinenplatz was a large circus at the hub of several converging roads. At that time only five spacious houses lined its circumference. These were owned by such members of the Bavarian establishment as Count Montgelas and (while he was Crown Prince) Ludwig himself, but were all leased to tenants, including foreign embassies. The Russian Embassy had occupied No. 3 since its move from Herzogspitalstrasse in 1825. No. 5 was home to the French Embassy, while the Papal Nuncio had his residence at No. 4. The only building to survive, with alterations, to the present day is No. 5.[20] The Tyutchevs' new home at No. 1 belonged to the sculptor Joseph Heinrich Kirchmayer, who in order to ensure light for his studio on the ground floor had commissioned the architect Karl von Fischer to design an unusual eight-sided building with many windows. The Tyutchevs occupied the first-floor apartment.[21] They were not the first Russians to live there. Inviting her brother-in-law Nikolay to stay soon after they had moved in, Eleonore wrote: 'do not be alarmed, my friend, you will find us in Kirchmayer's house on Karolinenplatz where Uncle Nikolay once stayed, and then later the Kireyevskys; but everything has been whitewashed and cleaned.'[22]

Here Eleonore and Tyutchev did their best to entertain in a style commensurate with his position as Second Secretary. Their soirées were attended by society acquaintances and members of the diplomatic corps, including their near neighbours the Papal Nuncio and French Chargé d'Affaires.[23] 'A teapot and two wax candles on the table, and agreeable conversation: such is the ambience of their little salon', wrote Pyotr Vyazemsky after attending one of these gatherings during a stay in Munich.[24] On occasion they may have stretched to musical entertainment. Another visitor, Aleksandr Turgenev, records that he waltzed with Eleonore at one of their soirées, but does not reveal if anything more ambitious than a piano was involved.[25] In fact on the whole he seems to have found their household decidedly modest, even describing it as 'poor' on one occasion.[26]

This is not surprising. For several years they had been living beyond their means, amassing substantial debts in the process.[27] A growing family and a complement of servants and nursemaids which seemed to increase with every year, not to mention what Eleonore calls 'the requirements of our position',[28] were all quite beyond what little ability or inclination to cope the ever unpractical Tyutchev may have had. Despite efforts made by Potyomkin on his behalf, there was little hope of promotion. The Russian diplomatic service as a whole was subjected to severe budgetary constraints during these years, and the few openings which did arise were usually allocated to staff affected by cutbacks at other missions.[29] For those like Tyutchev without powerful patrons in high places the prospects were especially bleak. In 1831 Potyomkin recommended him for accelerated promotion to the rank of Collegiate Assessor, arguing that his 'rare talents' promised well for the future.[30] This was not granted. In a despatch to Nesselrode the following year Potyomkin requested a cash bonus for both Tyutchev and Krüdener, pointing out that for many years salaries had not increased despite rises in the cost of living.[31] With the despatch he enclosed a private letter to Nesselrode, offering in Tyutchev's case to forego part of his own salary if that was the only way such a payment to him could be financed. This, he wrote, would help Tyutchev escape from the 'financial embarrassment' in which he found himself.[32] The Ambassador's noble gesture was ignored in St Petersburg. 'As for the *bonus* which we awaited with more impatience than all the rest,' Eleonore wrote nine months later, 'it has not arrived; we shall have to wave goodbye to it.'[33]

On top of all this came the unwelcome prospect of losing their champion and friend Potyomkin. In May 1832 he received official notification that he was to be posted to the Hague as Ambassador, and was reluctantly forced to accept. At the same time Nesselrode asked him to stay in post in Munich until the following year to oversee the installation of King Ludwig's son Otto as King of Greece.[34] 'This is one of the most disagreeable things that could happen to me,' wrote Tyutchev, for whom Potyomkin was 'a perfect gentleman', 'a *rara avis* among the Russians'.[35] There was some talk of him accompanying Potyomkin to the Hague as First Secretary,[36] but nothing came of it. Another possibility — that Krüdener would receive a promotion to Vienna, vacating the post of First Secretary in Munich for him to inherit — also failed to materialise.[37] This would become a constant refrain in Eleonore's letters over the coming years, as Tyutchev saw his hopes of stepping into Krüdener's shoes repeatedly dashed.

There was one bright ray amidst the gloom. Having returned to active service on the general staff at the beginning of the previous year, in May 1832 Nikolay began a tour of duty as Military Attaché at the Russian Embassy in Vienna.[38] Opportunities for him and Tyutchev to travel as diplomatic courier between Vienna and Munich now offered the real possibility of a reunion. Eleonore was as delighted as her husband at the news. She wrote urging Nikolay to come as soon as possible (adding that Clotilde was due to leave for a visit to the country soon and would be 'most annoyed' to miss him).[39] The three-year-old Anna could not remember her uncle and seems to have confused him with the somewhat forbidding St Nicholas of German folklore. '*Was ist das für ein Nicolas, er thut mir doch nichts?*' ('Who is this Nicholas, he won't do anything to me, will he?') she anxiously asked her mother, to be reassured that on the contrary he would come bearing sweets and a doll for her.[40] In the event it was August before Nikolay managed to obtain a mission as courier to Munich.[41]

By the beginning of 1833 Eleonore realised that after years of living beyond their means the financial situation had reached crisis point. 'One problem leads to another,' she wrote to Nikolay in April, 'and the only way to live on so little would be [...] to observe the most rigorous discipline. I have been trying in vain to achieve this for five years, and now I see only too clearly that without drastic remedies I shall never find a way out.'[42] Drastic remedies were indeed called for. The 'background of debt' to which Eleonore refers in the same letter amounted later that year to 12,000 roubles, twice the annual allowance Tyutchev received from the family estate.[43] By then they were in the embarrassing position of being unable to pay the rent.[44]

Characteristically it was Eleonore who showed herself prepared to take matters in hand. As a first step she turned to the practical Nikolay for the advice and support her husband was unwilling or unable to provide. For some time she had wanted Tyutchev to appeal to his parents for assistance, but he was reluctant to broach such a delicate issue with them and had always raised various objections.[45] Nikolay advised her to ignore these and write to them herself, making a clean breast of her and her husband's predicament.[46] This she did; Nikolay also wrote in support of her plea. Unfortunately Ivan and Yekaterina Tyutchev were by no means free of financial troubles themselves. The revenue from their estate had been falling year by year, and most of that was already earmarked for the allowances paid to their sons, not to mention the dowry they would one day have to provide for Darya.[47] In 1831 they had been forced to downsize, selling the house in Armenian Lane where Tyutchev had grown up and buying a much smaller house in the same street.[48] Even so they declared themselves willing to help. They were unable to pay off the whole debt at once, but agreed to make monthly repayments to the Tyutchevs' main creditor, a Viennese banker.[49] By the end of 1833 the immediate crisis had been resolved. 'You ask Théodore to tell you of our affairs,' Eleonore wrote to Nikolay early in the new year, 'and I think it would do no harm for me to do so in anticipation of this. What you obtained from Papa has been sufficient to remove our gravest concerns.'[50] Throughout the whole business Tyutchev appears to have remained aloof, leaving it to his wife, brother and parents to sort things out between them.

Meanwhile Eleonore had set about tackling the problem from another angle. First impressions of Prince Grigory Gagarin, who took over from Potyomkin in June 1833, confirmed her and Tyutchev's worst fears. 'It is the beginning of the end,' she wrote to Nikolay.[51] Compared with the affable and easy-going Potyomkin the new Ambassador appeared stiff, reserved and cold, and intent on maintaining the niceties of deference to rank. To Eleonore he seemed the very model of a St Petersburg bureaucrat. She feared that this would make it particularly difficult for Tyutchev to get on with his new boss — and that the fault would not lie entirely with Gagarin. Her letter to Nikolay continues:

> Given the temperament of your brother with which you are familiar, I fear that such a manner will poison their relations; with reserve and coldness establishing themselves on both sides, any further rapprochement will become impossible. I find this prospect distressing. On the other hand I have noticed that there are moments when Gagarin is quite free and open in his behaviour towards others, even towards me, and the blame for his reserve cannot be laid entirely at his door. You know how it is: once wounded by someone or prejudiced against them, Théodore is no longer himself; his stand-offish, offended demeanour, his caustic phrases or sulky silence: all this distorts the way he behaves, and I can well understand that he appears disagreeable. So from both sides it is a vicious circle [...][52]

Sensing that she could handle Gagarin more effectively than the prickly Tyutchev, Eleonore decided to take take the bull by the horns. Two or three weeks after the new Ambassador's arrival she made use of Tyutchev's absence to approach Gagarin for a frank conversation.[53] 'At last I have willy-nilly broken down that barrier of timidity, or perhaps of a sense of propriety, which up to now prevented me from taking an active hand in Théodore's service affairs,' she reported back to Nikolay. 'Just between us, my friend, I felt extremely uncomfortable during this début. Even while speaking I felt I was foolishly taking upon myself a right of protection or guardianship over my husband [...].'[54] She was relieved to find that Gagarin actually approved of her démarche. Indeed, it seems she soon had the aloof Ambassador eating out of her hand: 'Gagarin spends every evening at my house: it has become his habit to visit nobody but me; my conversations have had such an effect on him that it would be quite easy now to make him believe or do anything.'[55] And Eleonore's efforts soon bore fruit: in August, following representations from Gagarin, Tyutchev's salary was raised from 800 to 1,000 silver roubles a year.[56] In only a brief space of time the feared new arrival had done more for them than the well-intentioned Potyomkin had ever managed to achieve.

Eleonore had received scant support from Tyutchev in her struggle to save the family from ruin. The practical Nikolay seems to have been particularly unimpressed with his brother's performance. 'Fyodor, what a useless fellow you are!' he exclaimed on a visit to Munich not long after these events. 'And how true that is!' Tyutchev later commented with a laugh, recounting these words to the Ambassador's nephew Ivan Gagarin.[57] According to the latter, Tyutchev 'fully accepted the justice of this criticism, but was in no way humiliated by it, just as a nightingale is not humiliated by the fact that it cannot do the work of an ox or donkey.'[58]

Ivan Gagarin's characterisation, though undoubtedly faithful to the truth as he saw it, tells only part of the story. There was more to Tyutchev's paralysis of will than mere fecklessness or the charming eccentricity of a poet. For some time Eleonore had been growing increasingly alarmed at the state of her husband's mental health. Although there are hints of this in previous letters, it was not until September 1833 that she took advantage of Tyutchev's absence to confide her fears to Nikolay in full:

> I need to tell you things which are difficult to write about, but which are important for you no less than for me. I need your advice — perhaps there is after all some remedy? What I am speaking of has nothing to do with our [financial] affairs... I do not know how best to write about it: even as I speak to you I sense that I cannot express my thoughts. No doubt you will have guessed that it is only Théodore who could cause me such anxiety. It is his health of which I speak. Not that he is ill, no: he is about as well as usual; but there is within him a mental disorder which is making rapid and frightening progress. [...] You must know what I am referring to: I believe he inherited this legacy of suffering from your mother. Tell me what I must do: whenever I think about it, or experience such moments face to face, I feel as if I could die of fear and distress. Do you think it advisable to consult a doctor? Yet his general health is better than usual during these attacks of melancholy. But it is not just melancholy, a sense of disgust with everything, and incredible despair at the world and above all himself, it is also — and this is what terrifies me most — what he himself calls *l'idée fixe*. An idea — the most insane, most absurd imaginable — which torments him to a state of feverishness and tears [...].[59]

All the available evidence points with a reasonable degree of probability to Tyutchev's 'mental disorder' being a form of manic-depressive illness (or, in the currently preferred clinical terminology, bipolar affective disorder). Eleonore's statement that he inherited it from his mother is significant, as bipolar disorder is known to be one of the most genetically determined of the psychiatric illnesses.[60] The well-established link between manic-depressive states and artistic (especially poetic) creativity is also clearly relevant.[61] When the illness first struck is difficult to determine. In another letter to Nikolay at about this time Eleonore writes of it appearing as 'passing attacks, more or less', but that it 'keeps returning, and has certainly been getting noticeably worse for a year now': in other words, since the autumn of 1832.[62] That Tyutchev may have suffered mild depression and mood swings already in the late 1820s is suggested by one or two poems written then, which include the following:

> Just as when laid on glowing coal
> A parchment smokes and smoulders on,
> While muffled fire about the scroll
> Devours each word till all are gone —
>
> So too my life burns on each day,
> Breathed out as smoke that curls and drifts —
> Inexorably I fade away
> Amidst grey gloom that never lifts...
>
> O Heaven, could the flame for one
> Brief instant freely but ignite —
> And I, ablaze with glory bright,
> Burn out, all grief and torment done![63]

However, it is Eleonore's letters of September 1833 that provide the first evidence of a serious attack. By now the relatively cheerful tone of her correspondence with Nikolay the year before has given way to one of deep anxiety and helplessness, to a sense of despair at 'not being able to do anything, anything to combat this misfortune'.[64]

Tyutchev was left feeling equally helpless and defeated. According to Eleonore, during such attacks he repeatedly told her 'that he would much rather undergo a fatal illness than suffer like this, without hope of deliverance'.[65] The limited treatments then available — taking the waters, exercise, fresh air — were all tried and may even have helped to alleviate the worst of the symptoms. The writing of verse itself provided — as it has for other poets before and since — a form of therapy, both through the spontaneous expression of mental and emotional turmoil ('the lava of the imagination whose eruption prevents an earthquake', as Byron put it), and the more conscious effort of creating a formal poetic structure (Tennyson's 'sad mechanic exercise,/ Like dull narcotics, numbing pain'.)[66] That Tyutchev was aware of this palliative and healing function is evident from one of his few comments on the art of poetry:

> *Poetry*
>
> Amidst the toils and storms of life —
> A sea in raging turmoil, rife
> With passions violently clashing —
> Descends to us, the sons of earth,
> A vision, of celestial birth,
> Her gaze a heavenly radiance flashing,
> And onto waves in fury thrashing
> Pours balm that reconciles all strife.[67]

184

We are left to ponder the fact that Tyutchev's manic depression (for such it appears to have been) helped him create some of the most powerful and moving lyric verse ever written. The modern mind struggles to accept the idea of creative genius linked to mental aberration (a reservation shared implicitly, as we have seen, by certain critical interpretations of the poem 'Madness'). Indeed, the very concept of genius has become suspect, its almost total devaluation now apparently assured through constant and indiscriminate attribution to anyone and anything. Yet there are some still prepared to endorse the ancient understanding of it as a divine bestowal, at once blessing and curse, and to see the mental suffering entailed as an unavoidable price to be paid for the intellectual and spiritual advancement of mankind. There are even those willing to accept the bitter cup. Tyutchev was not one of them. Had treatment with modern drugs been available, he would surely have submitted to it gladly, foregoing the poems, whose fate was in any case of such little concern to him. As it was, he suffered at intervals for the rest of his life, and left us with the rich legacy of his art. Perhaps the least we can do in return is for once to ignore the shallow conventions of the age and allow him and others touched with genius some understanding for the all-too-human flaws inherent in their condition. Eleonore was certainly prepared to do this: 'when I think of that poor man,' she once wrote of him, '— nobody suspects, nobody can imagine what he is suffering — and to say that it is his own fault is merely to apportion blame where pity is due'.[68] For her the poems — an unknown quantity as far as she was concerned — did not even enter the equation. Can we who know them afford to be less magnanimous?

iii Greek Affairs

In the summer of 1833 Tyutchev was offered an important mission to Greece. In a letter to Nesselrode he was later to portray himself as the Embassy's expert on the Greek question, claiming that both under Potyomkin and Gagarin he had been entrusted with compiling all the despatches on this subject.[69] Although this was something of an exaggeration[70] (understandable perhaps in a letter angling for promotion), it is true that he took a particular interest in Greece's new-found role on the European stage. One instance of this — his encouragement of journalistic efforts to defend Russian policy in the area by the prominent Philhellene Friedrich Thiersch — has already been mentioned. His role in a much more far-reaching initiative by Thiersch can now also be examined.

Since achieving independence in 1829, Greece had fallen prey to rivalry between its protecting powers Britain, France and Russia, and to dissension from warring factions within. Thiersch had foreseen such problems from the beginning, and had early on conceived the idea of providing the fledgling state with a king chosen from one of Europe's existing ruling dynasties. He argued that — unlike a Greek, who would inevitably be seen as representing one or other of the rival factions — a ruler from outside could stand above the fray, and so provide a focus of allegiance to unite the country. To overcome Greek resistance to the idea of a foreigner ruling them, he suggested as ideal monarch a minor who could be educated in the Greek language and traditions, so becoming acceptable to the people as a whole. A Regency appointed from the monarch's own country would rule until he came of age. He even had a candidate for the post: King Ludwig of Bavaria's son Otto, then aged fourteen.[71] These proposals were first outlined by Thiersch in a letter to King Ludwig in September 1829.[72]

The King approved the plan, but made it clear that it would be inappropriate for him to propose his son as King of Greece. Thiersch realised that the key to getting his scheme approved by the protecting powers lay in the person of Tsar Nicholas. Accordingly in November 1829 he fleshed out his proposals in more detail in a memorandum addressed for the sake of appearances to another influential Philhellene, the Swiss banker Jean-Gabriel Eynard.[73] In fact the memorandum was intended for Nicholas I. Reasoning that it would have greater impact if sent with official endorsement, Thiersch gave a copy to his friend at the Russian Embassy, Tyutchev, who received it enthusiastically and undertook to sound out the Ambassador.[74] Potyomkin appears to have viewed the venture with approval to begin with, but then began to backpedal.[75] The most likely explanation is that King Ludwig (whom Thiersch had kept fully informed of his démarche) became concerned that he himself might be suspected as the initiator of the plan if it were presented through official channels, and that he informed Potyomkin of his reservations.[76] Thiersch in any case now had an opportunity to write to Nicholas in his capacity as representative of the Bavarian Greek Committee to thank him for his gift of plate and vestments for the newly inaugurated Greek Orthodox church at the Salvatorkirche. Taking advantage of this to enclose a copy of his memorandum, he appears to have sent the letter by normal post (Potyomkin having declined to forward it through diplomatic channels).[77]

The seeds were sown, but it took nearly three years for Thiersch's plan to come to fruition. The assassination in October 1831 of the autocratic and pro-Russian first President of Greece, Kapodistrias (the same who had once been Foreign Minister to Alexander I), threatened to plunge the country into civil war. Britain, France and Russia had agreed from the outset that Greece should be ruled by a monarch, but their first choice for the post, Prince Leopold of Coburg, had already withdrawn his candidacy. These were the circumstances in which Thiersch's proposals became acceptable to all three protecting powers, and on 8 August 1832 Otto was confirmed as King by the Greek national assembly. As recommended by Thiersch, Ludwig appointed three Bavarians as Regents to rule until his son came of age, presided over by the former Finance Minister, Count Josef von Armansperg. On 6 February 1833 King Otto (known as Otho to his Greek subjects) arrived in Nauplia (present-day Nafplion), the then capital of Greece, accompanied by the members of the Regency and some 3,500 Bavarian troops.

Tyutchev's role in all this was of course peripheral. Crucially, he had been unable to obtain his Ambassador's official backing for the plan; yet his own (and, as he reported, Potyomkin's) enthusiasm no doubt encouraged Thiersch to persevere in submitting it to the Tsar in a private capacity. Tyutchev had at best assisted as spear-carrier on the stage of history; yet once again he could count himself 'thrice-blessed' for having 'visited this world at times of destiny'.

If Nicholas and his ally Ludwig had hoped the Regency would respect Russian interests in Greece, they were soon disappointed. Armansperg had insisted on the Regency's complete independence from the Bavarian government as a condition of his appointment.[78] Once installed in Nauplia, he and his fellow-regents set about implementing policies clearly slanted towards British and French interests and against those of Russia. The final straw for St Petersburg came in July 1833, when reports began to circulate of French attempts at negotiations with the Regency for a marriage between Otto and a daughter of King Louis Philippe.[79] (A recently discovered French diplomatic document appears to confirm that these reports were not unfounded.)[80] Foreign Minister Nesselrode instructed Grigory Gagarin, his new Ambassador in Munich, to inform King Ludwig of these developments and suggest that he prevail upon his son to withstand French intrigues.[81] As Nesselrode was well aware, a personal union with the upstart July monarchy was the last thing Ludwig wanted for the house of Wittelsbach. At an audience granted to Gagarin on 27 July, the King expressed his shock at the reports of French marriage proposals, to which he said he was decisively opposed. He would write to Otto at once, but was worried the message might not get through. As he confided to the Ambassador, 'I cannot guarantee that [Armansperg] does not open my letters and suppress whatever does not suit him'. Gagarin then offered a secure channel: one of his diplomatic staff could deliver the letter to Nauplia, where the Russian Ambassador, Katakazi, would hand it to Otto in person. Ludwig readily agreed to this.[82] He no doubt also approved Gagarin's choice of Tyutchev as courier. The young Second Secretary was familiar enough from court and diplomatic functions, and was known to take a particular interest in Greek affairs. Ludwig had been informed of Tyutchev's enthusiasm for the plan to make Otto King of Greece, and may even have recalled Thiersch's personal recommendation of him as 'a young man wholly reliable and equally excellent in education as in character and way of thinking'.[83]

News of this audience (granted unusually to the as yet unaccredited Russian Ambassador at the King's summer residence) and of Tyutchev's imminent departure for Greece provoked much speculation in the Munich diplomatic corps. The French were particularly suspicious. Ambassador Vaudreuil insisted to Paris that Tyutchev was veiling his mission in secrecy, and that it must have some important objective other than the routine delivery of despatches. He conjectured that he could be the bearer of a proposal to marry Otto to the daughter of Tsar Nicholas, or that he had been given the task of presenting Russia's grievances to the Regency.[84] Later Vaudreuil made a further stab in the dark: Tyutchev was to make representations on the continuing presence of French troops in Greece.[85] Such speculation, echoed by other Western diplomats in Munich,[86] may even have been encouraged by Gagarin to divert attention from the true purpose of the mission. Confirmation for at least the second of Vaudreuil's speculations might appear to be given by a letter written many years later by Gagarin's nephew Ivan, who in the summer of 1833 had just taken up his post as trainee diplomat at the Embassy. In this Ivan recalls that he had been keen to undertake the mission to Greece himself, but that his uncle had told him that Tyutchev, 'who knew the members of the Regency personally, would be better able to explain in talks with them what exactly in their conduct of affairs had given grounds for displeasure'.[87] Yet this sounds more like the Ambassador letting his keen but inexperienced young nephew down gently (and perhaps in the process releasing disinformation which he calculated would spread to Vaudreuil and others). In fact no attempt was ever made by Tyutchev to engage in such 'talks', and forty years on Gagarin junior remained just as much in the dark as to the actual purpose of the mission as he had been at the time.

Just what that purpose was behind all the smoke and mirrors emerges from the now available texts of Russian diplomatic documents and of Ludwig's letters to his son.[88] Quite simply, Tyutchev was to deliver diplomatic mail to Katakazi, including the letter from King Ludwig to his son, maintaining secrecy throughout. Katakazi would then ensure the letter was handed to Otto in person. It was to be expected that there would be a reply (in his letter Ludwig expressly orders his son to hand this to Katakazi and no-one else), and that Tyutchev would take this back with other despatches to Munich. In other words, his role was that of courier. There is no mention of any of the various démarches suggested by Vaudreuil and others, which in any case it would have been highly irregular to entrust to such a junior official over the head of Katakazi, the senior man on the spot. No doubt Tyutchev was also told informally by Gagarin to keep his eyes and ears open and report anything of interest on his return, but this would have been no more than standard procedure.

According to Ivan Gagarin, Tyutchev accepted the mission with pleasure.[89] Eleonore too was happy for him to go. For some time he had been suffering deep depression, and although somewhat concerned at the idea of him travelling alone in such a state, she felt sure the journey and change of scenery would eventually lift his spirits.[90] The plan was to travel to Venice and there embark on a ship leaving for Nauplia.[91] In Venice there would be the prospect of a brief reunion with Nikolay, who was apparently taking advantage of his posting in Vienna to do some sightseeing before returning to Russia on leave. This prompted Eleonore to offer to accompany her husband as far as Venice, from where she could return to Munich with Nikolay on the first leg of his journey to Russia. Apart from anything else, this would allow her to unburden herself freely to him of her grave concerns for Tyutchev's mental health.[92]

iv Mission to Nauplia

Leaving the children in the care of Clotilde and Aunt Karoline Hanstein, Tyutchev and Eleonore left Munich on 4 August, accompanied by his manservant Joseph. Eleonore would later write of the 'misadventures' which dogged them on their journey.[93] These began in Venice when they discovered there were no sailings to Greece in prospect,[94] forcing them to head for Trieste, the alternative port of embarkation. Whether for this or some other reason, they missed their rendezvous with Nikolay.[95] Now Eleonore would have to find her own way back to Munich. In Trieste, where they arrived about the 12th,[96] the only vessel available was the *Carolina*, a corvette of the Austrian navy, on which arrangements had been made for the new Bavarian Chargé d'Affaires to Greece, Gasser, to travel to Nauplia. Learning of the predicament of Tyutchev and two Bavarian officials similarly stranded, Gasser persuaded the ship's commander to take them as well. However, the *Carolina*'s departure was delayed, first by illness affecting her commander, then by strong headwinds and high tides holding up an ammunition supply vessel from Venice.[97] It was not until first light on 1 September that the *Carolina* weighed anchor and slipped out of harbour with Tyutchev and Joseph on board. Eleonore was left standing 'alone and abandoned' on the quayside, as she later wrote to Nikolay, 'with an indescribable feeling of pain and distress'.[98] The ill-starred journey and enforced wait in Trieste had done nothing to improve her husband's mental state. She returned to Munich alone.

A day out of Trieste the *Carolina* ran into stormy weather, but battled on for another three days, an experience which can only have worsened Tyutchev's already wretched state of mind (he does at least seem to have been spared the added misery of seasickness).[99] Eventually they were forced into harbour on the island of Lusina (the present-day Croatian Hvar) off the coast of Dalmatia,[100] where the corvette sheltered from 5 to 8 September. From here Tyutchev wrote two letters to Eleonore. Although these have not survived, the first was by her account so revealing of his mental turmoil and anguish that he himself begged her in conclusion 'for pity's sake not to show it to anyone, not even to my brother'.[101] It was probably at this low point that, as Gasser later reported, Tyutchev considered abandoning his mission altogether and returning to Munich.[102] However, his spirits evidently lifted with the weather; the remainder of the voyage was in Gasser's words 'very fortunate'.[103] After possible stops at Corfu and Patras (as on the return journey), they reached their destination at the head of the Gulf of Argos on 17 September, only two days behind schedule.[104] First sightings of Nauplia from the sea — the Palamedi fortress towering above the town on its rocky prominence, and the fortified island of Bourtzi in the bay — gave visible reminders of the period of Venetian rule.

Once ashore, Tyutchev reported to Katakazi, to learn of yet another setback to his mission. Otto had left the capital four days previously on a royal progress through his kingdom and was not expected back for over a month.[105] Katakazi also informed him that in three days' time the *Carolina* would take Armansperg and Gasser on to Marathon, where the King was due to arrive on 25 September.[106] Before leaving, Armansperg appears to have received Tyutchev (the only time the two met in Nauplia, according to one source).[107] It will have been no more than a courtesy call. Even if Katakazi considered what might have seemed the obvious step of sending Tyutchev to Marathon to deliver the letter to King Otto, he evidently made no attempt to follow it through. Armansperg had been forewarned by the French about the young Russian envoy and his supposedly nefarious designs, and Katakazi no doubt reasoned that the wily President of the Regency Council would have no difficulty coming up with a diplomatically plausible reason for declining Tyutchev's company on board the *Carolina*. In any case it would be almost impossible to deliver the letter securely with the suspicious Armansperg hovering in attendance. There was nothing for Tyutchev to do but kick his heels in Nauplia for the time being.

Very much an interim choice as capital (already in 1834 the court and government were to move to Athens), Nauplia was in truth a small provincial town uncomfortable at finding itself thrust into the limelight of international politics. Some idea of life there at the time emerges from letters written to his parents by Dmitry Polenov, Legation Secretary at the Russian Embassy from 1832 to 1835, whom Tyutchev got to know during his visit. Polenov describes Nauplia as having only two paved roads, while 'all other parts of the town become so muddy after the slightest rainfall that they are impassable'. Guests invited to the first ball in honour of King Otto had to trudge there on foot through the muddy streets; only the King and Armansperg had carriages. As the orchestra struck up, 'the walls of Nauplia shook as they heard this unfamiliar noise ring out through its streets for perhaps the first time'.[108] A similar picture is painted by the Prussian diplomat Friedrich von Tietz, who arrived some months after Tyutchev:

Recent accounts have designated Napoli as the Paris of Greece. As far as respects the many narrow and offensive streets contained in the French capital, this comparison may be correct. But beyond this, we would recommend its authors to be more moderate in their similies [*sic*]. Napoli is a small town which at first sight resembles an Italian city with its flat roofs and open coffee-houses, but there the resemblance ceases.[109]

Poverty and desolation, the lack of anything approaching civilised living conditions, the enervating heat, dust, voracious insects — such are the elements of life in Greece emphasised by Tietz in his memoir. And in the midst of all this the Prussian notes with distaste the extravagant imported luxury enjoyed by Armansperg and lavished on his guests, all paid for from state funds which in Tietz's view would be better used to help the poor and needy.[110] Not surprisingly, Armansperg's house was one of the largest in Nauplia, and certainly the most lavishly appointed. The Russian Embassy, described as handsome and of solid construction, stood opposite the royal Palace, a low building only five windows in width dating from Kapodistrias's rule.[111] From the Palace, the street named Otho Street

> extends the entire length of the town [...] to the so-called Platane square, which is the evening resort of the citizens. Platanes are certainly not to be met with, but only sundry heaps of dust and rubbish, which, with the ruins of a once noble Venetian building, bound this square on one side. Another side includes a range of stone-built barracks, whilst a third is occupied by restaurateurs and coffee-houses. Amongst the former is a celebrated house kept by two sisters from Vienna, which furnishes an important chapter in the *chronique scandaleuse* of Napoli.[112]

In the absence of the King and Armansperg, Tyutchev's social life will have revolved mainly around the receptions held each evening in turn by the various embassies. Like others new to the country, he was no doubt bemused by the informal atmosphere of these, with guests smoking long Turkish pipes or sitting in shirt-sleeves on the hot September evenings.[113] Tietz describes one soirée at the Prussian Embassy at which the roof began to leak during a downpour, obliging the guests to hoist umbrellas.[114] In these circles Tyutchev could learn much of the power struggle being waged beneath the veneer of diplomatic niceties. No doubt his colleagues filled him in on Armansperg's style of government, and on the insidious role played by his wife (the 'evil spirit of Greece', as the British had dubbed her).[115] She and her salon were generally considered to be at the centre of a web of intrigue entangling the seat of government. The seventeen-year-old King was no match for such skilled operators as Armansperg and his wife. Freed from parental restraint, the young monarch was in Polenov's words 'a great lover of amusements',[116] and the Armanspergs took advantage of this, providing him with all manner of diversions to deflect his attention from more serious political matters. As Württemberg's Ambassador in St Petersburg informed his government on the basis of private reports from Nauplia: 'The Russian party in Greece observes with displeasure the King being taken from one ball to another, while [...] no fitting opportunity has been found to honour the memory of Count Kapodistrias [...] and the

King has not visited a single church of the predominant religion'.[117] The Bavarian Chargé d'Affaires Gasser also remarked on the over-familiar tone adopted towards the King in Madame Armansperg's salon, criticising in particular the attentions paid to him by the Armanspergs' eldest daughter.[118]

All of this and more Tyutchev picked up during his rounds of the diplomatic colony. At the Russian Embassy he no doubt warmed to Katakazi, who like himself was 'an arch wit', and given to 'sarcastic remarks'.[119] He also seems to have got on well enough with Polenov, whose family in Russia he apparently knew. Polenov later wrote to his parents describing Tyutchev as 'a very decent fellow', and mentioning an unspecified gift inside a red morocco casket which Tyutchev had asked him to send to them as 'a surprise'.[120] Unlike Katakazi, who had arrived only recently, Polenov had been in Nauplia since the previous year and would have been able to show his colleague from Munich around. Among other sights Tyutchev no doubt visited the church of St Spyridon. Its Venetian portal bore traces (still visible today) from the bullet which had killed Kapodistrias two years before on his way into the church. A further reminder of the first President of Greece was the Café Liberal, founded by him. Tietz describes this as 'a very elegant coffee-house, built like an Italian villa, from the balcony of which there is a delightful and extensive view, commanding the capital, the ocean, the plain of Argos, its city, and the mountains rising behind it'. Frequented by the King's uncle, Prince Eduard of Sachsen-Altenburg, it was the kind of fashionable gathering-place Tyutchev (who appreciated good coffee) would have been drawn to. Here, as Tietz says, listening to the military band and 'with some good coffee and a long Turkish pipe, an hour in Napoli may be whiled away delightfully'.[121] Perhaps it was from here that Tyutchev watched the sun setting over the bay and the mountains beyond, a sight which so impressed him that years later he could still recall its vivid colours in conversation with his daughter Darya.[122]

The *Carolina* returned from her trip to Marathon on the evening of 5 October with Gasser (and presumably Armansperg) on board, and remained in port until due to depart for Trieste via Patras on the 8th.[123] Aware that King Otto's itinerary would find him in Patras at about the same time as the *Carolina*, Katakazi decided to act. As he explained in despatches to Nesselrode and Gagarin, away from the capital it should be easier to deliver King Ludwig's letter to his son 'without arousing the curiosity and perhaps suspicion of the Regency by requesting a personal audience with the young Monarch.'[124] However, he realised that going to Patras himself 'would have given rise to rumours and interpretations among the public which it seemed to me more prudent to avoid'.[125] He therefore sent Tyutchev instead, instructing him to deliver the package with the letter to the King in person, 'without any intermediaries'.[126] From Patras Tyutchev would return to Trieste on the *Carolina*, and no doubt it was understood that he would if requested take on to Munich any reply from Otto.

Gasser confessed himself 'very unpleasantly surprised' on 7 October by the news that Tyutchev was about to leave Nauplia. This had left him only a day to complete a report for King Ludwig, part of the diplomatic mail his Russian colleague was to deliver to Munich.[127] Tyutchev left Nauplia the following day,[128] which was also when the *Carolina* set sail. The most obvious course of action would have been for him to travel on her to Patras, where he would presumably have had time to go ashore and deliver the letter before re-embarking for the onward voyage to Trieste. However, Tatyana

Dinesman has recently suggested that he travelled to Patras by an overland route instead.[129] Her evidence is Katakazi's despatch to Nesselrode of 30 September/ 12 October, where he writes of having instructed Tyutchev to return to Munich 'via the Morea [i.e. the Peloponnese], Corfu and Ancona', delivering the letter to King Otto in Patras on the way.[130] Yet the phrase 'via the Morea' could be taken to refer to the circuitous sea passage around the southern Peloponnese which all shipping between the Aegean and Adriatic was obliged to take until the opening of the Corinth Canal in 1892. (The rest of the itinerary detailed by Katakazi is certainly that followed by the *Carolina*.) Dinesman suggests the reason for taking the arduous route across country may have been to allow Tyutchev to arrive in Patras ahead of the *Carolina*, giving him more time to complete his mission there.[131] This is doubtful. From Nauplia to Patras by sea was a voyage of some 300 miles, which the *Carolina* could have completed in three to four days in reasonable conditions. Even by the fastest overland route, Tyutchev could hardly have expected to reach Patras much earlier. The first few miles to Argos would have been covered quite speedily (the road there from Nauplia, built by Kapodistrias, was said by Tietz to be 'the only one passable for carriages throughout Greece').[132] From then on it would have been a much slower and altogether more uncomfortable trek on horseback for the remaining 35 miles or so to Corinth. After passing by the ruins of Mycenae, the road became in Tietz's words 'nothing more than a narrow mountainous pass, over which a Greek horse or ass alone can go with safety'.[133] In these circumstances it would have been difficult to reach Corinth in less than two days. From there it was another 80 miles to Patras. Although this final stretch of the journey could probably have been completed by boat in 24 hours (much faster than on the poor roads along the southern shore of the Gulf of Corinth), Tyutchev would still have taken three days in all to reach his destination. This is without allowing for any hold-ups or misadventures on the way. And if the purpose really was to steal a march on the *Carolina*, why did Tyutchev wait until she left Nauplia, instead of setting off for Patras a few days earlier? In any case, it cannot be simply assumed that the *Carolina* made only a brief stop at Patras, a point on which no information is available. For all we know, she may have spent several days in port there (which might indeed help to explain why her return voyage from Nauplia to Trieste took ten days longer overall than the outward trip). In this case Tyutchev could have sailed on her to Patras, with ample time to go ashore and deliver the letter.

If Katakazi did send Tyutchev overland, it must have been for a quite different reason. It was after all vitally important that the letter be delivered to Otto in secret, without the knowledge of the Regency. Yet it it was to be expected that Armansperg would have agents on board the *Carolina*, primed to keep a close watch on Tyutchev and report on his mysterious mission. In Patras they would follow him ashore and dog his steps, making it extremely difficult to deliver the letter away from prying eyes. In these circumstances Katakazi may have calculated that sending Tyutchev overland offered a better chance of his slipping into Patras and approaching the King undetected, before embarking on the *Carolina* for the remainder of the voyage to Trieste. However, we have no way of knowing if this is what happened.

Dinesman quotes a further piece of evidence in favour of the overland route. Some nine months after returning from Greece, Tyutchev spoke of his visit there to Friedrich Lindner, whom he had met in Karlsbad. The only detail of the conversation recorded by Lindner is that Tyutchev was 'full of enthusiasm for the sight of the Gulf of Lepanto' (as the long stretch of water separating the Peloponnese from the rest of mainland Greece was then known).[134] It is certainly tempting to see this as confirmation that he traversed what is now the Gulf of Corinth while travelling overland, and to speculate that what fired his enthusiasm (as it had Byron's before him) was the magnificent scenery, with Mount Parnassus glimpsed across the blue waters

> Not in the fabled landscape of a lay,
> But soaring snow-clad through thy native sky,
> In the wild pomp of mountain majesty![135]

However, he would have seen the western extremity of the Gulf of Lepanto (now the Bay of Patras) in any case while travelling by sea. And here too, where in 1571 an Austrian-led fleet had decisively defeated the Turks at the great naval battle of Lepanto, there was more than enough to inspire admiration in one so alive to the resonances of the past.

More important than how Tyutchev got to Patras is the fact that he failed in his mission there. Katakazi appears to have foreseen this possibility, and to have taken the precaution of sending another member of the Embassy staff with him to bring the letter back to Nauplia if necessary. It was in fact finally delivered to Otto in secret via his adjutant on 23 October, soon after the young King had returned to the capital from his royal tour. In a despatch on this to Gagarin, Katakazi states merely that Tyutchev 'was unable to deliver' the letter in Patras, without going into further detail.[136] Clearly Armansperg was aware of Tyutchev's activities, and had managed to foil what he saw as an attempt to buttonhole the King behind the backs of the Regency. The French Ambassador in Munich, Vaudreuil, later reported on the basis of information from Nauplia that Tyutchev 'pursued King Otto in a vain attempt to meet His Majesty'.[137] That Vaudreuil's ultimate source for this was Armansperg himself is strongly suggested by his next despatch, in which he quotes verbatim from a letter from Armansperg: 'M. de Tutschef conducted himself very badly in Greece, but obtained nothing'.[138] Given the widely held if incorrect belief that Tyutchev had been sent to Greece as a royal marriage broker, Armansperg's indignation at his 'bad behaviour' is perhaps understandable.

Ignoring Ludwig's express instructions, Otto sent his reply not via Katakazi, but through the usual channels.[139] In view of the inordinate time taken to deliver his father's letter (nearly three months), he obviously considered the service offered by the Russians too unreliable. No doubt Armansperg also had a part to play in his decision.

Nothing is known of Tyutchev's sea voyage from Patras to Trieste beyond Katakazi's statement that Corfu and Ancona lay on the route. The *Carolina* reached Trieste on 3 November, nearly four weeks after setting sail from Nauplia.[140] Here another setback lay in wait. Because of a cholera epidemic, the ship's passengers had to spend a week or so in quarantine. As Eleonore later reported to Nikolay, conditions in the hospital where they were confined were 'disgusting in every respect'. Worst of all, Tyutchev had to witness the death of his manservant Joseph.[141]

It must have been with a sense of great relief that he finally reached Munich just after the middle of November.[142] He had been away for over three months. Soon afterwards King Ludwig will have received Gasser's despatch of 27 October from Nauplia, in which the Bavarian Chargé d'Affaires advises his monarch to find out via Gagarin 'exactly what M. Tutscheff saw and observed here'.[143] That Ludwig followed this up is suggested by the existence of a report on the situation in Greece commissioned by Gagarin from Tyutchev. It is — to put it mildly — an unusual document. Instead of the measured official briefing required by Gagarin, Tyutchev produced a brilliant satirical essay more suited to the columns of the political press. The opening gives a foretaste of what is to come:

> Fairy tales sometimes depict an enchanted cradle, around which gather the newborn child's guardian spirits. After these have bestowed their most beneficial charms on the privileged infant, without fail an evil fairy appears, to cast over the infant's cradle some fateful spell which destroys or impairs the dazzling gifts just lavished on it by friendly powers. Such, more or less, is the history of the Greek monarchy.
>
> It cannot be denied that the three great powers which took the monarchy under their wing endowed it most handsomely. But by what strange misfortune did it fall on this occasion to the King of Bavaria to play the role of evil fairy? A role of which he acquitted himself only too well in casting over the destinies of the newborn monarchy the evil spell of *his Regency*. For a long time to come Greece will remember this New Year's gift of the King of Bavaria.[144]

Most of what follows is devoted to criticism of the Regency's conduct of diplomatic affairs. Tyutchev picks on their granting of precedence to the British Ambassador above that of Russia, although the latter had been accredited earlier, pointing out that this conflicted with internationally agreed procedure and had almost led to a breach of diplomatic relations. 'A bizarre state of affairs!' he comments: throughout the long period of Ottoman rule Russia had maintained the closest and most benevolent relations with the subjugated Greeks, yet now 'it has taken the national government of liberated Greece but a few months to bring about what three centuries of foreign domination failed to achieve'.[145]

Next he turns his withering sarcasm on the Regency's decision to propose a British General, Sir Richard Church, as Greece's Ambassador to Russia. This, he says, at least kills two birds with one stone, managing to insult Greece and antagonise Russia at the same time. But why stop there in the pursuit of economy? Why not simply appoint some junior official from the British Embassy in St Petersburg, thus saving on removal expenses as well? He adds that the Russian government would be within its rights in rejecting Church's appointment. If that happened — a clear warning to King Ludwig — the blame would fall on the innocent head of Otto, whom the Regency would make their whipping boy ('*enfant de fouet*').[146] The message is clear: it was Ludwig who appointed the members of the Regency council, and it was for him to reassert his authority over them.

The report concludes with three specific proposals. Firstly, King Ludwig should revoke the *carte blanche* given to the Regency in its conduct of foreign affairs and insist that he and his son have the final say in this sphere. Secondly, the Russian government should exert strong pressure on the Regency (including if necessary the recall of Russia's Ambassador to Greece) to abandon its unilateral action in the matter of diplomatic precedence. Thirdly, Ludwig should be prevailed upon to appoint a suitable adviser to his son, who would act as a corrective to the Regency's anti-Russian tendencies and the pernicious influence of Madame Armansperg's salon.[147]

The report was never used as an official document. Ivan Gagarin later described it as a 'draft despatch' which his uncle refused to send because he found it 'insufficiently serious'. Indeed, it was only because the young Gagarin found the document amusing and decided to keep it for himself that it managed to survive at all.[148] The critic Georgy Chulkov suggested that Ambassador Gagarin's real reason for not accepting the report was that he feared the views so trenchantly expressed in it would displease Nesselrode, who — eager to satisfy Austrian interests in the Balkans — was supposedly striving 'somehow to rectify Russia's "mistake" of having supported Greece's struggle for national liberation'.[149] This reading of the situation (later repeated by Vadim Kozhinov)[150] seems unlikely. Although Nesselrode was certainly not one to condone rebellion against the established order, Greek independence was now a *fait accompli* and the Greek state a political reality with which he had to deal. It was no part of Tsar Nicholas's political philosophy to see Britain and in particular the France of Louis Philippe extend their influence in the area at the expense of Russia. Not surprisingly, Nesselrode's published despatches show him completely at one with his master in this respect. The pungently sarcastic tone apart, it is unlikely that anything in the substance of Tyutchev's report would have met with his disapproval. The proposal that King Ludwig appoint an adviser to Otto as a counterweight to the Regency's pro-Western policies had even been floated by Nesselrode himself in an earlier communication to Gagarin.[151]

The actual purpose of the document remains unclear. If it was a draft despatch (as claimed by Ivan Gagarin forty years after the event), it seems odd that Tyutchev should have included no details of his mission to Greece, and in particular no explanation of why he was unable to deliver the letter to Otto. On the other hand, the outspoken references to King Ludwig make it unthinkable that it should have been intended for his eyes. Perhaps, as previously suggested, it was more in the nature of an internal background report requested by Ambassador Gagarin prior to an audience with the King. Such an audience was indeed granted just before Christmas, and the record shows that 'Greek affairs' formed part of the discussion.[152] In any case we may assume that Ivan Gagarin was correct in recalling his uncle's displeasure at the report's flippant tone.

How successful had Tyutchev's mission been? King Ludwig's letter had been delivered to Katakazi, who eventually managed to pass it on to Otto. Secrecy had been maintained — over two months after Tyutchev's departure from Nauplia the French Ambassador there was forced to admit to his superiors in Paris that both he and his counterpart in Munich were still in the dark as to 'the real purpose' of the mission.[153] On the other hand the whole process had taken three months, and Tyutchev had been unable to bring back Otto's reply. Any hope of opening an alternative channel of communication between Otto and his father seemed to have been dashed. This was largely due to circumstances beyond Tyutchev's control and might not have reflected too badly on him, had he not submitted his facetious report, annoying Gagarin and reinforcing the perception of him as lightweight and unreliable.

As for the wider implications of Ludwig's letter, it seems its belated delivery did not do too much harm. In his despatch to Gagarin on 12 November, Katakazi stated that the mission entrusted to the French Ambassador in Nauplia had apparently so far met with 'not the slightest success'.[154] From the context it is clear he means the proposed dynastic union with France so vehemently opposed by Ludwig. Otto eventually married neither a French nor a Russian royal, but a German princess, a choice in which he was no doubt guided by his father.

On a personal level Tyutchev must have been left with mixed feelings about his journey to Greece and the country itself. Plagued as he was on the outward voyage by a whole series of adversities, including major depression, he is unlikely to have gone so far as one of Tietz's fellow-passengers on the ship from Constantinople to Nauplia, a well-educated young man who 'declaimed verses from the Odyssey in the original, and was intoxicated with the idea of at last treading the classic soil of Greece'.[155] Even so, no European schooled in the history and culture of antiquity could be completely immune to such sentiments, and we may assume that Tyutchev too set foot on Greek soil with at least something of Byron's fervent awareness that 'Where'er we tread 'tis haunted, holy ground'.[156] How long that will have lasted is another question. Only a few, such as Byron himself, were unaffected by the stark dichotomy of ideal and reality. Most European visitors hoping to find something of the spirit of ancient Greece were soon disillusioned by the poverty, backwardness and political squabbling of a country devastated by years of war. (Tietz was no exception, his expectations taking a particularly hard knock from the sight of some beggars in the ruins of Mycenae. 'These were the descendants of *the Greeks!*' he expostulates, '— whom we have been accustomed to look upon as the most civilised and perfect of human beings'.[157] And even his euphoric onboard companion was to find Homer no antidote to disillusion-ment: Tietz tells us that after three weeks in Greece 'his enthusiasm was dissipated: and he assiduously counted the hours for his return'.)[158]

Tyutchev returned to Munich, in the words of the French Ambassador, 'extremely discontented with his voyage'. (Vaudreuil went on to comment that the voyage 'appears not to have had any result', a judgement evidently coloured by his own false conjectures as to the nature and purpose of the mission).[159] For some time afterwards Tyutchev seems to have found the whole experience so traumatic that according to Eleonore 'he had a horror of talking about it'.[160] After a while, however — perhaps as his general mood lifted — he began to recall some of the more congenial aspects of his travels. Two months after his return Eleonore could report to Nikolay: 'now that he has quite forgotten the fatigues and anxieties of the journey, he sometimes finds himself missing the sun and the images of that incommodious country, to the extent that he even says he would like to go back there in a few years!!! It's easy enough to say that.' Somewhat tartly (and with what could be interpreted as a reference to romantic adventures) she continues: 'Besides, do not imagine that he had so much to complain about: everything was favourable towards him; Providence took care of our little child, and everywhere he found somewhere to lay his head.'[161] Later, as we have seen, particular images of Greece such as the Gulf of Lepanto or the setting sun would return to delight his mind's eye.

Travel was for Tyutchev a major source of poetic inspiration, with much of his verse composed literally en route. For this reason alone we might expect his long and eventful voyage to Greece to have yielded at least several poems, yet strangely enough until now not one has been conclusively linked to the voyage.[162] The reason could simply be that none has survived. Towards the end of 1833 Tyutchev by his own account destroyed most of his poetic manuscripts, and these may well have included some inspired by his recent visit to Greece. As he told the story in a letter to Ivan Gagarin, this was purely the result of his own carelessness:

> On my return from Greece, having set about sorting my papers in the twilight, I destroyed the major part of my poetic efforts, and it was only much later that I noticed this. I was somewhat put out at first, but was not slow to console myself by thinking of the great fire at the Library of Alexandria. — Amongst all this was the whole first act of *Faust*, Part Two, in translation. That was perhaps the best of the lot.[163]

Several scholars have been uneasy with this version of events. Gregg for instance claims that 'the burning of a large and bulky mass of verse by the poet himself (a circumstance which alone might well put us on guard) was no accident'. He sees the incident rather as a 'cathartic-destructive' act of self-disgust, citing in justification Tyutchev's revealing response to a request from Gagarin for poetic manuscripts: 'I have seized this opportunity of getting rid of them. Do with them as you please. I have a horror of old paper that's written on, particularly by me. It has a rancid smell about it, enough to turn one's stomach...'.[164] Kozhinov relates the 'accident' to Tyutchev's psychological state at the time, and suggests it could have been 'an act, perhaps even only half-conscious, of self-immolation'[165] Even the usually circumspect Pigaryov refers to it on one occasion as 'an *auto da fe* carried out by the poet himself '.[166] We have to concur. Although an accident cannot be entirely discounted, it does seem much more likely that Tyutchev destroyed his poems deliberately during a severe bout of depression, and that his later account of events to Gagarin was an attempt to gloss over this.

And yet two poems inspired by the voyage to Greece do appear to have survived, albeit unnoticed by critics. If Tyutchev has left no poetic depiction of the sunsets which so impressed him, in one of these poems he gives instead a vivid and dramatic account of daybreak at sea, evidently as seen from the *Carolina*. It is one of those scenes of natural transition and evolution on which his artistic imagination fastened so readily, with a human figure in the foreground as focus or gathering-point for the all-pervasive cosmic forces at play. The young girl in the poem is clearly suffering the torments of love (we have only to recall the daybreak imagery of 'That day remains in memory...' to be persuaded of this). Whether this was true of her prototype, and whether Tyutchev's relationship to her was anything more than that of curious (one might almost say voyeuristic) observer to fellow-passenger, we shall probably never know.

> Pale showed the east... Our craft sped gently,
> Taut canvas jubilantly flapping...
> Like heaven upturned, the sea beneath us
> A-quiver, tremulously lapping...

Red glowed the east... She prayed intently,
Her veil flung back in supplication:
Petitions on her lips, her glances
Fraught with the heavens' exultation...

Bright flared the east... Now diffidently
She bowed her head, as in confusion:
Her neck pearl-white, her young face streaming
With fiery droplets in profusion...[167]

The second poem is also set at dawn, this time apparently in Nauplia. Tyutchev describes the world awakening and stirring into life 'like a bird'. He alone has not slept, and although morning now cools his dishevelled hair, 'I languish still beneath the burden/ Of yesterday's fierce heat and dust'. Already he longs for the 'protecting veil' of night, for its 'tranquil darkness and fresh dews', and shrinks from the coming day:

How loathsome it all is, how strident,
How alien in every way —
The noise and tumult, shouts and babble
Of this new, incandescent day...

The final stanza of the poem has been seen by some critics (especially those of a 'progressive' or Marxist bias) as an expression of Tyutchev's alienation from the socio-historical developments of his age. According to them, the 'remnants of past generations,/ Outstripped by time's advancing tide' are those representatives such as the poet himself of a class doomed to extinction. But there is no need for such a contrived interpretation if we accept that the poem was conceived at Nauplia. In that case the reference is more obviously to those physical ruins of ancient civilisation seen by Tietz and others as a painfully ironic reminder of how far in their eyes the present inhabitants of Greece (the 'new people' of the poem) had fallen from former glory. The very nobility of the ruins is said to stand as a 'reproach' to the present day: one which Tyutchev finds in general 'justified', even if (presumably in that it takes no account of historical considerations) technically incorrect, or 'misinformed':

You remnants of past generations,
Outstripped by time's advancing tide:
However misinformed your strictures,
Still their reproach is justified!
What torment — like a washed-out spectre,
With faltering step, all vigour spent —
To have to follow a new people
On sunlight and endeavour bent!..[168]

8 Ernestine
(Munich, 1833-1837)

i Faux Frères

In January 1833 Baron von Dörnberg and his wife arrived in Munich from their home in Regensburg for the Carnival season. The city was in the grip of a typhus epidemic, and under normal circumstances this alone might have deterred Friedrich von Dörnberg, who was approaching middle age, from what would be a hectic round of social activity. However, he knew how much his young wife Ernestine loved to dance, and he was keen for her to shine in the ballrooms and salons of the capital. Nor was he disappointed. Her striking beauty, natural charm, refinement and intelligence soon made her a welcome guest at the most prestigious balls and banquets, including those given by the King himself.[1]

Ernestine (Nesti or Nesterle to her intimate circle) had managed to preserve or achieve a surprising serenity of spirit, given her troubled upbringing. Her mother had died when she was a year old, soon after the birth of her younger brother Karl. Their father, the Bavarian diplomat Christian Hubert von Pfeffel, was a cold and remote figure. After being looked after for some time by their grandmother, Nesti and Karl were put in the care of an over-strict English governess, whom their father later married. They were then sent to boarding schools. Baron von Pfeffel's ambassadorial duties (first in London, then Paris) kept him abroad for most of the time, but even the brief periods spent together as a family were overshadowed by his and his second wife's lack of any love towards them. The two neglected children soon developed a mutual bond of affection which was to last throughout their lives. Once when their father and stepmother were out, Nesti and Karl made preparations to run away from home, to be prevented only by their parents' return. In 1830, aged twenty, Ernestine married Baron Friedrich. As she later admitted, it was not so much a love match as a means of escape from her unhappy family background. He was some fourteen years older than she.[2]

Nesti's brother was the same Karl Pfeffel who had got to know Tyutchev as a student in 1830. It was no doubt through him that Tyutchev first became acquainted with the Dörnbergs during the Carnival season of 1833. Ernestine's reminiscence of one particularly memorable encounter at a ball about the middle of February was recorded many years later by her stepdaughter Darya:

> Mama [i.e. Ernestine] was dancing, and her husband, feeling unwell, decided to leave the ball, but didn't want to spoil his wife's enjoyment.. When he approached her, she was talking to a young Russian. He told her that she should stay and that he would leave on his own, and then turned to the young man and said: 'I entrust my wife to you'.[3]

The young Russian was Tyutchev. When Ernestine returned from the ball to where she and her husband were staying (almost certainly the *Goldener Hirsch* at 18 Theatinerstrasse, near the Odeonsplatz, then considered the best hotel in Munich),[4] she found the Baron had taken to his bed with typhus. A few days later he was dead.[5] After the funeral Ernestine went back to Regensburg, accompanied by Karl. Here he too fell ill with typhus, but recovered.[6] Pfeffel returned to Munich on or about 16 March to find the epidemic still raging. Meeting Tyutchev in the street, he found him 'most concerned' about Ernestine and her plans for the future.[7] Perhaps the Baron's final words to him at the ball had in hindsight taken on a fateful and prophetic ring. Certainly he now began to cultivate Pfeffel's friendship as a way of maintaining contact with Ernestine. A week after their meeting, Karl received an invitation to dinner from the Tyutchevs.[8] He himself was to date his closer friendship with Tyutchev from this time.[9]

Among the many carried off by typhus that year was the young playwright Michael Beer. He had been eagerly anticipating a journey to Greece, even learning some modern Greek in preparation.[10] Now his friends, who included Tyutchev, mourned a young life and a talented career cut short. In many ways Beer's moderate political views were close to those of Tyutchev. A convinced monarchist, he had been repelled by revolutionary excesses witnessed at first hand in Paris in 1830. According to Eduard Schenk, he 'largely shared [...] the views of his Doctrinaire friends in Paris, and with them considered the best constitution to be a monarchy limited and guaranteed by the representative system'.[11] On 25 March Tyutchev, Pfeffel and Schenk were among the throng of friends and admirers to accompany the torchlit funeral procession on foot as far as the Jewish cemetery outside the city.[12] Describing the scene in a letter to Ernestine, Pfeffel noted that Tyutchev, 'who has to see everything and know about everything, even wanted to be present at the interment ceremony'.[13]

Beer's was not the only funeral attended by Tyutchev that spring. On 30 May the 68-year-old Prussian Ambassador, Johann Emanuel von Küster, died of causes unrelated to the typhus epidemic. On such occasions it was customary for the diplomatic corps to turn out in force for the funeral, and we can be sure that Tyutchev, who was in Munich at the time, was among those attending. The Protestant ceremony took place at the city's 'alter Südfriedhof' cemetery on 2 June; the officiating pastor is likely to have been the Lutheran Dean of Munich, Friedrich Boeckh, who had a certain reputation as a preacher.[14] Soon afterwards Tyutchev described the scene in a poem combining a gently ironic reflection on the Christian faith with the affirmation of an alternative, pantheistic religion of nature:

> And now the coffin has been lowered...
> And all around in packed array
> Crowd mourners: jostling, loath to breathe in
> The stifling odour of decay...
>
> And by the open grave the pastor —
> A man of learning and repute —
> Begins his funeral oration
> In words well-chosen and astute...

He speaks of man, ordained to perish,
The Fall, Christ's blood that washes sin...
Each listens to these words of wisdom
And weighs them for himself within...

And all the while the sky so boundless
Shines with a pure undying light...
And all around us birdsong endless
Sounds from the blue unfathomed height...[15]

Meanwhile in Regensburg Ernestine was struggling to come to terms with the sudden loss of her husband. His death had come as a terrible shock, even if she had never loved him deeply. On 1 May she recorded her feelings in the album of pressed flowers and other mementoes, accompanied by dated notes, which provides a valuable if often enigmatic record of her inner life during these years. She writes that after the death of 'a loved one' everything connected with him becomes 'precious': 'His last words, his last actions — these are painful memories, but at the same time our heart finds in them an especial fascination'. Coming across long-forgotten personal belongings of the deceased is particularly poignant: 'the very fact of our forgetting makes them more precious to our heart than that which every day reminds us of him who is no more'.[16] The restrained and generalised nature of these remarks, written only two months after her husband's death, is eloquent enough. Having married for reasons other than love, it was perhaps inevitable that Ernestine would never feel much more than respect and a certain degree of affection towards him.

On the weekend of 15-16 June Tyutchev travelled to Eglofsheim, the country seat of the von Cettos to the south of Regensburg.[17] He was sent by Ambassador Gagarin to deliver a message to Krüdener, who with Amélie was staying there at the time. Tyutchev was only too glad of such an opportunity to combine business with a few pleasurable days spent in congenial company ('he would have gone there anyway', Eleonore commented in a letter to Nikolay).[18] Among those staying at Eglofsheim was Ernestine, as is clear from entries in her flower album. One commemorates an excursion to Donaustauf on Monday 17 June, no doubt organised by the Cettos for their guests including the newly arrived Tyutchev. And (as convincingly argued by Svetlana Dolgopolova) it was almost certainly this nostalgic return in Amélie's company to the ruined castle above the Danube that inspired Tyutchev to compose his bitter-sweet poetic evocation of an earlier visit in that long-lost 'golden time' of innocence and happiness.[19] Another poem set in the area, a kind of mock-ballad in which the Danube appears as a legendary realm of fabulous river-maidens, knights in armour and medieval castles, was more likely written during Tyutchev's visit to Eglofsheim the following year. Its ironic final twist in the manner of Heine returns once more to the theme of a lost golden age, and clearly derives from personal observation:

All is vanished: you too had to
Bow to fate as years went by,

And, O Danube, river steamers
Now your gleaming waters ply.[20]

Ernestine seems to have been at Eglofsheim throughout Tyutchev's stay. A further entry in her album shows that she was still there on 25 June.[21] Yet although he was no doubt keen to pursue her, there is nothing in the album entries to indicate that she felt anything for him at this stage.

While Tyutchev was away, Eleonore wrote to Nikolay that she hoped her husband would soon be able to visit him in Vienna. Her letter continues:

> I shall in any case not be sorry to send him on his travels for a while; he is, I believe, misbehaving [*il fait des sottises*], or something very like it. Idleness is indeed a perfidious thing. My friend, don't think of taking seriously what is, thank God, nothing but a joke. All that I really think is that Théodore allows himself without thinking to become involved in little society intrigues which, however childish they may be, could lead to unpleasant complications. I am not jealous, nor do I believe I have reason to be, but I am concerned to see him acting like a fool in this way: such behaviour can so easily lead to a fall.[22]

It had always been tempting for Eleonore to slip into the role of protective mother and see her husband's misdemeanours as no more than the antics of a wayward child. Yet on this occasion there is more than a hint of despair behind the bright façade. Perhaps by now she sensed that Tyutchev's '*sottises*' and 'intrigues' were in some way connected with the deterioration she had observed in his mental health over the previous months. Ernestine will have been the least of her worries, even assuming that she knew of her presence at Eglofsheim. Their paths appear to have crossed soon afterwards (just where is not known; probably not in Munich), for on 13 July Pfeffel wrote to his sister that Eleonore 'seemed most delighted to have seen you again'.[23] Eleonore had her eye on other, more serious threats, who may have included Amélie. Just a couple of months later Pfeffel would remark on Eleonore's jealousy of the French Ambassador's wife, Countess de Vaudreuil, who was said to receive guests at her salon in revealing attire ('*presque nue*', as Pfeffel puts it).[24]

In August Tyutchev left for Greece, returning only in mid-November. On 30 October Ernestine too returned to Munich for the winter season, moving into an apartment at 11 Schwabinger Landstrasse on which her brother had arranged a six-month lease.[25] The timing was purely coincidental, for at that time everyone in the capital from King Ludwig down was still in the dark as to Tyutchev's whereabouts.[26] Writing to Ernestine on 23 October, Pfeffel even light-heartedly suggested that, like Marlborough in the popular French song, he might not make it back at all.[27] It was a remark the sensitive Pfeffel would hardly have made had his sister, to whom he was very close, by then shown any sign of attachment to his friend.

After his return Tyutchev took every opportunity offered by the social round to meet Ernestine. The Carnival season began early that winter, ushered in by the marriage of the King's daughter Princess Mathilde to the heir to the Grand Duchy of Hessen-Darmstadt on 26 December.[28] 'Has Théodore told you of the exceptional animation of society this winter?' Eleonore wrote to Nikolay on 13 January. 'I do not go out myself, but apparently there are a great deal of pretty women, gossip, balls, etc., etc.'[29] Eleonore had good reason to keep herself apart from the hurly-burly, being six months pregnant — a circumstance which did nothing to deter her husband from the relentless pursuit of pretty women and gossip alike.

'Today, New Year's Eve, you will perhaps have thought of a certain ball at the Dönhoffs' in Munich,' Tyutchev wrote to Ernestine twenty years to the day after the event in question.[30] And from the rest of his letter it is clear that for him this ball at the house of the Prussian Ambassador on the last day of 1833 marked the beginning of their closer relationship. This is confirmed by a reference to Ernestine in a letter to his parents dated 18/30 December 1842, in which he claims that 'for nine years now' he has been 'the object of all her affections'.[31] Evidently his advances at the New Year's ball had not fallen on entirely stony ground. Like so many women before and after her, Ernestine was won over by his charm and eloquence, and in other circumstances might have surrendered more readily to his advances. Yet she was at least formally still in mourning for her late husband, and perhaps still too unsure of her feelings to embark on a serious relationship. More importantly, Tyutchev was not only married, but to someone Ernestine knew and respected, and who was currently expecting his child. It was enough to give her pause; especially as there was no lack of eligible bachelors willing to offer a union less fraught with complications.

Among these was Tyutchev's countryman Aleksandr Turgenev. Early on the morning of 27 March 1834 he arrived in Munich by coach from Augsburg and booked in to the same room at the *Goldener Hirsch* he had stayed in two years previously.[32] Now as then it was Schelling who drew him to the Bavarian capital. They had already developed close bonds after their first meeting in Karlsbad in 1825; the German philosopher valued Turgenev's intellectual ability, and would soon be professing an almost parental affection towards him.[33] Yet far from limiting himself to the rarefied atmosphere of Schelling's circle, Turgenev also plunged into the social whirl in which Tyutchev was so at home. And it was here — at balls, dinners and soirées hosted by the King, the aristocracy and diplomatic corps — that he encountered Ernestine and fell under her spell. On 4 April he attended a soirée at the Cettos', where (as he records in his diary) 'I exchanged pleasantries with the widow Dörnberg: Tyutchev had great difficulty in dragging me away'.[34] Soon he was to be found loitering in the Schwabinger Landstrasse at night, gazing up at her windows in the hope of a glimpse like some lovesick teenager.[35] Ernestine's varying response to his advances — now encouraging, now evasive — left him in a state of confusion and frustration. On 18 April he left a poetry reading given by August von Platen at the Schellings' 'to run to Cetto's, where I found the widow already, and exchanged pleasantries until 11.30. I accompanied her to her carriage: either she is toying with me, or she loves me: what will the one or the other lead me to?'[36] On another occasion at the Cettos' Ernestine was 'at first [...] amiable', but 'when others were present began to ignore me'.[37]

Turgenev could not help comparing Ernestine with the Countess Anna d'Arco-Valley, a more consistently serene young beauty who also appears to have caught his eye. One Sunday, seeing them both enter the Frauenkirche for mass, he slipped in and watched unobserved from behind a bronze statue at the back of the church. He was touched by the innocent sight of Anna, 'charming in her pious devotion'; but Ernestine seemed to display darker, more challenging depths. 'How ill prayer became the other one!.. yet I almost love her!' he confided to his diary later that day.[38] Elsewhere he likens Anna to 'the Madonna of Raphael', while Ernestine seems to him rather 'the Madonna of Mephistopheles'.[39]

All this served only to add to the fascination. He became more single-minded in his pursuit of her, encouraged among others by her brother. 'You are not forty yet', Pfeffel told him one day towards the end of his stay (the youthful-looking Turgenev was in fact ten years older). 'Why don't you get married? [...] You are wealthy!'[40] On 23 April Turgenev met Ernestine and Pfeffel in the street. He took a flower from the bouquet she was carrying; she smiled. He begged her for a meeting; at first she was evasive, then agreed to receive him at 3 p.m. the following day. 'I took her hand, pressed it with delight, and kissed it,' Turgenev writes in his diary. ' "In the street," she replied without anger. Her brother looked to one side. I was beside myself '.[41] Next day at the appointed time he presented himself at her apartment. Again his diary records their hour-long tête-à-tête:

> To begin with, an awkward conversation on trivial matters; then I took her hand and spoke of my feelings, kissing her hand three times with no resistance on her part. Afterwards she began to turn away and said she did not like it: I fell silent, then changed the subject [...]. Twice I wanted to take her handkerchief, but she would not consent; I spoke again only to say: '*Que cela reste*' ['Let it rest there']... I had achieved nothing. I don't know if I left more annoyance in her heart than... I left at four o'clock in a state of complete agitation and confusion.[42]

Returning that evening from the Schellings', Turgenev came across Ernestine sitting with her brother in her carriage (probably outside the Cettos' house, where she had spent the evening). He approached them, but received a cool reception from the woman he now regarded as 'the Empress of my thoughts';[43] it was left to Pfeffel to engage him in conversation.[44] As she later recalled, Ernestine had just learnt of the birth of a daughter, Darya, to Eleonore earlier that day. No doubt aware that Ernestine would be at the Cettos' that evening, Tyutchev had gone there too; he had mentioned the happy event only when asked by Countess Cetto how his wife was.[45] Never one to let the small matter of a birth in the family keep him from his social engagements, he was present (as was Ernestine) at most of the dinners and soirées attended by Turgenev over the following days.[46]

By now Turgenev seems more or less to have resigned himself to losing Ernestine. He had known all along that in May she intended to leave Munich to spend several months with her father, the Bavarian Ambassador in Paris. Following her there would have presented him with a serious dilemma. His brother Nikolay, sentenced to death *in absentia* for his part in the Decembrist conspiracy, had taken refuge in Paris, and Tsar Nicholas had exacted a solemn undertaking from Turgenev not to go there.[47] And in any case, after his declaration of love on 24 April Ernestine had (as he wrote not long after to Nikolay) 'suddenly changed towards me, and does not speak to or answer me'.[48] Most of all he was aware that he was twice her age. The day after their decisive meeting he went for a long solitary walk through the streets of Munich, to find that this merely 'increased my melancholy and despair, which are explicable only in terms of this late spark that has found its way into my heart... Will it too be extinguished, like the others?'[49] The next day he was writing to his brother that Ernestine 'has left a gaping hole in my heart; but we are no match, and I think we shall never come together in this life'.[50] As if to confirm this, he went out of his way to obtain a lithographic version of Stieler's portrait to remember her by. 'Now I have something to look at!' he wrote in his diary.[51]

It was also beginning to dawn on him that there was another, much younger and no doubt more determined, contender on the scene. Already on 19 April he had confided to his diary that Ernestine seemed to regard Tyutchev and himself as *'faux frères'*, apparently in the sense of rivals for her affection.[52] His eyes were finally opened on the eve of Ernestine's departure for Paris, when the Papal Nuncio, Count Charles d'Argenteau, hosted a farewell dinner in her honour. Tyutchev called for Turgenev at the *Goldener Hirsch*, and they went on to the Nuncio's together. Later Turgenev recorded the evening's events in his diary:

> It fell to me to partner [Countess] Braga. *She* sat separated from me by Braga and [Prince] Salm-Salm. She was flirting, smiling. The Nuncio wanted to drink to my health after hers; I said I drank to her: she gave a slight bow. [...] Her brother approached me several times. Both at my lodgings before the dinner and at the Nuncio's Tyutchev advised me to be bolder, to engage in repartee, and so forth. I replied that I did not want to: he appears to have a shrewd understanding of her, yet — loves her himself! We stayed on after her departure and exchanged pleasantries — at her expense![53]

Turgenev's bafflement is understandable. What induced Tyutchev to encourage his rival in this way? Did he perhaps hope Turgenev might succeed where he had failed, and at the last moment persuade Ernestine to stay in Munich? If so, his hopes were soon dashed, and the two frustrated suitors were left to seek some consolation in thoughts of sour grapes.

Next morning Turgenev rose before dawn to wait at the Maximilianstor for Ernestine's carriage on its way out of the city. At 5.30 he saw it approach, and halted it. His *'Bonjour'* was returned frostily; Ernestine ordered the carriage to drive on. *'Finita è la comedia!'* is the rueful comment in his diary. That evening he himself left Munich, heading in the opposite direction, towards Linz and ultimately Moscow.[54]

ii Intimate Diaries

Turgenev's diary provides us with a vivid and heartfelt account of his ill-starred love for Ernestine. Nothing comparable has survived to tell Tyutchev's side of the story. There is no diary, and any letters he may have written to Ernestine at this time were later destroyed by her.[55] The one intimate record we do have is in the poems addressed to or inspired by her.[56] The first (written apparently just before Turgenev's arrival in Munich) suggests that over three months after his declaration to her on New Year's Eve he had failed to receive more than an equivocal response. His longing for love and renewal is identified here with the forces of growth and becoming in nature, perhaps too with Christian faith in the Resurrection (as pointed out by Svetlana Dolgopolova, line 9 echoes a well-known Lenten contakion of the Russian Orthodox church).[57]

> The earth still wears a sombre air,
> Yet spring is in these breezes playing
> With boughs of stately firs and swaying
> The withered stalks in fields so bare —
> Still nature slumbers, although lighter
> Her sleep now, and through fading dreams
> She smiles with pleasure that spring seems
> About to waken and delight her...
>
> My soul, you too have slept, you too...
> But whence this sudden agitation
> That rouses you to delectation,
> Gilding your dreams with lustre new?..
> Snow thaws in gleaming liquefaction,
> Blue skies, resplendent, shine above...
> What is this, goading me to action:
> Spring fever — or a woman's love?...[58]

Yet at times Ernestine's cool and evasive attitude seems to have cast him into despair. Then he could even see in her, as Turgenev had, a 'Madonna of Mephistopheles' embodying the very negation of divine love:

> There is no feeling in your eyes,
> There is no truth in your replies,
> Your heart is cold and bare.
>
> O, courage! — would it were not true! —
> There is no God in heaven too,
> And so no point in prayer![59]

With her departure for Paris Ernestine was determined to draw a line beneath a growing attachment which troubled her in more ways than one; she remained adamant despite Tyutchev's emotional pleas. After a 'final farewell' (which in fact would be the first of several), Tyutchev had no option but to accept their separation as somehow ordained by fate. So much is evident from a poem written at the time. Although on the face of it a free translation of a piece by Heine,[60] Tyutchev's version expands the three stanzas of Heine's original to seven, adding much that is relevant to his own situation. The poem begins more or less in line with Heine's; yet even here the references to fate, to a 'final farewell' preceded by tearful scenes, and to the uncertain future are all Tyutchev's own:

> From place to place, from here to there,
> Fate, like a whirlwind, sweeps mankind;

Though some resist, she does not care,
But drives them on in fury blind.

The wind has carried to our ears
Love's last farewell (familiar sound)...
Behind us many, many tears,
Ahead, obscuring mists abound!..

In Heine's poem the voice borne on the wind is that of the woman he has left behind: 'O komm zurück, ich hab' dich lieb/ Du bist mein einz'ges Glück!' ('O come back, I love you/ You are my only happiness'). Tyutchev reverses the roles, recalling his own appeals to Ernestine to stay. In the process Heine's two lines of quoted speech are transformed into three stanzas:

'O stop, take counsel, and be wise:
Why run away, where will you go?..
Behind you love abandoned lies —
Where else has such delights to show?

'Behind you love abandoned lies,
Prostrate with heartache and distress...
O, spare your anguish, seize this prize:
The chance of lasting happiness!

'That sweet and poignant bliss recall,
The bliss that for so long you knew...
By going on you forfeit all
In life that was most dear to you!..'

Now that the die is cast, however, Tyutchev resigns himself to suppressing such memories, which like the memory of dead loved ones can bring only pain:

This is no time to call the dead —
With gloom enough the hour is rife —
Their image all the more we dread,
The more we held them dear in life.

From place to place, from here to there,
A mighty whirlwind sweeps mankind;
Should some resist, it does not care,
But drives them on in fury blind.[61]

But it was not so easy for him to forget Ernestine. Only a month later Karl Pfeffel wrote to her that Tyutchev was visiting him every two or three days to ask for news of her.[62] And another poem which seems to have been written at this time is indicative of the deep depression he had fallen into. The 'poor, pale flower' in verse four — perhaps

207

one he and Ernestine had picked together, now withered — can be seen as symbolic of their abortive relationship.

> I sit alone and contemplate
> The dying embers in the grate,
>   With tears half-blind...
> Thoughts of the past bring only pain,
> And, sunk in gloom, the words in vain
>   I seek to find.
>
> Did the past really once exist?
> And what is now — will it persist
>   Or disappear?
> Like all else that has gone before
> It slips into oblivion's maw
>   Year after year.
>
> Year after year, age after age...
> What use then if we rail and rage,
>   We mortal men?
> All flesh is grass that withers, yet
> We see each burgeoning spring beget
>   Green shoots again.
>
> For everything returns anew:
> The rose will bloom again, as too
>   Will briar and thorn...
> But you, my poor, pale flower, will not
> Come back to life: it is your lot
>   To lie forlorn.
>
> With what a bitter-sweet delight
> I plucked you and I held you tight
>   That fateful day...
> Now stay safeguarded on my breast
> Till love's last sigh has been expressed
>   And dies away.[63]

Ernestine's departure had been followed by a noticeable deterioration in his health (no doubt the two were connected), and Eleonore was concerned that this should be dealt with. A course of hydrotherapy at Marienbad in Austria (now Marianske Lazne, Czech Republic) was prescribed, and Eleonore wrote to Nikolay in Vienna asking him if he could accompany his brother there, 'as I for my part am absolutely unable to go with him, and you know what Théodore travelling on his own and taking a cure on his own would be like: it's enough to make one's hair stand on end'.[64] Before leaving for Marienbad, Tyutchev accompanied Eleonore and the rest of the family to Tegernsee,

208

where they were to spend the summer. From here on 6 July Eleonore wrote again to Nikolay: 'We have been here a fortnight, and although we have taken decidedly rustic accommodation in a thatched cottage, the fine weather, the superb landscape and carefree life are immensely beneficial.'[65] The clear waters of Lake Tegernsee, the pure mountain air and Alpine views all provided an ideal summer retreat from the dusty city for Eleonore, Tyutchev and the children, including the two-month-old Darya. No doubt Clotilde was also on hand to help with the children. For Tyutchev the fashionable resort had its own attractions. 'Théodore quite likes it here,' Eleonore reports in the same letter, 'and the prospect of seeing some of the *beau monde* arrive from Munich in a few days has decided him to stay until the end of the month'. Again she begs Nikolay to join Tyutchev in Marienbad, and hints that his illness may be at least partly psychological in nature: 'I must also confess to an ulterior motive, namely that your presence will save him from the dispiriting tedium of time spent at the spa. I am most fearful that otherwise he will not withstand this test of patience.'[66]

Far from staying until the end of the month, the restless Tyutchev was off on his travels just a few days later. Perhaps he had written to Ernestine in Paris and hoped to receive a reply or at least news of her in Munich, which lay on his route to Marienbad. Although none of their correspondence from this period has survived (he is known to have written nearly two hundred letters to her before 1840),[67] he would later remind her of the 'feeling of anguish, the heartache, the need for air, in other words the need to see you again at any cost' which her letters had often evoked in him during these early years.[68] Certainly the few days spent in Munich seem to have been particularly distressing. Towards the end of his stay there he was found lying unconscious in the Hofgarten, a public park.[69] Apparently he had not eaten for three days. He himself tried to make light of this, citing in mitigation his own absent-mindedness and ineptitude in practical affairs. As he later told it to Ivan Gagarin, one day he had been invited to dine at the Ambassador's, but got the times mixed up and arrived just as the meal was over; the following day, with the family away, there had been no servants at home to prepare dinner; then, on the third day, he 'simply lost the habit of eating' and ended up fainting.[70] Yet in view of the abundance of inns and restaurants in the city, we are entitled to query Tyutchev's account and wonder whether his collapse was perhaps more serious than he made out.

In any case he was soon well enough to resume his journey. The third week of July found him again at Eglofsheim, where he lingered for some days.[71] This time Ernestine was not there, but he was able to glean news of her from her brother Karl. In conversation with the Cettos' guests Tyutchev fell into his customary role of intellectual provocateur. 'Everyone has been thrown into disagreement here at Eglofsheim,' Pfeffel wrote to Ernestine a few days after Tyutchev's departure for Marienbad on 21 July. 'Monsieur de Tutcheff was the lump of sugar thrown into the kettle, and the political discussions continue with no end in sight, even though the prime mover has left.'[72]

A couple of days after leaving Eglofsheim he arrived in Marienbad, where he stayed for six weeks. Eleonore's fears for his peace of mind were probably exaggerated. Although it is not known whether Nikolay managed to join him, Ivan Gagarin was certainly there for the first half of his stay,[73] and there will have been a sufficient cross-section of international society taking the waters to keep boredom at bay. His course of hydrotherapy complete, he left on 3 September to rejoin the family at Tegernsee.[74]

At the centre of the resort's lively social life stood its impressive castle, a former Benedictine monastery acquired by the Bavarian royal family in 1817 and at this time occupied by Queen Karoline. She had moved there towards the end of the 1820s, finding life at her first dowager residence in Würzburg uncongenial. Writing of a stay at Tegernsee a few years later, Tyutchev described Karoline as 'the most amiable and hospitable hostess', adding that there had been 'often more society, festivities and amusements than one would have desired'. As always the Queen Mother was attended by her faithful chaplain Pastor Schmidt, who is said to have enjoyed the company of his patroness's many interesting guests, and whose services in the castle were, as once in Munich, open to all, there being no Lutheran church in the vicinity.[75]

Unlike Anna and Darya, who had been baptised into the Orthodox Church, the Peterson boys were being brought up in the faith of Eleonore and her first husband. On Sunday 28 September she welcomed the opportunity of taking them to one of Schmidt's services at the royal residence. Ever the curious if sceptical observer of religious practice, Tyutchev tagged along as well. The austere little chapel, lacking all the ornate trappings of an Orthodox or Catholic church, seemed to him like an empty house, its tenants about to depart. Perhaps memories were aroused of his and Eleonore's move from the apartment in Ottostrasse over two years before. And as he pondered the symbolism of this, the lines of a poem began to form in his mind:

> I love the Lutheran service, with its simple
> And solemn rite, austere and dignified —
> And understand the lofty creed implied
> By these bare walls, this empty, sombre temple.
>
> Do you not see? Faith, taking up position
> To leave, for one last time confronts you there:
> Still standing in the doorway, in transition,
> Although her house is empty now, and bare —
>
> Still standing in the doorway, in transition,
> The door still open, though the time is nigh...
> The hour has struck... Now pray with expedition:
> Soon you shall pray no more to Him on high.[76]

'[Tyutchev's] religion was the religion of Horace', Ivan Gagarin later recalled.[77] The scepticism underlying the poem is evident enough. Yet interfusing what would otherwise be satire is, as Richard Gregg puts it, 'an elegiac note so strong that it lifts the poem into an entirely different mode of expression'.[78] As a result it becomes more than anything a lament for the erosion of faith (and this must include the author's own) by the forces of rationalism. Earlier that year, in March, Tyutchev's attention will have been drawn to the first of a series of articles by Heine published in the influential Paris journal *Revue des Deux Mondes* under the title 'De l'Allemagne depuis Luther' (parts two and three appeared later, in the November and December issues).[79] Tyutchev will have agreed with Heine's argument in this first article that the Reformation had established the principles of reason and freedom of thought, and that this had led directly to the development of German philosophy. The implication (not spelled out by Heine) is that the Lutheran and other Protestant faiths bear within them the seeds of their own destruction. This certainly became Tyutchev's view. 'Protestant-ism with its numerous offshoots, having just about survived for three centuries, is dying of decay in all the countries where it had reigned until the present time', he was to write some years later.[80] Where he would part company with Heine (as is evident already in this poem) was in regretting the apparently inexorable process of cor-ruption, and dreaming that somehow, somewhere, it might be reversed.

Soon after writing the poem he returned with his family to Munich. In November there was a chance to meet the poet Pyotr Vyazemsky and his wife, who were travelling to Rome in the hope of curing their daughter Polina's tuberculosis. They spent a week in Munich, putting up at the *Goldener Hirsch*.[81] Vyazemsky was not impressed by the hotel ('the best in town, but pretty well the worst in Germany, at least of those we have seen so far');[82] more so by the city itself: 'The artist-king and poet-king (not so much for his verse as his deeds) is much engaged in improving the city's appearance and enriching it with artistic monuments from classical antiquity and the German past. [...] Munich can be acknowledged as a preparatory course for Rome.'[83] Vyazemsky met the Tyutchevs socially, and visited their home more than once.[84] Yet nowhere in his letters or notebooks of the time is there any hint that poetry was discussed, or even that he realised he was talking to a fellow poet. Hardly any of Tyutchev's verse had been published since the demise of *Galateya*, and Vyazemsky had most likely forgotten his own brief favourable mention of it in a review some four years previously; Tyutchev would of course have been the last person to remind him.

On 13 November the Vyazemskys set off on the next stage of what was to prove a fruitless mission. Years later Tyutchev remembered calling on them at their hotel in Munich: 'In the room a poor young girl was lying on a couch, coughing terribly. This was the daughter who died not long afterwards in Rome.'[85]

Among the names recorded in Vyazemsky's notebook of those he met in Munich is 'M-me de Darenberg [*sic*], a dark-eyed widow, daughter of the Bavarian Ambassador in Paris'.[86] Ernestine had originally intended to spend four months with her father in Paris,[87] and indeed an entry in her pressed-flower album records her as still there on 22 August, visiting the grave of Jean-Jacques Rousseau in nearby Ermenonville.[88] Presumably she returned to Munich soon afterwards, at the beginning of September as planned. Not long after Vyazemsky met her there, distressing news of her father prompted her to travel to Paris again. Whether she arrived before his death on 11 December is not known.[89] On a courier mission to Vienna in February Tyutchev was able to inform Aleksandr Turgenev that Ernestine's inheritance from her father, added to that from her husband, had left her a wealthy woman.[90]

As was her custom in Bavaria, Ernestine spent the summer months of 1835 in the Regensburg area. One day while staying with the Cettos at Eglofsheim, she pressed freshly-picked flowers in her album and wrote underneath: 'Souvenir of the happy days spent at Eglofsheim!! Flowers picked on 5 June 1835.' Kirill Pigaryov quotes this and later entries as probable evidence of his great-grandparents' blossoming romance.[91] It seems that Tyutchev again stopped at Eglofsheim on his way to the spa in Austria, and that during his stay he and Ernestine became closer than ever before.

On this occasion Tyutchev took the waters at Karlsbad (now Karlovy Vary, Czech Republic), 20 miles or so to the north-east of Marienbad, where he had been the previous summer. The Krüdeners were also there, together with other representatives of Munich society. Max von Lerchenfeld had come with his new wife Isabella (they had been married in Munich on 14 May).[92] Prominent among the international array of notables was the Russian Foreign Minister Count Nesselrode, relaxing before important talks between Tsar Nicholas, the Emperor of Austria and the King of Prussia to be held at Toeplitz (now Teplice) later that summer.[93] It was just the kind of milieu in which Tyutchev could shine as wit and raconteur. Writing to Amélie after resuming ambassadorial duties in St Petersburg later that year, Lerchenfeld recalled for instance 'Tyutchev's exclamations on the subject of Bibikov' as one of several abiding impressions of their time together at the spa that summer.[94]

Tyutchev seized the opportunity to plead his case for advancement with Nesselrode, who gave what was no doubt his standard response to such requests by promising to bear the supplicant in mind should any vacancies arise.[95] Amélie, Krüdener and Lerchenfeld had more success in negotiating a promotion for Krüdener to a post in St Petersburg, official confirmation of which reached Munich in the middle of October.[96] Here at last was the long-awaited chance for Tyutchev to inherit Krüdener's post as First Secretary; he immediately sent off a letter to Nesselrode staking his claim. Written in his usual elegant and polished French, the letter begins by reminding Nesselrode of the assurances he had given at Karlsbad, then goes on to list his qualifications for the post. These include a sound knowledge of diplomatic practice and of Bavarian and German affairs, acquired during thirteen years' service there. Tyutchev also claims (with 'a certain degree of exaggeration' as one authority generously puts it)[97] that in the years since Potyomkin's departure he had been entrusted with composing most of the despatches on political affairs from Munich. (Since Gagarin's arrival as Ambassador Tyutchev had in fact, in the words of the same authority, taken 'practically no part in the work of the Embassy'.)[98] Perhaps unwisely in this context, he also reminds Nesselrode of his involvement in the Greek question. In an attempt to evoke sympathy for his financial problems he writes of being 'reduced to the sad necessity of serving for a living', and of having a wife and two children to support, while hastening to add that he has no-one to blame for this but himself: 'in such a precarious and subordinate position as mine marriage is the most unpardonable of imprudences. I know, as I have been expiating it for seven years now. But I confess I should be profoundly unhappy if the expiation of this wrong should extend to three individuals who are completely innocent of it.'[99] Perhaps the most compelling reason for wanting the post — that it would enable him to stay near Ernestine — could of course not be mentioned.

He also enlisted Amélie and Krüdener to make representations on his behalf, but three months later Nesselrode replied to his letter that cutbacks in the Foreign Service ordered by the Emperor had made it necessary to allocate any posts falling vacant to diplomats made redundant elsewhere, and that as a result he was unable to offer him the position. To sugar the pill he announced that the Emperor had agreed to promote him from his honorary court rank of Gentleman of the Chamber to that of Chamberlain.[100] Soon afterwards came official notification that Apollonius von Maltitz, Russian Chargé d'Affaires in Brazil, had been appointed as Krüdener's successor.[101]

It was a severe blow to Tyutchev's pride, let alone his hopes of financial salvation. For all his disdain of careerism in any shape or form, and despite the maverick qualities often displayed in his professional life, he was well aware of his own ability and even had what Eleonore once called 'his dreams of ambition'.[102] 'My lot at this Embassy is rather strange,' he wrote bitterly to his parents. 'It has fallen to me to survive everyone here, and to inherit no-one's position.'[103] And his resentment is barely masked by the flippant tone adopted in a letter to Ivan Gagarin: 'Never having taken the [Foreign] Service seriously, it is only just that the Service should also make fun of me. [...] I do not have the slightest rational motive for persevering in a career which offers me no chance of a future.'[104]

It has been suggested that Tyutchev's slow progress up the diplomatic ladder was the result of deliberate blocking by Nesselrode, who (so it is claimed) was both suspicious of Tyutchev's political views and jealous of his talent. Proponents of this thesis draw a parallel with Nesselrode's treatment of the outstanding diplomat Aleksandr Gorchakov, who despite being held back by Nesselrode went on to become Foreign Minister under Alexander II.[105] In fact there is no evidence to support such a claim, at least not for this stage of Tyutchev's career. Certainly the constraints on the Foreign Service referred to by Nesselrode were real enough. In November 1835 Max von Lerchenfeld warned Amélie from his vantage point in St Petersburg that her and Krüdener's attempts to intercede on Tyutchev's behalf would probably come to nothing, as there was no shortage of diplomats senior to him applying for the post.[106] This indeed proved to be the case.

The setback in Tyutchev's career prospects had come hard on the heels of a more personal blow in September, when Ivan Gagarin left to return to Russia. As Gagarin later recalled, he had spent his two years as trainee diplomat in Munich 'in the closest intimacy with Tyutchev',[107] and had grown 'very fond of him'.[108] Arriving to take up his post just before his nineteenth birthday, this serious and idealistic youth must have reminded Tyutchev in many ways of the fledgling diplomat he had once been himself. Like him, Gagarin was devoted to intellectual pursuits, in particular literature and philosophy; he too attended lectures at Munich University and became personally acquainted with Schelling and other professors.[109] Politics was another consuming interest which they shared. The more Gagarin learned in Munich about the revolutionary and republican movements of France in particular, the less enamoured of them he became, and eventually he more or less abandoned the wildly utopian liberal views he had brought with him from Russia.[110] In this he was probably guided by his older friend. Tyutchev's influence in general on him at this time was according to Gagarin 'very great, and possibly had a decisive effect'.[111] In common with other Russian intellectuals of the day, Gagarin began to query what had set his country apart from the rest of Europe, and like Tyutchev found the answer in the schism between Rome and Byzantium. They would eventually draw diametrically opposed conclusions from this, with Tyutchev propounding a Slavonic reincarnation of the Eastern Empire and Gagarin entering the Jesuit priesthood. Yet at this time such unexpected developments could not be foreseen. Indeed, Gagarin later admitted that under the influence of German philosophy (and, no doubt, Tyutchev's example) he was 'never so far from religion as during those two years spent in Munich'.[112]

All these topics and more were discussed during regular cosy chats over tea and cigars at the Tyutchevs' house.[113] It is almost certain that Tyutchev felt able to confide details of his love life to Gagarin (whom he later complimented, albeit in another context, for being 'indulgent and *understanding*').[114] Their conversations, like their correspondence, will have been conducted in French, a language each spoke more easily than Russian.[115] This in no way prevented them from sharing an enthusiasm for Russian literature. Gagarin was one of the very few to whom Tyutchev showed his poetic manuscripts, and one of even fewer who recognised their true worth. He even harboured literary ambitions of his own for a while, before being forced to accept that his gifts were unequal to the task. ('O Poetry! Why do you not wish to accept me as your priest!' reads one despairing entry in his diary.)[116] Yet he remained an astute judge of the work of others, and of Tyutchev's in particular, which he did much to bring to wider attention.

The loss of such a congenial companion was felt deeply by Tyutchev. Writing to his 'very dear friend' more than six months after his departure, he confessed that 'since the moment of our separation not a day has passed without my missing you. Believe me, my dear Gagarin, there are few lovers who could in all conscience say the same to their mistress.'[117]

In the summer and autumn of 1835, after their days together at Eglofsheim, Tyutchev and Ernestine's relationship developed into a full-blown affair. Eleonore was pregnant again (always a dangerous time for their marriage); on 8 November she gave birth to their third child: another daughter, Yekaterina, or Kitty.[118] By this time Tyutchev's affair was known both to Eleonore and their immediate circle in Munich, to judge from a passage in one of Max von Lerchenfeld's letters from St Petersburg. Amélie had apparently written to him with news of the Tyutchevs' new baby and the birth of a child to the Hollensteins, who lived not far from them in Munich. However, her letter (which has not survived) evidently contained more than these bald facts, for on 15/27 November Max replied: 'Reinhard, who is fairly unknown here, blushed deeply when I told him of the birth of the Hollensteins' offspring. As for Madame Tyutchev's confinement, presumably she was the only one it caused to blush.'[119] The implication of Max's first remark (that a certain Reinhard, then keeping a low profile in St Petersburg, was known or suspected to be the father of the Hollenstein baby) seems clear enough. His second remark is more enigmatic. Is he suggesting that Tyutchev was not Kitty's father? But then why would this cause Eleonore *alone* to blush? A more likely explanation is that Max realised how embarrassing it must have been for Eleonore to give birth to Tyutchev's child at a time when he was known to be carrying on with another woman.

Two love poems, both clearly addressed to Ernestine, have been dated to this period. The first could have been written at any time between June 1835 and April 1836. The dark expressive eyes familiar from Ernestine's portraits were to become a leitmotif in Tyutchev's poems to her.

I love your eyes, their look supreme
Of smouldering flame that flares and dances...
When suddenly raising them, you seem
To burnish all who meet your glances
With lightning's pure celestial gleam...

But there's enchantment more beguiling:
In eyes cast down when keen desire
Erupts in kisses fraught with feeling,
Their pendent lashes the dull fire
Of heartsick passion half-concealing.[120]

The second shows strong parallels with a poem by Vladimir Benediktov, as originally pointed out by Kirill Pigaryov.[121] Benediktov's poem was included in a volume of his verse sent to Tyutchev by Ivan Gagarin at the end of October 1835, and it would seem safe to assume that Tyutchev's poem was written not long afterwards.[122] Although it is coloured by stylistic borrowings from Benediktov, the underlying experience is manifestly Tyutchev's own:

Last night, in reverie enchanted —
The moon's last pallid, languid beams
Upon your eyelids gently playing —
You sank into belated dreams...

The silence all about grew deeper,
And darker still the louring gloom,
The measured breathing of your bosom
Distinct now in the soundless room...

But not for long did night's pitch-darkness
Seep through the curtains' flimsy screen,
While drowsily your tossing ringlet
Toyed with some fantasy unseen...

For through the window swiftly gliding
Now all at at once slipped in with ease
A misty-white ethereal vision,
As if blown in upon the breeze...

Like some weird apparition, scurrying
Across a floor but dimly lit,
It reached the bed, snatched at the covers,
And seemed intent on mounting it...

Up like a wriggling snake it clambered,
And once on top, for all the world
Like ribbon stirred to fluttering motion,
Between the canopies unfurled —

> Where, touching all at once your bosom
> With radiance vigorous and bold,
> It forced with crimson shout of triumph
> Your silken lashes to unfold![123]

Richard Gregg refers to 'an indefinable erotic quality [...] in these lines, which the "events" described, namely, dawn awakening a sleeping woman, cannot wholly account for'.[124] His analysis of this quality centres on Tyutchev's choice of a snake to represent the ray of sunlight which interrupts the woman's sleep. It is of course a textbook phallic symbol, and in this case Gregg's Freudian sleuthing appears to have hit the mark. He aptly concludes that 'in the final synesthetic image of light breaking across the barriers of flesh we have a symbol for sexual union as old as Zeus' shower of gold, and as modern as Dylan Thomas's "Light Breaks Where No Sun Shines" '.[125] The whole poem could indeed be taken as an illustration of Tyutchev's own dictum that 'in verse, as beneath a mask, one can say almost anything with impunity'.[126]

The affair continued into the New Year, and is almost certainly reflected in more notes beneath flowers and leaves preserved in Ernestine's album: 'Memento of Sunday 7 February 1836'; 'Memento of 20 March 1836!!!'[127] By now the strains were beginning to tell. Tyutchev wrote to Ivan Gagarin of 'a winter spent in constant friction, for which none but I know the reason'.[128] His secretiveness can only have added to Eleonore's mental anguish. To complete their woes, by winter's end he was once again suffering from deep depression.

iii An Unforeseen Event

On 14 April half the population of Munich turned out to welcome King Ludwig and his consort on their return from a five-month visit to Greece. Buildings along the route of the procession were decorated with flags and bunting, and well-wishers packed the streets despite falling snow.[129] All the Tyutchev household went except for Eleonore. She had been in delicate health since the birth of Kitty and could not risk exposing herself to the unseasonably cold weather. Alone in the house, she poured out her anxieties in a letter to Nikolay, then in Moscow on leave from his post in Warsaw. Her first concern was for her husband: 'Théodore's health [...] is deteriorating from day to day. O my friend, this is what oppresses me more than anything, I cannot conceal it from you — nothing is more distressing than to see poor Théodore's physical — and, as a consequence — mental decline'. She knows his illness to be 'to a great extent haemorrhoidal', but this is only part of the story: 'He is a man stricken by the strangest imaginable paralysis of forces, preoccupied and consumed by an almost continual unease, this deadly torpor giving way only to fits of despair and futile rage.' She goes on to detail his 'attacks of frenetic irritation, followed by this listlessness, this perpetual anxiety, this depression — these strange ideas, to put it no more than that'. He himself repeatedly tells her that 'he would rather undergo a fatal illness than suffer in this way, with no hope of escape'. None of the prescribed remedies has done any good; his doctor has recommended a change of climate and sea bathing, but this is beyond their means, and in any case no leave would be forthcoming until Maltitz arrived. Eleonore is in despair: 'Ah, dear Nikolay, have pity on me, comfort me if you can'.

216

Such selfless concern for her 'Théodore's' health, coupled with the absence of any reference to her own, is characteristic. Yet the letter is shot through with other anxieties too, not least the suspicion that she was being kept in the dark on a series of matters. She writes for example that Tyutchev is most concerned to know if Nikolay received his last letter, for 'it seems to me that he would not much care for it to fall into hands other than yours. I do not know the reason for this, but would ask you to reassure him, for if it arrived after your departure [from Moscow], they will probably have opened the package.' Next she queries a suggestion made by Nikolay in his last letter: 'Tell me why you think it desirable that Théodore should go to Moscow, for even though this is almost impossible from a practical point of view, I should like to know the object of such a proposal.' Finally, and most intriguingly: 'You speak to us in veiled and unintelligible terms of things you have heard in Moscow. We are disturbed by this; why this reticence [— — —]'[130]

Just how the letter continues at this point must remain a mystery, for the following six lines in the manuscript have been heavily deleted in ink, evidently by someone other than Eleonore.[131] As a result we can only speculate as to the gossip or rumours Nikolay appears to have heard in Moscow. Could they have concerned Tyutchev's affair with Ernestine? Whatever their nature, Eleonore's response clearly contained material revealing and embarrassing enough to merit being removed from prying eyes by a member of the Tyutchev family at some later date.

The letter was a cry from the heart, a plea for support and reassurance addressed to one who, even at a distance, was more able to offer them than her husband. In similar circumstances (Tyutchev was suffering from depression again) Eleonore would later write to his mother: 'my heart is filled with cares, and in the state Théodore is in, I do not even dare speak to him about them, or ask for his advice and support'.[132] Now too he was oblivious to the warning signs. And just two weeks after Eleonore's distraught letter to Nikolay he was by his own account bowled over by an 'unforeseen event, potentially hideous in its consequences,' which 'very nearly turned my life upside down'.[133]

On the day in question he left the house at about four in the afternoon. He told Eleonore he was going to dine in town; she may well have suspected a rendezvous with Ernestine. About an hour later she suddenly felt (as she subsequently told him) 'her brain as if invaded by a rush of blood, and all her ideas became confused, leaving her with nothing but a feeling of inexpressible anguish and the irresistible urge to free herself of this at any cost'. Feverishly rummaging through some drawers, she found a small fancy-dress dagger from the previous year's Carnival. According to Tyutchev's account, 'the sight of steel fixed her thoughts, and in an access of complete frenzy she stabbed herself several times in the chest. Fortunately none of the wounds was serious'. With no-one to restrain her (Clotilde and Aunt Karoline were out at the time), she ran downstairs and out through the front door. Still losing blood, she staggered along one of the streets radiating from the Karolinenplatz, before finally collapsing '300 paces' (perhaps 200 yards) from the house. She was brought home by servants of their neighbours the Hollensteins.[134]

The unsuspecting Tyutchev returned to find his wife lying in her room, 'bathed in her own blood'. As he wrote to Gagarin a few days later, 'For twenty-four hours her life was in imminent danger, and it was only after bleeding her and applying 40 leeches that [the doctor] managed to restore her to reason... Now she is over the worst of it, but the nervous shock will make itself felt for a long time yet.'[135]

What had driven Eleonore to such extremes will have been clear enough to those in the Tyutchevs' immediate circle. Munich society at large appears to have jumped to a different conclusion. In a letter dated 12 May Franz von Baader reported a widely held view that 'complete financial ruin' lay behind the suicide attempt.[136] Either way it was a scandal the prim and proper Russian Ambassador could do without. When Krüdener left with Amélie on 3 May to take up his new post in St Petersburg, among the routine diplomatic mail carried by him was a letter from Ambassador Gagarin to Nesselrode requesting Tyutchev's transfer. In it Gagarin informed the Foreign Minister that Krüdener would on arrival brief him in detail on Tyutchev's 'unhappy and desperate position, and of the most urgent necessity of extricating him from it'. The letter praises Tyutchev's ability and intellect, but claims that 'because of the awkward and false situation he has placed himself in through his disastrous [*funeste*] marriage, [he] is presently unable to carry out his duties as Legation Secretary'. There is also a request for a grant of 1,000 (presumably, silver) roubles to enable Tyutchev to pay off his debts before moving on. Keenly aware of his staffing problems with Krüdener now gone and his replacement not expected until the autumn, Gagarin reports that he has asked the Russian Ambassador in Vienna to let his (Gagarin's) son Yevgeny, currently serving there, come to Munich to help him out, for (as he writes) 'nothing can be expected of Monsieur Tutscheff '.[137]

In the event no precipitate action was taken. There seems to have been some delay in seconding Yevgeny Gagarin to Munich, although he was there by the end of the year.[138] Even so, until Maltitz arrived the Ambassador had to rely on Tyutchev's help. In the quiet period of July and August he even took over as Chargé d'Affaires for eight weeks while Gagarin was away at Karlsbad.[139] Perhaps partly in recognition of this, at the end of July a generous grant of 1,000 *chervontsy* to pay off his debts was belatedly authorised 'in recognition of zealous service'.[140]

None of this was to be foreseen in May, however. At that time the prospect of a sideways transfer seemed imminent, and filled Tyutchev with misgiving. Although recent events had reconciled him to the idea of leaving Munich, pride demanded that it be for a more senior post elsewhere.[141] News of Eleonore's suicide attempt would soon reach St Petersburg, and the rumour mill would set to work on it. Indeed, his parents in Moscow were very soon shocked to hear garbled reports emanating from the capital that Nelly had actually succeeded in killing herself.[142] Tyutchev's main concern was that these wagging tongues could seriously harm his career prospects.[143] Although the Krüdeners would no doubt stand his corner once they arrived, additional damage limitation was called for. Having failed to reply to any of the several letters Ivan Gagarin had sent since returning to Russia, he decided that now was the time to write to his young friend. The version of events given in his letter lays great stress on physiological factors: Eleonore's health had suffered after the birth of Kitty; by the middle of April, when she had weaned the baby from breast-feeding, she seemed better, but the doctors had awaited the return of her periods 'not without some concern'; these had begun again 'with extremely violent cramps' on the morning of her suicide attempt; even the mental anguish which drove her to stab herself later that day was according to Tyutchev physiological in nature. He concludes: 'This is the *absolute truth* of the matter: the cause was purely physical. It was a rush of blood to the brain.' Then comes the nub of his letter: 'And if it should happen that someone seeks in your presence to give a perhaps more romantic, and yet completely false, colouring to the whole affair, I expect you as a friend, my dear Gagarin, to deny such absurd versions quite openly.'[144]

Although no reply to this has survived, the quandary it must have put Gagarin in is easy enough to imagine. He knew the score with regard to Tyutchev and Ernestine, and must have been convinced of those very aspects of the whole sorry affair he was now being asked to deny. Tyutchev's implied request that he publicly represent Eleonore's emotional distress as no more than symptoms of 'women's troubles' will have been particularly distasteful to Gagarin, who had come to feel great sympathy and affection for her during his time in Munich. There is some evidence that he did in fact ignore his friend's request. Later that year, on 17/29 December, Aleksandr Turgenev noted in his diary in St Petersburg: 'Pr[ince] Gagarin told me about the little widow made pregnant by Tyutchev'.[145] (The 'little widow' — *vdovushka* — is how Turgenev habitually refers to Ernestine in his diaries, so there can be no doubt as to who is meant.) If anyone had a right to know this, it was Turgenev, and on this occasion at least Gagarin had clearly decided that openness was more important than loyalty to a friend. There is of course the question of how reliable Gagarin's information can be considered. Although he must have received it at second hand, he is unlikely to have relayed such sensitive matter to Turgenev, of all people, if he suspected it to be no more than unsubstantiated tittle-tattle. Apart from which, he will have been aware that Turgenev would at some stage be able to verify the facts with Tyutchev himself (they did in fact meet some six months later). The presumption must be that Gagarin was satisfied as to the reliability of his source (who could, for instance, have been the Krüdeners). The editors of Turgenev's diaries appear to have reached the same conclusion. They state: 'We have no grounds for doubting the authenticity of the fact of which Turgenev was informed on 17 December' — and go on to suggest it may even have been the devastating news of Ernestine's pregnancy that proved the breaking-point for Eleonore, driving her to her desperate act of self-mutilation.[146]

A month after that act Eleonore took advantage of an invitation from her sister Louise to stay with her and her husband Count Ludwig at Burgfarrnbach near Fürth. Her doctors had recommended a stay in the country to recuperate, and now in the Pückler Limpurgs' palatial home with its extensive grounds she and the children could enjoy fresh air, solitude and freedom from the social constraints of the capital, not to mention the support and sympathy of her sister and in-laws. After four weeks there she could write to Tyutchev's mother that she felt 'very well, and even better than before my illness' (discretion or loyalty evidently dictating that she go along with her husband's gloss on events).[147] She had timed her departure from Munich at the beginning of June to coincide with Tyutchev's on a routine courier mission to Vienna.[148] However, he was back again by about the 23rd,[149] and for some three weeks after this he and Ernestine were both in Munich. Although Eleonore knew this, she stayed on at Burgfarrnbach, returning to Munich only at some time between 20 and 24 July.[150] By then Ernestine had left. To judge from the entry in her flower album, it was no routine leave-taking: 'Memento of my departure from Munich!! Monday 18 July 1836'.[151] Presumably she and Tyutchev had — for a second time — taken a 'final farewell' of each other; after this there is no evidence of their having met for over a year. If Ernestine was indeed pregnant, she will presumably have arranged to go somewhere, probably abroad, where she could remain incognito for the latter stages of the pregnancy and the birth, after which the child could be given away for adoption. Whether this is what actually happened we shall probably never know. Ernestine's flower album, which might be expected to provide clues as to her whereabouts that summer and autumn, is silent on the subject. However, it is silence of a particularly eloquent kind, for the entry following that for 18 July has at some stage been carefully cut out of the album.[152]

iv Poems Sent from Germany

When they set out on 3 May 1836 for their new life in St Petersburg, Amélie and Krüdener were carrying private correspondence from Tyutchev to his parents and sister, the letter to Ivan Gagarin quoted above, and a fairly bulky package, also addressed to him. This contained the manuscripts of all Tyutchev's poems that had escaped destruction in 1833 or been written since, sent in response to a request from his young friend.

After leaving Munich, Gagarin had spent some months in Moscow, then at the end of 1835 gravitated to St Petersburg, where before long he found a niche as Third Secretary at the Foreign Ministry.[153] Almost immediately he plunged into the social and artistic life of the capital, establishing close contact with the literary world, in particular its leading lights Pushkin, Zhukovsky and Vyazemsky.[154] Learning that Pushkin was planning to publish a new literary journal, *Sovremennik* (*The Contemporary*), he sensed an opening for Tyutchev and wrote asking him to send some of his poems. So it was that Tyutchev parcelled up all the poetic 'scribblings' ('*paperasses*') he could lay his hands on, glad of an opportunity, not to win literary fame but rather (as he wrote in the accompanying letter) to rid himself of tiresome clutter. 'Do with them as you will,' he instructed Gagarin.[155] It was another cathartic clear-out, if on a somewhat more modest scale than that of 1833.

What Gagarin received was an assorted bundle of 65 poems in both draft and fair copies, often in more than one version. Tyutchev had made no effort to sort or edit the manuscripts. Despite this, Gagarin wrote back that he had spent 'the most delightful hours' reading them, and now wished to share his 'enthusiasm' with others.[156] But first they had to be put into a more presentable and legible form. He spent some time carefully copying out most of the poems into a notebook, and gave this to Vyazemsky to read.[157] At this stage he was still concerned that feelings of friendship might have distorted his critical judgement.[158] He need not have worried. A few days later (as he reported to Tyutchev) he called unannounced on Vyazemsky towards midnight (it was the season of 'white nights'), to find him and Zhukovsky 'reading your verses and completely under the spell of the poetic sentiment which they breathe'. It was decided there and then that Pushkin should be asked to print 'a selection of five or six poems' in his journal, and that steps be taken to publish a separate collection of the verse in book form. Pushkin was also impressed by what he read in the notebook passed on by Vyazemsky and Zhukovsky. Gagarin, who saw him soon after he had been given the poems, reported to Tyutchev that 'he spoke to me of them with a just and heartfelt appreciation [*avec une appréciation juste et bien sentie*]'.[159] Another witness would write two years later of the 'heartfelt emotion [*umileniye*]' with which the great writer had read Tyutchev's poems.[160]

Pushkin decided to publish, not just the half dozen poems originally suggested, but twenty-five. The first sixteen appeared that autumn in prime position on the first pages of issue No. 3 of *Sovremennik*, followed by another eight in No. 4, all under the heading 'Poems Sent from Germany' and with the attribution 'Munich. F.T.'. The censors had rejected one poem in entirety, as well as two stanzas of another, 'Nature is not what you would have it...'; Pushkin insisted against their wishes on printing the latter with rows of dots to indicate the missing verses.[161] A further fourteen poems by Tyutchev were published in *Sovremennik* between 1837 and 1841 by the editorial team which took over after Pushkin's death.

Writing to inform Tyutchev of these developments, in particular the planned volume of his poetry, Gagarin concluded with the request: 'Entrust me with the honorary mission of being your publisher, send me some more poems, and endeavour to come up with a suitable title'.[162] Tyutchev's reply must have surprised him: 'I doubt very much that the scribblings I sent you merit the honour of being printed, especially as a separate volume. Every six months now things are being published in Russia which are infinitely better.' (He goes on to praise at some length the *Three Tales* of Nikolay Pavlov, which had recently caused a stir for their implied criticism of serfdom.) Nevertheless he agrees that as his 'rhymes' are now Gagarin's property, he can do with them as he pleases. As for sending more poems, he cannot, as he destroyed most of his 'poetic elucubrations' at the end of 1833, but ('if you persist in your ideas of publication') suggests Raich may still have some of those sent to him for *Galateya*.[163]

There is of course a certain element of self-parody in all this, with Tyutchev slipping into the role of self-deprecating aristocrat-dilettante. Yet the fact that he even manages to get the name of Raich's journal wrong — calling it '*Babochka*' ('*Butterfly*') from the emblem on its title page — suggests a genuine indifference towards the publication of his poetry. It is an impression which his actions (or rather lack of them) only help to confirm.

Following up Tyutchev's lead, Gagarin contacted Raich via Shevyryov, from whom at the beginning of November he received a package of 52 poems. He then set about the task of sorting the manuscripts and listing the 117 poems now in his possession.[164] In June or July 1837, while Tyutchev was in St Petersburg, Gagarin drafted two versions of a list of contents for the proposed book.[165] This was as far as the project was to get. On 27 July/ 8 August Gagarin was sent to London on Foreign Ministry business and then took up a junior diplomatic post in Paris, returning to Russia on leave only two years later.[166] Such a prolonged absence from Russia must have upset his publishing plans; in any case, the almost total lack of critical response to the poems in *Sovremennik* hardly augured well for the success of a separate volume. Despite the space and prominence allotted to the poems in Pushkin's journal, the concealment (presumably at Tyutchev's own request) of his identity behind the initials 'F.T.', or in later issues 'F.T-v.', did nothing to promote his literary fame. Only a small circle of initiates knew who this 'F.T.' from Munich was;[167] the wider reading public, unable to associate the poems with a name, soon forgot them. Yet they were at least there in print; eventually they would be rediscovered, and this in turn would establish his reputation as a major poet. For this reason alone Gagarin's role was pivotal: without him Tyutchev's poetry may well have been doomed to oblivion.

Time and absence inevitably weakened the bonds of friendship between Tyutchev and Gagarin. The younger man in particular grew into new enthusiasms and sought out new mentors. As early as January 1837 Tyutchev was asking his parents if they had any news of Gagarin, complaining (somewhat hypocritically) that his friend had stopped writing.[168] Perhaps the events surrounding Eleonore's suicide attempt had forced Gagarin to see his hero in a new and less flattering light. The following year Tyutchev, now serving at the Russian Embassy in Turin, wrote encouraging him to apply for a post which had fallen vacant there. 'Keep well, and retain a modicum of friendship for me,' the letter ends.[169] As far as we know, Gagarin never followed up this opportunity to be reunited with him. In 1843, a year before Tyutchev's final return to Russia, Gagarin was ordained as a Jesuit priest and settled in Paris, where he remained until his death in 1882. On leaving Russia he took with him all the manuscripts received both from Tyutchev himself and from Raich, and took care to preserve them. After the poet's death in 1873 he returned them to the family, and many previously unpublished poems appeared in print as a result. Gagarin's collection was to become the bedrock of later editions of Tyutchev's verse, at least for the period up to 1837.

v End of an Era

For Tyutchev life went on after Ernestine's departure from Munich in the summer of 1836. Just days later he was writing to Ivan Gagarin how much he missed Amélie...[170] He and Eleonore did their best to patch things up. It seems that some sort of line was drawn under the affair with Ernestine and plans made for a fresh start. Eleonore wanted them to leave Munich, and Tyutchev agreed they would spend the coming winter with his parents in St Petersburg, where with the Krüdeners' help he could press his case for a new and improved posting. His parents very much hoped they would settle in Russia for good. After the marriage of their daughter Darya to the writer Nikolay Sushkov earlier that year, Ivan and Yekaterina Tyutchev had let their house in Armenian Lane and moved to the family estate at Ovstug for the summer.[171] Writing to Tyutchev from there, his mother reportedly spoke of feeling 'completely forlorn' now that their last child had flown the nest.[172] Her letter has not survived, but was evidently in the same vein as another written to Darya at about the same time:

> it would be good if Fedya managed to obtain a post in Petersburg: his wife would be glad because all her sons are in Petersburg, and we should be able to live with them, and in the summer they could come to Ovstug for two or three months — it would be a great comfort for us in our old age to have one of the children with us.[173]

Eleonore was overjoyed at her mother-in-law's proposal. She wrote back to her from Burgfarrnbach, where Tyutchev had forwarded the letter:

> Dear Mama, there are words in your letter which made my heart pound and brought tears to my eyes. Could it be possible that we shall be reunited this

winter in St Petersburg? [...] I confess that at this moment this possibility seems more attractive to me than ever; I do not know if it is because of the bad days I had in Munich, or all that is so disagreeable and false about Théodore's situation, but living in Munich has become a cruel burden to me, and my only hope is that one way or another everything must change.[174]

At the beginning of September, after returning from Karlsbad, Ambassador Gagarin requested leave of absence for Tyutchev for the coming winter, citing family circumstances which required his return to Russia.[175] This was granted in October.[176] All seemed to be going to plan; but then Gagarin's health took a turn for the worse, and with still no prospect of Maltitz arriving he asked Tyutchev to stay on until the spring.[177] Disappointed, Eleonore resolved to travel to St Petersburg with the children on her own, but was persuaded against this. Soon afterwards she was glad she had stayed, for Munich was hit by a cholera epidemic, and as she wrote to her mother-in-law, 'knowing Théodore to be on his own here, I should have reproached myself every moment of the day'.[178]

The cholera went on claiming victims until well into the New Year. Tyutchev found its effects on the social life of the capital particularly irksome. 'Munich, never entertaining at the best of times, is now almost unimaginably dull and dreary,' he wrote to his parents in January.[179] Eleonore's account was more sober: 'We have never seen a winter more sadly silent than this one; most of society has abandoned the city, many families are in mourning'.[180] Tyutchev and his family were not affected by the disease, but by the New Year he was suffering from 'his usual complaint' (haemorrhoids), as well as 'a rheumatism of the head, which torments him greatly'.[181] Eleonore was also distressed by a renewed deterioration in his mental health. He had sunk into such a deep depression that, as she wrote to Nikolay, 'there are days when even I do not recognise him any more'. In what had by now become a familiar story she describes 'his insane irritability, his angry outbursts, his ideas which are almost absurd, and finally this utter depression which renders any distraction impossible for him'.[182] More than ever she was convinced that a complete change of scene was needed. In February she wrote to his mother:

> If only you could see him, dear Mama, as he has been for a year now — depressed, downhearted, ill, entangled in countless oppressive and disagreeable relationships, from which some kind of moral inertia renders him incapable of freeing himself — then you would be persuaded, as I am, that to get him away from here by whatever means will be to save his life. I cannot tell you any more — there are so many things which are difficult to say, and even more impossible to write [...].[183]

Tyutchev too seems to have realised that only drastic measures would ever free him from the 'oppressive and disagreeable relationships' to which he seemed addicted. Constitutionally incapable of committing himself to one woman, he could nevertheless respond at least with gratitude to Eleonore's continuing love in the face of all he had done to betray it, and even guiltily acknowledge that some concessions were called for on his part. In order to escape what Eleonore called the 'disastrous rut' they were in,[184] he gave her his solemn undertaking that they would leave Munich for good just as soon as possible.[185] And writing to his parents in April, he paid her this heartfelt tribute:

> [...] there is in this poor woman a strength of spirit commensurate only with the tenderness of her heart. I have my reasons for saying this to you. Only God who created her knows all that is of worth within her soul. But I want you who love me to know that never has a human being been loved by another as I have by her. I can say, almost from experience, that for eleven years now there has not been a single day of her life when, in order to assure my happiness, she would not have consented to die for me without a moment's hesitation. That is something indeed sublime and indeed rare, when it is not just an empty phrase.
>
> What I say must seem strange to you. But, I repeat, I have my reasons. This testimony of my appreciation is but a poor attempt at expiation.[186]

Throughout the winter their plans for leaving had been on hold. On top of everything else Ambassador Gagarin had become seriously ill; by January it was clear that he would not survive.[187] As a result most of the day-to-day running of the Embassy fell on Tyutchev's shoulders, at least until the long-awaited arrival of Maltitz on 9 February.[188] Just two weeks later the new First Secretary had the sad duty of informing his superiors in St Petersburg of the Ambassador's death.[189] With the appointment of Dmitry Severin as Gagarin's successor Tyutchev was at last free to take the leave due to him. 'I cannot wait to get away from here,' he wrote to his parents on 15 April. '[...] Before leaving I shall sell all my furniture here. For whatever happens, I am firmly resolved never to return.'[190]

His parents sent money to cover the cost of the journey.[191] About the middle of May Eleonore went on with the children and maids to her sister at Burgfarrnbach, hoping to rest a little after the upheaval of moving.[192] On the 19th she was joined there by Tyutchev. Two days later the family set off in a hired carriage to catch the steam packet leaving Travemünde on 3 June.[193]

9 Fair Prospects (Turin, 1837-1838)

i Death of a Poet

After the publication of Tyutchev's poems in *Sovremennik* a meeting with Pushkin had seemed inevitable. Yet this was not to be. Towards the end of February (NS) startling news from St Petersburg reached Munich in a despatch sent by Maximilian von Lerchenfeld:

> Russia has just lost its greatest man of literature, Mr. Alexandre Pouschkin, the most famous Poet it ever had. He died at the age of thirty-seven, at the apex of his career, after being gravely wounded in a duel. The details of this catastrophe, unfortunately provoked by the dead man himself with a blindness and a kind of frenetic hatred well worthy of his Moorish origins, have for days been the sole talk of the town here in the capital. His opponent in the duel was his own brother-in-law, Mr. Georges de Heeckeren, French by birth and adopted son of Baron Heeckeren, the Dutch ambassador. The younger Mr. Heeckeren, formerly known as d'Antès [*sic*], was an officer in the '*chevalier gardes*' and had recently married Mrs. Pouschkin's sister.[1]

The news soon spread through the diplomatic community in Munich; couriers and any other visitors from St Petersburg were no doubt questioned on the background to the bare facts outlined by Lerchenfeld. The story that emerged, for all its twists and turns, seemed on the face of it a straightforward case of jealousy and slighted honour.[2] Pushkin's beautiful young wife Natalya had for some time been amorously pursued by Georges d'Anthès, a legitimist refugee from the France of Louis Philippe serving as an officer in the Russian Chevalier Guards, an élite regiment which provided the imperial bodyguard. Although Natalya had not allowed things to go beyond the accepted norms of salon flirtation (and certainly not as far as Pushkin was prepared to take his own extramarital affairs), d'Anthès had become obsessed with her and was not easily dissuaded. He was encouraged in his persistent wooing of Natalya by his adoptive father, the Dutch Ambassador Jacob van Heeckeren. Things came to a head on 4/16 November 1836, when copies of a scurrilous anonymous 'diploma' admitting Pushkin to 'the Most Serene Order of Cuckolds' were received in the post by him and several of his acquaintances. This was in all probability no more than a malicious prank of a kind popular with young blades at the time, and at first Pushkin seems to have been prepared to shrug it off; however, it led him to question Natalya, who revealed the full story of d'Anthès's harassment of her. Although he was totally convinced of her innocence in the matter, his sense of honour was outraged at this assault on both his wife's and his own reputation, and he challenged d'Anthès to a duel. Intervention by

Heeckeren and Pushkin's friends — Zhukovsky in particular — persuaded him to agree to a two weeks' postponement. During this period Heeckeren let it be known that his adopted son was really in love with Natalya's younger (and less attractive) sister Yekaterina, and on 17/29 November their engagement was officially announced. Pushkin now withdrew his challenge, convinced that public opinion would revile d'Anthès as a coward for resorting to marriage to save his skin. This did not happen: on the contrary, d'Anthès attracted widespread admiration for what was interpreted by many in society as a noble act of self-sacrifice on his part to save the reputation of either Natalya or Yekaterina, or possibly both. After marrying Yekaterina on 10/22 January he continued his pursuit of Natalya quite openly. Goaded beyond endurance, Pushkin sent Heeckeren a highly insulting letter accusing him of orchestrating the whole business. The challenge which the letter was clearly intended to provoke came not from Heeckeren himself, but d'Anthès. The duel took place on 27 January/ 8 February. D'Anthès was only slightly injured, but Pushkin received a severe gunshot wound to the stomach from which he died two days later.

Huge crowds flocked to Pushkin's apartment on the Moyka canal to pay their last respects. The authorities feared with some justification that this unprecedented outpouring of popular feeling could turn against them. Newspapers were forbidden to print anything but a brief dispassionate report of Pushkin's death, with no mention of the duel; recriminations followed for the one or two eulogies which managed nevertheless to slip through. The venue for the funeral service was switched at the last moment to a smaller church, after which the coffin was spirited away at dead of night and under police escort to a monastery near the poet's family estate in Pskov province, with only his friend Aleksandr Turgenev to accompany him on this final journey. Here he was buried in a low-key ceremony attended by no more than a few mourners.

Even now many in high society continued to take d'Anthès's side and to condemn Pushkin for unreasonable and hot-headed behaviour which they unthinkingly attributed to the 'Moorish origins' cited by Lerchenfeld (Pushkin himself had always taken great pride in his maternal great-grandfather Gannibal, an African negro slave presented as a gift to Peter the Great while still a boy, who went on to achieve high rank and ennoblement for his outstanding services to the state). However, Pushkin's friends, who had also been puzzled and exasperated by his intransigence before the duel, now found among his effects a copy of his letter to Heeckeren and the draft of another (which in the event he had never sent) to the Chief of Police and Head of the Third Section, Count Benckendorff. In both letters Pushkin claimed to have incontrovertible evidence that Heeckeren was responsible for the notorious 'diplomas'. In this he was almost certainly mistaken, but the apparent strength of his conviction persuaded Zhukovsky, Vyazemsky, Turgenev and others that there could have been more to the whole affair than they had suspected. Copies of the letters were passed from hand to hand in the city, and speculation and conspiracy theories ran wild in the officially imposed information vacuum. The names of other enemies Pushkin had made at court were bandied about, including Count and Countess Nesselrode and the Minister of Education Sergey Uvarov, until the public imagination was filled with a whole gallery of sinister plotters who had supposedly conspired to bring about Pushkin's downfall. In impassioned verses a young Cornet of Hussars, Mikhail Lermontov, directly accused court circles of complicity in Pushkin's death:

> You who surround the throne in ravening collection —
> Butchers of Freedom, scourge of Genius and Fame —
>   Now cloak yourselves in all the law's protection
>   To stamp out Truth and Justice's pure flame!

The poem concludes with a warning to these unnamed luminaries that, for all their power to subvert earthly justice, they will one day have to answer to a higher instance: 'And all your black gore will not serve to make atonement/ For this, the poet's righteous blood!'[3]

Capturing the mood of bitter discontent with Nicholas's 'iron winter', Lermontov's 'Death of a Poet' spread rapidly through the city in handwritten copies, forcing the authorities to take action. On the Tsar's orders the author was arrested and medically examined for signs of insanity before being transferred to a regiment in the Caucasus.[4]

Heeckeren's recall to The Hague, without the audience normally granted by the Tsar to departing ambassadors, provided further fuel for speculation. Having already made himself unpopular with both Nicholas and his own monarch, he now found himself the object of the Tsar's displeasure for his role in encouraging d'Anthès's pursuit of Natalya; in any case the public scandal surrounding the duel had made it impossible for him to stay on. On 21 March/ 2 April, shortly before Heeckeren's departure, d'Anthès had also left the country in disgrace. Found guilty by a court martial of the nominally capital offence of duelling, he had as was usual in such cases been handed a more lenient sentence. The Tsar had decreed that d'Anthès be reduced to the ranks and, as he was not a Russian subject, deported.

Far from the fevered atmosphere of St Petersburg, Tyutchev too composed a poetic response to the death of Pushkin:

29th January 1837

> Whose hand unleashed the lead that shattered
> Our poet's heart for evermore?
> Who smashed that fragile, precious store
> And all its sacred essence scattered?
> Be now his guilt or innocence
> Before our earthly laws contended,
> A higher judgement seat has branded
> Him regicide for all time hence.
>
> But you, denied your rightful lease,
> Consigned to darkness cold and final:
> To your remains be peace eternal,
> To you, the poet's shade, be peace!
> Transcending gossip vain and spurious,
> To sacred, lonely heights you soared:
> For gods you were a sounding-board,
> Yet flesh and blood... blood hot and furious.

And to assuage your thirst for honour
In that most noble blood you paid —
And on your bier the people laid
Their grief to form a hero's banner.
Let Him condemn your rush to vengeance
Who sees all strife and knows all pain:
In Russia's heart you shall remain
As radiant as first love's remembrance!⁵

Given that Tyutchev's poetic response to events tended to be immediate, there is no reason to disagree with Georgy Chulkov's suggestion that these lines were written soon after the news of Pushkin's death reached Munich.⁶ Indeed, in some ways the poem reflects the line taken by Lerchenfeld in his despatch. He acknowledges Pushkin as Russia's 'greatest man of literature [...], the most famous Poet it ever had', while at the same time blaming him for provoking the duel 'with a blindness and a kind of frenetic hatred'. As might be expected, Tyutchev is more appreciative of Pushkin the poet; yet he too cites Pushkin the man's 'rush to vengeance' and 'blood hot and furious' as factors contributing to his downfall. Even so — uncomfortably aware perhaps of his own experience of the mismatch between poetic genius and moral virtue — he is careful to leave any judgement of such human failings to the Almighty.

The first four lines of the poem have been claimed by some to hint at the supposed conspiracy against Pushkin more openly alleged by Lermontov.⁷ Why, they ask, should Tyutchev query the identity of Pushkin's killer, unless it be to imply that d'Anthès was no more than a willing tool in the hands of others? However, lines 5 to 8 narrow down these supposed instigators to one at most (Heeckeren, say): hardly a major conspiracy. And even that seems a highly contrived reading. On the other hand, if we accept Chulkov's suggestion that the poem was written in Munich at a time when very little was known yet about d'Anthès beyond his name, Tyutchev's rhetorical questions make much more sense. And indeed, there is strong internal evidence in favour of Chulkov's dating. The lines 'Be now his guilt or innocence/ Before our earthly laws contended' can only have been written *before* about the middle of March (NS), when news of the court martial's verdict on d'Anthès (delivered on 19 February/ 3 March) would have reached Munich, rendering any further speculation on that score pointless.

ii Back in St Petersburg

Fate had denied Tyutchev a meeting with Pushkin. The best he could do was seek out those friends of the dead poet who had helped to see his work published in *Sovremennik*. Arriving in St Petersburg on or just after 25 May/ 6 June,⁸ he learnt that of these only Vyazemsky was in town. Ivan Gagarin would return from a visit to Moscow a week later,⁹ but Zhukovsky was away for the duration of Tyutchev's stay, accompanying the heir to the throne, Grand Duke Alexander, on a tour of Russia.¹⁰ Vyazemsky was — with Zhukovsky, Andrey Krayevsky and Pyotr Pletnyov — one of the collective editorial team which had taken over the running of *Sovremennik*. He appears to have encouraged Tyutchev to carry on contributing to the journal, which published nine new poems by him over the next three years. He also gave him the latest issue, a special edition dedicated to Pushkin's memory. It contained previously unpublished works by the dead poet, including one of his masterpieces: the narrative poem *The Bronze Horseman*, heavily cut to satisfy the censors. There was also an account by Zhukovsky of Pushkin's last moments, which again in deference to the censorship was bizarrely obliged to omit any reference to the cause of death. A few days later Tyutchev sent Vyazemsky a note of thanks for his copy of the journal, writing that it contained 'sad and beautiful pieces. It is truly, in the words of Chateaubriand, a book *from beyond the grave*, and I can add in all sincerity that the fact of having received it from your hands gives it renewed value in my eyes.'[11] Tyutchev will have been interested to learn more about the duel affair from Vyazemsky, who had been close to events, and who in later years hinted darkly that he knew or suspected more than he was able to disclose in public. No doubt Tyutchev (who was to become his close friend) was either now or later made aware of these suspicions, but how he reacted is not known. Nothing has survived among his recorded utterances to suggest what he thought of the various conspiracy theories which arose after Pushkin's death, and which have persisted and been elaborated on down to the present day.

Tyutchev will also have discussed the affair with Ivan Gagarin when the latter returned from Moscow. He gave him a copy of '29th January 1837', which Gagarin added to those already in his collection, including it in the list of contents drawn up at this time for his proposed edition of Tyutchev's verse.[12] However, Gagarin had much less to tell. Despite rumours which had arisen in the febrile atmosphere after Pushkin's death that he had been involved in preparing the notorious 'diplomas', he had in fact remained largely on the periphery of events. Already alerted to the rumours, Aleksandr Turgenev had carefully observed Gagarin's demeanour at Pushkin's funeral service, to be reassured by the young man's apparently genuine grief as he approached the bier to pay his last respects.[13] Subsequent testimony and research have tended to confirm Turgenev's instinctive judgement, clearing Gagarin of any involvement in the affair.[14] If Tyutchev knew of the accusations, he appears to have given them no credence, relying no doubt on his own judgement of the man, perhaps also on the opinion of Turgenev and others. Certainly he continued to associate with Gagarin in St Petersburg, and a year later was still writing to him in the friendliest of terms.[15]

To judge by Gagarin's recollections of him that summer, Tyutchev was every bit as keen to shake the dust of his native soil from his feet as on his previous visit seven years before. He 'didn't like being in St Petersburg, and longed only for the moment when he could go abroad again'. 'It's not *Heimweh* I'm suffering from, but *Herausweh*,' he told his friend.[16] The only conversation Gagarin was able — many years later — to recall them having about Pushkin's duel and death was very much in the same vein. One day on Nevsky Prospekt their talk turned to the sentence of deportation imposed on d'Anthès. Hinting that he would not be averse to such a 'punishment' himself, Tyutchev quipped that he too intended to kill a poet — Zhukovsky — at the earliest opportunity.[17]

More serious discussions of the events surrounding Pushkin's death could be had with others who had witnessed them at first hand. Count Michal Wielhorski, a close friend of Pushkin who had been at his bedside when he died, was visited by Tyutchev on at least one occasion.[18] But perhaps the most informed account came from Aleksandr Turgenev, who was in St Petersburg from 10/22 June to 19 June/ 1 July.[19]

He met Tyutchev and Eleonore several times, and 'Pushkin' is listed in his diary as one of the topics discussed. They also talked about 'Chaadayev and his punishment etc.',[20] a *cause célèbre* which clearly interested Tyutchev. The previous autumn one of Pyotr Chaadayev's *Philosophical Letters* — copies of which in the French original had been circulating among his friends for some time — had appeared in Russian translation in the Moscow journal *Teleskop*. It amounted to a comprehensive and damning critique of the whole of Russian history and Russian culture. Belonging neither to the East nor the West, according to Chaadayev Russians lived 'outside history', untouched by all the great political, social and cultural developments experienced by other nations. Russia was an 'empty page' in the history of mankind. Why should this be so? Because Russia had sided with 'decadent, generally despised Byzantium' at the time of the great Schism, thus cutting herself off from most of Europe. Even the programme of westernisation initiated by by Peter the Great had proved to be no more than a slavish imitation of externals, lacking in inner conviction. What was the solution? Russia must wholeheartedly embrace western values, which in practical terms could be done only by converting to Catholicism. For, unlike Orthodoxy, the Catholic faith embodied those social and political ideals of justice, prosperity and harmony on earth which alone could guarantee genuine progress.

The article was a blatant affront to the official doctrine of 'orthodoxy, autocracy and nationalism'. The journal was closed down and its editor, Nadezhdin, exiled to a remote location west of the Urals, some six hundred miles from Moscow; the censor who had approved the article was dismissed; Chaadayev was officially pronounced insane and placed under medical supervision in his own home, and all his papers were confiscated.

Both Turgenev and Ivan Gagarin were close to Chaadayev and could supply Tyutchev with details of the affair (and no doubt illicit copies of the *Philosophical Letters*). If on leaving Munich Gagarin had lost a guide and mentor in Tyutchev, he had found a new one in Chaadayev, becoming his devoted pupil and often acting as his intermediary to others such as Pushkin and Schelling. It was for instance via Gagarin that Chaadayev sent a copy of his *Teleskop* article to Pushkin in St Petersburg.[21] Gagarin later testified to Chaadayev's 'huge influence' on his development at this time: 'I owe everything to that man', he wrote.[22]

Despite the efforts of the authorities, the article in *Teleskop* had in Aleksandr Herzen's words shaken the educated public like 'a gunshot ringing out in the darkness of night'.[23] Chaadayev had fired the starting-pistol for heated debates about Russia's place in the world which would continue for years to come. Some would maintain with him that Russia must adopt the values of the West; a few, including Gagarin, would go so far as to embrace the Catholic faith. Others, while largely agreeing with Chaadayev's devastating critique of Russian conditions, would propose a way forward for their country distinct from that followed by the West. To these belonged Tyutchev. Yet for all their ideological differences, he and Chaadayev would in later years develop a cordial personal relationship founded on mutual respect.

After an absence of seven years Tyutchev had been reunited with most of his family. His parents had recently moved to St Petersburg to be near their daughter Darya and her husband Nikolay Sushkov, who were expecting their first child. Only Nikolay was missing: he did manage to join the rest of the family on leave from Warsaw later in the year, but after Tyutchev had left. The original plan had been for Tyutchev to obtain an overland courier mission to St Petersburg, leaving Eleonore to take the children and servants by sea. Apart from cutting down on costs, this would have provided an opportunity for him to meet up with Nikolay in Warsaw.[24] However, for whatever reason he had changed his plans at the last moment and travelled with Eleonore.[25]

The dramatic events in his personal life may have cast something of a shadow between him and his brother; this also appears to have been true of the rest of the family. Further bouts of depression and irritability did nothing to help. 'I realise how often I was truly unbearable,' he wrote to his parents soon afterwards. 'Do not attribute this to anything other than the strange half-abnormal state of my health — this said not as an excuse, but in explanation.'[26] Relations with his new brother-in-law Nikolay Sushkov were particularly strained. Although they had exchanged cordial letters on the occasion of his marriage to Darya,[27] now in St Petersburg Tyutchev took against him, believing him to be a schemer on the make ('un intrigant').[28] This turned out to be just another of those 'wild imaginings' testified to by Eleonore: much later he was forced to acknowlege that due to 'circumstances at the time and the state of my health' he had completely misjudged Sushkov.[29]

Apart from being reunited with his family, the main purpose of the visit as far as Tyutchev was concerned was to seek a new and improved posting away from Munich; to this end he began to cultivate his contacts in St Petersburg. Dmitry Durnovo, the senior court official the Tyutchevs had got to know in 1830, was now dead; but his son Pavel called on them not long after their arrival, after which Eleonore is known to have visited the salon of Pavel's wife Aleksandra.[30] Pavel Durnovo, an official in the War Ministry, was a frequent guest at the house of Count Nesselrode, while his wife was the daughter of Prince Pyotr Volkonsky, Minister of the Imperial Court.[31] These were useful people to know. Even more useful was Amélie Krüdener, also in St Petersburg with her husband at this time.[32] It was undoubtedly in large part thanks to her influence at court that on 3/15 August Tyutchev was appointed Senior (i.e. First) Secretary at the Rusian Embassy in Turin.[33] At the same time he volunteered for a courier mission to Turin, due for departure in the next few days. This would help to pay their travelling expenses; Eleonore could follow on with the children in due course. She was in any case in no hurry to leave St Petersburg, where she had been reunited with members of her own family: her sons Karl and Otto, now junior officers after passing out from the Naval Academy; probably also her brother Felix von Bothmer, who had entered service in Russia and was acting as guardian to his two nephews.[34] Her youngest son Alfred, now twelve, had also been brought with them from Munich, for it was intended that he should follow in his older brothers' footsteps as a naval cadet. The arrangements for this would take time: he was eventually enrolled at the Academy only the following January.[35]

On 8/20 August Tyutchev embarked at Kronstadt on the steam packet *Alexandra*, due to leave early the following morning for Travemünde. That night he was woken in his cabin by a messenger bearing news that Darya had given birth to a son. There was just time to write a brief note of congratulation to Darya and his parents before the ship weighed anchor.[36] Severe storms in the Baltic made for a trying passage, bringing back unpleasant memories of his voyage to Greece on the *Carolina* four summers before. The *Alexandra* finally limped into port on the evening of 26 August (NS), nearly three days behind schedule.[37] From Lübeck he wrote to his parents, thanking them for the love and solicitude shown towards him during his stay, and entrusting Eleonore and the children to their care. 'Love them for my sake. I confess that sometimes I feel very sad for my wife. No-one in the world but I can know what must be troubling her heart...' Turning to his career prospects, he recommended that Eleonore continue to cultivate her acquaintances in St Petersburg society, and in particular get to know Countess Nesselrode if at all possible. 'I have now learnt from experience just how necessary such contacts are in our service,' he added.[38]

From Lübeck his mission took him via Berlin to Munich, where he had despatches to deliver. These being apparently not too urgent, he economised by using stage coaches, reaching Munich only on 6 September. Here he spent several days, putting some unspecified family affairs in order and accepting invitations to dinner from the dowager Queen and the new Russian Ambassador, Dmitry Severin. At Severin's he met the writer and journalist Nikolay Grech, who was currently travelling around Europe.[39] Grech had abandoned his earlier liberal convictions after the failure of the Decembrist revolt, and was now co-editor with the notorious Faddey Bulgarin — whose activities on behalf of the Third Section were public knowledge — of *Severnaya pchela* (*The Northern Bee*), a conservative and pro-government journal.[40] Just a few months previously Grech had been in Paris, sent by the Third Section to offer monetary inducements to journalists to take a more pro-Russian line; unfortunately this secret mission had to be abandoned after his lack of discretion had brought it squarely into the public domain.[41] Although evidently aware of these bungled efforts, Tyutchev seems to have found Grech an amusing enough dinner companion at Severin's, characterising him in a letter to his parents as 'an excellent fellow, an ardent patriot and great talker'.[42] Two years later Grech would be one of the first to reveal in print the identity of the 'F.T' whose 'fine poems' (his words) had appeared in Pushkin's *Sovremennik*.[43]

From Munich Tyutchev informed his parents that he planned to meet up with Potyomkin on the way to Turin. Recently appointed Ambassador in Rome, his old friend and patron was currently staying in Switzerland to avoid an outbreak of cholera affecting southern and central Italy.[44] Tyutchev left Munich a few days after writing to his parents on 10 September[45] and headed for Lindau on the shores of Lake Constance, from where a ferry could be taken to the Swiss side. His onward route is uncertain, given that nothing is known of Potyomkin's exact whereabouts in Switzerland, but in any case the first part will have taken him either through or very close to Konstanz. And it is surely no coincidence that an entry in Ernestine's flower-album places her in that town on 16 September, at just about the time Tyutchev would have been in the area.[46] Their rendezvous must have been arranged by correspondence; yet as Ernestine later destroyed all their letters from this period, we can only speculate as to what if any encouragement hers may have given Tyutchev at this time. All that is certain is that already in Munich he had a change of heart about Eleonore following him to Turin that autumn.

Before setting out from there for Lindau and Konstanz he wrote Eleonore 'a long letter' outlining what he saw as 'serious objections' to her returning from Russia 'at this time of year and under present circumstances'.[47] That letter too has disappeared; but

Tyutchev repeats his case in another, surviving missive to his parents, clearly intended to enlist their help in dissuading Eleonore from travelling. His first argument concerns her health, which for some time has been 'far from robust'; what would be best for her now, he claims, is not 'new exertions and new upheavals', which 'will ruin her health completely', but rather 'several months of rest and tranquillity' in St Petersburg. Secondly, at this late stage in the season any unforeseen delay might prevent her from crossing the Alps before the weather deteriorated; she would then have to spend the winter in Munich, which would be 'very annoying for her and very unpleasant for me, and cause both of us considerable inconvenience'. Thirdly and finally, before Eleonore could think of leaving St Petersburg it was vital to obtain — 'with Amélie Krüdener's help' — a grant from the Foreign Ministry towards the cost of setting up home in Turin; without this they would find themselves 'plunged into new difficulties'.[48]

Tyutchev's second argument in particular is hardly convincing. It is difficult to see what additional distress or inconvenience either he or Eleonore would have suffered if she had been obliged to spend the winter with her sister and aunt in Munich, rather than in St Petersburg. There would even have been some advantages: the cost of living there was much lower than in St Petersburg, as Tyutchev himself concedes in the same letter; and the long and exhausting journey to Turin would have been broken into two, with a long period in between for Eleonore to rest and recover her strength. Indeed, Tyutchev's whole case smacks of special pleading, inviting suspicions that his true motive was to have Eleonore out of the way while he resumed his affair with Ernestine. This is indeed exactly what happened.

iii A New Start

'I have the honour to inform the Department that Court Councillor Tyutchev, appointed Senior Secretary to the Embassy in my charge, arrived in Turin on the 13/25th of this month of September'.[49] Thus Aleksandr Obrezkov, Russian Ambassador to the Kingdom of Piedmont-Sardinia, reported the arrival of his new deputy.

Tyutchev had received a general briefing on Russian policy towards Sardinia from Nesselrode before leaving St Petersburg;[50] now in Turin the Ambassador no doubt filled him in with more details of the situation on the ground. Relations between the two countries were inevitably those of a major power vis-à-vis a smaller and much weaker player on the European scene. In the post-Napoleonic settlement Russia had been largely instrumental in securing the throne of Piedmont-Sardinia for the ruling House of Savoy against Austrian claims, and had ever since assumed a debt of gratitude and loyalty in return. Strategically positioned between France to the west and Austrian-ruled Lombardy to the east, the kingdom was seen by Russia and her allies as having a key part to play in Italy as a whole, acting both as a buffer against revolutionary doctrines emanating from France and a reinforcement of Austrian influence in the region. The specific tasks of the Russian Embassy in Turin were stated by Nesselrode in a confidential memorandum to Obrezkov's successor as being 'to maintain and affirm the links which bind the court of Turin to the Holy Alliance'; 'to fortify the King in his wise decision courageously to resist offers of friendship and threats alike on the part of France'; and to encourage him to 'place his confidence in the friendship of Austria, which is for him the best guarantee of his peace'.[51] However, all this was easier said than done. King Carlo Alberto — or Charles Albert, as he was better known on the international stage — directed all aspects of foreign policy in person, leaving his Foreign Minister, Count Solaro della Margherita, little more to do than act as secretary and spokesman. A stickler for court etiquette, and quick to resent any slight, real or imagined, to his country's prestige, Charles Albert maintained a defiantly independent line in foreign affairs, especially with regard to Austria. Consequently it was not only Russia's diplomats who found the touchy Sardinian monarch difficult to deal with.

To begin with Tyutchev found himself scarcely involved in these problems on a practical level. Indeed, for the first eight or nine months his new position proved to be something of a sinecure. After settling in he wrote to his parents: 'As a post, as a job — in a word, as a way of earning one's living — Turin is undoubtedly one of the best postings there is. For a start, as far as work is concerned, there is none.' Promotion to First Secretary had brought an improvement in his financial affairs, which were now 'in the most splendid condition': he was even planning to put money aside for when Eleonore and the girls rejoined him. All in all, he concluded, it was 'a most comfortable way of earning 8,000 roubles a year'.[52] This was a somewhat optimistic estimate: according to official documents his annual salary as First Secretary was 1,500 silver roubles, or 6,222 roubles in paper money.[53] Even so, it was a welcome advance on the 1,000 silver roubles he had earned in Munich.

With Obrezkov in overall control, most of the donkey-work of the Embassy was done by Second Secretary Miklashevsky, assisted by a young supernumerary Attaché, Ernest Tom-Have, who reported for duty not long after Tyutchev.[54] It is perhaps indicative that only one diplomatic document in Tyutchev's hand (that announcing his own arrival) has been discovered for the whole of his first nine months in Turin. His main function appears to have been to stand by to take over from Obrezkov if and when required. Weary of life in Turin after five years there, the Ambassador had already signalled his intention of taking a year's sabbatical leave from the autumn of 1838, leaving Tyutchev as Chargé d'Affaires.[55] Such a prolonged stint as acting Head of Mission would be financially rewarding, and could well open the doors to higher things. Not for nothing do Tyutchev's letters to his parents and Eleonore from Turin dwell on the importance of cultivating those in St Petersburg with the power to further his career.[56]

For the moment, however, he could adjust to his new surroundings at leisure. For the first couple of months, while waiting for his main baggage to arrive and be cleared through customs, he booked into a hotel; after this he moved into two furnished rooms, with a box-room for his manservant.[57] During these early weeks in Turin he had time to write what he himself described as 'five or six — not letters, but tomes' to Eleonore (none has survived),[58] and others to his parents. His mornings were generally taken up with reading and walking.[59] The Embassy received copies of French, Russian and other international newspapers; and in addition to books readily available in Turin there were those in Russian he had brought with him, with others sent on later by his parents.[60] The city of Turin was there to explore, with its gridwork pattern of wide airy boulevards and arcaded squares, its baroque churches and palaces, its museums, art gallery and university. There were pleasant walks along the banks of the Po and out into the surrounding hills, with distant views of the Alps. 'The surroundings of Turin are magnificent, and the weather is still fine,' he wrote to his parents in the middle of November. 'Blue skies every day — and there are still leaves on the trees'. In the late afternoon he would usually dine with the Ambassador and his wife. 'This is the most agreeable part of the day,' he wrote. 'I stay talking to them until 8 or 9 p.m., then return to my room, do some more reading, and go to bed'.[61] It was hardly a punishing routine.

Obrezkov had a reputation for being unsociable, abrasive even; yet Tyutchev found himself treated well by his new chief and got along amicably with him. The Ambassador had struggled to engage with Turin society during his years in the city. Although he and his attractive wife entertained lavishly in an official capacity, hosting frequent balls and dinner parties, on the more personal level he complained it was impossible to get enough people together for a friendly hand of whist.[62] No doubt his own attitude towards the locals was partly to blame (according to Tyutchev 'he does little to disguise the lack of sympathy they inspire in him and his extreme desire to get away from them');[63] yet the root cause seems to have been what struck Tyutchev too as 'the inhospitable and unsociable habits' of the Piedmontese, and 'the customary reserve attributed to [their] character'.[64] Nor does Obrezkov's experience appear to have been unique: if we are to believe Tyutchev, few of the foreign diplomats in Turin had any contact with local society or saw their service there as anything but an exile to be endured.[65]

The effect on Tyutchev, to whom the social round was the breath of life itself, was predictable enough. After a couple of months he had reached the rueful conclusion that 'as a place to live [...] Turin is one of the dreariest and most dismal created by God', being 'as regards society and sociability in every way the opposite of Munich'.[66] In November he reported that he had made the acquaintance of some foreign diplomats and even a few members of local society, but grumbled that 'it is all so incoherent, so disconnected'.[67] Despite continued efforts to widen his circle (to include, as might be expected, several 'amiable women'), by the end of the year he was beginning to despair. The Advent period was particularly depressing. Thanks to the all-pervasive influence of the Catholic Church a ban was in place on all theatrical productions, balls and concerts; consequently 'the whole city resembled a monastery', the only 'entertainment' on offer being a daily programme of fire-and-brimstone church sermons. At least after Christmas the theatres opened again; but here too Tyutchev had been warned not to expect too much. Throughout the Carnival season social life centred exclusively on the theatre, where during a typical performance members of the audience would circulate from box to box with complete disregard to what was happening on stage. For two months this represented the sum total of social life in Turin.[68]

On Christmas Day Tyutchev wrote to his parents: 'I should very much like to be able to say that I am beginning to enjoy life here in Turin — but that would be to tell a great lie. No, the truth of the matter is that I do not like it here one bit, and it is only absolute necessity that reconciles me to such an existence. It is void of any kind of interest, and seems to me like a poor theatrical performance, all the more intolerable for being boring when its sole merit should be to entertain.'[69]

iv Final Farewells

Some relief from the boredom came soon after the middle of November with a trip to Genoa, the chief port of Piedmont-Sardinia. It was the King's custom to spend the month of November there, accompanied by his court and the ambassadors of foreign powers.[70] Tyutchev had been left to mind the shop in Turin; his visit to Genoa was no doubt undertaken to deliver and collect despatches and instructions, and to prepare himself for his expected duties as Chargé d'Affaires the following year. It would be a welcome change of scenery; but there was another, far greater attraction: Ernestine had agreed to meet him there. The entry 'Genoa. 24 November 1837' in her flower-album most likely records the date of their reunion.[71]

Over the next few days they took advantage of the mild Mediterranean climate to explore Genoa and its surroundings on foot, no doubt discussing at some length what was to be done about the intractable situation in which they found themselves. On one of their wanderings they came across and entered an old villa, long since abandoned and yet wondrously preserved in the warm southern air. A poem commemorating the scene depicts a timeless idyll shattered by the lovers' intrusion:

Italian Villa

So, having turned aside from life's upheavals,
Sequestered by a cypress grove opaque,
The villa, like some shade in fields Elysian,
    Once closed its eyes, no more to wake.

Two centuries or more have passed unnoticed
Since, ringed about as if by magic skill,
It fell asleep in its enchanted valley,
Surrendering to the heavens' changing will.

But here the heavens treat earth with such indulgence!..
Above this roof have winged in languid file
So many summers and warm southern winters —
Yet none has left its mark in all that while.

Still now the fountain babbles in its corner,
Beneath the ceiling breezes gust around,
A swallow darts in, fluttering and chirping...
Yet nothing can disturb this sleep profound!

We entered... All within was dark and tranquil,
And seemed as now forever to have been...
The fountain splashed... Quite still outside the window,
A stately cypress gazed in on the scene...

. . . .

All suddenly was thrown into confusion:
The cypress shook with vehemence intense;
The fountain ceased its chatter but to whisper,
As if through sleep, strange sounds bereft of sense.

What was this? Could it be that not for nothing
The life that held us then so much in sway —
That evil life, with its unruly passion —
Crossed a forbidden threshold on that day?[72]

The poet Afanasy Fet and the critic Richard Gregg have both pointed out the lack of artistic coherence between the first five stanzas and the final two (which Fet even thought would have been better omitted for the sake of homogeneity).[73] The thrust of Gregg's criticism (and it could be applied to other poems by Tyutchev) is that the imagery of the concluding section is too impenetrably private to stand on its own, requiring a biographical footnote to become fully clear:

the 'evil life' mentioned in these lines is of course the same stormy, pain-inflicting passion which 'flowed' in the adulterous poet and his mistress as they entered the villa. And so deeply did Tiutchev feel this guilt that it did not seem necessary to objectify it poetically. The poet, in short, took for granted what the reader cannot; and the poem fails artistically thereby.[74]

It is a just comment. Yet for all its artistic flaws, 'Italian Villa' remains invaluable precisely as a biographical document, faithfully mirroring Tyutchev's and Ernestine's innermost thoughts and feelings at the time. They must have been tempted to continue their liaison in Turin, and it would certainly have been easy enough to do so if Tyutchev's own description of the permissive moral climate prevailing there is anything to go by. In one of his letters to his parents he writes that the surest way to cure anyone suffering from 'a romantic imagination' would be to send them to Piedmont, for 'that which everywhere else is the subject of romance, the effect of some passion which throws a person's whole existence into disarray and ends by ruining it, is here the result of an amicable arrangement and disturbs the habitual order of life no more than lunch or dinner'. He claims never to have heard anyone speak of 'fallen women': on the contrary, a woman's lover or lovers would be pointed out to him 'quite openly and without the slightest hint of scandal, just as someone might say of a carriage passing in the street: That's Madame So-and-so's carriage'.[75]

However that may be, he and Ernestine agreed in Genoa to finish their relationship. The feelings of guilt attested by 'Italian Villa' clearly outweighed all other considerations, especially for Ernestine. She no doubt also wished to draw a line under an affair which had brought her little but emotional anguish and suffering. They parted on 1 December; soon afterwards Tyutchev was back in Turin on his own. So much is evident from another poem written at the time:

1st December 1837

Here then it is that we were fated
To say our poignant last farewells...
Farewell to all that captivated —
And brutally the life so mutilated
     That in your tortured bosom dwells!..

Farewell... With sorrow and despair
In years to come you will remember
This land, these shores and this eternal southern splendour
     Where nature blossoms late and fair —
     And with their fragrance in December
     Last fading roses warm the air...[76]

    In this poem the wild swings of emotion which threaten the artistic unity of 'Italian Villa' are equally apparent, if more successfully contained from a poetic point of view. The lovers are renouncing a passion which 'captivated' them and yet at the same time is acknowledged to have devastated ('mutilated') Ernestine's emotional life. No wonder that she is imagined years hence looking back at this time 'with sorrow and despair', or that the final images of sunshine and roses in December have — with their strangely unsettling sense of dislocation — something darkly ironic about them.

    Now that the die was cast, Tyutchev appears superficially to have demonstrated a quite uncharacteristic decisiveness. In reality it would be nearer the mark to speak of a recklessness born of mental and emotional upheaval. As if resolved to make his and Ernestine's decision public, he sent the two poems inspired by their meeting in Genoa to the editors of *Sovremennik* for publication. That anyone in St Petersburg who read them and recognised the cryptonym 'F. T-v.' could bring them and their content to Eleonore's attention was by now irrelevant, for he had also decided he must see her as soon as possible.[77] There was so much he needed to tell her, and to hear from her, that could only be said face to face. Probably while still in Genoa he obtained the indulgent Obrezkov's consent to a courier mission to St Petersburg in January, and in a state of inner turmoil wrote to Eleonore of his plan. He instructed her not to breathe a word of his 'project' to his parents: presumably they would not have understood. At the same time he wrote to inform Nikolay, whose leave in St Petersburg was about to end, that he would be able to visit him in Warsaw on his way to the capital. The two letters (neither of which has survived) were sent together, arriving in St Petersburg towards the end of December (NS). As she read hers, Eleonore was alarmed and disturbed not just by the content, but by a tone of nervous agitation, verging on the manic, which pervaded the whole letter. By now it was too late to send a reply before Tyutchev set out on his ill-considered journey; while Nikolay, to whom she instinctively turned for advice and reassurance in such situations, had already left to return to Warsaw. All she could do was forward Tyutchev's letter to him, together with one from herself:

Here is a letter which , if the one I received at the same time is anything to judge by, is not calculated to put you in a good humour. You who alone are able to speak to him and make him see reason — write to him without delay, for pity's sake, try to make him understand that his overheated imagination is turning his whole life into a fit of high fever. O, Nicolas, when I think of that poor man — nobody suspects, nobody can imagine what he is suffering — and to say that it is his own fault is merely to apportion blame where pity is due. I am now seriously afraid that he will carry out his insane project of coming here as a courier in February. He writes to me of it as something already decided. He has got Obrezkov to make the necessary arrangements — and provided there are no unforeseen obstacles he really will undertake this terrible journey in the depths of winter and in the state he is in — for he is ill, I recognise his illness well from the cruelly overwrought excitement [of his letter]. He tells me that if his plan succeeds he will travel to Vienna in January. Please write a few lines to him there — for it is from there that he wishes to take a courier mission to St Petersburg. He forbids me to tell his parents of his plan, so do not say anything about it either. I have no need to tell you that in writing to him it is necessary above all and in everything you say to administer *tranquilliser*. Tell him I am well and lack for none of the essentials, and that he should bear in mind that the only consequence of this whole terrible journey he wants to undertake would be to see me two months earlier, for I am waiting only for the moment to leave. If I had a good carriage, and money (that accursed thing, money!) I think I would travel to him. Farewell, Nicolas, love me, take pity on me. I have told you so little, but even so I know you understand what my life is like; I should gladly sacrifice the half of it to buy some peace and tranquillity for the remainder.[78]

Although Eleonore is understandably reticent as to why Tyutchev should want to see her so urgently, certain phrases ('nobody can imagine what he is suffering — and to say that it is his own fault is merely to apportion blame where pity is due'; 'I have told you so little, but even so I know you understand what my life is like') suggest that in his letter he had made a full confession of his meetings with Ernestine and their decision to end the relationship.

Some distraction from his own problems came in helping to sort out a friend's troubled affairs of the heart. Maltitz had written in some despair from Munich of his feelings for Clotilde, who unfortunately was failing to respond to his suit. Tyutchev wrote back with advice on how best to proceed: he was after all an acknowledged expert in such matters, as well as being in this particular case rather more than an impartial observer. On Christmas Day he informed Eleonore of these efforts in a postscript to a letter to his parents. He also complains of delays in their correspondence (her letters to him were sent in the diplomatic post via Félix-Édouard de Sercey, an old friend from Munich now serving at the French Embassy in St Petersburg), and briefly mentions his forthcoming 'project'. Despite the inevitably guarded tone of the postscript, which he knew his parents would also have sight of, it is worth quoting in full as the only scrap of his correspondence with Eleonore to have survived.

Now I come to my wife. Patience, my friend! I shall write to you in a few days. But what I can tell you already is that the belated arrival of your letters is causing me some very unpleasant moments. The last but one was from 13

November, and only on 23 December did I receive the last, dated 16/28 November. All those which you wrote to me via *Sercey* come from Paris and arrive here only after 22 days. Such are the joys of absence. In my next letter I shall write to you in detail about my condition both external and internal. Suffice it to know that there is not a moment in the day when I do not miss you. I should not wish it upon anyone to experience for himself all that is contained in those words. I have told you of my *project*. In a few days I shall know from replies from Rome and Naples whether it can be put into practice. If *not*, I have another proposition to make to you. Take good care of your health. Do you go out into society? To Countess Nesselrode, for instance? Please do that. It is of vital importance to me. Have the matters regarding money been settled in the way I wanted? How are the children? What are the *Krüdeners* doing? Enclosed with my next letter to you will be one to Amélie. I have had news from Maltitz. He is very unhappy with the situation he finds himself in. Clotilde has, I believe, gone with her aunt to Farnbach. In my reply to him I wrote much on the subject of your sister, and am curious to see what effect this will have.

Goodbye, my friend, until we meet again soon. O, absence, absence!

And to you too, dearest Papa and Mama, goodbye. I kiss your hands.[79]

Soon afterwards the arrangements for his courier mission were complete. On or just after 9 January he left Turin for Munich on the first stage of his planned journey to St Petersburg. Together with the Russian diplomatic mail he carried a despatch from Solaro to the Sardinian Ambassador in Vienna.[80] Crossing the Alps at this time of year — most likely by mail coach via the Mont Cenis Pass — was a cold and arduous business. Surrounded by a mountainous wilderness in the grip of ice and snowstorms, he remembered basking in the Mediterranean warmth and sunlight of Genoa just weeks before. Despite all the painfulness of that occasion, he now looked back on it with longing, feeling the icy cold penetrating him to the bone to be a portent not only of the Russian winter ahead, but of a whole future without Ernestine. These thoughts and feelings found immediate expression in a characteristic 'journey' poem:

> O blessèd South, was it but lately
> That I beheld you face to face —
> That you revealed your godly splendour
> To me, a stranger in that place? —
> And — not exultant, and yet quickened
> By other feelings new to me —
> I listened spellbound to the singing
> Of waves on your majestic sea?

In a fairly clear reference to erotic encounters with Ernestine he goes on to stress the 'harmony' of the waves' song, a harmony unchanged since those 'days of yore' when Aphrodite herself rose fully-formed from these very waves. And although he knows them even now to be glinting in the sun and singing their beguiling refrain, while 'sacred ghosts' of antiquity continue to haunt their azure expanse, for him they have become but a fabled memory to be conjured up against the harsh reality of the present:

240

But I have bade farewell and left you —
The North has claimed me back once more...
Its leaden skies, so grey and cheerless,
Weigh down upon me as before...
The air is biting here... Each valley,
Each peak with snow lies thickly decked...
Cold, the all-powerful enchanter,
Reigns here with tyranny unchecked.

Yet far from 'this realm of blizzards', there 'in the south so bright and golden', 'on the cusp of land and sea', the waves of the Mediterranean still beckon him:

More wondrous yet your silver sparkle,
Your vivid azure, fresh and clear —
And more harmoniously than ever
Your murmurings fall upon my ear![81]

Reaching Munich on 19 January, he handed the packet destined for Vienna to the Sardinian Ambassador to Bavaria, Marzano, explaining that he was not yet sure when or even if he would be proceeding to the Austrian capital.[82] On 4 February Marzano reported to Turin that he had forwarded the document in question to Vienna with a Russian courier. He does not name the latter, making it seem on balance unlikely that it was Tyutchev.[83] Certainly he could have gone no further than Vienna, for by March he is known to have been in Munich again. We can only speculate as to what led him to abandon his plans. Possibly by now the rigours of travelling in winter had begun to dampen his enthusiasm; there may have been letters from Nikolay and Eleonore waiting for him in Munich or Vienna which persuaded him to go no further; or perhaps there was simply no courier mission available to St Petersburg. And always pulling him in the other direction was the vague but cherished hope of seeing Ernestine for one more time. While in Munich he commissioned a portrait of himself by the accomplished amateur painter Hippolite von Rechberg. The young widow of Count Anton von Rechberg, an important court official who had died the previous year, Hippolite was a society acquaintance of both Tyutchev and Ernestine. The portrait, subsequently dated by Ernestine '9 March 1838',[84] was in fact intended as a parting gift to her, a memento of their time together. Of course, he would have to present it to her in person...

He was not expected back in Turin for some time yet, and was certainly in no hurry to return. During March he spent much time with Maltitz and Clotilde, whose romance had taken a more favourable turn: soon afterwards they announced their engagement, and in just over a year's time would become man and wife.[85] On the face of it Tyutchev and Maltitz appeared to have much in common: both were diplomats in Russian service; both were poets with a deep knowledge and love of literature, one writing in Russian, the other in German; soon they would be related by marriage. They could exchange their reminiscences of common acquaintances: Prince Kozlovsky, for instance, under whom Maltitz had served as a young diplomat in Stuttgart, and whose influence on him, as on Tyutchev, had been considerable;[86] or Heine, whom Maltitz had known in Berlin in the early 1820s.[87] Yet in character and temperament they were almost exact opposites. There was about Maltitz a certain self-satisfaction and philistine acceptance of the benchmarks of worldly success which would eventually alienate Tyutchev. A self-declared disciple (more accurately, epigone) of Goethe and Schiller, Maltitz was far more prolific as a poet than Tyutchev, producing verse epics and tragedies as well as shorter lyrics; yet his verse is on the whole derivative and now largely forgotten. Ironically, his most lasting achievement may be to have translated a few Russian poems into German, including two by Tyutchev.[88]

Given what we know of Tyutchev's feelings for Clotilde, it is likely that his ostensible blessing on her new-found happiness with Maltitz concealed a certain amount of private regret. Such at least would appear to be the sentiments of a poem written at about this time:

> O maiden, do not trust the poet,
> Or think him yours, all else above;
> And more than any blazing anger
> Be fearful of a poet's love!
>
> Your soul so innocent will struggle
> To make his heart your own in vain;
> The virgin's flimsy veil will never
> That all-consuming fire contain.
>
> The poet's powers elemental
> To all things but himself extend:
> He cannot help his laurels scorching
> A maiden's tresses in the end.
>
> In vain the common herd belittles
> Or praises him unthinkingly...
> The heart he stings not like an adder,
> But sucks its life-blood like a bee.
>
> The poet's pure hand will not sully
> That shrine so holy in your sight —
> But may, unwitting, crush you lifeless
> Or bear you off in heavenward flight.[89]

Clotilde and Maltitz provide the most obvious models for the poem's maiden addressee and her poet suitor (although, written in Russian, it was clearly never intended for her to read). At the same time Tyutchev projects onto these two figures so much of a view of poetry as divine, 'elemental' possession (comparable to that laid out in the piece on Pushkin's death), and so much of his own emotional life as 'wayward poet', that the identity of their prototypes becomes in the end a question of purely biographical rather than literary concern.

If anything, the poem demonstrates just how engrossed Tyutchev had become in his own emotional dilemmas. Some time after the middle of March he appears to have received a letter from Obrezkov warning him of an unfortunate diplomatic crisis which had blown up, necessitating his return to Turin.[90] He knew that Ernestine was in Geneva (she had arrived there from Cannes at the beginning of the month),[91] and the prospect of making a brief detour to see her on his way back to Turin was tempting in the extreme. This time he arranged a courier mission with the Sardinian authorities to cover travelling expenses and left Munich on 3 April, bearing a despatch from Ambassador Marzano to Solaro.[92] To while away the hours spent travelling by carriage he read a recently published volume of poems by Maltitz — no doubt a gift from the author. One of the more accomplished of these, 'The Swan',[93] seems to have particularly impressed him. Its use of the contrasting images of swan and eagle, symbolising the contemplative and active elements of human existence, was taken up and developed further by him in a poem with the same title which has been recognised as a variation on Maltitz's theme.[94] On the evening of 4 April he stopped at Lindau, from where he sent Maltitz another poem — in French, their common language — reflecting on the time they had spent together in Munich:

> Nous avons pu tous deux, fatigués du voyage,
> Nous asseoir un instant sur le bord du chemin —
> Et sentir sur nos fronts flotter le même ombrage,
> Et porter nos regards vers l'horizon lointain.
>
> Mais le temps suit son course et sa pente inflexible
> A bientôt séparé ce qu'il avait uni, —
> Et l'homme, sous le fouet d'un pouvoir invisible,
> S'enfonce, triste et seul, dans l'espace infini.
>
> Et maintenant, ami, de ces heures passées,
> De cette vie à deux, que nous est-il resté?
> Un regard, un accent, des débris de pensées. —
> Hélas, ce qui n'est plus a-t-il jamais été?[95]

The metaphorical 'voyage' from which he and Maltitz had rested for a while is the journey of life, conceived here in bleakly fatalistic terms — as in the earlier 'From place to place, from here to there...' — as little more than an enforced trek 'beneath the whip of an invisible power'. Man 'founders' in the infinity of space and time, his existence dwarfed into such insignificance and unreality that even its rare moments of apparent respite and comfort must be counted an illusion. It is Pascal's vision, stripped of the consolations of religious faith.[96]

Sending the poem to Maltitz, he appended a note which begins with an apparent acknowledgement of his own culpability in returning to Ernestine (an admission somewhat tempered by the implied plea of diminished responsibility): 'Goodbye. What a child I am, what a weakling [*Que je suis enfant, que je suis faible*]. All day today I did nothing but read you and think of you. — My heartfelt regards to Clotilde. May she be happy, and you too.'[97]

Hastening on, he reached Geneva on or around the seventh.[98] He booked into the hotel Ernestine was staying at, on the banks of the Rhône, and spent about a week there. Some years later, in the summer of 1846, a chance meeting with a native of Geneva brought back fond memories of the place. 'Geneva, Hotel des Bergues, the Rhône, you, I — eight years ago', he reminisced in a letter to Ernestine describing the encounter.[99] Happiness at being reunited was clouded by the imminence of what really had to be the very last of their 'final farewells'. Soon the Gulf of Finland would reopen for navigation and Eleonore would be on her way to join him in Turin, after which any further assignations would be out of the question. The gift of his portrait betokened not just gratitude for what had been, but closure. And now, as if to mock them, burgeoning signs of nature's spring awakening confronted the lovers at every turn. It inspired in Tyutchev a deeply-felt poetic reflection on man's longing to escape the pain of consciousness and timebound existence and find healing in the timeless and unconscious world of nature. Which of us (the poem asks) can fail to be moved by the arrival of spring, regardless of any personal distress or misfortune we may be suffering at the time? Nature herself on the other hand has no awareness of our individual woes. 'To her own laws obedient', she is oblivious to human concepts of time and decay. The poem concludes:

> Not for times gone do roses sorrow
> Nor nightingales their passing mourn;
> Not for the past does pale Aurora
> Shed fragrant tears before the dawn —
> And fear of death's untimely coming
> Has never yet torn leaf from tree:
> Their life lies spilt out in the present
> As one vast never-ending sea.
>
> O plaything of the self's delusion,
> Throw off the senses' masking cloak
> And into this life-giving ocean
> Plunge briskly, boldly: at a stroke
> Cleanse in its pure ethereal waters
> Your anguished breast of care and strife —
> And know, if only for an instant,
> Its godlike all-embracing life![100]

His departure could be delayed no longer. Apart from being expected back in Turin, he had diplomatic mail to deliver too. Leaving Geneva about 15 April,[101] he was in Turin by the 24th.[102] He had been away for over three months.

The serious diplomatic row between Sardinia and Russia which demanded his return had arisen from the most trivial of causes. Early in March Obrezkov's wife had appeared at court in the newly approved form of dress for wives of Russian diplomats. Loosely based on Russian peasant costume, this included a headdress with white lappets or streamers. The Sardinian court immediately took offence, deeming such lappets to be the preserve of ladies of royal birth. A stiff directive was circulated to all embassies, laying down the permitted dress code for ladies at court. Obrezkov took this as an insult to himself both personally and as representative of a great power, and in a despatch to St Petersburg requested his own recall. To Tsar Nicholas the whole affair seemed a nonsense; deciding nevertheless that Turin's 'not very friendly' handling of it 'deserves a lesson', he recalled the Ambassador and signalled his disinclination to nominate a successor. Obrezkov now found himself officially ostracised by the Sardinian authorities. By the time Tyutchev returned, relations between the two countries were at breaking-point.[103]

There was no doubt that Obrezkov's dislike of Turin and its inhabitants and his somewhat abrasive temperament had helped to aggravate the dispute. Yet most agreed that the chief blame lay with King Charles Albert, whose insistence on rigid adherence to the letter of court etiquette was notorious. The Dutch envoy, Heldewier, reported that the King's actions in the matter had been perceived as a gratuitous insult not just to Obrezkov, but to the whole diplomatic corps.[104] As he prepared himself for a protracted spell as Chargé d'Affaires in rather different circumstances from those originally envisaged, Tyutchev realised that his first duty would be to mend fences between the two countries. Thus — although privately critical of the King's conduct in what he called 'this puerile dispute'[105] — in public he was, according to Heldewier, 'very careful not to speak up too vigorously in support of his chief '.[106] Confirmation from Nesselrode of his appointment as Chargé reached Turin towards the end of May.[107] However, unforeseen events were to delay his accreditation at court for a further two months or more.[108]

10 The Hand of Fate
(Turin, 1838-1839)

i Into the Abyss

The future looked bright for Eleonore as she prepared to leave St Petersburg to join her husband. His promotion to Chargé d'Affaires should at last provide him with a challenging and satisfying role commensurate with his abilities and interests, leaving little time for that idleness ('*désœuvrement*') which she knew to have such a pernicious effect on him.[1] There would also be a substantial increase in salary, from 1,500 to 2,000 silver roubles per annum.[2] Perhaps at last they could hope to overcome their financial and emotional problems, enabling Eleonore to achieve that 'peace and tranquillity' for which she had declared herself prepared to sacrifice half her life. Certainly she would do all in her power to support him in his new position. Even before leaving St Petersburg she was at pains to assure the Sardinian Ambassador of her and her husband's 'keen desire to make themselves agreeable to [his] government', and to point out that Tyutchev 'greatly prides himself on his relations with [the Sardinian Foreign] Ministry'.[3]

She embarked on the first steam packet of the season, the *Nicholas I*, which left Kronstadt for Travemünde on 15/27 May 1838.[4] Travelling with her were her three young daughters Anna, Darya and Yekaterina, their Swiss governess Katharina Jardin, and two servants.[5] Among the other passengers was at least one familiar face, that of Vyazemsky; there were probably others. New acquaintances were in any case easily made in the sociable atmosphere on board. These included the nineteen-year-old Ivan Turgenev (no relation of Aleksandr), who was on his way to study in Germany. Like other young men before him, the future novelist appears to have fallen rather heavily for Eleonore's maternal charms, finding in them perhaps a substitute for those lacking in his own cold and domineering mother.[6] However — despite efforts by some commentators to inflate Turgenev's romantic aspirations into a shipboard 'affair' or 'liaison'[7] — there is absolutely no evidence to suggest that Eleonore's response was anything other than correct.

Three days into the voyage, on the evening of 30 May, Eleonore joined the children in their cabin, hoping for a good night's sleep before the *Nicholas I* docked at Travemünde early next morning. Ahead of them lay the long and arduous journey to Turin in hired carriages. In the early hours of the morning they were awoken by shouting: the ship was on fire.[8] They rushed on deck, dressed only in their night-clothes. Fires were a common enough hazard on these early steamers due to their timber construction: in this case a blaze had broken out in the furnace room and spread rapidly to other parts of the vessel. According to one account the ship was carrying too heavy a load, and combined with the use of poor quality coal wet from sea water this had caused the whole system to overheat. In their panic some of the passengers attempted to launch lifeboats themselves, but succeeded only in wrecking them. Fortunately for all concerned the German captain kept a cool head. After posting sailors with drawn cutlasses to guard the remaining two lifeboats, he decided not to attempt to douse the flames with pumps powered by the ship's engine — which would have meant stopping, and in any case offered little chance of success — but instead to head for shore with the intention of running his vessel aground. By now the rear end of the ship was ablaze, and most of the passengers were gathered in the bows. Turgenev managed to reach safety only by jumping from one roof to another of the passengers' carriages loaded on the ship, some of which were already burning from beneath. 'Nearly all the passengers were assembled there,' he later recalled. 'Some sailors, under the supervision of the captain, were busy lowering one of the two remaining lifeboats, fortunately the largest one. Across the other side of the vessel I could see, brightly lit by the glare of the fire, the line of steep cliffs stretching away to Lübeck. They were certainly almost two kilometres away. I could not swim; and although the place where we had gone aground was probably not very deep (for gone aground we had, without even noticing it), still the waves were very high.'[9] Women and children were let into the lifeboats first, some clambering down ropes, others simply jumping. Small children were lowered or dropped into the arms of those below.

Eventually all the surviving passengers and crew had been ferried to a sandbank near the shore, from where they waded or were carried the last two hundred yards or so. As they looked back, they saw the *Nicholas I* at first 'no more than a great mass of flames lying motionless on the sea, etched with the black outlines of funnels and masts, and with seagulls wheeling about it in slow and impassive flight; then a vast mound of ash speckled with tiny sparks, which came shooting out in long curving trajectories onto the now less turbulent waves.'[10] The vessel was totally burnt out above the waterline, yet thanks to Captain Stahl's decisive actions only five of the 170 men, women and children on board had lost their lives. Turgenev later recalled coming across Eleonore on the shore with her three daughters (he mistakenly remembers four): 'Among the ladies rescued from the shipwreck was Madame T..., very good-looking and charming, but encumbered by her four little daughters and their nurses; consequently she had been left abandoned on the beach, barefoot, her shoulders scarcely covered.' Turgenev gallantly surrendered his jacket, cravat and even boots to the shivering Eleonore.[11]

The disorientated survivors found they had come ashore only seven miles from their destination. Local villagers drove them in farm carts to Travemünde, where they rested before proceeding to Lübeck and Hamburg. Eleonore had to abandon any thought of her original plan of travelling to Turin via Paris.[12] From Lübeck on 1 June she wrote in a shaky hand to reassure her various relatives; only her note to her sister-in-law Darya Sushkova has survived: 'Dear Dorothée, We are alive! The children are unharmed, only I am writing to you with an injured hand... We managed to escape only with our lives... Papers, money, belongings — everyone lost everything, but there were only five fatalities! [...] Never will you be able to imagine that night of horror and agony!'[13] In a letter to Tyutchev's parents she reportedly wrote that she had sustained injuries to her left arm and back, while the children had only some bruises on the legs; she also asked for financial assistance.[14] Further letters were sent to Tyutchev and Clotilde. Turgenev in his account praises the courage and resolution shown by many of the women passengers;[15] Tyutchev too later acknowledged that only through Eleonore's 'presence of mind and courage' had her and the children's lives been saved. 'One can quite truthfully say that the children owe their lives twice over to their mother,' he wrote to his parents once he had been told the full story of what had happened.[16]

As if the physical and psychological effects of the disaster were not enough, Eleonore now had serious financial problems to contend with. Except for their furniture, which they had sold before leaving Munich, she had set off for their new home in Turin with all the family's personal and household effects, including clothes, silver and other valuables.[17] All this was now lost. Only recently she had taken receipt of over 3,000 roubles paid by the Foreign Ministry to cover their removal expenses;[18] presumably most of this too went up in flames. Among the papers lost was diplomatic mail she was carrying for the Sardinian authorities.[19] Other losses were beyond monetary value: these include her collection of Tyutchev's letters.

As luck would have it, Nicholas I was in Berlin at the time; on learning of the disaster he sent his aide-de-camp to Hamburg with money to cover the survivors' most pressing needs for clothing and travelling expenses. Eleonore wrote to the Emperor pleading her own case for support, and in the meantime borrowed money on credit.[20] Count Nesselrode, travelling with the Emperor, also came to Hamburg; he promised Eleonore he would do what he could in the way of compensation.[21] She was anxious to leave as soon as possible, concerned at how news of the disaster would affect her husband,[22] but was laid low for several days when a chill, aggravated by shock and general exhaustion, developed into 'something like a nervous fever'. Still not fully recovered, she set out for Munich with the children and servants, stopping in Berlin only to receive a sum of 200 louis d'or granted by the Emperor in response to her request.[23]

Far off in Turin, Tyutchev remained blissfully ignorant of the disaster until 11 June. On that day he was sitting quietly in his room when someone came to tell him of reports in the latest French newspapers that the *Nicholas I* had been destroyed by fire. He was thrown into despair. News had reached him only days before of the death of Darya's little son Vanya, born as he had left St Petersburg on the *Alexandra* the previous summer; now this seemed a terrible omen, strengthening his fears that Eleonore and the children could have been among the five deaths reported in the press. He asked Obrezkov to be allowed to go to Munich, where more up-to-date information would be available. It was not the most convenient of times to make such a request (his formal accreditation as Chargé d'Affaires was expected any day), but the sympathetic Obrezkov agreed that in the circumstances he should leave without delay, and reassured him there would be no repercussions for his career.[24] Tyutchev set off the same day, accompanied by his manservant Matthias Hölzl; travelling post-haste, he reached Munich on 16 June. His first call was at the boarding house at 4 Brienner-strasse kept by Eleonore's aunt Karoline von Hanstein.[25] He was immensely relieved to learn from her and Clotilde, who lived with her, that his loved-ones had all survived; there was even a letter for him from Eleonore.[26] Baroness von Hanstein refused to hear of him putting up at a hotel, insisting that he stay at her house.

A week later Eleonore and the children arrived: 'You may imagine our reunion', she wrote to Tyutchev's parents.[27] Although Tyutchev found her in better spirits than he had feared,[28] it soon became clear that she would have to rest before travelling on to Turin. Three days later a letter from Obrezkov reassured them that there was no need to hurry back; this was just as well, for Eleonore herself admitted to being still 'very unwell'.[29] Nevertheless she pressed for their departure, concerned that further delay would be damaging to her husband's career; it was left to him and the doctors attending her to persuade her that this would be folly.[30] Equally mindful of his career, Tyutchev pointed out that Amélie von Krüdener was expected in Munich soon and that it could only be to their advantage to see her.[31] Perhaps he already calculated that with her help he stood a chance of landing the ambassadorship in Turin once Nicholas had decided Charles Albert had learnt his lesson. No doubt finding the accommodation at Aunt Karoline's somewhat cramped, on 2 July they moved to new lodgings on nearby Wittelbacherplatz.[32] For a while Eleonore continued taking 'all sorts of remedies', but put her foot down when the doctors recommended she take a cure at Bad Kissingen: knowing that Tyutchev would not agree to leave her and go on alone, she insisted that they set out for Turin together come what may.[33] They left with the children on 10 July.[34] 'Because of my poor state of health, this final stage of the journey was particularly trying for me', she wrote afterwards.[35]

In Turin, where they arrived about 17 July,[36] she at once found herself plunged into a new sea of cares and anxieties. Suitable accommodation proved difficult to find, and for the time being they had to make do with rooms in a hotel. Tyutchev had already warned her that no furnished houses were available for rent in Turin,[37] so in the meantime she had to bustle around to sales and auctions in search of second-hand furniture. Money was again a problem: they had just about managed to pay their way as far as Turin, and now Tyutchev was forced to request an advance payment of salary.[38] The change of climate and surroundings proved a shock to Eleonore's system, wearing her health down even more. 'The city is beautiful, if somewhat monotonous and boring, and the countryside is picturesque,' she wrote to her parents-in-law after a month in Turin, 'but the suffocating heat and dust do not allow one to enjoy them [...]. All of us, even the children, are oppressed and exhausted by this fiery atmosphere.'[39]

There were also her husband's moods to contend with. He had finally been accredited as Chargé d'Affaires on 3 August,[40] and despite the summer absence of King and court was fairly occupied in his new role. Aware that 'the demands of his position make this disorder and lack of money doubly disagreeable to him', Eleonore was selflessly concerned to spare him as far as possible all the 'petty domestic cares which he finds distressing but can do nothing to remedy'. Yet despite all this she found herself admitting to his mother: 'I dare not speak to Théodore of my worries, as I find him depressed enough as it is. I do not know if it is due to the climate or the really very solitary kind of life he has to lead here, but taken together both of these aggravate that tendency of his to irritability and melancholy with which you are so familiar [...].'[41]

Although she had hoped to go to the Valle d'Aosta to take the waters,[42] by the middle of August they found an inexpensive house to rent in the suburbs, and she had to prepare herself instead for the upheaval of moving in. Yet in a letter to her mother-in-law on 16 August, Eleonore — ever the uncomplaining 'embodiment of meekness' — makes no mention of her own state of health, showing more concern for that of her husband: 'I find Théodore's health rather better than worse, and since he has been taking the hydropathic cure there has been an evident improvement. I hope he will have the determination to continue with this so simple remedy, for drinking plenty of water, rising early and bathing frequently can never do any harm, although it is clear that this can cure a long-standing complaint only slowly. As to the internal consumption of water, that is certainly very beneficial for him.'[43] Immediately after she had written this came good news: the Emperor had approved a grant of 800 *chervontsy*, worth 8,480 roubles in paper currency, to cover their losses in the fire.[44] Then, just two days later, she fell seriously ill. The exact nature of her illness is unknown: Solaro, the Sardinian Foreign Minister, wrote of her falling victim to 'a treacherous germ' ('*un faux germe*'), suggesting some kind of viral infection;[45] pneumonic complications have also been suspected.[46] Whatever the immediate cause, it is clear that the fire and shipwreck had so weakened her, both physically and mentally, that she was no longer in any state to resist. There followed 'three weeks of the most terrible suffering'.[47] On 8 September it was all over: death had claimed her at the third attempt.

Tyutchev, who had been with her to the end, was inconsolable in his grief. Later the story would be told in the family of how his hair turned grey overnight as he kept vigil by her coffin.[48] Years afterwards he spoke of Eleonore's death to their daughter Anna, who recorded his words in her diary. It seems old wounds had been reopened by thoughts of the disaster on the *Nicholas I*, the anniversary of which was only two weeks away. He began by saying that Eleonore — now no more than a 'vanished shade' — had once been 'life itself' for him, and 'so necessary to my existence that to live without her seemed to me as impossible as living without a head on one's shoulders'. At this point the raw emotion of his grief came flooding back, breaking down the barriers of his habitual reserve. 'Oh, how terrible death is! How terrible!' he exclaimed. 'A being whom you had loved for twelve years, whom you knew better than yourself, who was your life and happiness — a woman you had seen young and beautiful — laughing, loving and tender — and suddenly: dead, motionless, disfigured by corruption. That is terrible, terrible! There are no words to convey it. Only once in my life have I seen someone die... Death is terrible!' Shocked and upset as she was by this uncharacteristic outburst of her father, who had always seemed to her 'reticent by nature, and hating anything which shows the slightest sign of sentimentality', the seventeen-year-old Anna was nevertheless grateful for this rare insight into his innermost feelings.[49]

Eleonore was buried in a cemetery on the outskirts of Turin, in the present-day suburb of Torre Sellice.[50] There was apparently no money for a lavish funeral. Visiting her mother's grave over thirty years later, Darya Tyutcheva was surprised to find no more than a simple marble slab, neglected and overgrown, with no headstone or cross. The inscription in French had evidently been chosen by Tyutchev: 'She will come to me no more, but I am on my way to her'.[51] The grave has long since disappeared.[52]

Like Anna eight years later, Tyutchev's contemporaries in Turin were taken aback by his uninhibited manifestations of grief. According to the Bavarian Ambassador, he 'almost terrified Turin with displays of a despair which seemed to border on madness'.[53] Six weeks after the event he could write to his chief, Count Nesselrode: 'I am nothing any more, I can do nothing. This test has been beyond me... I feel completely destroyed...'[54] Doubtless his grief was compounded by agonies of remorse. Had Eleonore come to Turin the previous autumn as planned, she would have avoided the ordeal of fire at sea and shipwreck and would probably still be alive. Yet he had dissuaded her from this so that he could be with Ernestine...

On 17 October Tyutchev learned that Grand Duke Alexander, the twenty-one-year-old heir apparent to the Russian throne, then touring Italy, had arrived in Como. The following day (the eve of what would have been Eleonore's thirty-eighth birthday) he wrote to Alexander requesting an audience, as well as to the Grand Duke's tutor Zhukovsky, who was accompanying him. He hoped that meeting them — and especially Zhukovsky, who had known Eleonore in St Petersburg — would bring some comfort.[55] The letter to Zhukovsky was in Russian, his instinctively preferred language at such times of emotional crisis:

There are terrible moments in the life of a human being... To outlive everything that we lived by — *lived* for twelve whole years... What is more common than such a fate — and what more terrible? To outlive everything, and still to be alive. There are words we use all our lives without understanding them. And then suddenly we do... and in a single word — as if in a chasm , as if in an abyss — everything is swallowed up and disappears. At times of misfortune the heart believes, that is, understands. And for that reason I cannot but believe that a meeting with you at this moment — the most bitter, the most unbearable moment of my life — is not the gift of blind chance. For me it is not fortuitous that you have crossed the Alps... You have brought with you that which, after her, I love most of all in the world: our native land, and poetry... Was it not you who said somewhere: *There is much else apart from happiness that is noble in life*? In that dictum is contained a whole religion, a whole revelation.... And yet it is terrible, unspeakably terrible for the poor human heart to renounce happiness for ever. Farewell. My belief will not deceive me. We shall meet...[56]

Having received permission from Grand Duke Alexander, Tyutchev set out for Como, where he met Zhukovsky on 25 October.[57] They spent much of the next two weeks in each other's company, first in Como and then Milan, where Alexander moved with his entourage on 3 November.[58] It was the first time they had met since Tyutchev's youth. Zhukovsky listened sympathetically while the younger poet spoke at length of his bereavement, knowing that this could only help to relieve the burden of pain. One day, during a trip by steamer on Lake Como organised by Alexander, Zhukovsky conducted a 'pleasant conversation' with Tyutchev while sketching the passing landscape. At one point Tyutchev gazed wistfully towards the northern edge of the lake. 'Beyond those mountains lies Germany,' he said. Zhukovsky — 'In spirit [...], like a dove,/ Pure and intact', as Tyutchev would later describe him[59] — picked up the reference, and was disturbed by it. 'He is grieving for his wife, who died a martyr's death, yet they say he is in love with someone in Munich', reads the puzzled comment in his diary.[60]

Much of their conversation will also have been devoted to poetry and literature. It was Zhukovsky's first opportunity to discuss with Tyutchev the 'Poems Sent from Germany', published in Pushkin's journal. No doubt talk also turned to the subject of Pushkin's death, of which Zhukovsky had much to tell. And it may have been here in Como that Tyutchev was encouraged to pour his grief into the previously quoted 'Day and Night', a bleak poetic reflection on the metaphysical realities of existence.[61] Whereas in earlier poems he had frequently portrayed night as an emollient veil, descending upon and cancelling out the brash substantiality of day, it has been noted that here for the first time the roles are reversed: night is now the terrible reality, and day the healing veil — but one so flimsy as to be almost unreal, so that its apparent concealment of the 'abyss' is seen to be no more than a hollow pretence.[62] The experience of Eleonore's death had turned Tyutchev's world upside down — including, it seems, his poetic world. The image of the abyss as a metaphor for ultimate reality can of course (as discussed in Chapter 5) be shown to derive from Schelling's philosophy; yet for such 'borrowed' imagery to rise above the level of mere semantic representation it must first take on and develop a poetic life of its own. If our dating of 'Day and Night' is correct, it was composed almost immediately after Tyutchev had included in his letter to Zhukovsky the observation that we blithely use a word like 'death' without really understanding it, and that only direct experience of the reality, when 'in a single word — as if in a chasm, as if in an abyss — everything is swallowed up and disappears', can teach us its true meaning. In later poems and letters too he would often use the term 'abyss' in its various Russian or French forms ('*bezdna*', '*propast*' ', '*abîme*', '*gouffre*') as an image of death, extinction or separation.[63] The death of his wife had brought intimations of a metaphysical reality perceived not as some abstract philosophical concept, but as a palpable and terrifying fact.[64] Brute experience had taught him the meaning of the word; he could now imbue its poetic image with all the felt pain of his own existence.

After Tyutchev had left the imperial party on 10 November to return to Turin, Zhukovsky wrote to the current editor of *Sovremennik*, Pyotr Pletnyov: 'in Como and Milan I spent much time with Tyutchev, who is worthy of his poems.'[65] In a letter to Tyutchev's aunt Nadezhda Sheremeteva he was more expansive: 'Previously I knew him as a child, and now have come to love him as a mature adult; he is grieving for the loss of his wife. To him too, it seems, fate has not been very kind. He is an uncommonly brilliant person, and very good-natured, someone after my own heart.'[66]

Tyutchev had been favourably impressed by the young Grand Duke's 'natural dignity' and 'heartfelt kindness', and was gratified on leaving Milan to be told by Alexander that he hoped to visit Piedmont the following March.[67] From Milan he returned briefly to Turin before travelling on to Genoa, where King Charles Albert had as usual taken up residence for the month of November.[68] In the meantime his family had rallied round to give what support they could in his hour of need. As soon as his parents had learnt of Eleonore's death they had written offering to take Anna, Darya and Yekaterina into their care.[69] In the meantime Clotilde and Aunt Karoline declared themselves willing to look after them in Munich until the spring, when it would be easier for them to travel to Russia.[70] The girls left Turin with their governess Katharina Jardin while Tyutchev was in Como, and on 7 November moved into Aunt Karoline's house in Munich.[71] Nikolay left Warsaw as soon as he could obtain leave, and on 7 December was reunited with his brother in Genoa. He found Tyutchev in better physical shape than he had feared, but — as he reported to their parents — still 'in very low spirits': 'his nerves are so weakened that the slightest recollection of the past upsets him for days at a time.'[72]

There was no end in sight to his all-consuming grief and remorse. Even a year later he would write to his parents: 'there are things about which it is impossible to speak; memories which continue to bleed and will never heal.'[73] And although with

Ernestine's help he would gradually learn to live with his loss, it had changed him profoundly. In particular, he had all but lost his poetic voice. Two poems — 'Day and Night' and another yet to be discussed — were apparently written in the weeks and months immediately after Eleonore's death; yet over the course of the following ten years he would produce only four more lyric poems, together with half a dozen or so minor items (political verse and poems in French). Critics and biographers have generally been at a loss to explain this extended period when (to quote Richard Gregg) 'Tiutchev the poet had fallen strangely silent'.[74] Dmitry Blagoy suggested he had become disheartened by the lack of critical response to his 'Poems Sent from Germany'.[75] Yet for a good two years after these had appeared in *Sovremennik* he continued writing poems and sending them off for publication in that journal. In fact the chronology suggests a quite different explanation. The long hiatus which had begun with Eleonore's death ended in 1848 with two poems evidently intended to mark the tenth anniversary of her passing. One is a straightforward dedication to her,[76] the other — 'Now holy night has claimed the heavenly sphere...' (quoted in full in Chapter 5) — a conscious reworking of 'Day and Night'.[77] These inaugurated a period of renewed and sustained inspiration, resulting in some forty or more poems over the following three years (and thus, *pace* Blagoy, clearly *preceding* the renewal of critical interest in Tyutchev, which is generally accepted to have begun with the poet Nekrasov's appreciative article in *Sovremennik* in January 1850). During Eleonore's lifetime he appears to have addressed scarcely any poems to her; even the rare surviving exceptions — 'To Two Sisters', 'Autumn Evening' — fall far short of expressing all that now, too late, he felt for a wife whose love for him had been unbounded and unconditional. Perhaps it was no more than justice that his poetic voice had fallen silent; perhaps it would be restored only when he could manage somehow to atone for his neglect. Ten years later he found the words, and the spell was broken:

> Still love torments me with a vengeance,
> Still now my soul cries out to you —
> And through the veiled mists of remembrance
> Still shines your image, bright and true...
> An image treasured and pervasive —
> Unfading, never lost to sight,
> Unchanging, hauntingly elusive:
> A star set in the vault of night...[78]

Tyutchev had kept a lock of Eleonore's hair plaited into a bracelet, a relic which he evidently cherished over the years. It can still be seen in the Tyutchev Museum at Muranovo.[79] The need to be reassured of her continuing presence and closeness, so poignantly expressed in the lines just quoted, would be a leitmotif of later poetic tributes to her as well.

ii Diplomatic Diversions

At his lowest moments he had considered resigning his post and moving back to Munich. He wrote as much to Nikolay on 18 October, the same day on which he poured out his despair in letters to Nesselrode and Zhukovsky. His brother replied that this would be disastrous for his career, and that Munich would in any case hold many more painful memories of Eleonore than Turin. Far better to stay where he was and throw himself into his work.[80] This sensible advice was followed.

His immediate task as Chargé d'Affaires was to repair the damage done to Russo-Sardinian relations by the affair of Madame Obrezkova's headdress. In view of a new directive expected from St Petersburg instructing all wives of diplomats to appear at court in national dress, he had been relieved to hear from Eleonore that according to Nesselrode's assurance to her in Hamburg Western apparel would continue to be acceptable pending any official announcement. This would at least allow her to be presented at court without the notorious lappets sparking off a further diplomatic row. On the other hand, Madame Obrezkova — newly returned from Berlin, where she had met Tsar Nicholas — claimed to have it on the Emperor's own authority that national dress was already *de rigueur*, and that Eleonore must therefore wear it for her official presentation. One of Tyutchev's first deeds as acting Head of Mission was to write to Nesselrode for clarification in this 'unfortunate question of costume', a problem 'not of my creation, but which I have inherited'.[81] Nesselrode's reply was overtaken by events: Eleonore died before she could be presented at court.

A more serious opportunity to improve relations was provided by the visit of Grand Duke Alexander to Piedmont-Sardinia from 16 to 24 February 1839, the possibility of which Tyutchev had broached with the Tsarevich in Como. This passed off well, if not without the odd discordant note. Alexander declined for instance the King's invitation to stay in the royal palaces on the rather implausible grounds that he was travelling incognito; learning that the Governor of Genoa, Paulucci, had arranged a ball in Alexander's honour on the first Sunday in Lent, the strictly religious Charles Albert commanded him to cancel it (Paulucci pretended not to have received the King's decree and went ahead anyway); finally, Alexander was pointedly not awarded the Sardinian order customarily received by visiting dignitaries of his rank.[82] Yet apart from this the Tsarevich was accorded the warmest of welcomes. In a despatch to Nesselrode Tyutchev tried to explain the King's apparently inconsistent behaviour. Charles Albert, he wrote, 'is a fiery person beneath a cold exterior: in his passion there is calculation, but sometimes passion perverts his calculation'; what is more, he 'is vexed by the absence of a Russian ambassador at his court'.[83] Despite all this the Grand Duke's visit to Sardinia was judged by both sides to have done much to heal the rift between the two countries, and the Emperor let it be known that he appreciated Tyutchev's 'zeal and devotion' in helping to ensure its success.[84]

The visit also brought him together with Zhukovsky again. As before, Zhukovsky was impressed by the younger man, whose wit and erudition seemed to him very much in the spirit of the great Karamzin.[85] Tyutchev introduced Zhukovsky to some of his Turin acquaintances, including the Italian patriot and poet Silvio Pellico. Incarcerated by the Austrians for ten years for suspected membership of the Carbonari movement, Pellico had subsequently published an account of his experiences, *Le mie prigioni* (*My Prisons*), which proved hugely damaging to the Austrian authorities, not least because of the spirit of Christian forgiveness in which it was written. Tyutchev appears to have respected the convictions of this 'man of great suffering' ('*mnogostradalets*'), as he described Pellico to Zhukovsky; he was in any case never one to let ideological differences stand in the way of personal friendship or admiration. He and Zhukovsky visited Pellico on the afternoons of 20 and 21 February, staying for an hour or so on each occasion. [86]

During his eleven months as Chargé d'Affaires in Turin Tyutchev sent a total of 45 official despatches to Nesselrode or his deputy, all couched in his usual elegant French.[87] In these, as well as dealing with such routine matters as the issuing of passports, financial transactions, assistance to Russian nationals in Piedmont and the like, he had ample opportunity to apply his keen analytical mind to weightier political issues. One of his despatches — on a trade agreement recently concluded between Sardinia and the USA — concludes with a wry apology for its 'length and dryness'. Yet in it he gives an impressive analysis of the economic and geopolitical implications of the treaty, including penetration of the northern Italian, Swiss and German markets by US trade, and 'the strengthening and ultimate establishment of [...] the USA in the Mediterranean'.[88] Similarly, a threatened breakdown in trade relations between Sardinia and Spain (later averted) is not only traced back to its political causes (injudicious remarks made in his official capacity by the Sardinian Governor of Nice to some Spaniards), but also — in view of 'the revolutionary posturing of the Madrid government' — shown to be fraught with the danger of military conflict.[89] And when what he calls on one occasion 'the fortunate sterility of events'[90] leaves little or nothing to report from Piedmont-Sardinia itself, he is quite happy to turn his attention to the wider international scene.[91] The language and approach of these despatches may be more conventionally restrained than that of the report on Greek affairs rejected by Ambassador Gagarin; yet there is still the same sense of a brilliant if somewhat erratic political intellect reaching always after the broader context. Reporting the Turin government's concern in April 1839 at events in France, where conflict between King Louis Philippe and Prime Minister Thiers seemed about to escalate into a more serious political crisis, he finds some reassurance in the assertion that 'fifty years of revolutionary debauchery have used up all this country's energies, leaving it capable of no more than impotent stirrings of desire'.[92] It was a witty analogy, no doubt, but one which the events of 1848 would prove spectacularly wrong.

Tyutchev also shows himself to be a keen observer of Sardinian internal politics. The picture painted in his despatches is of a powerful conservative and 'ultra-religious' clique at court, led by Solaro and backed by the Catholic hierarchy, which is slowly but surely extending its influence over the ailing and reclusive King. Inspired by a 'spirit of bigotry', this party is keen to neutralise or remove the few supporters of progressive policies (or 'rational ideas', in Tyutchev's more cautious terminology) still remaining at court. The latter include the Governor of Genoa, Paulucci, and the Minister of the Interior, Pralormo. As a friend of Russia (he had formerly spent over twenty years in Russian service, rising to become Military Governor of Riga and Governor-General of the Baltic provinces),[93] Paulucci is singled out as worthy of particular support in the power struggle taking place. Tyutchev concludes that it would be disastrous if the clerical party prevailed, for 'the greatest misfortune for a country is to have a government which is no more than the instrument of a particular party'. What is more, for such an administration 'any considerations of a political or conciliatory nature in dealings with governments which do not have the good fortune to be Catholic will come to be regarded as the beginnings of heresy'. As one commentator on these despatches has pointed out, this contains a fairly clear warning that a fundamentalist Piedmont-Sardinia could reject Russian influence and move closer to Catholic France.[94]

Foreshadowing Tyutchev's later critique of the Roman Catholic Church in general are his comments in one despatch on the Archbishop of Turin, who had publicly denounced the government of Prussia for its differences with the Vatican: 'Unfortunately, for all its fulminations against the spirit of the age, the Catholic clergy remains unaware that it is itself much more seriously and deeply infected by that spirit than it imagines, and that what it considers to be religious fervour is most often no more than that same spirit of revolt against power, that hatred of all authority, which are the chief malady of the present age'.[95]

Of especial interest are Tyutchev's reports on various programmes of reform then under way in Piedmont-Sardinia. He gives for instance a detailed account of reforms to the penal system designed to reflect the most progressive practice of other countries, in particular Switzerland. Carried out under the auspices of Minister of the Interior Pralormo, these measures represent in Tyutchev's view 'genuine progress, which although admittedly of little interest to the daily press, nevertheless deserves to be brought to the attention of an enlightened government'.[96] Clearly he hoped his despatches might help to further the cause of reform in Russia. This was particularly true of Sardinia's proposed abolition of feudal servitude, which in his view 'may inaugurate a new era' for that country.[97] Support for the abolition of serfdom in Russia was growing, despite the opposition of highly-placed diehard conservatives such as Count Uvarov and Prince Aleksandr Menshikov. Tsar Nicholas himself had declared the institution to be a 'flagrant evil' in principle, although in practice he baulked at what he saw as insuperable political obstacles to a programme of general emancipation. One of his most able administrators, Minister of State Domains Pavel Kiselyov, was a committed opponent of serfdom. In 1839 he submitted proposals for regulating the relations between landowners and serfs, including the terms under which serfs could be emancipated by mutual consent with their masters. Much watered down, these proposals formed the basis of a law promulgated three years later, which however did little to tackle the basic problems of serfdom and indeed remained largely a dead letter. Kiselyov was more successful in improving the status and welfare of the state peasants directly under the control of his ministry, especially in the field of education.[98] In 1839, apparently as part of a fact-finding exercise, he sent Nesselrode a set of questions to be circulated to Russian embassies on the organisation and administration of state domains in the particular country for which they were responsible. One of Tyutchev's last acts as Chargé d'Affaires was to reply with a memorandum he had compiled on the situation in Piedmont-Sardinia. According to his accompanying despatch, this dealt largely with what he saw as the most important question he had been asked to address, namely that of land ownership.[99] Tyutchev's attitude towards serfdom is unlikely to have changed materially since his and Sverbeyev's attacks on it in 1823; certainly he later welcomed and supported the reforms of Alexander II. Unfortunately his memorandum of 1839, which might provide further evidence of his views on the matter, has still to be traced.[100]

iii Second Marriage and Flight

'Today's date is a sad one for me: 9 September,' Tyutchev wrote to Ernestine on the fifth anniversary of Eleonore's death. 'That was the most terrible day of my life, and *without you* it would probably have been my last.'[101] During the darkest hours his one ray of hope had been the thought of seeing Ernestine again. They were reunited in Genoa on 30 November, almost a year to the day after they had made their 'last farewell' there.[102] Tyutchev in particular must have been struck by the coincidence of time and place: was it not an omen of their intended destiny? Many years later he would look back on their strolls together 'along the walls of the Genoa fortress, overlooking the beautiful waves of the Mediterranean, now calm, now raging', and wonder ruefully if they could ever again, as in those blissful days, 'belong completely to one another'.[103] Within a week they had resolved to marry just as soon as the social decencies allowed. Ernestine informed her brother Karl of their decision by letter on 9 December;[104] no doubt they also told Nikolay, who had arrived two days earlier, but otherwise kept the engagement to themselves for the time being. Quite apart from what society at large might think, their own rejoicing was inevitably overshadowed by the tragic circumstances which had brought them together. Tyutchev had a double burden of remorse to bear, for he knew that his love for Ernestine had caused her almost as much suffering as it had Eleonore. This found expression in a poem written apparently at this time or soon after, in which the beginning of his and Ernestine's passionate affair — what he would later call 'our mythological times'[105] — is recalled in the light of all that had happened since, including the death of Eleonore:

> With what sweet tenderness, what lovesick melancholy,
> On him would rest your gaze of languishing desire!
> And you: bewildered, speechless, like one struck insensate
>   By lightning's pure celestial fire!
>
> And there were times you'd fall upon your knees, all trembling,
> And weeping — all the turmoil of your heart revealed...
> But soon by carefree, childlike sleep most mercifully
>   Your silken lashes would be sealed —
>
> And, sinking into his receiving arms, you'd slumber,
> He cradling gently as a mother your dear head...
> Your groans would cease, your laboured breathing become calmer,
>   And peacefully you'd sleep instead.
>
> But now... O, had your dreams then shown you but some portent
> Of what the future still for us two held in store,
> You would have woken with a scream, as if tormented —
>   Or else slept on, to wake no more.[106]

Already on 5 December King Charles Albert and his court had left Genoa for Turin after the usual month's stay. They were followed by the diplomatic corps, with the exception of some envoys who (like that of Russia) were also accredited to the minor court of Parma, and who now took the opportunity of paying formal respects to the ruling Archduchess Marie-Louise. Tyutchev reported to Nesselrode that although he had intended to join them, poor health had obliged him to postpone the visit until another occasion.[107] No doubt he relied on the same excuse to justify staying on in Genoa with Ernestine and Nikolay until after Christmas. He returned to the capital just before the New Year, accompanied by Nikolay, who was duly presented to the King and introduced to Solaro and several of the foreign envoys.[108]

Ernestine stayed on in Genoa until the end of February, then moved to Turin, remaining there throughout March and most of April.[109] By now Tyutchev's domestic arrangements had given their marriage plans an unexpected urgency. The girls seemed to have settled down well enough in Munich, but in March Clotilde wrote to say she would be unable to look after them for much longer. She and Maltitz were due to be married on 6 April, after which they were hoping to move to The Hague.[110] The girls could stay on with with their great-aunt Karoline for the time being, but she could not be expected to look after them indefinitely, even with the help of a governess or nanny. Ernestine declared that she would be only too happy to take on the role of mother to the girls herself; apart from anything else this would avoid having to send them to their grandparents in Russia as originally planned. First, of course, she and Tyutchev would have to be wed. On 13 March Tyutchev wrote to Nesselrode asking for permission to marry, explaining that although he had been 'firmly resolved to defer this step for a long time to come', the family circumstances just outlined now rendered it necessary. At the same time he requested leave 'for several months', claiming that the various arrangements he had to make would involve 'absences and numerous journeys'. In this connection he delicately reminded Nesselrode of the latter's assurance to him earlier that winter, conveyed via Amélie von Krüdener, that he would not object to him 'temporarily' absenting himself from his post.[111]

The logistical problems Tyutchev faced in arranging his second marriage were as daunting as the first time round. To be valid in Russian law, their marriage had to be concluded in an Orthodox church, while Ernestine's faith also required a Catholic ceremony. Neither denomination had any objection in principle to a double consecration, but the Church in Italy would perform the ceremony only on condition that children from the marriage be raised as Catholics. However, as a Russian subject Tyutchev was barred by law from giving any such undertaking. The only way out of the impasse would be to marry somewhere outside Italy — perhaps Switzerland, where the Catholic authorities were thought to take a more relaxed view on the religious upbringing of children.[112] First of all, of course, they would need official permission from St Petersburg.

In the meantime life went on. On 22 April Tyutchev set off on his postponed official visit to Parma. He left Second Secretary Aleksey Bogayevsky (who had taken over from Miklashevsky the previous year) in temporary charge at the Embassy. At about the same time Ernestine also left Turin, heading for Florence, where her brother Karl had moved with his wife and children for a protracted stay. It is likely that she and Tyutchev travelled together for the first part of their journey. After visiting Parma he hoped to join her and the others in Florence for a while.[113] However, they had probably got no further than Alessandria, half-way to Genoa, when he was surprised to see Tom-

Have appear. The young Attaché had been sent in hot pursuit of him with an urgent message from Bogayevsky. Just after Tyutchev's departure a personal letter from Tsar Nicholas to King Charles Albert had arrived, expressing gratitude for the reception accorded to Grand Duke Alexander on his recent visit. There were also instructions from Nesselrode to Tyutchev to deliver the letter in person if possible, and at the same time to give oral assurances to the King or Solaro of the 'sincere friendship and community of principles' which the Emperor trusted would now inform relations between the two courts.[114] There was nothing for it: he had to abandon his journey to Parma and return to Turin. Here on 24 April he took Nicholas's letter to Solaro and said it would be a great honour to be permitted to deliver it to the King in person. Solaro pointed out that such a presentation by a mere Chargé d'Affaires was strictly against etiquette, but agreed to find out whether Charles Albert, about to leave Turin for several days, would make an exception when he came back.[115]

Tyutchev settled back to wait for the King's return. In the meantime, on 27 or 28 April, news arrived in the form of a despatch from Nesselrode that Nikolay Kokoshkin, up to then Chargé d'Affaires at the Russian Embassy in Florence, had been appointed as the new Ambassador to Piedmont-Sardinia and would be arriving to take up his post in the near future. Tyutchev was instructed to carry on in charge of the Embassy in the meantime.[116] He had hoped to step into Obrezkov's shoes himself, and made no attempt to conceal his disappointment. Reporting Kokoshkin's elevation, the Bavarian Ambassador von Olry commented:

This appointment seems to have dashed the hopes which M. de Tustschew [sic] apparently conceived for himself. However that may be, if this diplomatic agent applies the mobility of his genius just as readily to the chances of fortune as he does to his amorous liaisons, he will have little cause for regret. Indeed, having on the tragic death of his wife almost terrified Turin with displays of a despair which seemed to border on madness, he has just astonished society here by the rapidity with which a new attachment impels him towards a second marriage, to Baroness Dörnberg. He speaks of nothing else but this impending union and the obstacles which, spurred on by his impatience, he is passionately seeking to overcome in order to speed its conclusion.[117]

The disheartening news from St Petersburg left Tyutchev feeling disinclined to hang around indefinitely for Charles Albert to return. He was also annoyed that he had still received no reply to his request for leave in order to marry and settle his family affairs; he reminded Nesselrode of this in a despatch acknowledging notification of Kokoshkin's appointment, adding: 'My most cherished interests, both now and in the future, depend on the favour which I ask.'[118] Postdating this and four other despatches to 1 May, when the quarterly Russian courier from Naples and Rome was expected to pass through, he set out once more for Parma on 29 April.[119] When the very next day Charles Albert arrived in Turin and indicated his willingness to receive Nicholas's letter from the Russian Chargé d'Affaires in person, it was of course too late. There appear to have been no recriminations. According to Tyutchev the King had read and been 'deeply moved' by the letter already before leaving the capital.[120] This appears to be confirmed by a report from the French Chargé d'Affaires dated 25 April that Nicholas's letter had been received by the Sardinian court with 'very great joy'.[121] And Tyutchev's failure to appear for a purely formal presentation could if necessary be justified in terms of conflicting claims on his presence: his courtesy visit to Archduchess Marie-Louise was long overdue, and had already been twice postponed.

In Parma he was warmly received by the Archduchess, who regretted that only poor health had prevented her from extending an invitation to Grand Duke Alexander on his recent tour of Italy.[122] As widow of the Emperor Napoleon, she will have provided fascinating conversation; but Tyutchev's thoughts were elsewhere, and as soon as he could he left Parma and hurried on to join Ernestine in Florence. After he had been obliged to turn back to Turin on 23 April, she had continued her journey via Genoa. On the 25th she wrote to Pfeffel that her arrival in Florence would be delayed.[123] This may be connected with her later recollection of having nearly drowned while attempting to cross a swollen stream in northern Italy, although whether that was on this occasion is not absolutely clear.[124] In any case she was in Pisa by 2 May and reached Florence two days later.[125] Tyutchev joined her there soon afterwards, and certainly no later than the 10th.[126] He was in no hurry to return to Turin, calculating that his visit to Parma, followed by the Sardinian Foreign Minister's absence for several weeks to attend canonisation ceremonies in Rome, would in conjunction furnish a plausible excuse for his failure to communicate with St Petersburg.[127]

The four weeks or so they spent together in Florence that May were later remembered by Ernestine as the happiest time of her life. In conversation with her stepdaughter Darya in 1857 she recalled that 'every day there were festivities and such gay processions in the outlying parts of the city, and in the evenings, when [we] strolled through the outskirts of Florence, it was as bright as day with glow-worms.' Recording these words in her diary, Darya comments: 'Everything around you seems beautiful when you are in love. How much more so that which was truly beautiful must have seemed to Mama, with her poetic, refined and feminine nature, when she was in love.'[128] Together they made excursions into the surrounding countryside: to Bello-sguardo Hill just outside Florence, where they could walk through grassy meadows along the Via Piana, enjoying views of the city below; to Fiesole, an ancient settlement with Etruscan and Roman remains including a temple and amphitheatre; and to the magnificent villas of Castello and La Pietra with their ornately laid out gardens, built on the lower slopes of Monte Morello as retreats for the Medici.[129] They stayed at a hotel in Florence, but spent much time with the Pfeffels.[130] For Karl in particular it was an opportunity to cement his friendship with his future brother-in-law. Writing to Ernestine after she and Tyutchev had left, he recalled with gratitude 'the friendliness shown towards us by Mr Tyutchev. His intellect, his amiable conversation and easy manner — these are what we shall recall with particular pleasure when returning in thought to those days spent by you in Florence. [...] I thank Heaven for having granted me this opportunity to come to know him and esteem him according to his deserts.'[131]

One of the topics discussed with the Pfeffels will have been the wedding plans. Tyutchev had already set the wheels in motion for them to be married in the Orthodox church attached to the Russian Embassy in Berne, followed by a Catholic ceremony, also in Switzerland. He hoped to receive definite confirmation of this, and news of Kokoshkin's arrival, on the way back to Turin.[132] Then — assuming Nesselrode had agreed to his request for a lengthy period of leave, which was surely a formality — they would be free to marry. At some stage they would have to go to Munich to collect the girls, although Aunt Karoline seemed to be coping well enough for the moment, as a letter from Anna had confirmed.[133] As for future plans, they would spend part of the summer in Switzerland, after which Tyutchev hoped to obtain a new and improved posting elsewhere. Turin offered no chance of promotion now, and in any case was too full of painful memories. Grand Duke Alexander himself had offered to help further his career, and it would be easy enough to remind him of this via Zhukovsky.[134]

They were in no great hurry to return to Turin as they bade farewell to the Pfeffels and left Florence on 4 June.[135] They lingered for some days in ancient Lucca with its picturesque town walls, not neglecting to visit the famous curative springs and baths about an hour's drive away.[136] On the way to Lucca they are almost certain to have made the short detour to Pisa, which Ernestine had visited on her journey to Florence, and where she later recalled being charmed, not so much by its individual architectural treasures — the leaning bell-tower, the Romanesque cathedral, the Campo Santo cemetery — as by the general atmosphere of a place where 'everything reminds one of a glorious past, with no interference from the hustle and bustle of the present day; where grass grows in streets lined on both sides by uninhabited palaces; where one can stroll without meeting a living soul to distract one from immersion in times long past.'[137] Leaving Lucca on 10 May, they took the coastal road via Carrara, Portovenere and La Spezia, and arrived in Genoa on the 13th.[138] From here three days later Tyutchev thought it advisable to send two despatches to Nesselrode, with excuses for the interval of over six weeks since his last.[139]

They were back in Turin by the end of June.[140] Here at last Tyutchev found waiting for him the reply to his request for permission to marry and take leave. Dated 15/27 April, it must have arrived at the Embassy not long after he reached Florence. Nesselrode informed him there was no objection to his marrying, subject to 'the formalities prescribed by law in the case of marriage between a Russian citizen and a national of another country, and also in the case of a difference in the religion of the spouses'. However:

As for the leave for which you apply, Sir, in order to go to Munich to fetch your children, I regret that I cannot grant it to you at present. Mr Kakoshkin [sic] has only just been appointed Minister Resident at the Sardinian Court and I consider it my duty to instruct you to postpone your journey until his arrival and entry into service, especially as he will not delay in proceeding to the place of his new appointment, of which I already informed you in my despatch of 1[13] April 1839.[141]

Nesselrode's ruling was predictable enough. It was after all presumptuous to assume that his informal agreement to a temporary absence in response to Amélie's intercession could be taken as *carte blanche* for extended leave. What were all these journeys Tyutchev claimed were necessary to sort out his family affairs, and why should they take several months? Let him get married by all means, but he must stay at his post until Kokoshkin arrived.

But waiting indefinitely for Kokoshkin (of whom there was still no news) was no longer an option. The prenuptial honeymoon in Tuscany had borne fruit: by the beginning of July Ernestine knew or at least suspected that she was pregnant.[142] Tyutchev decided to ignore his chief 's explicit instructions and go ahead with the wedding in Switzerland as planned. At first the risks involved may not have seemed too great. The summer political break had begun on 1 July with the King moving to his summer residence at Racconigi, and other diplomats in Turin would be taking advantage of his absence over the coming two months to go away themselves.[143] In these circumstances it seemed safe enough to leave the Embassy in the hands of his second-in-command, Bogayevsky, as he had done throughout May and June.

However, there was a problem. For Bogayevsky, already keen to leave Turin, the prospect of having to stay on as unacknowledged dogsbody for the rest of the summer while his comparatively well-paid superior went swanning off again may have proved the final straw. Whatever the reason, he appears to have abandoned Turin at about the same time as Tyutchev, formally resigning his post later that autumn.[144] The only other stand-in available was the Attaché, Tom-Have. To leave such a lowly trainee with no diplomatic accreditation in charge of an embassy was unthinkable; Tyutchev decided to do it anyway. After dictating four despatches to be picked up by the next official courier, he left for Switzerland with Ernestine on 7 July.[145] Just over a week later the Austrian Ambassador, Meysenbug, reported to Vienna that Tyutchev 'has gone to Switzerland, leaving here only an Attaché, charged with the duty of stamping pass-ports. As Mr Tyutchev seems to have the intention of retiring from the Service, it is probable that he will not return here again.'[146] Meysenbug may have misinterpreted Tyutchev's no doubt forcefully expressed intentions. Although he was clearly set on resigning as First Secretary in Turin, he evidently had no plans to retire from the Foreign Service altogether, but rather to seek preferment elsewhere with the help of highly-placed contacts. He was certainly under no financial pressure: as a wealthy heiress, Ernestine had declared herself prepared to support him and his daughters after their marriage, not to mention paying off his debts of 20,000 roubles.[147] Knowing this may of course have encouraged him to take risks with his career.

If Tyutchev hoped that his dereliction of duty would go undetected, he was mistaken: there would be serious consequences. The whole affair was to provide the stuff of widespread gossip and legend during his lifetime, much of which can be discounted as demonstrably inaccurate in essential details. However, one later account deserves to be considered, if only because the scholar who recorded it, Yevlaliya Kazanovich, heard it from an unnamed source who in turn claimed to have had it from Tyutchev's own lips. According to this, Tyutchev, 'taking the diplomatic codes with him, set out for Switzerland with his future wife, [...] married her there, and lost the codes and other important official documents in the confusion of the wedding and journey.'[148] Sensitive diplomatic documents were routinely coded, and the keys for their decipherment were vitally important documents. They were changed regularly to foil potential code-breakers: tables containing the new key would be distributed to the heads of foreign missions, who were under an obligation to return the superseded tables under equally secure conditions. In response to an instruction from the Foreign Ministry to return two such tables, on 1 May Tyutchev had undertaken to send them with the next official Russian courier calling from Naples and Rome.[149] His very last despatch before leaving Turin in July (No. 28) states that he was sending with the courier 'tables No. 153, 154 and 155, now superseded'.[150] Although the Foreign Ministry had apparently requested two tables, Tyutchev writes of returning three. Did he perhaps send back one of the new tables by mistake? This would have caused problems for the new Ambassador, at least for a while, and might have formed a basis for the story, garbled over the years, quoted by Kazanovich. Or did he indeed take the new ones with him rather than entrust them to Tom-Have, and then lose them somewhere? The fact that he returned the superseded tables tells us of course nothing of what he may have done with the new ones. For this reason it is impossible to concur with the recently made assertion that despatch No. 28 'throws into question the firmly entrenched legend of Tyutchev having lost the diplomatic codes "in the confusion of the wedding" '.[151] The existence side by side of the despatch and of the account quoted by Kazanovich must rather be considered at the very least a remarkable coincidence.

After crossing the Mont Cenis pass into France on 8 July,[152] Tyutchev and Ernestine made their way through Savoy and into Switzerland. By the 21st they were in Fribourg,[153] where their hopes for a Catholic consecration of the marriage in Switzerland were dashed. 'I was greatly distressed by the Bishop of Fribourg's incomprehensible behaviour towards you,' Pfeffel's wife Carolina wrote in reply to Ernestine's account, now lost, of their interview with him.[154] There were no problems with the Orthodox wedding, which went ahead as planned in the church of the Russian Embassy in Berne on 29 July. Acting as witnesses were the Russian Ambassador to Switzerland, Baron Paul Ludwig von Krüdener (no relation of Amélie's husband), and his First and Second Secretaries.[155] In the meantime they had made enquiries about a Catholic consecration in the Grand Duchy of Baden. This time there was no trouble obtaining permission: the ceremony took place on 10 August at what is now the Holy Trinity church in Konstanz, just over the border from Switzerland.[156]

Meanwhile back in Turin Tom-Have was finding he had more to cope with than the routine stamping of passports. On 21 July he was obliged to write to Solaro on behalf of three Russian officers seeking official permission to visit fortresses in Piedmont-Sardinia.[157] This opened an exchange of notes between the Foreign Minister and Russia's supernumerary representative which continued well into August.[158] On 8 August the French Chargé d'Affaires, Chatry, reported that Tyutchev had 'taken up residence' in Switzerland, 'leaving here only an Attaché with no accreditation whatever, who finds himself fairly embarrassed by this irregular situation'.[159] To make things worse, there was still no sign of Kokoshkin.

Having evidently got wind of Tom-Have's predicament, Tyutchev decided he must return to Turin temporarily. Leaving Ernestine in Konstanz, he arrived in the Sardinian capital at some time between 22 and 25 August.[160] He appears to have stayed no more than a week or two, just long enough to put in a token appearance and deal with outstanding paperwork, and perhaps to reassure himself (and Tom-Have) that Kokoshkin was at last on his way. However, eager to join Ernestine in Munich, where they had decided to spend the winter, he was in no mood to hang around for the new Ambassador. By the time Kokoshkin finally arrived in the last week of September,[161] Tyutchev was already in Munich.[162] It was another serious failure of judgement on his part, for which he would pay dearly in due course.

On 18 October he wrote to Nesselrode formally resigning from his post as First Secretary in Turin. He also requested leave to spend the winter in Munich, as it was now too late in the year to contemplate travelling with his children to Russia. He undertook to return to his native country the following spring, if possible to settle there permanently.[163] This implied that he hoped for a Foreign Ministry post in St Petersburg, but the wording was vague enough to leave other options open. There were no objections from Nesselrode, who was still evidently unaware of his wayward diplomat's escapades. As Tyutchev later told his parents, the Foreign Minister replied 'most obligingly', agreeing to his request.[164] The official documents show that Tyutchev and Bogayevsky were to be kept on the Foreign Ministry staff without pay until new appointments had been agreed. They were both granted four months' leave from 10/22 November, with permission to stay abroad. The staff changes in Turin brought good news for Tom-Have: he was appointed to replace Bogayevsky as Second Secretary .[165]

11 In Search of a Role (Munich, 1839-1844)

i Home Life

Tyutchev must have felt he had come full circle after the upheavals of Turin. The first-floor apartment he and Ernestine rented at 18 Briennerstrasse, situated where that street meets the eastern side of the Karolinenplatz, was next door to the house he and Eleonore had left two years before, determined never to return.[1] Clotilde and Maltitz were just a couple of minutes' walk away at 4 Ottostrasse: recently renumbered from 248, this was the same house where Tyutchev and Eleonore had begun their official married life together, and where Anna had been born.[2] Anna, Darya and Kitty left the Maltitzes and moved in with their father and Ernestine, who rapidly established a close bond with at least the two younger of her stepdaughters.[3]

For the first few months Tyutchev and Ernestine led (in his words) 'a very secluded and quiet life', their social contacts restricted largely to their own family, the Maltitzes and Clotilde's relatives: her ageing father, Count Karl, now in the care of his daughter and son-in-law; Aunt Karoline von Hanstein; and the four of Clotilde's surviving brothers — Friedrich, Hippolyt, Karl and Maximilian — then living in Munich.[4] Outside the family circle Tyutchev found he got on surprisingly well with the Russian Ambassador Dmitry Severin, whose appointment two years before had been one of his stated reasons for leaving Munich.[5] From Maltitz he was pleased to learn that Shevyryov was at nearby Dachau for the autumn and winter and could be expected in Munich soon. Maltitz wrote to Shevyryov that Tyutchev had conceived ambitious literary plans to rival their own, involving the translation of Latin poetry into Russian.[6] Nothing came of these pipe dreams. Nor did Shevyryov's visit to Munich in October spark off any of the poetic creativity their meetings on Ischia had generated ten years previously. Instead, Tyutchev grumbled at being named as a 'Russian poet' in an article by Shevyryov's friend Nikolay Melgunov, recently published in Germany. 'How ridiculous Tyutchev is with his diplomatic modesty!' Melgunov retorted in a letter to Shevyryov, pointing out that his poems were already in the public domain.[7] He had always cultivated the image of poetic dabbler; now, it seems, even that was beneath him.

His immediate plan was to spend the rest of his leave that winter in Munich,[8] after which he was under an obligation to return to St Petersburg to apply for a new diplomatic posting. With the confidence of one who believed his misdemeanours to have gone undetected, he talked of accepting nothing less than Legation Councillor, or failing that a 'reasonably acceptable' Foreign Ministry desk job in St Petersburg, as a condition of remaining in service. Of course, part of him recognised that he could not expect Ernestine to support him and his daughters out of her own capital indefinitely (his private income — the 6,000 roubles a year from the family estate — was a drop in the ocean).[9] Yet as long as she was prepared to do so, he was only encouraged in his tendency to procrastinate and muddle through. He failed to report for duty in St Petersburg in 1840, partly no doubt through plain inertia, but partly for more genuine reasons. At the end of February the family moved to a larger apartment at 6 Otto-strasse, next door but one to the Maltitzes;[10] a week later, on 6 March, Ernestine gave birth to a daughter, Maria.[11] Soon afterwards she was laid low for several weeks after complications with breast-feeding and was advised to spend the summer at Tegernsee to recover her health.[12] There could be no question now of her travelling to Russia, and Tyutchev seems to have been unwilling to go without her.

His superiors in St Petersburg were evidently still unaware of his dereliction of duty in Turin, for his progress up the career ladder continued unaffected. In November 1839 he was awarded the customary decoration for fifteen years' unblemished service (a silver-gilt clasp displaying a Roman numeral garlanded with oak leaves); in January 1840 he was promoted (with effect from 31 December 1838) to Collegiate Councillor, equivalent to the army rank of Colonel.[13] He might even have got away with his transgression, had he not in February made the fatal mistake of sending the Foreign Ministry a reminder that he was still owed salary for the last five months of his service as Chargé d'Affaires. The period claimed was from 1/13 May to Kokoshkin's formal assumption of the duties of Ambassador on 29 September/ 11 October 1839.[14] No doubt he needed the money, but he must at least have suspected that St Petersburg would check with Turin. This was indeed the case. Kokoshkin reported back on the basis of information from Tom-Have and the Embassy's banker Travi that Tyutchev 'left Turin on 25 June/ 7 July and travelled via Switzerland to Munich, from whence he did not return to his post again' (his brief visit in August appears to have been overlooked). Tyutchev duly received the salary owing to him up to this date, but in return he had given the game away about his misconduct.[15]

In the autumn of 1840 Ernestine became pregnant again; the following June she was delivered of a healthy child: a boy this time, christened Dmitry in deference to his godfather, Severin.[16] Once again family circumstances had given Tyutchev an excuse to postpone the required visit to St Petersburg, now more than a year overdue. In July he wrote to his parents that he might travel to Russia that autumn;[17] but even if he was serious, he had left it too late. On 16 August 1841 he was summoned to the Embassy by Severin to be informed of a directive which had just arrived from St Petersburg: in view of his 'protracted failure to report back from leave' Tyutchev was no longer to be considered on the staff of the Foreign Ministry;[18] he was also stripped of the title of Chamberlain.[19]

According to Severin, Tyutchev heard his 'sentence' read out with 'a profound sense of mortification'.[20] Yet it was no more than could have been expected in the circumstances. There is certainly no reason to follow Vadim Kozhinov in supposing political reasons for his dismissal.[21] His unauthorised abandonment of the Turin Embassy against express instructions, apparent loss of secret documents, false salary claim and failure to return from leave were more than sufficient grounds. If anything he could count himself fortunate to have retained the status of civil servant, as acknowledged by his transfer to an obscure revenue department later that year.[22] Indeed, one is tempted to wonder with one of his biographers whether patronage in high places may have helped him avoid even more severe punishment.[23]

Tyutchev's dismissal from the Foreign Service left him even more at sea than before. The thought of retiring into private life in Russia — let alone running the family estate at Ovstug — filled him with dread.[24] At the same time he was alienated by the rising tide of Russophobia in the West, and had no great desire to stay in Munich. During a lengthy stay in the Bavarian capital in 1841 Karl Pfeffel formed the impression (as he later recalled) that Tyutchev had become disillusioned with living there. Political and cultural developments seemed to have run out of steam as King Ludwig pursued a new reactionary course, reversing earlier enlightened reforms and strengthening the hand of the ultra-conservative clerical party. The death of Montgelas in 1838 and Schelling's departure for Berlin in 1841 had deprived Tyutchev of much-needed intellectual stimulation.[25] And with the promotion of Maltitz to the post of Chargé d'Affaires at the court of the Grand Duchy of Sachsen-Weimar-Eisenach in May 1841 he lost a further congenial companion.[26]

Yet in many ways his personal life during these years in Munich was happier than it had been for a long time. He was married to the woman who despite everything would remain the great love of his life. She bore him children, including a son and heir, while treating the daughters from his previous marriage no differently than her own. Perhaps for the first time he began to appreciate the joys of family life. And thanks to Ernestine he was at last free of financial worries. They were able to send Anna, Darya and Kitty to the prestigious Royal Institute for girls,[27] to move to more spacious accommodation as the family grew, eventually taking an apartment on the fashionable Ludwigstrasse,[28] and to indulge their shared passion for travel. Tyutchev's health too had shown a significant improvement. Over a year after settling in Munich he wrote to his parents that he had succeeded in strengthening his nerves through a regime of bathing in cold water, and that he now realised his previous ills to have been the result of 'major nervous debilitation'.[29] Although he does not say so, it seems clear that Ernestine's calming influence had been at least as effective as the cold baths. In fact there is no evidence during these years for the disabling attacks of depression to which he had once been so prone. This may be yet another reason why he turned away from poetic composition, no longer needing its therapeutic effect.

Ernestine by contrast suffered several health setbacks. Following the postnatal problems already mentioned, in the winter of 1841-42 she fell victim to a viral epidemic which claimed more lives in Munich than the cholera five years before. She recovered, but was left so weakened that her doctors prescribed a cure at Bad Kissingen, followed by sea-bathing.[30] Rheumatism was also to become a problem requiring visits to spas in the years to come.[31] In the early summer of 1842 she and Tyutchev went to Bad Kissingen for six weeks so that she could take the waters as recommended.

During their stay he took the opportunity to travel on alone to Weimar to spend a few days with the Maltitzes and see his daughter Anna, who had been sent to live with her Aunt Clotilde and Uncle Apollonius the previous November.[32] She had found it difficult to adjust to a stepmother, and Ernestine's naturally placid and easy-going temperament was not ideally suited to dealing with a fractious pre-adolescent.[33] All had agreed that Anna would be better off in the care of Clotilde, to whom she had always been close.[34] In the event she stayed nearly two years (and according to Maltitz 'felt much happier with us than in her own home').[35] Tyutchev's visit to Weimar in the summer of 1842 was not his first: he had gone there, again on his own, the previous September, hoping for a convivial reunion with the Maltitzes and with high expectations of the little town, famous for its association with Goethe and Schiller.[36] He was disappointed on both counts. Very soon he was counting the days for his departure, repelled by the 'provincial and pedantic pettiness' which seemed to him to permeate the place. He was also irritated by the Maltitzes' rather suspect displays of marital bliss, with Clotilde showing herself as 'aggressive and cantankerous towards the world at large' as she was 'idolotrous of her husband'.[37] Given what we have learnt of his earlier feelings for Clotilde, it is easy enough to detect a note of jealousy. On his second visit he even began to speculate on darker reasons for her habitual bad temper. 'Unless I am much mistaken, the poor woman has some sad secret,' he confided in a letter to Ernestine. 'It is probably that she has no children, and moreover finds her husband much less amorous towards her than would be necessary for her to have any hope of seeing her wish fulfilled.' And (in a shaft aimed as much at Maltitz's literary pretensions as his lack of ardour): 'Alas, when one's in bed with one's wife, it's not enough just to read her verses by Schiller.'[38] The one redeeming feature of Weimar in his eyes was the presence of Grand Duchess Maria Pavlovna, sister of the Emperors Alexander I and Nicholas I and consort to Karl Friedrich, the reigning Grand Duke of Sachsen-Weimar-Eisenach. A cultured woman who had known and been admired by Goethe, she was a great patron of the arts. Tyutchev met her several times during his two visits and was cordially received.[39]

While making his way back from Weimar to Munich in September 1841, he experienced his first railway journey of any length. Boarding the train in Leipzig at three o'clock in the afternoon, he reached Dresden in time to visit the theatre that evening, and was immediately converted to this novel form of transport. 'One has to agree,' he enthused to Ernestine, 'that steam is a great magician; there are moments when one's movement is so swift and devouring, when space is so completely conquered and annihilated, that it is difficult not to experience a slight feeling of arrogance.'[40] And to his parents he predicted that 'Thanks to the railways, very soon the whole of Germany will occupy no more space on the traveller's map than one of its provinces does today.'[41]

In Dresden he sought out a colony of Russians he knew to be living there, many of them friends and relatives he had not seen for years. Among them was his second cousin Yelizaveta Yazykova, sister of the exiled Decembrist Vasily Ivashov whose marriage to Camille le Dantu he had played some part in facilitating eleven years before. Yelizaveta told him that both Vasily and Camille had died in Siberia, that her parents were also dead, and that she herself was wasting away with consumption.

Such stark reminders of mortality and the ravages of time made him even more eager to be reunited with Ernestine in Munich.[42] His letters to her on the relatively few occasions they were apart during these years are full of tender affection and concern for his 'darling' ('*ma chatte chérie*'), as he invariably addresses her ('I kiss your dear eyes and embrace all the rest' is a typical signing-off); at the same time they are permeated with a clearly genuine, almost paranoid horror of being separated from her. Without her he feels 'like an infant that has just been weaned', or (revealing once more the amputation complex noted by Gregg) 'quite one-armed [*manchot*], quite incomplete'; elsewhere he complains of 'my complete inability to exist by myself '. He needs the constant reassurance of her love to hold him together as a human being: 'I absolutely need your presence to make my own endurable. When I cease to be *the one so loved*, I am but the poorest of wretches.' Absence itself takes on the attributes of some malevolent force of nature or fate: it is 'a kind of non-being which is conscious of itself '; the distance separating him from Ernestine is perceived to be a 'chain growing heavier and heavier as it lengthens'; no longer 'the object of a constant preoccupation, of a so loving concern', he feels that 'the objects which surround me [...] interpose themselves like a wall between me and that adored life which I have left behind me and is now receding into the distance to such an extent that it seems to me impossible that I should ever succeed in regaining it.'[43]

For the roots of this almost pathological insecurity we need search no further than the deep-seated feelings of guilt he undoubtedly still had for his deliberate decision in Turin to prolong his separation from Eleonore, a decision for which he had paid the most terrible price. In one of his letters to Ernestine he gives a revealing explanation for his fear of absence: 'It seems to me that all the powers of nature are on the alert, watching only for the moment when I turn my back in order to checkmate me.'[44] And in a short poem in French enclosed with another letter to her the themes of absence and the fragility of human existence are similarly linked:

> Que l'homme est peu réel, qu'aisément il s'efface! —
> Présent, si peu de chose, et rien quand il est loin.
> Sa présence, ce n'est qu'un point, —
> Et son absence — tout l'espace.[45]

Before going on alone to Weimar in September 1841, Tyutchev had visited Prague with Ernestine. The city left an indelible impression on him during the few days they spent there. He felt immediately at home at this crossroads of the Slav and Germanic worlds, which he told his parents reminded him in some ways of Moscow (Prague Castle towering above the river Vltava, or Moldau, mirroring in his mind's eye perhaps the Kremlin as seen across the Moskva).[46] 'It is a magical city, this Prague!' he wrote later, recalling his visit: 'one cannot help but feel at every step that on these hills, beneath the semidiaphanous veil of a great past, an even greater future is working its way to fruition!'[47] These words are from a letter to the Czech philologist and patriot Vaclav Hanka, whom Tyutchev had met during his stay in Prague. A professor at the Charles University, or Karolinum, Hanka was a leading figure in the Czech national revival, a movement supported in the main by academics and intellectuals, including the poet Jan Kollar, the philologists Josef Dobrovsky and Pavel Safarik, and the historian Frantisek Palacky. These Czech nationalists saw the other subjugated Slav peoples as natural allies in their country's struggle for liberation from German political and cultural domination; some, including Hanka, also looked to Russia for inspiration and support. Tyutchev may well have met some of the other members of the movement in Prague, but it was certainly Hanka who made the strongest impression. In a later article, recalling his visit in 1841, he comments on the 'unwavering esteem in which Russia, the Russian name, her glory and her future have continued to be held by those of a national persuasion in Prague', while at the same time 'our faithful ally Germany' had allowed itself to be swayed by Polish émigré propaganda into 'stir[ring] up the whole of European public opinion against us'. The one criticism of the Russian government he remembers hearing from the Czech nationalists was that in adhering to the doctrines of the Holy Alliance it had been obliged to demonstrate official 'reserve and indifference' towards the national aspirations of the Czechs. Hanka — 'the most national of that country's patriots' — had urged a more robust stance towards Austria, particularly as regards the latter's Polish territories. 'Bohemia [i.e. the Czech lands] will only be free and independent,' he told Tyutchev, 'will only enjoy full autonomy, when Russia has regained possession of Galicia.'[48]

Such sentiments were music to Tyutchev's ears, confirming his own views on the future of the Habsburg Empire and of the Slav nations in general. Before leaving Prague he presented Hanka with a poem inscribed to him which reflects their cordial and intense discussions:

> Must we stay apart forever?
> Now is time to make amends:
> To reach out to one another —
> To our kinsmen and good friends...

For centuries (the poem continues) the Slav nations have lived as if in darkness, either separated from each other or, in the case of those under foreign domination, forced to engage in internecine strife. But:

> Now in this long night of darkness,
> Here on Prague's commanding height,
> Unassuming in his valour,
> One has lit a beacon-light.

Hanka's scholarship and engagement have dispersed the gloom, so that 'All the homeland of the Slavs' — from the Neva to Montenegro, from the Carpathians to beyond the Urals — lies clearly exposed before us:

> And all accents of our native
> Word once more we understand...
> And our heirs shall see enacted
> What their fathers dreamed and planned...[49]

ii The Project

Tyutchev's growing faith in Panslavism and Russia's imperial destiny coincided with his need, not just to find a new role in life, but to support a growing family too. Reinstatement as a diplomat seemed out of the question for the time being, at least at the kind of level required to satisfy his financial demands. Perhaps instead he could offer his services at doing what he knew best: defending the Russian cause in the West, and persuading others to do the same in print? He was of course motivated by patriotism: but it was patriotism of a distinctly critical and even dissident variety. After all, he knew that articles published in the Western press could raise issues forbidden by the Russian censorship yet still enjoy wide clandestine circulation among influential figures and educated readers inside Russia.[50] What better way to combine his own political agenda with service to country and earning a living (not to mention the attractions of a continued life in the West)?

To have any chance of succeeding with his 'project' (as he came to call it) he needed to cultivate those highly-placed contacts who alone could facilitate his return to government service. An auspicious start had been made in September 1840 with the arrival in Munich for the winter of the 21-year-old daughter of Tsar Nicholas, Grand Duchess Maria Nikolayevna, who had married King Ludwig's nephew the Duke of Leuchtenberg the year before. Tyutchev was presented to her in Munich, after which both there and at Tegernsee he and Ernestine met her socially on several occasions.[51] A lover of poetry, the Grand Duchess one day expressed her admiration of his 'Autumn Evening', which had recently appeared in *Sovremennik*; to her it seemed a perfect reflection of the autumnal scene at Tegernsee.[52] He responded with a poem specially dedicated to her. It begins:

> With gracious, heartfelt recognition
> From one whom birth has set apart
> Do not, I beg, perturb the poet
> Or conjure dreams within his heart...

Having so recently rejected the public persona of 'Russian poet', Tyutchev is happy to slip into something of a masquerade version of the role for the Grand Duchess's benefit. The poet, he continues, spends his life 'lost in the common crowd' and 'rarely serves the powers-that-be': he passes by 'earthly idols' with bowed head, or stands before them 'confused and proudly shy'. Yet if suddenly 'a heartfelt word' should fall from their lips, and 'through the mask of earthly grandeur/ A woman's tender charm shine forth',

> O, how his heart is filled with ardour —
> With sentiment sublime and sweet —
> And though of love may be no question,
> Still he may worship at their feet...[53]

It is an accomplished enough piece, but with nothing at its heart. 'I cannot say it cost me any great effort; I was after all addressing a woman,' Tyutchev later boasted of an extravagantly fulsome letter he had composed to request a favour of Maria Niko-layevna.[54] He might well have said the same of this poem. In the event his charm offensive paid off, for she was to prove a valuable patron over many years.

Earlier the same year he had been able to renew another useful contact. Staying at Tegernsee with Ernestine and the children that summer, he had been delighted to find Amélie von Krüdener there with her husband. No doubt there was discussion of his career prospects and of ways in which she might help, although he learned that her position at court was no longer as assured as it had been.[55] Tsar Nicholas had apparently tired of her feminine charms and, in his own expression, had 'relinquished his place' to Count Benckendorff.[56] Even so, as Head of the Third Section Benckendorff wielded considerable political power in his own right; he was also far more besotted with Amélie and malleable to her persuasion than the Tsar had ever been.[57] Amélie was able to give Tyutchev inside information relating to her new admirer and patron. Some of this shed light on the mystery surrounding an anonymous German brochure entitled *Die europäische Pentarchie* (*The European Pentarchy*), published in Leipzig the previous year, which had caused a considerable stir both in Germany and Russia.[58] Its author argued that each of the five major European powers (the 'pentarchy') should be allocated its own sphere of influence. The most controversial proposal was that lesser German states such as Bavaria should come under the aegis of Russia rather than of Austria and Prussia: this challenged the official policy of the Holy Alliance that the two major German-speaking states should be the sole arbiters of German affairs. Alarm bells rang for Metternich when reliable intelligence reached him that the author of the brochure was a certain K.-E. Goldmann, a German serving as a Russian official in Warsaw. As Goldmann was known to be a protégé of Meyendorff, the Russian Ambassador in Berlin, who in turn was a confidant of Benckendorff, Metternich not unnaturally suspected Third Section involvement. Amélie revealed that Metternich had sent a sharp letter to Benckendorff demanding an explanation. Benckendorff had claimed ignorance in the matter; he had passed the brochure to Amélie's husband for evaluation, and was said to have shown surprise when Krüdener reported it to have been written in Russia's interest. To this day it is unclear to what extent if any Goldmann received official encouragement or support for his initiative.[59]

All this was meat and drink to Tyutchev. Although in a subsequent article he felt obliged to repeat the official line that Goldmann's thesis was in no way a reflection of Russian policy,[60] there can be no doubt that he agreed with it in private. As he later recalled on the eve of the Austro-Prussian war of 1866, throughout his time in Germany he had 'constantly repeated to the Germans that the Thirty Years' War lay, so to speak, at the root of their historical situation, and that only Russian guardianship temporarily restrained the logical development of this ever-present force. [...] Only under this most benign and mildest of guardianships could there be unity between Austria and Prussia, i.e. could Germany exist.'[61]

From Amélie and also from Severin Tyutchev was able to learn much about the rivalry between Benckendorff and Nesselrode, and in particular their disagreement over a major issue of policy. In 1832, following the crushing of the Polish revolt, the Third Section had for the first time extended its operations beyond the borders of the Russian Empire. Apart from monitoring the activities of Polish and other émigrés hostile to the regime, one of the aims was to counter the increasingly anti-Russian tenor of the Western press. In charge of undercover propaganda operations in Germany was Baron Karl von Schweizer, based in Berlin, who paid journalists to peddle a line favourable to Russia and the Holy Alliance (notable among his clients was Charles Durand, editor of the French-language *Journal de Francfort*). A similar action was mounted in Paris (following Grech's abortive attempt in 1837) by Yakov Tolstoy. Nesselrode, however, was opposed to the Third Section's propaganda activities abroad, seeing them as a violation of diplomatic convention, not to mention a serious encroachment on his own sphere of competence; in any case, he believed the work of 'hired pens' had little effect on public opinion, and that the current wave of Russophobia would eventually subside of its own accord.[62]

Germany became the arena in which this dispute between the Tsar's two chief ministers was played out, with Russia's ambassadors taking opposing sides. In 1839 Severin (who supported Nesselrode's position) gave Aleksandr Turgenev details of how his Berlin opposite number Meyendorff was attempting to extend his control of Third Section operations throughout Germany. He told Turgenev for instance that the previous year Meyendorff had sent an agent to Bavaria to gather information on Poles living there; Severin had stood firm and had the spy expelled.[63] In 1841 Severin complained to Nesselrode of the presence in Munich of Benckendorff's man Schweizer, who appears to have been putting out feelers to an influential daily paper.[64] True to their chief's directives, Severin and his deputy Viollier limited themselves to official protests at anti-Russian articles in the Bavarian press, coupled with requests for greater restrictions on freedom of expression.[65]

Such were the circumstances in which Tyutchev conceived his 'project'. He always believed that purely repressive measures of the kind advocated by Nesselrode achieved nothing in the great battle of ideas: on the contrary, it was necessary to meet the enemy head-on in open combat. Nor was there much to be said for Benckendorff's policy of bribing hacks to churn out the official line, or editors to suppress hostile material. What both lacked, he felt, was a positive and all-embracing political vision, a faith in Russia's historical mission which could be proclaimed to the world. He began to dream of a grand campaign to win hearts and minds involving active encouragement and support for Western opinion-makers sympathetic to the Russian cause. Of course, such a scheme would require the Tsar's approval; and realistically that could be gained only through Nesselrode or Benckendorff.

Meanwhile the Russophobia Nesselrode had hoped would go away continued to grow in strength. Already hostile towards Nicholas after his suppression of the Polish revolt, now in the so-called 'Eastern question' Western public opinion suspected him of expansionist ambitions at the expense of Turkey in the Balkans and Bosphorus. These suspicions were reflected in the German press, notably in the internationally respected Augsburg *Allgemeine Zeitung* (*Universal Gazette*), published by Baron von Cotta and edited by the talented journalist Gustav Kolb, a friend of Heine. Early in 1841 Tyutchev will have been disturbed to read a contribution by Heine from Paris which commended the 'religious zeal' of the Muslims as 'the best bulwark against the aspirations of Muscovy, which is planning no more or less than obtaining on the shores of the Bosphorus, whether through conquest or stratagem, the key to world domination.'[66] In an earlier article another acquaintance of Tyutchev's, Jakob Philipp Fallmerayer, had warned of 'the growing danger from Slavic-Greek churchdom' led by Russia and prophesied a coming struggle to the death between the Catholic West and Orthodox East.[67] Such articles in the *Allgemeine Zeitung* merely reflected the wider state of public opinion, as reported by Nikolay Nadezhdin from Vienna in 1841: 'Throughout Germany the alarm is being sounded; rumours, fears and suspicions are being spread; there are general calls for mobilisation against a bogeyman christened with the mystical name of *Panslavism*.'[68] Only a few isolated voices in Germany were prepared to speak out on Russia's behalf. In December 1840 Tyutchev delivered a note by hand to his close neighbour Friedrich Thiersch congratulating him on an article he had published anonymously in the *Allgemeine Zeitung*.[69] This defended Nicholas I's policies as 'high-minded' and dismissed as a 'phantom' the idea that Russia was bent on world domination.[70] Tyutchev thanked Thiersch for 'the first words of reason and truth about Russia to have been spoken in the European press', adding that reading the article had been for him like 'seeing the first large drops of rain after three months of drought'.[71] That he knew Thiersch to be the author of the anonymous publication suggests he had discussed it with him in advance; he may even have had some influence on the writing of it. Some passages in the article certainly appear to reflect his views: for instance, Thiersch's assertion that Russia is 'one of the most powerful and influential guarantors of Germany's independence and security'.[72]

Among the other spa visitors during Tyutchev's and Ernestine's stay at Bad Kissingen in the early summer of 1842 was Aleksandr Turgenev. His letters and diaries record lengthy discussions with Tyutchev over a period of two weeks, centring largely on Russian foreign policy and the growing hostility to Russia in the Western press. Turgenev wrote to his brother that Tyutchev had proved 'a rich source' of information for him on these and other matters.[73] The question of influencing or infiltrating the Western press evidently came up, for Turgenev reported a claim apparently made by Tyutchev that the *Allgemeine Zeitung* had repeatedly offered to carry pro-Russian articles, but that Nesselrode had refused to follow this up.[74] (Evidence from another source suggests it was Cotta, rather than his editorial staff, who was willing to co-operate in this way.)[75] Tyutchev even had a candidate in mind as provider of such articles. In letters to his brother, Turgenev refers to 'a certain Fallmerayer', author of a book 'written completely in our interest', 'who was described to me in Kissingen as a person capable of serving our interests in the German newspapers, but whose services are not being made use of in Russia.'[76] As subsequent developments show, only Tyutchev could have described Fallmerayer in these terms.

Jakob Philipp Fallmerayer had risen from humble origins in the Tyrol to become a brilliant classical scholar and teacher. In 1828, like Heine, he found his way to a professorship at Munich University barred by conservative Catholic circles to whom his national-liberal views were unacceptable; seven years later he was appointed Professor at the Munich Academy of Sciences. He made his name with the book mentioned by Turgenev, the two-volume *Geschichte der Halbinsel Morea während des Mittelalters* (*History of the Morea Peninsula During the Middle Ages*), published in 1830 and 1836.[77] This caused great controversy (and outraged the Philhellenes) with its claim that the present-day population of Greece was predominantly of Slav origin. Several protracted journeys through the Near and Middle East enabled him to pursue philological and historical researches in the field of orientology. The first, lasting three years, was undertaken as private secretary to Count Osterman-Tolstoy, whom he had got to know in Munich in 1831. It seems likely that Fallmerayer already knew Tyutchev at that time, and may have been introduced to Osterman-Tolstoy by him. Another acquaintance in common was Friedrich Bothmer, who like Osterman-Tolstoy became a lifelong friend to Fallmerayer.[78]

Apart from his learned publications, Fallmerayer gained the reputation of a brilliant and incisive commentator on current affairs through regular contributions to the *Allgemeine Zeitung*. One, a review of *The European Pentarchy* in 1840, will hardly have escaped Tyutchev's attention.[79] Fallmerayer interprets the book's advocacy of

Russian guardianship over the central German states as the latest evidence of the 'fanatical quest for hegemony [*Alleinherrschafts-Fanatismus*]' displayed by 'our enemy' Russia (162). At the same time he is highly critical of the West, where a 'wretched shopkeeper existence' has weakened the moral fibre of European nations, leading to a general 'revulsion, world-weariness, suicide and despondency of spirit despite groaning tables and bursting coffers'. Russia by contrast is 'a universal, militarily disciplined, colossal theocratic state, a joyless house of correction [*eine Buß- und Thränenanstalt*] dedicated to the moral regeneration of a world that is corrupt and gradually foundering in the slough of material interests' (165). He finds the hostility between Russia and the West deeply rooted in history, in particular 'the struggle between the holy sees of Rome and Byzantium'. Military campaigns against Russia from the thirteenth century on by Teutonic knights, Poles, Swedes and others had been given Rome's blessing to convert the Orthodox faithful by force. Napoleon's invasion of 1812, which 'the devout Russian people perceived as a war of religion', was but the last and most cataclysmic attempt by 'the Latin West' to subdue its vast neighbour to the east. And the character of the Russian nation could only be properly understood in the context of this history: 'That is why an indissoluble cement of blood, victory and religious fervour binding the spiritual and secular powers will continue to give the Empire of Muscovy sustenance and strength for the foreseeable future' (166). Nor is the homogeneous and monolithic nature of the Russian state — its 'unity of will' — so much imposed from above by autocratic rule, as something that 'flows from within': from the commonly held beliefs and attitudes of the Russian people (167).

Fallmerayer reminds his readers that after the crushing of Poland by her eastern neighbour, Germany now finds herself as Europe's first line of defence against Russia. It falls to Germans, 'the bearers of Latin Christianity and its intellectual heritage', to decide 'the question of the century'; yet they are 'incurably divided by religion and politics', so that as the battle lines are drawn up we see 'a conglomeration against a tight-knit unity, tired Rome against a Neo-Byzantium crowned with the laurels of victory and in the first full flower of youth' (168). He identifies two main causes or symptoms of the West's decay: firstly, revolution, any resurgence of whose 'spirit of destruction' would, as in 1812, serve only to strengthen Russia's position of dominance in Europe (169); and secondly, the 'theoretical fragmentation' caused by German philosophy, which from Kant onwards had taken the sovereignty of the individual to be axiomatic, thus endorsing the proliferation of conflicting opinions (170). He calls on the Germans to abandon the abstract realm of philosophical speculation and devote themselves, like the Russians, to the rougher and more practical arts of warfare, diplomacy and politics: 'do as they do, fight them with their own weapons'. Germans must become single-minded, united in a common creed and cause, and at the same time 'clever, cunning, slippery, artful'. Be prepared, he says, to 'die for your faith and your fatherland with the same devotion as the Russians'. 'Power,' he concludes, 'has always belonged to the clever, the resolute, the strong and active' (174). And although he does not spell it out in so many words, it is clear that the common cause he believes capable of uniting his fellow-countrymen and inspiring them to greater things is that of German unification.

With the benefit of hindsight it seems an all too depressing analysis, foreshadowing the history of Europe for a century and a half to come, and illustrating how from the early ideologues through to Hitler and Stalin Pan-Germanism and Panslavism would continue to mirror and feed off each other. It is easy enough to see why such an analysis should have appealed to Tyutchev at the time, despite its overall anti-Russian tenor. He will have been impressed by the grand Hegelian sweep of Fallmerayer's historical approach, with its reduction of surface events to the underlying clash of opposing principles in a process seen as both inevitable and providential. This chimed very much with his own view of history, and indeed several of Fallmerayer's specific points would be repeated by him in later articles. These include the tracing back of present antagonisms to the schism between Rome and Byzantium; the attribution of present German disunity to the Reformation and religious wars; and the picture of a spiritually 'corrupt' West, its social fabric allegedly disintegrating from the corrosive effects of revolutionary practice and philosophical theory. He will also have noted Fallmerayer's undoubted talent as a propagandist; for instance, the way in which he manages to appeal to raw emotion (the fear of an external threat) as a means to a political end (German unity), while cloaking the whole exercise in the appearance of intellectual respectability. These were invaluable skills, if only they could be harnessed to the Russian cause. Most of all, he was drawn to Fallmerayer's vision of Russia as a rising new civilisation, at once forbidding and vital, to be feared and yet also emulated by the West. Here he found perfectly mirrored his own deeply ambiguous feelings towards the land of his birth.

Apart from Turgenev, Tyutchev also met the liberal writer and publicist Karl August Varnhagen von Ense at Bad Kissingen in 1842. Varnhagen may well have been singled out as another possible recruit for the 'project', for he was highly regarded for the power of his pen, and both Metternich and the Prussian government had unsuccessfully attempted to enlist his services.[80] Sympathetic towards the Russians since 1813, when he had fought under their command in the Prussian War of Liberation, he had subsequently translated Pushkin and other Russian writers into German and in general acted as a cultural mediator between the two nations. On 5 July he recorded in his diary having met 'Heine's friend, the Russian poet' Tyutchev. (The second of these designations in particular is most unlikely to have come from Tyutchev himself, suggesting that Varnhagen already knew of his work, whether directly or by reputation.) Over the next two days they had long and 'intellectually stimulating' conversations, Varnhagen finding Tyutchev 'a splendid person' with 'the gift of an all-embracing view of things'.[81] Before leaving Bad Kissingen, Tyutchev presented his new acquaintance with a short poem in Russian entitled 'The Banner and the Word', in which he celebrates Varnhagen's military and literary connections with Russia.[82]

After their stay in Bad Kissingen that summer Tyutchev and Ernestine headed for Ostend, where it was hoped sea-bathing might alleviate the stiffness in her joints. In Frankfurt they were joined by Nikolay.[83] He had arrived in Munich earlier that year, having recently retired from the army with the rank of Colonel, and now planned to spend some time abroad before taking over the running of the family estate at Ovstug.[84] Travelling on from Frankfurt together, they took a steamer down the Rhine, an area new to Tyutchev, who was pleased to find that its scenery of craggy gorges and towering medieval castles 'fully lived up to my expectations'.[85] Passing the Lorelei rocks no doubt brought to mind Heine's poem about the legendary siren, by then already a popular song in the well-known setting by Friedrich Silcher. From Cologne they were able to travel to Ostend by train, breaking the journey with a week's stay in Brussels. Tyutchev was again impressed by the speed of rail travel, while Ernestine found it 'a fairly inexpensive form of transport, but disgusting — dirty and exhausting'.[86]

At Ostend — then a fairly fashionable resort with a cosmopolitan mix of summer visitors — they were met by Karl Pfeffel, who had arrived ahead of them. From here Tyutchev had planned to accompany Nikolay to St Petersburg by steamer. The six-day sea voyage certainly looked to be a convenient and relatively comfortable way of effecting his long-delayed trip to Russia; however, news from passengers just off the boat that his patroness Grand Duchess Maria Nikolayevna had left St Petersburg for Italy was enough to persuade him to abandon the idea and stay with Ernestine.[87] In view of this Nikolay too postponed his return; but finding Ostend 'a rather dreary place', he hopped on a cross-channel steamer in search of livelier diversions in London and was away for some two weeks.[88] Tyutchev also relieved the boredom with a short visit to Brussels in Pfeffel's company for a performance by the renowned French actress Rachel (Élisabeth Rachel Félix), on tour that summer to the Belgian capital.[89] Ernestine conscientiously pursued her course of sea-bathing, hoping it would prove more beneficial than the somewhat ineffective cure at Bad Kissingen. Tyutchev took a few dips with her, 'purely out of curiosity, without any need whatsoever', and at the end of their month's stay was able to report a gratifying improvement in his wife's health.[90]

Back in Munich that September he was pleasantly surprised to find Amélie spending a few weeks in the city on her way to Paris for the winter. She was travelling with her friend Anna Sheremeteva, a distant relative of Tyutchev's aunt Nadezhda Sheremeteva with whom he could remember playing as a child in Moscow. Earlier that year at Bad Kissingen Tyutchev had apparently talked to Aleksandr Turgenev of the relationship between the two women, for in a letter to his brother Turgenev claimed on the basis of what he had heard that 'Countess Sheremeteva has passionate feelings for her [Amélie] to the point of obsession, and is jealous of her, like a lover [...]. She writes her passionate notes, and if she finds even another woman with Madame Krüdener she weeps with vexation and jealousy.'[91]

It may be, as suggested by Aleksandr Ospovat,[92] that Tyutchev discussed his 'project' with Amélie; he may even have sounded her out on gaining Benckendorff's support. What is certain is that he lost no time making a first approach to Fallmerayer, back in Munich after a two-year visit to the Balkans and Constantinople, from where he had contributed a series of articles to the *Allgemeine Zeitung*.[93] On 9 November Tyutchev invited the now celebrated writer to his home at 7 Ludwigstrasse, and they talked at some length. According to Fallmerayer's diary, Tyutchev praised his guest for being 'alone among all the publicists of the West' in his understanding of the true nature of Russia and Byzantium, before launching into what Fallmerayer describes as a 'percipient examination' of his published books and articles.[94] The next meeting noted by Fallmerayer took place on 12 March 1843 at the same venue. On this occasion Tyutchev was full of praise for Fallmerayer's latest article in the *Allgemeine Zeitung*, predicting that it would go down well in Russia, where people 'were counting on' him. He stated that it was Fallmerayer's 'achievement to have brought into circulation the idea of a great and self-sufficient eastern Europe in antithesis to the western one'. Developing some of his own ideas on the subject, Tyutchev commented on a map in a recent publication by the Prague scholar Pavel Safarik showing the full extent of Slav settlement in Europe, and predicted a 'wretched fate' for Austria once its mainly Slav subject peoples had freed themselves from German domination. He also strove to defuse some of the hostility shown towards Russia by Fallmerayer in his articles. He pointed out that Western antagonism towards, and aggression against, his country had always proved counter-productive, serving only to strengthen and consolidate the power of the 'hated rival'. As for the widespread suspicion that Russia was bent on world domination, nothing was further from the truth: 'We want only to exist'.[95]

The theme of Slav unity had been taken up by Tyutchev the previous September in lines to the Polish poet Adam Mickiewicz. In voluntary exile since 1829, Mickiewicz had from 1840 been lecturing on the history and culture of the Slav peoples at the Collège de France in Paris. His lectures caused controversy among his fellow-countrymen for their balanced and non-polemical treatment of Russian cultural and historical achievements. Tyutchev managed to get hold of some transcripts of Mickiewicz's lectures circulating at the time, and was so impressed that he sent him an epistle in verse.[96] He hails the Polish poet both as a 'man of reconciling love' who 'by praeternatural effort' has 'healed the enmity within', and as the 'prophet' of a dawning new age of Slav solidarity:

> We sense the Light — the Time approaches —
> The final barrier is down —
> Arise, ye several scattered nations,
> Unite as one to seize your crown —
>
> Arise — not Poland, and not Russia —
> But one great Slavic Family!
> Awake — and for the first time ever
> Declare yourself for all to see! [97]

We have to remind ourselves that these are lines from one poet of genius to another. As with so much of Tyutchev's verse of this period there is a dispiriting sense of creative energy draining away from poetic inspiration to be lost in the seductive void of ideology.

iii Journey to Russia

On 30 or 31 May 1843 Tyutchev set off at last on his much-postponed journey to Russia.[98] Concern for the children and renewed health problems prevented Ernestine from accompanying him; instead, she spent the summer at Tegernsee. In Vienna he was joined by Nikolay, who had spent the winter there, and they travelled to Moscow together. Apart from being reunited with his parents and sister and sorting out family financial affairs, Tyutchev's main aims in visiting Russia were to clarify his somewhat shadowy status as a civil servant and if possible win official support for his 'project', both seen as first steps towards reinstatement in the Foreign Service. At the same time he was under no illusion as to the obstacles to be overcome following the disgrace of his dismissal two years before. From Vienna he wrote to Ernestine of the 'host of embarrassing impressions, misunderstandings and contradictions' he expected to encounter in Russia, and which he would have his work cut out to dispel.[99]

The first hundred miles or so from Vienna were covered by train in a few hours; the remaining nine hundred would take at least two weeks by horse-drawn carriage. Cracow, where they stopped for two days, seemed to Tyutchev a last outpost of the 'picturesque' West before the vast 'Scythian plain' stretching ahead. In Warsaw they bumped into 'the inescapable Turgenev' on his way from Moscow to Bad Kissingen, 'his notebook in his hand'. ('One would, I think, have to travel as far as China in order to avoid him,' Tyutchev commented.)[100] Their talk was of a recent publishing sensation, *La Russie en 1839*, by the French traveller and writer the Marquis de Custine.[101] The book combined a lively and frank account of a visit to Russia with a damning critique of autocracy from one whose initial theoretical enthusiasm for it as a form of government had been rudely shattered by the reality encountered. Already in Vienna Tyutchev had handed his copy of the work to the Bavarian Ambassador to read and then forward to Ernestine at Tegernsee, evidently foreseeing that it would be confiscated at the Russian frontier.[102]

On 26 June/ 8 July Tyutchev and Nikolay arrived in Moscow to an emotional welcome from their parents and Darya. Yekaterina Lvovna wept as she embraced the prodigal sons, their long absence and sporadic correspondence forgiven and forgotten in the joy of the moment. Having sold their second house in Armenian Lane, she and her husband were living in rented accommodation at 25 Sadovaya-Triumfalnaya Street, in what was then a quiet, almost rural suburb; Tyutchev and Nikolay stayed in rooms taken for them by their parents in the same house. Darya and her husband Nikolay Sushkov were also living in Moscow, Sushkov having resigned as Governor of Minsk two years before. Two or three times a week the whole family dined together at their house, just ten minutes' walk from Sadovaya-Triumfalnaya at what is now 11 Staropimenovsky Lane (*Pereulok*). Darya had recently given birth to a son, named Ivan in memory of the child they had lost five years previously (tragically, he too would die before reaching his second birthday). In contrast to the negative impression gained on his previous visit, Tyutchev took a liking to Sushkov, and was impressed with the efficient and helpful way in which he helped to mediate an agreement on the running of the family estate. They also had literary interests in common, for Sushkov was himself a published poet and critic.[103]

It was eighteen years since Tyutchev had been in what he always considered his home town, and he took pleasure in reacquainting himself with 'the city in all its immense variety', savouring its '*genius loci* ', its 'certain intangible air of power and serenity'.[104] A few days after arriving he wandered round the Kremlin, a 'spectacle without parallel in the world', as he wrote to Ernestine, referring her to the awestruck description given by Custine, 'who cannot be suspected of bias'. From the Kremlin he made his way through narrow winding streets lined with buildings in a bewildering variety of styles and dominated at intervals by the golden domes of ancient churches and monasteries, to find at length the turning into Armenian Lane. Standing before the old family house at No. 11, now used as a home for the widows and orphans of priests, he was lost in poignant memories of childhood and youth. 'It was like a dream,' he wrote to Ernestine, 'and how old and worn out I felt when I awoke from it. I had to remind myself that I have you to stop myself feeling that my heart was failing and melting away.'

Even more distressing was 'the terrible sorcery' wrought by time on the features of old friends. Meeting Raich again for the first time in 21 years he was shocked to see his sometime tutor 'with the shrunken face of an old man, almost bereft of teeth, presenting so to speak a crude caricature of his former appearance'. 'I have still not recovered from the shock,' he wrote to Ernestine the following day, and added: 'You too will grow old. And I feel that in my absence you are more completely, more irresistibly subject to the hideous action of this disease called time.'[105]

There were other, politically more interesting encounters: with the Westerniser Chaadayev for instance;[106] and, at the salon of Avdotya Yelagina, with leading figures in the nascent Slavophile movement.[107] In a letter to Ernestine, Tyutchev mentions having met 'some of my university friends who have made a name for themselves in literature and become truly distinguished men'.[108] These included Pogodin, now Professor of History at Moscow University, whom he saw soon after arriving,[109] and another prominent Slavophile, the poet and religious philosopher Aleksey Khomyakov.[110] (Shevyryov, who on 19/31 July wrote to Pogodin from outside Moscow that he still hoped to meet Tyutchev, had not been a contemporary of his at university).[111] From Pogodin Tyutchev learned of two official reports his old friend had written at the request of the Minister of Education Sergey Uvarov on journeys made by him to the Slav lands in 1839 and 1842. These predicted the disintegration of the Austrian and Ottoman Empires and called for a vast federation of Slav nations under Russian hegemony to be built from the ruins. Pogodin also advocated mounting a propaganda campaign in the Western press to explain government policy and counter the growing wave of anti-Russian sentiment.[112] Tyutchev was pleased to find such confirmation of his own ideas in discussions with Pogodin and others of similar persuasion.[113]

Remembering the urbane and somewhat lightweight young wit of liberal opinions he had known in his youth, Pogodin on the other hand was startled to hear this 'European' expatriate propound views almost identical to his own. Years later he was still at a loss to explain the transformation: 'how could he, an aristocrat by birth, a sybarite by force of habit, lazy and insouciant by nature, feel to such a degree — preserve and develop within himself — the purest Russian and Slavonic principles and aspirations?'[114] To Pogodin it seemed as unexpected and miraculous an assertion of those principles as Natasha Rostova's famous Russian dance in *War and Peace*.[115] It can hardly have been Tyutchev's intellectual evolution itself that came as a surprise to such as Pogodin (many of whom had after all — as conceded by one of their number, Aleksandr Koshelyov — themselves started out as 'fervent Westernisers' before becoming Slavophiles).[116] What was so unusual in Tyutchev's case was that he had apparently developed his ideas in isolation from the mainstream of Russian intellectual life, and that while holding them he never attempted to deny or discard the outward attributes of Europeanism acquired in his youth.

Tyutchev's first impression of his father on arriving in Moscow was that he looked much older and weaker.[117] In October he would be celebrating his seventy-fifth birthday, reason enough to think of putting the family's financial affairs in order.

Darya had already received a handsome dowry in cash, land and serfs from her parents on marrying Sushkov.[118] Ivan Nikolayevich now announced to his sons that he was transferring two-thirds of the remaining estate to them in common ownership, leaving it to them to decide how they divided the revenue. Inevitably it was the practical Nikolay — now retired, and unencumbered by family ties — who would have to shoulder the day-to-day responsibilities of a country squire, and in recognition of this Tyutchev agreed to accept no more than a third of the income. Even so, he reckoned this should amount to somewhere between 10,000 and 12,000 roubles a year, nearly double the allowance received hitherto.[119] Writing of all this to Ernestine, he acknowledged the great sacrifice his brother was making for the sake of the family. Nikolay would find living in Russia 'even more disagreeable' than he did (as Ernestine herself had once pointed out), and could only regard the prospect of spending most of the year at Ovstug as 'a sentence of exile'; and yet, resigned by now to bachelordom, he had set himself the goal of leaving the estate as a thriving concern for his nephew Dmitry to inherit one day.[120]

After six weeks with the family in Moscow it was time for Tyutchev to move on to business matters in St Petersburg. On the morning of his departure, Sunday 8/20 August, he attended mass with his mother and father at their local church, followed by a visit to the wonder-working icon of the Virgin Mary in the Iverian Chapel by Red Square to pray for a safe and auspicious journey.[121] For the sceptical Tyutchev, unlike his devout parents, the Orthodox Church and its rite could never be the focus of a profound personal faith. He would always perceive Orthodoxy (and religion in general, which he once defined from its Latin etymology as 'the tie which for every historical society secures and binds the fasces')[122] almost exclusively in terms of its historical, political and social significance. Now too, writing of the scene in church to Ernestine, he portrayed it as representing an unbroken historical tradition, older and more authentic than that of the Western church, and portentous of the great imperial mission inherited by Russia from ancient Rome and medieval Byzantium. And to this he added the revealing comment that 'for anyone who has but a passing involvement with it and can take from it what he will, there is in these so profoundly historical forms, this Russo-Byzantine world where life and religion are one, [...] an incomparable poetic grandeur, a grandeur capable of disarming the fiercest hostility'.[123] As Boris Kozyrev has pointedly asked, whose hostility can be meant here if not Tyutchev's own, 'disarmed' now by the compelling poetic myth of Russia's destiny in which he had put his faith?[124]

The whole family came to see him off from the coach station at Hotel Shevaldyshev in Tverskaya Street. He reassured them (his mother in particular, whose farewells he found embarrassingly emotional) that he hoped to return the following year.[125] In his pocket as he boarded the coach was a letter from Ernestine which had just arrived, and which he looked forward to reading as a 'pick-me-up' ('*réconfortatif* ') for the three days of 'horrible existence shut up inside the diligence' which lay ahead. Instead he was upset to find her letter 'one of the coolest and calmest you have ever written me'. It seems (as suggested by his characteristically unrepentant reply) that she had complained of his extramarital adventures. From St Petersburg he wrote back:

Know, my dear friend, that I find absence exasperating in the extreme, that it is a long time since I saw you and that I find it hard to get used to this privation. I tell you this, casting all dignity aside, because I know very well that *at the present time* I can no longer count on reciprocity. I know this, I feel it. But what does that matter? I am too old to start loving again — and whether I like it or not, I must get used to the idea of making do with at best a mutual affection. As for myself, do you know, I have to tell you in all honesty that there is no-one in the whole world but you that I truly love. All the rest is purely incidental. All the rest is outside of me. Whereas you are my own self, and my love is only so true because it is egoism of the purest kind.

So when I read your last letter, which betrays not a hint of the agonies of privation, the memory of your past letters rose to seize me by the throat, and I understood perfectly what an old man feels on happening to rediscover his portrait as a young man. — Time, time! The word sums up everything.[126]

Arriving in St Petersburg on the afternoon of 11/23 August, he booked into Demouth's, the best hotel in town (just off Nevsky Prospekt, on the Moyka Canal), but was soon obliged to move to a cheaper establishment.[127] He was in some doubt as to what his visit might usefully achieve. Both Severin and Nikolay had advised him to seek attachment to the Munich Embassy as a first step towards reinstatement, but this was more than his pride could swallow. On the other hand he knew he had forfeited the right to expect anything more elevated. All he could do was request a testimonial certifying that he was, technically speaking, still in government service.[128] The required document, 'couched in perfectly honourable terms', was fairly easily obtained with help from a well-placed relative, Mikhail Muravyov (husband of Tyutchev's cousin Pelageya, née Sheremeteva).[129] Apart from listing his various posts and promotions, it certified that 'showing commendable conduct, Collegiate Councillor Tyutchev has fulfilled the duties assigned to him with zeal; he has never been tried or found guilty of any offence, and has been attested competent and worthy of promotion'. The reasons given for his dismissal in 1841 merely repeat those stated at the time: 'protracted failure to report back from [...] leave' and 'lack of information as to his whereabouts'.[130]

Circulating among the foreign diplomats in St Petersburg brought him back in touch with European affairs. He also met Vyazemsky and visited the Grand Duchess Maria Nikolayevna.[131] Yet his most auspicious encounter was with the Krüdeners, then staying outside the capital at Peterhof. Visiting them, he was introduced for the first time to Amélie's lover Count von Benckendorff, to whom he was able to outline his plan of recruiting prominent figures to defend the Russian cause in the German press. Benckendorff was sufficiently impressed with his ideas to discuss them with the Emperor the following day, and after his interview assured Tyutchev that they had been received 'rather favourably', giving 'cause to hope that they could be followed up'. He also invited Tyutchev to accompany him and the Krüdeners to his castle at Fall, near Reval (now Tallinn), travelling by sea from Kronstadt.[132] Over five days, from 29 August/ 10 September to 2/14 September, Tyutchev discussed with Benckendorff how best to proceed with his 'project'.[133] It was agreed that pending the Emperor's formal consent there was nothing to stop him sounding out possible recruits such as Fallmerayer or contributing articles to the German press himself. An immediate priority was the need to repair or limit the damage inflicted by Custine's book. He undertook to meet Benckendorff the following year to report back on progress and hopefully put his 'project' on a more regular footing. Leaving Reval on 4/16 September to return to Germany, he was gratified to have received this 'tacit authorisation' from such a powerful figure. He had even found the feared Head of the Third Section quite affable and forthcoming on a personal level, although he recognised that this had been 'largely on account of Madame Krüdener' and only to a lesser degree 'out of personal sympathy'.[134]

iv A Doomed Campaign

From Reval he took a series of steamers calling at various Baltic ports, and after an 'Odyssey' of some ten days finally disembarked at Stralsund. He was able to board a train on the recently opened line to Berlin, arriving there on 26 or 27 September.[135] Already on the 29th he began his assault on German public opinion with a call on Varnhagen von Ense. After some opening compliments ('He assures me that the Russians appreciate me and are grateful to me,' Varnhagen noted in his diary) Tyutchev turned the conversation to Custine's *La Russie en 1839*. According to Varnhagen's account, he took a 'fairly calm view' of the book, 'correcting much of it, but also recognising its virtues', and even asserting that in Russia 'all educated and intelligent people agree more or less with the author's assessments; hardly anyone disapproves, and there is praise for the tenor of his exposition'. He followed this up with a tempting journalistic titbit for his host: 'Even General von Benckendorff told the Emperor frankly: "Monsieur de Custine has merely formulated ideas which the rest of the world has had about us for a long time, and which we have ourselves." However, the Emperor is indignant that the author should attempt to divide the sovereign from his people.' He then widened the conversation, impressing Varnhagen with the 'uncommon percipience' of his views on Russia and the Slavs — their 'languages, customs, forms of government' — and revealing 'a broad historical awareness' of 'the ancient dispute and ethnic struggle between the Greek and Latin churches'.[136]

Evidently on this occasion he refrained from presenting Varnhagen with a direct proposition, limiting himself instead to the arts of persuasion and advocacy. His chief concern was to draw some of the sting of Custine's book (which he would later attack head-on)[137] by playing down the reaction to it inside Russia. Whether or not there was a follow-up visit to press matters further (none is recorded in Varnhagen's published diaries), it is clear that Tyutchev made no headway with the German publicist, who remained as strongly opposed to the Russian autocratic system as he had been hitherto.[138]

While in Berlin he paid several calls on the Russian Ambassador Meyendorff, who as the main conduit for Benckendorff 's influence in Germany was almost certainly made aware of the 'project'. Visits to his old friend Max von Lerchenfeld — now Bavarian Ambassador in Berlin — and his wife Isabella will have been of a more purely social nature.[139]

Back in Munich on 8 October,[140] Tyutchev closed in on his main quarry: three days later Fallmerayer was invited to his house in Ludwigstrasse. This time there was no beating about the bush. 'This evening tea at Tyutchev's,' Fallmerayer wrote in his diary for that day; 'lengthy secret discussions and formal proposals to defend the * * cause in the West with my pen, i.e. to make the West aware of how things really stand in the Eastern question, as hitherto, without violating my own convictions; Benckendorff would arrange further developments next year.'[141] (As observed by Yevlaliya Kazanovich, in this context the asterisks can only be deciphered to mean 'Russian'.)[142] Fallmerayer gives no indication of how he responded; perhaps, reluctant to offend his host, he asked for time to consider the proposition. On 14 November he paid a second visit. This time his diary reports only a general discussion of politics and current affairs; there is no further mention of Tyutchev's proposal.[143] Like Varnhagen von Ense, Fallmerayer was too independent a figure to contemplate becoming a hired pen, least of all for such a paymaster as the Third Section. Two years later he turned down an invitation from the Bavarian Crown Prince Max-Josef, whom he greatly admired, to enter his service on a regular basis. 'It is impossible to be free and at the same time be paid to serve the great,' he commented in his diary.[144] If the patriotic Fallmerayer would not be in the pay of a German prince, it is not surprising that he refused to take the Tsar's silver.

If anything, Tyutchev's approach had backfired, for Fallmerayer's warnings to his fellow-countrymen about the perceived threat from the east grew even more strident. In the introduction to his book *Fragmente aus dem Orient* (*Fragments from the Orient*), published in 1845, he claimed to know of a secret Russian 'plan of conquest' for the German states that involved buying off the various ruling princes, whose loyal subjects could be expected to go along with whatever their masters decided.[145] 'Our natural enemies, our most venemous opponents and slanderers are in any case the Russians,' he writes. 'Between such peoples hatred is instinctive and any understanding impossible.'[146]

With Varnhagen von Ense and Fallmerayer out of the picture, the 'project' as originally conceived was already in ruins. A further possible candidate, the tried and tested Thiersch, seems to have been rejected by Tyutchev as a spent force ('no-one attributes the slightest significance to Thiersch's articles about general European policy,' he had told Aleksandr Turgenev already in the summer of 1842).[147] This left him with what had always been the more realistic option suggested by Benckendorff, namely to write articles for the German press himself. Throughout the winter of 1843-1844 he conducted what was by his own account a 'more active than usual' correspondence with 'St Petersburg'.[148] Although none of this has survived, it appears to have been mainly with Amélie, Benckendorff and even Nesselrode, and was no doubt largely connected with the progress of his 'project' and the prospects of a return to government service.[149] In February or March Benckendorff wrote to say he would be coming to Germany that summer for a health cure and would be glad of the opportunity to meet him.[150]

Contemporary reports suggest that by this time Tyutchev may have already published several pieces in the German press, although searches have so far failed to identify any of these.[151] His first known contribution was in response to an article on conditions in the Russian army in the Caucasus which appeared in the *Allgemeine Zeitung* over three days, from 16 to 18 March 1844. One of a series entitled 'Letters of a German Traveller from the Black Sea', the article referred to the Russian practice of sentencing criminals to long periods of service in the army, and contrasted this with

France, where the same crimes would not only be punished with a term in the galleys but disqualify a man from military service.[152] This brought the usual official protest to the Bavarian government from the Russian Embassy,[153] but on this occasion also — perhaps by arrangement — an unofficial response in the form of a letter from Tyutchev to the editor of the *Allgemeine Zeitung*. Identifying himself only as 'a Russian', Tyutchev complained that the article in question seemed to be based on the premiss that 'the Russian soldier is often the equivalent of a French convict sent to the galleys'; he pointed out that it was these 'galley slaves' who had liberated Germany from the Napoleonic yoke, and went on to mount an impassioned defence of the courage, discipline and humanity of the common Russian soldier and to accuse certain sections of German society of ingratitude.[154] The *Allgemeine Zeitung* printed his letter on 21 March, together with an editorial disclaimer to the effect that their correspondent from the Black Sea had in no way intended to liken Russian soldiers in general — 'whose courage, modesty and perseverance he extols' — to convicts. It also made the not unreasonable point that enlisting convicted criminals was common practice in other countries such as Britain.[155]

Tyutchev's letter did not go unnoticed in the German press. Writing in the *Allgemeine Zeitung* some time later, the author of the article attacked by him accused Tyutchev of having completely misunderstood it, and supposed that this must be due to his poor command of the German language.[156] (In fact, although he claimed to speak German badly,[157] Tyutchev's reading knowledge of the language was clearly competent, as shown by his translations of both poetry and official documents. It would be truer to say that he had misrepresented the article deliberately in order to sharpen his polemical attack on it.)[158] The letter also sparked off a fairly protracted row between the *Allgemeine Zeitung* and the *Kölnische Zeitung*, with the latter accusing its Augsburg rival of pro-Russian tendencies, and each trying to outdo the other in affirmations of patriotic zeal.[159]

Immediately after the publication of his letter Tyutchev sent the editor of the *Allgemeine Zeitung* a second and much longer contribution examining the phenomenon of Russophobia in the German and Western press against a wider historical and political background, once again stressing that he was writing in his capacity as a private Russian citizen.[160] Continuing the theme of his first missive, he argues that Russia's great role in the Napoleonic wars had been to uphold the principle of 'historical legitimacy' against the forces of revolution and anarchy (20). (The period 1807-1811, when as Napoleon's ally Russia had been able to annex Finland, is conveniently ignored.) Germany in particular had benefited from the ensuing peace, which stabilised and held in check the 'terrible propensity for disintegration' seen by Tyutchev as marking that nation's whole history, most notably during the Thirty Years' War (15). Yet despite the relative unity and prosperity enjoyed by the German states over the past three decades, certain sections of the press had come to see Russia not at all as a benefactor, but as 'the ogre of the nineteenth century' (14-15). Why should this be? The answer could only be that the West in general was fearful and distrustful of a newly established power which it did not understand and felt to be alien to its own common traditions and culture.

Only a few 'rare intelligences' — two or three in Germany, one or two in France — had managed to 'lift one corner of the veil' and see Russia for what it really was, but by and large their words had gone unheeded (17). They evidently did not include Custine, whose book comes in here for none of the cautious praise Tyutchev had been prepared to accord it in private conversation with Varnhagen von Ense; on the contrary, he now says it can be taken no more seriously than a newspaper critic's review of a vaudeville show. At the same time he is contemptuous of the 'self-proclaimed defenders of Russia' (unnamed, although he clearly had Grech in mind, among others) who had rushed into print in the West with earnest denials of what was after all a piece of nonsense best ignored; they remind him of nothing more than 'people who in an excess of zeal would hasten to open their parasols to protect the summit of Mont Blanc against the heat of the day'. Russia, he says, has no need of such apologias; that is provided by history itself (12). Just as Columbus's contemporaries had once denied his discovery of the New World, believing America to be no more than an extension of the continent they already knew, so for centuries the West had refused to accept the existence of 'another Europe, Eastern Europe, the quite legitimate sister of the Christian West and, like it, Christian: not feudal and not hierarchical, it is true, but by that very token more deeply Christian'. For long ages Russia, the 'principal motor' of this separate and self-sufficient world, had seemed enveloped in a thick fog of chaos and stagnation. That all changed at the beginning of the eighteenth century, when 'the hand of a giant swept the fog aside, and the Europe of Charlemagne found itself face to face with the Europe of Peter the Great...' (17-18).

Tyutchev makes the sweeping claim that Russia's territorial expansion over the centuries had not been achieved through violent conquest, but had been 'the most organic and legitimate piece of work ever accomplished by history', representing 'an immense restoration', a reassimilation of the Slav peoples into that 'other Europe' embodied by Russia. This is why, for instance, Poland had had to disappear — 'not, God forbid, its uniquely Polish ethnic quality, but the false civilisation, the false national character that had been imputed to it'. He implies that the process will continue, extending to the Slav peoples under Austrian and Turkish rule. And somewhat undermining his own claims of peaceful territorial expansion, he asserts that all that remains to be decided in the Eastern question is whether Russia will obtain what is rightfully hers through 'the natural course of events', or whether she will in the end have to resort to force of arms 'at the risk of the greatest calamities for the world' (18-19).

Gustav Kolb, the editor of the *Allgemeine Zeitung*, did not publish the article, no doubt feeling that to do so would expose his newspaper to yet more charges of pro-Russian bias. Showing far more concern for the dissemination of this political tract than he had ever done for his lyric verse, Tyutchev had it printed privately in brochure form under the title *Lettre à Monsieur le D-r Gustave Kolb, rédacteur de la Gazette Universelle*.[161] It was published anonymously and enjoyed only a limited circulation, with Aleksandr Turgenev taking the lead in publicising it; there appears to have been no echo whatsoever in the German press.[162] Yet if the article failed in its express purpose of enlightening German public opinion, it succeeded in another. Among the brochure's readers was Tsar Nicholas, who had been shown a copy by Adjutant-General Lev Naryshkin. According to Naryshkin, the Emperor declared it to be in agreement with his own thinking and was curious to know who the author was.[163] Such an endorsement could only help Tyutchev in his campaign to be rehabilitated.

The whole of the summer of 1844, from the middle of May to the end of August, Tyutchev and Ernestine spent in France: first Paris, where Ernestine had for some time been planning to consult specialists for her anchylosis (stiffness of the joints), then Vichy, where she took the waters.[164] Paris was much changed since Tyutchev's last known visit in 1828. The freedoms brought by the July Revolution had made the city, in Heine's phrase, a 'new Jerusalem'[165] for political dissidents and revolutionaries of every stamp, in particular those seeking refuge from more oppressive regimes east of the Rhine. It would be strange if Tyutchev had not at some stage sought out his old friend Heine, who is known to have been in Paris throughout the ten weeks he was there.[166] If they did meet, a further intriguing possibility arises: that Heine might have introduced Tyutchev to a new friend and journalistic colleague of his in Paris, Karl Marx. The young Rhineland émigré was already hard at work applying Hegel's philosophical method to the study of economic theory and revolutionary practice, as if intent on vindicating the prophetic claim made by Heine and Tyutchev alike that German idealist philosophy bore within it the seeds of revolution.[167]

Among those Tyutchev definitely did meet in Paris were Aleksandr Turgenev and his brother Nikolay, the émigré Decembrist.[168] Aleksandr was pleased to see the 'clever and knowledgeable' Tyutchev and his own old 'Munich passion' Ernestine once more,[169] and interested to hear his account of his visit to Russia the previous year. Perhaps unwisely, this included details of the undertaking to 'write about Russia abroad' agreed with Benckendorff.[170] The liberal Turgenev now saw Tyutchev's brochure, which he had spent some time and effort publicising, in a new light. In letters to Vyazemsky, while continuing to describe it as 'well written', he reported that it had had a mixed reception in Paris, and suggested that if Tyutchev really wanted to 'edify Europe on our account', he would do better to write 'in greater accordance with his European way of thinking'.[171]

In France the question of whether to spend the coming winter in Russia continued to be for Tyutchev and Ernestine, as she wrote to Karl Pfeffel, 'the subject of our heart-to-heart conversations and even matrimonial quarrels'.[172] Although Tyutchev had left his parents with the impression that they would see him again the following year, and had dutifully reiterated this intention in a letter to them in March,[173] he now insisted to Ernestine that he 'did not want this journey at all'.[174] There seemed little point, now that he could receive further instructions regarding his 'project' from Benckendorff at one of the German spas. Ernestine on the other hand had set her heart on spending the winter in Moscow, which he had described to her in such glowing terms, and where she would at last be able to get to know his family. It would also be more economical to live there than in St Petersburg: an important factor as far as Ernestine was concerned, whose capital had been eaten into by four years of supporting an unemployed husband.[175] The hoped-for increase in his income from the family estate had failed to materialise; indeed, in Paris they received a letter from Nikolay regretting he would have to postpone any payment to his brother for another six months, as to date all the revenue had gone towards paying off the mortgage. No doubt Ernestine felt such matters needed to be sorted out with 'the fat colonel' (as she called Nikolay) in person.[176] Both were in any case keen to get away from Munich ('we have both had enough of the place,' he had written to his parents in March, 'and my wife is perhaps even more tired of it than I am'),[177] and in the end her arguments won the day.

In July Tyutchev wrote from Paris to Anna at the Max-Josef-Stift, or Royal Institute, in Munich: 'We are more than ever minded to travel to Russia this year, and I should not hesitate to take you with us if I thought we were going to stay there for good'. However, since 'it is more than probable that this will not be the case, and that we shall return to Germany next spring', he felt it would be better for his daughters to continue their studies uninterrupted in Munich. On the other hand, 'if it should happen that we decide next winter to settle in Russia for some years, I shall not fail to send for you and your sisters or come to collect you myself next spring.'[178] This seems to have been added merely as a reassurance to his daughters, for he clearly still hoped to receive formal authorisation to continue with his 'project' in Germany. Thus on 4 August Ernestine wrote from Vichy to ask her brother Karl in Munich 'whether Madame Krüdener will be staying in Germany for some time longer, and what she knows about Benckendorff. All this interests Tyutchev greatly.'[179]

Tyutchev and Ernestine arrived back in Munich on 30 August, and a little over two weeks later set off for Russia with little Maria (or Marie, as she was usually known) and Dmitry, leaving Anna, Darya and Kitty at the Max-Josef-Stift as planned.[180] Ernestine's carriage also remained in Munich,[181] again suggesting the absence as yet of any firm intention to settle permanently in Russia. On 18 September they arrived at Eglofsheim and stayed overnight with the Cettos. Also there was Amélie; she told them that Benckendorff 's course of treatment in Germany had done nothing to improve his health and that, fearing the worst, he was already on his way back to Russia. Leaving Eglofsheim, they travelled by rail from south of Leipzig via Berlin to Stettin, where they transferred by boat to the steam packet *Nicholas* docked at Swinemünde. On 20 September/ 2 October they arrived at Kronstadt. Only after disembarking in St Petersburg at noon the following day did they learn that Benckendorff had died over a week before while returning by naval vessel to Reval. Amélie was being accused by Benckendorff 's widow and family of having relieved him of most of his fortune, leaving them with practically nothing to inherit; she was also widely criticised in St Petersburg society for abandoning her lover in his final illness, leaving him to die a lonely death at sea. Moreover there were strong (and on the available evidence quite credible) rumours that she had secretly converted Benckendorff, a Lutheran by birth, to the Catholic faith.[182] Amélie's position at court, already insecure, now became practically untenable; soon, as we have seen, the Emperor and Empress would attempt to remove her by appointing Krüdener Ambassador to Sweden.

All this could not have come at a worse time for Tyutchev. The 'project' on which he had pinned his hopes for remaining in the West was surely doomed, now that its powerful sponsor was dead and his protectress fallen from favour. By an irony of fate the self-proclaimed patriot found himself stranded on the very shores he had hoped to avoid.

Plate 1
The reconstructed manor house at Ovstug, now a museum devoted to Tyutchev.

Plate 2
12 Herzogspitalgasse, Munich, the first floor of which housed the Russian Embassy from 1808 to 1825.

Plate 3
Schloss Köfering near Regensburg, seat of the Counts von Lerchenfeld.

Plate 6
Donaustauf around the middle of the 19th Century. Note the river steamer, as described in one of Tyutchev's poems.

Plate 7
View of the Danube from the ruins of Donaustauf castle.

Plate 8
Tyutchev's first wife Eleonore
at about the time of their
marriage in 1826.

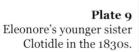

Plate 9
Eleonore's younger sister
Clotidle in the 1830s.

Plate 10
Ernestine von Dörnberg, 1833.

Plate 11
Tyutchev, March 1838.

Plate 12
Yelena Denisyeva, late 1850s.

Plate 13
Tyutchev, 1850 - 1851.

Plate 14
Ernestine Tyutcheva, 1862.

Plate 15
Nikolay Tyutchev, brother of
the poet, 1856.

Plate 16
Anna Aksakova, Tyutchev's eldest
daughter, 1864.

Plate 17
Tyutchev in 1867.

12 The Return
(St Petersburg, 1844-49)

i Reinstatement

Tyutchev booked himself and the family into the Hotel Coulon on Mikhaylovskaya Street (the site of the present-day Hotel Europe), intending to stay in St Petersburg no longer than absolutely necessary before moving on to Moscow. Apart from petitioning for reinstatement in the Foreign Service he hoped to rescue something of his 'project', and with Benckendorff dead this could now be achieved only with Nesselrode's support.[1] Unfortunately the Foreign Minister was away from the capital,[2] and nearly a month went by before he returned and was able to grant Tyutchev an interview. When they finally met just after the middle of October, Tyutchev was pleasantly surprised to find his former chief well-disposed towards him and apparently already informed about his 'project'. Without much further ado Nesselrode invited him to return to the Foreign Service, at the same time explaining that it would be necessary for him to stay on in St Petersburg until a specific posting could be found. Tyutchev accepted on the spot, gratified — as he reported to his parents — 'less on my own personal account than for that cause which alone interests me'.[3]

Prepared now for a longer stay, Tyutchev and Ernestine left the Hotel Coulon for more affordable furnished accommodation on the English Embankment.[4] They threw themselves into the social life of the capital: balls, dinners, theatre and opera, but above all soirées where conversation was the main attraction. 'I rarely return home before two in the morning', Tyutchev wrote to his parents after a couple of months of this.[5] Ernestine soon felt very much at home in St Petersburg; to her brother Karl she remarked on the 'kind and friendly reception' they had met with, and contrasted 'the simple and free-and-easy manners adopted in society here' with 'the stiffness of Munich drawing-rooms'.[6] As for her husband, she reported that he 'is completely reconciled to his native land', where he 'enjoys huge success', adding somewhat revealingly that 'it would be ungrateful [of him] to detest it as before, since he is liked and appreciated here as nowhere else'.[7]

Among those he impressed with his wit, intellect and breadth of knowledge was the Foreign Minister's wife Countess Nesselrode, who took him and Ernestine under her wing and later used her influence to further his career.[8] One particularly opportune society encounter that winter was with the Emperor's daughter Maria Nikolayevna. She remembered Tyutchev from her lengthy stay in Bavaria four years before, when she had taken a liking to his poetry and shown a benevolent interest in his career. Now she told him her parents were interested in meeting him, and said she would arrange this.[9] The following spring she duly presented Tyutchev and Ernestine to her mother the Empress, and also offered help in finding suitable educational places for his daughters in St Petersburg.[10]

Another renewed acquaintance was with the poet Vyazemsky. 'I am very glad that Tyutchev is here,' Vyazemsky wrote to Aleksandr Turgenev at the beginning of October, describing the new arrival as 'a charming *causeur* like the late Kozlovsky, but with firmer ideas and principles'.[11] By January he was hailing him as 'the lion of the season'.[12] The qualities that so captivated the salons of St Petersburg that winter are apparent from a memoir by the writer Vladimir Sollogub, at whose soirées Tyutchev was to become a frequent and popular guest. Tyutchev, he recalled,

would sit on a sofa in the drawing-room, surrounded by fascinated listeners male and female. I have had much occasion in my life to converse with and listen to renowned speakers, but none of them has ever made such a bewitching impression on me as Tyutchev. From his lips, like pearls, scattered words that were witty, tender, caustic and kind in turn. He was perhaps the most urbane person in Russia; but urbane in the fullest sense of the word. Every evening he needed, like the breath of life itself, the bright light of chandeliers and lamps, the gay rustle of expensive ladies' gowns, the chatter and laughter of attractive women. At the same time his own appearance ill accorded with his tastes: he had no looks at all, was sloppily dressed, and was clumsy and absent-minded. But all this disappeared as soon as he began to speak, to hold forth; immediately everyone would fall silent, and throughout the whole room only Tyutchev's voice would be heard. I think his chief fascination in this instance was that his accounts and observations '*coulaient de source*', as the French say: there was nothing prepared, rehearsed or contrived about them. His rival in the salon stakes, Prince Vyazemsky, was certainly endowed with a rare attraction; but he could never lay claim to the simplicity of enchantment that was such a distinguishing feature of Tyutchev's intellect.[13]

The two 'rivals', who had known each other only superficially before, soon became the best of friends. In Vyazemsky Tyutchev discovered a kindred spirit with whom he could talk freely of politics, history and of course literature. In a letter to him at the end of 1844 Tyutchev discusses for instance an article on 'The Greco-Slavonic World' recently published in the Paris journal *Revue des Deux Mondes*, enquires about Vyazemsky's campaign to have a monument erected to the writer of fables Ivan Krylov, and asks if he might borrow one or two volumes of Gogol's *Collected Works*.[14] Perhaps it was discussions of this kind — perhaps even Vyazemsky's active encouragement — that provided Tyutchev with the stimulus for a brief return to poetic creation in the autumn of 1844. So ephemeral was this that it appears to have gone unnoticed at the time (Pletnyov, who as editor of *Sovremennik* had continued publishing Tyutchev's verse for as long as the supply held up, reported with some disappointment after meeting him that autumn that he 'doesn't like poetry any more').[15] And yet the two poems which resulted are undoubtedly the highlight of an otherwise barren decade.

The first, dated 21 November 1844, is one of Tyutchev's meditations on the theme of north and south.

I stood beside the broad Nevá,
And through the fog so raw and bitter
Glimpsed great St Isaac's dome: a glitter
Of dull gold looming from afar.

Into the wintry night-dark sky
Clouds hesitantly rose unbidden...
Beneath me deathly-pale and and leaden
I saw the frozen river lie...

And thought with silent, sad regret
Of lands where summer had not ended:
Of Genoa and its gulf so splendid,
Ablaze with brilliant sunlight yet...

Have you bewitched me with your arts,
O North, magician undisputed,
That I must linger, as if rooted
To unyielding granite, in these parts?

O that some breeze in passing flight
Through all the darkness here persisting
Might swiftly bear me, unresisting,
There, there, where still the South glows bright!..[16]

'There, there...': the echo of 'Dahin, dahin!..' in Mignon's song is unmistakeable and almost certainly deliberate (Tyutchev was to make his own translation of Goethe's poem some years later).[17] Clearly the unwonted rigours of a Russian winter (his first for nearly 20 years) had done much to bring on this new bout of *Herausweh*. A couple of weeks later he wrote to his parents in Moscow that 'this terrible climate is decidedly contrary to my nature', and complained that the warm clothes he and Ernestine had brought with them from Munich were no match for the freezing temperatures[18] (they responded by sending him a fur-lined coat).[19] The second poem, 'Columbus', is the presumed thinly-veiled tribute to Schelling, inspired by Odoyevsky's *Russian Nights* (then the talk of St Petersburg salons), which has been mentioned earlier.[20]

The poems proved to be a momentary if powerful flash in the dark: apart from one piece in French, nothing would be written for a further three years. Taken together (and assuming that 'Columbus' was indeed addressed to Schelling) they indicate that Tyutchev's heart that autumn was still very much in the West. Intellectually it was a different matter. Early in 1845 he decided to submit (presumably with Nesselrode's blessing) a memorandum to the Tsar outlining his views on Russia's place in the world and reiterating his proposals for a campaign to defend his country's cause in the Western press.[21] The first four-fifths is devoted to painting a picture of Western 'proselytism' over the centuries in Eastern Europe, said to have been spearheaded by the Church of Rome and motivated by a conviction that 'any society not made in the exact image of the Western variety is not worthy of life' (34). Rome is branded 'on principle the personal enemy of the Slav race' and accused of having 'engaged in a war to the death against their nationality'(31), ignoring the fact that 'historically speaking' the Slav peoples belong to Russia 'as living limbs belong to a body of which they form part' (36). The Church of Rome is further accused of having broken away from the only true 'universal Church' (that of Eastern Christianity) and of having exerted a disastrous political influence in the countries under its spiritual authority.

The reason for this extended diatribe becomes clear towards the end of the memorandum, when Tyutchev turns to his cherished 'project'. Claiming that Russia's case against the West's propaganda onslaught had up to then gone largely by default, he asks: 'is it necessary to recall the recent deplorable and scandalous apostasy, as much political as it was religious in nature... and would such apostasies have been possible had we not voluntarily and gratuitously yielded the monopoly of discussion to enemy opinion?' (39). Any direct reference to Benckendorff's credibly rumoured conversion would have been out of the question — and if forced into a corner he would no doubt have protested that he was writing here of Ivan Gagarin, who the previous year had become a Jesuit priest, committing himself to the cause of converting Russia and the Slavs to Catholicism.[22] Yet the implied message to Tsar Nicholas was clear enough: if even the head of his security services could be 'turned' in this way, surely the case for a vigorous counter-propaganda campaign was incontrovertible.

Tyutchev concludes by offering his loyal services abroad as resident press co-ordinator of the journalistic 'auxiliary forces' on whom he still seems to have believed Russia could rely (40-41). The prospects for such a campaign are, he believes, good. He claims that many in the West have grown weary of the 'fragmentation' of conflicting interests and opinions into which their own society has fallen and would gladly exchange this for the monolithic unity and power represented by Russia. More than that: 'In the present state of minds in Europe public opinion, undisciplined and independent as it may seem, asks basically for nothing more than to be violated with grandeur' (40). It might be inferred that this curious formulation is more indicative of Tyutchev's own psychological attitude towards the Russian colossus than of any objective reality.

There is no direct evidence of how Nicholas reacted to the memorandum. It is true that on 16 March 1845 Tyutchev was officially reinstated in the Foreign Service, although still without any post or salary, and a month later his title of Chamberlain was restored by imperial decree.[23] Yet even if the memorandum was submitted before these events (and we cannot be sure it was), it is unlikely to have been a decisive factor in his rehabilitation, which Nesselrode had in any case more or less promised already the previous autumn. If anything, Tyutchev's Panslavist sentiments are unlikely to have gone down well, clashing as they did with the official policy of entente with Austria and co-operation with Turkey. As for the claims made for his 'project', these must have seemed unrealistic given the precious little he had achieved so far. The sceptical Nesselrode evidently had no difficulty persuading his sovereign to dismiss the whole scheme, for nothing more was heard of it. Some months later Tyutchev was told that in the coming winter he would be allocated a temporary post in St Petersburg at a salary of 1,500 silver roubles until such time as a suitable diplomatic posting could be found abroad.[24]

On 20 May he was granted five months' leave and a few days later left for Moscow with Ernestine and the children for the much-delayed reunion with his parents and sister.[25] Ernestine was favourably impressed by her in-laws, whom she now met for the first time. She wrote enthusiastically to her brother Karl of the kindness and hospitality shown towards her and the whole family by Tyutchev's 'dear elderly parents', adding that in general she had found Russia far more agreeable than Germany as a place to live.[26]

During their two-month stay in Moscow Tyutchev showed Pogodin and others the memorandum he had sent to the Tsar, and it began to circulate in handwritten copies.[27] While Pogodin and the Slavophiles no doubt approved of its sentiments, the reaction of the Westernisers was understandably negative. Chaadayev dismissed it as 'a house of cards'.[28] Aleksandr Turgenev found in it only 'ill-founded fantasies contrary to his [Tyutchev's] former convictions',[29] and sending a copy to his brother Nikolay in Paris claimed that Tyutchev had been rewarded for writing it with the prospect of a diplomatic post abroad and a 'retainer' of 6,000 roubles[30] (evidently a misunderstanding of the salary promised for the coming winter). Nikolay too was dismayed by the memorandum. He wrote back: 'Russians whose hearts beat with love for their country would do well to think not in terms of *us* and *them*, or the history of Byzantium and its legacy, but of hunger and cold, of beatings and the knout: in a word, of serfdom and its abolition.'[31] And in correspondence with Vyazemsky (who defended Tyutchev) Aleksandr expressed his fears that such 'fantasies' — harmless enough when confined to the Slavophile salons of Moscow — would if published in the West merely fan the flames of Russophobia and help to provoke a build-up of military forces on both sides.[32]

Just weeks after writing these prophetic words Turgenev was dead. Despite their ideological differences, Tyutchev felt the loss of his old rival in love and intellectual sparring partner. 'You will of course have been sorry to hear of Turgenev,' he wrote to his aunt Nadezhda Sheremeteva. 'For all his superficiality and idle talk there was in him much kindness, much warmth of heart.'[33]

Returning to St Petersburg at the beginning of August, he and Ernestine prepared for another winter in the capital.[34] Already in Moscow he had made arrangements for Anna, Darya and Kitty to be brought to St Petersburg; they arrived by steamer on 16 September, accompanied by their half-brother Karl Peterson.[35] With help from Grand Duke Alexander and his sister Maria Nikolayevna, Darya and Kitty were admitted that autumn to the Smolny Institute, Russia's most prestigious educational establishment for daughters of the nobility. Anna, already too old to apply for a place, moved in with her father and stepmother.[36] Problems with finding suitable accommodation obliged the family to spend the winter in rooms at Hotel Demouth, later recalled by Anna as expensive, dirty and generally unpleasant.[37]

The post promised by Nesselrode finally materialised on 15 February 1846. Tyutchev was appointed Special Assignments Officer to the State Chancellor[38] (the Foreign Minister had been honoured with this rarely awarded rank, the highest in the state service, the previous year). The impressive job title was in fact, as he had himself foreseen, little more than 'a pretext to give me several thousand roubles'.[39] The favour enjoyed by Tyutchev in royal circles had obliged Nesselrode to offer him this sinecure, but it soon enough became clear that there was no serious intention of re-employing him as a diplomat.[40] The salary of 1,500 silver roubles, the first he had received in nearly seven years, was certainly welcome, even if it did seem a 'beggarly' sum to Ernestine when set against the exorbitant cost of living in the capital.[41] Her concern is understandable, given that she was expecting another child, and it was no doubt a relief when in mid-March they were offered rent-free accommodation in an apartment owned by Yevtikh Safonov, a distant relative of Tyutchev.[42]

At the beginning of May he received news that his father had died on the family estate at Ovstug. Although not unexpected (Ivan Nikolayevich was in his seventy-eighth year and had been increasingly frail for some time), this came as 'a terrible blow' to him.[43] He went through the range of emotions common to those who have lost a parent: a sense of 'abandonment and desertion'; a feeling of having 'aged by twenty years' and 'moved a whole generation closer to the fatal limit';[44] and guilt at having neglected over the years to show his father 'those proofs of affection which he so appreciated'.[45] His grief reopened the wound of Eleonore's death, and he poured out his heart to Anna; she was shaken by the unprecedented display of raw emotion from her father as he anguished over the horror of death, the loss of youth, the loss of love...[46] His sister Darya and Sushkov had gone to be with their mother at Ovstug (Nikolay was abroad, his whereabouts unknown), and much as he wanted to join them, he knew his place must be with Ernestine, then in the final stages of pregnancy.[47] On the afternoon of 30 May she was successfully delivered of a boy, christened Ivan in memory of his late grandfather.[48]

Tyutchev waited until Nikolay could be informed of their father's death and had returned from abroad before setting off with him for Moscow at the beginning of August.[49] They found their mother (who had moved in with the Sushkovs) in better spirits and health than expected; but without his father Moscow seemed to Tyutchev this time 'like a magic lantern whose light has been extinguished'.[50] From now on Nikolay would be running the family estate from Ovstug, and at the end of the month Tyutchev accompanied him there, planning to stay a few days. He had low expectations of this sentimental journey to his birthplace, which by his own admission he had 'left 27 years ago and so little regretted'. As he wrote to Ernestine before setting out, 'none of my living memories relate to the period I was last there. My life began later, and everything other than that life is as foreign to me as the day before I was born.'[51] With overnight stops and on primitive roads it took them a good four days to reach Ovstug from Moscow (longer than the journey by sea and rail from St Petersburg to Berlin). By the end of it he felt himself to be somewhere in 'the antipodes' and longed for Ernestine's presence to 'fill the abyss and renew the chain'.[52]

The day on which they arrived — 28 August — was the anniversary of Eleonore's death (9 September NS); memories of this, followed by the sight of his father's study with the couch on which he had died, were enough to make him feel he had arrived in a 'land of shades'. A new house now stood in place of the one where he had been born and spent his earliest years, but his father had thoughtfully left the shell of the old building standing for him to see on his return. Contemplating this or wandering through the familiar grounds of the estate, he felt himself for a while plunged in 'that enchanted world of childhood, so long since obliterated and destroyed'. However, 'the spell was not long in evaporating', to be replaced by 'a feeling of complete and definitive boredom'.[53] A week in the country, cut off from the intellectual stimulation of the city, was about as much as this incomparable poet of nature could ever stand. On 8 September he bade farewell to Nikolay in Bryansk and made his way via Moscow to St Petersburg, arriving home on the 20th.[54]

The legal settlement of the estate was completed in February 1847. Ivan Niko-layevich had already transferred part of it to his sons in 1843, and as the older of the two Nikolay was entitled to two-thirds of the remainder. However, in recognition of his brother's family commitments Nikolay generously agreed to split the total estate (1,244 male serfs and their families settled in various villages and hamlets of the Bryansk district) in such a way that each received a roughly equal share of land and serfs.[55] Ovstug itself went to Nikolay, and from now on he would divide his time largely between there and Moscow. They both relied for the running of their estates (the absentee landlord Tyutchev almost entirely so) on the family steward Vasily Strelkov, a former serf granted his freedom and an education by their father (and rumoured by some to be the latter's natural son).[56]

By the summer of 1847 Nikolay was able to report that Tyutchev's share of the estate was producing an annual income of 5,000 silver roubles. Ernestine calculated that with her husband's salary and the income from her own capital they now had 12,000 silver roubles a year, but still felt this was scarcely enough to make ends meet in St Petersburg.[57] Her own preferred option was to move to Moscow, where the cost of living was much lower.[58] However, this would have meant him having to resign from the Foreign Service, which he was reluctant to do.[59] Perhaps he still dreamed of a plum diplomatic posting abroad; his more realistic wife knew this to be wishful thinking and resigned herself to life in St Petersburg.

ii A Western Odyssey

Despite the improvement in their material circumstances, by the spring of 1847 Tyutchev had fallen into one of his recurrent depressions. Ernestine even hoped for some dramatic political development to shake him out of his state of 'lethargy and dejection'.[60] In the event it was the offer from Nesselrode of a courier mission to Berlin and Zürich which provided the necessary stimulus. It was exactly 25 years since he had first set foot on German soil as a young trainee diplomat, and he must have welcomed the prospect of marking the anniversary in this way. There were more practical considerations too. For a start, Ernestine would be away for most of the summer undergoing mud-bath treatments at the Baltic resort of Hapsal (now Haapsalu, Estonia).[61] In addition, he had hopes of finding an opening for Anna as Maid of Honour at the imperial court and reasoned that leaving her with the Maltitzes at Weimar for the duration of his trip would allow her to make a favourable impression on the Grand Duchess Maria Pavlovna, sister of the Tsar.[62] In the same cause (and no doubt that of his own career) he also planned to pay his respects to Countess Nesselrode, who was spending the summer at Baden-Baden.[63] Then there was the carriage Ernestine had left in Munich: without any great hope of success she asked her impractical husband to arrange for this to be shipped to St Petersburg.[64] He was also keen to see Karl Pfeffel again, having missed his company in Russia. He knew his brother-in-law would be leaving Munich with his family to spend the summer at Ostend, and wrote suggesting they meet somewhere in the Rhineland, or failing that

Ostend itself. At all events he intended to avoid Munich, claiming that even after three years' absence the city still aroused in him 'a feeling of satiety'.[65] (The prospect of having to deal with Ernestine's carriage may also have played its part.)

On 21 June, ten days after Ernestine had left for Hapsal with the younger children, Tyutchev and Anna embarked on the steamer *Prussian Eagle* for the passage to Stettin.[66] He let Anna have their cabin and slept on deck, where he was soaked by a fine drizzle of rain and (for the first time in his life, according to him) suffered from seasickness. Arriving at Stettin on 24 June/ 6 July, they were able to reach Berlin by train the same day. Next morning he delivered despatches to the Russian Ambassador, Meyendorff, who invited him to dine. Also at the dinner was one of his oldest friends in Germany, Max von Lerchenfeld, now Bavarian Ambassador to Prussia. It was only natural that they should celebrate their first meeting a quarter of a century before, recalling together the events of that long-lost 'golden time': 'a whole world of familiar impressions took shape around me once more,' Tyutchev wrote to Ernestine, adding: 'I am not at all adverse to such resurrections; far from it — they renew the chain.'[67]

Next day it was on by train to Weimar. Clotilde and Maltitz were proud to have moved into Goethe's old house, renting what had been the servants' quarters on the second floor,[68] but spending a night under the great poet's roof appears to have left no great impression on Tyutchev. His account to Ernestine speaks only of finding Weimar an 'abominably dreary' place; while the self-opinionated Maltitz seemed to be 'at the same point I left him four years ago. Still the same old song'.[69] Next morning he hurried on to Zürich, leaving Anna in the Maltitzes' care. Travelling by train wherever possible, he reached Zürich by about 2/14 July and delivered his remaining despatches to the Russian Ambassador Paul von Krüdener (the same who had assisted at his and Ernestine's Orthodox wedding ceremony in Berne eight years before).

His official duties complete, he was now free to devote himself to private business. Travelling by train had left him with a healthy profit on his courier's expenses, and with money in his pocket he was in no hurry to return. After a couple of days with the Krüdeners (who betrayed their non-Russian origins by serving him 'execrable' tea),[70] he made his way to Baden-Baden, stopping overnight in Basel and Strasbourg. Countess Nesselrode, the object of his journey, had in the meantime moved to Bad Wildbad, a smaller and more remote spa some fifteen miles to the east; yet despite this and the apparent lack of any society of note to detain him (he had expected 'something more glittering, more comprehensive' in this respect),[71] he lingered in Baden-Baden for eleven days, from 6/18 to 17/29 July. Bad Wildbad when he eventually reached it seemed to him a 'wild location' peopled largely by invalids and overrun with wheelchairs, and he was not surprised to find the Chancellor's wife 'somewhat disheartened by her isolation' there.[72] Over the following week he turned the situation to his advantage, assiduously cultivating her company in the furtherance of both his and Anna's careers.

Leaving Bad Wildbad, he made for Frankfurt, with stops in Heidelberg and Darmstadt on the way. In Frankfurt he hoped to find a letter giving details of the Pfeffels' movements; but he had written asking for these only after reaching Baden-Baden, and Pfeffel's reply, though prompt, was still in the process of being sent on from there. Knowing that Zhukovsky and his wife were staying at Bad Ems, six hours from Frankfurt by rail, he decided while waiting to visit the revered elder poet. He found Zhukovsky working on his translation of the *Odyssey*, and the next six days 'from morning to evening' were spent reading and discussing this monumental labour and talking on 'all manner of subjects'. 'His *Odyssey* will truly be a great and beautiful work,' Tyutchev wrote to Ernestine, 'and thanks to him I rediscovered within myself that faculty, dormant for so long, for wholehearted participation in enjoyments of a purely literary nature.'[73]

From Bad Ems he spent a leisurely three or four days following the course of the Rhine before returning to Frankfurt on or about 8/20 August. Here he was pleasantly surprised to find his brother waiting for him. After first calling on Ernestine at Hapsal, Nikolay had come to Frankfurt via Berlin, Vienna and (probably) Munich on his way to join the Pfeffels at Ostend. The vexed question of Ernestine's carriage, which seems hardly to have occupied Tyutchev up to then, was now settled in short order. 'After mature reflection,' Tyutchev wrote to her, it had been decided 'by my brother and myself ' to have her carriage shipped down the Rhine to Rotterdam and from there by merchant vessel to Kronstadt. This would be far cheaper than his original plan of taking it with him by rail to Stettin to be loaded on the Kronstadt steam packet.[74] Although Tyutchev does not say so, the suspicion must be that Nikolay had already on his own initiative brought the carriage from Munich to Frankfurt to be sent down the Rhine as described. What is certain is that the detailed arrangements betray Nikolay's hand rather than that of his impractical younger brother.

Also waiting in Frankfurt was Pfeffel's long-awaited reply to his letter. Now he knew where the Pfeffels were, but he still needed to go to Weimar, and time and money were running out. He decided not to accompany Nikolay to Ostend, but stayed on in Frankfurt until his brother's departure two weeks later. On 16/28 August he was visited by Zhukovsky and dined with him at the Hotel de Russie. Aware that it was 98 years to the day since Goethe had been born in the city, they celebrated the occasion in fitting style, at the same time marvelling to find themselves apparently 'the only two individuals in Frankfurt to have had the goodness to recall this illustrious anniversary'.[75]

On or about 23 August/ 4 September he left for Weimar, the last station of any length on his journey. Much of his stay of some twelve days was spent in the company of Grand Duchess Maria Pavlovna, who promised to support his bid to have Anna appointed Maid of Honour, and in particular to raise the matter with her nephew Grand Duke Alexander and his wife when they visited Weimar later that month. This left him feeling confident that his efforts on Anna's behalf would 'not be without result'.[76] Leaving Weimar on 6/18 September, he and Anna arrived in Dresden by train the same day, intending to return home by the land route via Warsaw. However, in Dresden he suddenly changed his mind ('as constantly happens with him,' Anna complained in her diary)[77] and decided to take the steamer instead, travelling to Stettin by rail via Leipzig and Berlin. They disembarked in St Petersburg on 16/28 September.

For over two months he had immersed himself once more in that world to which — whatever his political theories might suggest — he would always be inexorably drawn. On many occasions what he called his 'Western streak'[78] had responded with enthusiasm to sights and scenes encountered on his travels: whether the 'splendid and magnificent panorama' of lake and mountains seen from his hotel room in Zürich[79]; or

Basel cathedral rising above a huddle of medieval buildings on the far bank of the Rhine as the river flowed past at his feet, 'singing' in the evening twilight;[80] the wild scenery of the northern Black Forest around Bad Wildbad, which prompted him to write: 'I am reassured to find that there are still mountains in this world. May God bless and preserve them';[81] or the valley of the Neckar snaking sinuously into the far distance, viewed from the hills above Heidelberg. 'Ah, this beautiful country!' he exclaimed, describing this last scene to Ernestine. 'But to speak of it is an absurd substitute for being there. It is like trying to express music in words.'[82]

Epiphanies of this kind could once have been counted on to inspire a whole crop of characteristic 'journey' poems. Yet even Zhukovsky's reawakening of his slumbering literary interests was not enough to break the long poetic silence. It seems that 'expressing music in words' had, as he himself implied, slipped for the time being beyond his grasp. At least such experiences helped to 'renew the chain' connecting him to his Western past — even if, without Ernestine at his side, the comparison between then and now often proved to be painful. At Strasbourg he searched for a lilac bush they had seen flowering near the cathedral three years before, and was saddened to find it had gone.[83] Visiting some gothic church or ancient ruin on his own would be enough to remind him of Ernestine and 'the abominable nightmare that is absence'.[84] Writing to her at one of these low points, he attempted to put his mental distress into words:

> It is the conviction which flows from everything as far as I am concerned that my time is over, and that nothing in the present can be called my own. These countries I have seen again are no longer the same. Can I forget that in years gone by — when I visited them for a first, a second, a third time — I was still young, and was loved? — And now I am old — and alone, very much alone.[85]

At such moments he felt the whole journey, with its scurrying back and forth to dance attendance on individuals 'of as little consequence to me as I am to them',[86] to be as sterile as 'the pointless toing-and-froing at a masked ball'.[87]

The few political comments he made on what he had seen in the West are surprisingly positive. He was much impressed by Europe's industrial and economic achievements, particularly the rapidly growing rail network, an 'admirable thing' which helped to ease his travels in more ways than one ('it reassures my imagination in the face of my feared enemy, *space*: that terible space which on ordinary roads engulfs one body and soul').[88] The 'prodigious material growth' in evidence everywhere was 'admirable', 'staggering' even. That 'its ever accelerating speed gives one in spite of oneself forebodings of an impending catastrophe' was the only somewhat reluctant qualification he felt obliged to make.[89] In Switzerland he learned of political tensions which some believed could erupt into civil strife, but he was unconvinced it would come to that. 'I have never seen a country with a more placid, more easy-going countenance,' he wrote to Pfeffel, adding that in his view both here and elsewhere in Europe 'revolutionary yearnings' were the preserve of a few isolated individuals, and that the masses were too inert to be roused. Which of these two tendencies finally prevailed was not, he believed, something he or Pfeffel would live to see.[90]

iii Hortense

There is an intriguing and in some respects still enigmatic footnote to Tyutchev's trip abroad. It seems that somewhere on his travels through Germany he became involved with a young Frenchwoman, Hortense Lapp, and persuaded her to return to Russia with him. The main evidence for this is found in a letter she wrote many years after Tyutchev's death to none other than Leo Tolstoy, details of which were first published by Georgy Chulkov.[91] Archival records add a few scant details to her biography. She was a native of Strasbourg, born in that city as Joséphine Hortense Romer on 3/15 June 1824; her father's occupation is given as dyer.[92] There too on 28 November/ 10 December 1844 she married Laurent Lapp, described as a landlord ('propriétaire'), the son of a linen merchant from the nearby village of La Wantzenau.[93] After the wedding they made their home in Strasbourg, where Laurent earned a living as proprietor of a small bar ('limonadier'). Within the year, on 21 October/ 2 November 1845, Hortense gave birth to a son, whom they named Jules.[94]

As we have seen, Tyutchev passed through Strasbourg in the summer of 1847, but is most unlikely to have met Hortense there: he stayed only one night (5/17 - 6/18 July), and in any case she is quite specific in her account that they met in Germany. The most likely venue would appear to be Baden-Baden, the closest point (some 30 miles) to Strasbourg on Tyutchev's itinerary. It is worth recalling in this context his otherwise inexplicably lengthy stay there from 6/18 to 17/29 July, despite the pressing need to join Countess Nesselrode at Bad Wildbad and the apparent lack of interesting society to detain him. Unlike Tyutchev, Hortense is not listed among the spa visitors to Baden-Baden at the time; yet someone of her social background is in any case unlikely to have gone there to take the waters.[95] We are left to speculate that some family drama had led to a rift with her husband (her eventual readiness to go to St Petersburg certainly suggests this), and that she had been drawn to the fashionable resort of Baden-Baden in search of work: no doubt in one of the large hotels catering for international guests where her native command of French would have been an asset. Where else indeed at that period can one easily envisage the wife of a bistro proprietor and daughter of a dyer engaging an aristocratic Russian courtier in conversation? A casual encounter between hotel guest and chambermaid or barmaid would seem on balance the most likely scenario. But let us turn to Hortense's own much later account of events:

> In 1847 I became acquainted with F.I. Tyutchev in Germany. As soon as he saw me he took a great liking to me, and asked me to go to St Petersburg with him. I refused point-blank, in no way attracted to the idea of living in such a harsh climate as that of St Petersburg — I, who am so sensitive to and afraid of the cold. However, Tyutchev gave me not a moment's peace, but begged and implored me to go with him, making the most tempting promises and saying I should not have cause to regret it. Finally I gave in to Tyutchev's entreaties and went with him, and lived with him for 25 years, until his death.[96]

What exactly were the 'tempting promises' which apparently persuaded Hortense to change her mind? Although here again we can only speculate, it is difficult to see what Tyutchev could realistically have offered other than a post on his domestic staff.

His youngest son Ivan was then just over a year old and would soon need a nanny proficient in French. Some years before he had in his wife's absence interviewed a prospective nanny for their then one-year-old son Dmitry: a Frenchwoman who — as he reported approvingly to Ernestine — 'speaks her language purely'.[97] On that occasion he had left the final decision to Ernestine; now he no doubt felt able in the circumstances to justify presenting her with a *fait accompli*. If he did offer Hortense employment in this way, it might explain her otherwise puzzling statement that she subsequently 'lived with him for 25 years'. At the time it would also have provided him with a perfect excuse for travelling in the company not just of his manservant Emmanuel Tuma, but of a presumably attractive 23-year-old Frenchwoman as well. Perhaps he even hoped to take in Ernestine with this deception.

Whether Hortense took her infant son Jules with her to St Petersburg is not known. What is certain is that after settling there she gave birth to two more sons, Russian subjects who became army officers and were killed within weeks of each other during the Russo-Turkish war of 1877-1878. So much is evident from letters sent to her by comrades of one of these after he had fallen in action, copies of which she enclosed with her letter to Tolstoy.[98] Both sons were illegitimate (Hortense was barred from re-marrying as French law at that time did not permit divorce), and the question naturally arises whether Tyutchev could have been the father. In the case of one, Nikolay Lapp-Mikhaylov, the surname would appear to suggest otherwise. By the same token it cannot be ruled out that the other, referred to simply as Dmitry Lapp, was his son. Indeed, there is strong evidence that he was. Less than a month after Tyutchev's death his daughter Darya wrote to Kitty of their sister Anna's concern for the welfare of Hortense's children, and reported that Ernestine had agreed to relinquish her own widow's pension in favour of their mother.[99] In the letter to Tolstoy Hortense also refers to this arrangement, complaining that she had not received the pension payments for some years (not surprisingly, given that Ernestine had died six years previously). We have to conclude that these payments were intended to replace financial support provided during his lifetime by Tyutchev himself, presumably in recognition of the fact that he was father to at least one of Hortense's children and to ensure her continued discretion in the matter.

Although Ernestine later accepted responsibility for Hortense's welfare, it must at the time have been a hurtful shock to discover the young Frenchwoman's relationship with her husband, and we can only imagine the marital discord and recriminations which resulted. That this occurred quite soon is suggested by what would appear to be Tyutchev's attempt at reconciliation, a poem composed only some three weeks after his return in the autumn of 1847. Written in French with the title 'Un rêve' ('A Dream'), it is unusual in being the first poetry of any kind known to have come from his pen in almost three years, and can be seen as the first of a series of 'penitential' pieces dedicated to Ernestine throughout the rest of their married life. Ernestine later told her stepdaughter Darya how it came to be written, as recorded by her in a note appended to a copy of the poem. According to this, Ernestine had already in advance decided she would be unable to give Tyutchev anything for his birthday that year, claiming that she could not afford to do so. Feeling upset, she went to bed that night and had a dream in which she presented her husband with a rose and a carnation from her album of dried flowers, which as soon as he took them were miraculously transformed into the fragrant living blossoms they had once been.[100] One suspects that Ernestine's claimed lack of money may have been an excuse devised to satisfy Darya and the rest of the family and divert attention from emotionally more charged reasons. Certainly the dream enacts her deepest longings in a particularly vivid way, as Tyutchev makes clear in his own account of it:

> Et consultant d'une main bien-aimée
> De votre herbier maint doux et cher feuillet,
> Vous réveillez dans sa couche embaumée
> Tout un Passé d'amour qui sommeillait...
>
> Tout un Passé de jeunesse et de vie,
> Tout un Passé qui ne peut s'oublier...
> Et dont la cendre un moment recueillie
> Reluit encore dans ce fidèle herbier...

Just as in the dream, she gives him a rose and a carnation, and he holds them close to the fire. For one brief instant they appear to flower anew: their colour returns, and they are 'bathed in flame and scent'. He explains to her the symbolism of this 'strange mystery':

> Lorsqu'une fleur, ce frêle et doux prestige,
> Perd ses couleurs, languit et se flétrit,
> Que du brasier on approche sa tige,
> La pauvre fleur aussitôt refleurit...
>
> Et c'est ainsi que toujours s'accomplissent
> Au jour fatal et rêves et destins...
> Quand dans nos cœurs les souvenirs pâlissent,
> La Mort les fait refleurir dans ses mains...[101]

The intended message of the poem is clear. Tyutchev is appealing to Ernestine to recall and revive their past love, which, although 'slumbering', 'cannot be forgotten'; and he urges that they do this now, for otherwise their love will one day be brutally and painfully reawakened by death, when (as he knew from bitter experience) it would be too late for anything but regrets.

Very little is known of Hortense's later life. According to her own account, at some time after the death of Nikolay and Dmitry she emigrated to America with another son (Jules?) and settled in the old French quarter of New Orleans. By October 1900, when she wrote to Tolstoy, she was back in Europe: her letter was sent from an address in Vienna. After this we lose track of her, and nothing is known of when or where she died. Hortense's affair with Tyutchev may have been brief, its only lasting legacy the no doubt unwelcome birth of at least one child; she may as far as we can tell have inspired none of his poetry; yet she surely deserves more than the almost total neglect she has suffered at the hands of Tyutchev's biographers.[102]

iv 1848

On 1 February 1848 Tyutchev was appointed a Senior Censor at the Foreign Ministry with a rise in annual pay to just over 2,400 silver roubles.[103] Nesselrode's ministry was responsible for the censorship of books and periodicals imported from abroad and of items in the Russian press concerning foreign affairs. For Tyutchev it was a sideways step, more or less precluding any return to diplomatic service. On the other hand it appealed to his interest in matters of the press, while the unrestricted access to foreign publications allowed him to keep abreast of European affairs. The appointment was followed by promotion (his first in nearly ten years) to the rank of State Councillor.[104] His duties hardly appear to have been onerous. Indicative (though possibly exaggerated) is Ernestine's claim that they took up on average no more than half an hour a day, and then only every other week.[105] This may be due in part to the remarkably liberal view he took of the censor's role. One newspaper editor later recalled that he 'passed for publication everything sent to him for approval';[106] and from other sources too it is clear that he genuinely detested the harsh censorship regime of Nicholas I's final years and did all in his power to subvert it, often incurring official displeasure as a result.[107]

Just weeks after his appointment word reached St Petersburg of the February Revolution in Paris which had swept Louis Philippe from his throne and inaugurated a republic based on universal suffrage. This did not come as a bolt from the blue for Tyutchev, whose close reading of European developments had already persuaded him to revise his earlier more sanguine view of the revolutionary danger. The civil war he had so confidently discounted for Switzerland the previous summer had in fact broken out soon after his return to St Petersburg; by the end of 1847 the nationalist opposition in Hungary under Lajos Kossuth was demanding radical political reforms and greater autonomy from Vienna; at the beginning of 1848 revolts in Italy forced the rulers of Sicily and Tuscany to agree to constitutions; and even Pope Pius IX had to concede reforms in the governance of the Papal States. Throughout Europe the rigid structures imposed by the settlement of 1815 seemed to be giving way under the accumulated pressure of 30 years of rapid social and economic change. In the first weeks of 1848 Tyutchev's insistent predictions of a coming crisis fell on deaf ears in St Petersburg. He advised Ernestine to move her investments to Russia; she did nothing, and later had to admit ruefully to his 'truly extraordinary powers of divination'.[108]

From Paris the bushfire spread rapidly to other parts of Europe. After a popular uprising led by professors and students in Vienna on 1/13 March a revolutionary government was proclaimed, and Metternich had to flee the country. The mighty Austrian Empire seemed on the verge of collapse as Czech, Magyar and Italian nationalists agitated for independence. Similar revolts brought liberal politicians to power in Prussia and throughout Germany, and a national assembly was convened at Frankfurt to deliberate on uniting the various scattered principalities into a single German state.

Although Tyutchev had predicted the crisis, he was deeply shaken by the extent and violence of it when it came. Ernestine reported him 'excessively moved and saddened' by the proliferation of events;[109] Vyazemsky observed him 'seething and holding forth', and for a time was even concerned that his friend might 'collapse under the weight of impressions and shattering blows'.[110] Tyutchev's immediate reaction to events was expressed in letters to friends. In March he warned Pfeffel that Western civilisation, weakened by the disease of individualism, was quite possibly in its death throes. Revolution, previously assumed to be no more than a growing pain, could now be seen for what it was: a deadly cancer. The only hope lay in radical surgery, but even then there was no guarantee of success. In the meantime Russia must prepare to defend herself against a military crusade mounted by Western revolutionary forces on the scale of 1812.[111] In a letter to Vyazemsky the same month he argued that they and their countrymen had long made the mistake of equating civilisation with Europe and now needed to develop a Russian alternative. In his view at present 'no real progress is possible except through struggle', and consequently revolutionary Europe's hostility 'is perhaps the greatest service it could render us'. Indeed, that hostility must be seen as 'providential'.[112]

In April he submitted a memorandum on the crisis to Tsar Nicholas.[113] Its tone is apocalyptic and dogmatic. For some time, writes Tyutchev, only two political forces, representing diametrically opposed principles, have contested the field in Europe. They are Russia and Revolution. Russia is above all 'the Christian empire', its people Christian not just in a formal sense, but by virtue of 'that faculty for renunciation and sacrifice which forms as it were the basis of their moral nature'. Revolution by contrast is essentially anti-Christian in its idolatrous apotheosis of the individual, 'that absolutism of the human ego elevated into a political and social right'. Today these two great powers or principles stand face to face; tomorrow they may already be engaged in open warfare. On the outcome of this struggle to the death — 'the greatest conflict the world has ever witnessed' — will hang the political and religious future of mankind for centuries to come (42-43).

It may at first seem odd to find Tyutchev's dualistic analysis of the situation after 1848 endorsed (albeit with positive and negative poles reversed) by one of the founders of Marxism. In March 1853 Friedrich Engels declared that 'on the continent of Europe there exist in fact only two forces: on the one hand Russia and absolutism, on the other revolution and democracy'.[114] Sharing as they did Hegel's view that history progresses through the inexorable clash of opposing principles, for the proponent of absolute monarchy as for the Marxist there could be no room for a third, more pragmatic way involving compromise. In his memorandum Tyutchev accordingly scorns attempts to placate the revolutionary impulse by conceding political reforms, most notably that made in France under Louis Philippe. He believes quite simply that there can be no truck with revolution, and praises Tsar Nicholas for not being taken in by 'the great illusion of 1830' (44-45). Democracy in general — the assumption that effective policy-making can arise from the will of the majority — is dismissed as 'one of the most foolish illusions of our epoch' (46). And not surprisingly he considers the Frankfurt parliament — a 'conglomeration of journalists, lawyers and professors' displaying the 'kind of ineptitude peculiar to German ideologues' — bound to fail in its aim of uniting Germany (48).

So far Nicholas will have found little to disagree with in the memorandum. The next section, dealing with the situation in central and eastern Europe, was more controversial. Tyutchev argues that (always excepting 'factiously Catholic' Poland, the 'fanatical accomplice of the West and always a traitor to its own') the Slav peoples will be rendered immune to the cosmopolitan lure of revolution by their nationalist aspirations. He points to the pro-Russian sympathies of Hanka and other leaders of the Czech liberation movement, and in effect calls on the Tsar to support their demands, arguing that Russia's previous policy of upholding the status quo in Europe is no longer appropriate in a context of revolutionary advances and the likely collapse of the Austrian Empire (50-51). He warns against the growing power of an independent or autonomous Hungary, which of all Russia's enemies 'is perhaps the one that hates her most passionately'. The Magyar people, 'in whom by the strangest of combinations revolutionary fervour has just been added to the brutality of an Asiatic horde', find themselves surrounded by Slavs whom they despise and see it as their mission to subjugate in order to create a bulwark against Russia's legitimate claims in the region. Formerly Hungary's expansionist ambitions had been kept in check within the Austrian Empire, but without Vienna's restraining hand Tyutchev now fears 'the most reckless adventures' (52-53).

He concludes with a rousing affirmation of Russia's ability to defend herself and her brother-Slavs against the onslaught of revolutionary forces: 'Russia, land of faith, shall not be found lacking in faith at the supreme hour. She will not flinch from the grandeur of her destinies or hold back from her mission.' And when, he asks, has that mission been clearer than now, with the whole of Western civilisation lying in ruins? 'One could say that God is writing it in signs of fire on the storm-blackened skies. [...] And when above all this vast wreckage we see floating aloft like a Holy Ark this even vaster Empire, who will then question that Empire's mission, and is it for us, her children, to show ourselves sceptical and faint-hearted?..' (54).

Sentiments very similar to these were expressed by him in verse at about the same time. 'The Sea and the Cliff ', widely acknowledged as one of his most effective political poems, conjures up a scene of furious waves vainly battering a massive granite cliff:

> See the ocean hurl its breakers
> Ceaselessly to strike and pound —
> Roaring, whistling, howling, hissing —
> At a bluff on rocky ground.

By the final stanza it is clear that the sea and the cliff of the title are intended to represent on the one hand the chaotic forces of Western revolution and on the other the implacable and invincible strength of the Russian autocracy:

> Stand fast, cliff so tall, so mighty! —
> And within the briefest space
> You shall see the waves grow weary
> Of assaulting your proud base...
> Worn out by their sport malicious,
> They will ease off by and by,
> And — subdued, no more seditious,
> No more wayward and capricious —
> At your heel defeated lie...[115]

After reading Tyutchev's memorandum the Tsar is said to have asked for it to be published abroad.[116] Despite any reservations he may have had about its Panslavist views, he no doubt felt a certain amount of sabre-rattling vis-à-vis the revolutionary West — and especially the Hungarians — was just what the current situation called for. In May Ernestine sent a copy of the memorandum to Pfeffel, with a letter informing him of the Emperor's wish.[117] While approving of the document's anti-revolutionary tenor and admiring its polemical brilliance, Pfeffel was disturbed by its preaching of expansionist aims. He told Ernestine the *Allgemeine Zeitung* would certainly 'grasp it with both hands', but that publishing it in Germany would only provide Russia's enemies with ammunition. Instead he circulated the document privately among foreign diplomats and other influential individuals in Munich.[118] By this time it was circulating in Russia too and had become the subject of heated debate in Moscow and St Petersburg salons. Even the Westerniser Chaadayev found much to praise in it, although he wondered ironically why so few in Russia seemed to be aware of the great mission claimed for their country by Tyutchev;[119] while for the Slavophiles Shevyryov welcomed it as containing 'simply a declaration of war against the Germans on behalf of the Slavs'.[120]

Among those who read the memorandum in Munich was the French Ambassador Paul de Bourgoing, who knew Tyutchev personally from the latter's time in that city. As part of a campaign for his own advancement (he apparently hoped to be appointed Ambassador to Russia) in May 1849 Bourgoing published privately in Paris a brochure containing most of Tyutchev's memorandum, accompanied by his own commentary.[121] Tyutchev is not named as the author of the document, which is given the title 'Memorandum Presented to the Emperor Nicholas After the February Revolution by a Russian, a High-ranking Official in the Ministry of Foreign Affairs'. Bourgoing had only twelve copies of the brochure printed, which he sent to the President of the Republic Louis Bonaparte, the former Prime Ministers Thiers and Molé, and other influential politicians and journalists.[122] In his commentary Bourgoing describes Tyutchev's text as 'a kind of manifesto' sent to Germany 'with the tacit agreement' of the Russian government and claims that it 'very accurately reflects the mood of the St Petersburg cabinet'.[123] He praises the author for his breadth of knowledge and skilful command of French, at the same time describing him as 'more absolutist than the absolutist Emperor' and dismissing his 'Panslavism' as a 'fantasy of gigantic proportions [*rêverie gigantesque*]'.[124]

About a month later a review of Bourgoing's brochure by the journalist Eugène Forcade containing lengthy quotations from Tyutchev's memorandum appeared in the journal *Revue des Deux Mondes*.[125] Soon afterwards the *Allgemeine Zeitung* printed extensive extracts from the memorandum in German.[126] Both publications repeat the title given to it by Bourgoing. Forcade describes it as 'a quasi-official document', 'the veritable manifesto of Muscovite Panslavism', which had been deliberately leaked to diplomatic circles in Germany by means of 'a skilfully calculated indiscretion'.[127]

Concerned that the title Bourgoing had given the memorandum could lead to misunderstanding, Pfeffel suggested to Ernestine that Tyutchev send the editor of the *Revue* a note denying in effect that the document represented official Russian policy.[128] Ernestine's reply — that her husband considered this unnecessary — suggests that his journalistic démarche continued to enjoy support at the highest level.[129]

Tyutchev's immediate predictions of apocalypse for the West had in the meantime proved unfounded. In France elections based on the principle of universal suffrage so unacceptable to him produced a national assembly reflecting the conservative views and interests of millions of newly enfranchised peasant farmers; armed with this mandate, the government was able to crush left-wing insurrections in Paris and elsewhere. The Austrian and Prussian governments reasserted their authority in Vienna, Prague, Berlin and the lesser German states, and dispersed the Frankfurt parliament (Fallmerayer, who was one of the delegates, had to flee to Switzerland to escape arrest).[130] The Hungarian revolt under Kossuth was put down by Austria, assisted by an army of some 170,000 sent by Nicholas. Resistance was also crushed in Austria's rebellious Italian provinces; King Charles Albert of Piedmont-Sardinia, who had declared war in support of the insurgents, was heavily defeated and forced to abdicate. The newly elected President of France, Napoleon's nephew Louis Bonaparte, intervened militarily to overturn the Roman republic and reinstate Pope Pius IX to temporal power, thereby assuring himself of the Catholic and conservative vote at home. By the summer of 1849 the forces of order (or reaction, depending on one's view) had won the day throughout Europe.

None of these developments did anything to shake Tyutchev's belief that the West was fundamentally doomed. Writing to Pfeffel three years after what he termed 'the catastrophe of February', he admitted that at the time the 'unforeseen violence' of events had led him to believe the end would come much sooner. Whereas the revolution had seemed to him then to be 'the prelude to a general cataclysm', it must now be viewed rather as 'the starting point of a long and slow process of disintegration'.[131] Towards the end of his life he still maintained that although predicting the immediate future may be as difficult as forecasting the weather a week ahead, the final outcome of a historical process 'can be calculated in the same way as an eclipse 500 years in the future'.[132] It is the classic argument of those whose predictions of the end of the world have had to be postponed indefinitely.

v Russia and the West

In the autumn of 1849 Tyutchev decided to expound his views in more detail in a major work to be entitled *La Russie et l'Occident* (*Russia and the West*). He sketched out chapter notes for the book and began dictating the text in French to Ernestine. In the event only three chapters were completed; yet from these and his surviving notes — supplemented by evidence from letters and elsewhere — we can gain a clear enough picture of the planned work.[133] It is first and foremost a dogmatic statement of Tyutchev's political faith, but also contains much astute observation and analysis. The general tone is oracular, the text peppered with such terms as 'providence', 'providential', 'the hand of God', 'divine chastisement'.

Tyutchev begins with a general evaluation of the current European situation. He welcomes the suppression (partly, as he points out, with Russian assistance) of the 1848 revolution, but is convinced that this has done no more than put off the final day of reckoning. He compares that revolution to an earthquake which has left buildings standing but so weakened that their collapse can be expected at any time (81). The deadly force that has unleashed such devastation is Western individualism, in particular the idea of the sovereignty of the people, tantamount in his eyes to the dictatorship of the majority: the '[sovereignty] of the human ego multiplied by numbers — that is, backed by force' (61). He also condemns what he calls 'the fetishism of Westerners for all that is form, formula and political mechanism' (57).

Turning to the situation in individual European countries, he dismisses the movements for German and Italian unification as based on 'utopian' schemes dreamt up by small groups of liberal intellectuals hopelessly out of touch with the silent majority (83, 85-86). Delegates to the Frankfurt parliament had debated the relative merits of the 'greater German' and 'little German' models for unity: the former with Austria, the latter without. Both are rejected as impracticable by Tyutchev. A renewed German Empire including Austria would, he claims, fall prey to the same religious and cultural conflict that had split the nation since the Thirty Years' War; while a 'little' Germany (inevitably dominated by Prussia) would lack any juridical or historical legitimacy as successor to the Holy Roman Empire. His own preference is for what in fact came about soon afterwards, namely the re-establishment of the pre-1848 German Confederation, with Russia acting as honest broker between Austria and Prussia (86).

In the case of Italy he similarly rejects as utopian the idea supported by many patriots at the time that their country could be united under the leadership of a reinstated and politically reformed Papacy (67-68). While in favour of freeing Lombardy and Venetia from 'German' (that is, Austrian) rule, he is prepared at most to endorse a loose confederation of independent Italian states (83).

The most controversial section of the book deals with Austria. Tyutchev takes sharp issue with the so-called Austroslavists, led by the liberal Prague historian Frantisek Palacky (and supported among others by Pfeffel),[134] who believed that on the basis of constitutional concessions already granted Austria could evolve into a federation in which the Slavs would dominate by sheer force of numbers. This seems a nonsense to Tyutchev. Now that Vienna has regained the upper hand, he argues, the German-speaking ruling class will have little hesitation in rescinding paper rights yielded to the Slavs under revolutionary duress. After all, does not the whole *raison d'être* of Austria lie in the domination of Slavs by Germans? 'Can Austria cease to be German without ceasing to be altogether?' The Slav populations will respond by asserting their nationality in renewed revolutionary activity, and the Empire will disintegrate in 'permanent civil war' (87-88).

It might be thought he would have welcomed such a process, yet in his notes for this chapter he writes of the 'serious inconveniences' and 'dangers' it would hold for Russia (88). He expands on this in a letter written at the time, pointing out that it would be a disaster if the Slavs — hitherto neutrals in the epoch-making struggle between Russia and Revolution — were to be 'infected' by the revolutionary principle, for they would then by definition be lost to the Russian cause.[135] It follows from this that he was absolutely opposed to fomenting or even condoning revolutionary uprisings in the Slav countries as a means of detaching them from Austria. Such a policy would in his view have resulted in a bloc of independent Slav states 'infected' with Western liberalism and thus hostile to Russia — scarcely a desirable outcome in the 'supreme struggle' between East and West. What he appears to have envisaged on the contrary was a direct incorporation of the western and southern Slavs into the Russian Empire on the existing Polish model. This is clear from the stark choice offered in his book to the Czechs, Slovaks, Poles and Croats of Austria: 'either to remain Slavs in becoming Russians, or to become Germans in remaining Austrians' (89). Or, as we find in the notes to another chapter: 'No political national identity possible for the Slavs outside Russia' (90). This conviction that the future of the Slavs lay with — indeed, within — Russia was to remain an inalienable part of his political credo.

But how was this to come about? Although he does not go into detail in the outline notes for his book, it must be assumed that — as neither revolution nor democratic evolution from within was an acceptable option — what he envisaged was armed intervention, no doubt on some such pretext as restoring order or coming to the aid of Russia's brother-Slavs. He had indeed already hinted as much in his 'Lettre à M. le Docteur Gustave Kolb' of 1844.[136] Some commentators have attempted to play down the more wildly expansionist and bellicose features of Tyutchev's *Realpolitik*, claiming that his grand Panslavist vision is no more than a mythopoetic construct and therefore not to be taken too literally.[137] Yet there is always something ominous about the coupling of 'poetic' utopia and concrete political plan. Like most ideologues, he was fixated on the magnificent dream and none too fastidious about the methods required to achieve it. One witness (A.V. Meshchersky) recalls him already in the winter of 1844-45 expounding at a fashionable St Petersburg salon 'very warlike plans for the pacification of all the Slav peoples by annexing them to the Russian crown by force of arms, something he described as both an inevitable fact and a quite easily achievable goal'.[138] Nor was this an isolated case of political intransigence. On other occasions Tyutchev was prepared to justify Peter the Great's poisoning of his son Alexis as 'a terrible necessity',[139] and on similar grounds to support the brutal suppression of the Polish revolt of 1863.[140]

In the final section of his book Tyutchev turns to the future and to the all-important role allotted to his country by Providence. He sees the historical reality of Russia as determined by two major elements or principles: the Slav race and the Orthodox faith (89). These can be said to represent the body and soul respectively of the Russian Empire (91). The concept of Empire itself is universal: it has always existed, and is handed on from one nation to another. After the four great Empires of pagan times (Assyria, Persia, Macedonia, Rome) arose the fifth and 'definitive' Christian one inaugurated by Constantine (93). And he reaffirms the late medieval Russian doctrine of 'Moscow the Third Rome' in claiming that this 'legitimate' Empire continued as Byzantium, its title passing to Russia after the fall of Constantinople to the Turks in 1453 (90-91).[141] The Papacy and the Holy Roman Empire of Charlemagne are dismissed as illegitimate usurpations of that title, and are seen as ultimately responsible for the gradual decay of authority and the growth of individualism in the West (59-60, 93). The revolutions of 1848 represent the final agony of Western civilisation resulting from that deadly virus; they will be followed in the near future by 'two great providential acts' which will 'bring to a close for the West the revolutionary interregnum of the last three centuries and inaugurate a new era for Europe'.

One of these will be 'the constitution of the great Orthodox Empire, the legitimate Empire of the East' — that is, the Russia to come — 'accomplished by the absorption of Austria and the retaking of Constantinople' (95). This vast new Empire would include all the Slav and Orthodox peoples of Europe, with the Orthodox faith taking precedence as a unifying factor over purely racial (in other words, Slav) determinants (90). Ethnic groups such as the Magyars who fitted neither category but found themselves part of the Empire would simply have to accept a 'subordinate place' in the new order (88). Such an aggrandised Eastern Empire would inevitably dominate the whole of Europe. Tyutchev envisages in particular the 'submission' to it of the German and Italian states (including the German-speaking rump of Austria), representing between them the historical remnants of the old Holy Roman Empire (94).

Related to this is the second of the 'providential acts' to be accomplished soon: the reunion of the Eastern and Western Churches (95). He sees the hand of Providence at work in the erosion by revolutionary forces of both the Papacy's temporal power and its spiritual authority. It was, he argues, Rome's usurpation of temporal power that had separated it from the universal Church; and with that barrier removed, the Church could be one again, its spiritual authority restored (72-73, 94). And in a letter written at the time he makes it clear that he sees the reunion being achieved not through joint deliberations of the two Churches, but by Rome's return to the Orthodox fold.[142]

He concludes that the coming establishment of a universal Orthodox Empire and the reunion of the Churches are the two sides of a single momentous working-out of Providence which can be summed up as: 'An Orthodox Emperor in Constantinople, master and protector of Italy and Rome. An Orthodox Pope in Rome, subject of the Emperor' (95).

Further details of Tyutchev's grandiose vision emerge from political poems of the period. 'Russian Geography' cites biblical authority (a prophecy in the Book of Daniel) for his dream of a vast Empire with joint capitals in Moscow, Rome and Constantinople and stretching 'From the Nile to the Neva, from the Elbe to China, / From the Volga to the Euphrates, from the Ganges to the Danube'.[143] And in 'Prophecy' he predicts the birth of that Empire for 1853, when he believes Russia will liberate Constantinople from the Turkish yoke to coincide with the 400th anniversary of the city's fall.[144]

By the beginning of October 1849 he had finished dictating to Ernestine the second chapter of his book, 'The Roman Question'. With its sharply critical view of the Papacy and its proposal for the return of the Catholic Church to Orthodoxy it was calculated to provoke controversy in the West. Encouraged by the polemical response to the publication of his memorandum to the Tsar (and no doubt having first assured himself of official approval), Tyutchev sent a copy of the chapter to Pfeffel in the hope that it too would find its way into print. As on previous occasions, part of his calculation was almost certainly to appeal to public opinion inside Russia: as a censor at the Foreign Ministry he was well aware that (as Ernestine put it in a letter to her brother accompanying the chapter) 'in Russia people like reading and trust only that which originates from abroad, especially from Paris', and that contraband copies of banned foreign publications were passed eagerly from hand to hand.[145]

Just a few weeks later, towards the end of 1849, he abruptly abandoned all further work on the book. Ernestine was puzzled, for up to then he had insisted it would be 'the end of the world' if he failed to complete it. In a letter to Pfeffel she tentatively attributed her husband's sudden volte-face to his mood-swings and lack of self-discipline, aggravated by 'irritability' and a 'constant state of depression'. Only a sharp polemical response to 'The Roman Question' in the West, she believed, might now goad him into completing the work.[146] This was certainly forthcoming. Pfeffel had sent the chapter to the *Revue des Deux Mondes* in Paris, which published it on 20 December 1849/ 1 January 1850. Although Tyutchev's request for anonymity was respected, the article was printed under the title 'The Papacy and the Roman Question. From the Point of View of St Petersburg', prefaced by remarks hinting that it was by the same Russian diplomat who had written the memorandum published by Bourgoing.[147] Once again the perception of Tyutchev's article as a quasi-official statement of Russian policy created something of a sensation in the West. In St Petersburg too, as predicted by Ernestine, it was widely read and debated.[148] As before, Pfeffel worried that he could have inadvertently helped to compromise Tyutchev with his superiors;[149] however, Ernestine reassured him that her husband should have no trouble proving that the disputed subtitle was an editorial addition beyond his control.[150]

'The Roman Question' provoked a far more vigorous, extensive and protracted response in the West than all of Tyutchev's previous articles put together. The attack was led over the years by such prominent figures as the journalists Pierre Laurentie and Eugène Forcade and the historian Jules Michelet, with many others including Pfeffel and Ivan Gagarin joining in the public debate. The bulk of the critical reaction came from France, but with significant contributions also from Germany, Britain, Belgium and the Polish territories under Prussian and Austrian control. Controversy surrounding the article flared up again at the time of the Crimean War and rumbled on well into the 1860s, by which time Tyutchev had long since been publicly revealed as the author.[151]

Here, it seemed, was the stimulus Ernestine had hoped would induce Tyutchev to take up his pen once more. François Buloz, the editor of the *Revue des Deux Mondes*, let it be known that he would welcome further contributions;[152] Pfeffel had already offered the prospect of 'Europe-wide fame as a political writer'.[153] Yet despite all this Tyutchev made no attempt to return to the polemical fray or to resume work on his hastily abandoned book. This might be attributed to his notorious detestation of the physical process of writing, were it not that in this case all he had to do was dictate the remaining chapters to Ernestine ('as if [...] reading from an open book', according to her), using his existing notes as a guide.[154] A more likely reason was indicated by Ernestine in January 1850 in a letter to Pfeffel conveying her husband's decision not to supply Buloz with further material for the *Revue*. She explained that 'the question of Austria necessarily occupies an enormous place' in his thinking, and that his view on this subject, 'by virtue of the fact that it emanated from St Petersburg, would immediately be taken as the official view and would alarm all Western governments'. What is more, 'this view would not be supported here, for to express it publicly would be to encroach upon an area forbidden to a subject of His Majesty the Emperor of all the Russias'.[155] The clear implication is that Tyutchev's authorisation to publish abroad — especially on matters concerning Austria's Slav population — had been suddenly withdrawn in the changed political climate of late 1849. After their joint suppression of the Hungarian revolt in the summer, Russia and Austria were on course for renewed collaboration in foreign affairs, and Nesselrode in particular was determined that nothing should be allowed to damage relations with Vienna.

A straw in the wind is the fate of a memorandum on Austria which the economist Ludwig Tengoborsky, a former diplomat at the Russian Embassy in Vienna, attempted to submit to the Tsar via Nesselrode. At the beginning of December 1849 he sent a copy to Tyutchev, who found in it 'words of gold' and 'glowing confirmation of all that I have thought, that is to say sensed and conjectured, on the subject of Austria', in particular his own conviction of 'the intimate and inexorable solidarity which ties the destinies of these races [the Austrian Slavs] to those of Russia'.[156] Nesselrode apparently decided to suppress Tengoborsky's memorandum; certainly a month after receiving it he had still not forwarded it to the Tsar.[157]

It is almost certain that Tyutchev's book was vetoed in the same way, and that this is why — denied any hope of seeing it published — he decided to abandon it.[158] Even the relatively tame article on the Papacy and the first reviews of it in French and Belgium newspapers caused some of his close friends in St Petersburg to be alarmed on his behalf. 'Truly, fear — inexplicable and unreasoning fear, the constant sense of some indeterminate danger that has no name — dominates all minds in this country,' commented Ernestine.[159] Soon afterwards Tyutchev poured all the feelings of anger and frustration aroused by Nesselrode into a vicious lampoon of the slight figure — slight in every sense in his eyes — whose cautious foreign policy seemed to him to be denying Russia the greatness that was hers by right:

> No, no, my dwarf ! unrivalled coward! —
> Though you may twist and turn about,
> You'll not convert our holy Russia
> To your dull creed of wavering doubt...
>   [...]
> No matter who believes in Russia
> If she but to herself stay true —
> And God will not postpone her triumph
> To satisfy a cowardly few.
>   [...]
> Byzantium's holy crown and sceptre
> From Russia you shall not withhold!
> No — you are powerless to hinder
> A destiny long since foretold![160]

In poems such as this and his political writings Tyutchev showed himself to be indeed, in Bourgoing's telling phrase, more absolutist than the Emperor. Yet in his zealous preaching of the 'Russian idea' as an antidote to corrupt Western values he seemed remarkably prone to the very failings of which his opponents stood accused. He dismissed as utopian the ideals of German and Italian nationalists and of Western revolutionaries in general;[161] yet what could be more of a 'monstrous utopia' (to quote Pigaryov)[162] than his own imperial and Panslavist dream? Was it not hopelessly unrealistic to imagine that the Slavs already chafing under Austrian rule would take any more kindly to Russian domination than the Poles had done before them? Similarly, critics within or sympathetic to the Orthodox tradition have rightly taken him to task for harbouring the same Caesaropapist delusion — the same denial of

Christ's 'my kingdom is not of this world' — of which he accused the West.[163] Above all, perhaps, we search his political writings in vain for those virtues of 'renunciation and sacrifice' seen by him as central to the moral nature of the Russian people;[164] too often what we find instead are precisely the proselytising fervour and hubristic self-righteousness claimed to be characteristic of revolutionary Europe. Reviewing the impact of Tyutchev's published articles on Western public opinion, Ronald Lane concludes that 'they did not build bridges between Russia and Europe, but rather burned them'.[165] Perhaps it was as well for international relations that his political *magnum opus* remained unfinished.

13 Poetic Rebirth, Last Love (St Petersburg, 1849-1854)

i A Poet Through and Through

For a decade after the death of Eleonore Tyutchev's poetic inspiration had lain dormant; it was, as we have seen, only with a piece evidently written to mark the tenth anniversary of that event ('Still love torments me with a vengeance...') that he appears finally to have broken the spell. Another poem of this period, 'Now holy night has claimed the heavenly sphere...', seems in returning to the theme of 'Day and Night' — one of the last poems before the long hiatus — a similar attempt to pick up where he had left off (to 'renew the chain', as he himself was fond of saying). The philosophical assumptions linking these two pieces on the night theme have already been examined.[1] Less obvious perhaps are the biographical connotations they may have in common.

'Day and Night', it will be recalled, appears to reflect Tyutchev's dark night of the soul after Eleonore's death, and the later poem can be read in much the same way. It is full of a sense of disorientation, of being left as a 'homeless orphan' (one of Tyutchev's favourite images of separation), cut off from what was once 'bright' and 'alive' and is now no more than a 'phantom', a 'long-gone dream'. In this context even the dark 'abyss' becomes a disturbing metaphor for loss and grief. Indeed, one is tempted to wonder whether this poem (dated 1848-1849 by Pigaryov)[2] might in fact have been conceived as a companion piece to 'Still love torments me...'.

Richard Gregg adds a further layer of biographical significance by finding echoes of 'Holy Russia' in the phrase 'holy night' and arguing that the vanished 'golden day' stands for the 'golden time' of Tyutchev's youth in the West. Gregg sees the poem as an inner psychological commentary on Tyutchev's political beliefs in which his return to the darkly forbidding Russian fold (the 'native legacy' of the final line) is revealed to be an act of penance and expiation.[3]

The two interpretations are by no means mutually exclusive. Eleonore would always remain closely associated in Tyutchev's mind with the 'golden time', and his feelings of guilt for her death undoubtedly resulted in the need for expiation of some kind. As for the political connotations suggested by Gregg, at the very least the poem offers a revealing glimpse into inner doubts and a profound existential unease lurking beneath all the confident outward bluster of such contemporaneous pieces as 'Russian Geography' and 'Prophecy'.

For a time it was not clear whether 'Still love torments me...' and 'Now holy night...' heralded a new beginning, or whether they would remain an isolated outburst comparable to that of 1844. That question was decided in the summer of 1849. Ernestine had originally wanted the family to spend several months at Ovstug. As well as wanting a break from St Petersburg society, she saw this as a way of achieving much-needed economies. Tyutchev on the other hand flatly refused either to immure

313

himself in the depths of the countryside for months on end or to be separated from her for any length of time. Eventually a compromise was reached: they would travel to Ovstug together but stay only a few weeks.[4] They left St Petersburg on 21 May, and after some ten days with family and friends in Moscow headed on towards Ovstug.[5] North of Bryansk on 6 June they ran into a passing storm. Ever sensitive to displays of transience and ephemerality in nature, Tyutchev was fascinated by the sudden eruption of thunder and lightning, followed by torrential rain whipping up dust from the parched fields and the almost as sudden return of calm and sunshine. As he observed this drama from his carriage, lines of verse began to form in his mind:

> Hesitantly, diffidently
> From above the sun looks down...
> Suddenly a clap of thunder
> Causes all the earth to frown.
>
> Intermittent gusts of warm air,
> Distant rumbling, spots of rain...
> Rich the green of unripe cornfields,
> Set against the sky's dark stain.
>
> From behind one cloud a steel-blue
> Streak of lightning slithers out,
> Briefly compassing with pallid
> Fire its contours all about.
>
> Raindrops scatter with a vengeance,
> Hurling dust into the air;
> Peals of rattling, echoing thunder
> Their defiant wrath declare...
>
> Once again the sun, uncertain,
> Glances at the fields below,
> Bathing all the earth's disordered
> Travail in a radiant glow.[6]

They reached Ovstug the following day. The mixed emotions that Tyutchev had expressed in letters to Ernestine on his visit three years before were now poured into verse:

> And so once more I find myself confronted
> With native haunts, long-lost and yet unmourned,
> Where thought and feeling first within me dawned —
> And where now, as I look on, disenchanted,
> While all around the daylight fades and dies,
> My childhood stares at me from misted eyes...

Poor, wretched phantom, fleeting and inconstant,
Of that remote, forgotten happiness!
With what misgiving and half-heartedness
I gaze at you, my guest for this brief instant!
To me you seem as distant as must be
A brother who expired in infancy...

Not here, not in these tracts unpopulated,
Are ties of birth I find still meaningful:
Not here was wondrous youth's great festival
In all its burgeoning glory celebrated...
And in another soil was laid, not here,
All that I lived for, all that I held dear.[7]

It is a paradoxical confession for one about to embark on a major treatise arguing his country's superiority over the decadent West. For all his cerebral faith in Russia, his heart still drew him to places where he had first experienced the joys and sorrows of life to the full. And prominent among these markers on his journey would always be (as the closing lines of the poem tell us) Eleonore's modest grave on the outskirts of Turin.[8]

Despite these initial feelings of alienation Tyutchev seems to have adapted tolerably well to the routines of country living. He had arranged to have newspapers and journals sent, including the *Allgemeine Zeitung*, so was able to keep track of ongoing counter-revolutionary actions and other political developments in Europe.[9] Ernestine had taken an immediate liking to Ovstug and its surroundings, and would return regularly in the years to come. 'I love the Russian countryside,' she wrote on a later visit; 'these vast plains, undulating like great waves on the open sea, these limitless spaces, immeasurable to the eye — all is filled with grandeur and never-ending sadness.'[10] To judge by his poetry, that summer at Ovstug some of Ernestine's enthusiasm for his 'native haunts' must have rubbed off on Tyutchev too. The green corn battered by storms in early June had ripened by the end of their stay; the sight of it rippling in the breeze by moonlight one summer night inspired a memorable picture in words:

On a still night, late in summer,
How the stars appear to smoulder:
Ripening cornfields in their glimmer
Seem asleep to the beholder...

How hypnotically all glitters
In the silence of the night:
Wave on wave of golden wheat-ears,
By a harvest moon washed white...[11]

He had produced concise landscape sketches of this kind before (a useful example for purposes of comparison would be 'Evening', written in the mid-1820s).[12] Where this one differs is in its use, or rather non-use, of figures of speech. Metaphor, simile and personification, freely deployed in the earlier poetry to suggest the underlying unity and living force of nature, are here almost totally absent. The stars appear to 'smoulder', and the cornfields seem 'asleep'; yet even these isolated and restrained metaphors have little purpose beyond the creation of atmosphere. Tyutchev is concerned here to summon up a specific scene, free of all 'cosmic' overtones. Even the choice of words (the rippling corn 'washed white' by the moon) hints at painterly aspirations. From now on in general his nature poetry would tend towards what could best be termed poetic realism, shedding in the process much of the metaphysical and symbolic baggage of his earlier, 'Western' period.

Six weeks in the country was more than enough for Tyutchev, and towards the end of July, with his leave nearly at an end, he was preparing to return. Ernestine had originally intended to stay on at Ovstug without him, but he appears to have persuaded her to change her mind. They reached St Petersburg soon after the middle of August to unwelcome news of the death abroad of his patroness Countess Nesselrode.[13]

The talk of St Petersburg later that autumn were two stars of the operatic firmament, Giulia Grisi and Giovanni Mario, who had arrived for a season with the city's Italian company. Longtime partners in life as well as on the stage, the celebrated soprano and tenor took the capital by storm. Tyutchev went to hear them on several occasions, partly to remain *au courant* with society gossip, but also because (as Ernestine put it) 'he loves music as such, albeit with the incomparable naivety and artlessness of one who knows nothing about it'.[14] An undoubted further attraction in his eyes will have been that Grisi was not just an accomplished singer and actress, but a beauty of some renown. It is even quite likely that he met her socially, perhaps at soirées given by the music-loving Count Michal Wielhorski, which featured 'all the famous singers, composers and actors', and which he is known to have attended regularly in the second half of the 1840s.[15]

One of Grisi's most outstanding performances that autumn and winter was in the title role of Bellini's *Norma*, one which she had made very much her own. As Ernestine commented, 'there is no other Norma like Grisi: she says it herself, and I think she is right'.[16] Set in Roman-occupied Gaul in the first century BC, Bellini's opera will have appealed to Tyutchev's sense of history. Its portrayal of the Gauls as noble savages, morally superior to their civilised rulers and destined one day to succeed them in the wider scheme of things (already in the opening scene the druid priestess Norma prophesies the fall of Rome), had certain resonances with 'Russia and the West', on which he was then working. But it was echoes of his own life in the love triangle at the centre of the opera which will doubtless have affected him most.

As the action develops it becomes apparent that for some years Norma has been married to the Roman Proconsul Pollione, managing to keep this secret despite the fact that they have children. To achieve this she has relied heavily on help with child-rearing from a young companion named Clotilde (a coincidence Tyutchev can hardly have failed to miss). Now, however, Pollione has turned his attentions to a young novice priestess, Adalgisa. At the beginning of Act II Norma appears with a dagger, intent on committing suicide after first killing her sleeping children rather than let Pollione abduct them to Rome. Although she is eventually persuaded against this course of action, the highly dramatic scene must inevitably have aroused painful memories for Tyutchev. Grisi's performance certainly struck a chord with Ernestine: 'I marvel at how accurately she portrays the pangs of jealousy tormenting a passionate and resolute heart,' she wrote after seeing her in the role.[17] Throughout the opera Bellini and his librettist, the poet Felice Romani, contrast the possessive and ultimately destructive love of Pollione with an altogether more altruistic and self-sacrificing variety displayed by the two women Norma and Adalgisa. At the very end in an act of renunciation and purification Norma chooses to join the now captive Pollione on the pyre where he is to be burnt for pursuing Adalgisa. Too late now as death approaches, Pollione recognises Norma's sacrifice and acknowledges what a 'magnificent woman' ('*sublima donna*') he has lost in her. All this cannot have failed to arouse in Tyutchev memories of himself, Eleonore and Ernestine more than a decade before.

The scholar Gennady Chagin makes a convincing case for Giulia Grisi being the previously unidentified addressee of a poem written by Tyutchev that autumn or winter.[18] If he is right, it could even be that the title 'Memory' used in one of the manuscript versions[19] was suggested by a particular moment in *Norma* (Act I, scene 2) when, recalling the early days of her love for Pollione, the heroine twice repeats the poignant phrase '*Oh rimembranza!*' In the poem Grisi's 'southern gaze' (assuming it is she) evokes similarly poignant memories of Italy, the lost paradise once inhabited by Tyutchev's supposed ancestors the Dudgi.

> Once again my eyes encounter
> Yours, and all this wintry haze —
> All our northern gloom and darkness —
> Flee before your southern gaze...
> And another land — that cherished
> Homeland — rises into view:
> Paradise, which guilt ancestral
> Means its sons must now eschew...
>
> Shapely laurels, gently swaying,
> Stir the blue untainted air,
> While the ocean's measured breathing
> Dissipates all heat and glare;
> All day long in sun-drenched vineyards
> Ripen grapes of golden cast,
> And arcades of ancient marble
> Breathe tales of an epic past...
>
> Like some hideous dream the fateful
> North is banished from my sight;
> Far above, the dome of heaven
> Floats, ethereally fair and bright;
> Once again I drink the healing
> Light with eager, thirsting eyes,
> And in its pure rays a magic
> Realm once more I recognise.[20]

317

The surge of creativity experienced at Ovstug had shown no signs of abating after his return to St Petersburg. Over the two and a half years from the summer of 1849 to the end of 1851 he would produce (not counting purely political and other occasional verse, translations and pieces in French) some 40 lyric poems, making this one of the most prolific periods of his life. In this new verse, together with the move towards poetic realism and away from 'cosmic' themes already mentioned, there was what Boris Kozyrev has identified as a greater emphasis on 'the human soul with its sins and atonements, its joys and sufferings'.[21] Tyutchev's own experiences in the intervening years had evidently made him more sensitive to the tribulations of others. A good example is a poem conceived one evening in the autumn of 1849 during a journey home by cab (an open drozhky) in heavy rain. He arrived wet through to be greeted at the door by one of his daughters. Telling her he had just composed 'a few rhymes', he proceeded to dictate them to her while being helped out of his soaking outer garments.[22]

> Tears of humanity, tears of humanity,
> Flowing eternally early and late...
> Flowing invisibly, flowing in secrecy,
> Ever abundantly, ever unceasingly —
> Flowing as rain flows with autumn finality
> All through the night like a river in spate.[23]

Another poem in this vein, 'To a Russian Woman', may have been written already at Ovstug. Here Tyutchev muses on a young life wasting away in an atmosphere of provincial philistinism, conformity and banality:

> Far from the sun and far from nature,
> Far from society and art,
> Far from life and from love's allure,
> Your youthful years will pass unnoticed:
> Still-born the stirrings of your heart,
> Once cherished dreams a hope no more...

She is doomed to live a life of anonymous obscurity in this 'unpeopled, nameless land', after which all trace of her will vanish like smoke in a dark autumnal sky.[24] We do not know the name of the young provincial woman who inspired these lines (one version has the title 'To my Fellow-countrywoman', the original Russian implying someone from Tyutchev's native region).[25] What is remarkable — and new in Tyutchev's work — is his compassionate awareness of another's misfortune. Certainly there is nothing here of that 'erotic attachment to the spectacle of feminine suffering' rightly identified by Gregg as a feature of the earlier poems.

Solidarity with suffering humanity is also evident in an important poem written the following year (1850):

Two Voices

1

Be valiant, my friends: fight the fight and show mettle,
Though hopeless the fray and unequal the battle!
Above you the stars keep their silence on high,
Beneath you cold graves just as silently lie.

Let gods on Olympus enjoy ease of living:
Immortal, they know neither toil nor misgiving;
Those curses afflict only mortals below...
No victory theirs: death is all they shall know.

2

My friends, show your mettle: fight on, lion-hearted,
Though fiercely the battle may rage all around!
Above you mute stars in their courses uncharted,
Beneath you graves hearing and speaking no sound.

Let Zeus and his kin watch with envy unending
The struggle of resolute hearts here below;
Who, vanquished by Fate alone, falls while contending
A victor's crown snatched from the gods' hands may show.[26]

In the stars above and graves below we see contrasted the immutability of fate and the ephemeral fragility of our existence. It is a mystery we can never hope to penetrate: both stars and graves respond to our questions with silence. The image has been shown to derive from Goethe's 'Symbolum', a poem on the masonic vocation which also contains a reference to the victor's crown, yet in general theme has little in common with Tyutchev's lines.[27] Much closer in spirit, as noted by Aleksandr Neuslykhin, is the poem 'Hyperions Schicksallied' ('Hyperion's Song of Fate') by Hölderlin, in which the enviably ordered life of the gods ('Free of fate, like a slumbering/ Infant, breathe the celestial ones') is contrasted with the lot of 'suffering' men, who find themselves falling 'Blindly from hour to/ Hour, tossed like water/ From one stony cliff to/ Another, and on down/ Into the unknown, year after year.'[28] The first of Tyutchev's 'voices' (verses 1-2) similarly asserts that, unlike the immortal gods, humanity is doomed to failure in its unequal struggle with fate. Here he conjures up once more that mythopoetic world — the world of Goethe and Hölderlin among others — which he had embraced as a young man in Munich. Then in 'Cicero' too he had portrayed the gods as all-powerful masters of fate whose earth-born minions may at best hope to be granted a tantalisingly brief taste of the immortality denied to them in principle. Voice one essentially reaffirms this view: subject to death, humans can never be victorious in their 'hopeless' struggle against fate and must therefore be considered inferior to the immortal gods. Voice two (verses 3-4) seems at first merely to repeat voice one; yet on closer examination it becomes clear that through subtle variations, like a composer reworking an earlier theme, Tyutchev has in fact stood everything on its head. Voice two makes no reference to the struggle being 'hopeless'; despite being subject to death, mortals are now said to be vanquished 'only' by fate; and the gods look on as if from the sidelines, 'envious' of the unyielding courage shown by men and forced in the final analysis to cede the victor's crown to them. The gods, it seems, have become superfluous to the great tragic drama; after this they would make no further appearance in Tyutchev's lyric verse.

Boris Kozyrev has observed that 'Two Voices' represents a major turning-point in Tyutchev's development, signalling the abandonment of the ecstatic pantheism of his youth in favour of a closer concern with the vicissitudes of the human soul, adrift in an inhospitable universe.[29] This darker, almost existentialist vision is reflected in several other poems of the time.[30] Never again would Tyutchev portray nature as a 'life-giving ocean' in whose waters we may heal the wounds inflicted by a malevolent fate.[31] More often it appears as a blind, meaningless force, itself an agent of that fate (in one of his letters he even writes of nature as an implacable opponent in some cosmic game of chess, always seeking to catch the unwary individual off guard and deliver check-mate).[32] Of course he would continue to celebrate its surface beauty (albeit in more elegiac and muted tones), but its underlying chaos would appear increasingly destructive rather than creative, senseless rather than purposeful.

For Tyutchev this renewed burst of creative energy was essentially a private matter. There seemed in any case little point in attempting to reach out to a wider public. Poetry had fallen out of fashion to such an extent that by the middle of the 1840s it had more or less disappeared from the major literary journals.[32] Particularly influential in this respect was the foremost critic of the time, Vissarion Belinsky, who saw prose as on the whole a more suitable medium for the politically and socially engaged naturalism he was keen to promote in literature. In 1846 one of his associates, Nikolay Nekrasov, became publisher and editor of *Sovremennik*, and continued to maintain the journal as a forum for progressive literature and ideas in the Belinsky tradition after the latter's death in 1848. Himself a poet, Nekrasov was dedicated to creating a new kind of 'civic' verse dealing with social and political issues, but realised there would be little point in this unless the public could first be won over to the idea of reading poetry again. With this in mind, from the beginning of 1850 he began publishing in his journal a series of articles under the general title 'Minor Russian Poets' (a term he explained as including those whose neglect was in his view quite unjustified).

The first was devoted to the enigmatic 'F.T.' or 'F.T-v' whose poems had appeared in *Sovremennik* between 1836 and 1840.[33] The identity of this person was clearly a mystery to Nekrasov, as was the question of why he had apparently written so little verse, or indeed whether he was still alive (90, 109). (Kirill Pigaryov supposes that Nekrasov must have been surprised to discover in due course that 'F.T.' was in fact the well-known society figure and salon wit who lived just a few streets away[34] — and who by the strangest of coincidences had only recently returned to poetic creation in earnest after an interval of ten years.) Even more puzzling to Nekrasov was why these poems, judged by him some of 'the few brilliant phenomena in the field of Russian poetry' (91), should have suffered such critical neglect. In an attempt to right that wrong his article reproduced in full 24 of the poems printed in Pushkin's journal, interspersed with his own comments. (Regrettably, he took it upon himself to 'improve' on the original texts in places, whether hoping to make them more accessible to his readers or from misguided aesthetic considerations is not clear. Whatever his motives, he set an unfortunate precedent for others to follow.) The article singles out Tyutchev's depiction of nature for special praise, in particular his ability to express 'its most subtle, elusive features and nuances' (91). Favourable comparisons are repeatedly drawn with Pushkin and Lermontov (90, 93-94, 98, 99), culminating in the assertion that — the title of the article notwithstanding — 'we have no hesitation in ranking Mr T-v among the major Russian poetic talents' (108). Nekrasov concludes with a call for the poems to be published as a book, declaring that this could take its place in any library 'next to the best products of Russian poetic genius' (109).

To the small circle of initiates who knew the true identity of 'F.T.' Nekrasov's ringing endorsement came as a call to action. Writing to St Petersburg soon after the article's publication in January 1850, the Slavophile and poet Aleksey Khomyakov asked the recipient of his letter to convey to Tyutchev the 'vexation' he and others in Moscow had felt on reading the poems: 'Everyone is delighted with them and indignant with him... Is it not shameful to be silent when God has given one such a voice?' Tyutchev, he added, is 'a poet through and through' in whom 'the poetic source cannot run dry'.[35] Not long afterwards Khomyakov's associate Pogodin managed to persuade Tyutchev to send some of his latest pieces for publication in his journal *Moskvityanin* (*The Muscovite*). Enclosed with one manuscript Pogodin found a characteristically self-deprecating note from his old friend: 'You flatter me with your encouraging remarks and might easily rekindle my interest in versification, but what use can there be in a galvanised muse?'[36] Starting with the April issue, *Moskvityanin* published sixteen poems during the course of 1850 and five in 1851. Two more were included in the 1850 issue of his almanach *Kievlyanin* (*The Kievan*) by another old university friend, Mikhail Maksimovich.[37] To begin with Tyutchev insisted on anonymity, although in an editorial note Pogodin playfully invited his readers to guess the identity of a poet 'very well-known to all lovers of Russian literature' (evidently a broad hint at Nekrasov's article).[38] No doubt aware that he was fighting a losing battle, Tyutchev eventually agreed to his name being disclosed in the July 1850 issue of *Moskvityanin*.[39] Public recognition as a poet appears to have brought him little personal satisfaction. As before, in 1836, he had stepped into the limelight unwillingly, pushed forward by others.

ii Yelena

At the end of 1849 Ernestine had cited a 'constant state of depression' as one of the possible reasons for her husband's abandonment of 'Russia and the West'. This appears to have proved a more serious and protracted episode than any he had suffered for some years. As so often, he sought relief in a hectic rush of social activity. Early in 1850 Pletnyov grumbled that because of his 'intemperate' lifestyle it was hardly ever possible to find him at home, even at times agreed in advance.[40] Many years later Tyutchev admitted that at the time he had been in the grip of a suicidal despair, to which he might well have succumbed 'if it had not been for *Her*. Only she alone — inspiring, investing my lifeless, moribund soul with the breath of that infinitely alive, infinitely loving soul of hers — was able to put off the fateful outcome.'[41] 'She' was not Ernestine, but a young woman of 24, Yelena Aleksandrovna Denisyeva.

Yelena (Lyolya to those who knew her well) came from an old landowning family which had fallen on hard times. Her father, a retired army Major, had been obliged to take employment as an estate manager in the provinces. Born in 1826, Yelena lost her mother at an early age and was put in the care of her maiden aunt Anna Dmitrievna Denisyeva, who was Deputy Head of the Smolny Institute in St Petersburg. Although never officially enrolled as a pupil, Yelena was permitted to attend classes there on an informal basis while continuing to live in her aunt's service apartment. Anna Dmitrievna was a strict disciplinarian in the classroom, but appears to have let things slip somewhat on the domestic front. Yelena was allowed to skip classes, and in general enjoyed far greater freedom than her classmates. Anna Dmitrievna would take her young niece to society gatherings, leaving her unattended while she herself played cards, and even allowed Yelena to stay unchaperoned as a guest in aristocratic households of sometimes dubious repute.[42] In later years Tyutchev would seek to play down his role in Yelena's seduction by hinting that she had already been corrupted by such disreputable company, in particular that of the writer Count Vladimir Sollogub, a notorious ladykiller who according to Tyutchev 'had a bad influence' on her.[43]

When Tyutchev's daughters Darya and Kitty entered the Smolny Institute in November 1845 they found themselves in the same class as Yelena's half-sisters Marie and Anna (her father having remarried after the death of his first wife).[44] Yelena, still living with her aunt, took her half-sisters' new classmates under her wing, and it was only natural that on visiting days the Tyutchevs should develop friendly relations with the Deputy Head ('an excellent person' in Tyutchev's initial estimation)[45] and her niece. Before very long the Denisyevs were being invited to their home and seen as family friends.[46] There will also have been opportunities to meet the twenty-year-old Yelena in society, where she already enjoyed great success and was surrounded by admirers. Quite apart from her obvious beauty — she was a vivacious, attractive brunette, slim and shapely, with large dark eyes and expressive features — she displayed intelligence, wit, and depths of powerful unaffected emotion. So much is evident from her surviving portrait and photographs, and from the reminiscences of her brother-in-law Aleksandr Georgievsky.[47] Certainly it is easy to believe the latter when he writes that among Yelena's many admirers at this time was Tyutchev himself. Gradually admiration deepened into something more serious, as in Georgievsky's words Tyutchev, 'valuing her charming company, developed ever closer relations with Lyolya and became more and more infatuated with her'.[48]

But there was to be no easy conquest. Indeed, ungratified desire may well have been a contributory factor in the suicidal depression later admitted by Tyutchev himself. The evidence for this is a poem which can be dated to the years 1849-1850. Entitled 'Twins', it begins with a fairly conventional celebration of the divine 'twins' Sleep and Death before going on to examine a more unusual coupling: there is, we are told, in the whole world 'no pair more splendid' than these, nor 'any charm more dread' than that which 'renders hearts their slaves'. Their identity is revealed in the final stanza:

Who in the grip of strong emotion,
When passion shows its darker side,
Has never known the twin temptations
Of those two — Love and Suicide![49]

Critics have commented on the poem's anticipation of Baudelaire and the Decadents[50] (although the theme itself is at least as old as Petrarch); its biographical significance appears on the other hand to have gone unnoticed. Much the same applies to another piece dated July 1850:

Lord, grant to him Thy consolation
Who in the summer heat and glare
Must like a beggar trudge the highway
Outside a parkland cool and fair —

Who casts a furtive glance through railings
At grassy combes and shady trees,
Or at the tantalising freshness
Of radiant, richly verdant leas.

For him in vain the branches fashion
Their canopy of welcoming green,
For him in vain the soaring fountain
Descends in mists of drops unseen.

The clouded azure of the grotto
Cannot command his downcast gaze,
Nor will the fountain's jetting waters
Bedew his head with cooling haze...

Lord, grant to him Thy consolation
Who, doomed upon life's path to fare,
Must like a beggar trudge the highway
Outside a parkland cool and fair.[51]

This is clearly meant to be understood metaphorically. The man is said to be not an actual beggar, but *like* one: a comparison evidently referring to his inner state of mind rather than to any outward similarity. The degree of empathy shown towards him suggests indeed that Tyutchev is writing about himself. And towards the end we learn the true nature of his journey: it is (in the one variant phrase of the otherwise repeated final stanza) 'life's path' that he treads. It is possible to interpret the poem (like the earlier 'Madness', with which it shows certain parallels) as an expression of man's perennial longing for spiritual sustenance. In this case, as the prayer at the beginning makes clear, it seems to be specifically the gift of Christian faith for which the beggar-like poet pleads. What can be seen as essentially the same statement, supported by similar imagery, is made more explicitly by a poem written about a year later. This identifies a spiritual disintegration eating away at the heart of intellectual enlightenment as the central dilemma of 'Our Age' (the title of the poem). Modern man is said to be 'scorched by the withering blight of unbelief'; he 'knows his lot to be but pain and grief' and 'thirsts for faith', but standing before the 'bolted door' is too proud to beg for admittance by repeating the words from St Mark's gospel: 'Lord, I believe; help Thou my unbelief!'[52]

However we choose to interpret 'Lord, grant to him Thy consolation...', the prayer with which it opens is undeniably a new departure for Tyutchev. On the few occasions that overtly Christian imagery had previously appeared in his original verse it had either provided a target for irony or scepticism,[53] or (in the political verse) remained largely rhetorical in function.[54] Now for the first time we have an expression of piety that manifestly comes from the heart, and this would be repeated in subsequent poems.[55] Tyutchev had turned away from the 'religion of Horace', seeking to regain the Christian faith from which he had lapsed (and which would in fact remain stubbornly denied to him). What could have brought about this change of heart? Two likely causes are suggested by Boris Kozyrev: a growing sense of personal guilt, and the influence of the deeply devout Yelena.[56]

Yet while the prayer undoubtedly expresses Tyutchev's newly found religious aspirations, the interpretation of the rest of the poem suggested above is not the only possible one. As well as spiritual desolation, images of unbearable heat or burning in his verse often denote unfulfilled, unproductive or destructive love.[57] It is therefore equally possible to see the beggar-like figure as Tyutchev himself in the toils of frustrated desire for Yelena. Interestingly enough, it is not for admittance to the luxuriant world on the other side of the railings that he prays, but for *consolation* in his predicament. In other words, he appears to accept that the bliss for which he thirsts is inaccessible because forbidden by divine law. Yet if this is what Yelena had told him, she was about to execute a remarkable *volte face*.

By the summer of 1850 Ernestine had grown increasingly concerned about her husband. For some time there had been a certain chill in their relations. The Hortense Lapp affair had not helped and is unlikely to have been the last of his infidelities. On reaching her fortieth birthday in April 1850 Ernestine may well have wondered how much longer she could retain the affections of her notoriously wayward spouse. Tyutchev for his part will have noted how the previous summer she had proposed spending several months apart from him at Ovstug. This year he had been promised a courier mission, but she had declined to accompany him abroad.[58]

At the end of June he told her that Nesselrode had unexpectedly withdrawn the offer of foreign travel.[59] On 2 July she wrote to Vyazemsky that the constant state of expectation had had 'an agitating effect' on him, and that in order to 'relieve his need for a change of place' he had for two weeks been commuting back and forth on what was then Russia's only working railway, twenty miles of track connecting St Petersburg with the imperial palaces of Tsarskoye Selo and Pavlovsk. The second of these belonged to the Tsar's recently deceased younger brother Grand Duke Michael and his wife Yelena Pavlovna, a Princess of the Württemberg royal family; it also boasted a pleasure garden or so-called 'Vauxhall' and was a popular destination for trippers from the capital. Ernestine told Vyazemsky that Tyutchev had even rented a room near the station at Pavlovsk and had stayed there overnight on several occasions.[60] Any suspicions she may have had on this score are discreetly passed over in her letter. That suspicions there were is clear from Georgievsky's account, which reveals that at about this time Ernestine was concerned at her husband's amatory pursuit of certain unnamed society beauties. According to Georgievsky, she even made an effort to divert him from such worldly-wise rivals by encouraging what she saw as a fairly harmless flirtation with the young and innocent Yelena Denisyeva.[61] In her letter to Vyazemsky she expressed her confident expectation that a trip to Lake Ladoga with Anna and Yelena planned by Tyutchev for the near future, followed in all probability by a visit to Moscow to see his mother, would put an end to the 'entertainment' on offer at Pavlovsk; after this 'autumn will be upon us and everything will fall back into place'.[62]

It was a vain hope. Just two weeks later, on 15 July, Tyutchev and Yelena became lovers. We know this from a poem entitled '15 July 1865'. Never intended for publication, it commemorates the fifteenth anniversary of that 'fateful day of bliss divine/ When first into my soul she poured her being/ And breathed her very spirit into mine'.[63] A more immediate account of these first intimate encounters is given by a poem written at the time:

> Though the sultry heat of midday
> Breathes in at the open pane,
> Here in this calm sanctuary,
> Where deep shade and silence reign,
>
> And aromas quick and fragrant
> Roam throughout the darkened space,
> Let sweet somnolence enfold you
> In its gentle, dark embrace...
>
> In one corner, never tiring,
> Sings a fountain night and day,
> Moistening the enchanted shadows
> With unseen reviving spray...
>
> And a love-struck poet's daydream
> Seems to haunt the unlit room:
> Hovering, fraught with secret passion,
> Lightly in the shifting gloom...[64]

Composed already in July 1850, this is now generally accepted as one of the earliest items in the remarkable 'Denisyeva cycle'. As a compellingly candid poetic diary of the affair with Yelena this 'cycle' (a convenient scholarly designation: there is no evidence that Tyutchev ever conceived of the poems as such) remains unsurpassed. Critics have variously described it as 'a novel in verse'; 'a human document, shattering in the force of its emotion'; and 'a few songs without comparison in Russian, perhaps even in world poetry'.[65] Unfortunately there is no overall agreement as to the exact contents of the cycle, even if its core components are beyond dispute. Certainly a case could be made for including — if only as a kind of prologue — 'Twins' and 'Lord, grant to him Thy consolation...'. Indeed, 'Though the sultry heat of midday...' can be read as a sequel to the second of these. The mendicant poet, his prayers apparently answered, has now been granted refuge from the midday sun in the soothing shade of the 'sanctuary'; there is even a cooling fountain nearby to mirror that glimpsed from afar in the earlier poem.

If, as seems likely, religious scruples had for some time held Yelena back from adultery, what persuaded her eventually to ignore them? A possible explanation is given by Georgievsky, to whom she later more than once expressed her firm belief that the union she and Tyutchev had embarked on was a true marriage in the eyes of God if not of man, and that this outweighed any legalistic objections. One particularly emotional affirmation of this was recorded verbatim by Georgievsky:

> I am more of a wife to him than his previous wives, and no-one in the world has ever loved and valued him as I do — every sound and intonation of his voice, every expression, every line of his face, every glance and smile; I live in him completely, I am completely his, and he is mine: 'and two shall become one flesh', but he and I are one spirit. [...] Isn't that then the essence of a marriage blessed by God Himself: to love one another as I love him and he loves me, and to be as one instead of two separate individuals? Am I not then married to him, is ours not a true marriage?[66]

Faced with such unshakeable conviction, neither Georgievsky nor the various priests she consulted on the subject had the heart to contradict her. Nor, apparently, did Tyutchev. Aware that a fourth marriage was forbidden by the Orthodox Church, he seems to have deliberately left her with the impression that Ernestine was his third wife. 'His previous marriage is already dissolved as a result of his having entered into a new marriage with me,' Yelena later told Georgievsky, 'and that he doesn't ask for the Church's blessing on this marriage is purely because he has already been married three times [...]. But such is the will of God, and I humbly submit to His holy volition, although not without at times bitterly lamenting my fate.'[67]

Tyutchev was both flattered and alarmed by the sheer power of Yelena's love. His own initial reaction to their intimacy had been — as he guiltily recalled in a poem the following year — little more than 'pride' in his 'conquest'.[68] But if he imagined this would be just another 'fleeting passion' he had reckoned without Yelena. In her he encountered 'so deep and self-denying, so passionate and powerful a love that it engulfed his whole being too'.[69] These are the words of Georgievsky, who believed it was only by virtue of this unconditional love that she was able for so many years to retain the affections of such an 'easily enamoured and inconstant poet'.[70]

In July 1850 such considerations still lay in the future. For the moment there was only the euphoria of new-found love, not to mention the excitement of clandestine assignations. On the evidence of a poem written that month, these included nocturnal boat trips on the Neva:

On the Neva

Once again a star-glow quivers,
On the rippling tide afloat;
Once more to the waves delivers
Love its enigmatic boat.

And as in a dream the vessel
Glides on between tide and star,
And two spectral forms that nestle
In the craft are borne afar.

Is it idle youth partaking
Of the night's enchantments here?
Or two blessed shades forsaking
This world for a higher sphere?

White-fledged waves so fleet and nimble,
Trackless as unbounded seas,
Shelter in your void this humble
Craft and all its mysteries![71]

The journey by steamer to Lake Ladoga and the Konevets and Valaam monasteries went ahead as planned from 4 to 9 August. Anna shared a cabin and a monastery cell with her friend Yelena, evidently unaware of what had transpired between her travelling companions.[72] Stormy weather encountered at one point during the voyage inspired a poem ('Whipped up by a gusting sullen/ Squall, the waves grew dark and swollen,/ Glinting with a leaden sheen').[73] The circumstances of its composition might make this seem an obvious candidate for inclusion in the 'Denisyeva cycle', but in fact it is a purely descriptive piece containing no reference to Yelena.

By September Yelena realised that she was pregnant. Despite this they managed to keep the affair secret until the following March, when the Smolny bursar came across evidence of their illicit meetings at a flat rented for the purpose near the Institute and reported this to his superiors. For Yelena's aunt Anna Dmitrievna in particular the resulting scandal could not have come at a more awkward time. It was shortly before the annual leavers' ceremony, a grand occasion customarily attended by members of the imperial family at which '*chiffres*' (diamond brooches in the shape of the Empress's monogram) were awarded to girls who had graduated with distinction. Anna Dmitrievna had been in charge of the current leavers' class for several years, in recognition of which she had been expected to receive an honour and to see her niece Yelena appointed a Maid of Honour at court. Among the leavers that year were Tyutchev's daughters Darya and Kitty and Yelena's half-sister Marie. Denisyev *père* had come up specially for the ceremony from the provinces with his second wife, and his public outburst of rage on learning of the affair only helped to give it wider currency. Anna Dmitrievna was obliged to accept retirement on a fairly generous pension and vacate her official quarters at the Institute. Yelena's fate was much harsher. Disowned by her father, who forbade her sisters any contact with her, and shunned by most of her former friends and acquaintances, she became totally dependent on Anna Dmitrievna, with whom she continued to live and who supported her financially.[74]

The events of March 1851, and their devastating effect on Yelena, are recalled in one of the poems of the 'Denisyeva cycle':

> That which you gave your adoration
> And prayers, and cherished as divine,
> Fate yielded up to desecration
> By idle tongues quick to malign.
>
> The mob broke in and violated
> The shrine within your heart concealed,
> And you must see, humiliated,
> Its sacred mysteries revealed.
>
> Could but the soul, serenely flying
> Above the mob on wings so free,
> Escape from all this world's undying
> Vulgarity and bigotry![75]

Georgievsky maintains that Tyutchev had to flee abroad to escape the wrath of Yelena's father.[76] This is clearly a distortion of actual events: Tyutchev may well have found it advisable to go into hiding for a while, but is known to have stayed in Russia throughout 1851. More credible is a related claim made by Georgievsky: that at the time 'poor Lyolya was abandoned by everyone, the first to do so being Tyutchev himself '.[77] That this indeed happened is suggested by a poem which has long puzzled scholars:

> Those eyes... I loved them to distraction —
> God knows, they held me in their sway!
> From their dark night of wondrous passion
> I could not tear my soul away.
>
> Their gaze, impossible to fathom,
> Laid bare the life within entire,
> Revealing an unending chasm
> Of grief and smouldering desire.
>
> Beneath her lashes' silken glory
> They brimmed with pensive, mournful life,
> Like pleasure, languorously weary,
> Like suffering, fraught with tragic strife.

And at such moments of rare wonder
Not once was it vouchsafed to me
To gaze unmoved upon their splendour
Or stem the tears that flowed so free.[78]

Line 9 leaves us in no doubt that Tyutchev has one particular woman in mind. Editors from Chulkov on agree that in view of the poem's intense emotional charge and date of composition (before the beginning of 1852) that woman can only be Yelena; yet all are troubled by the fact that she should be referred to throughout in the past tense.[79] If Georgievsky is right and Tyutchev felt obliged or was persuaded to break off relations with Yelena after the débâcle of March 1851, the apparent inconsistency is resolved. Convinced that he and Yelena had parted for ever, he would quite naturally write of their passionate encounters in the past tense. In the event it would prove to be just another of his 'final farewells', no more enduring than its predecessors. They would stay together for fourteen years, during which time she would bear him two more children.

One of these, Fyodor, later claimed that Tyutchev too found himself shunned by society and the court, and that his career was blighted as a result of the affair.[80] Pigaryov has shown this to be completely untrue. There was no change in the pattern of his promotions, and he continued to be received at court and in polite circles as before.[81] Although there was no doubt individual disapproval of what he had done, the unthinking double morality of the time ensured that it was the woman who had to bear the full weight of social disgrace. It was Yelena who suffered, not Tyutchev. This despite the fact — apparent even to such a sympathetic observer as Georgievsky — that if blame had to be apportioned between them, he clearly deserved the major share for his seduction of an impressionable young woman half his age, and for making her pregnant. According to Georgievsky, he accepted as much himself.[82] His feelings of guilt and self-reproach first came to a head in the immediate aftermath of March 1851, as is clear from a poem written at that time. This is also of interest for providing further apparent evidence of an abortive 'final farewell' (see in particular verse 5, and the phrase 'ask, and discover' in line 7):

O, how our love breeds ruination:
How we unerringly destroy
In passion's blind intoxication
Our heart's desire, our deepest joy!

When you first claimed her as your lover,
What pride that conquest roused in you!
A year's not passed... Ask, and discover
What now survives of her you knew.

The roses in her cheeks have vanished,
Her carefree smile, her gaze so clear...
All these by withering dews were banished —
By tears, hot tears that scorch and sear.

Do you recall that fateful hour
When you two first met — you and she:
Her words, her glance of magic power,
Her laughter like a child's so free?

And now? Has all been dissipated?
For how long did the vision last?
Like northern summer, a belated
And transient guest, it swiftly passed.

For her your love was retribution
Wrought by a vengeful destiny;
It stained, as with a vile pollution,
Her blameless life with infamy...

A life of bleak renunciation,
Of suffering... And when she turned
To memories for consolation,
Here too her faith and hope were spurned.

Now she has felt life's charms expire
And views the world as one apart...
The mob burst in and through the mire
Trod all the flowers of her heart.

And what is left for the retrieving,
Like ashes, from her long ordeal?
Pain, bitter pain of rage and grieving —
Pain without hope or tears to heal!

O, how our love breeds ruination!
How we unerringly destroy
In passion's blind intoxication
Our heart's desire, our deepest joy![83]

iii Portrait of a Marriage

On 20 May 1851 Yelena gave birth to a daughter.[84] She was christened Yelena after her mother, who in keeping with what she believed to be her true marital status insisted on the child's surname being recorded as Tyutchev. This brought no tangible benefits, as in such cases the law denied the child any right to membership of the nobility or inheritance of property, the father's name not even being entered on the register. Tyutchev went along with the charade out of deference to her feelings.[85] Never before had he felt the need to mark the birth of a child with a poem, but now the sight of the hapless young mother and her child 'without a name' (because illegitimate) moved him

330

to express in verse his feelings of guilt towards them both:

> 'I am unworthy of your loving':
> How often you have heard that phrase.
> Although your love was my creation,
> How poor I seem in its bright rays...
>
> In that pure light examination
> Of my own heart is hard to bear —
> I stand in awe and veneration
> And worship you in silent prayer...
>
> And when at times with such emotion,
> With such a piety sincere,
> As if impelled to make devotion,
> You kneel before that cradle dear,
>
> Where *she*, your first-born, gently slumbers —
> Your cherubim without a name —
> Know too why I should feel so humble
> Before your loving heart's true flame.[86]

We do not know when exactly the full extent of Tyutchev's infidelity first became known to Ernestine, but by all accounts she reacted and continued to react with great dignity and outward restraint. Members of the family later recalled that to them and others she 'never even once revealed that she knew of her husband's affair'.[87] Only alone with him, away from the gaze of others, will she have felt able to give vent to her emotions. He weakly attempted to placate her with offerings in verse. One in French, dated 12 April 1851, describes listening to her reminiscences of childhood, which have always delighted him with their 'freshness', 'mystery' and sense of spring ('Je croyais sentir dans une brise/ Glisser comme un printemps voilé').[88] Aware of his wife's efforts to learn the language of her adopted country, he also wrote a poem in Russian on a scrap of paper torn from the same sheet and slipped it into her flower-album with a note in French: 'For you (to decipher all on your own)'. There it lay unnoticed for a quarter of a century. Ernestine finally chanced upon it only two years after his death, and was deeply moved to read this message from beyond the grave:[89]

> I do not know if grace will condescend
> To touch this soul that sin has robbed of merit —
> If I shall rise again and know an end
>   To this long darkness of the spirit...
>
>   But if my soul is ever meant
> To know peace here on earth, then you beside me
>   Could bring me grace — you who were sent
> To be my earthly providence and guide me!..[90]

331

Tyutchev's inability to break with Yelena had been a blow to Ernestine. The birth of his illegitimate daughter finally impelled her to escape what had become an intolerable situation: just over two weeks later, on 6 or 7 June, she left the capital for Ovstug. He accompanied her as far as Moscow, from where a few days later she and the younger children travelled on without him.[91] She had for some time set her heart on a lengthy stay in the country; perhaps now she also felt a separation would help to decide things one way or the other. In a letter to her soon afterwards Tyutchev wrote that during their last few days together in Moscow he had been 'mad, or rather ill', in a state of 'fever and unreason', and that now in recollection every detail connected with her departure 'has a quite physical effect on me, as certain odours do on the nerves'.[92] He hung on in Moscow for about a month, prevented at first from travelling by a severe case of haemorrhoids, then increasingly like Buridan's ass dithering between its two bales of hay. Although none of his correspondence with Yelena has survived, we may safely assume letters from her urging his speedy return. From Ernestine he received expressions of injured reproach. His fervent declarations that he still loved her must, she felt, be no more than the product of overwrought nerves, the self-delusion of a sick imagination. If he really meant it, why was he still in Moscow and not with her at Ovstug? Stung by one such missive, he replied with a confused mixture of self-accusation and self-justification:

What must have happened in the depths of your heart to make you doubt me — to make you no longer understand, no longer feel that for me you are *everything*, and that compared with you all the rest is *nothing*? — I shall leave tomorrow if possible to rejoin you. I should be prepared to go not just to Ovstug but to China if necessary to ask you if you really doubt me in earnest and whether you by any chance imagine that I could live with such doubt. You see, my darling, there is in the idea that you doubt me something that could drive me mad.

So, my love for you is nothing but a question of nerves — and it is with an expression of resigned conviction that you tell me such nonsense. Don't you know that since your departure I have despite everything been unable for two hours at a time to consider your absence acceptable? In vain have I accused myself of faint-heartedness, of madness, of illness, of anything you like. All to no avail. It is stronger than me. I have had the bitter satisfaction of sensing within me something that survives indomitably through all the travails and inconstancies of my foolish nature. And do you know what has aggravated even more this bitter instinct, which is as strong and egoistic as that of life itself? I'll tell you quite bluntly. It is the impression, the simple impression that it was a question of making a choice: just the shadow of such an idea was enough to make me aware of the abyss that exists between you and everything that is not you. Not of course that I needed any enlightenment on that score, rather it was that the pride of my affection for you felt offended.

Alas, my darling, I have been much in the wrong [*j'ai eu bien des torts*]... I have behaved stupidly, shamefully... Only with regard to you have I never been in the wrong [*Vis-à-vis de toi seule, je n'ai eu aucun tort*], for the very good reason that it is quite impossible for me to be so with regard to you...

I shall be coming, then, and by the shortest route possible...
I cannot wait to have lunch with you on your balcony...[93]

Particularly startling here is his disclaimer of guilt vis-à-vis Ernestine. What he appears to be saying (and she herself must have puzzled over the wording) is that the wrongs she had suffered had been beyond his control or at least not of his choosing. He was probably quite sincere in this. For all his poetic gestures in the direction of Christianity, in matters of personal morality he seems on the whole to have been guided by a principle which according to his son Fyodor he himself termed 'pagan forbearance' ('l'indulgence païenne'), and which he was careful to differentiate from its Christian counterpart. As explained by Fyodor, 'pagan forbearance' derived from 'a profound understanding of the recesses of the human soul and a recognition that on this earth things can be no different from the the the way they are'.[94] Tyutchev's principle may well enjoin understanding or even forgiveness for the failings of others; more importantly perhaps as far as he was concerned, it also conveniently sanctions an acceptance of one's own failings as inevitable and incorrigible. This effectively does away with the need for repentance — but also with any prospect of coming to terms with one's guilt through atonement. Tyutchev was well aware of this. As he later wrote to Ernestine: 'I am often deeply disgusted with myself while at the same time perceiving this feeling of disgust to be sterile, as this impartial assessment of myself comes purely from the mind; the heart has nothing to do with it, for there is no admixture of anything resembling an impulse of Christian contrition.'[95]

On 6 July, four days after unburdening himself to Ernestine, he was shown a letter his sister Darya had received from her. This provoked a further outburst:

Your letter to my sister very nearly had the effect of launching me like a projectile towards Ovstug. That you should say such stupid things when addressing me I can tolerate... But to read these same things stated to a third party in a tone of resigned conviction — and by you, who are far from voluble on such intimate matters — was a hundred times more than enough to shatter my nerves. There is in particular one line, one phrase, which whenever I repeat it to myself (as I do continually) has on me the effect of a razor-blade slicing into an eyeball. All this, you must agree, is not calculated to let me suffer my ailment with patience... You claim that all my attachment for you is no more than an illness, and that the first distraction to appear on the scene would be sufficient to distract me from it... [...] You know very well that for me your absence, whether from a psychological or physical point of view, is unbearable — and it is at such a moment that you write all these fine things to my sister... that you were able to write to her for instance that *if I were to lose you*, once the first moment had passed *it would not be long before all traces of your memory were painlessly erased*... If some practical joker had thrust a burning coal down my neck it could not have burned me more than this sentence. And what leads you to assume such a reaction on my part? Clearly the thought that I should be left with other affections to console me. Yet if they were able to console me with your loss, how can it be that they are not enough to help me endure two or three months of absence?[96]

He did not go to Ovstug that summer, nor did a visit tentatively proposed for later in the year materialise. By the beginning of July his leave had expired and he made no attempt to extend it. Just after the middle of the month he returned to St Petersburg and into the arms of Yelena.[97] For her this was a minor victory, but even so the continuing uncertainty of her position made for a volatile relationship. She was, as Tyutchev himself once described her, 'of an impetuous and extremely hot-tempered nature' ('*d'un caractère violent et emporté au plus haut degré*'), capable during one of their domestic arguments of hurling a heavy bronze ornament at him (it narrowly missed, knocking several tiles out of the stove). And although he later told Georgievsky that he valued such outbursts as evidence of her devotion, Georgievsky himself came to believe that equally important with love as a binding factor in their relationship was his fear of what lengths such a passionate woman might resort to if he ever attempted to leave her.[98] There was certainly also an element of guilt at his own inability to match the almost frightening intensity of her love; this runs as a leitmotif through the 'Denisyeva cycle'. One poem from this time declares love to be a 'fateful duel', an 'unequal struggle' in which the one whose affections are the stronger is 'doomed to suffer and succumb'.[99] In another we seem to hear him speak directly to Yelena:

> Though I have earned them, spare me from your shafts of rancour!
> That your part is more enviable none can deny:
> Your love burns truly, brightly as a flame, but I —
> I see you and am racked by jealousy's vile canker.
>
> Without belief I stand, a pitiful magician,
> Before a world of wondrous dreams by me devised —
> A lifeless image, by your pure soul idolised:
> This I now see with shame to be my true condition.[100]

And in a remarkable companion-piece we eavesdrop on Yelena confiding her woes to a third party in the voice once described by Tyutchev as 'never [...] devoid of emotion' when speaking to him:[101]

> Do not say that his love for me is undiminished —
> That, as before, he cares for me...
> No: ruthlessly he wears me down, would see me finished —
> Although the knife shakes in his hand, I see...
>
> Now weeping, now incensed — indignant, wretched, lonely,
> A prey to violent passion, wronged, abased —
> I live in constant torment — live for him, him only...
> But O, this life!.. How bitter is its taste!
>
> He measures out the air I breathe in meagre ration...
> Who'd treat their fiercest enemy so ill?
> Still I draw breath — though painfully, in laboured fashion —
> And yet to live have neither cause nor will.[102]

Yet although altercations of this kind may have erupted from time to time, there can be no doubt that being with Yelena helped Tyutchev to cope with Ernestine's absence after his return to St Petersburg. The evidence is in his letters. As indicated by the extracts quoted above, those written to Ernestine from Moscow had been anguished and at times incoherent; they are peppered with plaintive references to 'the emptiness left by your absence' and 'my continual anxiety of spirit', and gloomy pronouncements of the sort: 'for me absence is a state of non-being'.[103] Now in St Petersburg they become calmer and more rational in tone; more space is devoted to society gossip, and there are even flashes of humour. The change in mood can hardly have escaped Ernestine's notice. Despair at her absence seems to have given way — quite unreasonably in the circumstances — to sentiments of irritation and anger. 'I positively protest at your absence,' he grumbles on 31 July. 'I will not and cannot put up with it.'[104] Three days later he claims to find it 'an unexpected revelation' that she is apparently quite able to do without him: 'I should be no more astonished now if one fine day my head were to leave my shoulders and take itself off for a walk on its own without a care as to what was happening to me...'[105] And in one letter he included a short poem in Russian which can have offered little comfort once she had laboriously deciphered the sense:

> There is a higher truth in separation:
> Love, though it last a lifetime or a day,
> Is but a dream of momentary duration
>   For which awakening means cessation —
> And, summoned to awake, no man may disobey...[106]

'Here, my darling, are some bad verses expressing something even worse,' he comments in the letter.[107] Ernestine returned to St Petersburg at the end of September.[108] If she hoped to find the affair had burnt itself out, she was disappointed: Tyutchev was still deeply entangled, unable and unwilling to choose between the two women in his life. It must have been a miserable winter for all concerned. Some insight into his state of mind is provided by a poem written in November 1851:

> Day turns to evening, dusk draws nigh,
> Deep shadows from the mountain spread,
> Clouds darken all the fading sky...
> The hour is late. Now day is fled.
>
> Yet I'll not mourn for day's decline,
> And night's dark terrors shall not fear,
> If only, magic spirit mine,
> You'll comfort and stay with me here...
>
> Enfold me with your wings, to calm
> My troubled heart and make me whole:
> Their shadow will as healing balm
> Bring peace to my enchanted soul.

335

Who are you? Are you progeny
Of earth, or sent from heaven above?
An aerial spirit you may be —
But one aflame with woman's love![109]

The mountainous terrain hinted at in the first stanza is far removed from the actual place and time of composition. In fact, as suggested by the strong echoes of 'A golden time still haunts my senses...' in these opening lines, we appear to be back in the mythological 'golden time' of the poet's youth in Bavaria.[110] In that earlier poem his nostalgia had fixed on a particular moment from those years, his visit to Donaustauf Castle with Amélie in the spring of 1824. Now the yearning and regret are more generalised, the waning day, darkening sky and ominous shadows more clearly metaphorical as he contemplates the loss of youth, the passing of time and the approach of death. Who exactly is the enigmatic 'aerial spirit', 'aflame with woman's love', for whose soothing influence on his 'troubled soul' he longs? Could she be Yelena? Had he perhaps been forced to take another 'final farewell' of her that autumn? But there is no evidence for this, and in any case what would be the point of the 'golden time' allusions? She could equally be Ernestine, as argued by one commentator,[111] although this would mean having to accept that the poem was written during her long absence at Ovstug, and that the date printed in the first published version (1 November 1851) is spurious. Then there is Eleonore, in some ways a perfect fit for the mysterious protecting spirit under whose wing Tyutchev seeks refuge. In one of his letters he had written of being moved by the anniversary of her death on 28 August (9 September NS),[112] so she was clearly in his thoughts that autumn. But appealing as the idea may be of Eleonore's ghost as some kind of celestial referee in the tussle between Ernestine and Yelena, we have in the final analysis to ask if Tyutchev has any particular woman in mind at all. Certainly he himself professes not to know who or what this angelic vision is ('Who are you? Are you progeny/ Of earth, or sent from heaven above?'). The poet Blok may have come closest to the truth in seeing her as the 'great shadow of the feminine':[113] something akin to Goethe's 'eternal feminine', perhaps, or — put more mundanely — an amalgam of the various objects of Tyutchev's affections. If so, she provides an apt image indeed for the confusion and indecision bedevilling his love life at this time.

By the spring of 1852 Ernestine had decided to return to Ovstug with Anna, Darya, Kitty and the younger children (apart from the ten-year-old Dmitry, who was at a boarding school in St Petersburg) with the intention this time of spending a whole year there. This was largely for reasons of economy (Darya and Kitty had just completed an additional one-year course at the Smolny Institute and were living at home again, placing further strains on the already stretched family budget).[114] Ernestine also hoped to restore her health, for she had been weakened by a viral infection and developed a worryingly persistent cough, and needed to escape the treacherously damp climate of St Petersburg.[115] In any case she had by her own admission come to love Ovstug, where she found inner peace in the vastness and seclusion of the Russian countryside.[116] Above all she needed to be far from St Petersburg and all it had come to mean. At the end of May the family vacated the apartment near the Anichkov bridge on Nevsky

Prospekt (now No. 68) which had been their home for nearly two years and took the newly inaugurated train service to Moscow. Tyutchev accompanied them on to Ovstug, but stayed only a couple of weeks, returning to St Petersburg by the end of June.[117]

There now began a period of well over two years almost nine-tenths of which he and Ernestine would spend apart, coming together only on four occasions for between three and six weeks at a time. It must have seemed to Yelena that she had won. No doubt it was at this time that the ideas later asserted so forcefully to Georgievsky became finally fixed in her mind, in particular her conviction that the marriage to Ernestine had been effectively 'dissolved' and that although she and Tyutchev might possess no scrap of paper declaring them man and wife, theirs was in every other respect a 'true marriage'.

From July to September 1852 Tyutchev rented a dacha on Stone Island (Kamenny Ostrov), one of several leafy islands in the Neva delta favoured by the wealthy as a summer retreat from the dust and heat of the city. His accommodation on the ground floor of what he described to Ernestine as 'a fairly agreeable hovel [*masure*]' was more than adequate for a man living on his own: a drawing room flanked by conservatories on either side, with another three or four rooms to the rear.[118] In fact we can assume that he was joined, at least for part of the time, by Yelena. A poem addressed to her bears the inscription: 'Stone Island. 28 July.'

> The sun gleams brightly, waters sparkle,
> All nature smiles, all life is new,
> Trees quiver with elation, bathing
> Their branches in the radiant blue.
>
> Trees sing, the waters glint with sunlight,
> The air is touched with love's caress,
> And all the flowering life of nature
> Is drunk with life in sweet excess.
>
> Yet in all this exhilaration
> There is no joy that can compare
> With one brief smile of tender pathos
> Wrung from your heart in its despair...[119]

The enduring world of nature in all its fascination and vital power is familiar to us from so many of the earlier poems. Yet here, as in other verse of the period, we sense that a radical shift in perception has taken place, exemplified according to Boris Kozyrev in the poem's 'purely Christian' affirmation that 'the human soul afflicted by sorrow' is 'stronger than all the abundantly burgeoning power of nature'.[120]

It is thanks to Kozyrev's critical insight that a poem written in April 1852 must now also be considered part of the 'Denisyeva cycle':

You, my wave upon the ocean,
Creature of caprice and whim,
Whether resting or in motion,
With what wondrous life you brim!

Laughing in the sunlight, flashing
Heaven's mirrored edifice,
Or in frenzy tossing, thrashing
In the turbulent abyss —

How you charm me with the gentle
Murmur of your love-filled sighs —
Move me with your elemental
Raging, your prophetic cries!

Be you by the rip-tide shaken,
Be your aspect dark or bright,
Yet keep safe what you have taken,
Guard it in your azure night.

To your gentle undulation
Votive offering I made:
Not a ring was my oblation,
Neither emerald nor jade —

In that fateful moment, carried
Onwards by enchantment rare,
In your depths not these I buried,
But my heart, that beats yet there.[121]

To summarise Kozyrev's argument: the epigraph ('mercurial as a wave') reveals the subject of the poem to be a metaphor for something else; to judge by the third stanza in particular, that something would appear to be a woman; and the only woman to match these characteristics is Yelena, whose emotional volatility and temperamental out- bursts are well documented in Georgievsky's memoirs and Tyutchev's letters. The 'fateful moment' refers unmistakeably to their first intimate encounter, while the final two stanzas as a whole are Tyutchev's coded justification for his inability to offer her marriage in the conventional sense: he declares that what he has given her — his heart (or soul in the original) — is far more important than the mere token of a ring.[122]

The poems inspired by Yelena are sometimes also referred to as the 'Last Love' cycle. The title is taken from one of the poems which perhaps more than any could be seen as representative of the whole cycle. It was written at some time between the middle of 1852 and the beginning of 1854.

O, how at life's ebb-tide love seems
To hold both tenderness and foreboding!
Shine on, last love — shine, parting beams,
Till forced to scatter at nightfall's bidding!

Dark shadow fills half heaven's vault;
Westward alone does an afterglow linger...
Day, pause in your flight, if you cannot halt:
Enchantment, stay a little longer!

Though thinly now the blood may course,
The heart with tenderness brims over...
O last love, doomed to be the source
Of joy and hopelessness interwoven![123]

The same images of evening, sunset and encroaching darkness encountered in 'Day turns to evening, dusk draws nigh...' are here linked quite explicitly to 'life's ebb-tide' (even the irregularities of metre seeming to reflect a now uncertain, faltering pulse of vitality). With all the unassailable confidence of youth Tyutchev had once celebrated first love as a 'golden dawn', a 'new world', an unlimited realm of future possibilities.[124] Last love by contrast is frighteningly aware of its own vulnerability, the inevitable facts of mortality and fading powers lending to it a bitter-sweet tenderness and at the same time an obsessive sense of foreboding that all could end at any moment.

After leaving the Islands towards the end of September, Tyutchev moved first into a hotel and then into furnished rooms.[125] This was typical of the semi-nomadic or (as he called it) 'bohemian' existence which he once complained to Ernestine of having to lead in her absence,[126] but which seemed in fact not altogether unsuited to his temperament. He and Ernestine continued to write to each other about once a week on average, as they did throughout their long separation. He kept her up to date with society news and gossip, and reported on his efforts to obtain positions at court for his daughters. Concerned for Ernestine's health, he tried to persuade her to accompany him abroad for the winter, but this foundered on her objections to the expense.[127] Already at the beginning of August he was writing to Anna: 'I feel the impossibility of living at Ovstug begin to pale before the impossibility of living at a distance from Mama';[128] yet December found him still in St Petersburg. 'But why am I still here?' he asks in one of his letters to Ernestine. 'What is this paralysis which has taken hold of me? What am I doing here? What interest could be so powerful that it compels me to subordinate to it the only real interest of my life?.. There is nothing I can do, I sense the hand of fate in these absurd delays.' If not exasperated by this, Ernestine may even have derived a certain wry amusement from it. The letter continues:

No, once again, we should not have separated... It is a crime against ourselves which I should never have allowed to be committed... It is very good of you to love me as you do. Just between ourselves, I know of no creature in the world less worthy of affection than myself. What is more, all the affections which have happened to stray in my direction have always seemed to me the result of a misapprehension, yours alone excepted. For I am aware that you know me through and through, and this makes me feel your love to be like the grace of God. I am hardly deserving of it... And yet, my darling, I sense that it is impossible for you not to love me... Impossible. Never mind all the follies, contradictions and inconsistencies I have managed to amass. There is in my whole being nothing real apart from yourself...[129]

One genuine reason for staying in St Petersburg was his continuing campaign, actively supported by Grand Duchess Maria Nikolayevna, to have his older daughters appointed Maids of Honour.[130] There is also no doubt that (despite protestations to the contrary to Ernestine) he was enjoying the social life of the capital to the full, with little regard to the expense involved.[131] In December Ernestine received a sobering letter from her brother-in-law Nikolay in Moscow containing a breakdown of her family's income and outgoings for that year. Nikolay warned that Tyutchev's profligate personal expenditure (which presumably included the upkeep of his second family) was undermining all her attempts at economy, with the result that she and the children might well have to stay at Ovstug indefinitely.[132] Earlier her brother Karl too had urged her to make her husband see sense and start living within his means, abandoning unrealistic 'illusions' of social prestige.[133] He also appears to have sent an outspoken letter on the subject to Tyutchev himself.[134]

On Christmas Eve Tyutchev finally received official confirmation that Anna had been appointed Maid of Honour to the Grand Duchess Maria Aleksandrovna, wife of the future Tsar Alexander II; a few days later he left for Ovstug.[135] It was his first visit to the area in winter since childhood. New Year's Eve found him in high spirits, driving by sleigh through sunlit snowy forests not far from his destination. The beauty of the scene inspired one of his more cheerful 'journey' poems:

> Spellbound by that dark magician
> Winter see the forest now:
> An unmoving apparition,
> Mute and robbed of all volition,
> Sparkling snow on every bough.
>
> So it stands, bereft of motion,
> Neither living nor yet dead:
> Drugged as if by magic potion,
> Shackled by the witching notion
> Of light snow as steely thread...
>
> Should the winter sun with squinting
> Rays the sleeping woods caress,
> They — unstirring, never hinting
> At arousal — flare up, glinting:
> Radiant in their loveliness.[136]

He reached Ovstug during the all-night vigil service to mark the turn of the year. The initially happy atmosphere of the reunion turned sour over the next few days as underlying differences between him and Ernestine erupted into what Anna in her diary describes as a 'row', leading to 'serious exchanges' between them. The apparent catalyst was Ernestine's insistence that he should accompany Anna back to St Petersburg, where she was to take up her new duties almost immediately, and his indignation that she should even think of his leaving again so soon after their six-month separation. 'I love nobody in the world more than you, and yet, and yet, not the way I used to!' Anna heard her stepmother exclaim during one altercation. Things were eventually smoothed over by Anna herself volunteering to travel without her father, chaperoned by her maid and the estate manager Vasily Strelkov.[137] After her departure on 4 January some degree of harmony was restored. Tyutchev expressed concern at how much weight Ernestine had lost, while she, worried by his unkempt appearance, enjoined Anna by letter to make sure he was fitted out with new clothes on his return. There were walks in the snow, and in the evenings the family gathered for readings by Tyutchev in his 'soft, sonorous voice' from Pushkin's verse drama *Boris Godunov* and other works in Russian and French. Ernestine was particularly pleased at how much of the Russian she could understand.[138] By now she and Tyutchev were 'like turtle-doves', as Kitty was happy to report to Anna.[139]

He left on 21 January. 'Ah, my darling, how much more enjoyable was my awakening yesterday, with your dear figure glimpsed through the screen,' he wrote to Ernestine the following morning from Roslavl, where he had spent the first night en route. 'Now they are over, those three weeks seem to me like an oasis of calm and happiness...' He hoped they could now agree to leave the 'desert' of separation behind them and 'return once and for all to inhabited territory'.[140] But of course it was not as simple as that. Writing to her in February, he expressed himself saddened by, and at the same time unable to deny the justice of, 'a sentence in one of your recent letters in which you say how satisfied I must have felt on returning to St Petersburg to be back at my old habits again, safe in the knowledge of having done a good deed, namely of having come to see you...'[141]

'Habits' was the euphemism occasionally used by Ernestine to denote her husband's liaison with Yelena; it was the closest she ever came in her recorded utterances to mentioning the unmentionable. Although she had come to love Russia, she was now beginning to think the only way to break him of these undesirable 'habits' was for them to return to the West, at least temporarily. For a start they could go abroad together that summer. Tyutchev himself had been keen on the idea for some time, and her sacrifice in taking the family to Ovstug did after all now seem to be making it affordable. Already in February she was preparing to return to St Petersburg the following month before their planned departure abroad in May.[142] At about the same time Tyutchev was annoyed to learn of a concerted effort by friends including Count Bludov and Severin to obtain a foreign posting for him. As he informed Ernestine, Severin had succeeded in persuading Nesselrode to offer him the fairly insignificant post of Consul-General in Leipzig, 'only in some more acceptable form, giving the appointment the appearance of a kind of literary-diplomatic mission'. On the face of it this seemed the kind of job promoting Russia's interests in the Western press that he had angled for in the past; but he was probably right to suspect it as no more than window-dressing designed to lure him away from St Petersburg. Both Severin and Bludov knew Ernestine and no doubt sympathised with her desire to break her husband of his bad 'habits'. To add insult to injury, the man he would be replacing in Leipzig was none other than Tom-Have, his former assistant in Turin. Tyutchev decided to put paid to what he called this 'plot' hatched by well-meaning friends. He asked Severin to inform Nesselrode that regrettably his present circumstances would allow him to consider nothing less than an ambassador's post (something he knew was out of the question), but that in view of the Chancellor's evidently favourable disposition towards him he would be grateful for a courier mission to Paris in May, combined with extended paid leave.[143] This was readily granted.

Towards the end of March Ernestine arrived in St Petersburg with Darya, Kitty, Ivan and Marie. The family were able to stay rent-free in the same house on the Field of Mars (Marsovo pole) where they had lived from March 1846 to June 1847, again courtesy of Tyutchev's distant relative Yevtikh Safonov. A fairly modest suite of rooms was made available for Ernestine and the children on the ground floor, while Tyutchev moved into separate accommodation on the first floor, claiming shortage of space.[144] To judge from the observations of Anna, who visited them from time to time, their renewed family life was far from idyllic. 'My misfortune is my family,' she wrote in her diary on 5 May. 'The prevailing spirit in it is one of gloom, negation and depression, making life one continuous ordeal.' She confessed herself dismayed at the 'continual complaints and permanent bad mood' of Darya and Kitty, 'Mama's depression' and 'the sophistries of my father, who is paradox personified'. And again on 15 May: 'Meetings with my family upset and torment me'.[145]

On 10/22 June 1853 Ernestine left by steamer for Lübeck, taking Ivan and Marie with her. Dmitry was still at his boarding school, and it had been arranged for Darya to stay with Anna at court. Kitty went to the Sushkovs, her uncle and aunt in Moscow, where she fitted in so well that from now on this became her permanent home. Tyutchev had to hang on for a few days for important despatches announcing Russia's imminent occupation of Moldavia and Wallachia. He left on the Stettin packet on 13/25 June and proceeded via Berlin to Paris, delivering diplomatic documents in both capitals. He had arranged for Ernestine and the children to meet him at Cologne and accompany him on the final stage of his journey. They spent the whole of of July (NS) in the Paris area: he in the city itself, she and the children in a house formerly owned by her mother at Franconville just outside. From time to time they visited each other. She found him bored and restless: most of society had left the capital for the summer, and he grumbled that even the Russian Ambassador Kiselyov had afforded him scant hospitality.[146]

One person Tyutchev did manage to see was his old friend Heinrich Heine. For five years Heine had been confined to his house in the rue d'Amsterdam, slowly dying from a wasting disease now thought to have been a form of tubercular meningitis. Like other visitors, Tyutchev will have been shocked by his first sight of the German poet. Emaciated, partially paralysed and blind in one eye, he lay on a pile of mattresses to ease the agonising pain in his spine, for which opium had constantly to be administered. Yet as eyewitness accounts testify, this frail body still contained an alert mind that had lost nothing of its incisive wit or creative power.[147] Tyutchev too later told Maltitz that he had found Heine 'full of life'.[148] Their conversation no doubt centred on politics, in particular the growing conflict between Russia and the West which was about to escalate into full-scale war, and regarding which they found themselves on opposing sides. Yet if Ronald Lane is correct in identifying Tyutchev as the unnamed addressee of a letter from Heine (and his arguments are convincing),[149] political differences appear not to have affected the warmth of their personal relationship. Dated 28 July 1853 (NS), Heine's letter begins: 'My dear friend' and was sent with the gift of several books on German and Austrian history.[150]

On 18/30 or 19/31 July Tyutchev and Ernestine left to join the Pfeffels at Lindau on Lake Constance.[151] Tyutchev would later recall the four weeks spent in their company as 'one of the most agreeable memories of my life'.[152] He particularly enjoyed the intellectual stimulus of conversation with Karl, whose character, 'so full of sensitivity and at the same time so strongly attached to order and rule' inspired in him (perhaps because so removed from his own) 'a profound sympathy'.[153] During this time the two families made a trip into Switzerland, where Tyutchev was as always captivated by the beauty and grandeur of the mountains (they stayed at Goldau, a resort at the foot of the Rigi near Lake Lucerne). He was afterwards moved to declare that 'the moonlight of Goldau will illuminate my memories for a long time to come';[154] and even a year later on receiving a letter from Pfeffel said it was 'like a breath of last summer coming from the lakes and mountains of Switzerland'.[155]

On 19/31 August Ernestine and Pfeffel accompanied Tyutchev by lake steamer from Lindau to Friedrichshafen, where they parted company: Ernestine and her brother to rejoin his family at Lindau for what was left of the summer, Tyutchev to head back to St Petersburg via Stuttgart, Baden-Baden, Frankfurt, Weimar (where he stayed with the Maltitzes), Dresden, Breslau and Warsaw.[156] It appears to have been an amicable parting dictated by nothing more than Tyutchev's need to return from leave, with no hint at this stage of undue marital discord. On the contrary, Ernestine assured Anna by letter soon afterwards that, while enjoying the company of her 'dearly beloved' brother and his family, she missed her husband, 'for nothing and nobody can replace him in my heart'.[157] She appears to have told him as much too: 'So it is true that you still love me a little,' he wrote, thanking her for her first letters from Lindau.[158]

He spent two days waiting at Kovno (now Kaunas, Lithuania) to report on his courier mission to Nesselrode, who was expected to pass through on his way to Warsaw (the Chancellor eventually granted him an interview in his carriage lasting all of five minutes: 'just long enough for us to communicate what we had to say to each other' in Tyutchev's sardonic estimation).[159] It was at Kovno that Napoleon had crossed the Neman to invade Russia in 1812; and here, sensitive to the distant rumblings of an approaching new conflict, Tyutchev filled the time by composing a stirring evocation in verse of that fateful event which, published some months later on the eve of the Crimean War, would be seen as something of a call to arms.[160] Yet it was typical of him that such public expressions of sentiment should go hand in hand with a more jaundiced private view of the realities of Russian life. Just days before composing these lines he had complained to Ernestine of the sudden deterioration in hotel standards after crossing the frontier. 'It is not without a kind of melancholy,' he commented sarcastically, 'that I took my leave of the *corrupt* West with all its cleanliness and comfort to return to the filth, full of such promise for the future, of our own dear country.'[161] And re-encountering the Russian landscape, in which only clouds could provide some pale simulacrum of the mountains left behind, he was prompted to pun: 'how could the Great Poet who created the Rigi and Lake Lucerne put his name to such platitudes?'[162]

He arrived back in St Petersburg on 9 September (OS) to find their rooms at Safonov's taken and the furniture in storage, and for the time being booked himself into the Hotel Klee at 12 silver roubles a week.[163] Five days later he wrote to Ernestine to say he had found suitable alternative accommodation for the family, but there was only room for the two of them plus Ivan and Marie. Darya and Kitty would have to stay where they were: this was, he said, 'my *ultimatum*, my *ultimatissimum*, and the condition *sine qua non* to my agreeing to your return'. The attempt at humour appears to have misfired. Ernestine must have resented the implication behind the cod diplomatic jargon that he was not too concerned whether she came back or not, an impression only reinforced by a passage later in the letter advising her that if travelling overland she could quite conveniently delay her return until early November (OS) and thereby 'cut short the *longueur* of a winter in St Petersburg'.[164] She wrote back that he clearly no longer loved her, and that she would be spending the winter in Munich in the company of her brother Karl and his family. For Tyutchev this came as a bombshell, as can be judged from his reply:

> What is the meaning of the letter you wrote in reply to my first letter from St Petersburg? Have we really reached the point of misunderstanding each other so badly? Or is it all a dream? Can you not see that everything is under threat now, everything? Ah, Nesterle, this is more distressing, more painful, more terrible than words can express. [...] Misunderstanding is a terrible thing, and it is terrible to feel it growing deeper and wider between us — terrible to feel with one's whole being, as I do, that at any moment it could swallow up the last remnants of our family happiness — all that remains to us in our final years of happiness, of love, and indeed of self-esteem ... not to mention everything else...[165]

One of her reproaches he had found particularly hurtful:

> You say you no longer believe anything, and make the terrible assertion that as far as I am concerned you are no more than an old decayed tooth: painful at the moment of extraction, but with the pain soon replaced by an agreeable sensation of emptiness...[166]

It was now that their marriage came closest to breaking-point. As he indicated to her in one letter at this time, Ovstug had been bad enough, but Munich, where she felt at home and was surrounded by those she knew and loved, might well tempt her to stay away for good.[167] Particularly so if she continued to feel (as her letters made plain) that he had 'plenty of strings to [his] bow' and would survive well enough without her.[168] On 10 October he told her flatly: 'I cannot accept a new separation of 8 or 9 months, for that would be a *final* separation.'[169] She hastened to reassure him that, whatever his feelings for her might be, she still loved him. This did something to restore his composure. 'May God bless you; thank you for everything that you say to me,' he wrote back after receiving her letter on 26 October. '[...] since realising that I still retain my former place in your heart and that my absence leaves a void in your life, all is well.'[170] But on the main question dividing them she would not relent, and this continued to alarm and anger him. 'Papa is in despair because Mama will not be returning this winter,' Anna reported to Kitty at the end of October. 'He bitterly regrets the disintegration of our family.' A few days later she added: 'He wanders about like a lost soul and shows no interest in anything but the question of Mama's possible return.'[171]

Anna also informed Ernestine of her father's depressed state, and suggested that one way out of the whole sorry business might be for the family to spend some years abroad.[172] Ernestine needed no persuasion on that score: 'for a thousand reasons it is imperative that he break with certain habits which have arisen in St Petersburg,' she replied in January 1854, 'and I see no other way of achieving this than by removing him from there — removing him for several years.' She even asked Anna to enlist the support of his friends in renewed attempts to obtain a foreign posting for him, stipulating that this should be for no more than two or three years, since 'the last thing on my mind is any thought of leaving Russia for good'.[173] At times of frustration with official Russian policy he even seemed amenable to such a scheme himself. After clashing head-on with his superiors in the Censorship Department in July 1854 for instance he wrote despairingly to Ernestine: 'it was you who brought me to this country, it's for you to get me out of here'.[174] But two things held him back: a fierce sense of loyalty to his country in time of war and his continuing love for Yelena. As a result nothing came of Ernestine and Anna's project.

Nor in the event did it come to the final rupture so dreaded by Tyutchev. Ernestine left Munich on 17/29 April, just as British and French declarations of war against Russia were coming into effect.[175] She arrived back in St Petersburg on 11 May, 'calm and serene, restored both in mind and body' according to Anna, and told Tyutchev (who seemed not unduly put out) that she would be spending the summer at Ovstug.[176] The fact that he had rented only a small flat for her and the children and intended to stay in a hotel himself may have contributed to her decision.[177] Two weeks later they travelled to Moscow together, and on 1 June Ernestine went on with the children to Ovstug.[178]

When she returned to the capital in October,[179] it was to a fine apartment she had had her eye on for several years, and which Tyutchev (no doubt anxious to avoid a recurrence of the Munich episode) had at last made efforts to secure. Situated on the third floor of a substantial building at what is now 42 Nevsky Prospekt, next to the Armenian church and opposite the Gostiny Dvor market, it consisted of fourteen rooms with parquet flooring throughout. The annual rent was advertised at 1,500 silver roubles inclusive of firewood, water and use of a stable and outhouse, although Tyutchev believed he could negotiate a reduction on this from the owner, Khristofor Lazarev, an old friend of the family from earlier days in Armenian Lane.[180] Ernestine found the climb up 78 steps to reach the apartment no deterrent, for she had long dreamed of a home where she could (as Tyutchev put it) 'soar at a certain height above the importunate crowd'.[181] After a restless decade of migration from one temporary address to another both were ready for a more settled existence and would in fact stay at 42 Nevsky Prospekt for the remainder of their life together.

With the move to Lazarev's house something in the nature of a marital truce or *modus vivendi* appears to have been reached, marking the end of their long separation. From this point on a clear pattern emerges, with Ernestine spending half the year (typically, November to April) in St Petersburg and the other half (May to October) at Ovstug. During the summer months Tyutchev would usually remain in town with Yelena. It seems Ernestine had decided to put the interests of the family first and accept her husband's 'habits' as an irrevocable fact of life.

iv One Small Volume

After a brief period in the spotlight following Nekrasov's article and the new poems in *Moskvitayanin* Tyutchev's poetic reputation seemed once again in danger of sinking into obscurity. In his almanach *Raut* (*The Rout*) for 1851 Sushkov included a translation by his brother-in-law of Schiller's 'Das Siegesfest' ('The Victory Celebration');[182] this was followed by five poems in the 1852 issue, together with an announcement that an edition of his collected poems would appear later that year.[183] To this end Sushkov set about compiling a notebook with texts copied from published sources and from manuscript versions in albums kept by Ernestine and other members of the family.[184] In its final form the 'Sushkov notebook' contained 93 poems. There were the usual copyists' errors; more seriously, Sushkov like Nekrasov before him took it upon himself to 'improve' on the originals in places by smoothing out the metre or replacing what he evidently considered archaic or unusual vocabulary. Tyutchev did at some stage have sight of the notebook, as shown by amendations to one or two of the poems made in his hand, but this inspection appears to have been at best cursory and can in no way be seen as marking his approval of Sushkov's alterations.[185]

For reasons which are not absolutely clear the project was never completed. One of Anna's letters documents problems with copying texts from the various family albums caused by the prolonged absence of Ernestine and the older daughters at Ovstug.[186] The decisive factor was more likely indifference and lack of co-operation on the part of Tyutchev, described by the exasperated Sushkov at this time as 'the laziest and most insouciant of poets'.[187] Fortunately a saviour appeared on the scene in the shape of Nekrasov's journal *Sovremennik*. Having himself earlier called for Tyutchev's poems to appear in book form, it was only natural that in 1852 Nekrasov should give his blessing to Sushkov's publishing venture in the columns of that journal.[188] Towards the end of 1853, when it was clear that the project had stalled, matters were taken in hand by one of his collaborators on *Sovremennik*, Ivan Turgenev (the same who had once so gallantly donated his jacket and boots to the shipwrecked Eleonore).

Now an established writer, Turgenev had been exiled to his country estate in May 1852 for expressing liberal views in defiance of the censorship. His collection of stories *Zapiski okhotnika* (*A Huntsman's Notes*) had achieved great popularity and was widely interpreted as an implicit attack on serfdom. Tyutchev admired the stories for a poetic vision akin to his own, finding in them 'a quite remarkable fullness of life and strength of talent' and a no less remarkable combination of 'human reality at its most intimate and the intimate reality of nature at its most poetic'.[189] He was delighted to hear that Ernestine, spending the winter at Ovstug, was also reading and enjoying the stories in Russian and that she even expected a visit from the exiled author (his estate,

Spasskoye-Lutovinovo, was to the north of Oryol).[190] Although the proposed visit never took place, in December 1853 Turgenev was allowed to return to the capital, and soon afterwards at the salon of his patroness Princess Sofya Meshcherskaya met for the first time since being shipwrecked with them Tyutchev's daughters Anna and Darya (both of whom the Princess tried unsuccessfully to marry off to him). He was also introduced to Tyutchev, whose poetry he had admired for some time. 'Papa and he are the best of friends,' Anna wrote to Kitty on 28 December, 'and spend whole evenings in each other's company whenever they meet. They are such a good match — both of them witty, affable, lethargic and untidy.'[191] Little more than a month later Turgenev was able to report to Sergey Aksakov: 'I have persuaded Tyutchev [...] to publish his collected poems'.[192] (He later gave Fet to understand that this had been achieved with 'great difficulty', and in impromptu verse boasted of having induced Tyutchev to 'unbutton').[193]

An editorial team was set up consisting of Turgenev, Nekrasov and the writer and critic Ivan Panayev.[194] They worked at a remarkable pace, undoubtedly helped by the preliminary labours of Sushkov, several of whose wilful amendations they adopted word for word.[195] The collection of 111 poems (88 of which had appeared in print previously) was published first as supplements to the March and May editions of *Sovremennik*, and then in June (with the exception of one, 'Prophecy', to which the Emperor had taken exception) as a separate volume, *Poems by F. Tyutchev.*[196] The April issue of the journal also contained a critical appraisal by Turgenev entitled 'A Few Words on the Poems of F.I. Tyutchev'.[197] In it Turgenev hails 'one of our most remarkable poets, bequeathed to us as it were with the seal of Pushkin's approval' (112). This connection with the golden age of Russian poetry provides the main thrust of the article: Tyutchev 'belongs to the previous generation' (112); he alone among living poets 'bears the stamp of that great epoch' dominated by Pushkin' (112); his works show 'the influence of Pushkin' (113); there is even a particularly revealing reference to 'the almost Pushkinian beauty of his phrasing' (114). Along the way Turgenev makes some astute critical remarks. According to him the intellectual content of Tyutchev's verse 'never appears to the reader in its naked abstract form, but always merges with some image taken from the world of the soul or of nature, penetrated by and itself penetrating that image inseparably and indissolubly' (114). He considers that 'Mr Tyutchev's shortest poems are almost always the most successful' (114), while the political verse — those pieces 'not drawn from his own wellspring, such as "Napoleon" and others' — he finds 'less appealing' (115). And he predicts that because of its subtlety and the demands it makes on the reader Tyutchev's poetry will never achieve wide popularity: 'A violet does not fill the air with its scent for twenty paces around: one must draw closer to catch its fragrance' (115).

Of particular interest are Turgenev's reservations. In Tyutchev's verse, he writes, 'we often come across archaic expressions, pale and feeble lines; he seems sometimes to fall down in his command of the language' (114). And although as critic he hastens to add that such 'external' shortcomings are redeemed by the sheer genius of Tyutchev's inspiration, as editor he evidently felt it his duty to rectify them in a misguided attempt to make the texts both more 'Pushkinian' and more acceptable to public taste. (All that can be said in Turgenev's defence is that such practice appears to have been fairly widespread at the time. Tyutchev was by no means innocent of it himself, having some years previously persuaded Vyazemsky and Pletnyov to publish his own 'improved' version of a poem by Zhukovsky without the latter's approval.)[198] Tyutchev himself appears to have taken no interest whatsoever in the editorial process, engrossed as he no doubt was in other and to him more important matters (Ernestine's return from abroad and the beginning of the Crimean War). This is clear from the editors' admission in their Introduction that they have included early items by Tyutchev 'which he himself would probably now reject'.[199] In other words there had evidently been no consultation on the matter, despite Turgenev's regular social contacts with him. We can only assume that he gave his editors the same *carte blanche* earlier accorded to Ivan Gagarin, and (as is well attested for a later edition of his verse)[200] probably did not even bother to glance at the proofs. His remarkable lack of interest in the whole venture is further demonstrated by the complete absence at the time of any recorded comment by him on such an important milestone in his poetic career. Only much later is he reported to have pointed out some of the unauthorised alterations in conversation with the poet and writer Pavel Kovalevsky, who noted his versions of how the passages in question should read in his own copy of the poems. Unfortunately this volume has never been traced.[201]

The cumulative 'improvements' of various editors succeeded on the whole in producing only the kind of 'pale and feeble lines' criticised by Turgenev himself. The poet Afanasy Fet (who had to endure similar over-editing of his own work at Turgenev's hands) later complained that as a result Tyutchev's 'diamantine verses appeared replaced with paste'.[202] These corrupt versions were perpetuated by later editions until half a century after the poet's death, when scholars returned to the autograph manuscripts and earlier published versions of the poems in an attempt to establish authoritative texts. Their task was complicated by the discovery of indirect but apparently incontrovertible evidence that Turgenev and his colleagues must have had access to manuscripts, since lost, of at least some of the poems in later redactions made by Tyutchev.[203] Consequently the 1854 edition could not be rejected out of hand; instead, editors were obliged to judge each variation from the existing manuscripts on its own merits in a painstaking and delicate procedure likened by Kirill Pigaryov to the restoration of old paintings, each accretion having to be removed with the utmost care lest anything be lost of the masterpiece underneath.[204] Thanks to the outstanding textological work of such scholars as Pigaryov, Georgy Chulkov and Aleksandr Nikolayev we can now be fairly certain that, with the exception of a handful of relatively insignificant still disputed phrasings, what we see on the page is what Tyutchev intended us to read.

Turgenev's prediction that Tyutchev's collected verse would not achieve widespread popularity proved to be sound. Although with one notable exception it received favourable reviews,[205] its print-run was not large, and by the end of the 1850s it appears to have sold out.[206] At the time of Tyutchev's death it was already considered a bibliographical rarity.[207] In 1859 Fet remarked that on its publication the book had caused a stir 'among the narrow circles of those who appreciate the refined' and regretted that now, five years later, it 'still enjoys so little currency among the mass of the reading public'.[208] Poetry was in any case falling out of fashion, and this change in public taste was reflected in the publishing practice of the literary journals. In 1857 one of the original editorial team for the collected poems, Ivan Panayev, informed

Turgenev that Tyutchev was prepared to submit some of his latest verse for publication in *Sovremennik*; yet nothing came of this.[209] Paradoxically, having done so much to rescue Tyutchev's poetic legacy from oblivion, the journal never again published any of his work.[210] However much Turgenev and Nekrasov may have appreciated his poetry, they evidently saw it as belonging to the past.

For all its shortcomings, the edition of 1854 brought together for the first time between the covers of one book a representative collection of Tyutchev's poems, which up to then had lain scattered over the pages of various periodicals, many of them obscure and forgotten. The survival of his poetic reputation was assured, and for that at least Turgenev deserves our gratitude. The number of readers reached by the book and later editions based on it may have been small, but these were often figures of some influence in the literary world. They included major writers such as Tolstoy, Dostoyevsky and the Symbolists, all of whom came to recognise and proclaim Tyutchev's genius as a result. One of his warmest admirers, Afanasy Fet, inscribed a later edition of the poems with a tribute in verse which could equally be applied to that of 1854. He sees the book as a 'patent of nobility' bestowed upon its readers by the author, and for him it will always be the preserve of a discerning few. His poem concludes:

> But let upon the scales of justice
> The immortal muse make her assay:
> And we shall see this one small volume
> Innumerable tomes outweigh.[211]

14 New Beginnings
(St Petersburg, 1854-1864)

i Cretins Versus Scoundrels

Less than two weeks after Tyutchev's return from abroad in September 1853 Russia and Turkey were at war. This in itself was not so remarkable: conflicts between the two countries had been breaking out every twenty years or so since the time of Peter the Great. What made this one different was that for the first time Turkey could rely on the military backing of major European powers. The war had its origins in a protracted and seemingly trivial dispute between the Greek and Roman Churches over the custodianship of shrines in the Holy Land, in the course of which Russia had sought clarification of her long-standing but ill-defined treaty rights of protection over the Sultan's Christian subjects. In the ensuing diplomatic discussions Turkey, encouraged by assurances from Britain and France, took an obstructive attitude. In July 1853, in a heavy-handed attempt to exert pressure, Nicholas I occupied the Turkish-controlled Danubian principalities of Moldavia and Wallachia. His refusal to withdraw until a satisfactory solution had been arrived at prompted Turkey to declare war.

Although the Sultan's intransigence and Tsar's sabre-rattling were undoubtedly the immediate causes of the Russo-Turkish war, lurking beneath the surface were serious and deep-seated rivalries between the great powers which would turn this localised conflict into the longest and bloodiest war to afflict Europe between 1815 and 1914. The governments of Britain and France hastened to prop up Turkey — the 'sick man of Europe' in Nicholas's phrase — against the perceived threat of Russian expansion in the region. They were supported by public opinion in their own countries, which had come to see the Tsar's authoritarian and militaristic regime as an outdated obstacle to the spread of progressive democratic ideals. The wider European conflict, when it came, was as much a clash of ideologies as a struggle for predominance in the Near East.

For Tyutchev the outbreak of war seemed to offer the fulfilment of all his prophecies and hopes for a resurgent Slavdom led by Russia. On 16 November he wrote to Ernestine: 'That which has just begun is not war, not politics: it is a world in the process of formation, which in order to exist must above all rediscover its lost consciousness of itself...'[1] He even found confirmation of his ideas from a surprising source. Spiritualism, mediums and 'turning tables' were all the rage in St Petersburg society that autumn, and Tyutchev was swept up in the general enthusiasm. 'He is completely obsessed with the tables,' Anna wrote of her father at this time, 'not only the turning variety but those that prophesy as well.' She was amused to note how the utterances of his medium invariably replicated his own predictions of victory for the Slav idea: 'Strange that the spirit of this table and that of my father should be as alike as two pins: the same political viewpoint, the same play of imagination, the same style.'

He had, she said, been 'terribly angry with me for my scepticism'; she for her part saw his preoccupations as no more than to be expected of a mind which, though 'brilliant' and 'incisive', was 'not firm in the realm of religious convictions and moral principles'.[2]

Undeterred, he continued to aver that (as he wrote to Ernestine some time later), '*the Supernatural*, to call it by its name, has entered into the affairs of this world like the Commendatore's statue'.[3] Were Russian troops not at that moment on their way to free Constantinople, as predicted by him for the 400th anniversary of that city's fall? Were the hosts not already assembling in Europe for the final showdown between East and West? As Britain and France made diplomatic and military moves to intervene on Turkey's behalf, the tone of his utterances became increasingly apocalyptic. What lay ahead was 'one of the most dreadful crises ever to have shaken the world', 'something even more formidable than 1812';[4] it was 'quite simply the end of the world, or at least the beginning of the end'.[5]

Now and throughout the conflict he kept in close touch with those who, like him, believed the government was pursuing the cause of Russia and the Slavs with insufficient vigour. On visits to Moscow he met and discussed the war with Pogodin, Samarin and other members of the Slavophile circle based there.[6] And with Anna's assistance he was able to bring letters and memoranda emanating from what he called 'the national party' to the attention of the heir to the throne. In March 1854, for instance, he warmly endorsed a proposal by the historian Aleksandr Popov for an independent newspaper under the Tsarevich Alexander's protection to promote the Russian national cause more robustly than the official press was able.[7] (Although nothing came of this, at about the same time Tyutchev appears to have embarked on a separate journalistic venture of his own, of which more below.) He was also active in circulating among figures of influence at court a wide-ranging series of unpublished articles by Pogodin in the form of letters (two addressed to him) which criticised the pre-war policy of adherence to the Holy Alliance, attacked the existing system of government and called for immediate reforms.[8]

For some time those of a Slavophile or 'national' bent (the 'Moscow opposition', as Anna called them)[9] had been viewed with distrust by the authorities and kept under close surveillance.[10] In the aftermath of 1848 some had even been arrested and interrogated on suspicion of harbouring revolutionary sympathies.[11] While no-one could possibly suspect Tyutchev of that, his political agitation during the war made him highly unpopular in certain influential quarters. On a visit to Munich in March 1855 Nesselrode's son made it clear to Karl Pfeffel that his father took as a personal affront the 'opposition to the government' evinced by Tyutchev in 'excessively impassioned speeches' to St Petersburg salon audiences.[12] Fortunately for Tyutchev, Anna's position at court offered him a degree of protection, while Nesselrode's star was by then in any case beginning to wane.

During the early stages of the war Tyutchev writes only admiringly of Nicholas in his private correspondence. He praises the 'calm and dignified' bearing displayed by the Emperor[13] and commends his avowed 'love of peace', which will nevertheless not prevent him from calling upon Russia's vast military resources as necessary.[14] In stark contrast with this veneration of the Tsar is his jaundiced view of government circles at large: misled by an 'inconceivable infatuation', ministers and bureaucrats are said to have aimed only at being the West's 'understudy' instead of seeing it as Russia's 'natural and necessary adversary'.[15] He is particularly dismissive of Nicholas's manifesto to the nation on the outbreak of war as drawn up by the Foreign Ministry — 'pale and colourless, like everything emanating from there' — and looks forward to the more persuasive eloquence of big guns.[16] Soon he is writing to Ernestine with all the relish of an armchair warrior about Russia's early military successes. Contrasting the admirable 'relentlessness' of the ordinary Russian footsoldier with the 'softness' of his political masters, he recounts how on 19 November General Bebutov's troops 'cut to pieces' 35,000 Turkish soldiers, taking only thirteen prisoners (the rest were bayonetted as a reprisal for earlier Turkish atrocities).[17]

A great and unexpected blow to Nicholas's plans was the hostile stance taken by Austria and Prussia, his partners in the Holy Alliance. Having helped the Emperor Franz Josef to suppress the Hungarian uprising in 1849 and supported him in a dispute with Turkey over Montenegro only the previous year, Nicholas naturally assumed his young protégé would allow him a free hand against Austria's ancient enemy. Nor did he expect trouble from his brother-in-law, King Friedrich Wilhelm IV of Prussia. Yet although the two German-speaking powers remained technically neutral throughout the conflict, Austria in particular would pursue, in the words of one historian, 'a definitely anti-Russian policy which brought her twice to the verge of war and facilitated the victory of the coalition'.[18] On 28 March/ 9 April 1854 — just before the British and French declarations of war took effect — Berlin and Vienna formally condemned Nicholas's occupation of the Danubian principalities and called for the removal of Russian troops. In June Austria went further, threatening to enter the war on the allied side if Russia did not comply.

Tyutchev's letters reflect the acute sense of betrayal shared by most Russians. Already in February he has written off Austria and Prussia, describing their policy towards Russia as 'wretched and nauseating'. He even welcomes the prospect of war on another front, convinced that the Austrian Empire, 'whose whole body is nothing but one Achilles' heel', will disintegrate as its Slav population rises in revolt.[19] In April he fulminates against the Germans' ingratitude for services rendered in the past, discerning a national propensity to 'bear a grudge longer for a good deed than for a grievous insult'.[20] When Austria's June ultimatum arrived in St Petersburg, Russia's Ambassador to that country, Prince Aleksandr Gorchakov, was in the city for con-sultations. He knew Tyutchev well, and before returning to Vienna revealed to him the instructions he had been given in response to the ultimatum. He was apparently to tell the Austrians that Russia had no desire to fight them, but that if they should declare hostilities, 'we shall engage in total war against them, a war of extermination, using every means available'. Tyutchev liked the sound of this, even if it was little more than a diplomatic feint. 'Please God that it should be so,' he commented, reporting the news to Ernestine, 'but I don't believe a word of it... Not yet...'[21]

It was during this period of mounting tension between Russia and Austria that several inflammatory extracts from Tyutchev's private letters were published in the Western press. Earlier that year in Munich Ernestine had shown some of his correspondence to her brother Karl, who had forwarded copies of passages dealing with the international situation to the editor of the *Revue des Deux Mondes* in Paris.[22] As with Pfeffel's previous approaches to the *Revue*, it seems unlikely he would have done this without authorisation from Tyutchev. Certainly there is no hint of surprise or displeasure in Tyutchev's subsequent comments on the publications to Ernestine; on the contrary, it is almost with an air of pride that he announces 'a certain sensation' caused by one of them in St Petersburg, claiming that this 'could almost have tempted me to write something more developed and coherent on the subject as a whole' had she, his former assistant on such projects, not been away at Ovstug.[23] Nor did Ernestine have any qualms about supplying Pfeffel with further extracts from Tyutchev's letters after her return to Russia (none of which, however, appears to have found its way into print).[24]

The published extracts appeared in the *Revue* between April and June 1854 in two articles by Charles de Mazade and one by Eugene Forcade .[25] The author of the letters is identified only as an eminent Russian diplomat 'placed at the heart of the Russian government, an enthusiastic supporter and eloquent defender of the Emperor Nicholas's policies' (Forcade),[26] whose writings are said to express 'in *all its plenitude* Russian thinking on this whole lengthy crisis' — thinking which here 'avows without prevarication the ambitions it publicly denies', thereby revealing 'the secret long-term aims of Russian policy' (Mazade).[27] It was of course not the first time that his personal views had been offered in the Western press as a reflection of official government policy.

The most substantial of these articles, and containing the most extensive extracts from Tyutchev's letters, is Forcade's of 20 May/ 1 June on Austria's policy towards Russia in the current crisis.[28] One of the passages quoted (from a letter to Ernestine of 2/14 February) bitterly denounces Austrian and Prussian declarations of neutrality as no more than a first step towards open hostility; asserts that 'quite apart from racial antipathy' towards Russia, the two German powers 'have over forty years contracted too many obligations not to be impatient to seize the first favourable opportunity to take their revenge for them'; and predicts that their 'defection' from the Holy Alliance, far from ensuring their independence, will submit them to the 'revolutionary influence' of France. In all this Forcade detects 'resentment' in Russian governing circles at the failed attempt to get Austria on side. He goes on to quote further examples of 'violent outbursts' and 'braggadocio' in the letters, including Tyutchev's claim that the war is a 'supreme struggle' between East and West, from which Russia will emerge triumphant no longer as herself but transformed into 'the great Graeco-Russian Eastern Empire'.[29]

A few days later the explosive letter extracts from Forcade's article were reprinted in the *Allgemeine Zeitung*, arguably the most influential and respected newspaper of the German-speaking world.[30] It is difficult to know what effect such alleged revelations of Russia's 'secret long-term aims' may have had on the Austrian authorities at a time of heightened tension between the two countries. At the very least they cannot have helped. Pfeffel was justifiably concerned that the affair could land Tyutchev in trouble with his boss, the pro-Austrian Nesselrode;[31] fortunately for him, his identity as author of the letters appears to have remained undiscovered in St Petersburg.[32]

For all his threats of 'total war', Nicholas found himself obliged to comply with Austria's ultimatum. By September Russian troops had been withdrawn from the Danubian principalities and, with Turkey's agreement, replaced by Austrian forces. Tyutchev fulminated against what he saw as an 'appalling disgrace', 'one of those acts of public infamy which for nations usher in the period of their final decline'. He excoriated the 'cowardice, ineptitude, infamy and stupidity',[33] the 'unspeakable, incomparable mediocrity' of the ministers and bureaucrats charged with the destinies of Russia: 'all that pack of idiots who, in spite of everything and on the ruins of a world they will have caused to collapse under the weight of their own stupidity, are fatally condemned to live and die in the final incorrigibility of their idiocy'.[34] If this was the best Russia could offer against the 'shameless deceit'[35] of the vast Western 'conspiracy'[36] ranged against it, then God help Russia. It was, he punned in French, *'la guerre des crétins contre les gredins'* ('the war of the cretins against the scoundrels').[37]

In fact it is difficult to see how else the hard-pressed Russian government could have responded to the ultimatum. The military campaign against Turkey had already run into difficulties, and a substantial British and French fleet stationed in the Gulf of Finland was by now effectively blockading the capital. One evening in June Tyutchev stood on the jetty at Peterhof, gazing towards the setting sun and picturing, just beyond the range of vision, 'this armada, the most formidable ever to have appeared on the seas': 'the entire West coming to show its denial of Russia and bar her way to the future'. For one who evidently concurred with Hegel's dictum that periods of peace and tranquillity are but empty pages in the history of mankind there was a certain thrill to be had (as he wrote to Ernestine) in witnessing 'one of the most solemn moments in the history of the world'.[38]

The war entered a new phase in the autumn of 1854 when an allied expeditionary force landed in the Crimea and laid siege to the main Russian naval base at Sevastopol. Poorly equipped, inefficiently led and plagued by cholera as the British and French troops were, they encountered an enemy even more severely handicapped by internal weaknesses of the autocratic system. In particular, the longstanding failure to build good roads or any railway line at all south of Moscow brought major logistical problems. Immediate disaster was averted by the garrison and population of Sevastopol, whose heroic resistance managed to withstand the siege for a whole year. The worsenng situation shook Tyutchev's confidence further. Already in June he had admitted to Ernestine to feeling at times like someone descending a steep slope in a carriage who suddenly realises there is no-one in the driving seat.[39]

In February 1855 Tsar Nicholas contracted influenza. Within a week he had developed complications and become seriously ill. He died on the morning of 18 February.[40] Later that day Anna dined with her parents and was able to give them her account of events as seen from inside the palace. She found them already shaken by the news. 'It's like being told that God is dead,' commented Tyutchev.[41] Two days later in a letter to Pfeffel he reiterated his belief that the good intentions of 'our dear late Emperor' had been constantly thwarted by 'the false system, the inept and anti-national system' under which Russia had laboured for the past forty years.[42] The arrival of the Austrian Archduke Wilhelm for the Tsar's funeral was widely seen as adding insult to the injury his country had inflicted on Russia's war effort — injury which many felt had even helped to hasten Nicholas's demise.[43] Tyutchev dashed off a philippic in verse attacking the Austrian 'Judas Iscariot' for this affront to the Emperor's 'sacred shade';[44] capturing the general mood, it circulated widely in manuscript copies.[45]

Tyutchev was pleased that in his accession manifesto the new Tsar, Alexander II, declared his intention to pursue the war.[46] At the same time Alexander authorised

Gorchakov in Vienna to continue with peace negotiations reluctantly entered into by Nicholas in November.[47] In March Anna reported her father as 'anxious, worried and [...] in a very sombre mood' about the course of these discussions, the substance of which was being kept secret.[48] As the year went on, further setbacks in the Crimea led him to conclude that the incompetence blighting the Foreign Ministry had spread to all branches of the administration, including the military. Nor was this surprising in a system whose guiding principle for many years had been the repression of thought. 'The effects of such a system could not be kept limited or confined,' he wrote to Ernestine — 'everything has been subjected to it, everything has undergone the same level of repression, everything without exception has sunk into the same state of idiocy.'[49] Now, like many of the Slavophiles, he awaited with a certain grim satisfaction the coming crisis 'which, like a broom, will sweep away all this decay and infamy'.[50]

In August he travelled to Ovstug to spend a couple of weeks with Ernestine and the family. After leaving Moscow he observed the telegraph wires lining the road south and wondered what ominous news they might be bearing from the Crimea. In a poem composed en route he describes 'prophetic birds' alighting on the wire every so often. One, a black raven, seems particularly attracted to it:

> Crowing gleefully, it hovers,
> Keeps the wire in constant sight:
> Does it smell perhaps the bloodstained
> News of Sevastópol's plight?..[51]

Returning to Moscow on 3 September, he received from his brother Nikolay the 'overwhelming', 'staggering' information that Sevastopol had fallen to the French a week before.[52] Anna was also present; fully expecting her father to explode with anger, she was surprised and relieved to see him take the news in tearful silence.[53]

For the many Russians eager to find a scapegoat for the disaster the late Emperor presented an easy target. Tyutchev too rounded on the man he had so recently revered as the divinely anointed scourge of revolution. Writing to Ernestine just two weeks after learning of the fall of Sevastopol, he inveighed against 'the monstrous ineptitude of that ill-fated man who, having had during thirty years of his reign the most con-stantly favourable opportunities, missed and squandered them all, only to engage in hostilities under conditions that were quite simply impossible'. Nicholas's miscon-ceived foreign policy had condemned Russia to fight Britain and France with one hand while the other was pinned down by Austria. In short, he had acted like a man who goes about entering a house by first bricking up all the doors and windows and then attempting to knock a hole in the wall with his head.[54] Karl Pfeffel was moved to protest at this attack on Nicholas after receiving a copy of the letter from Ernestine.[55] It is not difficult to see why. Tyutchev had himself for years consistently defended the alliance with Austria and Prussia, while adopting towards the West as a whole a public stance not far removed from that of a bar-room brawler threatening (in his case in the most elegantly turned French) to take on all comers.

It seems to have been at this time that Tyutchev composed his devastating epitaph on the late Emperor:

Throughout your reign you served nor God nor Russia,
But simply followed your own star —
Your deeds, both good and bad, mere empty masquerading,
The falsest of façades, a mockery degrading:
You were an actor, not a Tsar.[56]

Russia fought on, incurring further losses. In October Tyutchev was still writing bleakly in terms of 'the final, decisive battle' between East and West on which depended the very existence of the Slav peoples led by Russia: '*to be* or *not to be, us* or *them...*'[57] He was whistling in the dark. In December the Austrian government called on Russia to accept peace terms dictated by Britain and France, threatening in the case of refusal to enter the war on the allied side. This second Austrian ultimatum was the final blow as far as Alexander and his ministers were concerned; on 4/16 January 1856 they signalled their acceptance.[58] Tyutchev had been in favour of fighting to the bitter end as in 1812; according to Ernestine, he 'went quite mad with rage' on learning of the capitulation.[59]

The Crimean War ('a mad enterprise' in the judgement of one eminent British historian,[60] 'a foolish expedition to the Black Sea' in that of another)[61] was over. Under the main terms of the Treaty of Paris Russia was obliged to cede part of Bessarabia to Moldavia, abandon her claim of protection over the Sultan's Orthodox subjects and recognise the Black Sea as a demilitarised zone barred to warships of any nation. Diehards like Tyutchev on both sides regretted that the war had not been fought to the finish. More reasonable voices pointed to what had been gained: a more equitable balance of power in Europe; the collapse of that great bulwark of reaction, the Holy Alliance; in Russia itself, the prospect of reform and greater freedom of expression. Others wondered if it had all been worth the loss of over half a million lives.

ii The Thaw

It soon became apparent that in response to popular demand the new Tsar Alexander II was minded to soften the rigours of his father's regime, and in particular to allow greater freedom of expression (or *glasnost'*, as it was known even then). Realising that the long 'iron winter' was over, Tyutchev began to speak of a 'thaw' ('*ottepel'*'), a term which rapidly caught on.[62] (A hundred years later it would be revived to denote a similar period after the death of Stalin.) Yet only with the end of the war in March 1856 did Alexander feel able to proceed in earnest. Hardly was the ink dry on the Treaty of Paris when he announced his intention to abolish serfdom and inaugurate a programme of reform. This was followed by two highly symbolic measures: the dismissal of Nesselrode as Foreign Minister and appointment of Russia's Ambassador to Austria Gorchakov as his successor; and an amnesty for the surviving Decembrists, who were at long last permitted to return from their Siberian exile.

In common with the overwhelming majority of Russian intellectuals, Westernisers and Slavophiles alike, Tyutchev welcomed and in general supported the 'Tsar-liberator's' reforms. At times he chafed at the slow progress being made to implement them,[63] and was aware of the obstructive tactics used by reactionary ministers and officials, many of whom had managed to survive in office from Nicholas's reign (like, he once said, the hair and nails continuing to grow on a corpse after its burial).[64] And he was at one with the Slavophiles in regretting what he saw as the government's lack of inner rapport with the national soul and spirituality of Russia, leaving it solely reliant on the external mechanisms of power as a means of achieving reform.[65]

All this exercised Tyutchev greatly in connection with the central reform, the Emancipation of the serfs. Visits to Ovstug in the summers of 1855 and 1857 gave him a chance to test the mood of the countryside at first hand. In 1855 he arrived just in time for the Festival of the Assumption of the Blessed Virgin on 15 August and appears to have entered into the spirit of the village celebrations, enjoying the peasants' impromptu songs of praise to himself and Ernestine and responding with humorous speeches in Russian.[66] But already on his way to Ovstug he had noted the signs of poverty and backwardness everywhere in evidence, and this had deepened his pessimism about the war, then still in progress. How could such a run-down, ill-used land hope to prevail against the material might of the advanced West? Yet if the seeds of regeneration lay anywhere, then surely in the very spirit and faith of these humble peasants seen from the windows of his carriage: smarting under the injustices of serfdom, governed from afar like colonial subjects by a corrupt clique of Europeanised incompetents, they alone in fact represented the future of Russia. There and then he put these thoughts and feelings into a poem which was to be well received by the Slavophiles (and, later, Dostoyevsky, who quoted it several times in his works):[67]

Villages of mean appearance,
Nature's gifts at their most frugal —
Land of infinite endurance,
Homeland of the Russian people!

Foreign eyes so proudly gazing
See you, but remain in darkness,
Blind to the veiled light suffusing
All your nakedness and meekness.

As a lowly pauper, bowing
Low beneath the cross's burden,
Once your length and breadth, bestowing
Blessings, walked the King of Heaven.[68]

Two years later he was again in Ovstug on 15 August. This time as he watched the villagers celebrating his thoughts turned to the proposed Emancipation:

This crowd of the obscure, low-born,
Long-suffering, gathered here in number:
Shall Freedom come to shake their slumber,
To rouse them with its golden dawn?..

357

It shall — and in that dawn shall be
Dispersed these dank fogs of inaction...
But wounds grown foul with putrefaction,
The scars of ancient injury,

The emptiness that long has gnawed
At souls, corrupting thought and feeling —
Who will bind these up, and bring healing?..
Thou, stainless robe of Christ our Lord...[69]

This too found a resonance among the Slavophiles. Ivan Aksakov saw in it an answer to those who feared the abolition of serfdom would 'merely arouse the savage instincts of the lower orders and provoke them to revenge'. He characterises the poem as reflecting both Tyutchev's 'deeply held faith in the Christian element of the Russian national spirit' and his conviction that 'a massive historical injustice could not be expunged by external, formal legislation alone — that a solution to the problem was not just a matter of precise regulations and accurate accounting'. According to Aksakov, he understood that the decisive factor in reaching an accommodation between land-owners and peasants 'must be and would be the very spirit of the people, the spirit of that land through which, in Tyutchev's own words, "As a lowly pauper, [...] bestowing/ Blessings, walked the King of Heaven..."'[70]

The Emancipation manifesto was eventually promulgated on 19 February 1861. Tyutchev addressed a brief tribute in verse to the Emperor in commemoration of that momentous day, which had 'In freeing mankind from the marks of bondage,/ Restored our younger brethren to the fold'.[71] Although Alexander was reported to have been 'moved' by the poem,[72] Tyutchev was realist enough to know that it was force of cir-cumstance rather than inner conviction that had driven him to free the serfs. In private he joked that Alexander no doubt felt like someone who realises he has mistakenly handed a beggar a gold coin instead of a copper one but is too embarrassed to ask for it back.[73] (He may have been speaking from experience. The story was told of how once, accosted by a beggar woman and finding he had only a large banknote on him, he had absent-mindedly asked her to go and change it for him. She had been only too happy to oblige, and of course was never seen again.)[74]

Tyutchev was called upon to translate the Emancipation manifesto into French for the government publication *Journal de St.-Pétersbourg*,[75] but apart from this had no official involvement. His main contribution to the wider reform programme was through his work as censor. His attempts to undermine the 'censorship terror' introduced after 1848 have already been mentioned; these continued until the end of Nicholas's reign, earning him on occasion official reprimands from his superiors at the Foreign Ministry. One such carpeting in July 1854 pushed his patience to the limit: 'if I were not so needy,' he fumed to Ernestine, 'what an intense feeling of pleasure it would have given me at that precise moment to fling the salary they pay me back in their faces and walk away with impunity from all that pack of idiots [...] and these are the people one has to submit to being lectured to and hauled over the coals by, in return for a pittance.'[76] By now it must have been clear to the censorship gamekeepers that they had a poacher in their midst. It was after all only a few months since the publication of

Senior Censor Tyutchev's poem 'Prophecy' had incurred the wrath of the Tsar himself. Yet despite repercussions from that affair involving Nesselrode, the Minister of Education and the Head of the Third Section,[77] he managed to hang on to his post.

Things changed for the better with the accession of Alexander II, in particular after the replacement in April 1856 of Nesselrode with Gorchakov, who according to Ernestine was already 'well disposed' towards her husband.[78] Tyutchev associated frequently with his new chief, and by the following year was able to report to Ernestine that they had become 'the best of friends'.[79] Born in 1798, Gorchakov had attended the prestigious Lycée at Tsarskoye Selo as a classmate of Pushkin before embarking on a diplomatic career. Despite showing a great flair for his chosen profession, his liberal views and opposition to Nesselrode's pro-Austrian foreign policy made him increasingly unpopular with his chief. He was dismissed from the service in 1838, managing to achieve reinstatement only three years later. In July 1854, when the bankruptcy of Nesselrode's policies had already become apparent, Gorchakov was appointed Ambassador to Austria by Nicholas against his Foreign Minister's objections.[80] Gorchakov's human failings included vanity and a hugely inflated sense of self-importance, features almost bound to provoke the ridicule of Tyutchev,[81] who nonetheless recognised genuine ability beneath all the flim-flam, not to mention 'national' political aspirations in some ways akin to his own. 'He is no ordinary character,' he told Ernestine. 'With him the cream is on the bottom and the milk on top.'[82]

Under the new Foreign Minister Tyutchev's own stalled career began to pick up. In April 1857 he was promoted for the first time in nine years, to Active State Councillor (grade 4 in the Table of Ranks).[83] This entitled him to parity of esteem with a Major-General, but brought no change in duties or pay (soon afterwards indeed he was complaining to Ernestine of having to set aside nearly a third of his current annual salary of 2,400 silver roubles for the new uniform required at court).[84] Later that year Gorchakov invited him to write on foreign affairs for the newspaper Le Nord, a mouthpiece for the Russian government published in Brussels. He declined on the grounds that he would be unable to express his views freely in such an organ.[85] By this time the Tsar and his ministers were becoming alarmed at the growing success of Kolokol (The Bell), an independent Russian weekly newspaper published in London by the émigré radical publicist Aleksandr Herzen. In the new climate of freedom no amount of border controls seemed able to prevent large numbers of this being smuggled in and avidly read by Russians eager for any free expression of ideas. Wary of relaxing the censorship any further, the Emperor sanctioned instead a plan to counter Herzen's newspaper with a rival literary periodical sponsored and financed by the government but having all the outward appearance of an independent publication.[86] Gorchakov was keen on the idea and in the autumn again approached Tyutchev, this time offering him a post on the editorial board of the proposed organ. Tyutchev again refused, and for the same reasons. In November he spelled these out in a memorandum on the subject of censorship addressed to Gorchakov, but also intended for the Emperor's eyes; at the same time copies were circulated fairly widely in St Petersburg and Moscow.[87]

Couched in suitably diplomatic language, Tyutchev's memorandum is in fact a powerfully argued plea for greater freedom of expression. The rigid censorship under

Nicholas I had, he asserts, been 'a veritable public disaster' (103). Russia's humiliating defeat in the Crimea was the final proof that 'one cannot subject minds to a restraint or restriction that is too absolute and too prolonged without causing severe damage to the entire social organism' (96). Surrounding itself in this way with 'a desert, a vast intellectual void', the central power finds itself acting without external checks or guidance and ends by 'falling into confusion and collapsing under its own weight even before it succumbs to the fatality of events' (97).

Tyutchev pays tribute to measures taken by the present Emperor 'to relax the excessive rigour of the previous system and to restore to minds the air they were lacking'; literature in particular had benefited greatly from 'the day when freedom of expression was restored to it in certain measure' (97). Yet in these conditions of increased freedom the government cannot continue to rely on censorship alone, which by its nature is a purely negative instrument: 'Censorship is a matter of limitation, not of guidance. Yet what is needed in our country, in literature as in everything else, is not so much repression as leadership. Strong, intelligent, self-assured leadership: that is what the country is calling for, that is the watchword of our whole present state of affairs' (99). Tyutchev is in effect advocating that the government learn how to manage a free press. He points to the experience of the German states, where governments bitterly attacked by the press in 1848 had since contrived to enlist that same press as 'an auxiliary force', making of it 'an instrument adapted to their own use' (99-100). How much easier, he argues, it will be in Russia, where loyalty to Tsar and antipathy to revolution are so deeply entrenched, for the central power to 'take upon itself the direction of the public spirit' and 'assert its right to govern the minds of men' (100). Even so, this must be coupled with a recognition that public opinion in Russia has come of age and that people deserve to be treated as adults. What is more, the central power must itself be 'sufficiently persuaded of its own ideas, sufficiently imbued with its own convictions, to feel the need to spread their influence in the wider world and let them seep, like an element of regeneration, like a new life, into the very depths of the national consciousness' (101). In short, both government and people need to accept that 'the destinies of Russia are like a ship run aground which no effort on the part of the crew will ever manage to shift, only the rising tide of national life being able to lift and refloat her'. And for this to happen, 'freedom of discussion' must be allowed as far as is reasonably possible (102).

Turning to Gorchakov's specific proposal, Tyutchev argues that nothing effective in that line will be possible until the Russian government 'has essentially changed the way it views its relationship with the press'. Any hope of influencing public opinion under an unreformed system of officially sanctioned publications must remain 'an illusion' (103). It is not the actual views expressed in Herzen's newspaper that have attracted so many readers, but the fact that they are freely expressed. And if the periodical proposed by Gorchakov is to have any chance of combating those views, it must be allowed the same degree of editorial independence as its adversary. Only then will journalists gladly form themselves into an 'intellectual militia' devoted to the Emperor and the national cause, rather than turning away, as at present, from what must essentially be seen as a 'police operation' (105-106).

Tyutchev's proposals met with a mixed reaction in government circles. Aleksandr Timashov, Executive Director of the Third Section, strongly criticised them in an internal memo, arguing against any further relaxation of the censorship.[88] Gorchakov on the other hand was evidently impressed, and soon afterwards had an opportunity to help his protégé fill a senior post to which his talents, experience and interests were ideally suited. The vacancy had arisen through the death of the reactionary Aleksandr Krasovsky, Chairman of the Foreign Censorship Committee, which was responsible for censoring all publications imported into the Russian Empire. On 17 April 1858 Tyutchev was appointed his successor, remaining in the employ of the Foreign Ministry although the committee itself came under the jurisdiction of the Ministry of Education.[89] We have the testimony of a committee member sympathetic to Tyutchev that the post of chairman was 'a kind of sinecure and was always filled by individuals with connections and patronage in high places'.[90] Certainly the duties appear to have been, as admitted by Ernestine, 'not onerous', generally making few demands on her husband's time.[91] The committee met only every Wednesday from two to four,[92] and most of the routine work was dealt with by administrative staff. For this Tyutchev received an initial annual salary of 3,430 silver roubles (an increase of 1,000 on his previous job), rising to 4,000 by 1860.[93] From October 1858 he was also granted a supplementary salary of 1,143 silver roubles by the Foreign Ministry in recognition of his long service in that department.[94] None of this should be taken to imply that he was content to coast along as a mere figurehead or token head of department. On the contrary, he clearly relished the access to foreign publications and influence over censorship policy afforded by the post, and comments made by members of his family suggest that he both enjoyed the work and devoted a fair amount of attention and energy to it.[95]

His right-hand man was the committee's secretary Mikhail Zlatkovsky. He and the other office staff welcomed their new chief as a breath of fresh air after the reactionary Krasovsky. 'Tyutchev's appointment was a total revolution in the inner life of the committee,' Zlatkovsky later recalled. 'As for Fyodor Ivanovich's personal influence on the whole staff, I can only say that all were christened with a new spirit'.[96] In Zlatkovsky's memoir Tyutchev appears as 'an enemy of all petty bureaucracy': a broad-brush administrator who trusted his staff to handle details while he dealt with the wider issues. He is said for instance to have made it almost a point of honour to be 'not particularly versed in paperwork', leaving to his secretary the detailed framing of documents, which he would then sign after the briefest of oral summaries.[97] The committee had its own offices and was assisted in its work by subordinate committees and individual censors in Moscow and other provincial cities. Its members were appointed for their expertise in foreign languages and allocated publications to assess on that basis.[98] More than once in his letters Tyutchev emphasises the cordial working relationship he enjoyed with his team of censors;[99] in some cases this developed into personal friendship.

When Tyutchev took over the committee, the draconian system of foreign censorship Alexander II had inherited from his father was still technically in operation. Customs officials had orders to confiscate all books, periodicals and brochures from incoming travellers at the border (only personal Bibles and prayer books were exempt). These were sent to the nearest censorship office for vetting, together with printed matter intercepted by the postal authorities and books imported by the retail trade. The process of reclaiming approved titles was so complicated that many travellers simply gave up.[100] In practice it had become fairly easy during the period of the 'thaw' to circumvent the law through smuggling and bribery, leading to a flood of illegal imports available (at a price) on the black market. In 1857 Alexander ordered a review of the cumbersome and by now ineffective legislation, stipulating that any new proposals conform to the principle of 'reasonable vigilance'.[101] Opinion was divided in government circles between those like Tyutchev who wanted a more liberal regime and those who felt things had already got too much out of hand and wanted to tighten the reins. The debate dragged on for years, and a new statute was finally approved only in 1865.

Tyutchev's committee made several submissions on foreign censorship during this time, suggesting among other reforms that the practice of banning publications outright be scrapped and only the lesser sanction of restricted access retained; that technical and academic works be exempt from censorship; and that travellers be permitted to bring in single copies of foreign works (unless in Russian).[102] Tyutchev also strongly (and, for the time being, successfully) opposed a proposal to introduce 'dual' censorship, a belt-and-braces system that would have provided for legal sanctions after publication as a back-up to the existing preliminary censorship.[103] He found these struggles highly frustrating. Trying to persuade those in power of the virtues of free speech was, he once said, about as easy as getting a group of deaf people with no conception of music to perform a Haydn oratorio.[104] He found a friend and ally in Aleksandr Nikitenko, a Professor of Literature at St Petersburg University who also worked as a censor. In the spring of 1858 Nikitenko was entrusted by Minister of Education Kovalevsky with drafting the new censorship statute required by the Tsar, but soon found his attempts to guarantee the principle of free speech frustrated by the Third Section and hardline government ministers. At their meetings he and Tyutchev would compare notes, discuss tactics and commiserate over their boss Kovalevsky, who seemed unwilling or unable to match rhetoric with action on the subject of reform.[105]

Among those inclined to favour a cautious approach on censorship was the Emperor himself. Soon after Tyutchev's appointment Kovalevsky proposed him, Ivan Turgenev and other literary figures as candidates for a new committee which, like Napoleon III's *bureau d'ésprit public*, would be given the task of ensuring the press kept within official guidlines and reflected government thinking. Alexander is reported to have been angered by Kovalevsky's suggestions. 'What good are these writers of yours?' he snapped. 'There's not one of them can be relied on.' Instead he appointed a hardline triumvirate including Timashov of the Third Section.[106] A further ominous development was the Tsar's decision at the beginning of 1863 to transfer jurisdiction over censorship from the Ministry of Education to that of the Interior.

Some interesting insights into Tyutchev's philosophy and practice as censor are provided by annual reports on the work of the committee compiled under his direc-tion. In the first of these he states his aim as having been 'to put the committee's operations on a more rational footing'. 'Wishing to satisfy the needs of the reading public,' he writes, 'and taking the development of Russian literature into consideration, I have endeavoured to grant more latitude to foreign literature as well'.[107] Figures given in the report for 1863 show that despite an almost threefold increase in book imports over the preceding decade (from just under a million volumes to nearly three million), the number of titles banned had dropped from 464 in 1853 to 142 in the current year (a further 87 having been approved with pages excised or passages blacked out). This trend Tyutchev attributes both to 'our government's more liberal view of Russian and foreign literature' and to the wider effects of the reforms, many of the publications imported being of a scientific or technological nature.[108] Works by writers such as Byron, Shelley or Balzac, previously banned as politically subversive, were now passed by the committee, sometimes against the recommendation of the individual censors reporting on them. Heine was a difficult test case: the committee felt able to approve only some of his writings, continuing to ban others or permit them only with excisions.[109] Being obliged to treat his old friend in this way clearly rankled with Tyutchev: in one of his submissions on censorship reform he made a plea for exempting *in toto* the works of writers who had achieved the status of classics, specifically naming Heine as a case in point.[110]

Perhaps the pithiest statement of his philosophy as censor was given by him in verses inscribed in the album of a colleague in 1870:

> Commanded at the highest level
> To mount a guard on thought and art,
> We strove to be not over-zealous —
> Though, armed with rifles, looked the part.
>
> We bore our weapons with reluctance,
> Few charges we coerced or cowed:
> The role of *prison guard* disdaining,
> As *guard of honour* we stood proud.[111]

Tyutchev's other political involvement during these years was in the field of foreign affairs. What influence he had was achieved mainly as a result of his association with Gorchakov, and to a lesser extent through Anna, who as Maid of Honour to the Empress continued to champion the 'national' cause at court. The Crimean disaster had forced him to move his predictions of a great Slav-Orthodox Eastern Empire into a distant and uncertain future. Napoleon III and Alexander II were now described ironically as 'the Emperor of the West and the Emperor *manqué* of the East'.[112] In a letter to the writer and traveller Yegor Kovalevsky (brother of the Education Minister) in 1860 he inveighed against recent moves by 'that beast Napoleon' and the British government to extend their influence over the Ottoman Empire at Russia's expense. Even if those 'two dogs' ended up fighting over the Turkish bone, he believed Russia would be in no position to benefit: 'We are so morally and spiritually impotent, so unutterably insignificant! [...] Never has a state — and what a state: a whole world! — lost its sense of *historical self-knowledge* to such a degree.' It was Russia's destiny and mission to free the Slavs from Western domination. 'But who in Russia feels this, who understands it? You, myself and 10 other individuals, but not of course the Tsar, nor the Prince [Gorchakov].'[113]

Like others of the 'national' persuasion he rejoiced at Austria's defeat in 1859 at the hands of France and Piedmont, which had joined forces in the cause of Italian unification. He saw the Italians' successful struggle for independence not only as just retribution for Austria's perfidy towards Russia, but as a promising omen for the still subject Slavs.[114] In the run-up to the conflict he had been concerned that certain powerful figures at court might sway the Russian government into returning ('like a dog to its vomit', as he later put it)[115] to the old pro-Austrian alignment. By letter and at personal meetings he worked assiduously on Gorchakov, flattering him as 'the man who is necessary, irreplaceable for the country' and stiffening his resolve against any support for Austria.[116] Fortunately, the Emperor showed himself equally opposed to such a rapprochement.[117]

The rail link from St Petersburg had made it much easier to visit Moscow, and during these years he made it his habit to spend a few weeks there at least once a year, usually in the summer. Here he felt close to the true national spirit of Russia and relished the intellectual company of those such as Pogodin and the leading Slavophiles (Khomyakov, Samarin, the Aksakovs) in whom that spirit seemed to speak most clearly. 'Here I see much more intelligent society in two weeks than during six months in St Petersburg,' he wrote to Ernestine on one of his visits.[118]

The question of Tyutchev's precise relationship to the Slavophile movement has been a matter of much debate. Some have quite rightly pointed out aspects of his thought which set him apart from the Slavophiles. He steadfastly refused for instance either to demonise Peter the Great or to idealise pre-Petrine Russia. Nor is there any evidence of interest on his part in their social theories, in particular their promotion of the traditional peasant commune or *obshchina* as a viable native alternative to Western forms of society. Indeed, although their veneration of the peasantry met with his theoretical approval, in practice his whole temperament and way of life made it quite impossible for him to share their enthusiasm for country ways. Never in a thousand years would he have contemplated donning peasant dress or growing a beard, as many of the Slavophiles did to advertise their 'national' sympathies. Yet as far as the central articles of their faith was concerned — the unity of the Slav peoples; the need for an alternative to the rationalism and materialism of the 'corrupt' West; the special character and destiny of the Russian people and of Orthodox spirituality — he was undeniably at one with the Slavophiles. They for their part welcomed him as an ally in their cause, while he expressed his admiration for the leading figures of the movement,[119] associated with them and attended their gatherings. On occasion, it is true, he found himself bored and irritated by what he saw as the parochial nature of their discussions ('always the same thing over and over again'),[120] and claimed that their obsession with such 'puerile' matters rendered them deaf to 'the great events brewing without'.[121]

In short, Tyutchev was too much his own man ever to think of himself as a fully subscribed member of the movement. (Significantly, in a letter to Ivan Aksakov commending him for a series of articles on Slavophilism he refers to the latter throughout as '*your* doctrine' and '*your* faith', and repeats these phrases in later correspondence with him.)[122] Aksakov himself concluded after years of close friendship that Tyutchev's world-view, 'if not directly linked to [Slavophilism], has mutual affinities with it'.[123] Perhaps it would be most appropriate to think of him as the movement's unofficial and always independent-minded adviser and spokesman on foreign affairs.

All these 'national' thinkers, not least Tyutchev, had long been exasperated by one glaring discrepancy in their grand equation: the Poles. In January 1863 that fractious nation once again cocked a snook at the concept of Slav brotherhood by rising in arms against Russian rule. That they had evidently drawn inspiration and encouragement from the Italian Risorgimento can only have rubbed salt in the wound as far as Tyutchev was concerned. 'What a wretched breed these Poles are, though, for all their bravery!' he fumed in one letter to Ernestine.[124] And in another: 'The paroxysm of fury and madness of this whole race is something unimaginable.' And he hinted that the Poles would have only themselves to blame if their insurrection were to escalate into a major new war between Russia and the West, resulting in 'the mass extermination of a whole race of men'.[125]

Ivan Aksakov's Slavophile Moscow newspaper *Den'* (*The Day*) asserted that the uprising had been instigated by the westernised Polish nobility and clergy, and that the broad mass of the peasantry remained true to its Slav roots. Aksakov and other Slavophiles argued in *Den'* that the rebellion should be put down swiftly before the Western powers had a chance to intervene, while initially at least pleading for reconciliation and the granting of a degree of cultural autonomy once things had returned to normal. Their support for armed intervention was matched and even exceeded by many of the Westernisers, who argued somewhat bizarrely that in fighting the insurgents the Russian government was defending its programme of reform against the forces of reaction. The hitherto liberal journalist Mikhail Katkov took a particularly harsh line in his newspaper *Moskovskiye vedomosti* (*Moscow News*), demanding the extension of military government from the Lithuanian provinces chiefly affected to the whole of Poland, rejecting any concessions to cultural autonomy and even calling for an offensive war against France and the other Western powers.[126]

In May 1863 the government minister Mikhail Muravyov was appointed Governor-General of Vilna with dictatorial powers to crush the rebellion. These he made full use of, earning himself the nickname 'Hangman Muravyov' in the process. Tyutchev had known him since childhood days in Moscow, when their families had been close and Mikhail on visits to the house in Armenian Lane had met, fallen in love with and eventually married Tyutchev's cousin Pelageya, daughter of Nadezhda Sheremeteva. Now in St Petersburg Tyutchev called on Pelageya to hear at first hand of the energetic measures taken by her husband,[127] and in letters to his family expressed full support for the 'punitive exterminations' carried out by 'the Archangel Michael'.[128] A poem by him published in Aksakov's *Den'* in August paints a ghastly vision of the insurgents as the dead of 1831 newly risen from their graves:

> A fearful, gruesome nightmare weighs upon us,
> A nightmare filled with suffering and pain:
> Knee-deep in blood, we battle against corpses
> Arisen to be buried once again.[129]

Although Prussia under its new Prime Minister Otto von Bismarck supported Russia's actions, Britain, France and Austria applied diplomatic pressure on behalf of the Poles. By March Tyutchev was convinced that those nations would use Poland as the pretext for an all-out war against Russia.[130] On 11 June the Russian government received separate notes from the three powers demanding that the Polish question be decided by a general European conference.[131] The following day Tyutchev left by train for what had now become his regular summer visit to Moscow.[132] Before leaving he had been asked by Gorchakov to make contact there with Katkov and Aksakov, acting as (in his words) 'a kind of official intermediary between the press and the Minister of Foreign Affairs'.[133] In lengthy discussions with them he personally found Aksakov's views on the Polish question more congenial than Katkov's hardline approach.[134] However, it was the influential Katkov that Gorchakov was particularly keen to gain as an ally in the press. Acting on his chief's instructions, Tyutchev urged the editor of *Moskovskiye vedomosti* to moderate the tone of his leading articles on foreign affairs, in particular to drop his demands for an offensive war, which were threatening to derail Gorchakov's attempts to reach a diplomatic solution of the crisis.[135] He was undoubtedly helped in this by Yelena Denisyeva's brother-in-law Aleksandr Georgievsky, by this time a close friend, who as Katkov's assistant editor frequently wrote the newspaper's leading articles.[136] In return Katkov was offered exclusive access to confidential documents and briefings from the Foreign Ministry. Even so, Tyutchev's efforts appear to have been only partially successful: while accepting the privileges offered, Katkov did nothing to tone down his editorial line until November, by which time any immediate danger of war had in any case disappeared.[137]

Gorchakov had asked Tyutchev to impress on Katkov, Aksakov and others in Moscow that his reply to the Western notes would be robust and uncompromising.[138] He was true to his word. On 1 July he informed the French, British and Austrian governments that Russia would agree to confer only with the two other powers directly concerned, namely Austria and Prussia, and then only after order had been restored in Poland, regarding anything beyond this as unwarranted interference in Russia's internal affairs. Tyutchev was delighted with the text of the note (published on 10 July as an exclusive in Katkov's *Moskovskiye vedomosti*) and immediately congratulated Gorchakov by letter.[139] Presented with the alternative of declaring war or backing down, the Western powers discovered they had little stomach for another adventure of Crimean proportions and not for the first or last time abandoned the Poles to their fate. By the end of the year the insurrection was largely over. It was also clear that Gorchakov's diplomacy had managed to avert the wider European conflict which so many had feared. 'Here is a man who has of late grown enormously in stature,' Tyutchev wrote admiringly of him in November.[140]

The other hero of the day, for some at least, was Mikhail Muravyov. For his name-day in November 800 or so representatives of St Petersburg society, including Tyutchev, clubbed together to send him a silver-gilt panel depicting St Michael. Among those approached to sign the accompanying letter of tribute was the city's liberal-minded Governor-General Prince Aleksandr Suvorov (grandson of the famous general, who in 1794 had defeated a similar uprising by occupying Warsaw). Suvorov caused outrage in the 'national' camp by making it known that he would have nothing to do with any tribute to 'such a cannibal' as Muravyov.[141] Tyutchev responded by attacking him in verse:

> Humane descendant of a noble grandsire,
> Dear Prince, forgive us for our foolish ways:
> That we as Russians, not consulting Europe,
> Should heap a Russian cannibal with praise...

Tyutchev goes on to laud Muravyov, 'Who, sacrificing all to his dear people,/ Saved and preserved as whole our Russian land', and so on in much the same vein.[142] Circulated in manuscript copies, the poem caused a 'great sensation' in St Petersburg, reportedly incurring the Tsar's displeasure.[143] A copy reached Herzen in London, who (no doubt to its author's embarrassment) printed it in his journal as evidence of disarray in Russia's governing circles. 'What has become of Tyutchev's once fine verse? What has become of his talent?' Herzen mused in an accompanying note.[144] It was a fair question. In fact before long he would be creating some of his finest poetry, but in circumstances he can never have envisaged or hoped for.

iii A Double Life

The move to a more settled existence in the autumn of 1854 did nothing to clarify Tyutchev's confused domestic arrangements. His life was now divided effectively between two wives and two families. On the one hand was his legitimate family, centred on Ernestine and their comfortable new apartment at 42 Nevsky Prospekt; on the other Yelena, claiming to be his real wife in all but legal title and condemned by financial straits to constant migrations with her aunt and young daughter from one set of shabby rooms to another ('all the poor circumstances of her domestic life' deplored by Tyutchev himself on one occasion).[145] He would visit them when he could, perhaps two or three times a week. Their daughter Yelena, or Lyolya, grew up in the belief that her parents were married, her father's frequent absences being explained to her as due to the demands of his work.[146] Compared with the often tempestuous atmosphere at the Denisyevs', that at the apartment on Nevsky tended to be cool, if not frosty. Anna once remarked in her diary that the English word 'cheerless' summed it up perfectly, going on to describe it as 'gloomy and oppressive, like somewhere where the sun never shines'.[147] She invariably found her father 'very morose' on her visits home: 'usually we see him only asleep. As soon as he wakes up he leaves the house. [...] I always return from there with a heavy heart. It is as if the breath of life has abandoned [the house]'.[148]

From about May to October Ernestine would regularly decamp to Ovstug with the younger children, leaving the field free for her rival. Yelena and her aunt were in the habit of moving to a dacha on the city outskirts for the summer months, partly no doubt as an economy measure.[149] This was evidently the case in 1855, to judge by two poems written by Tyutchev in July of that year. The first was apparently occasioned by a fire in the dacha settlement:

> Flames leap upwards, incandescent,
> Scattering sparks that dart and gleam,
> While a cool breath from this garden
> Wafts to them across the stream.
> Here deep shade, there heat and clamour —
> Dazed, I wander aimlessly,
> Conscious now of one thing only:
> You are with me, part of me.

Smoke on smoke, fire spits and crackles,
Chimneys stand bereft and bare;
While, serene, in calm indifference,
Leaves stir, rustling, in the air;
By their gentle breath enveloped,
Now I hear your fervent speech;
Thanks to God: with you beside me
Heaven itself is within reach.[150]

'You are with me, part of me' seems to echo the line 'All within me, I in all' in the earlier poem 'Shadows fall, dove-grey, and mingle...' (more obviously so in the original Russian: '*Vsyo vo mne, i ya vo vsyom*'; '*Ty so mnoy i vsya vo mne*'). The critics Vasily Gippius and Boris Kozyrev (who appear to have noted the contrasting parallel independently of each other) both see the lines as epitomising the two distinct periods of poetic output to which they belong: the earlier one pagan, 'I'-centred, 'cosmic'; the later one more compassionate, 'you'-centred, *almost* Christian.[151]

The second poem written in July 1855 makes no direct reference to Yelena. Whether or not (as argued by Richard Gregg)[152] this debars it on technical grounds from inclusion in the 'Denisyeva cycle' is a fairly arcane point that need not detain us for long. Tyutchev is known to have presented the manuscript to Yelena, and the poem (considered by Pigaryov to be 'internally linked' with the piece just discussed)[153] is surely infused with her unseen presence. Apart from Gregg, all critics from Chulkov on have accepted it as part of the canon.

How rarely we encounter them —
    Moments beyond compare
That bring us, as we enter them,
    Release from earthly care!
Above me I hear murmuring
    The crown of tree on tree,
And only songbirds clamouring
    On high commune with me.
All that is false and odious
    Is far away from here;
The unhoped-for, the harmonious
    Now seems so real, so near.
Contentment and tranquillity
    With inward joy unite;
Sweet somnolence envelops me —
    O time, pause in your flight![154]

Here too Kozyrev makes fruitful comparisons with 'Shadows fall, dove-grey, and mingle...', arguing that although both poems would appear to describe a similar experience of self-oblivion and oneness with nature, the later (and in his view 'much weaker') piece again reveals Tyutchev's leanings towards Christianity. Because of these 'there can of course no longer be any question of "tasting annihilation" — things go no further than the exclamation: "O time, pause in your flight!" ' (an echo, Kozyrev points out, of the undertaking made by Goethe's Faust to forfeit his soul if ever tempted to ask the fleeting moment to stay).[155] This is undoubtedly true; yet one wonders whether in this case the concession to Christian belief was made, consciously or otherwise, in deference to the poem's dedicatee, Yelena. Tyutchev's Christianity would always remain more a matter of aspiration than of achieved faith, as is evident from another poem written in 1855:

> O my prophetic soul! O heart
> In thrall to anguish and disorder,
> That pulses on the shifting border
> Between two lives lived out apart!..
>
> In two divided worlds you dwell:
> Your day is passion, agitation,
> Your dreams a tangled divination
> Of what the spirits seem to tell...
>
> Though fateful passions with fierce heat
> This lacerated breast be filling,
> My soul, like Magdalene, is willing
> To cleave forever to Christ's feet.[156]

Through renewed echoes of *Faust* ('Zwei Seelen wohnen, ach, in meiner Brust') and the direct quote from *Hamlet* in the opening line[157] Tyutchev hints that his own predicament is but part of the wider spiritual malaise suffered by modern man, as embodied by those two literary archetypes. Torn between the higher imperatives of the soul and what in an earlier poem he had called the 'evil life' of the senses, he declares himself 'willing' to renounce his sinful ways and, like Mary Magdalene, follow Christ. This seems already a tacit acknowledgment of failure: in his case intention alone was never to prove sufficient for the leap of faith.

There are also poems reflecting periods of relative happiness spent with Ernestine, particularly at Ovstug, one of the few places where she could have him to herself. Although even now he could never bring himself to stay more than a couple of weeks at a time, his attitude towards his birthplace seems to have mellowed with the years. 'And the lilacs, are they already in flower? And are the nightingales singing?' he asks wistfully in one letter to Ernestine.[158] His visits in 1855 and 1857 have already been mentioned. On the first he was met on the highway from Roslavl by Ernestine and Darya, who had set off by barouche in anticipation of his arrival. Ernestine's reaction when they caught sight of his carriage approaching is described by Darya in a letter to Anna: 'The horses were reined in, Mama jumped straight down into the dust, and if you had seen her joy, her happiness, you would have been deeply moved. She had something like a fit of hysterics, which she attempted to conceal with bursts of laughter.'[159] Tyutchev soon settled into the leisurely pace of country life, enjoying long walks with Ernestine and Darya and spending his evenings in conversation or reading with the family. On occasion he voiced his old sense of unease at having the ideal Ovstug of childhood memory rudely confronted with the unvarnished reality of the present; but there were lighter moments too. Unused to equestrian pursuits, he volunteered one day to join Darya on a ride. She reported that she 'nearly died laughing' at the sight of her father bouncing precariously up and down on a little nag borrowed from Marie, he and the serf accompanying him the very picture of Don Quixote and Sancho Panza.[160]

Ovstug and the surrounding area inspired some of the finest nature poetry of Tyutchev's later years. Leaving there in the summer of 1857 he was accompanied by Darya, and from Moscow she wrote to Kitty that he had spent part of the journey talking at some length about Ernestine. We might assume that this included the delicate question of his relationship with Yelena; certainly Darya felt unable to reveal the details of their conversation in writing, telling her sister she would save them for when they next met face to face. 'We passed through the estates of our friends the Breverns in tears: he was speaking of Mama,' she added. 'It was so sad to see his old man's eyes filled with tears.'[161] Their mood was reflected by the signs of autumn's onset around them, caught by him in a poem composed and with Darya's help committed to paper in the jolting carriage:[162]

> There comes with autumn's first appearance
> A brief spell full of wonder and delight:
> Whole days of crystalline transparence
> And evenings luminously bright...
>
> Where once the sickle strode through wheat-ears tumbling
> An air of space and emptiness reigns now;
> Only a wisp of cobweb, trembling,
> Gleams on the idle furrow's brow.
>
> The empty skies fall still as birds forsake us,
> Yet distant still is winter's first unruly storm,
> And, seeping from above, a blueness pure and warm
> Is added to the drowsing acres...[163]

This was another of Leo Tolstoy's favourites. He particularly admired lines 7-8, where a few deft strokes (Tolstoy singles out the evocative use of 'idle') are sufficient to create a whole picture of rural tranquillity and repose following the hectic activity of the harvest. 'The art of writing poetry lies in the ability to find such images, and Tyutchev was a great master of that,' he commented.[164] He first got to know both the man and his poetry in St Petersburg towards the end of 1855. The 27-year-old veteran of Sevastopol had arrived from the Crimea in November to find himself famous as the author of stories based on the epic siege which had appeared in *Sovremennik*. It was the editors of that journal — 'Turgenev, Nekrasov and Co.' — who, as Tolstoy recalled much later, 'persuaded me with difficulty to read Tyutchev'. As he did so, Tolstoy was by his own confession 'simply overwhelmed by the greatness of his poetic talent'.[165] It was the beginning of a lifelong fascination with a poet he always considered to be at least the equal of Pushkin, and of whom he once said quite simply: 'One cannot live without him'.[166]

At one of their first meetings Tyutchev told the young writer how much he admired his Sevastopol stories and launched into a detailed discussion of them. Tolstoy was later to recall his surprise at encountering such 'sensitivity to the Russian language' in one 'who spoke and wrote French more fluently than Russian'.[167] Two years later they very nearly became related through marriage. Tolstoy, then in Moscow in search of a bride, met Kitty at the Sushkovs' salon and for a time became quite enamoured with her. He considered proposing, but eventually decided against it on the grounds that she was too much the cosseted aristocrat to share his chosen life as a working writer.[168] Despite this he and his father-in-law *manqué* remained on the best of terms. While shunning the literary scene as such, Tyutchev was always happy to associate with writers on an individual basis. Vyazemsky was by now an old friend, and apart from Tolstoy and Turgenev, in the second half of the 1850s he developed cordial relations with the poets Apollon Maykov and Yakov Polonsky (both of whom served as censors on his committee) and Afanasy Fet.

In 1858 Tyutchev's thoughts turned to another of the women in his life as the twentieth anniversary of Eleonore's death began to loom. The day itself — 28 August (9 September NS) — found him at Ostankino near Moscow, where the court was then gathered, he himself having arrived in Moscow from St Petersburg only the previous day. His main purpose in going to Ostankino was, he told Ernestine, 'to see Anna', and no doubt he derived some comfort from his daughter's presence on that day.[169] Old enough to remember her mother, she was a living link with that aspect of his past and could sometimes find herself privy to his innermost thoughts on the subject. 'Papa visited me the other day,' she reported to Kitty on a later occasion. 'He spoke to me of our mother, of that sad and heartrending past! I wept for a long time after he left.'[170]

After two weeks in Moscow Tyutchev took his leave of his aged mother, wondering as always now if he would see her alive again. Back in St Petersburg these apprehensions, exacerbated by the recent reopening of old wounds, found expression in a letter to Ernestine:

> It is extraordinary how everything in life is repeated, how everything seems as if it must last eternally and be repeated to infinity, until a certain moment when suddenly everything is swallowed into the abyss and vanishes, and that which seemed so real, that which one felt to be as solid and immense as the ground beneath one's feet, becomes a dream with no existence other than in memory, and which memory itself struggles to recapture. [...] After this one sleeps only with one eye shut and in spite of oneself; one feels oneself to be living only from day to day.[171]

Already earlier that year (perhaps with the anniversary in May of the *Nicholas I* disaster in mind) he had composed a poem in memory of Eleonore. The opening harks back to periods of emotional anguish and despair in his life:

At those times when the bosom
Is weighed with thoughts of doom,
The heart has grown despondent,
And all ahead is gloom —

one may (he continues) be granted moments of relief, sudden lightenings of mood as inexplicable as the workings of divine grace:

A sunbeam may unbidden
Steal in on our despair
And touch the walls with radiance:
A cheerful, sparkling glare.

So to a heightened degree was for him was the effect of Eleonore's love:

A hundred times as bounteous,
Ethereal, bright and free,
A hundred times more welcome
Was your dear love to me...[172]

Vadim Kozhinov has plausibly suggested that the opening lines refer specifically to Tyutchev's suffering after being rejected by Amélie;[173] they could equally recall in more general terms his many documented episodes of depression. On either reading the poem is a heartfelt and poignant expression of thanksgiving for Eleonore's healing love. Written at about the same time, and published in the same issue of the Moscow journal *Russkaya beseda* (*Russian Symposium*) in May 1858, was a poem about an unnamed woman whom some critics have claimed to be Ernestine, and others, Yelena.[174] A third and altogether more plausible possibility, given the circumstances of the poem's composition and publication, is Ronald Lane's suggestion that it was conceived as a companion piece to 'At those times when the bosom...' to mark the forthcoming anniversary of Eleonore's death, and that she is the woman remembered here:[175]

To sort a pile of letters, on
The floor she sat, all unregarding,
Like ash from which all heat has gone
Now handling them, and now discarding.

On each familiar leaf she took
Her gaze, so strange and distant, rested;
So too departing souls must look
Upon the shell just now divested...

O, how much life lay buried there,
Life lived and now beyond retrieving —
How many moments of despair,
Of love and joy transformed to grieving!..

I stood unspeaking and apart,
And would have knelt — the impulse filled me —
And more than heavy was my heart,
As if a dear shade's presence chilled me.[176]

On this supposition the poem was conceived by Tyutchev as an act of expiation towards his first wife and recalls a painful incident from their marriage which evidently arose from his liaison with Ernestine. Eleonore is preparing to destroy letters from him of a personal and intimate nature (as indicated by verse 3), while he stands aside, silent and helpless to intervene, overcome by a guilt-stricken impulse to fall upon his knees. Tyutchev's recollection of the scene is darkened even further by his knowledge of what happened since: the imagery of the 'departing soul' and 'dear shade' point ahead unmistakably to Eleonore's death.

In August 1858 Anna was appointed governess to the Tsar's five-year-old daughter Maria Alexandrovna, and the following month the post of Maid of Honour she had consequently vacated was filled by her sister Darya.[177] With two daughters close to the throne reinforcing his own position as Chamberlain, Tyutchev was now firmly established at court. Encounters with the 'Tsar-liberator' confirmed his opinion of Alexander's general good will and affability, even if he seemed somewhat lacking in certain other qualities. 'Whenever the Emperor converses with a man of intellect,' Tyutchev once mischievously observed, 'he takes on the appearance of a martyr to rheumatism forced to stand in a draught.'[178] Why the divine embodiment of autocracy should display such manifestly human failings was, he believed, a paradox explicable only in terms of some mysterious 'ulterior motive' on God's part.[179]

Temperamentally Tyutchev was quite unsuited to the role of courtier. Witnesses agree on his disdain for rigid court etiquette, his dislike of ceremony and his refusal to see class or rank as anything more than an accident of birth.[180] There are many anecdotes illustrating his disregard for such outward trappings of court life as ceremonial uniforms, medals and decorations, and indeed for accepted conventions of dress in general. Leaving Anna after visiting her at Peterhof one chilly summer evening, he found he had forgotten to bring an overcoat. She easily persuaded him to borrow one of hers, and was reduced to laughter at the sight of him striding towards the ferry in this incongruous garb 'with all the dignity of a Roman senator'.[181] On another occasion he appeared at a ball given by the Grand Duchess Yelena Pavlovna in the threadbare livery jacket of his burly manservant Emmanuel, which he had mistaken for his own tail-coat. The spectacle of the slightly-built Tyutchev wearing a servant's uniform several sizes too large for him caused much amused comment, dismissed by him as the usual tiresome carping at his appearance to which he had grown accustomed over the years. Only on returning home did he realise what had happened, but even then was quite unperturbed, insisting it was a mistake anyone could have made.[182] Even in the appropriate dress he managed to look scruffy, and was well aware (but quite unconcerned) that the Emperor must regard him as some kind of 'holy fool'.[183]

Further anecdotes attest to the boredom and absent-mindedness induced in him by elaborate court rituals. Deputed on one occasion to carry the train of a Grand Duchess, he brought the whole procession to a halt by stopping to chat with a bystander of his acquaintance. Another courtier had to prise the train from his grasp before the cortège could proceed, leaving Tyutchev still deep in conversation.[184] During a long church service to celebrate the Emperor's name-day he and the poet Aleksey Tolstoy wandered off to the Metropolitan's private quarters in search of a cup of tea.[185] Writing of the even more interminable consecration ceremony for St Isaac's Cathedral, he himself describes how he simply walked out and in full court regalia made his way home on foot through the bemused crowds in search of 'my room, my dressing gown and my dinner, of which I was in urgent need'.[186] In the end all these eccentricities were overlooked at court in favour of his ability to entertain any gathering with the sparkling brilliance of his wit and eloquence.

Towards the end of the 1850s he was increasingly plagued by painful attacks of gout which sometimes left him immobile for weeks on end. Doctors recommended taking the waters in Germany or Switzerland, and in the summers of 1859, 1860 and 1862 he spent lengthy periods abroad. The two ministers to whom he reported showed themselves ready to help: Gorchakov with courier missions, Kovalevsky and his successor Aleksandr Golovnin with generous allowances of paid leave. In 1859 he was away for almost six months, from May to November.[187] After delivering diplomatic mail in Berlin he headed for Munich to join Ernestine and the children, who had left Russia a few days ahead of him, and travelled on with them to Bad Reichenhall in the Bavarian Alps. A couple of weeks later he left them to begin a course of spa treatment at Bad Wildbad, with brief stops on the way at Tegernsee, where he met up with the Pfeffels, and again at Munich. Booking in at the newly-built Hotel Vier Jahreszeiten on Maximilianstrasse, he found little in the Bavarian capital to evoke the 'golden time' of his youth. All the old haunts had lost their magic and struck him now (as he wrote to Ernestine) as oddly unreal and 'completely strange'. He left the city after two nights, as far as is known never to set foot there again.

The three weeks spent taking curative baths at Bad Wildbad brought little improvement in his health, but he consoled himself with the active social life of the spa, meeting many fellow-countrymen including the Vyazemskys and his brother Nikolay, who was travelling in Europe on his own. Towards the end of his stay came disturbing news that while attending the Empress his daughter Darya had suffered a serious nervous breakdown, for which treatment abroad was required. He at once changed his plans, applying for and receiving an extension to his leave in order to be with her. On 13/25 July he met up with Ernestine and the children at Heidelberg, and they travelled on together via Frankfurt and Wiesbaden to Bad Ems, where Darya had meanwhile gone in the company of Tyutchev's cousin Pelageya and her husband Mikhail Muravyov. From there Ernestine took the children on to Blankenberge on the Belgian coast for sea-bathing. The consensus of medical opinion at Bad Ems was that Darya should continue with treatment there and in Switzerland, followed if possible by a winter spent somewhere in the sun.

Throughout his travels Tyutchev had followed with great interest the course of France's successful military campaign in support of Italian independence from Austria. At this point his incorrigible urge to be on hand at the great moments of history outweighed all other considerations. Reassuring himself that Darya was in the safe care of the Muravyovs, on 21 July/ 2 August he set off alone for Paris to witness Napoleon

III's triumphal entry into the capital at the head of his troops. The three-hour parade of some 80,000 troops convinced him both of the Emperor's popular support and of the likelihood that he would be tempted to make further use of such overwhelming military might. He spent nearly two weeks in Paris, always one of his favourite cities, unexpectedly bumping into Nikolay again for the third time that summer (he had also popped up in Wiesbaden). There was a characteristic upset when the rail journey back to rejoin Darya took nine days instead of the expected two, during which time he failed to make contact with his family, causing general concern as to his whereabouts and safety. (He subsequently explained that exhaustion had forced him to take things easy.) From Frankfurt, where Darya had gone to meet him, they travelled to Baden-Baden for further medical consultations.

The dowager Empress Alexandra Fyodorovna had meanwhile agreed for Darya to be transferred to her service and accompany her to Nice, where she would be spending the winter, an arrangement strongly endorsed by the specialist consulted in Baden-Baden. They accordingly made for Vevey on Lake Geneva in time for the Empress's arrival on 10/22 September en route for the south. They were warmly received by Alexandra Fyodorovna, who during her two and a half weeks at Vevey frequently invited Tyutchev to her gatherings and even requested a copy of his collected poems (some of which at least she apparently came to admire). She left for Nice with her retinue on 29 September/ 11 October. Tyutchev took an affectionate leave of his daughter, who was touched and perhaps a little surprised to see him bless her with the sign of the cross. There was nothing now to keep him in the West (Ernestine and the children had already returned to St Petersburg), but he lingered around Lake Geneva (Lake Léman in French) and in Geneva itself for another two weeks before heading back home by land via the 'necropolis' of Weimar (where he met the Maltitzes), Berlin and Königsberg. He arrived in St Petersburg on 2/14 November.

While still surrounded by the magnificent scenery of lake and mountains at Vevey, he had shivered at the thought of leaving 'this enchanted spot', 'this blessed land'[188] — of being forced to 'pass the icy sponge of a St Petersburg winter over these splendours'.[189] From Berlin he contemplated the gloomy prospect of 'launching myself, not into eternity like those condemned to hang in England, but into infinity like those who journey to Russia'.[190] And after Königsberg, as the vast 'Scythian plain' opened up before him, he wrote this:

On the Return Journey

I

Joyless scene and joyless hour —
Journey's end is still so far...
Like some spectre freed at last
From its grave, the moon through wreathing
Mists now lights this empty land...
    Far, so far — be not downcast...

And to think that at this hour
There where we no longer are,
Mirrored in Léman so vast,
This moon is alive and breathing...
Joyful scene and joyful land —
    Far, so far — forget what's past...

II

Familiar sights again... this smoke-grey awning
    Where massive, leaden snow-clouds loom,
And in the dull-blue distance, as in mourning,
    Dark forests wrapped in autumn gloom...
A drab and silent world too vast to reckon:
    All empty, arid, untraversed...
Just here and there, half-glimpsed through bush and bracken,
    The glint of ice on water, winter's first.

No sound, no colour here: all is arrested,
    All life extinguished, gone; man here, it seems —
Resigned to fate, his mind numb and exhausted —
    Must see himself as if in his own dreams,
And, eyes grown dim in twilight evanescent,
    Cannot believe that yesterday he knew
A land where mountains, rainbow-iridescent,
    Gaze on themselves in lakes of deepest blue...[191]

The following year saw another lengthy stay abroad for reasons of health, from late June to the beginning of December (OS).[192] On this occasion he was accompanied on all his travels by Yelena. They spent roughly the first half of this period at Wiesbaden, where he took the waters, after which on the advice of doctors they moved to Geneva for some two months so that he could benefit from a diet of fresh grapes.[193] In his first letter to Ernestine after arriving in Wiesbaden he told her he had just missed meeting Ivan Turgenev in Frankfurt, and that this had sparked memories of reading his new novella *First Love* earlier that year:

> I began reading it, lying on my chaise-longue next to the window, with you sitting not far away on the sofa by the door to my room. It was a moment to relish. Through my reading I could feel your presence and see everything around me enveloped in the pink glow of a beautiful sunset. I felt so happy and deeply loved.[194]

We almost have to remind ourselves that he wrote these words to his wife while holidaying with his mistress, and that Ernestine read them in her now annual self-imposed exile at Ovstug. Yelena was in her element throughout these months spent together: they signed in at hotels as 'M-r et M-me Tutcheff ', and for a few months at

376

least she could live out the fantasy of being his wife.[195] There was another, more practical reason for her presence: she had become pregnant, and it was no doubt considered advisable for the birth to take place as far as possible from the wagging tongues of St Petersburg.

Their idyllic holiday from reality was not without the usual quasi-marital tiffs later witnessed by Georgievsky. One particularly tempestuous row erupted in Baden-Baden, where they spent a week or so between Wiesbaden and Geneva. Out walking with him one day, Yelena let drop that she would like him to bring out a second edition of his poems. This immediately put him on his guard, for as he later recalled, 'she didn't give a brass farthing for poems, even mine — she only liked those in which my love for her was expressed — expressed publicly and for all to hear.' Indeed, she went on to demand not only the inclusion of such intimate verse, but that the volume be dedicated to her rather than Ernestine. He retorted that she was being selfish — that knowing as she did how completely he was hers, it was unreasonable to ask for further declarations in print which could only offend Ernestine. Her voice trembling with emotion, she declared that one day when she was dead he would bitterly regret what he had said. At the time this struck him as such an empty threat from one so full of youthful vitality that he dismissed it from his mind as mere histrionics on her part. All her cries and protestations were met with the reply, 'You are asking for the impossible...'[196]

They reached Geneva on or about 13/25 September, a month before the baby was due.[197] There was a Russian Orthodox church for Yelena to attend, where the young priest in charge, Afanasy Petrov, will soon have been confronted with the delicate issue of her views on marriage. He seems to have taken a sympathetic pastoral approach, and before long he, his wife and Yelena had become the best of friends.[198] Tyutchev, impressed by Petrov's 'exceptional intellect', was also happy to associate with him, and in general enjoyed being welcomed into the lively atmosphere of Geneva's artistic and literary circles.[199] On 11/23 October Yelena gave birth to a son who was christened Fyodor after his father.[200] As with their first child, Yelena insisted on his surname being entered in the register as Tyutchev.

In the summer of 1862 Yelena again accompanied Tyutchev abroad, this time together with her aunt Anna, the children and a nurse for little Fedya.[201] On this occasion they were away from Russia for less than three months, from the end of May to the middle of August (OS). After two weeks in Wiesbaden (from where Tyutchev was able to visit Karl Pfeffel in nearby Bad Homburg) they had originally intended to proceed to Baden-Baden for further medical consultations, but decided at the last moment to spend the rest of their time on the shores of Lake Geneva.[202] In a letter to his daughter Darya Tyutchev said he had recoiled at the thought of having to mingle with the hordes of rich and famous in Baden-Baden, preferring instead the natural glories of lake and mountains.[203] No doubt Yelena's wishes had also carried some weight. They arrived in Montreux at the eastern end of Lake Geneva on or just before 19 June/ 1 July, and for the first few days are known to have stayed at nearby Vernex.[204] Soon afterwards Tyutchev set off on a two-week tour of the Bernese Oberland with a certain Korsakov, a young Russian artillery officer only recently discharged from a mental asylum, whose acquaintance they had apparently made at Vernex.[205] Left to her own devices, Yelena will have found it easy enough to renew her friendship with the Petrovs in Geneva thanks to a new railway line running the length of the lake along its northern shore.[206] Tyutchev and Korsakov travelled via Martigny and Sion to Leukerbad (Loèche-les-Bains), and from there on foot over the Gemmi Pass to Kandersteg, 'one of the most difficult and hazardous passages of the Oberland Alps' according to Tyutchev. At over 2,000 metres he viewed the spot where the previous year a Frenchwoman's mule had stumbled, hurling her to her death a hundred feet below. The 'absolute silence' of these uplands he found 'of inexpressible beauty', and not for the first time he felt the mysterious attraction of 'this world apart which no longer belongs to the living'.[207] Two years before in Switzerland he had written:

> Although my home is in the valley,
> I sometimes cannot help but sense
> The pure life-giving force of breezes
> That roam about those peaks immense —
> And know the breast's eternal longing
> To struggle free from stagnant air:
> To leave all that is earthbound, stifling,
> And soar on high to summits bare...
>
> Those inaccessible expanses
> I watch, engrossed, for hours on end...
> What cooling dews in raging torrent
> Or rushing stream to us they send!
> And sometimes too we catch a glitter
> Of flame-light as their virgin snow
> Is touched by feet of heavenly angels
> Who unseen through the ice-fields go.[208]

From Kandersteg they pushed on to Interlaken and Lakes Thun and Brienz. There was a comic interlude at the Hotel Bellevue in Brienz when some English guests were able to decipher only the final words of Tyutchev's scrawled entry in the hotel register announcing him as Chamberlain of His Majesty the Emperor of Russia. The rumour rapidly spread that the Tsar himself was staying incognito at the hotel, to the extent that at dinner that evening Tyutchev and Korsakov were surprised to be greeted by the strains of their country's national anthem from the hotel orchestra. After this they headed back to Lake Geneva via Berne and Fribourg (where the sound of the cathedral organ he and Ernestine had heard 21 years before overwhelmed Tyutchev with 'a sadness which no human words would be capable of expressing').[209]

'Ah, how happy one could feel in this beautiful country, if one were not what one is,' he had written to Ernestine from Vernex before setting off on the tour. Yet being what he was, he had to steel himself for a return to 'the frightful St Petersburg winter' which lay ahead; he even confided to her that he would be returning earlier than planned.[210] The reason was not far to seek. One of his chiefs, Minister of Education Kovalevsky, had recently been replaced with an unknown quantity, Aleksandr Golovnin. Previously Tyutchev had always been able to leave his committee in the capable hands of his deputy Yegor Komarovsky, but this time Golovnin had rather ominously insisted on appointing his own nominee to run things in the chairman's absence. In addition moves were already afoot to transfer overall responsibility for censorship from Golovnin's ministry to that of the Interior. In such a climate of uncertainty it would be inadvisable to stay away from his post for too long.[211] He made sure he was back in St Petersburg on 15/27 August, several days before his leave officially expired.[212]

Soon after their return Yelena and her aunt were paid an unexpected visit at their flat in Kirochnaya Street (now 14 Saltykov-Shchedrin Street)[213] by Aleksandr Georgievsky, the husband of Yelena's half-sister Marie. A young history professor at the Odessa Lycée, Georgievsky had recently been seconded to a special committee of government officials and academics set up to draft a new and more liberal charter for Russia's universities. Feeling at a loose end in the big city (his wife and children were still in Odessa), he had decided to make himself known to his sister-in-law and her family. He received a warm welcome and was asked to stay for dinner that evening, when he also met Tyutchev for the first time. Although he already knew and admired his poetry and some of his political writings, Georgievsky had formed a negative opinion of his character from what he had heard from his wife about the affair with Yelena. Yet at this first meeting all was forgotten in the discovery of common interests and attitudes, and from then on Georgievsky was happy to accept invitations to dine with them whenever his duties permitted, usually once or twice a week. It was the beginning of a long and cordial friendship.[214]

In October Tyutchev spent ten days in Moscow, apparently accompanied by Yelena.[215] Soon after their return they were saddened to learn that they would be losing the company of their new friend, who had been offered the post of assistant editor on Katkov's *Moskovskiye vedomosti*. In the middle of November Georgievsky left for Moscow to start work there.[216] At the beginning of May 1863 Tyutchev suffered a serious attack of gout which kept him confined to bed for over a month. As Ernestine had already left for Ovstug and Anna and Darya were busy at court, Yelena took charge of his care, dividing her time between the apartment on Nevsky and a dacha in the Chornaya Rechka district where her aunt and the children had moved for the summer.[217] On 12 June, still not fully recovered, he left by train for Moscow.[218] He took furnished rooms at what is now 5 Bolshoy Gnezdnikovsky Lane (*Pereulok*), just off Tverskaya Street.[219] Yelena followed discreetly some days later with Lyolya and little Fedya and stayed in the Georgievskys' vacant apartment.[220] Her in-laws had moved into a summer dacha at Butyrki on the northern ouskirts of the city, from where Georgievsky commuted daily to work on the newspaper.[221]

Tyutchev's two months in Moscow were partly spent, as already mentioned, liaising with the press on behalf of the government, a task undoubtedly made easier by his now close ties with Georgievsky. (Yelena too appears to have done her bit, at least on a social level, to establish cordial relations with Katkov.)[222] He also had meetings with Slavophile friends and contacts with his own family to occupy him. Yet there were ample opportunities for himself, Yelena and the children to spend time with Georgievsky's wife Marie and their children, with Aleksandr joining them whenever the demands of his job allowed.[223] One Sunday the two families went on a picnic to Tsaritsyno, an estate with picturesque ruins, lakes and summer houses on the outskirts of Moscow once belonging to Catherine the Great.[224] The following day (15 July) they celebrated the name-day of the Georgievskys' young son Volodya together, followed by

Marie's on 22 July and Aleksandr's on 1 August.[225] It also seems likely that Yelena would have accompanied Tyutchev on a pilgrimage made by him at the beginning of July to the great Trinity Monastery at Sergiev Posad outside Moscow.[226]

At the same time he was paying regular visits to the Sushkovs, where he could also see his mother and Nikolay.[227] They were all well aware that Yelena was with him in Moscow. Nikolay had seen her, and was reported to be none too happy at her presence. His sister Darya was more forthright in her disapproval, flatly refusing to go near Tyutchev's rented rooms, where in her words 'a certain individual continues to occupy the place usurped by her'. 'All this angers me beyond measure,' she wrote to Kitty. In Darya's eyes Yelena was very much the cunning predator and Tyutchev her helpless victim. 'My poor brother,' she laments in one letter to Kitty: 'he seems to be completely under the influence of that individual, who should be living a life of humility and repentance instead of treating another woman's husband as her own.' 'What a joy it would be,' she writes in another, 'if only he could put an end to this awful way of life.'[228] One of the more trying aspects of that life as far as Tyutchev was concerned was the constant need to maintain a strict *cordon sanitaire* between not only the two objects of his affection but their respective families too. Thus in Moscow he continued to correspond regularly with Ernestine, but was obliged to do so furtively from his sister's address lest the jealous Yelena discover what to her would have seemed an act of infidelity.[229]

On or about 10 August, after two months away, Tyutchev and Yelena returned to St Petersburg (again no doubt by separate trains).[230] It must have been soon afterwards that their third child was conceived. Later that autumn, following concerted persuasion by Marie, Yelena and Tyutchev (and some string-pulling on the latter's part), Georgievsky accepted a post with the St Petersburg newspaper *Russky invalid* (*The Russian Invalid*) and moved with his family to the northern capital.[231] For Yelena in particular this more than made up for Ernestine's return from Ovstug towards the end of November.[232] That winter she and Tyutchev frequently entertained, and were entertained by, the Georgievskys, contacts which helped her not only to overcome something of her sense of social isolation, but also to feel more closely involved in Tyutchev's political interests and pursuits.[233]

As Yelena's pregnancy drew to an end they discussed the question of names. For her it was self-evident that like its elder siblings the baby should be registered with Tyutchev's surname. He made a feeble attempt to persuade her otherwise, but was met with such a storm of tearful rage (it was the memorable occasion when she damaged the stove by throwing an ornament at him), that he was forced to give in.[234] On 22 May 1864 she was delivered of a boy, Nikolay.[235] Just twelve days before (the timing is unlikely to have been coincidental) Ernestine had left by train for Bad Kissingen with their now 24-year-old daughter Marie.[236] Tyutchev's own preference would have been to go abroad with them,[237] but in the circumstances he had no choice but to stay. Apart from anything else, Yelena's health had for some time been giving cause for concern. A worrying chest complaint meant that windows had to be kept closed against the damp St Petersburg air, and in the evenings her aunt fretted about her sitting too close to smoking candles.[238] For more than a week after giving birth she felt too weak to get up and, when she eventually did, had to take to her bed again the following day.[239] Tyutchev seems to have been more concerned at this stage at the lack of congenial company now that most of his acquaintances had left for the summer.[240] Yelena wrote to the Georgievskys that her 'little God', her 'unamusable Louis XIV' was complaining of boredom.[241] While she struggled to regain her health, he was off joyriding around the Islands every evening with their daughter Lyolya, who had just turned thirteen. Taking advantage of the 'white nights', they would finish off their jaunts with an ice cream together, returning home after midnight.[242]

Further disappointments conspired to prevent Yelena's recovery. After only a few months in St Petersburg, Georgievsky decided to accept an attractive offer to return to Katkov's *Moskovskiye vedomosti*; he, Marie and their children made their farewells and departed for Moscow on 31 May, leaving Yelena inconsolable at the loss of her companions.[243] At about the same time Tyutchev received a message that Nikolay needed to see him in Moscow on family business. 'All this is exasperating, and prevents me from getting any better,' Yelena wrote to her sister.[244] Despite her pleas, on 13 June Tyutchev set off for Moscow. It was a tearful parting on both sides. As Yelena was too unwell to leave the house, Lyolya saw him off at the station instead.[245]

Just over two weeks later, while Tyutchev was still away, Yelena and her aunt moved house. It was at least the fourth time in under two years that financial constraints had forced them to seek cheaper accommodation, and the worry and upheaval must have taken a further toll on her fragile health.[246] A few days later, on 4 July, Tyutchev was back in St Petersburg. He had timed his return to coincide with that of Gorchakov, hoping that in the meantime Yelena's condition would have improved sufficiently for him to be able to apply for a courier mission abroad.[247] Instead he was deeply shocked to see how much she had deteriorated. Consumed with remorse at ever having abandoned her, he now spent every day at her side. On 17 and 18 July Kitty saw her father briefly while passing through on her way abroad and found him very despondent. He told her Yelena was 'very ill' and that he feared for her life.[248] The outlook was indeed bleak, for she had contracted tuberculosis of the lungs, a disease for which there was then no widely accepted treatment.[249]

By the beginning of August Yelena's life had begun to slip away. A priest was summoned to hear her confession and administer the last rites.[250] Tyutchev has left us a record of her final hours:

> All through the day unconscious she had lain,
> And now dark shadows covered her completely.
> Outside upon the leaves warm summer rain
> Was falling — singing softly, sweetly.
>
> And slowly she revived — at length came round,
> And heard the raindrops' gentle sussuration;
> And listened long, enchanted by the sound,
> The while absorbed in lucid contemplation...
>
> Then, as if speaking to herself, she said
> These few words, spoken lucidly and clearly
> (For I was there, alive though surely dead):
> 'All this I loved, I loved so dearly!'

* * * * * * * * * * * *
* * * * * * * * * * * *

You loved, with love as deep as the abyss —
For you that matchless love was all that mattered —
O Lord, that I should live on after *this*...
That still my heart beats on and has not shattered...[251]

Yelena died on 4 August 1864. Three days later she was buried in St Petersburg's Volkovo cemetery. Her gravestone bore the words Tyutchev had heard her utter not long before her death: 'Lord, I believe, and confess my sins...'[252]

15 The Final Years
(St Petersburg, 1864-1873

---

i A Broken Spring

The last word the Georgievskys in Moscow had had of Yelena was a letter from her dated 5 June. Hearing no more, they assumed all must be well.[1] The news of her death, in a distraught and incoherent letter from Tyutchev, came as a bolt from the blue:

St Petersburg. 8 August

Aleksandr Ivanych!

It's all over — yesterday we laid her to rest... What it's all about, what's happened, what I'm writing to you about — I don't know. — Everything inside me is dead: thought, feeling, memory, everything... I feel a complete idiot.

Emptiness, terrible emptiness. — Not even in death can I see any prospect of relief. Oh, I need her here on earth, not somewhere up there...

My heart is empty — my brain exhausted. — Even remembering her — summoning up in memory her living image as she was, looked, moved and spoke — is beyond me.

It's so dreadful — unbearable — I have no strength to write any more — in any case, what is there to write?..

F. Tchv.[2]

With his family scattered abroad (Ernestine and Marie at Bad Kissingen, Darya and Kitty at Arcachon on the Côte d'Argent, Anna touring Germany with the Empress and her retinue), and even neighbours from the other apartments away, Tyutchev had only the remaining servants to keep him company in the big house.[3] He turned all visitors away apart from Polonsky, to whom he had unburdened himself shortly before Yelena's death, and who now did what little he could to comfort him.[4] An exception was also made for Fet, who happened to be in St Petersburg. He arrived to find Tyutchev stretched out on a couch, his head and shoulders swathed in a shawl, shivering uncontrollably with grief. 'At such times there is nothing one can say,' Fet later recalled. 'After a few minutes I pressed his hand and left quietly.'[5]

In his reply to Tyutchev's letter Georgievsky promised to join him just as soon as he could get away. 'Oh, come, come, for the sake of God, and the sooner the better!' Tyutchev wrote back. 'Thank you, I thank you from the bottom of my heart. Perhaps you will be able to lift, if only for a few minutes, this terrible burden, this burning stone which weighs down on me, suffocating me...'[6] Georgievsky arrived on 16 August and spent a few days with his friend. He encouraged him to speak at length of Yelena and his feelings for her, and Tyutchev found some relief in recalling their years together and pouring out his feelings of guilt at having, as he saw it, brought about her ruin. Together they visited the various stations of her life: houses where she had lived, dachas on the Islands, the flat (still home to her aunt Anna Dmitrievna) which had seen her final days, and of course her still fresh grave.

Georgievsky strongly urged Tyutchev to go back with him to Moscow. He would be able to stay at the Sushkovs' house (they had left for the country), spending as much time as he wanted with the Georgievskys, who lived nearby. At such a time he clearly needed to be in the bosom of his family. The question was, which one? He had already informed Ernestine of Yelena's death and made arrangements to join her in Switzerland. Although seriously tempted by Georgievsky's proposal, he decided to stick to his original plan, and Georgievsky returned to Moscow alone.[7]

Tyutchev could count on the sympathy of his immediate family. Ernestine later told one of her stepdaughters: 'for me his grief is sacred, whatever its cause may have been'.[8] There were even expressions of pity for Yelena, now that she was no longer there to appreciate them. 'Poor, poor woman!' the hitherto censorious Darya Sushkova was moved to write. 'May the merciful Lord receive her, she has paid in full for the error of her ways!'[9] Hidden beneath such conventional decencies was a general sense of relief which could be acknowledged only in the most oblique terms. Kitty was presumably not alone in feeling that 'what has happened will have a salutary effect on the life of our family', and in predicting that 'Mama will be very kind to him at this difficult time, first and foremost from the goodness of her heart, but also because this will give her the opportunity of binding him to her more firmly and more genuinely than ever before.'[10]

The family were much exercised by the delicate question of what to do about Tyutchev's illegitimate offspring. On her deathbed Yelena had made him promise to remove Lyolya from her aunt Anna's care; now he appealed to his daughters to make arrangements for all three children. The general consensus was that a sound middle-class upbringing by foster-parents in Switzerland or Germany would provide these unfortunates with a suitable grounding for their future station in life and ensure they avoided the social pretensions which, it was felt, had led to their mother's downfall. However, neither Tyutchev nor Anna Dmitrievna was likely to agree to such a radical separation at the present time, and in any case events had already been partly forestalled by a well-meaning friend of the family, Countess Yulia Stroganova, who shortly after Yelena's death arranged for Lyolya to enter Mlle. Trouba's boarding school in St Petersburg.[11] Lyolya's placement at this fashionable establishment for daughters of the aristocracy was also supported (and possibly paid for) by the school's patroness, Grand Duchess Yelena Pavlovna.[12]

Within a few days of Georgievsky's departure Tyutchev set off for Switzerland.[13] In response to a letter from Anna waiting for him in Berlin he made a detour to see her at Jugenheim near Darmstadt, where she was staying with the Empress.[14] Anna was shocked by her father's appearance: he was mere skin and bone and seemed to have aged by some fifteen years in a matter of weeks. His psychological state struck her as being 'close to madness'; she even feared that he was not long for this world. She found the three days spent with him 'mental torture'.[15] From Jugenheim he travelled in Vyazemsky's company to Geneva, where he was met at the station by Ernestine and

Marie.[16] According to an eyewitness, husband and wife embraced 'with passionate tenderness'.[17] After three weeks at Ouchy near Lausanne, on 26 September/ 8 October they moved into the familiar Hôtel des Bergues in Geneva, occupying the same suite of rooms they had taken as lovers in March 1838. Here Tyutchev found himself surrounded by familiar faces, for the Pfeffels were staying at the same hotel, and they were soon all joined by Kitty and Darya from Arcachon. The two families enjoyed walks and meals together, often rounding off the day with a hand or two of whist.[18] Among other Russians of their acquaintance staying in or near Geneva were the Vyazemskys, Antonina Bludova, Gorchakov and Grand Duchess Yelena Pavlovna.[19]

None of this could distract Tyutchev from his all-consuming grief. 'I can't go on, my friend Aleksandr Ivanych, I can't go on,' he wrote to Georgievsky after ten days in Geneva. 'The wound is festering, not healing... [...] Only with her and for her was I able to be somebody, only in her love, her boundless love for me, was I aware of myself... Now I am something existing to no purpose, a kind of living, doleful nonentity...' He had, he said, tried every known remedy: nature, the society of others, the love and sympathy of his family; but like opium they had only deadened the pain for a while before wearing off. 'The only small ray of comfort I have known is when — as for example with the Petrovs here, who loved her so well — I have been able to speak of her to my heart's content'.[20] He had agreed to a regime of prayer and fasting under Father Afanasy Petrov's spiritual guidance to prepare him for confession and holy communion, something last undertaken after the death of Eleonore.[21] Clearly he was struggling under the same weight of guilt as then. A few hours before making his confession he wrote to Darya (then still in France): 'Oh, pray for me. Ask God to grant me grace, grace, grace! [...] Oh, may she herself intercede for me, she who must feel my distress, my anguish, my despair, and must suffer in consequence — she who prayed so much — prayed so much during her life on earth, which I filled with bitterness and grief and which despite this never ceased to be a prayer — a tearful prayer to God.'[22]

On 12/24 October, after nearly six weeks in Switzerland, they left Geneva and headed for Nice, where the imperial family were wintering.[23] The natural splendours of lake and mountains, so appealing in the past, had brought him as little consolation as his attempts at religious observance. The day before their departure the chill north wind which had blown for some time dropped suddenly; the sun rose in a clear sky, and as morning wore on it seemed for a moment as if summer had returned in all its glory. He took a last walk by the lake, enjoying the unexpected warmth, the autumnal colouring of the trees, the clear views across calm azure waters to distant peaks as far as Mont Blanc. All this transient beauty he captured in verse, as if wishing to preserve it for ever. Yet even now all was overshadowed by thoughts of Yelena. The poem ends with the poignant cry:

> Here all the pain and the distress
> Could swiftly from my heart be banned
> If only in my native land
> I knew there to be one grave less...[24]

At Nice they were reunited with Anna, already there in her capacity as governess to the imperial couple's daughter, while Darya resumed her duties as Maid of Honour.

Kitty had meanwhile returned to Russia.[25] The winter that followed should by any normal reckoning have been one of the happier times in Tyutchev's life, offering all the glitter, gossip and political interest of the Russian court, transported as if by magic from the icy cold of St Petersburg to the balmy shores of the Mediterranean. Now all these delights were as ashes in his mouth. Anna found her father, if not as overwrought as at Jugenheim, 'still immersed in the same misery of painful regrets, the same desolation at the loss of earthly joys', and was distressed to see his grief provoke him into 'irritation, acrimony, injustice towards his wife and the rest of us'.[26] Already in Geneva he had found the impossibility of discussing his grief with Ernestine deeply frustrating, and had upset her by confiding in his daughters instead.[27]

But it was only in letters to the Georgievskys and Polonsky that he was able to vent his feelings of despair and hopelessness to the full. 'My friend, now everything has been tried. — Nothing has helped, nothing has brought consolation, — I can't go on — can't go on — can't go on...' Life had become an 'incessant torture', a 'mutilation',[28] bringing only the 'torments of hell', of which he had previously had as little conception as of life beyond the grave.[29] The feeling that he had been condemned to a kind of living death pervades these letters from Nice. Attempts to digress on current political developments are broken off with such comments as: 'enough of trying to galvanise my dead soul... It cannot be brought back to life';[30] or: 'I have been stupidly distracted into discussing matters of concern to the living, but of none to me. Tomorrow, 4 February, it will be six months since I ceased to be one of their number.'[31] Yelena's death, he declared, had quite simply 'broken the spring of [my] life'.[32]

By the end of the year he was bitterly regretting his decision not to go to Moscow. Too late now he persuaded himself that there, supported by Georgievsky's family and involved in his journalistic activities, 'I should have been able somehow to work my way through the pain of my grief'; whereas in Nice, surrounded by those to whom any mention of Yelena was unwelcome, 'I have simply driven the illness inside my organism and made it incurable.'[33] All he yearned for now was to return to 'where something of her still remains: her children, her friends, all the poor circumstances of her domestic life, in which there was so much love and so much grief'.[34] Ernestine noted this quite uncharacteristic impulse, the reasons for which can have been no mystery. 'My husband [...] does not like Nice and is homesick for Russia,' she wrote to her brother Karl in December.[35] Tyutchev himself acknowledged that 'no amount of bright December sunshine, nor this clear warm sky, nor this sea, these olive and wild orange trees can blot out the feelings of alienation and forlornness.'[36]

It was barely four years since Nice had been ceded to France by the kingdom of Piedmont-Sardinia, and it struck him as a cruel irony of fate that his suffering should be played out not only in what had been the imagined land of his ancestors, but in that part of it associated with the other great loss endured by him. 'Italy has played a curious role in my life,' he wrote soon after leaving the area. 'Twice it has appeared to me as a funereal vision after the two greatest sorrows it has been my lot to experience... There are countries where mourning is worn in bright colours. It seems that I hail from those countries...'[37]

But it was in poetry that the agony of that winter found its most striking expression:

386

This Nice, this fabled southern winter...
This glare that leaves me pierced and battered...
Like some poor victim of the hunter
Life struggles feebly on, though shattered...
All hopes of flight extinguished, huddling
With broken wing and trailing feather,
It cowers in the dust, still trembling
With pain and helplessness together...[38]

At the end of December Tyutchev sent this and two other poems dedicated to Yelena's memory to Georgievsky, requesting that all three be published in Katkov's journal *Russky vestnik* (*The Russian Messenger*). One was the poem recalling Yelena's last hours ('All through the day unconscious she had lain...'), another his evocation of Lake Geneva in autumn, its beauty now forever vitiated by thoughts of her grave.[39] Soon afterwards he added a fourth, a picture in words of the Mediterranean by night composed at the beginning of January.[40] Here, as before in 'You, my wave upon the ocean...', the fathomless sea with its shifting moods and powerful allure conjures up the essence of Yelena herself. The final stanza echoes that of the earlier poem, although now with much darker and perhaps more literal connotations:

All in the midst of this turmoil, this splendour,
As in a dream I stand — lost, loath to go —
Would that I could to their beauty surrender:
Would that my heart I could drown far below...[41]

In letters to Georgievsky Tyutchev emphasised that he saw the printing of these tributes to Yelena's memory as an act of atonement and restitution. He could not forget how four years before at Baden-Baden he had fallen out with her over the question of publication, and now he felt driven to make symbolic amends.[42] Usually so indifferent to the fate of his verse, he took for once an uncharacteristically active approach, even stipulating the order in which the poems were to be printed. He also insisted that they be published as they stood, without cuts. 'Any who may take offence at them will offend me even more,' he declared in a clear reference to his own family. He asked for his name to be given in full as author, agreeing to the abbreviation 'T.' after representations from Georgievsky and Katkov only because he knew it would prove a fairly transparent disguise.[43]

As was to be expected, the quartet of poems ruffled some feathers when published in the February issue of Katkov's journal. Ivan Aksakov resented his own *Den'* being passed over for poems of such quality and had to field awkward questions on the subject from friends and sympathisers unaware of Tyutchev's quasi-familial relationship to Katkov's assistant Georgievsky.[44] Anna and Kitty no doubt reflected the wider views of the family in their expressions of displeasure. For Anna the publication was all of a piece with her father's behaviour in Nice, where she was pained to see 'how incontinently he gives way to his despair, making no attempt whatever to conceal or control it, even before strangers'. He in turn took umbrage at being expected to exercise more self-control, perceiving this as a callous response to his plight.[45] Such tensions within the family made Anna only too glad that, like Darya and Kitty, she had already flown the nest. She felt sorry for the remaining daughter, Marie, whom she saw 'suffering and withering away in this closed circle of mutual incomprehension'.[46] Yet unknown to anyone Marie had already decided on a way out. According to the construction later put on events by Tyutchev, she had found 'her existence in the parental home so perfectly dull — despite all the affection with which she was surrounded there — that in order to escape she rushed headlong into the most absurd of marriages.' All this he blamed on Ernestine's placidity and lack of sociability, conveniently overlooking any characteristics of his own which may have played a part.[47]

Marie's choice had fallen on a forty-one-year-old naval officer and aide-de-camp to the Tsar, Nikolay Birilyov, who commanded a frigate in the naval squadron then anchored off Nice in connection with the imperial family's visit. A veteran of the Crimean War, he had been decorated for valour during the defence of Sevastopol. Unfortunately, severe shell shock had permanently impaired his mental faculties and left him subject to epileptic fits. At the Admiral's New Year ball Marie danced through the night with him, captivated by his tales of the Sevastopol campaign, and returned home to tell her parents she had met the man of her dreams.[48] Three weeks later Birilyov formally asked for Marie's hand in marriage. According to Anna, her parents 'agreed to everything in mute rage, our simpleton noticed nothing of this, and now poor Marie has to endure the most terrible scenes.' Ernestine found it impossible to relate to this straightforward military man's lack of breeding and social graces, not to mention his insistence on speaking Russian, while Tyutchev was more concerned about the brain damage.[49] He later told Polonsky (who in the spring of 1864 had himself unsuccessfully proposed to Marie) that he could not understand what his daughter saw in Birilyov, whose injuries had made him 'quite simply an idiot'. It had been clear to him from the start that her desire to mother an invalid was no foundation for marital happiness, but Anna and more importantly the Empress had championed Birilyov's cause, making it difficult for him to withhold consent.[50] Marie also stood her ground, and on 5/17 February, little more than three weeks after announcing their engagement, she and Birilyov were married at Nice.[51] By the following year, as his condition deteriorated further, Marie was regretting her hasty decision. Her diary for May 1866 contains the heartfelt cry: 'Mama was right, right, right!'[52]

On 3/15 March, Tyutchev and Ernestine left Nice for St Petersburg. It was time to return: apart from anything else, the new censorship statute, so long in gestation, was about to be promulgated, and it seemed advisable (as Gorchakov pointed out) for Tyutchev to be at his post at what could be a time of sweeping administrative changes.[53] Ten days spent en route in Paris were a kind of homecoming for Tyutchev after the exile and alienation of Nice, a town summed up by him as 'no more after all than the most picturesquely poetic, most resplendently fragrant backwater'.[54] From the French capital he wrote to Anna: 'It is true that in Paris the *genius loci* has always looked kindly on me. I love this place.' Conversations with figures of influence at the court of Napoleon III and attendance at a session of parliament brought him up to date with latest developments.[55] He met Ivan Turgenev at a pavement café and was overcome with grief while speaking of Yelena; as they parted, Turgenev noticed that the front of Tyutchev's shirt was soaked with tears.[56] He also arranged a meeting with

Aleksandr Herzen.[57] It would be fascinating to know what exactly the chairman of the Foreign Censorship Committee and the publisher of the banned expatriate newspaper *Kokokol* found to talk about, but no detailed record survives. Possibly they thought it best to stick to the neutral ground of French politics. All that Herzen later revealed of their conversation was that Tyutchev told an anecdote ridiculing Napoleon III's measures against alleged 'conspirators';[58] in view of his liberal attitude towards political dissent, this was perhaps one area where he and Herzen could agree.

There was distressing news for him when he and Ernestine arrived in St Petersburg on 26 March/7 April: little Lyolya, now nearly fourteen years old, had contracted the same disease that had carried off her mother.[59] Placing her at Mlle. Trouba's boarding school had, as predicted by Tyutchev's family, not proved to be the wisest of decisions. After her mother's death she had continued to believe what she had always been told, namely that her parents were legally wed and that Anna, Darya and Kitty were her half-sisters from a previous marriage. Not unnaturally, she made a point of telling her aristocratic classmates that two of her sisters were Maids of Honour at court, and even claimed to have received gifts from the Empress's daughter via Anna. When word of this reached Alexander and his consort in Nice, they let their anger be known to Anna, who feared for her position and was strengthened in her resolve to move Lyolya to Switzerland.

Before any steps could be taken in that direction there was a further mishap at the school, this time with more serious consequences. An aristocratic lady came to visit her daughter after a lengthy absence abroad and was introduced to her classmate and friend Lyolya Tyutcheva. She asked Lyolya why she was in mourning, and was perplexed when told it was for her mother, for she had seen Ernestine in good health only days before (presumably in Nice). Further questioning left no doubt in the lady's mind as to the scandalous truth; she turned on her heel and walked away without a parting word. Deeply upset, Lyolya confronted her great-aunt Anna, who was forced to admit to the pretence kept up for so many years. Lyolya refused to return to Mlle. Trouba's and went into a decline, sobbing for hours at a time, not sleeping and refusing to eat. Georgievsky believed it was this emotional upheaval that triggered the tuberculosis already dormant within her and allowed it to develop unchecked.[60] Whatever the truth of this, she seems also to have infected her infant brother Kolya (Nikolay), who was still less than a year old. Both children died on the same day, 2 May 1865, and were buried next to their mother in the Volkovo cemetery.[61] Their four-year-old brother Fedya was spared.

Tyutchev had been sustained throughout his wretched exile abroad by the thought of seeing his and Yelena's children again, in particular Lyolya, whom according to Georgievsky he 'especially loved and even spoilt, sometimes to the detriment of sound educational requirements'.[62] Now even that consolation had been snatched from him. A few weeks after their death he turned up at Polonsky's door looking frail and unsteady. 'The poor old man had come to see me,' Polonsky told a friend, 'evidently not knowing what to do with himself from emptiness of spirit and grief.' Tyutchev recalled the events of the previous summer: Yelena's illness, his abandonment of her to go to Moscow, Lyolya seeing him off at the station. 'And now none of them is alive!' he exclaimed. 'Yet a year ago their disappearance seemed as impossible to me as that of the sun, the moon, and blessings of that sort.'[63] Not long afterwards he confessed in a letter to Marie Georgievskaya that since Yelena's death not a day had dawned without his feeling 'a certain amazement that a person can carry on living after his head has been cut off or his heart torn out'.[64] Daily he dragged himself to the apartment of Yelena's aunt Anna, each time dreading a return to the scene of his beloved's final days and hours, yet still preferring the searing pain of reawakened memories to the blank deadness of spirit that had become his usual state. What drew him there was little Fedya, cared for by a nanny under Anna Dmitrievna's direction. He kept a watchful eye on the boy, relieved that he showed no signs of the dreaded disease. Desperately clutching at any link with Yelena, he also sought out former friends and classmates who had stuck to her during the years of social ostracism; but as with everything else, he found this brought little relief.[65]

15 July was the fifteenth anniversary of that 'fateful-blissful day' when he and Yelena had become lovers. He commemorated the event in a poem intended apparently only for Georgievsky's eyes (it remained unpublished for nearly four decades).[66] Just over a week later he and Ernestine left for Ovstug with the Birilyovs.[67] He had not visited his birthplace in eight years and had no great desire to do so now, but financial losses incurred by the sugar-beet refinery on the estate demanded urgent attention. An expert hired to look into matters on the spot had reported abuses by Vasily Strelkov, the estate manager.[68] Rumoured to be the illegitimate son of Tyutchev's father, who had freed him from serfdom and appointed him estate manager in the first place, Strelkov was now apparently busy lining his pockets at his employers' expense (in the event he was dismissed and the refinery leased to a local factory-owner).[69] For Tyutchev, never a devotee of rural seclusion, the prospect of having to sort out such tiresome practical matters will scarcely have added to the appeal. One compensation was time spent in Moscow on both the outward and return journeys — some four weeks in total — when he was able to visit the Georgievskys regularly at their new apartment on Malaya Dmitrovka and enjoy social occasions and outings with them.[70]

He and Ernestine left Moscow on 3 August for the three-day journey by road to Ovstug.[71] That evening at one of the coaching stations on the Kaluga road he felt the need to stretch his legs after being cooped up in the carriage for hours on end. Most likely he chose as many travellers did then to walk on ahead while the horses were changed, instructing the coachman to pick him up further down the road. Although the fresh air and exercise were welcome, his mood was sombre, for tomorrow it would be exactly a year since Yelena had died. As he reflected on this in the gathering gloom, verses formed in his head to which he later gave the title 'On the Eve of the Anniversary of 4 August 1864'. Unpublished in his lifetime, the poem expresses his grief for Yelena perhaps more poignantly than any other in the Denisyeva canon. As Vadim Kozhinov has observed, we hear in it for the first time since her death 'the melody of sorrowful resignation'.[72] Tyutchev struggles to imagine her departed spirit watching over him, much in the same way as that of the woman (Eleonore?) in 'Day turns to evening, dusk draws nigh...' Yet whereas in that poem the thought had comforted him, here it serves merely to heighten his still acute sense of loss. On the other hand the raw feelings of anger and denial which had overwhelmed him at the time of Yelena's death appear to have subsided, replaced by the resignation spoken of by Kozhinov. Then he had railed: 'I need her here on earth, not somewhere up there'; now 'somewhere up there' has become the focus of his anguished yearning, while earthly existence is marked only by images of weariness, twilight and grief.

> Dusk falls as I trudge the lonely highway,
> All around is still as night grows near...
> Heavy is my heart, my limbs are weary...
> Oh, my dearest, can you see me here?
>
> Over me I watch the darkness gather,
> Watch day's last pale gleamings disappear...
> In this world we two once lived together:
> Dearest angel, can you see me here?
>
> Now a day of memory appalling,
> Given to prayer and grief, is drawing near...
> From wherever spirits have their dwelling,
> Dearest angel, can you see me here?[73]

ii By Faith Alone

The new law on censorship was promulgated on 6 April 1865, just a few days after Tyutchev's return from abroad, and came into force on 1 September. Eight years in the making, and originally intended as a comprehensive replacement for Nicholas I's statute of 1828, it turned out to be a confusing patchwork of what were said to be 'provisional' new measures superimposed upon others retained from the past. Those like Tyutchev who had argued for greater freedom of expression found it disappointing. Although preliminary censorship was abolished for books over a certain length and for periodicals published in St Petersburg and Moscow, the law provided an impressive array of post-publication sanctions for the government to call on as required. As far as books were concerned, the authorities were empowered to seize any deemed offensive, pending future legal action (which in practice rarely materialised). For periodicals a system of '*avertissements*' was introduced, based on that adopted by Napoleon III in France, which gave the Minister of the Interior powers to issue official cautions to newspapers and journals. After a third caution he could order the periodical in question to cease publication for a period of up to six months or apply to the Senate to have it closed down permanently. A special body, the Council on Press Affairs, was established to advise him in these matters.[74]

Tyutchev was at least relieved that his job had not disappeared. The Foreign Censorship Committee survived, and as its chairman he now found himself *ex officio* also a member of the new Council on Press Affairs. On 30 August he even received a promotion, his first in eight years, to the grade of Privy Councillor (third in the Table of Ranks, equivalent to Lieutenant-General).[75] This was to be the summit of his service career. Realising that much depended on the spirit in which the new censorship rules were applied, he and another member persuaded the Press Council at one of its first meetings to agree on a statement of intent emphasising the provisional nature of the new rules and distancing the Council from the arbitrary way in which the system of '*avertissements*' was applied in France. The members voted to publish the statement in the official press, but this was vetoed by the Minister of the Interior, Pyotr Valuyev.[76] Although Tyutchev hoped the Council would nevertheless be able to implement the guidelines it had adopted, too often in practice it was powerless to prevent cautions being served on the independent press. Eventually he was driven to protest to the Minister in person. He believed that banning subversive thought merely lent it a spurious glamour and authority out of all proportion to its true significance, and that it would soon wither if subjected to the glare of public debate. Unfortunately there was little sympathy for this view in ruling circles, even among those who, like Valuyev himself, claimed to be liberals.[77]

On 31 March 1866 Valuyev issued Katkov's *Moskovskiye vedomosti* with a caution for its attacks on the government, overruling an almost unanimous vote to the contrary by the Council on Press Affairs. Katkov defiantly refused to print the caution in his newspaper as required by law, aware that if he persisted he would have to pay a daily fine for up to three months, after which his publication would be closed down. Tyutchev wrote to Georgievsky urging that his chief swallow his pride and print the caution, as the loss of *Moskovskiye vedomosti* would be a disaster for the nationalist cause.[78] Katkov, determined by now on a duel to the death, ignored the advice. Then on 4 April a young radical extremist, Dmitry Karakozov, made an unsuccessful attempt on the life of the Tsar. The ensuing atmosphere of reaction encouraged Valuyev to step up his campaign against the press. On 7 May he called an extraordinary meeting of the Press Council and to the members' surprise took the chair himself, telling them they had been summoned to give legal sanction to the government's decision to close down *Moskovskiye vedomosti*. He announced that a second caution had already been issued the previous day and called on them to draft for his signature a third, which would result in the newspaper's closure for two months. They were also asked to approve similar measures against the journal *Sovremennik* and other periodicals. They proceeded to endorse the proposed action without further debate. The only dissenting voice was Tyutchev's: declaring his opposition both to the Minister's demands and the Council's decision, he stormed out of the room. One other member, the writer Ivan Goncharov, ran after him to shake him by the hand, saying he would gladly have joined his protest but could not afford to lose his job. Tyutchev went straight home and wrote Valuyev a letter of resignation from the Council. That evening he dined with the recently appointed conservative Minister of Education, Count Dmitry Tolstoy, who was outraged at what he heard and a few days later pleaded Katkov's case with the Tsar.[79] Tyutchev had already enlisted Gorchakov's support;[80] his cousin Mikhail Muravyov, now heading the commission of enquiry into the Karakozov affair, was also prepared to take Katkov's side.[81] The backing of these influential figures evidently persuaded the Tsar to reverse Valuyev's decision. At a personal audience granted to Katkov in Moscow on 20 June Alexander told him he was free to resume publication of his newspaper, which from now on would enjoy his, the Tsar's, personal protection. Within days *Moskovskiye vedomosti* was again rolling off the presses.[82]

On 30 June Tyutchev celebrated this 'complete victory' by resuming his place on the Council on Press Affairs.[83] Yet despite his role in Katkov's triumph he was beginning to cool towards him. Not only did he feel his intransigence in the affair had been counterproductive, but more importantly began to find himself frequently at odds with the line on foreign policy taken by *Moskovskiye vedomosti*.[84] He had in any case always been ideologically closer to Ivan Aksakov and his newspaper *Den'*. These ties were further strengthened in January 1866 when the prominent Slavophile became his son-in-law. For as long as possible Anna had put off revealing their desire to be wed, fearing (as in Marie's case) an adverse reaction from her father; but when eventually approached he was only too happy to give his blessing, relieved that his nearly thirty-seven-year-old daughter had at last found not just a partner, but one as eminently suitable in his eyes as Aksakov.[85]

Anna had to resign her post at court on marriage, and she and her husband settled in Moscow. At the same time, to Tyutchev's great regret, falling circulation and associated financial problems forced his new son-in-law to cease publication of *Den'*.[86] Before too long, however, Aksakov found himself involved in negotiations with representatives of Moscow's merchant community to publish a newspaper championing their interests. This was to have a business and financial bias, but would also contain a substantial political section reflecting Aksakov's views as editor. The new daily, *Moskva* (*Moscow*), began publication in January 1867.[87] Tyutchev actively collaborated in the enterprise, regularly supplying Aksakov with detailed analyses of foreign affairs and advice on leader articles, as well as inside information gleaned from his contacts in government circles. On at least one occasion this included secret intelligence obtained by the Foreign Ministry, which he was careful to stipulate should be used for background information only.[88] Correspondence between himself, Aksakov, Katkov and others had to be delivered by relatives or trusted acquaintances travelling between Moscow and St Petersburg, for the Third Section had reverted to old habits of intercepting mail.[89] Even before the first issue of *Moskva* appeared an official of the Finance Ministry was sacked after Aksakov had incautiously named him in a private letter as one of several government employees prepared to supply the newspaper with information. Count Pyotr Shuvalov, the new Head of the Third Section appointed in the wake of the Karakozov affair, was more than ready to co-operate with Valuyev in his campaign against the free press.[90] Yet despite these difficulties Tyutchev was able to keep Aksakov constantly informed and to influence the paper's editorial line on a number of important issues. One of the sources of information to whom he was closest, Gorchakov, was once even heard to remark with apparent naivety on *Moskva*'s accuracy in anticipating government policy.[91] (Whether Gorchakov had in fact sanctioned at least some of these leaks for his own political purposes we shall probably never know).

Having failed to silence Katkov, Valuyev had Aksakov firmly in his sights. Ignoring a vote against by the Council on Press Affairs, he served *Moskva* with its first caution less than three weeks after it had begun publication. Ironically, France had just recently abolished the system of '*avertissements*'; how long, Tyutchev wondered, would Russians persist in wearing this 'legislative crinoline' after it had fallen from fashion in Paris?[92]

Cautions continued to rain down on *Moskva* with depressing regularity: a total of nine over the 22 months of its existence (January 1867 to October 1868), during which period it was ordered to suspend publication on three occasions (for three, four and six months respectively). Following the third suspension it was closed down permanently after referral to the Senate.[93]

Tyutchev did what little he could behind the scenes to defend *Moskva*, but it was a losing battle, and he had ruefully to accept the role of 'a veritable Don Quixote' tilting ineffectively against 'this combination of stupidity and mediocrity armed with omnipotent and arbitrary power, of which the Press Council is after all no more than the figurehead.'[94] Although in practice most of his efforts were inevitably on behalf of Aksakov and other political allies, he fought for the principle of free speech as such and was equally prepared when necessary to take up the cudgels on behalf of his opponents.[95] He was in that respect more truly a liberal than many for whom the tag was little more than a badge of expediency during the period of reform. To the end he maintained his belief that freedom of expression and a free press were quite compatible with the principle of autocracy — but only in some ideal Russia in which autocracy was vested in the person of the sovereign alone and not the bureaucratic machine.[96] Whether this could ever have worked in practice is impossible to say. (The one serious historical experiment of the kind in Russia to date — Mikhail Gorbachov's attempt to combine *glasnost'* with one-party rule — would suggest the contrary, although of course undertaken in circumstances far removed from those envisaged by Tyutchev.)

Tyutchev's views on autocracy were very close to those of the Slavophiles. He defended it not as a universally applicable principle but a home-grown institution uniquely suited to Russia's historical and national characteristics. 'Only in our soil can it take root, outside of our soil it is simply inconceivable,' he once wrote of it.[97] For this reason he was quite happy to praise Thiers's efforts in establishing a republic after the fall of France in 1870, and indeed to predict that republicanism was the way ahead for the rest of Europe. Only in Russia did monarchy have a future, and only then if it 'becomes more and more national, for without national character — a vigorous and conscious national character — the Russian autocracy is a nonsense.'[98] Like the Slavophiles, he opposed any move to import parliamentary democracy, seeing it as an exotic growth unsuited to local conditions. A national representative council with purely consultative functions (something on the lines of the pre-Petrine *Zemsky sobor*, or Assembly of the Land) might well appear in the fulness of time, but it must do so *organically*, growing from within, and not be imposed from without.[99] Slavophiles liked to think of the state (as indeed did many Western conservatives) as a living organism developing over time according to internal laws of its own, rather than as a rational construct or mechanism of human design. For Tyutchev this is what set his ideal of Russian autocracy apart from the 'crudely materialistic and atheist absolutism' of Western origin which according to him was increasingly favoured by Russian ruling circles and even the Tsar himself.[100] In his view the only true and lasting authority was the moral variety that drew its strength from positive convictions and belief; that which grew only from the barrel of a gun was ultimately doomed to fail. One of his most prophetic political insights was that negative brute force alone, far from crushing sedition, succeeds only in fanning its flames. As he put it towards the end of his life: 'If for want of principles and moral convictions power resorts to measures of material repression, it becomes by so doing the most appalling accomplice of negation and of revolutionary subversion, but begins to be aware of this only when the evil is already irreparable.'[101] The relevance of this to the subsequent course of Russian history scarcely needs to be pointed out.

During his final years he witnessed the ominous first stirrings of forces that would eventually destroy everything he believed in. His comments on these are interesting in the extreme. Like many others at the time he mistakenly thought the lone would-be assassin Karakozov to be part of a wider conspiracy with its roots in the Polish émigré community. Yet although he favoured strong measures to combat such acts of terrorism, he also argued that any general return to the reactionary ways of Nicholas I would be a mistake: 'By forcibly suppressing thought — even in the area of nihilist teachings — we shall only exacerbate and add to the harm'.[102] In the summer of 1871 he took a close interest in the trial of 77 suspected revolutionaries, daily attending the court as a spectator. As the 'absolute insignificance of the individuals concerned and of their acts' became apparent to him during the proceedings, the large number put on trial ceased to be alarming and seemed instead merely ridiculous.[103] Welcoming as 'fair' the final verdict acquitting well over half of the accused, he commented: 'The evil is present, but where is the remedy? What can a power without any conviction of its own achieve against such misguided but fervently held convictions? In a word, all the insipid materialism of the government against this revolutionary materialism?' One bright spot in all this as far as he was concerned was the efficiency and impartiality of court proceedings as provided for by the legal reforms of 1864 (in the preparation of which his friend Count Dmitry Bludov had played a leading role). Here at least was one Western institution which seemed able to thrive in Russian soil. He was particularly impressed by the judges and lawyers, detecting in their professionalism 'the powerful germ of a new Russia, and the best guarantee of its future.'[104]

Yet all too often this 'new Russia' remained a distant and elusive goal. In August 1867 Marie wrote to him from Ovstug of increasing immorality and drunkenness among the local peasantry and priesthood, children dying from lack of care, and other social evils. He replied that what she described was unfortunately not confined to the environs of Ovstug: '*Dissolution* is everywhere. We are heading for the abyss, not as a result of recklessness but of indifference.' The 'vacuity and lack of conscience' ('*inconscience et manque de conscience*') of those in power had reduced the country's finances to a parlous state, inviting comparison with Hamlet's 'Something is rotten in the state of Denmark'.[105] Faced on another occasion with the same exasperating disparity between ideal and reality, he commented: 'One should understand once and for all that there is nothing serious in Russia but Russia itself. '[106] With some allowance for hyperbole we can accept Ivan Aksakov's assertion that Tyutchev's ardent faith in this mystical concept — this 'Russia itself ' — preoccupied him 'at the level of some elemental force, more compelling than any other, personal feeling.'[107] Only such an absolute, unquestioning faith could withstand the onslaught of discouraging evidence to the contrary registered by the intellect. That is the message of some epigrammatic lines written in November 1867 which both in Russia and beyond have acquired the distinction of becoming Tyutchev's most frequently quoted (and often parodied) utterance:

> Who would grasp Russia with the mind?
> For her no yardstick was created:
> Her soul is of a special kind,
> By faith alone appreciated.[108]

Not long after these lines were written Ernestine told her brother that Tyutchev was now content to live in Russia and no longer felt the urge to spend even short periods anywhere else. The unhappy experience of his last visit abroad, followed by renewed absorption in the cultural and intellectual life of his own country during the period of reform, had apparently cured him of his long-standing and persistent occidento-philia.[109]

At the same time he never turned his gaze inwards or ceased to ponder the question of Russia's relationship to the world at large. Foreign affairs had always been his his central and consuming passion, and this did not change. Having long predicted a struggle for hegemony between Prussia and Austria now that Russia, weakened by the Crimean defeat, was no longer able to exert a restraining influence, he was not surprised when war broke out between the two countries in June 1866 over Bismarck's proposals to unify Germany under Prussian leadership. He even welcomed the conflict, believing such internal strife between Western powers to be Russia's only certain guarantee against renewed attack, and was dismayed when the Tsar (motivated in his caustic judgement purely by 'affectionate solicitude for [his] poor German kinsfolk') made attempts to mediate.[110] He went so far as to draft a personal letter to Alexander strongly advising him against such a step (whether this was actually sent is not clear).[111] In the event the Russian government's proposal for a European congress to broker a peaceful agreement between Prussia and Austria foundered on lack of support from the other major powers. In Tyutchev's sardonic view Gorchakov and his fellow ministers had been saved from boarding the wrong train by arriving too late at the station.[112]

Immediately after Prussia's victory he predicted a coming war between that country and France, and again argued it was in Russia's interests to encourage 'such perpetual internecine war in the West'.[113] In this case he believed Russia should not remain neutral, but actively support Prussia against France and her likely ally Austria: this, he reasoned, would offer the chance of 'regaining' vital Slav territories from the Austrians, in particular Galicia and the Carpathian chain.[114] While accepting that after the Crimean setback a waiting game and the adoption of new and more subtle tactics were required, he never abandoned as long-term goal his dream of a great Graeco-Slavonic Empire under Russian domination. In January 1867 he criticised an article on the Eastern Question by the historian Sergey Solovyov in Aksakov's *Moskva* which argued that as the Ottoman Empire collapsed Russia should enable its Slav and Orthodox peoples to establish their own independent states. 'No, Russia's relationship to the Graeco-Slavonic world is not at all like that,' he wrote to Aksakov. 'It's not just a matter of a juxtaposition of parts, but of the living, mutual, organic interconnectedness of a single whole.'[115] The point had been made more clearly in a letter to Georgievsky the previous year. Here he maintained that throughout eastern Europe 'there can be no place for *separate sovereign states*, as in western Europe, — that for all these lands and peoples there is not and cannot be any lawful supreme power outside of Russia, outside of Russian autocratic rule'.[116]

While most of the Slavs looked to Russia as a powerful ally in their struggle for independence, few were prepared to endorse Tyutchev's blueprint for unification. This became particularly apparent during the so-called Slavonic Congress held in May 1867.[117] 84 delegates from the Slav lands — Czechs, Slovaks, Serbs, Croats, Bulgarians and others (but not the Poles) — were invited to spend nearly a month in Russia at the time of the All-Russian Ethnographic Exhibition in Moscow. Once the idea of such a congress had been given official blessing, it was enthusiastically promoted by Aksakov and others in the Slavophile press, while fundraising and practical arrangements were taken in hand by the Moscow and St Petersburg Slavonic Philanthropic Committees. The congress took place against a politically charged background as far as the Austrian Slavs were concerned. The authority of the Habsburg monarchy had been seriously weakened by successive military defeats at the hands of Italians, French and Prussians, forcing Austria's rulers to consider constitutional reforms as a way of preventing the break-up of their Empire. The most prominent Czech delegate to the congress, Frantisek Palacky, continued to advocate the 'Austroslav' model of a federation of equal states organised on ethnic lines. However, the predominance this would have given to the Slavs, who formed a majority of the Empire's population, was clearly unacceptable to the country's German-speaking rulers. At the beginning of 1867 they decided instead on the ingenious arrangement known as the Dual Monarchy, under which they agreed to share power with the Magyars. This left the Slavs subservient in both parts of the Empire, especially so in Hungary. 'You look after your barbarians, and we shall look after ours,' the new Hungarian Premier Count Andrassy is reported to have told Austria's Foreign Minister von Beust,[118] who in turn was credited with saying: 'The Slavs must be driven to the wall.' For the Czech delegates in particular, who formed the largest contingent, attendance at the Slavonic Congress became an act of political protest against the new dispensation.

During the time they were in Russia (from 8 May to 2 June, divided roughly equally between St Petersburg and Moscow) the delegates were treated to a programme of lavish hospitality and organised events somewhat reminiscent of the 'culture and friendship' jamborees of later Soviet times. On arrival at St Petersburg's Warsaw station they were greeted by a waiting crowd of about two thousand and after the traditional welcoming ceremony with bread and salt escorted to their accommodation in the city's best hotel, the Bellevue on Nevsky Prospekt. Both in St Petersburg and Moscow there were banquets with the obligatory toasts and speeches, guided tours of the sights, visits to theatres and concerts and meetings with a series of officials and groups. Resolutions were passed on the strengthening of cultural, scientific and economic ties.

Mindful of Austrian sensibilities, the organisers of the congress were initially at pains to stress its unofficial and non-political nature. This was not to Tyutchev's liking. He persuaded one of the chief organisers, the scholar and publicist Vladimir Lamansky, to invite the Minister of Education Dmitry Tolstoy to a banquet on 11 May, arguing that his presence would give the occasion 'that note of official character which is after all desirable'.[119] Tolstoy attended and gave a speech, and afterwards laid on two dinners for the delegates himself, all apparently with the Emperor's enthusiastic approval.[120] Even more significant was a reception for some of the delegates given by Gorchakov. He told them (no doubt with Tyutchev's prior encouragement): 'I as a Russian and a Slav shall always pursue a Slav policy and do all in my power to support Slav progress.' He also expressed the hope that his successors would be able to achieve more in this respect. Finally, on 14 May, the Tsar himself warmly welcomed 23 of the delegates at an audience at Tsarskoye Selo.[121]

At the banquet on 11 May, which Tyutchev also attended, a poem composed by him for the occasion was read out. Entitled 'To the Slavs', it welcomed the delegates to Russia not as guests but as members of one great family:

> You are at home here in our country:
> Much more, indeed, than in your own —
> Here, where subjection to those speaking
> A foreign tongue remains unknown

The Slavs were 'a single people', 'brothers', 'the offspring of a single womb'. Only the absent Poles — 'our Judas' — had deserted the family and gone over to the common enemy (a curious comment on a people which had suffered such even-handed depredations from its western and eastern neighbours alike). The poem concluded with a look forward to the glorious day of unification, when 'the cry "Tsar-liberator"/ Will echo beyond Russian soil.'[122] The reading was frequently interrupted by applause and cries of 'bravo!', and at the end Tyutchev was besieged by those wishing to embrace the author or shake him by the hand.[123] It was perhaps his moment of supreme fame for a kind of verse which he himself conceded in a letter to Aksakov to be 'worthless' and no more than 'empty rodomontade'.[124] Although he approved of the views expressed in them, Aksakov too was honest enough to admit the aesthetic inferiority of these rhymed tracts, large quantities of which Tyutchev churned out in the 'national' cause during the last years of his life.[125]

Why the author of 'Silentium!', 'Sea Stallion' and the Denisyeva poems should have stooped to such banalities is a question which has exercised the many critics and scholars who have agreed with Aksakov's judgement. A possible answer was hinted at by Tyutchev himself in a letter to Anna where, advocating verse as a particularly effective medium for the propagation of a political 'slogan' ('*mot d'ordre*'), he commented: 'You know the value I place on verse in general, and my own in particular. But one cannot evade the fact that there are still plenty of honest souls who to the present day are susceptible to the superstition of rhyme, — that rhyme still has the power to edify and persuade.'[126] To accusations that such propaganda exercises amounted to a desecration of his poetic craft and calling he would no doubt have replied that he thought this a sacrifice worth making in what for him was a higher cause.

By the time the delegates were ready to leave St Petersburg for Moscow Tyutchev had managed to form some picture of their general views. One close to his own way of thinking was the Galician academic and journalist Yakov Golovatsky. In a speech at the May 11 banquet he declared that for centuries his people had considered themselves Russian and called for their speedy reintegration into the Russian Empire. Writing to congratulate him the following day, Tyutchev assured him that the 'return' of Galicia (what is now the western Ukraine) was only a matter of time, and that 'only with this reunification shall we begin to see a decisive turn for the better in the destinies of the whole Slavonic world.'[127] Golovatsky paid dearly for his bold intervention: after his return the Austrian authorities stripped him of his academic status and functions, and later that year he emigrated to Russia.[128] However, his views appear to have been unrepresentative of the congress as a whole. Before the delegates left St Petersburg

Tyutchev wrote to Samarin that several of them considered Russia to be 'only a power — a friendly, allied, auxiliary power, but so to speak an *external* one'. He suggested that during their stay in Moscow Samarin and his associates make it clear to them that they, the Slavs, 'form *a single whole* with Russia'.[129] The point was repeated in a letter to Aksakov: it was vital that the delegates return home 'imbued to the core of their being' with the knowledge that the scattered Slav peoples were fractions of which only Russia could provide the unifying integer.[130]

He also sent Aksakov a second poem 'To the Slavs' which was read out at one of the banquets in Moscow. More overtly anti-Austrian than its predecessor, it takes as its epigraph von Beust's provocative declaration 'The Slavs must be driven to the wall', then turns the imagery of this around by depicting Russia's frontiers as the wall in question:

> Though rugged as a cliff of granite,
> This wall can stretch, and stretch again;
> Already one sixth of our planet
> Is held within its vast domain...

Let the Germans pin you to that wall's impregnable defences (he tells the Slavs), and they will soon realise their mistake:

> However much they may subject you
> To brutish insult and blind hate,
> This wall — your wall — will not reject you,
> Nor leave its own to meet their fate,
>
> But open wide to grant admission
> And then, a living bulwark, close
> Behind you, taking up position
> Within close quarters of our foes.[131]

This too was noisily acclaimed and by popular demand given a second reading.[132] Such manifestations were no doubt registered with disapproval in Vienna. They were also deplored by more disinterested observers. Shown a literal translation of the earlier and more moderate poem 'To the Slavs' by one of Tyutchev's daughters, Karl Pfeffel saw in its Panslavist message a threat to the stability not just of Austria. 'Don't we have enough causes for upheaval in Europe already?' he commented in a letter to Ernestine. 'Isn't there enough inflammatory material around, without having to throw these burning brands into it as well?'[133]

After the delegates had left Russia Tyutchev continued to fulminate against Palacky and other in his view 'stupid, obtuse, muddled' proponents of the Austroslav solution. Such intellectuals were, he fumed in a letter to Samarin, the Slavs' own 'worst enemy', failing as they did to understand the only possible 'correct relationship to Russia' of their various nations. That relationship could be summed up quite simply: 'To be reborn as Slavs they must first submerge themselves in Russia.'[134] It was a view he never abandoned to the end of his days.

In 1869 he welcomed the publication in serial form in the journal *Zarya* (*Dawn*) of Nikolay Danilevsky's influential work *Russia and Europe*, which was close in concept to his own ideas. A trained botanist (in which capacity he would later mount an attack on Darwinism), Danilevsky attempted to apply 'scientific' laws to the history of mankind. Just as living organisms are born, flourish and die, he argued, so too civilisations rise and fall, to be replaced by others. He identified ten such civilisations or 'cultural-historical types' to date, the last being the European, or as he preferred to call it, 'Romano-Germanic'. Russia and the Slavs formed no part of this 'type', and indeed Europe had always regarded them as enemies. Europe was now in irreversible decline, and its leading place in the world would be taken by a new and quite distinct Slavic 'type' to be forged in a cataclysmic war over the Eastern Question. Russia would be victorious, the Austro-Hungarian and Ottoman Empires would collapse and a new Slav federation emerge with its capital in Constantinople. He predicted that most of the Slav peoples would enter the federation voluntarily, as would the Orthodox and partly Slavic Greeks and Romanians. Only the Hungarians and Poles would have to be coerced, their territories being strategically too vital to abandon to the West. The new culture to emerge from this political union would be largely shaped by the Slavophile principles of autocracy, the Orthodox faith and the village commune.[135]

'A man of such absolute conviction has become a rare and refreshing phenomenon in our times,' Tyutchev wrote admiringly of Danilevsky. He was delighted to find such 'a zealous advocate in step with my own aspirations and claims' and went out of his way to establish personal contact with him.[136] No doubt there were certain points in Danilevsky's scheme with which he found himself in disagreement: the degree of internal autonomy apparently conceded to the Slav peoples, perhaps, or the insistence that there would be nothing 'European' about the envisaged new 'cultural-historical type' (Tyutchev preferred to think of his Graeco-Slavonic Empire as an alternative, Eastern variant of Europe). Yet these were questions of niggling detail on the one hand and abstruse philosophical definition on the other. In purely practical terms what Tyutchev and Danilevsky proposed was identical: the whole of Europe east of a line meandering down from the Baltic to the Adriatic brought under autocratic Russian domination.

The subsequent legacy of these and similar Panslavist ideas can hardly be described as benign. The emancipation of the Slavs from Ottoman and Austrian rule over the following half-century was inevitable in an age of nationalism and in itself would have caused little harm. What did the damage was the peculiar notion that peoples of widely differing cultural backgrounds should be welded into a single power bloc simply because they happened to speak related languages, and that this was to be achieved through a cataclysmic war between East and West. It required only a few fanatics in positions of power and authority on either side to believe in such wild prophecies for them to become self-fulfilling. When the great showdown between German and Slav finally came in 1914 (to be resumed in 1941), it swept away not only the Turkish and Austrian Empires, as predicted by the Panslavists, but also the Orthodox autocracy that stood at the the very heart of their political beliefs; while from the ruins of that devastating conflict arose totalitarianisms of right and left which racked the body of Europe for a further three-quarters of a century, and which Tyutchev for one would surely have condemned out of hand.

History usually manages to have the last laugh over those who claim to know her ways. The world-shaking revolution so confidently predicted for western Europe by both Marx and Tyutchev eventually came to pass not there but in Holy Russia, the place least expected by either. It was no Orthodox Tsar but the leader of that new revolutionary state who in 1939, colluding with his fellow-tyrant in a latest partition of Poland, achieved Tyutchev's cherished objective of Galicia's return to the motherland, thereby sowing the seeds of a present-day conflict of interests. And by the greatest irony of all it was Stalin too who finally established the great Slav empire, stretching from the Elbe to China, once dreamt of by the poet.

iii The Blue Unfathomed Height

Katkov's battles with the censorship hardly augured well for the future of *Moskovskiye vedomosti*, and with a wife and children to support Georgievsky had for some time been casting around for more secure employment in government service. In August 1866, largely thanks to Tyutchev's intervention with the new Education Minister Dmitry Tolstoy and his deputy Ivan Delyanov (an old family friend of the Tyutchevs who lived in the same building on Nevsky Prospekt), Georgievsky was appointed editor of that Ministry's official journal in St Petersburg.[137] Tyutchev was delighted to have the Georgievskys back in the capital and continued to enjoy their company over the following years, valuing them not just as good friends but for their connection to Yelena.[138]

His relationship with another living link, his and Yelena's son Fedya, was more problematic. The boy remained with his elderly great-aunt Anna, who was assisted by a children's nurse, and from time to time Tyutchev would visit to discuss his welfare and financial support. Fedya later recalled that on such occasions he was terrified of his father, who (one can only assume from feelings of guilt) would avoid speaking to him or even making eye contact. On one of these visits Fedya's abject fear and Tyutchev's legendary absent-mindedness combined to bizarre effect. Tyutchev was discussing the boy's upbringing with his nurse while they all took a stroll around the garden, he resting one hand on the back of Fedya's neck as they walked. Ever more engrossed in conversation, he unwittingly tightened his grip until the boy was in imminent danger of being throttled. Fedya was too scared to say anything, and it was left to the nurse to point out to Tyutchev what he was doing. 'Dammit!' he exclaimed. 'I thought it was my walking stick.'[139] In fact he was more concerned for his son than this might suggest. Just before the boy's eighth birthday he begged his daughter Kitty to ensure that 'poor Fedya' was not abandoned should anything happen to himself, and was profusely grateful when she promised to do so, telling her she had 'taken a great weight off his mind'.[140] Two years later the Aksakovs, themselves childless, offered to take on Fedya's upbringing, and he moved in with them in Moscow, attending a new grammar school founded by Katkov and an associate. Tyutchev expressed his appreciation to Anna, declaring that he could now depart this world 'with one pang of conscience less'.[141] He continued to take a close interest in the boy's progress. One of Fedya's last clear recollections of his father dates from the summer of 1871, when on a visit to Moscow Tyutchev came to visit him at his school and rather touchingly found himself surrounded by numbers of young enthusiasts for his lyric verse.[142]

Direct references to Yelena practically disappear from Tyutchev's correspondence (even his letters to the Georgievskys) from about the middle of 1865. Yet although the first anniversary of her death may on the surface have appeared to bring a certain degree of closure, inwardly he never ceased to grieve for her or to feel that with her some vital part of his own being too had died. During the white nights of June 1868, like a ghost returning to the haunts of a previous life, he stood gazing at the same waters of the Neva where as newly-fledged lovers in the far-off summer of 1850 he and Yelena had enjoyed clandestine boating trips together. His reflections on this scene bring the 'Denisyeva cycle' to a close at the very point where it had begun eighteen years before:

> Once more above Nevá's broad flow,
> As if life were not long since over,
> I stand as I stood years ago
> To gaze down at the slumbering river.
>
> No stars have pricked through heaven's blue;
> A pale enchantment stills each murmur;
> Only the moon's soft rays imbue
> The pensive waters with their glimmer.
>
> Am I but dreaming, by and by
> To wake, or truly now perceiving
> What by this same moon you and I
> Beheld while still among the living?[143]

His letters of the period reflect the same sense of world-weariness, of belonging to the dead rather than the living. Writing to Ernestine on one occasion, he happens to mentions that night is falling, and adds: 'I feel the same fading of the light in all my being [...]. For good or ill, I feel I have lived long enough'.[144] In a letter to Anna congratulating her on her new life after marriage to Aksakov, he comments: 'as for me — my own life is definitely finished, *dead* and *buried*.'[145] Elsewhere he writes of his 'profound conviction that my life is lived, and that I no longer have any reason to be in this world...'[146]

Politics and current affairs provided some diversion, as did the latest developments in Russian literature. A contemporary has left us a vivid picture of the regular salon confrontations between Tyutchev and Vyazemsky at this time. His dishevelled white hair flying in all directions, Tyutchev would launch into a disquisition on some topical theme, his 'drawling speech, in which every word was yet clearly articulated' becoming increasingly agitated; while Vyazemsky sat calmly listening, puffing his pipe and interjecting the occasional 'hm', before marking the end of the tirade with some brief reasonable comment which would only send Tyutchev, 'as if stung by such imperturbability', into further impassioned flights.[147] They usually clashed over politics, but at one of Vyazemsky's soirées in December 1868 Tyutchev sprang to the defence of *War and Peace*, the first three parts of which had just been published and which Vyazemsky had criticised in an article for what he considered its crude realism. According to an eyewitness, on this occasion their argument 'almost ended in a shouting match'.[148] At another gathering he was even prepared to defend *Crime and Punishment* against its author. Dostoyevsky had been speaking of his admiration for Victor Hugo's *Les Misérables*, which he said he thought better than his own novel. At this (Dostoyevsky later recalled) Tyutchev 'grew angry with me', arguing that *Crime and Punishment* was in fact 'incomparably superior'.[149] On the other hand he let it be known to Turgenev through a mutual acqaintance that he was 'very disappointed' with the 'lack of national feeling' in his novel *Smoke* when it appeared in 1867,[150] and mounted a public attack on it with polemical verses in the journal *Otechestvennye zapiski* (*Notes of the Fatherland*).[151] Not surprisingly, when he and Turgenev met at a dinner party some years later 'a heated argument about Slavophilism and Westernism' was said to have broken out between them, with each trying to shout the other down.[152]

Despite this keen and impassioned interest in the works of other writers he remained steadfastly indifferent to the public reception of his own lyric verse. In 1867 his son Ivan (newly graduated from law school) joined with Aksakov in preparing a new volume of his collected poems. We have Aksakov's testimony that he and Ivan were unable to persuade Tyutchev either to provide original manuscripts of hitherto unpublished poems or to check copies of these made by members of the family and others, which often contained errors or variant readings. 'There was nothing for it but to to select the best and print them without any involvement on the part of the author himself,' Aksakov recalled. 'Not only that, he was sent a complete table of contents for the proposed book: it stayed with him for a month and was returned unchecked; he had not even glanced at it.'[153] The volume left the printers in March 1868 in an edition of 1,800.[154] More than half of the 184 poems in it were reprinted from the 1854 edition; of the rest, 35 were published for the first time.[155]

Tyutchev was sent an advance copy but even then did not bother to examine it. His interest was aroused only when someone in the family pointed out the embarrassing presence of several impromptu lampoons originally intended only for private circulation.[156] According to Marie, her father was 'enraged' in particular by the inclusion of a poem attacking Vyazemsky.[157] He shot off a letter to Kitty in Moscow regretting 'the most unnecessary and pointless publication of this collection of doggerel fit only to be forgotten' and demanding that the offending verses be removed.[158] Aksakov managed to have four poems excised and the table of contents amended before the book was distributed.[159] Tyutchev's final verdict on the publication was inscribed in a copy sent to Pogodin:

> Accept this wretched catalogue of verses
> At which I haven't even deigned to look,
> Prevented by sloth's and inaction's curses
> From taking any interest in the book...
>
> Today verse has the life-span of a bubble:
> Conceived at noon, by evening it is dead...
> Correcting it seems hardly worth the trouble —
> Oblivion's hand will do the job instead.[160]

In a sense he was right. By the 1860s lyric poetry had become deeply unfashionable, and the book sank more or less without trace. It received only a couple of fairly cursory reviews, and even a decade later some of its modest print-run still remained unsold.[161] One of the few to recognise its true worth at the time was Pogodin. Writing to thank Tyutchev for his copy of the poems, he assured him that they would never die, because 'the feelings and thoughts that inspire them belong to the category of the eternal'.[162]

Yet not even such admirers as Pogodin could deny that most of Tyutchev's great poetic achievements now lay in the past. During his final decade he produced relatively few purely lyric pieces, and of these only the concluding items in the Denisyeva cycle and one or two others can really stand comparison with his best work. Many of the rest read like pale reprises or pastiches of earlier poems (a 'stylistic atavism' identified by Richard Gregg for the very end of Tyutchev's life but actually observable well before that).[163] There was even a nostalgic revisiting of bygone enthusiasms with translations of a poem by Goethe and another by Heine.[164] All too often one has the impression of old age striving to recreate the lost intensity of youth and managing only an uncomfortable parody.

Much the same could be said of his love life at this time. Yelena's death did not lead to a reconciliation with Ernestine. On the contrary, for her his continuing expressions of grief merely served to rub salt in the wound. She spoke unusually frankly of this in a letter to her stepdaughter Darya shortly after returning from Nice in the spring of 1865: 'Papa [...] claims to be the most hapless, the most unfortunate of people, subjected by Providence to the most undeserved afflictions. One could say much against that, but it is wisest not to interrupt his outpourings. As for myself, it has been some considerable time since I lost his affection irrevocably and learned to seek other remedies against disappointments of that kind.'[165] One of these remedies had been to spend half the year apart from him at Ovstug, a practice not abandoned after their return to Russia.

Tyutchev for his part appears to have resumed his inveterate 'habits', albeit with diminishing returns. Among the circle of Yelena's former friends with whom he maintained contact was a certain Yelena Bogdanova, who in his tortured imagination began to fill the role of surrogate for her dead namesake. Born Baroness Uslar (her father's family came originally from Germany), she was three and a half years older than Yelena Denisyeva, with whom she had first become friendly as a pupil at the Smolny Institute. She kept in touch with Yelena after leaving, and through her came to know Tyutchev already in the 1850s. She was twice widowed, her second husband having committed suicide in 1863 after running into financial difficulties. As a result she had to give up the family estate and move to more modest accommodation in St Petersburg, where she kept open house for a circle of writers and intellectuals who included Tyutchev, the novelist Ivan Goncharov, the poet Aleksey Apukhtin and her former teacher at the Smolny, the academic and censor Aleksandr Nikitenko. They all valued her as — in the words of her son — 'a woman of rare intellect and of vast erudition and memory, and who was invariably hospitable'.[166] Much admired as a beauty in her youth, she appears to have kept her good looks into middle age,[167] and we may assume it was as much these feminine charms as her intellect and artistic leanings that first attracted Tyutchev.

His surviving letters to her[168] contain no passionate declarations, limiting themselves to such occasional gallantries as a reference to 'your dear and beloved person' or the valediction 'permit me to kiss your fair hands with grateful devotion'.[169] Yet clearly discernible beneath the restraint is a strong if one-sided attachment. 'Do you miss me a little? — Don't be afraid to admit it to me,' he writes wistfully during a visit to Moscow.[170] In other letters he twice makes the pointed remark that she is far less susceptible than he to the pain of separation.[171]

Increasingly it was illness that prevented him from seeing her as much as he would have liked. From the spring of 1867 on he began to suffer recurrent attacks of gout and rheumatism lasting sometimes weeks or even months at a time. On good days he could rely on servants to carry him down the 78 steps from the apartment to his carriage, but mostly he was obliged to keep to his bed or chaise longue.[172] For one addicted to the lively glitter of society and the salon such involuntary confinement was a torment; but it was Yelena Bogdanova's company that he missed most of all, as his letters to her attest.[173] His hopeless devotion found expression in gifts of cream and butter (then something of a luxury in St Petersburg), the loan of his carriage and help with sorting out various legal and financial matters.[174] He also took a solicitous interest in her grown-up children, using his influence to further the career of one of her sons[175] and befriending and corresponding with another.[176]

The poetic fruits of this unrequited love affair were meagre: two fairly unremarkable poems, found among his letters to her. The more substantial of these is appropriately enough on the theme of separation, in particular doubts and misunderstandings arising from the loved-one's absence.[177] The other is an impromptu quatrain apparently taken down from his dictation while he was ill. In it he tells her he hopes one day to lie in his grave as he does now on his couch, for he would happily spend eternity listening to her in silence.[178]

In the summer of 1867 his doctors advised a cure at Toeplitz, but he declined. 'There was a time, about four years ago, when I should gladly have gone to the ends of the earth for treatment, but then I was *not alone*,' he explained to his brother.[179] The following year he refused again. 'He finds the idea of going abroad repugnant as never before,' Ernestine noted.[180] Instead he agreed to a course of treatment at Staraya Russa, a spa in Novgorod province.

The journey there by train, then river steamer along the Volkhov to Novgorod and across Lake Ilmen, he found 'truly of the most agreeable'.[181] 'Faced with the undefined and unlimited sweep of these horizons,' he wrote to Anna, 'with these far-flung expanses of water embracing and providing communications for such vast tracts of countryside, one instinctively feels that here indeed is the cradle of a Giant.'[182] At Novgorod he stopped off to view the historic town and nearby Yuryev Monastery, and was pleasantly surprised by Staraya Russa itself. He told Anna that his treatment there was going well and Ernestine that he thought the place as good as any of the smaller German spas with its well-tended parks, theatre and programme of concerts.[183] To neither did he mention what for him must have been one of the chief attractions: the presence there at the time of Yelena Bogdanova.[184]

The following summer he undertook a journey to Kiev. It was the first time in his life he had ventured south of Ovstug, and his original ambitious plan included Odessa and possibly the Crimea too. Before setting out he told Anna it was a region 'I wish to have seen before I die, as the setting for events of the not too distant future which, however, it will probably no longer be granted me to witness...'[185] No doubt he had in mind Russia's hoped-for restoration as a naval power on the Black Sea; he also appears to have envisaged Kiev as the future capital of an enlarged Russian Empire.[186] In the event he made it no further than Kiev, which he found 'one of the few things in this world which have not deceived my expectations'.[187] He saw the city illuminated for a visit by the Emperor on his way back from the Crimea, an unforgettable sight with the golden domes of its churches and monasteries reflected in the Dnepr. In general he felt that 'some new world, some new, distinctive Europe has suddenly appeared and spread throughout these broad Russian expanses',[188] and according to Ernestine returned 'full of enthusiasm for his journey'.[189]

While in Kiev he met his old childhood friend Andrey Muravyov, who after making a name for himself as a writer on the history and liturgy of the Russian Church now in retirement lived in a house overshadowed by St Andrew's Cathedral on its high bluff above the Dnepr. Tyutchev wrote a poem to commemorate their meeting beneath Rastrelli's 'temple wrought of air and light' which 'Rears up in wondrous elevation,/ As if vouchsafed the power of flight'.[190]

With advancing years his mystical faith in Russia as intellectual ideal was increasingly leavened by a more down-to-earth emotional attachment to his native soil. He kept up his tradition of visiting Moscow during the warmer months, drawn not just by the prospect of meetings with family and Slavophile friends, but also 'that atmosphere so dear to me of Moscow in summer, where there is so much air, so much light and ringing of bells'.[191] A favoured destination near St Petersburg was Tsarskoye Selo, especially in autumn when for him the park and lake with its swans took on a contemplative, almost magical air.[192] This he had described in verse already in 1858:

> I love, when autumn shades are falling,
> The grounds of Tsarskoye Selo —
> When tranquil twilight comes, enthralling
> The world to slumber deep and slow;
> While, languishing upon the clouded
> Glass of the lake, in waning light
> Glide white-winged spectres, as if shrouded
> In some dull torpor of delight...
>
> And at October days' brief ending
> Dark shadows claim the surfaces
> Of steps of porphyry ascending
> To Catherine's great palaces —
> And, as the sylvan park grows dimmer,
> Revealed against the star-set sky
> A golden dome's ethereal glimmer
> Seems witness to an age gone by...[193]

Even the once despised Ovstug was now 'that blessed piece of earth',[194] and an Indian summer in St Petersburg could summon up nostalgic thoughts of the same sun 'gilding the dead leaves on the trees and the glistening mud of the paths' in his distant native village.[195] In 1868 the railway reached Oryol, and the following year Bryansk,[196] and he took advantage of this to visit Ovstug more frequently. He was there in 1868, 1869 and 1871, although never for more than a week or so at a time. In July 1869 he found not only Ernestine there, but also Marie and her husband, for the ailing Birilyov had been prescribed rest in the country. Tyutchev was shocked to see how far his son-in-law's health had deteriorated. He had recently suffered 25 epileptic fits in just over two days, and his death now seemed imminent. It would be a release, and only Marie clung to the faint hope that he might survive (in fact he did, going on to outlive both his wife and father-in-law). Recounting this 'tormenting' drama in a letter to an acquaintance, Tyutchev commented: 'It is all as natural as these treetops bathed in light and this river flowing in the sun... And yet man will always doggedly persist in seeking the answer to a riddle in that which is overwhelmingly self-evident.' And as if recalling earlier attempts of his own to find such an answer, he went on to quote lines from a poem on the subject of death written by him many years before:

> And all the while the sky so boundless
> Shines with a pure undying light.[197]

In that poem, as throughout his Munich years, nature had still appeared as an object of worship, more worthy of devotion than any worn-out deity of conventional religion. Since then life had taught him to recognise beneath the decorative outward appearance a force more in tune with Schopenhauer's concept of the universal will: blindly relentless in its action, indifferent to human concerns and ultimately without purpose. Not long after setting down his thoughts in the letter just quoted, still at Ovstug, he expanded on them in verse:

> Nature, just like the Sphinx, contrives to set
> Mankind the deadliest test that ever was.
> Why do we always fail? Perhaps because
> She holds no riddle, and has never yet.[198]

His final visit to Ovstug, lasting barely a week, was in August 1871.[199] One day he and Ernestine went to call on a neighbouring landowner of their acquaintance, Vera Fomina. Her estate was at nearby Vshchizh, until the thirteenth century seat of one of the principalities of Kievan Rus, but by then no more than a village. On the way there the sight of ancient burial mounds by the roadside, relics of constant battles between Russians and nomadic steppe-dwellers in that distant age, inspired a further reflection on the mysteries of being. It is one of the very few undisputed masterpieces of his final years.

> Of all the life that raged so violently,
> Of all the blood that flowed in rivers here,
> What has survived, what traces persevere?
> Two or three burial mounds are all we see...

And on them oak-trees, fully-grown meanwhile,
Sprawl confidently; there, with branches stirring,
They stand in lofty majesty, not caring
Whose bones, whose memory their roots defile.

For Nature has no knowledge of the past —
Our phantom years do not concern or touch her;
And faced with her we dimly see at last
Ourselves as a mere fantasy of Nature.

When each has played its futile part in turn,
She gathers in her children to her bosom,
Where all without distinction come to learn
The healing stillness of that all-engulfing chasm.[200]

Three days later he left Ovstug, and from Moscow sent Ernestine a telegram with details of his journey: 'Tiring but not boring. Slept much. Pleasant meeting with author of War and Peace.'[201] Tolstoy had joined the train after visiting Fet at his estate near Mtsensk, and they had spent four hours in conversation. Describing this encounter to the literary and cultural critic Nikolay Strakhov, Tolstoy gave his assessment of Tyutchev: 'He is a brilliant and majestic child of an old man. Apart from yourself and him I know of nobody among the living with whom my thoughts and feelings would coincide to such a degree. Yet at a certain spiritual level such unity of views on life does not unite people for earthly goals, as is the case in lower spheres of activity, but leaves each independent and free. That I have experienced with you and with him.'[202]

The previous year, 1870, Tyutchev had made what would prove to be his last journey abroad. This he managed with unerring historical timing to synchronise with the Franco-Prussian War predicted by him four years previously.[203] Another disabling attack of gout that spring had led his doctors to recommend a course of treatment at Karlsbad and Bad Wildbad. He was most reluctant, protesting that salt baths and a diet of yoghourt at home would be equally effective; but Ernestine insisted. She and Marie were due to leave for Ovstug, and (as she indicated to Anna) she was unhappy about leaving him on his own amidst 'all the irresistible temptations' of St Petersburg (these no doubt included Yelena Bogdanova). To make absolutely sure he went, she and Marie accompanied him on the Warsaw train as far as Dinaburg (now Daugavplis, Latvia), from where they could take a convenient connection to Roslavl near Ovstug. Despite threats to leave the train with them and catch the next one back to St Petersburg, he travelled on to Warsaw.[204] It was here that he heard the news that France had declared war on Prussia. 'It is as if someone were to announce the beginning of the end of the world,' he wrote to Ernestine, adding that he expected to find Berlin 'in an inexpressible state of excitement'. He was evidently beginning to perk up at the prospect, for the letter concludes: 'My health is fairly good. The journey alone is already a cure for me.'[205] He reached Berlin on 6/18 or 7/19 July to find passenger trains cancelled as rolling stock was requisitioned to effect the meticulously planned mobilisation.[206] Somehow he managed to get across the border to Leipzig on 8/20 July and on to Karlsbad in neutral Austria, where he arrived one or two days later.[207]

His stay at the spa was not a happy one. On the 13th/25th he was informed by telegram that his son Dmitry, who had been suffering from a serious heart complaint for some time, had died suddenly two days before. Grief-stricken, he wrote the same day to Ernestine that he planned to leave Karlsbad immediately and join her at Ovstug.[208] This initial impulse appears to have weakened as he reflected that she had only herself to blame that he was so far away. 'I shall never forgive myself,' he wrote bitterly to Darya some days later, 'that I allowed myself to be bundled out of St Petersburg and escorted away just *nine* days before his death...'[209] So he stayed on at Karlsbad, although his treatment was not going at all well. On 21 July/ 2 August he took some satisfaction in informing Ernestine that the cure 'so warmly recommended' to him had actually made the neuralgic pains in his legs worse. He said he had received medical advice to try the baths at Toeplitz instead and would be going there 'in a few days'.[210] In fact there is sound evidence that he left almost immediately, but not for Toeplitz.[211] By 26 July/ 7 August he was briefly back in Karlsbad again, and only then or the following day did he travel on to Toeplitz (now Teplice, Czech Republic).[212]

Where had he gone between 22 July/ 3 August and 26 July/ 7 August? Almost certainly, as argued by the Tyutchev scholar Aleksandr Nikolayev, to the spa resort of Bad Kösen between Leipzig and Weimar, approximately eighty miles as the crow flies from Karlsbad. His reason for going was to meet his sister-in-law Clotilde Maltitz, recently widowed at the age of 61, who is known to have stayed there from 2/14 July to 1/13 October.[213] Nikolayev suggests that after arriving in Karlsbad Tyutchev learnt of her presence at Bad Kösen through letters from his daughters, with whom (Anna in particular) Clotilde had remained in correspondence throughout these years[214] (Darya was in Germany at the time, although whether she took the opportunity to visit her aunt is not known).[215] Tyutchev recorded his reunion with Clotilde in verse immediately afterwards. Meeting her again had evidently aroused not just memories of the 'golden time' in Munich, but long dormant affections too. The poem begins:

> We met — and all the past came flooding
> Into my frozen heart once more,
> Reviving it, as I remembered
> Those years, that golden time of yore...

Continuing with an evocation of the 'intense emotion of those years', the sudden recollection of which now seems like a breath of spring in autumn, it concludes:

> As in a dream I gaze upon you,
> As if across the years' divide —
> And now those sounds speak out more clearly
> That in my heart had never died...
>
> Not only memory is speaking:
> Life too proclaims itself once more —
> You have not lost that old enchantment,
> And still I love you as before!..[216]

The treatment he had undergone during his two and a half weeks at Toeplitz was a great improvement on that at Karlsbad. As he told Yelena Bogdanova (with whom he corresponded throughout his stay abroad), he felt the benefit from the very first bath.[217] Apart from this Toeplitz was 'a charming place to stay', with many other Russians to keep him company.[218] He left on 14/26 August and took a leisurely route back to Russia by rail, stopping off in Prague, Vienna, Krakow and Warsaw. In Smolensk he visited his son Ivan, now married and pursuing a legal career there, and on 7/19 September was reunited with Ernestine at Ovstug. Five days later he was off again, back to St Petersburg via Moscow.[219]

Throughout his stay abroad he had followed the unfolding events of the Franco-Prussian war, feeling as so often before that he was witnessing 'the staging of a great drama conceived and produced according to all the rules of art'.[220] Initial grim satisfaction at the prospect of an internecine war which would leave the West fatally weakened soon gave way to shocked fascination as news came in of one easy Prussian victory after another against a disorganised and demoralised French army, culminating in the decisive battle of Sedan at which Napoleon III was captured and forced to abdicate. Although Tyutchev believed the Germans to have right on their side, he could not help mourning 'the final collapse of France, that great and beautiful country whose name will have earned such glory in the history of the world'.[221] Yet she had only herself to blame. The disease of revolution, dismissed by many as no more than growing pains, had revealed itself to be a deadly cancer destroying France from within, and her defeat at the hands of Prussia amounted to a 'sentence without right of appeal passed by the Supreme Judge'.[222] Far from achieving his own imperial ambitions, that 'second-rate actor [histrion]' Napoleon III had merely succeeded in conjuring up a hostile new empire on France's doorstep.[223] Russia too would be vulnerable to the new united Germany under Prussian leadership that was an inevitable consequence of the war: free of any threat from across the Rhine, this resurgent power might easily turn its attention east and inflict on Russia even greater military disasters than those suffered by France.[224]

More than anything he was shocked by the 'moral impossibility' of what was taking place for all to see: a large-scale modern war in the very heart of civilised Europe. It was, he said, like 'a public display of cannibalism'.[225] The ruthless bombardment of Paris and other French cities with scant regard to civilian casualties prompted him to describe the Prussians as 'well-trained Huns', and in general he deplored the 'quality of barbarism', 'that element of the systematically ruthless', which had characterised the war.[226] A poem written while hostilities were still in progress paints a lurid picture of the West 'drowning' in the blood which now gushes from the 'brimming chalice of divine wrath'. The Slavs too — 'you, our friends and brothers' — are in danger of being engulfed, and Tyutchev enjoins them to 'close ranks' against the common peril. Bismarck ('the oracle of modern times') had spoken of forging German unity 'with blood and iron', but that of the Slav peoples will be forged with love. 'Let's see which stands the test of time,' the poem concludes.[227]

On 19/31 October the Russian government took advantage of the international turmoil to circulate to the Western powers and Turkey a note unilaterally repudiating the Black Sea clauses of the 1856 Treaty of Paris. This caused a sensation when published in the Russian press on 3 November. Tyutchev, who had despaired of ever seeing his country regain her vital strategic position in the south, immediately penned a letter to Gorchakov congratulating him on this 'stroke of daring', followed soon afterwards by a fulsome tribute in verse.[228] His elation was somewhat dampened by subsequent events. Loyal addresses to the Tsar in support of his government's action began to flood in from the municipal councils (dumy) established in major cities under recent local government reforms. Only the Moscow Duma failed to join in the chorus of orchestrated adulation. Ivan Aksakov, Samarin, Cherkassky and others of the Slavophile persuasion who predominated in the assembly welcomed the 'national' character of Gorchakov's declaration, but feared it could plunge the country into a disastrous war for which it was as ill-prepared as it had been in 1854.[229] In fact Gorchakov had judged his moment with great diplomatic skill: France was out of the picture as a military threat; Prussia and Austria had already offered their support for a revision of the Paris Treaty; and even Britain and Turkey seemed prepared to discuss the matter. The immediate sense of affront at Russia's breach of international law was in the event allayed not by war but the seven-power Treaty of London of March 1871, which gave de facto approval to Gorchakov's diplomatic coup.[230] Most of this was unknown to the 'Moscow opposition', whose failure to produce a public expression of support soon came to be seen in government circles as an act of insubordination. Encouraged by Tyutchev, they eventually agreed to submit an address which, drafted by Aksakov and approved by the Duma, was sent on 18 November. Unfortunately this not only congratulated the Tsar for throwing off the 'unlawful fetters' imposed by the Treaty of Paris, but had the temerity to praise his internal reforms and express the hope that these might extend to even greater freedom of thought, expression and religious belief. The word 'freedom' seems to have stung the Emperor, who was reported to be 'beside himself' and 'extremely angered' by the address. He was encouraged by his conservative advisers to see it as an unwarranted intrusion into matters which were his alone to decide, and even to detect in it 'constitutional and revolutionary aspirations'. The address was rejected, any publication of it forbidden and its instigators placed under Third Section surveillance.[231] In St Petersburg Tyutchev found himself virtually alone in publicly defending the Moscow address; in private he expressed disgust at the prevailing attitude there, even in 'national' circles, of servile conformity to the Emperor's prejudices.[232] Bitterly he had to conclude that 'attempting political manifestations in Russia is like trying to strike a light on a piece of soap.'[233]

Other political developments at this time were hardly more encouraging. Following on from an encyclical of 1864 denying freedom of conscience, in 1870 Pope Pius IX promulgated the dogma of papal infallibility. This seemed designed to confirm Tyutchev's view (shared by most Slavophiles from Khomyakov on) that Rome had turned its back on the Orthodox ideal of a 'community of the faithful freely united in spirit and truth under the law of Christ' to become instead 'an institution, a political power — a state within the state.'[234] He responded with polemical verses berating the 'Dalai Lama of the Vatican' for his 'blasphemy' in supposedly claiming divine powers.[235] Many Catholics were also unhappy with the Pope's controversial pronouncements, and for a time Tyutchev attached great significance to the breakaway Altkatholiken (Old Catholics) movement founded by Ignaz Döllinger and other prominent theologians at a congress in Munich in September 1871, hoping it would spread to the Czech and other Slav lands and induce Catholics there to look east to the Orthodox Church for a spiritual home. Together with the St Petersburg theologian Ivan Osinin (a personal friend who had attended the Munich congress as an unofficial delegate of the Russian Church) Tyutchev persuaded Ivan Aksakov to write an article proposing links between the *Altkatholiken* and the Eastern Church which (in Anna's German translation) was published as a brochure in Berlin.[236] It took the line propounded to Aksakov by Tyutchev that the only viable option open to the Catholic rebels was to return to the bosom of the 'Universal Church', in other words to Orthodoxy.[237] This was something which even many Slavophile sympathisers felt to be asking for the impossible.[238] There was no response from the *Altkatholiken*, who in any case failed to make any major impact; within a few years they had been virtually written off by Aksakov.[239]

There were renewed frustrations for Tyutchev in his work as censor too. The supposedly liberal Minister of the Interior Valuyev was replaced in 1868 by Aleksandr Timashov, formerly Executive Director of the Third Section. Of his new boss and other officials of the 'squalid' censorship department under his command Tyutchev wrote to his brother Nikolay: 'They are all more or less scoundrels; just looking at them is enough to make one feel quite sick, only unfortunately for us our feelings of nausea never actually result in vomiting.'[240] Having first failed to gain higher approval for a proposed full-scale revision of the 1865 censorship statute,[241] Timashov appears to have decided on salami tactics in his attempts to limit press freedom. In January 1872 he announced that all censorship matters still under the jurisdiction of the courts were henceforth to be dealt with by administrative and police bodies. The measure was approved by the Committe on Press Affairs, 'without any opposition' according to Tyutchev. His own protest was voiced in a letter to Anna. How could it be, he asked, 'that when it comes to harmful doctrines and pernicious tendencies we have nothing to pit against them but material repression? What has become of the true spirit of conservatism in our country?'[242]

Such disappointments can only have added to his general sense of weariness with the world. 'Ah, how insipid life is, when it is not distressing,' is the heartfelt cry of one of his letters to Ernestine at this time.[243] During these final years he would often be seen wandering the streets for hours on end, self-absorbed and oblivious to passers-by, a bizarre and somewhat pathetic sight as he plodded along with an invariably still partly collapsed opera hat perched on his head, the overcoat or plaid draped over his shoulders according to the season trailing behind him on the pavement.[244] Pogodin has left us a picture of this eccentric figure, 'with long and permanently unbiddable grey hair fanning out from his temples, dressed in slipshod fashion, with none of his buttons properly fastened,' slipping into some glittering hall where a ball or rout was in full swing. 'The little old man makes his way along one of the walls with unsteady gait, clutching his hat, which seems about to fall from his grasp at any moment.' Engaged in conversation by one of the guests, 'he gives a perfunctory reply out of the corner of his mouth... looks absently about him... seems already bored and may well be thinking of retracing his steps...' But then some piece of news or gossip is heard which stirs him into action: 'he becomes animated, and from his lips begins to pour a stream of oratory: fascinating, brilliant, a true improvisation...' Soon his latest *bons mots* are passing from mouth to mouth in the ballroom, and from there throughout the drawing rooms of the capital.[245] Yet even at such moments all was not as it seemed. A closer observer than Pogodin, Ivan Aksakov, noticed that 'quite often after some spirited humorous remark one might catch the sound of what seemed to be involuntary groans being wrenched from within his breast. His mind sparkled with irony, but his heart was aching.'[246]

In 1871 Tyutchev admitted to 'a sense of growing terror' at the spectacle of his generation dying off around him, his contemporaries disappearing one by one 'like the last cards in a game of patience'.[247] The deaths of Maltitz in 1870 and Sushkov the following year saddened him for the emptiness they left behind, but in both cases grief was tempered by a sharpened awareness of his own mortality.[248] A series of deaths in the family had begun in May 1866 with that of his mother which, though not unexpected (she was in her ninetieth year) hit him particularly hard.[249] The death of Marie's one-year-old daughter a year later, followed by Anna's delivery of a stillborn child, caused him to grieve more on behalf of his daughters.[250]

His inveterate fear of losing those dear to him extended to Nikolay, who was three years older than himself, and of whom for some time now he had seen little. He missed his brother's company, regretting that they appeared to be 'like two vessels which have allowed themselves to become ice-bound at a great distance from each other'.[251] Then in December 1870 came news that Nikolay had suddenly collapsed and died at his favourite haunt, the English Club in Moscow. Tyutchev and Ernestine left immediately to attend the funeral.[252] On the night train back to St Petersburg he began to drowse off, lulled by the motion of the carriage and the sight of snowflakes swirling past the window in the surrounding gloom. He had always been particularly open to poetic inspiration at such moments of sensory transition when the self is absorbed into the wider realm of the unconscious. Now too the verses came to him:

> Long my companion on life's thoroughfare,
> Dear brother, you have left for shores unknown...
> And on a summit desolate and bare,
> Encompassed by the void, I stand alone...
>
> How long must I remain, forsaken, here?
> A day, a year — then emptiness shall reign
> Where now into night's dismal gloom I peer,
> Bewildered at the causes of my pain...
>
> All passes — and how easy not to be!
> Without me, what would change? This blizzard still
> Would howl — this steppe, this bleak obscurity
> Would all the same the vast horizon fill.
>
> Days numbered, losses hard to count, I mourn
> The flower of life, long past and lost to view —
> And with no future, of illusion shorn,
> Take up my place to head the fateful queue...[253]

It had, he told Kitty at the end of 1870, been a 'terrible year'.[254] Yet there was worse to come. At the beginning of 1872 his daughter Marie was found to have tuberculosis. Ernestine took her to Bad Reichenhall in the Bavarian Alps in hope of a cure, but it was too late. Marie died there on 2/14 June 1872. Ernestine brought her body back for burial in St Petersburg's Novodevichy cemetery.[255] It was a mortal blow for Tyutchev. Early indications of Marie's illness he had described as 'the black spot growing larger on my horizon',[256] and he said the news in May that her condition was hopeless had struck him like his own sentence of death.[257]

In the autumn his own health took a sharp turn for the worse. By November he was complaining of persistent headaches, and at the beginning of December suffered what appears to have been a minor stroke that left him with impaired vision and a weakened left hand.[258] On 29 December the Russian press carried news that the former Emperor Napoleon III had died in exile in England. Tyutchev set about composing a poem to mark the occasion, a long rambling affair of little or no artistic merit.[259] The next day he dictated the text to Ernestine, his slurred speech and her partial deafness and inadequate knowledge of Russian making this a difficult operation which took up most of the day. Following a restless night he appeared sluggish, but was otherwise well enough to go out and celebrate New Year's Eve in the company of friends. On the morning of 1 January he called on his young friend Vladimir Meshchersky to offer him the poem for publication in his journal *Grazhdanin* (*The Citizen*). Discovery of a clerical error by Ernestine while reading the poem aloud sent him into a rage which appears to have triggered a second and more serious stroke. Meshchersky sent him home in a cab, where he arrived according to Ernestine 'in a terrible condition'. Doctors who came to examine him in the course of the day — including the eminent Dr Botkin, sent on the Empress's orders — agreed there was a good chance of survival, although his left side would remain paralysed, and advised that he refrain from speech or mental exertion. They might as well have asked him to stop breathing. When Aksakov arrived with Anna on the 3rd, he was greeted with the words 'This is my Sedan', followed by a lengthy disquisition on current affairs.[260]

Ernestine believed she could discern signs that her husband's illness had 'returned him to the path of faith abandoned by him in his youth'.[261] She and Anna found him for instance surprisingly amenable to their suggestions that he take communion, and on 5 January a priest was duly brought in to hear his confession and administer the sacrament. Afterwards Tyutchev summoned the family to his bedside and demonstratively embraced Ernestine with the words: 'This is the one whose forgiveness I should ask'.[262] One of his last poems, composed a few weeks later, is addressed to her:

> Of so much — health, sleep, will-power, even air —
> Through God's chastising hand I am bereft;
> Just you of all His blessings has He left,
> That I might still have cause for thankful prayer.[263]

Gradually his condition improved. By the end of January, though still bedridden, he was entertaining large gatherings of visitors (described by one of them as being 'like a rout').[264] In February he was able to get up and wash himself.[265] At the end of March he was already making plans to spend the summer at Tsarskoye Selo and even visit foreign spas.[266] There were still sparks of the old wit and repartee. Informed that the Emperor was minded to pay him a visit, he protested that this placed him in a somewhat difficult position, as he would surely be expected to expire promptly thereafter.[267] He continued to follow the latest political developments with great interest, including Russian military advances in central Asia and the so-called 'Kulturkampf' against the Catholic Church in Germany. While he found much to admire in Bismarck's new Reich (in particular, the way it managed to combined strong central authority with a relatively liberal censorship regime),[268] he was highly critical of what he saw as a determined attack by the state on freedom of conscience and religion. Such overzealous secularism could, he warned, 'precipitate Europe into a state of barbarism without precedent in the history of the world which will authorise all other forms of oppression'.[269]

By April he was well enough to get out and about in his carriage again, and to the dismay of his family resumed his hopeless pursuit of Yelena Bogdanova, picking her up every morning for joyrides around the city.[270] Yet he was under no illusion as to his prospects of recovery. That same month he wrote to Anna: 'I ought to think of myself as a spectator after the curtain has fallen who has nothing more to do but gather up his things and head for the exit.'[271] Of his many visitors one in particular gave him (as he wrote to Darya) 'a moment of poignant emotion'. On 31 March Countess Adlerberg — 'my dear Amélie Krüdener', as she would always be for him — 'wanted to see me one last time in this world and [...] came to take her leave of me.' Fifty years had somehow slipped by since they had first met and fallen in love. 'It was the past, the best years of my past, that came in her person to give me the kiss of farewell,' he told Darya.[272]

In the shadow of death he took stock of his life. Those like Aksakov who were close to him knew that for some time regrets about 'his wasted efforts, his failure to live up to his vocation and talents' had been causing him 'inner, secret anguish'.[273] Had his life really been frittered away in salon oratory? Two years before he had been astonished on meeting a Greek diplomat he had once known in Munich to be regaled with various witticisms of his own, uttered in that distant past and long since forgotten by himself. 'A whole life, then, spent in nothing but that,' he commented ruefully to Ernestine.[274] What would come to be seen as his lasting achievement — the 'one small volume' that 'innumerable tomes outweighs' — seems genuinely never to have occurred to him. As always it was the impact of his political writings, not his poetry, that concerned him. He was pleased when in April 1873 the journal Russky arkhiv (Russian Archive) published his 1857 memorandum on censorship in the original and in Russian translation.[275] Aware that the government was about to announce reactionary new press laws 'diametrically opposed' to those envisaged by his memorandum, he relished the controversy it was likely to stir up. He felt that his article was 'a landmark' ('une date'), and that it highlighted the 'retrograde path' taken in censorship matters in more recent times. He looked forward to Russky arkhiv publishing more of his political writings.[276]

On 19 May he and Ernestine moved out to his beloved Tsarskoye Selo, where they had rented a dacha for the summer in Malaya Street.[277] Here he could enjoy fresh air and, pushed by a nurse in his wheelchair, some of his favourite walks in the palace grounds. Predictably, he was soon complaining of loneliness, especially as many of his friends and acquaintances had departed for the summer. Above all he missed Yelena Bogdanova. Just a week after arriving at Tsarskoye he left Ernestine to return to the city for two days, accompanied by a nurse and his manservant. This was to say goodbye to Yelena, who was about to go abroad.[278] His daughter Darya, by then in Bad Kissingen, was outraged when she learned by letter of these goings-on. 'It was with a sense of horror that I read everything relating to Bogdanova,' she wrote back to Kitty. 'That individual is falsehood personified. Let Aksakov recall what Polonsky told him about the indignities she made Papa suffer this summer, and now she lays on an idyll. Poor Papa has lost his head. He seems as if scourged by passion. That individual is torturing him with slow fire — and to what purpose?'[279] On 30 May his close friend and censorship colleague Aleksandr Nikitenko visited him at Tsarskoye. The following day Nikitenko wrote to Yelena Bogdanova of the emotional turmoil Tyutchev was going through: 'He bitterly laments his solitude [...]. Most of all he rails against your absence. Your sympathy was a healing balm for him. [...] he continually appealed to you, complaining that you too have abandoned him.'[280]

Two weeks later, on 13 June, Tyutchev suffered another stroke which left him completely paralysed for several hours. When he regained the power of speech he enquired in a frail voice after the latest political developments. This was followed by a further stroke on 20 June. Now the end seemed near, and a priest was hastily summoned to administer the last rites. Later in the day his own confessor arrived, to be asked before he too could launch into prayers for the dying whether he had any news of the military campaign in central Asia ('I've already been buried today,' Tyutchev explained).[281]

He struggled on for another three weeks, constantly slipping into unconsciousness. Irreversible brain damage had made speech almost impossible, and towards the end he lapsed into silence. 'Oh, what torture to be unable to find the words to express one's thought!' he complained in a more lucid moment.[282] One of his last recorded utterances was to Anna or Kitty: 'Make a little life around me.'[283] For the last six days he was alone with Ernestine; she stayed with him day and night. He died on the morning of 15 July, 'quietly, without suffering, without complaints, without words' according to Aksakov.[284] Had he been aware of the date, he would surely have seen the hand of Providence at work: it was the anniversary of that 'fateful day of bliss divine' when Yelena had first 'breathed her very spirit' into his.

There was no lack of tributes, both public and private. Already on learning that Tyutchev was seriously ill, Leo Tolstoy had written to a relative that, although he had met him no more than ten times or so in his life, 'I love him and consider him one of those unfortunate people who are immeasurably superior to the crowd among whom they live and are therefore always lonely.'[285] Tyutchev remained Tolstoy's favourite poet, and to the end of his days he would continue to champion his lyric verse as at least on a par with that of Pushkin.[286] Meshchersky's journal Grazhdanin carried an obituary written by the editor, none other than Dostoyevsky, who hailed the deceased as 'a powerful and profound Russian poet, one of the most remarkable and original of those who continue the era of Pushkin';[287] in private correspondence Dostoyevsky subsequently referred to Tyutchev as 'our great poet'.[288] For Turgenev death cancelled out their recent differences. 'I deeply regret his loss,' he wrote to Fet. 'Dear, brilliant Fyodor Ivanovich, as brilliant as day itself! Farewell!'[289] Although Fet's own immediate reaction is not recorded, he would later call Tyutchev 'one of the greatest lyric poets ever to have existed on this earth'.[290]

The funeral took place on the morning of 18 July. It was a quiet family affair: most of St Petersburg was away for the summer, and a certain confusion over the arrangements may also have played its part. A notice placed in the newspapers the previous day invited mourners to join the cortège for its departure from the house in Tsarskoye Selo at 9 a.m. Aleksandr Nikitenko, who had visited Tyutchev faithfully throughout his final illness, arrived promptly to be told the funeral party had already left. He ran to the station, only to see the specially chartered train bearing his friend's coffin receding into the distance. That evening he recorded in his diary his bitter disappointment at having been prevented from paying his last respects to 'a person whom I loved, and who had shared with me alone the last poor crumbs of his life.'[291]

Tyutchev's coffin, swathed in flowers, travelled in the luggage van, and from the station in St Petersburg was conveyed by hearse to the city's Novodevichy monastery. Rapid decomposition of the body had made it impossible to observe the customary Orthodox practice of leaving the coffin open, to be nailed down during the funeral service. Otherwise everything will have been as usual, down to the chanted invocation by priest and choir: 'Give rest to the soul of Thy servant fallen asleep' and the singing by all of 'Eternal memory'. Afterwards the coffin was carried to the graveside, followed by a few family members and household retainers, among them no doubt Tyutchev's faithful manservant of many years Emmanuel Tuma. Ivan Aksakov comforted Anna as her father's remains were lowered into the freshly dug grave next to that of Marie. To himself he reflected how much easier and more natural it seemed to bury a loved-one at this time of year, the austere chanting of the priest lightened by singing birds and the murmur of leafy trees, the earth soft, warm, almost inviting. And as he pondered on this, lines written some forty years before came unbidden into his head:

> And now the coffin has been lowered...
> And all around in packed array
> Crowd mourners: jostling, loath to breathe in
> The stifling odour of decay... [...]
>
> And all the while the sky so boundless
> Shines with a pure undying light...
> And all around us birdsong endless
> Sounds from the blue unfathomed height...[292]

Already the poems had taken on a separate and enduring life of their own. But that is another story. Like most biographies of poets, ours has tended to present its subject's creative output as the result of specific circumstances, focusing on the outward events or conditions, inner emotional compulsions, impressions and intellectual stimuli attendant at the birth of this or that poem. The biographer can only hope that such rummaging in the minutiæ of the life may yield fresh insights into the verse, perhaps even a deeper understanding of it. In Tyutchev's case we have observed the confessional and cathartic role played by the poems at various stages in his life; taken as a whole they can certainly be seen, in the apt phrase of a contemporary, as 'the mirror of his soul'.[293] It was a mirror from which he himself habitually flinched, prompted no doubt, as suggested by Richard Gregg, by feelings of self-loathing and disgust;[294] almost certainly too by unease at the vertiginous depths revealed therein. This might help to explain why he sought the hectic social round as a form of escapism: a desperate attempt, as he once said, to 'avoid at any price any serious encounter with myself '.[295] Given his attitude towards his verse, we must count ourselves fortunate that any of it survived at all. And yet, paradoxically, what its rescuers found so worthy of salvage — what ensured its lasting fame — were those very depths he himself found so disturbing. All art can be said to deal in the scattered shards of experience; only great art vouchsafes us, reflected in them, glimpses of the absolute. Slight vessels that Tyutchev's short lyrics may seem at first sight, they are capable of transporting us effortlessly into far reaches of the infinite world-ocean. Nowhere has this quality of his verse been captured more vividly than in words written by Afanasy Fet, offered here as a fitting envoi to our exploration of the life and work of this great Russian poet:

> On a calm autumn night two years ago I stood in a dark passageway of the Colosseum, looking at the starry sky through one of the window apertures. The brightest stars gazed into my eyes, intently and radiantly; and with time, as I peered into the delicate blue of the heavens, others revealed themselves to me, gazing at me just as mysteriously and just as eloquently as the first. After them the faintest glimmers too appeared in the depths and gradually emerged in their turn. Restricted by the dark mass of the walls, my vision took in only a small part of the heavens, but I could sense that they were unbounded, and that there was no end to their beauty. It is with feelings similar to these that I open the poems of F. Tyutchev.[296]

APPENDIX I

ADDRESSEES AND DATINGS OF SOME POEMS BY TYUTCHEV

(i) A numbered sequence of seven poems from 1830

The poems are: 1. 'Across Livonia's fields I journeyed on my way...' ('Cherez livonskiye ya proyezzhal polya...'); 2. 'Knee-deep in sand our horses flounder...' ('Pesok sypuchy po koleni...'); 3. 'Autumn Evening' ('Osenniy vecher'); 4. 'Leaves' ('List'ya'); 5. 'The Alps' ('Al'py'); 6. 'Mal'aria'; 7. 'That day remains in memory...' ('Sey den', ya pomnyu, dlya menya...') (I, 124-131). Fair copies of these, all with autograph dating '1830' and numbered 1-7, are to be found on two manuscript sheets in the RGALI archive (505/13, sheets 2 & 3); surviving draft versions of nos. 1, 2, 5 , 6 and 7 are on a further two sheets (505/13, sheets 4 and 5).[1]

It is clear from Tyutchev's own dating that the poems were all composed in 1830, but when and where exactly is not immediately apparent. A clue is offered by the numbering in his fair copy, which on internal evidence appears to indicate the order in which they were written. Nos. 1 and 2 open the sequence with descriptions of the landscape in Russia's western Livonian territories, the second being marked 'on the journey' ('dorogoy'). These could have been written only after Tyutchev and his family left St Petersburg at the end of September (OS) on the return journey by land to Munich (the outward journey had been made by sea). The autumnal rural landscapes of nos. 3 and 4 could have been observed anywhere in the countryside between there and southern Germany. No. 5 describes dawn breaking over the Alps, which they would have seen towards the end of their journey. It seems reasonable to conclude that the numbering of the sequence is indeed chronological, and that nos. 6 and 7 — both 'non-journey' poems — were therefore most likely written soon after Tyutchev's return to Munich.

Kirill Pigaryov claimed on the other hand that three — nos. 3, 4 and 7 — were written during Tyutchev's stay in St Petersburg between the beginning of June and the end of September (OS). He offered no evidence for this assertion, nor did he explain why the poems are numbered as they are. Moreover, he supposed (again, it is not clear on what grounds) that the young girl recalled in no. 7 is the same person as the older of the sisters addressed in 'To Two Sisters' ('Dvum syostram', I, 116), contending that both poems were inspired by a supposed meeting with this hypothetical old flame in St Petersburg in the summer of 1830.[2] However, subsequent research has demonstrated that 'To Two Sisters' could have been written no later than March 1830, long before Tyutchev set out for St Petersburg.[3] Elsewhere I have argued that no. 7 was in fact written soon after Tyutchev's return to Munich on 13/25 October and that it refers to his first love Amélie.[4] As for nos. 3 and 4, it is of course possible to see them (as implied by Pigaryov) as reflecting autumnal scenes witnessed in a St Petersburg park or the grounds of some out-of-town palace such as Tsarskoye Selo. On the other hand a rural setting would seem if anything more plausible and certainly fits in with the idea of a chronological sequence.

(ii) 'Here, where heaven's vault looks down, lacklustre...' ('Zdes', gde tak vyalo svod nebesny...', I, 119)

Tatyana Dinesman has argued that this description of a bleak landscape was, like nos. 1 and 2 in the group just discussed, written while Tyutchev and his family were travelling through the Baltic provinces on their way back to Munich in the autumn of 1830.[5] However (as she mentions herself), one manuscript version is included in the so-called 'Raich collection', which means it must in fact predate March 1830.[6] Although marked '*V doroge*' ('on the journey') in the same manuscript, the reference is clearly to some previous journey. Kirill Pigaryov's suggestion that it was written in May 1830 on the journey to Russia has to be rejected on the same grounds.[7] Aleksandr Nikolayev speculated that it was written 'during [Tyutchev's] journey to Paris and Rome in October 1829'.[8] Although (as Dinesman points out) it is now known that Tyutchev did not travel to Paris in 1829 and by October of that year had already returned from Italy, other journeys to those destinations before 1830 must be considered a possibility. For the time being, however, the poem's genesis and exact dating remain unclear.

(iii) A sequence of six numbered poems (undated)

The poems are: 1. 'In the air's oppressive stillness...' ('V dushnom vozdukha molchan'ye...'); 2. 'Why, O willow, to the river...' ('Chto ty klonish' nad vodami...'); 3. 'Such a wet and gloomy evening...' ('Vecher mglisty i nenastny...'); 4. 'And now the coffin has been lowered...' ('I grob opushchen uzh v mogilu...'); 5. 'Pale showed the east... Our craft sped gently...' ('Vostok belel... Lad'ya katilas'...'); 6. 'Just like a bird, at break of day...' ('Kak ptichka, ranneyu zarey...') (I, 135-140).

The numbered autographs, on five sheets torn from a notebook, appear to be fair copies written within a short time of each other.[9] The suspicion must be that this 'cycle', like the group of seven numbered poems discussed above in (i), relates to a particular year, although in this case none is indicated in the manuscripts. Until now it has not been possible to date it any more accurately than to the first half of the 1830s.[10] However, internal evidence in 'Pale showed the east... Our craft sped gently...' (I, 139) suggests that the cycle was composed in 1833. This poem describes a sea voyage (as line 4 makes clear), only two of which Tyutchev is known to have made in the first half of the 1830s. The first, in June 1830 from Lübeck to St Petersburg, was by steamer; yet the poem clearly describes a sailing vessel (line 2). This can only refer to the second voyage, on the frigate *Carolina* to Greece and back in the summer and autumn of 1833. The identity of the girl depicted is unknown: possibly a daughter or servant of the Bavarian Chargé d'Affaires Gasser or of one of the other officials on board.

There is nothing in the other poems to contradict such a dating. 'Just like a bird, at break of day...' (I, 140), for instance, would appear to be set in the heat and dust of Greece in summer. 'And now the coffin has been lowered...' (I, 138) is at first sight not so easy to place. It describes what is evidently a Lutheran burial (the officiating priest is explicitly referred to as a 'pastor', and his graveside oration is recognisably Protestant in content and form). The only one of Tyutchev's Lutheran relatives by marriage who might possibly have died at this time was his stepson Alexander Peterson, the exact date of whose death has still to be established. Born in 1823 as one of Eleonore's four sons from her first marriage, he is last mentioned in a despatch from Foreign Minister Nesselrode to the Russian Ambassador in Munich dated 27 June/9 July 1833 agreeing to Eleonore's earlier request that 'because of his weak health' Alexander be allowed to stay abroad with her and not be sent to Russia for his education.[11] After this he drops out of the record. He evidently died at some time before 1845, for in a letter written to Anna that year Tyutchev refers first to 'your brother Charles' (i.e Karl) and then to 'your two other brothers Othon [Otto] and Alfred'.[12] As both Alexander's parents were Lutheran, he will have been brought up in that faith and given a Lutheran burial. It is just conceivable that he died at some time in 1833 between the (unknown) date of Eleonore's request to Nesselrode and Tyutchev's departure for Greece on 23 July/ 4 August, and that the funeral described is his. However, Eleonore makes no mention of a death in her five letters to Tyutchev's brother Nikolay covering this period. Also, if Alexander did die then, it was not in Munich, as his name does not appear in burial records of the Lutheran church in Munich for the years 1832-1836.[13]

Whose burial, then, does the poem record? A clue is offered in the Russian text, where those present are said to have 'crowded' ('*stolpilosya*') around the grave and even to be 'jostling' each other ('*tolkutsya*'). This would certainly have been the case at a diplomat's funeral, for on such occasions it was customary for the whole diplomatic corps to turn out in force.[14] The only Protestant funeral of this kind in Munich in 1833 was that of the Prussian Ambassador Johann Emanuel von Küster, who died on 30 May at the age of 68 and was buried on 2 June. Unlike many that year, he does not appear to have been a victim of the typhus epidemic: in his case 'narrowing of the intestinal tract' ('Verengung des Darmkanals') is cited as the illness causing death.[15] Tyutchev was in Munich at the time, as is clear from a despatch in his hand dated 20 May/1 June,[16] and will therefore have been expected to attend the funeral. The date accords well with the strong suggestion of spring or summer in the poem's final stanza; it also helps to confirm that the cycle is numbered chronologically. The burial will have taken place at what was at the time Munich's only cemetery; this still survives as 'der alte Südfriedhof'.

The officiating pastor is not named in the records. He is unlikely to have been Ludwig Schmidt (see pp.96-97, 210), who after the death of Maximilian I had largely retired from public duties to devote himself exclusively to his role as the dowager Queen Karoline's personal chaplain.[17] We should probably look rather to Friedrich Boeckh, Lutheran Dean of Munich from 1830 to 1848. Known for his impressive sermons and his publications on liturgical matters, he would appear to be a good match for the 'learned' ('*uchony*') pastor portrayed in the poem.[18]

(iv) 'Columbus' ('Kolumb') (I, 194)

The autograph manuscript is dated 1844 in Tyutchev's own hand.[19] The second verse has long been recognised as a paraphrase of the last two lines of a poem by Schiller with the same title;[20] the first is original (although containing, as we shall see, references to another work). The poem as a whole is therefore clearly no 'straight' translation, but rather one of Tyutchev's characteristic exercises in literary cross-reference and 'variations on a theme'.

What might have prompted Tyutchev to take up this particular theme at the time he did? Richard Gregg suggests an answer may be found in a reference to Columbus in his 'Lettre à M. le Docteur Gustave Kolb', written in Munich in March-April 1844.[21] Here Tyutchev derisively likens most Western commentators on Russia to those contemporaries of Columbus who believed he had discovered, not a new continent, but merely an extension of the familiar Eurasian continent.[22] Connecting this with a subsequent reference in the article to Peter the Great, Gregg concludes that in the poem too 'the discovery of the new world by Columbus stands for Peter's revelation of Russia to the West'.[23] However, it is worth noting that nowhere in the article does Tyutchev directly compare Peter the Great to Columbus; that the reference to Peter actually comes a whole page after that to Columbus (a fact somewhat obscured by Gregg's abbreviation of the passage in quotation); and that examined in context any connection between the two seems fairly tenuous.[24] In fact the reference to Columbus could with equal justification be linked to a passage immediately preceding it, in which Tyutchev excludes in advance from his strictures on Western Russia-watchers 'a few rare intelligences, two or three in Germany, one or two in France' who have 'lifted one corner of the veil' and understood the true essence and significance of Russia.[25] It could be argued that these individuals too (foremost among whom critics have identified Schelling)[26] are by implication being compared to Columbus. However, as with the parallel claimed by Gregg, nowhere is this made explicit.

A more promising immediate source for the poem would appear to be Vladimir Odoyevsky's *Russian Nights* (*Russkiye nochi*), published in St Petersburg in 1844. It is unlikely that Odoyevsky's book — a collection of stories told by a group of friends during St Petersburg's 'white nights' and linked by their imagined discussions — would have gone unnoticed by Tyutchev when he returned to Russia in the autumn of that year. According to one critic it made 'a huge impression' at the time, becoming 'the subject of fierce polemics and heated philosophical disputes'.[27] Tyutchev had most likely encountered Odoyevsky much earlier, either before leaving for Munich in 1822 or during his first home leave in 1825. In those days both had belonged to Raich's group and to the close-knit literary world of Moscow in general (Tyutchev perforce as a 'corresponding member' for much of the time). Exactly when they resumed or deepened their acquaintanceship after Tyutchev settled in St Petersburg is not known, but certainly by the second half of the 1840s they and their families were associating on a regular basis.[28]

The dialogues interspersing the stories in *Russian Nights* touch on themes which greatly interested Tyutchev at the time, not least the question of Russia's place in history and her role vis-à-vis what was seen to be a declining West. In a remarkable final peroration the leader of these discussions (who goes under the name of 'Faust' and is clearly a mouthpiece for Odoyevsky's own views) celebrates the 'all-embracing many-sidedness' of the 'Slavonic spirit' which he believes will heal the West of its deadly materialism, rationalism and internal contradictions; and he claims that the 'best minds' of the West (among whom he names Schelling and Baader) have themselves reached the same conclusion. Unlike the Slavophiles (but like Tyutchev), he praises Peter the Great, whom he sees as having skilfully 'inoculated' Russia with just enough of Western civilisation to rouse the giant from its centuries of torpor. The book concludes with one of Faust's young disciples quoting the words: 'The nineteenth century belongs to Russia!'[29] In view of these sentiments, it seems almost certain that the controversy surrounding *Russian Nights*, and indeed the book itself, had an impact on Tyutchev at the time.

In one of the earlier dialogues Faust/Odoyevsky recalls for his younger listeners a time when he and his contemporaries (clearly he has the 'Lovers of Wisdom' in mind) had fallen under the spell of Schelling's philosophy. He goes on to explain what it was that so fired their enthusiasm:

> At the beginning of the nineteenth century Schelling was what Christopher Columbus had been in the fifteenth: he discovered a part of man's world about which there had been only shadowy legends — *his soul*. Like Christopher Columbus he went in search of one thing and found another; like Christopher Columbus he aroused unfulfillable hopes. But like Christopher Columbus he gave a new direction to human enterprise! Everyone rushed to this magical, opulent land: some inspired by the intrepid navigator's example, some in search of knowledge, some from curiosity, some for profit. Some brought back great treasures, others only monkeys and parrots; but much too was lost at sea.[30]

This may have reminded Tyutchev of the link between Schelling and Columbus implied by his own article earlier that year. More to the point, he seems to have been reminded of Schiller's poem on the great explorer. Certainly in his own poem he chooses to paraphrase from Schiller precisely those lines which appear to echo both Schelling's '*Identitätsphilosophie*' and the latter's ideas on the intimate rapport between genius and nature: 'Mit dem Genius steht die Natur in ewigem Bunde:/ Was der eine verspricht, leistet die andre gewiss.' ('Nature and genius are joined in eternal alliance:/ What one [genius] promises, the other [Nature] unfailingly accomplishes.') (It is not suggested that Schiller was influenced by Schelling's philosophy in this case, merely that it was possible for Tyutchev to detect a similarity of ideas.)

If the second verse of Tyutchev's poem paraphrases Schiller, the first shows interesting parallels with the passage quoted from *Russian Nights*. Apart from the general similarity of tone (eulogistic throughout), it repeats one of Odoyevsky's key ideas in stating that the new world discovered by Columbus (or Schelling) was not only 'unknown' but 'unexpected' (compare in the passage by Odoyevsky: 'he went in search of one thing and found another'). As with so much of Tyutchev's lyric verse, there is throughout this stanza a tantalising sense of metaphorical depths lurking beneath the surface. There are various indications of this. We are told for instance that in order to 'accomplish the unfinished scheme/ Of world-creation' Columbus 'tore the veiling screen asunder/ [...]with godlike hand', descriptions which in content and phrasing seem also to hint at the function of the philosopher or artist as outlined by Schelling. And it certainly seems to be the case that Tyutchev intends the 'new world' discovered to be understood metaphorically. He tells us that Columbus 'plucked [it] forth', or, more strikingly in the original, 'brought [it] out into the world with [literally: "behind"] him' ('Na Bozhy svet [...] vynes za soboy'): hardly appropriate if applied to an actual continent. Could 'new world' perhaps refer synecdochically to the spoils of exploration? But then the epithets 'unknown, unexpected' would be strangely out of place. The only reading that can possibly make sense in the context is that Columbus brought back with him hitherto unknown and unexpected *knowledge* of a new world. And of course this is precisely what Schelling is said to have done in Odoyevsky's analogy. Significantly, too, Tyutchev states that Columbus brought this new world to public attention 'from mist-wreathed infinity' ('iz bespredel'nosti tumannoy'). On one level this can be taken as referring to the boundless seas on which the explorer set sail. Yet here too there are inescapable metaphorical overtones. Elsewhere in Tyutchev's poetry the sea often appears as a potent image for the vital force informing both nature and the soul or unconscious mind of man: in a word, for the metaphysical absolute or infinite, the 'universal soul' as posited by Schelling.[31] Moreover, the term *'bespredel'nost' '* ('boundlessness', 'infinity') and its related forms, together with its near-synonym *'neizmerimost' '* ('immeasurability'), are used by Tyutchev in several other poems in precisely this metaphysical sense.[32]

There remains one nagging question. If 'Columbus' was indeed intended as a celebration of Schelling's achievement, why should Tyutchev have gone to the trouble of encoding his eulogy so thoroughly as apparently to defeat the whole object of the exercise? In fact this can be answered quite simply. At the time of composition, the key to the cipher — Odoyevsky's *Russian Nights* — was being hotly debated in Russian intellectual circles. Writing as was his wont for the moment, with little or no regard to posterity, Tyutchev could be confident that his cryptic reference would be picked up by those in the know. And as with so much of his lyric verse, such fellow initiates seem ultimately to be the only readers he was really interested in.

(v) 'To sort a pile of letters, on...' ('Ona sidela na polu...') (II, 89)

This and the poem 'At those times when the bosom...' ('V chasy, kogda byvayet...') (II, 88) would appear to have been composed at much the same time: fair-copy autographs of them have survived, written in the same ink on matching halves of a sheet of paper torn in two. They were first published in an issue of the journal *Russkaya beseda* (*Russian Symposium*) approved by the censor on 17 May 1858 (OS), and are both dated 1858 by Aksakov and the poet's son Ivan in their 1868 collection of Tyutchev's verse.[33] As will become apparent, there is reason to assume that this reflects the date of composition rather than that of first publication. If so, both poems were written at some time between January and April 1858 (OS).

The scene portrayed in 'To sort a pile of letters...' is clearly a painfully recalled incident from one of Tyutchev's own troubled relationships. In verse 3 the poet tells us the letters being sorted through by the woman are witnesses to their earlier life together, now irrevocably past ('beyond retrieving'). That life had its 'moments of despair', yet also of 'love and joy', which, however, have been 'transformed to grieving' (in the original, 'killed' ['*lyubvi i radosti ubitoy*']). The one responsible for destroying their love in this way, for turning it into 'ash from which all heat has gone' (verse 1) appears to be the poet himself. In verse 4 he says he is ready to fall to his knees, evidently to beg the woman's forgiveness. Yet he does and says nothing, paralysed by feelings of guilt and remorse.

Kirill Pigaryov made the apparently reasonable suggestion that the woman was Ernestine, pointing out that she is known to have destroyed some of the correspondence in her possession.[34] That the woman intends to destroy the letters is in fact not stated directly in the poem, yet this is made clear enough through use of simile. In the second verse we are told that she looks at the letters (in literal translation) 'in a strange sort of way, as souls look from on high at the body they have abandoned'. Read in isolation, this certainly suggests that the letters no longer have any sentimental value for the woman and that she feels no compulsion to keep them, but not that she necessarily wants to destroy them. However, the simile does not occur in isolation, but comes almost immediately after another applied to the letters in verse 1, where the woman is described as handling them (again literally) 'like ashes which have grown cold'. As we have seen, this is on one level a fairly well-worn poetic image for burnt-out passion. What makes it original and remarkable is its parallel functioning as an example of prolepsis, or poetic prefiguring: the woman is seeing the letters as what she intends them to become.

This is why we sense instinctively from the third line on that the letters are to be burnt, and in that respect Pigaryov is surely right. On the other hand, his suggestion that the woman in the poem is Ernestine must be considered doubtful. Elsewhere he informs us that Ernestine destroyed all the letters (more than 190) written to her by Tyutchev before their marriage, while preserving nearly 500 from after that date.[35] Apart from the fact that we do not know when she destroyed these letters (the most likely time would have been after Tyutchev's death, which is when she is known to have destroyed her letters to him),[36] her motive for doing so was clearly to remove compromising evidence of their affair, conducted while Tyutchev was still married to Eleonore. The fact that she also carefully deleted certain references to these earlier years from his later, surviving letters reinforces the point.[37] Is this really what we are witnessing in the poem? We see the poet stricken with one-sided guilt, yet if the woman is Ernestine, destroying the evidence of their adulterous affair, why does no guilt seem to attach to her? On the contrary, she appears almost angelic.

Other critics have advanced Yelena Denisyeva as a more likely candidate.[38] This too seems doubtful. Although Yelena was a temperamental woman capable of impulsive acts when her temper was roused, she is also known to have been highly possessive of Tyutchev and of her relationship with him. It seems hardly credible that she would have destroyed any of his letters to her, documenting as they surely did his attachment — and certainly not in the calm, deliberate way depicted. In fact we have evidence that at least some such letters did survive both of them. In 1903 their son Fyodor wrote of the beginning of their relationship:

At that time he was getting on for fifty, but nevertheless had managed to preserve such freshness of heart and emotional integrity [...] that, reading his *passionate* [*dyshayushchiye strast'yu*] *letters* and poems, one simply refuses to believe that they were written, not by some twenty-five-year-old youth in love for the first time, but by an old man of fifty [...].[39]

From this it seems fairly clear that Fyodor must have had access to letters from his father dating from the early years of the relationship. In fact they were probably still in his possession in 1903, as were autographs or copies of five poems dedicated to Yelena which Fyodor published in his memoir for the first time. Unfortunately all these manuscripts have since been lost. It might be objected that the apparent survival of these letters does not in itself prove that Yelena never destroyed any others. Yet is it really likely that she would have done so as described in the poem, while sparing precisely these (on Fyodor's testimony) 'passionate' letters from the early years of their love?

If the woman sitting on the floor is neither Ernestine nor Yelena, who could she be? Given that the reference is clearly to one of Tyutchev's long-standing relationships, we are left with one other credible candidate: Eleonore, as suggested many years ago by Ronald Lane.[40] In fact a strong case can be made for her. To begin with the physical evidence of surviving letters, it is true that none of Tyutchev's letters to Eleonore has come down to us (apart from a note to her appended to a letter written to his parents while she was staying with them).[41] However, none of the letters written to her by other members of his family (in particular his parents and brother Nikolay) has survived either, although her letters to them are preserved in the Tyutchev family archive at Muranovo.[42] As pointed out by Pigaryov, this state of affairs is almost certainly explained by the loss of Eleonore's family papers and effects in the fire and shipwreck of the *Nicholas I* in May 1838.[43] And although as a result of that disaster we are now prevented from verifying whether or not she had at some earlier date deliberately destroyed letters from Tyutchev, at least such an event remains open as a possibility. In other words, on the best available evidence of surviving letters Eleonore cannot be ruled out as the woman in the poem. Ernestine and Yelena on the other hand, as we have seen, almost certainly can.

Further confirmation of Eleonore is found in the fact that the poem appears to have been written shortly before its first publication in *Russkaya beseda* in May 1858, twenty years to the month after the disaster on the *Nicholas I*, the effects of which on Eleonore's health did so much to hasten her death just over three months later. We know that Tyutchev was in the habit of marking such fateful anniversaries in verse.[44] The poem 'At those times when the bosom...', written like 'To sort a pile of letters...' soon before May 1858 and published with it in the same issue of *Russkaya beseda*, is known to be dedicated to Eleonore (there is a note to that effect appended to a copy of it made by Tyutchev's daughter Yekaterina).[45] It would be reasonable to conclude that 'To sort a pile of letters...' was written as a companion piece to it, and that both poems were conceived as expiatory tributes to Eleonore's memory. That the tragic events of 1838 were then very much on Tyutchev's mind is also suggested by a poem composed a few months after these two. 'Uspokoyeniye' ('Consolation'),[46] a free translation of 'Blick in den Strom' ('Gazing at the River') by Nikolaus Lenau, has been shown by Ronald Lane to contain clear echoes of those events, in particular in its variations on the original (for instance, references to 'what we called our own' having 'gone from us for ever', and to feeling 'oppressed', 'as if beneath a gravestone', none of which is in

426

Lenau's text). As Lane points out, the autograph is dated 15 August 1858 (OS) in Tyutchev's hand, and the poem was published soon afterwards in the August issue of *Russkaya beseda*, evidently to coincide with the anniversary of Eleonore's death on 28 August/ 9 September.[47]

Yet undoubtedly the most compelling evidence for Eleonore is contained in the text of 'To sort a pile of letters...' itself. The use of prolepsis in line 3, comparing the letters to ashes which have grown cold, has already been noted. This prepares us for two further examples of 'prophetic' simile later in the poem. In verse 2 Tyutchev describes the woman looking at the letters in a 'strange and distant' manner ('*chudno tak*'), and comments: 'So too departing souls must look/Upon the shell just now divested'. And as if to underline this, he concludes the poem by saying he was overcome by a terrible sadness, 'As if a dear shade's presence chilled me'. These two similes (cited by Lane as 'internal clues' pointing to Eleonore) can only be fully appreciated when we realise that Tyutchev's recollection of a painful incident from his first marriage is coloured here by the knowledge of his wife's subsequent death. The similes prefigure her death, and lose much of their emotional force (the second in particular becoming merely puzzling) if we assume that the poem refers to Ernestine or Yelena, both of whom were alive at the time of composition. Read in this light, 'To sort a pile of letters...' emerges — rather like that other 'memory' piece, 'A golden time still haunts my senses...' ('Ya pomnyu vremya zolotoye...') — as a complex tapestry woven from various distinct time-strands.[48] To the original simple opposition of narrator's present and recalled past event are added in the course of the poem a prehistory contained in the letters and, finally, the more recent past of the woman's death, eloquently suggested through the use of prolepsis.

Biographical indications, the evidence of surviving letters, the date of the poem, its imagery and even aesthetic considerations thus all point to Eleonore. The scene recalled presumably took place at some time in the mid-1830s, following the discovery of her husband's infidelity with Ernestine.

APPENDIX II

TYUTCHEV'S SERVICE CAREER

DATE (OS)	RANK	POST	SALARY*
21.02.1822	Provincial Secretary (XII)	Appointed to Foreign Ministry, awaiting posting	None
13.05.1822		Supernumerary Attaché, Munich Embassy	None
25.02.1825	Collegiate Secretary (X)		
25.02.1828	Titular Councillor (IX)		
17.04.1828		Second Secretary, Munich Embassy	800
25.02.1832	Collegiate Assessor (VIII)		
08.08.1833			1,000
31.12.1835	Court Councillor (VII)		
28.06 - 22.08. 1836		Chargé d'Affaires, Munich Embassy	
03.08.1837		First Secretary, Turin Embassy	1,500
22.07.1838 - 25.06.1839		Chargé d'Affaires, Turin Embassy	2,000
31.12.1838	Collegiate Councillor (VI)		
01.10.1839		Resigned from post of First Secretary, Turin Embassy	None

30.06.1841		Dismissed from Foreign Service
16.03.1845		Reinstated in Foreign Service
15.02.1846		Special Assignments Officer to State Chancellor	1,500
01.02.1848		Special Assignments Officer and Senior Censor	2,430
05.05.1848	State Councillor (V)	
07.04.1857	Active State Councillor (IV)	
17.04.1858		Chairman, Committee of Foreign Censorship	3,430
08.10.1858			4,573
30.08.1865	Privy Councillor (III)	

* Annual, in silver roubles. From 17.04.1858 Tyutchev's main salary was paid by the Ministry of Education, supplemented from 08.10.1858 by 1,143 silver roubles from the Foreign Ministry. By 1860 the Ministry of Education component had risen to 4,000, after which no further figures are available.

THE TABLE OF RANKS

Instituted by Peter the Great in 1722 as part of his policy of making service to the state compulsory for the nobility, the Table of Ranks (*Tabel' o rangakh*) remained in force virtually unaltered for nearly two centuries. It was abolished only after the October Revolution of 1917. During Tyutchev's lifetime the hierarchy of corresponding civil service and army ranks in operation was as follows:

GRADE	CIVIL RANK	ARMY RANK
I	Chancellor (*Kantsler*)	Field-Marshal
II	Active Privy Councillor (*Deystvitel'ny tayny sovetnik*)	General

III	Privy Councillor (*Tayny sovetnik*)	Lieutenant-General
IV	Active State Councillor (*Deystvitel'ny statsky sovetnik*)	Major-General
V	State Councillor (*Statsky sovetnik*)	- - - - - - - -
VI	Collegiate Councillor (*Kollezhsky sovetnik*)	Colonel
VII	Court Councillor (*Nadvorny sovetnik*)	Lieutenant-Colonel
VIII	Collegiate Assessor (*Kollezhsky asessor*)	Major
IX	Titular Councillor (*Titulyarny sovetnik*)	Captain
X	Collegiate Secretary (*Kollezhsky sekretar'*)	Staff Captain (*Shtabs-kapitan*)
XI	Ship's Secretary (*Korabel'ny sekretar'*)	- - - - - - - -
XII	Provincial Secretary (*Gubernsky sekretar'*)	Lieutenant
XIII	District Secretary (*Provintsial'ny sekretar'*)	Second Lieutenant
XIV	Collegiate Registrar (*Kollezhsky registrator*)	Ensign

SOURCES

Listed here, with abbreviations, are sources referred to frequently or in more than one chapter. Others are detailed as they occur individually in the Notes.

TYUTCHEV'S WORKS

The standard edition of Tyutchev's works referred to is: **F.I. Tyutchev, *Polnoye sobraniye sochineniy i pis'ma*, 6 vols., Moscow, 2002-2005.** This contains all Tyutchev's verse (vols. I-II), his articles and other writings on politics in French, with Russian translations (vol. III), and a wide selection of his letters in the original, with Russian translations where appropriate (vols. IV-VI). **All references to this edition are by volume and page number alone (e.g.: IV, 255).**

For the texts of Tyutchev's poems and commentaries on them the six-volume edition is largely indebted to the work of previous scholars, in particular G.I. Chulkov, K.V. Pigaryov and A.A. Nikolayev in *PSS* (1933), *Lirika* and *PSS* (1987) respectively (full publication details listed below). These major editions are also referred to in the Notes.

Many of Tyutchev's letters not included in the six-volume edition are in a variety of other publications referred to individually. One of the earliest, 'Lettres' (full details below), is by far the most significant in terms of size, but suffers from editorial shortcomings. It has been quoted from only in cases where no alternative text is available.

ARCHIVES

AVPRI: Arkhiv vneshney politiki Rossiyskoy imperii (Archive for Foreign Policy of the Russian Empire), Moscow.

AVPRI (K): AVPRI, *f.* 133 (Kantselyariya Ministra inostrannykh del), *op.*469 (Ministerstvo inostrannykh del).

AVPRI (M): Missiya v Turine: AVPRI, *f.* 196, *op.* 530.

LAELKB: Landeskirchliches Archiv der Evangelisch-Lutherischen Kirche in Bayern (Archive of the Evangelical-Lutheran Church in Bavaria), Nuremberg.

Muranovo: Muzey-usad'ba 'Muranovo' imeni F.I. Tyutcheva (Tyutchev Museum), Muranovo.

RGALI: Rossiysky gosudarstvenny arkhiv literatury i iskusstva (Russian State Archive of Literature and Art), Moscow.

RGB: Rossiyskaya gosudarstvennaya biblioteka (Otdel rukopisey) (Russian State Library, Manuscript Department), Moscow.

SK: Schlossarchiv Köfering, conserved at the Staatsarchiv Amberg, Bavaria. Archive of the Counts von Lerchenfeld (uncatalogued: no archival references available). I am grateful to the present Count von Lerchenfeld for permission to quote from documents in the archive.

TAS: Turin: Archivio di Stato.

UNPUBLISHED MATERIALS

Bothmer: 'Nachrichten aus dem Leben des Grafen Karl von Bothmer, von ihm für seine Kinder geschrieben in Karlsruhe 1827'. Autobiographical account by the father of Tyutchev's first wife Eleonore (surviving 52-page typescript copy from the original manuscript lost in 1945). I am grateful to Frau Henriette von Bothmer, for many years custodian of the Bothmer family archive, for permission to quote from this.

Köckenberger: Typescript copies of letters from Amélie von Krüdener to the Krüdeners' steward (*Haushofmeister*) Georg Köckenberger. I am grateful to the latter's great-grandson Dr Karl Köckenberger for permission to quote from these.

I am also greatly indebted to Dr Ronald Lane for making available the following materials from his collection:

1. Copies made by him at Muranovo of Eleonore Tyutcheva's letters (in French).

2. Typewritten transcripts made under the direction of, and corrected by, the late K.V. Pigaryov of nearly all Tyutchev's letters (in French) to his second wife Ernestine for the period 1840-1853.

3. Typescript Russian translations of 34 of the 45 diplomatic despatches sent by Tyutchev in his capacity as Russia's Chargé d'Affaires at Turin, 1838-1839. The originals are held in AVPRI (K), No. 212 (despatches for 1838) and No. 207 (those for 1839).

(Where available, archival references are given in the Notes for any previously unpublished quotations from Dr Lane's collection.)

PERIODICALS

AZ: *Allgemeine Zeitung*
RA: *Russky arkhiv*

BOOKS AND ARTICLES

A number of these items can be accessed online via links at:
www.tyutchev.ru
www.ruthenia.ru/tiutcheviana (click on the 'Bibliografiya' box)
http://community.livejournal.com/tiutchev/2806.html

Aksakov: I.S. Aksakov, *Biografiya Fyodora Ivanovicha Tyutcheva*, Moscow, 1886. Facsimile reprint: Moscow, 1997.

Arkhipov: Yu. Arkhipov, 'Svoyak Tyutcheva Apollony Petrovich Mal'titz', *TS* (1990), 312-319.

Aronson & Reyser: M. Aronson, S. Reyser, *Literaturnye kruzhki i salony*, Leningrad, 1929.

Barsukov: N.P. Barsukov, *Zhizn' i trudy M.P. Pogodina*, 22 vols., St Petersburg, 1888-1910.

Benn & Bartlett: Anna Benn, Rosamund Bartlett, *Literary Russia. A Guide*, London, 1997.

Berkovsky: N.Ya. Berkovsky, 'F.I. Tyutchev', in: F.I. Tyutchev, *Stikhotvoreniya* (ed. N.Ya. Berkovsky, N.V. Korolyova), Moscow & Leningrad, 1962, 5-78.

Binyon: T.J. Binyon, *Pushkin*, London, 2002.

Blagoy: D. Blagoy, 'Tyutchev, yego kritiki i chitateli', *TS* (1923), 63-105.

Brandt: R.F. Brandt, 'Materialy dlya issledovaniya "Fyodor Ivanovich Tyutchev i yego poeziya"', *Izvestiya otdeleniya russkogo yazyka i slovesnosti Imperatorskoy Akademii Nauk*, XVI (1911), Part 2, 136-232; Part 3, 1-65.

Briskman: M. Briskman, 'F.I. Tyutchev v komitete tsensury inostrannoy', *LN*, XIX-XXI, 1935, 565-578.

Chaadayev: P.Ya. Chaadayev, *Sochineniya i pis'ma*, 2 vols., Moscow, 1913-1914.

Chagin: G.V. Chagin, *'O ty, poslednyaya lyubov'...'. Zhenshchiny v zhizni i poezii F. I. Tyutcheva*, St Petersburg, 1996.

Chereysky: L.A. Chereysky, *Sovremenniki Pushkina* (2nd., revised ed.), Moscow, 1999.

Chulkov (1923): G.I. Chulkov, 'Lyubov' v zhizni i v lirike F.I. Tyutcheva', *TS* (1923), 5-32.

Chulkov (1928): G.I. Chulkov, *Poslednyaya lyubov' Tyutcheva*, Moscow, 1928.

Custine: Adolphe, Marquis de Custine, *Empire of the Czar. A Journey Through Eternal Russia*, New York, 1989. (Abridged translation of Custine's *La Russie en 1839*, 4 vols., Paris, 1843.)

Dewey: John Dewey, 'Tiutchev and Amalie von Lerchenfeld: Some Unpublished

Documents', *The Slavonic and East European Review*, LXXIX, No.1, January 2001, 15-30.

Dinesman (1999a): T.G. Dinesman, 'O datirovkakh i adresatakh nekotorykh stikhotvoreniy Tyutcheva', *Letopis'-1*, 277-290.

Dinesman (1999b): T.G. Dinesman, 'O nekotorykh faktakh biografii Tyutcheva', *Letopis'-1*, 298-304.

Dinesman (1999c): 'Tyutchev v Myunkhene. (K istorii diplomaticheskoy kar'yery)', *TS-II*, 121-201.

Dinesman (2004): T.G. Dinesman, *F.I. Tyutchev. Stranitsy biografii (K istorii diplomaticheskoy kar'yery)*, Moscow, 2004.

DN: 'Vy — moi yedinstvennye korrespondenty v Moskve...' (ed. G.V. Chagin), *Druzhba narodov*, 1999, No.4, 203-221. (30 letters from Tyutchev to A.I. & M.A. Georgievsky.)

Dok.: *F.I. Tyutchev v dokumentakh, stat'yakh i vospominaniyakh sovremennikov* (ed. G.V. Chagin), Moscow, 1999.

Dolgopolova: S.A. Dolgopolova, ' "Ya pomnyu vremya zolotoye" ', *Nashe naslediye*, 2003, Nos.67-68, pp.58-63

Dolgopolova & Tarkhov (1989a): S.A. Dolgopolova, A.Ye. Tarkhov, 'Istoriya tyutchevskogo memorial'nogo sobraniya', *LN-2*, 600-609.

Dolgopolova & Tarkhov (1989b): S.A. Dolgopolova, A.Ye. Tarkhov, 'Prizhiznennaya ikonografiya Tyutcheva', *LN-2*, 610-631.

Dudek: G. Dudek, 'Der philosophische und künstlerische Gehalt der Gleichnisformen in F.I. Tjutcevs Poesie', *Zeitschrift für Slawistik*, III, 1958, Nos.2-4, 494-519.

Ekshtut: S. A. Ekshtut, *Tyutchev. Tayny sovetnik i kamerger*, Moscow, 2003.

Ernestine: K.V. Pigaryov & L.N. Kuzina, 'Vospominaniya Ern. F. Tyutchevoy (v zapisi D.F. Tyutchevoy)', *LN-2*, 99-103. (Reminiscences by T.'s second wife Ernestine, as recorded by his daughter Darya in her diary for 2 & 23 June 1857 [OS]).

Fallmerayer: J.P. Fallmerayer, *Gesammelte Werke*, 3 vols., Leipzig, 1861. (Accessible online at: www.literature.at)

Fet (1859): A. Fet, 'O stikhotvoreniyakh F. Tyutcheva', *Dok.*, 121-139. (Reference is made to this edition in preference to the less accessible original publication in *Russkoye slovo*, 1859, No.2 [Feb.], 63-84.)

Fet (1983): A. Fet, *Vospominaniya*, Moscow, 1983.

Ficquelmont: *Il diario di Dar'ja Fëdorovna Ficquelmont (1829-1831)* (ed. N. Kauchtschischwili), Milan, 1968.

Fisher: H.A.L. Fisher, *A History of Europe*, 2 vols., London & Glasgow, 1961.

Florinsky: Michael T. Florinsky, *Russia. A History and an Interpretation*, 2 vols., New York, 1960.

Gagarin: I.S. Gagarin, *Dnevnik. Zapiski o moyey zhizni. Perepiska* (ed. Richard Tempest), Moscow, 1996.

Georgievsky: 'Iz vospominaniy A.I. Georgievskogo' (ed. G.G. Yelizavetana, K.V. Pigaryov et al.) , *LN-2*, 104-163.

Gippius: Vas. Gippius, 'F.I. Tyutchev', in: F.I. Tyutchev, *Stikhotvoreniya* (ed. Vas. Gippius, K. Pigaryov), Leningrad, 1936, 5-48.

Glasse: A. Glasse, 'Diplomaticheskaya missiya Tyutcheva v Gretsiyu', *LN-2*, 446-452.

Gol'denveyzer: A.V. Gol'denveyzer, *Vblizi Tolstogo*, 2 vols., Moscow, 1922.

Gregg: Richard A. Gregg, *Fedor Tiutchev. The Evolution of a Poet*, New York & London, 1965.

Grot & Pletnyov: *Perepiska Ya.K. Grota i P.A. Pletnyova*, 3 vols., St Petersburg, 1896.

Heine (1968): Heinrich Heine, *Sämtliche Schriften* (ed. Klaus Briegleb), 6 vols., Munich, 1968-1976.

Heine (1970): Heinrich Heine, *Säkularausgabe. Werke, Briefwechsel, Lebenszeugnisse*, Berlin & Paris, 1970- (27 vols. of works and correspondence published, vols. of commentary ongoing.)

Heine, *Briefe*: Heinrich Heine, *Briefe*, ed. Friedrich Hirth, 6 vols., Mainz, 1950-1957.

Herzen: A.I. Gertsen [Herzen], *Sobraniye sochineniy*, 30 vols., Moscow, 1954-1966.

HSH: *Hof- und Staats-Handbuch des Königreichs Baiern*, Munich (annual publication).

Hümmert: Ludwig Hümmert, *Zwischen München und St. Petersburg. Bayerisch-russische Beziehungen und Begegnungen 1799-1918*, Munich, 1977.

Ilyasova: T.A. Ilyasova: 'Minuvshim nas poveyet i obnimet...', *Nauka i zhizn'*, 1984, No.7, 122-127.

Jesse: Horst Jesse, *Die Geschichte der Evangelisch-Lutherischen Kirchengemeinden in München und Umgebung 1510-1990*, Neuendettelsau, 1994.

Kauchtschischwili: Nina Kauchtschischwili, *L'Italia nella vita e nell'opera di P.A. Vjazemskij*, Milan, 1964.

Kazanovich: Ye.P. Kazanovich, 'Iz myunkhenskikh vstrech F.I. Tyutcheva (1840-ye gg.)', *Uraniya*, 125-171.

Kelly: Laurence Kelly, *Moscow. A Traveller's Companion*, London, 1983.

Khomyakov: A.S. Khomyakov, *Polnoye sobraniye sochineniy*, 8 vols., Moscow, 1900.

Kommentariy: G.V. Chagin, V.N. Kasatkina, *Ivan Segeyevich Aksakov i yego biografiya Fyodora Ivanovicha Tyutcheva. Kommentariy*, Moscow, 1997. (Companion volume to the 1997 reprint of Aksakov.)

Kondrat'yev: I.K. Kondrat'yev, *Sedaya starina Moskvy*, M., 1999 (revised reprint of the 1893 edition).

Koshelyov: *Zapiski Aleksandra Ivanovicha Koshelyova*, Berlin, 1884. Facsimile reprint as: Alexander I. Koshelev, *Zapiski, 1806-1883*, Newtonville (Mass.), 1976.

Kozhinov: Vadim Kozhinov, *Tyutchev*, Moscow, 1988.

Kozyrev: B.M. Kozyrev, 'Pis'ma o Tyutcheve', *LN-1*, 70-131.

Lane (1971): R.C. Lane, 'The Reception of F.I. Tyutchev's Political Articles in Russia and Abroad, 1844-1858', *European Studies Review*, I (1971), No.3, 205-231.

Lane (1982): R.C. Lane, 'Pascalian and Christian-Existential Elements in Tyutchev's Letters and Poems', *Forum for Modern Language Studies*, XVIII, No.4, October 1982, 317-334.

Lane (1983): R.C. Lane, 'Anniversaries in Tyutchev's Poetry', *Scottish Slavonic Review*, No.1, 1983, 125-136.

Lane (1984a): R.C. Lane, 'Four Unpublished Letters of Tjutcev to F. Thiersch (1829-1840)', *Jahrbücher für Geschichte Osteuropas*, XXXII (1984), No.2, 224-233.

Lane (1984b): R.C. Lane, 'Hunting Tyutchev's Literary Sources', in: W. Harrison, A. Pyman (eds.), *Poetry, Prose and Public Opinion: Aspects of Russia 1850-1970*.

Essays Presented in Memory of Dr N.E. Andreyev, Letchworth, 1984, 43-68.

Lane (1987): R.C. Lane, 'Tyutchev's Service Absenteeism and Second Marriage in the Light of Unpublished Documents', *Irish Slavonic Studies*, No.8, 1987, 6-13.

Lane (1988a): R. Leyn [R.C. Lane], 'Publitsistika Tyutcheva v otsenke zapadnoyevropeyskoy pechati kontsa 1840-kh — nachala 1850-kh godov', *LN-1*, 231-252. (A revised and much expanded version in Russian of Lane [1971].)

Lane (1988b): R.C. Lane, 'Tjutcev's Mission to Greece (1833) According to Diplomatic Documents', *Russian Literature*, XXIII, 1988, 265-280.

Lane (1990): R.C. Lane, 'Tyutchev's Diplomatic Role in the Visit of Grand Duke Alexander to Turin, 1839', *Irish Slavonic Studies*, No.11, 1990, 79-89.

Lane (1994): R.C. Lane, 'F.I. Tyutchev's Diplomatic Career in Munich (1822-37)', *Irish Slavonic Studies*, No.15, 1994 (1996), 17-43.

Letopis' (Ch.): G.I. Chulkov, *Letopis' zhizni i tvorchestva F.I. Tyutcheva*, Moscow & Leningrad, 1933.

Letopis'-1, *Letopis'-2*: T.G. Dinesman (ed.), *Letopis' zhizni I tvorchestva F.I. Tyutcheva,* Parts 1 (*1803-1844*) & 2 (*1844-1860*), Muranovo, 1999, 2003 (ongoing).

Lettres: 'Lettres de Th. I. Tjutscheff à sa seconde épouse, née Baronne de Pfeffel', *Starina i novizna*, XVIII (1914), 1-63; XIX (1915), 104-193; XXI (1916), 155-243; XXII (1917), 245-277; 'Quelques lettres de Th.I. Tjutscheff adressées à son beau-frère Baron de Pfeffel', ibid., XXII (1917), 278-293.

Liberman: *On the Heights of Creation. The Lyrics of Fedor Tyutchev* (translated with introduction and commentary by Anatoly Liberman), Greenwich (Connecticut) & London, 1992.

Liedtke: Christian Liedtke, *Heinrich Heine*, Reinbek bei Hamburg, 1997.

Lirika: F.I. Tyutchev, *Lirika* (ed. K.V. Pigaryov), 2 vols., Moscow, 1965.

LN: *Literaturnoye nasledstvo*, Moscow, 1931- (ongoing series).

LN-1, *LN-2*: (With specific reference to:) *Literaturnoye nasledstvo*, Vol. XCVII (*Fyodor Ivanovich Tyutchev*, ed. S.A. Makashin, K.V. Pigaryov, T.G.Dinesman), Parts 1 & 2, Moscow, 1988-1989.

MAT: *Moskva. Atlas turista* (ed. S.V. Smigel'skaya; 2nd., revised ed.), Moscow, 1990.

Mazour: Anatole G. Mazour, *The First Russian Revolution, 1825. The Decembrist Movement*, Stanford, 1961.

MD: *Memuary dekabristov. Severnoye obshchestvo* (ed. V.A. Fyodorov), Moscow, 1981.

Mende: F. Mende, *Heinrich Heine. Chronik seines Lebens und Werkes* (2nd., revised and augmented edition), Stuttgart, Berlin, Cologne & Mainz, 1981.

Nikitenko: A.V. Nikitenko, *Dnevnik* (ed. I. Ayzenshtok), 3 vols., Leningrad, 1955-1956.

Nikolayev (1979): A.A. Nikolayev, 'Sud'ba poeticheskogo naslediya Tyutcheva 1822-1836 godov i tekstologicheskiye problemy yego izucheniya', *Russkaya literatura*, 1979, No.1, 128-143.

Nikolayev (1988): A.A. Nikolayev, 'Zagadka "K.B." ', *Neva*, 1988, No.2, 190-196.

Nikolayev (1989): A.A. Nikolayev, 'O neosushchestvlyonnom zamysle izdaniya stikhotvoreniy Tyutcheva (1836-1837)', *LN-2*, 503-529.

NPTT: P. Kirillov, Ye. Pavlova, D. Shakhovskoy (eds.), 'Neizdannye pis'ma Tyutcheva i k Tyutchevu', *LN*, 1935, XIX-XXI, 580-602.

OA: *Ostaf'yevsky arkhiv knyazey Vyazemskikh*, Vol. IV: *Perepiska P.A.Vyazem-skogo s A.I. Turgenevym (1837-1845)*, St Petersburg, 1899.

Oertzen: Augusta von Oertzen, *Die Schönheiten-Galerie König Ludwig I. in der Münchner Residenz*, Munich, 1927.

O.N.: [Ol'ga Nikolayevna, daughter of Nicholas I], *Son yunosti. Zapiski docheri Nikolaya I*, Paris, 1963.

Ospovat (1980): A.L. Ospovat, *'Kak slovo nashe otzovyotsya...'. O pervom sbornike F.I. Tyutcheva*, Moscow, 1980.

Ospovat (1986): A.L. Ospovat, 'Iz materialov dlya biografii Tyutcheva', *Izvestiya Akademii nauk, seriya literatury i yazyka*, XLV, No.4, 1986, 350-357.

Ospovat (1989): A.L. Ospovat, 'Neskol'ko zametok k literaturnoy biografii Tyutcheva', *LN-2*, 499-502.

Ospovat (1992): A.L. Ospovat, 'Novonaydenny politichesky memorandum Tyutcheva: k istorii sozdaniya', *Novoye literaturnoye obozreniye*, 1992, No.1, 89-115.

Ospovat (1994): A.L. Ospovat, 'Tyutchev i zagranichnaya sluzhba III Otdeleniya. (Materialy k teme)', *Tynyanovsky sbornik. Pyatye Tynyanovskiye chteniya* (ed. Ye.A. Toddes, Yu.G. Tsivian, M.O. Chudakova), Riga & Moscow, 1994, 110-138.

Ospovat (1999): A.L. Ospovat, 'Elementy politicheskoy mifologii Tyutcheva. (Kommentariy k stat'ye 1844 g.)', *TS-II*, 227-263.

Petrova: I.V. Petrova, 'Mir, obshchestvo, chelovek v lirike Tyutcheva', *LN-1*, 13-69.

Pfeffel-Z: K. Pfeffel, '[Zametka o Tyutcheve]', in: K.V. Pigaryov, 'Karl Pfeffel o Tyutcheve', *LN-2*, 33-36.

Pfeffel-Laurentie: Letter of K. Pfeffel to P. Laurentie (editor of the newspaper *L'Union*, Ostend, 6 Aug. 1873 (NS), Aksakov, 317-319 (reprint of the original French text as published on 13 Aug. in *L'Union*, here incorrectly named *L'Univers*). (For a Russian translation see Pigaryov [as previous reference], 36-37.)

Pigaryov (1935a): K.V. Pigaryov, 'Tyutchev i problemy vneshney politiki tsarskoy Rossii', *LN*, 1935, XIX-XXI, 177-256.

Pigaryov (1935b): K.V. Pigaryov, 'Sud'ba literaturnogo nasledstva F.I. Tyutcheva', *LN*, 1935, XIX-XXI, 371-418.

Pigaryov (1937): K.V. Pigaryov, 'F.I. Tyutchev o frantsuzskikh politicheskikh sobytiyakh 1870-1873 gg.', *LN*, 1937, XXXI-XXXII, 753-776.

Pigaryov (1965): K.V. Pigaryov, 'Poeticheskoye naslediye F.I. Tyutcheva', *Lirika*, I, 273-314.

Pis'ma: F.I. Tyutchev, *Sochineniya* (ed. K.V. Pigaryov), 2 vols., Moscow, 1984. Vol. II (*Pis'ma*).

Pogodin: 'F.I. Tyutchev v dnevnike i vospominaniyakh M.P. Pogodina' (ed. L.N. Kuzina), *LN-2*, 7-29.

Polonsky (1998): Arkady Polonsky, *Progulki s Tyutchevym po Myunkhenu*, Kiev, 1998.

Polonsky (2003): Arkady Polonsky, *'Zdes' Tyutchev zhil...'. Russky poet v Myunkhene* (4th., revised and augmented edition), Kiev, 2003.

Pratt: Sarah Pratt, 'The Metaphysical Abyss: One Aspect of the Bond Between Tiutchev and Schelling', *Germano-Slavica*, Fall 1982, IV, No.2, 71-88.

Pri dvore-1, Pri dvore-2: A.F. Tyutcheva, *Pri dvore dvukh imperatorov*, Parts 1

(*Vospominaniya. Dnevnik 1853-1855*) & 2 (*Dnevnik 1855-1882*), Moscow, 1928-1929.

PSS (1933): F.I. Tyutchev, *Polnoye sobraniye stikhotvoreniy* (ed. G.I. Chulkov), 2 vols., Moscow & Leningrad, 1933-1934. Facsimile reprint: Moscow, 1994.

PSS (1987): F.I. Tyutchev, *Polnoye sobraniye stikhotvoreniy* (ed. A.A. Nikolayev), Leningrad, 1987.

PTN: 'Pis'ma F.I. Tyutcheva k grafu K.V. Nessel'rode' (ed. L.V. Gladkova, Ye.N. Lebedev), *Tyutchev segodnya. Materialy IV Tyutchevskikh chteniy*, Moscow, 1995, 139-184.

PTR: ' "Ya zhiv i vas lyublyu"... Pis'ma F.I. Tyutcheva k roditelyam' (ed. L.V. Gladkova), *Nashe naslediye*, 2003, Nos.67-68, pp.43-57.

Pumpyansky: L.V. Pumpyansky, 'Poeziya F.I. Tyutcheva', *Uraniya*, 9-57.

Pushkin: *The Complete Works of Alexander Pushkin in English*, 15 vols., Downham Market, 2001-2003.

Raich: S.Ye. Raich, 'Avtobiografiya', *Dok.*, 22-37. (Reference is made to this edition in preference to the less accessible original publication in *Russky bibliofil*, 1913, No.8, 5-33.)

Rogov: Kirill Rogov, 'Variatsii "Moskovskogo teksta": k istorii otnosheniy F.I. Tyutcheva i M.P. Pogodina', *TS-II*, 68-106.

Rothe: Hans Rothe, ' "Nicht was ihr meint ist die Natur". Tjutcev und das Junge Deutschland', *Studien zu Literatur und Aufklärung in Osteuropa. Aus Anlaß des VIII. Internationalen Slavistenkongresses in Zagreb (Bausteine zur Geschichte der Literatur bei den Slaven*, 13), Giessen, 1978, 319-335.

Schelling: *Friedrich Wilhelm Joseph von Schellings sämmtliche Werke* (ed. K.F.A. Schelling), 14 vols., Stuttgart & Augsburg, 1856-1861.

Schmidt: 'Schmidt, Ludwig Friedrich von', in: *Allgemeine Deutsche Biographie*, 55 vols., Munich, 1875-1912. XXXIV, 722-728 (accessible online at: http://de.wikisource.org/wiki/ADB).

Smirnova-Rosset: A.O. Smirnova-Rosset, *Dnevnik. Vospominaniya*, Moscow, 1989.

Solovyov: V.S. Solovyov, 'Poeziya F.I. Tyutcheva', *Dok.*, 392-408. (Reference is made to this in preference to the less accessible original publication in *Vestnik Yevropy*, 1895, No.40, 735-752.)

Strémooukhoff: D. Strémooukhoff, *La poésie et l'idéologie de Tiouttchev*, Paris, 1937.

Sverbeyev: D.N. Sverbeyev, *Zapiski*, 2 vols., Moscow, 1899.

TPBF: *Fyodor Ivanovich Tyutchev v pis'makh k Ye.K. Bogdanovoy i S.P. Frolovu (1866-1871 gg.)* (ed. Ye.P. Kazanovich), Leningrad, 1926.

Tietz: M[onsieur] [Friedrich] von Tietz, *St. Petersburgh, Constantinople and Napoli di Romania in 1833 and 1834*, 2 vols., London, 1836. (Translation of Tietz's *Erinnerungs-Skizzen aus Russland, der Türkei und Griechenland*, published the same year in Coburg & Leipzig.)

TM: 'Tyutchev v Myunkhene. (Iz perepiska I.S. Gagarina s A.N. Bakhmetevoy i I.S. Aksakovym)' (ed. A.L. Ospovat), *LN-2*, 38-62.

Tolstoy: L.N. Tolstoy, *Sobraniye sochineniy*, 20 vols., Moscow, 1960-1965.

Toporov: V.N. Toporov, 'Zametki o poezii Tyutcheva. (Yeshcho raz o svyazyakh s nemetskim romantizmom i shellingianstvom)', *TS* (1990), 32-107.

TPD: 'Tyutchev v pis'makh i dnevnikakh chlenov yego sem'i i drugikh sovremennikov' (ed. K.V. Pigaryov, T.G. Dinesman et al.), *LN-2*, 171-432.

TS (1923): *Tyutchevsky sbornik (1873-1923)*, Petrograd, 1923.

TS (1990): *Tyutchevsky sbornik* (ed. Yu. Lotman), Tallinn, 1990, 312-319.

TS-II: *Tyutchevsky sbornik II* (ed. L. Kiselyova, R. Leybov, A. Yungren), Tartu, 1999.

Turgenev (A.I.): 'Tyutchev v dnevnike A.I. Turgeneva' (ed. K.M. Azadovsky, A.L. Ospovat), *LN-2*, 63-98.

Turgenev *S*, Turgenev *P*: I.S. Turgenev, *Polnoye sobraniye sochineniy i pisem*, 28 vols., Moscow, 1961-1968. Published in two sections with separately numbered volumes: *Sochineniya*, vols. I-XV; *Pis'ma*, vols. I-XIII.

Tynyanov (1922): Yu. N. Tynyanov, 'Tyutchev i Geyne', in: Tynyanov, *Poetika. Istoriya literatury. Kino*, Moscow, 1977, 29-37. (Reference is made to this edition in preference to the less accessible first publication in *Kniga i revolyutsiya*, 1922, No.4, 13-16.)

Tynyanov (1977): Yu.N. Tynyanov, 'Tyutchev i Geyne', in *Poetika. Istoriya literatury. Kino* (as previous item), 350-395. (This much more extensive essay on the theme of Tyutchev and Heine remained unpublished during Tynyanov's lifetime.)

Tyutchev (F.F.): 'Fyodor Ivanovich Tyutchev. (Materialy k yego biografii)', *Dok.*, 226-240. (Reference is made to this edition in preference to the less accessible first publication in *Istorichesky vestnik*, 1903, XCIII, No.7, 185-203.

Tyutchev (F.I. jr.): F.I. Tyutchev [grandson of the poet], 'F.I. Tyutchev i yego deti (1838-1852 gg.)', *Uraniya*, 180-218.

Tyutcheviana: *Tyutcheviana. Epigrammy, aforizmy i ostroty F.I. Tyutcheva* (ed. G.I. Chulkov), Moscow, 1922.

Tyutchevy: G.V. Chagin, *Tyutchevy*, St Petersburg, 2003.

Udolph: L. Udolph, *Stepan Petrovic Sevyrev 1820-1836. Ein Beitrag zur Entstehung der Romantik in Rußland* (*Bausteine zur Geschichte der Literatur bei den Slaven*, 26), Cologne & Vienna, 1986.

Uraniya: *Uraniya. Tyutchevsky al'manakh. 1803-1828* (ed. Ye.P. Kazanovich), Leningrad, 1928.

Varnhagen: Karl August Varnhagen von Ense, *Aus dem Nachlaß Varnhagen's von Ense. Tagebücher* (ed. Ludmilla Assing), 15 vols., Leipzig, Zürich & Hamburg, 1861-1870, 1905. (Vol. XV, 1905, is the index.)

Vyazemsky: P.A. Vyazemsky, *Zapisnye knizhki (1813-1848)*, Moscow, 1963.

Yashin: M. Yashin, 'K portretu dukhovnogo litsa', *Neva*, 1966, No.2, 169-176; No.3, 186-199.

Zavalishin: D.I. Zavalishin, *Zapiski dekabrista* (2nd. ed.), St Petersburg & Moscow, 1910. (The earlier Russian editions of 1906 and 1908 appear to have the same pagination as this.)

Zhizn': K.V. Pigaryov, *Zhizn' i tvorchestvo Tyutcheva*, Moscow, 1962.

Zhukovsky (1903): V.A. Zhukovsky, *Dnevniki*, St Petersburg, 1903.

Zhukovsky (1999): V.A. Zhukovsky, *Polnoye sobraniye sochineniy i pisem*, 20 vols., Moscow, 1999- (ongoing).

NOTES

Abbreviations used

Frequently cited publications, archives, etc. are referred to in abbreviated form. For the full version of these see the foregoing 'Sources' section.

Chapter 1. Childhood and Youth

1. S.P. Shevyryov, 'Obozreniye Russkoy slovesnosti na 1827 g.', *Moskovsky vestnik*, 1828, I, 62 (quoted in Udolph, 104).

2. 'Graf Osterman-Tolstoy', *RA*, 1878, I, 362 (quoted in *Tyutchevy*, 104-105).

3. Based on two later accounts by T. of an apparently unchanging pattern of religious observances followed when leaving his mother in Moscow (letters to Ern. T. of 14/26 Aug. 1843 and 11/23 Sept. 1858. IV, 258; Lettres, XIX, 186). For a description of the chapel (later demolished) see Kelly, 162-165.

4. For a description of the book and the history contained in its inscriptions see: N.P. Belevtseva, 'Knigi, prinadlezhavshiye Tyutchevu', *LN-2*, 636.

5. The doctrine of 'Moscow the Third Rome' was first formulated in 1510 by Filofey, a monk of the Lazarus Monastery at Pskov, in a missive to Grand Duke Vasily III of Moscow.

6. Aksakov, 6.

7. There is an account of the episode in N.M. Karamzin's *Istoriya Rossiyskogo gosudarstva* (Vol. V, SPb., 1817, 422-423), a work with which T. was familiar as a student (see Pogodin, 11-13 passim). For other accounts known at the time see *Zhizn'*, 7 (footnote 1).

8. Aksakov, 8; *Letopis'* (Ch.), 13.

9. *Zhizn'*, 7 (footnote 2).

10. B.O. Unbegaun, *Russkiye familii*, M., 1989, 293 (quoted in *Tyutchevy*, 6). For more on Russian names of Tatar origin see: Orlando Figes, *Natasha's Dance. A Cultural History of Russia*, London, 2002, 361-363.

11. This finds its clearest expression in lines 5-8 of the poem 'Vnov' tvoi ya vizhu ochi...' (I, 208).

12. *Tyutchevy*, 9.

13. Ibid., 21

14. Ibid., 17, 19.

15. Ibid., 19-20; Florinsky, I, 573.

16. *Tyutchevy*, 21-22.

17. Aksakov, 8. The eyewitness account is quoted in *Tyutchevy*, 22-23.

18. *Tyutchevy*, 380.

19. Ibid., 23, 380. Nikolay retired as '*sekund-mayor*', equivalent to the later rank of Captain.

20. Ekshtut, 22-24.

21. Ibid., 24; T. Tret'yakova, *Tyutchevy — myshkinskiye dvoryane*, Yaroslavl, 2003, 35.

22. *Tyutchevy*, 380-382.

23. Ibid., 25-26.

24. Ibid., 27; *Zhizn'*, 8.

25. 1776, the year of birth given in *Letopis'* (Ch.), 68, has recently been corrected by G.V. Chagin on the basis of archival documentation (*Tyutchevy*, 32-33).
26. Aksakov, 8-9; *Zhizn'*, 8; Ekshtut, 24-26.
27. *Tyutchevy*, 47.
28. J.P. Fallmerayer, 'Graf Ostermann-Tolstoi', in: Fallmerayer, II, 364; Florinsky, I, 458.
29. *Tyutchevy*, 48; Florinsky, I, 514, 540.
30. Aksakov, 9.
31. Ibid., 8-9.
32. *Zapiski, stat'i, pis'ma dekabrista I.D. Yakushkina* (ed. S.Ya. Shtraykh), M., 1951, 47-48.
33. 'Lyubeznomu papen'ke!' ('To Dear Papa!'), I, 11.
34. Aksakov, 9. T. himself refers to his mother's 'gratuitous lamentations' and 'fanciful apprehensions' in a letter to his second wife Ernestine dated 8/20 June 1861 (Lettres, XX, 185).
35. *Tyutchevy*, 384; *Letopis'-1*, 17. Tyutchev mentions the time of day when he was born in a letter written to Ernestine from SPb. on his 49th. birthday, 23 Nov./ 5 Dec.1852 (RGB. 308.1.20, *l.* 70-71*ob.*).
36. Aksakov, 9.
37. *Letopis'-1*, 17.
38. Aksakov, 11.
39. *Tyutchevy*, 386.
40. E.g.: F.I.T. to Vaclav Hanke, Mu., 16/28 Apr. 1843. IV, 227.
41. Quoted in: James H. Billington, *The Icon and the Axe. An Interpretative History of Russian Culture*, London, 1966, 1.
42. Charles Colville Frankland, *Narrative of a Visit to the Courts of Russia and Sweden in the Years 1830 and 1831*, 2 vols., London, 1832. II, 269.
43. Details from a mortgage deed for the property dated 1804: *Tyutchevy*, 49-50.
44. F.I.T. to Ern. T., M., 14/26 Aug. 1846. IV, 258.
45. *Letopis'-1*, 19, 20. For further relevant entries in the church's registers see ibid., 18-20. The church has survived, and was restored to use in the early 1990s. The Ostermans' house still stands, much altered and extended, at what is now 8, Maly tryokhsvyatitel'sky pereulok (*Tyutchevy*, 49).
46. F.I.T. to I.N. & Ye.L. Tyutchev, Mu., 17/29 June 1838. IV, 101.
47. F.I.T. to I.V. Sushkov, Mu., 21 June/ 3 July 1836. IV, 48.
48. Pogodin, 10 (diary entry for 9 Aug. 1820).
49. Reproduced in Dolgopolova & Tarkhov (1989b), 615, 619, with notes on the portraits (613-614).
50. Aksakov, 11.
51. See: *Letopis'-1*, 18, 19, 20, 328.
52. P.D. Tyutcheva to N.N. Sheremeteva, Znamenskoye , [late 1810]. IV, 482.
53. Aksakov, 11.
54. Ern. T. to K. Pfeffel, SPb., 14/26 May 1846. TPD, 217.
55. Gregg, 174.
56. Aksakov, 17; *Tyutchevy, 128*.
57. Aksakov, 17.
58. F.I.T. to N.I. Tyutchev, SPb, 13/25 Apr. 1868. VI, 322.
59. Aksakov, 9-10.
60. Leo Tolstoy, who first met T. in the 1850s, recalled that he 'spoke and wrote more fluently in French than in Russian' (Gol'denveyzer, I, 182-183). In a letter to his daughter Anna dated 22 Oct./ 3 Nov. 1871 T. himself admitted that he found it easier to express his thoughts in French than in Russian (quoted in *Letopis'* [Ch.], 221). For more on the use of French and neglect of spoken Russian by the aristocracy in the early 19th. century see Figes (as note 10), 55-57.
61. Aksakov, 11.
62. Ibid., 9.
63. Kozhinov, 28. On 25 August 1820 T.'s university friend Mikhail Pogodin noted in his diary: 'Conversed with Tyutchev *and his parents* about literature, about Karamzin, Goethe, Zhukovsky, about the university'. (Pogodin, 11. My italics.)
64. Osterman-Tolstoy's name appears in the records of Three Saints' Church as godfather to one of Anna's servants in February 1808 (*Tyutchevy*, 52-53).
65. Fallmerayer, 'Graf...' (as note 28), 364-366.
66. *Tyutchevy*, 212.

67. *Letopis'-1*, 20.

68. Ibid., 21; *Tyutchevy*, 55, 58-59.

69. *Tyutchevy*, 56-57. The print and a ground plan of the house are reproduced in *Kommentariy*, 96.

70. *Tyutchevy*, 58-59.

71. Ibid., 56-57, 82-83.

72. At Ivan Nikolayevich's death in 1846 his personal estate numbered only 615 serfs, but to this must be added the 629 serfs, with land, which he had given to his sons three years previously (IV, 555-557). Similarly, in 1836 Yekaterina Lvovna settled the lands and 509 serfs she had received from Anna Osterman on her daughter Darya as a dowry (*Tyutchevy*, 211-212).

73. It has been estimated that in 1834 only 3% of landowners in Great Russia itself (i.e. excluding Ukraine and Belorussia) owned more than 500 male adult serfs each (Florinsky, I, 575). At the time Yekaterina was just above this limit, Ivan comfortably so.

74. Prince Peter Kropotkin, *Memoirs of a Revolutionist*, London, 1899 (quoted without page reference in Kelly, 282).

75. *Tyutchevy*, 83.

76. Ibid., 57-58.

77. Ibid., 62-63; Kozhinov, 43; Kondrat'yev, 325-326.

78. Kozhinov, 35.

79. Benn & Bartlett, 114-115; *MAT*, 148.

80. Kozhinov, 42; Kondrat'yev, 323-324.

81. Benn & Bartlett, 43; *MAT*, 150.

82. Benn & Bartlett, 9-10, 25-26.

83. *MAT*, 148.

84. Ibid..; Kozhinov, 35; Robin Edmonds, *Pushkin. The Man and his Age*, London & Basingstoke, 1994, 37.

85. Kondrat'yev, 291-294; I.P. Mashkov (ed.), *Putevoditel' po Moskve. 1913*, M., 1998 (reprint of the 1913 edition), 114, 120-122; Kozhinov, 37; *Tyutchevy*, 57; Tamara Talbot Rice, *A Concise History of Russian Art*, London, 1963, 134-135.

86. Kondrat'yev, 277-278; *Putevoditel'* (as note 85), 332-333.

87. *Putevoditel'* (as note 85), 201; *MAT*, 167 (No.41).

88. *Putevoditel'* (as note 85), 149-151; Kondrat'yev, 298-299.

89. Quoted (without reference) in Kozhinov, 38.

90. Ibid.

91. Accounts of the same journey can be found in T.'s letters to his wife Ernestine of 31 Aug./ 12 Sept. (Ovstug) and 13/25 Sept. (Moscow) 1846, by which time travelling conditions had not materially improved (IV, 365, 368-369). Further details are taken from two unpublished letters to Ernestine from Moscow dated 18/30 June and 21 June/ 3 July 1851 (RGB.308.1.19, *l.* 3-4, 1-2*ob.*).

92. IV, 555.

93. G.V. Chagin, 'Rodina poeta', *LN-2*, 598-599.

94. F.I.T. to Ern. T., Ovstug, 31 Aug./ 12 Sept. 1846. IV, 365.

95. 'Itak, opyat' uvidelsya ya s vami...'. I, 204.

96. Aksakov, 12.

97. F.I.T. to Ern. T., Vienna, 13/25 June 1843. IV, 230.

98. Aksakov, 12.

99. 'Neman'. II, 60.

100. *Tyutchevy*, 37, 39.

101. Aksakov, 12.

102. Barsukov, I, 13-15.

103. Koshelyov, 4.

104. *Tyutchevy*, 384-386.

105. *Letopis'-1*, 22.

106. As note 95.

107. Kozhinov, 3; *Tyutchevy*, 68.

108. *Tyutchevy*, 64.

109. The figure quoted by Summerville in: General Count Philippe de Ségur, *Napoleon's Expedition to Russia* (ed. Christopher Summerville), London, 2003, 255.

110. *Tyutchevy*, 64.

111. Barsukov, I, 17.

112. Koshelyov, 5.

113. See: Aksakov, 12; *Zhizn'*, 10-11; Kozhinov, 40-42.

114. *Materialy dlya istorii Lazarevskogo instituta vostochnykh yazykov*, Part I, Moscow, 1914, 2-3 (quoted in *Tyutchevy*, 62-63).

115. *Zhizn'*, 10; de Ségur (as note 109), 124.

116. K.A. Polevoy, *Zapiski*, SPb., 1888, 100 (quoted in *Tyutchevy*, 65-66). Apart from Raich, T. is known for instance to have been taught French literature by the translator Pierre d'Inocourt in 1815-1816 (Raich, 30; *Letopis'-1*, 317). No doubt other tutors were hired on an ad hoc basis to teach those subjects required for university entrance (e.g., German, maths, geography — see *Letopis'-1*, 29) which Raich is unlikely to have taught.

117. Aksakov, 13.

118. Raich, 22-27.

119. Ibid., 31.

120. Ibid., 27-29.

121. Ibid., 29.

122. *Tyutchevy*, 63, 68.

123. Raich, 29.

124. Ibid.

125. Ibid., 24-25, 30.

126. D.F. Tyutcheva to Ye.F. Tyutcheva, Ovstug, 20 Aug./ 1 Sept. 1855. TPD, 276. Here Raich is not identified by name, but merely referred to (in the French original of Darya's letter) as T.'s '*menin*'. Pigaryov considered that this archaic term (formerly used for young noblemen appointed as companions to the Dauphin of France) could refer equally to Raich or Khlopov; he accordingly translates it into Russian as '*pestun, vospitatel'* ', i.e. 'governor, tutor' (*Zhizn'*, 12). The Russian version of the letter given in TPD allows for no such doubt, boldly rendering '*menin*' as '*dyad'ka*' (i.e. Khlopov), a distortion repeated by later scholars (*Letopis'-1*, 20; *Tyutchevy*, 66). Only Kozhinov translates it as '*nastavnik*' ('tutor'), evidently believing the reference to be to Raich (Kozhinov, 15). This seems a more credible assumption all round. Unlike Khlopov (then well into his forties), Raich in his early twenties fits easily into the ironically assigned role of young nobleman; T.'s composition of a poem for the 'funeral' provides a further unmistakable pointer to his tutor's guiding presence.

127. 'Lyubeznomu papen'ke!'. I, 11. This has been dated to 1813 or 1814 (I, 277).

128. As note 126.

129. *Tyutchevy*, 68.

130. References to Ivan Nikolayevich in surviving church records tell the story of his brief pre-war civil service career. In February 1809 he is still referred to as 'Lieutenant Tyutchev' (i.e., the rank at which he had retired from the guards). By September 1810 he is 'Collegiate Assessor' (grade 8 in the Table of Ranks), but in January 1811 already 'Collegiate Assessor (retired)'. (*Letopis'-1*, 20-21.)

131. As note 129.

132. Raich, 29-30; *Letopis'-1*, 23. Raich claims to have passed his finals after six months and to have been awarded his Bachelor's ('*kandidat*') degree after some delay in 1817; in fact he officially graduated on 20 Feb. 1818 (*Dok.*, 430).

133. Kozhinov, 61-62. G.V. Chagin quotes a document attesting that Nikolay passed an entrance examination for Muravyov's academy in ten subjects (*Tyutchevy*, 68-69), which implies that he too must have received a thorough education at the hand of tutors.

134. *Tyutchevy*, 42.

135. Raich, 29.

136. *Tyutchevy*, 43-45.

137. *Letopis'-1*, 24-25.

138. Raich, 30.

139. Ibid., 30-31; N.V. Sushkov, *Moskovsky blagorodny pansion*, Moscow, 1858, 92 (quoted in *Letopis'-1*, 24).

140. Raich, 30.

141. Ibid.

142. 'Na novy 1816 god'. I, 12-13.

143. Most of the others are occasional pieces composed to mark family events: 'Lyubeznomu papen'ke!'; 'Dvum druz'yam'; 'V den' rozhdeniya lyubezneyshego papen'ki!'; 'V den' rozhdeniya miloy mamin'ki' (I, 11, 15; IV, 480, 481). There is also a four-line epigram inscribed in T.'s own copy of *La Henriade*, defending the 'prodigious' Voltaire against attacks from envious critics: 'Puskay ot zavisti serdtsa zoilov noyut...' (I, 16). As shown by K.V. Pigaryov (*Lirika*, II, 327; *Zhizn'*, 30-32), this last piece is in fact heavily plagiarised from an epigram by I.I. Dmitriev.

144. *Tyutchevy*, 69.

145. A.F. Merzlyakov to P.A. Novikov, M., 3/15 July 1817. *Russkaya starina*, XXVI, 1879, No.10, 350 (quoted in *Letopis'-1*, 25).

146. *Tyutchevy*, 74-75.

147. Chulkov's suggestion, made in a note accompanying the first publication of 'Na novy 1816 god' (*Feniks*, M., 1922, Part I, 137) was subsequently endorsed by K.V. Pigaryov (*Zhizn'*, 13; *Lirika*, II, 325).

148. *Tyutchevy*, 76.

149. 'Poslaniye Goratsii k Metsenatu, v kotorom priglashayet yego k sel'skomu obedu'. I, 17-19.

150. Strémooukhoff, 31; *Zhizn'*, 16.

see *Letopis'-1*, 43, 55, 58.

152. Aksakov, 13. **151.** For details of further readings and publications of T.'s poems by the SLRL in 1821 and 1822

153. *Letopis'-1*, 27.

154. Ibid., 26; Mazour, 71; Kondrat'yev, 309.

155. Florinsky, II, 753, 879; Aksakov, 14.

156. Zhukovsky (1903), 52.

157. Ibid., 55.

158. Aksakov, 14.

159. Ibid., 16; '17-oye aprelya 1818'. II, 255.

160. 'Pamyati V. A. Zhukovskogo'. II, 55.

161. *Tyutchevy*, 92.

162. Ibid., 42, 70-71; *Letopis'-1*, 26.

163. Writing to his wife from Ovstug on 20 August/ 1 Sept. 1846, T. stated that he had last been there 27 years before (IV, 359). (The figure of 26 years mentioned in a letter to his mother eleven days later [ibid., 362] appears to be a slip of the pen, as the summer of 1820 was spent at Troitskoye: see *Letopis'-1*, 35-37.)

164. *Letopis'-1*, 29.

165. Kondrat'yev, 328; *MAT*, 166-167.

166. Ekshtut, 33. In 1824 Moscow University had 820 students, Kharkov 337, Kazan 118, and St Petersburg only 51 (Florinsky, II, 726).

167. *Letopis'-1*, 32-33, 45-46.

168. Yu.M. Lotman, *Besedy o russkoy kul'ture. Byt i traditsii russkogo dvoryanstva (XVIII - nachalo XIX veka)*, SPb., 1994, 323.

169. N.I. Pirogov, *Sobraniye sochineniy*, 8 vols., M., 1957-1962. VIII, 223-224 (quoted in *Tyutchevy*, 81-82).

170. Quoted in Ekshtut, 35.

171. M.A. Dmitriev, *Glavy iz vospominaniy moyey zhizni*, M., 1998, 121 (quoted in Ekshtut, 36).

172. Sverbeyev, I, 109.

173. N.V. Basargin, *Vospominaniya, rasskazy, stat'i*, Irkutsk, 1988, 305-306 (quoted in Ekshtut, 37-38).

174. Pirogov (as note 169), VIII, 223-224.

175. *Zhizn'*, 17; *Tyutchevy*, 101; *Letopis'-1*, 52.

176. *Letopis'-1*, 30-31, 32-33.

177. N.V. Sushkov, 'Oboz k potomstvu s knigami i rukopisyami', *Raut*, 1854, No.3, 263-264, 266, 270 (quoted in *Tyutchevy*, 77-78).

178. *Zhizn'*, 18.

179. N.I. Nadezhdin, in: *Teleskop*, Part II, 1831, No.5, 87 (quoted in *Zhizn'*, 18).

180. *Biograficheksy slovar' professorov i prepodavateley imperatorskogo Moskovskogo universiteta*, Part II, M., 1855, 96 (entry by S.P. Shevyryov) (quoted in *Zhizn'*, 18-19).

181. Koshelyov, 6.

182. Pogodin, 11 (diary entry, 13 Oct. 1820).

183. *Tyutchevy*, 80.

184. Koshelyov, 6.

185. I.A. Goncharov, *Polnoye sobraniye sochineniy*, 9 vols., SPb., 1896. IX, 111-112 (quoted in *Zhizn'*, 19).

186. *Letopis'-1*, 33-34.

187. Ekshtut, 34.

188. *Letopis'-1*, 34-35.

189. As pointed out by R.F. Brandt (Brandt, Part 2, 149), these lines closely echo Schiller's: 'Was wir als Schönheit hier empfunden/ Wird einst als Wahrheit uns entgegen gehn' ('What we have perceived here as Beauty/ Will one day approach us as Truth').

190. 'Uraniya'. I, 20-25.

191. *Letopis'-1*, 35.

192. M.N. Virolaynen, 'Molodoy Pogodin', in: M.P. Pogodin, *Povesti. Drama* (ed. M.N. Virolaynen), M., 1984, 3-18 (here: 4).

193. Ibid., 6.

194. Barsukov, I, 58; F.I.T. to M.P. Pogodin (2 letters): Troitskoye, second half of July & 8 Aug. 1820 (OS). IV, 9; Pogodin, 10 (diary, 9 Aug. 1820).

195. Pogodin, 24.

196. Pogodin, 10 (diary, 9 Aug. 1820).

197. Ibid., 11-12 (diary entries for 13 Oct., 26 Nov., 2 Dec. 1820)

198. Ibid., 12 (diary, 2 Dec. 1820); see also ibid., 18 (note 15).

199. See the entry from Pogodin's diary quoted (without date) in: Rogov, 99 (note 4). The diary page no. referred to suggests that the entry was made at some time in 1821.

200. Virolaynen (as note 192), 3.

201. Pogodin, 13 (diary, 30 Oct. 1821).

202. Ibid. (diary, 23 Jan. 1822).

203. Extract from Pogodin's unpublished autobiography. TPD, 182.

204. Rogov, 71 (Pogodin's diary, 9 Aug. 1820). (In the version of the same entry published in Pogodin, 10, this passage is omitted.)

205. F.I.T. to M.P. Pogodin, M., between 20 Feb. and 6 April 1821 (OS). IV, 10.

206. ' "Ne day nam dukhu prazdnoslov'ya"!..'. I, 35.

207. Pogodin, 13 (diary, 6 Dec. 1821).

208. Mazour, 68, 71-72; Florinsky, II, 740-741.

209. Florinsky, II, 740; N. Chulkov, 'Moskva i dekabristy', in: *Dekabristy i ikh vremya,* 2 vols., M., 1927-1932. II, 295 (quoted in Ospovat [as note 210], 237).

210. A.L. Ospovat, 'O stikhotvorenii "14-oye dekabrya 1825". (K probleme "Tyutchev i dekabrizm")', *TS* (1990), 233-251 (here: 237).

211. Pogodin, 12 (diary, 1 Nov. 1820).

212. Ibid., 7 (diary, 3 Oct. 1820).

213. Ibid., 8 (diary, 13 April 1824).

214. Ibid., 7 (diary, 24 Feb. 1821).

215. Ibid., 12 (diary, 16 March 1821).

216. Barsukov, I, 56.

217. Pogodin, 9 (diary, 19 Feb. 1822).

218. As note 211.

219. *Zhizn'*, 27.

220. 'Liberty. An Ode' (transl. Walter Arndt). Pushkin, I, 269.

221. 'K ode Pushkina na vol'nost''. I, 27. (The word printed as '*bednye*' in line 8 of this edition is a misprint for *blednye*'.)

222. V.P. Gorchakov, 'Vyderzhki iz dnevnika moikh vospominaniy o A.S. Pushkine i yego drugikh sovremennikakh', *Moskvityanin*, 1850, Part 2, No.7, April, Book 1, 190-192, 194 (quoted in Ospovat [as note 223], 70-71).

223. *Zhizn'*, 28-29; A.L. Ospovat, 'Tyutchev i Pushkin', *Tynyanovsky sbornik. IV-ye tynyanovskiye chteniya*, Riga, 1990, 71-72.

224. Ospovat (as note 223), 71-72. The source quoted by Ospovat for Pushkin's remark is: A.F. Vel'tman, 'Il'ya Larin', *Moskovskiy gorodskoy listok*, 1847, No.8 (10 Jan.), 30.

225. The allegation by the critic Yury Tynyanov of something approaching a feud between the two poets rests on very flimsy evidence. It is discussed in more detail in Chapter 8.

226. As note 211.

227. From Pogodin's unpublished draft memoirs of student life quoted in N.V. Korolyova, 'Tyutchev i Pushkin', *Pushkin. Issledovaniya i materialy*, IV, M. & L., 1962, 187.

228. As note 211.

229. Pogodin, 3.

230. 'Kharon i Kachenovsky'. I, 28.

231. *Lirika*, II, 332; *Zhizn'*, 20.

232. Pushkin, I, 283; ibid., II, 38, 80.

233. 'Vesna' (Lyubov' zemli i prelest' goda...'); 'A.N.M.'; 'Protivnikam vina'; 'Poslaniye k A.V. Sheremetevu'; 'Druz'yam pri posylke "Pesni radosti" — iz Shillera'. I, 29-30, 31, 36-37, 39, 44.

234. Strémooukhoff, 36.

235. *Dok.*, 430 (note 28); *Letopis'-1*, 29.

236. Raich, 33; A.N. Murav'yov, *Znakomstvo s russkimi poetami*, Kiev, 1871, 5; N. Putyaya, 'Zametka ob A.N. Murav'yove', *RA*, 1876, II, 357 (all quoted in Aronson & Reyser, 123-124).

237. K. Polevoy, *Zapiski*, SPb., 1888, 100-101 (quoted in Aronson & Reyser, 126-127); *Letopis'-1*, 278.

238. In addition to the three memoirs referred to in note 236, see: M.A. Dmitriev, 'Vospominaniye o S.Ye. Raiche', *Moskovskiye vedomosti*, 1855, No.141, Lit. otd.; Koshelyov, 11-12 (both quoted in Aronson & Reyser, 124, 125-126).

239. *Tyutchevy*, 96.

240. Toporov, 78-79; Koshelyov, 7; Udolph, 11; *Tyutchevy*, 94; Ye. Khin, 'V.F. Odoyevsky', in: V.F. Odoyevsky, *Povesti i rasskazy*, M., 1959, 3-38 (here: 5).

241. In a letter dated 16 April 1822 (OS) his cousin, the poet and future Decembrist Aleksandr Odoyevsky gently chided the seventeen-year-old Vladimir for his belief that in 'the incomprehensible Schelling's abstruse speculations is contained the sum total of human wisdom' (Khin [as note 240], 5). Not long afterwards Odoyevsky translated and read out to Raich's circle the chapter 'Nichts-Gott' ('Nothing-God') from Oken's *Lehrbuch der Naturphilosophie* (*Manual of Natural Philosophy*) of 1807 (ibid., 6; Aronson & Reyser, 268). Pogodin also read out to the circle his own translation of Schelling's 1807 speech 'Über das Verhältnis der bildenden Künste zu der Natur' ('On the Relationship of the Fine Arts to Nature') (Aronson & Reyser, 268-269).

242. Koshelyov, 8-9; Toporov, 79.

243. The years of birth of the leading '*lyubomudry*' are: 1804: Vladimir Odoyevsky and Nikolay Melgunov; 1805: Dmitry Venevitinov and Nikolay Rozhalin; 1806: Ivan Kireyevsky, Aleksandr Koshelyov and Stepan Shevyryov; 1807: Vladimir Titov; 1808: Pyotr Kireyevsky. (Some reference works give the year of Odoyevsky's birth as 1803. However, according to more reliable sources he was born either on 30 July or 1 August 1804 [OS], making him eight months younger than Tyutchev. See: Khin [as note 240], 4; Alfred Rammelmayer, 'V.F. Odoevskij und seine "Russische Nächte" ', in: V.F. Odoyevsky, *Russkiye nochi* / Vladimir F. Odoevskij, *Russische Nächte* [facsimile reprint of the Moscow 1913 edition], Mu., 1967, v-xxvi [here: vii].)

244. *Letopis'-1*, 32-33, 40-41. See also: F.I.T. to M.P Pogodin, M. 23 June 1821(OS). IV, 12-13.

245. F.I.T. to M.P. Pogodin, June (before 21st., OS) 1821. IV, 12 (No.9).

246. V.N. Toporov claims to have found a reference to Schelling in Pogodin's diary record of discussions with T. on 9 Aug. 1820 (Toporov, 79). This is puzzling, as the published version of this entry makes no mention of Schelling (see: Pogodin, 10). One can only assume that Toporov misread 'Schiller' (who is mentioned) as 'Schelling'.

247. F.I.T. to M.P. Pogodin: three letters of June (before 21st.) and one of 23 June 1821 (OS). IV, 12-13.

248. Pogodin, 24.

249. *Letopis'-1*, 45-46.

250. G.V. Chagin has speculated that T.'s parents — in particular his mother — may have wanted to send him abroad in order to extricate him from what they saw as damaging political and/or amorous involvements (*Tyutchevy*, 97). However, no evidence is produced for either hypothesis, the second of which seems particularly unlikely. If (as also suggested by Chagin: see below, note 284) the supposed liaison was with a serf girl, the natural solution for T.'s parents would have been to send her away rather than their son. Apart from anything else, the time scale involved (over a year between T.'s second application to to graduate early and his eventual departure for Munich) would have been far too long to offer any effective remedy.

251. *Letopis'-1*, 44.

252. Ibid., 323.

253. Ibid., 44-45.

254. Florinsky, II, 638-641.

255. Zavalishin, 174 (quoted in *Dok.*, 53: see also 443, note 4); D.I. Zavalishin, 'Vselensky orden vosstanovleniya i otnosheniya moi k "Severnomu taynomu obshchestvu" ', *Russkaya starina*, 1882, XXXIII, No.1, 20 (quoted in *Letopis'-1*, 54).

256. G.V. Chagin (*Tyutchevy*, 98) points out Yelizaveta Alekseyevna's family connections to Aleksandr Nikolayevich Golitsyn, but confuses the issue by describing her as his sister ('*sestra*'), a relationship evidently precluded by their differing patronymics. Perhaps he intended to say she was his cousin ('*dvoyurodnaya sestra*').
257. Pogodin was given details of this visit by Tyutchev on 9 August. See Pogodin, 12 (diary, 9 Aug.), 18 (note 23).
258. *Letopis'-1*, 47.
259. Virolaynen (as note 192), 4.
260. *Letopis'-1*, 49.
261. Aksakov, 16.
262. *Letopis'-1*, 51-54.
263. Ibid., 53.
264. As note 255.
265. Zavalishin, 19.
266. Lotman (as note 168), 368.
267. Zavalishin, 'Vselensky orden...' (as note 255), 20.
268. A.L. Ospovat cites an unpublished letter from Ya.N. Tolstoy to P.A. Vyazemsky (Paris, 24 Aug./ 5 Sept. 1853) as evidence that T. got to know Tolstoy in 1822 (Ospovat [as note 210], 236, 248 *n*.19). For biographical details of Tolstoy see Chereysky, 83.
269. Ospovat (1986), 351.
270. Ibid., 350-351; *Letopis'-1*, 55.
271. *Letopis'-1*, 55, 58.
272. D.I. Zavalishin, 'Vospominaniye o gr. A.I. Ostermane-Tolstom', *Istorichesky vestnik*, 1880, II, No.5, 96 (quoted in *Letopis'-1*, 54).
273. The practice is described (relating specifically to the year 1818) by a character in Pushkin's 'A Novel in Letters'. The same character states that a decade later (i.e. after the Decembrist revolt) it had fallen into disuse. (Pushkin, IX, 94.)
274. V. Bazanov, *Vol'noye obshchestvo lyubiteley rossiyskoy slovesnosti*, Petrozavodsk, 1949, 16 (quoted in Lotman [as note 168], 340).
275. Zavalishin, 10, 40 (quoted with these page references to the 1908 edition of Zavalishin's *Zapiski dekabrista* in Lotman [as note 168], 336, 368).
276. 'Stanzas to Tolstoy'. Pushkin, I, 307.
277. Aksakov, 16. A likely informant for this period in T.'s life would have been Pogodin, who was still alive when Aksakov wrote his biography.
278. Ibid., 41.
279. Ibid., 47.
280. Ibid., 16.
281. Tyutchev (F.F.), 235.
282. *Tyutchevy*, 25, 85-86.
283. Aksakov, 40.
284. The prominent Tyutchev scholar Gennady Chagin has claimed that documents from the church records of St Nicholas in Armenian Lane point to an affair with a certain Katya Kruglikova, a household serf two years older than T. who was in the employ of his parents. (*Tyutchevy*, 102-103). Chagin himself concedes that the evidence in question is circumstantial (ibid., 102), and it is certainly open to more than one interpretation. It consists of two entries over a year apart (17 April 1821 and 25 May 1822) for christenings of serf children at which T. and Katya are named together as godparents (ibid.; see also *Letopis'-1*, 43, 56). In fact it was not unusual for masters to act as godparents to the children of serfs (the fourteen-year-old T. and his sister Darya, then eleven, are recorded as having done so in 1818: *Letopis'-1*, 26), nor that they should share the honours with a non-noble (this had been so when T. was put forward as godfather at the ages of three and five respectively: *Letopis'-1*, 19, 20). Moreover, in all these cases the initiative was clearly taken by T.'s parents, and the same no doubt applies to his nomination as godparent with Katya at the age of seventeen. That he and Katya were invited to be godparents again a year later could be seen as nothing more significant than the repetition of a satisfactory precedent. Proceeding from the supposed liaison, Chagin next examines an entry in the church register for the birth of twins on 25 March 1823, nine and a half months after T.'s departure for Munich. Katya's father Ivan Kruglikov is named as the father (the mother's name, as was standard practice for non-noble births, is not recorded). The twins were christened Nikolay and Darya, the godparents being (for Nikolay) Aleksey Sheremetev and T.'s aunt Nadezhda Zavalishina, and (for

Darya) T.'s brother and sister Nikolay and Darya (*Tyutchevy*, 102). Chagin finds it odd that the father of a twenty-two-year-old daughter should want to have more children, and that these should be named after their masters and have members of the latter's family as godparents. The underlying assumption of the first of these points (that pregnancies at that time were usually planned) is easily dismissed. As to the second, all that can be reasonably deduced from the facts as they stand is that Kruglikov and his family clearly enjoyed their masters' particular favour. This is indeed confirmed by a further fact established by Chagin: that some years later the Kruglikovs were granted their freedom from serfdom (ibid., 103). Yet although this was usually a reward for services rendered, it is difficult to accept the implication that in Katya's case these included bearing T.'s children. Such a hypothesis would necessarily involve the following improbable chain of events: (1) the twins were fathered by T. on the very eve of his departure for Germany and were born somewhat overdue nine and a half months later; (2) on learning of Katya's pregnancy, T.'s parents agreed to let her give birth in their Moscow household, rather than send her away to the seclusion and anonymity of the country; (3) after the birth they persuaded Katya's mother and father to pose as the parents, and their parish priest to go along with this charade; (4) although the deception must have been immediately apparent to scores of people living in the house (family and relatives, servants, tenants), not to mention friends and neighbours, T. and Katya's secret remained safe. In the absence of any evidence to the contrary it would seem more reasonable to accept the facts as they stand and conclude that it was indeed Katya's mother (or stepmother) who gave birth to the twins.

285. *Letopis'-1*, 55. 'Embassy' is used throughout for simplicity (it was technically a Legation).

286. Zavalishin, 43, 50, 107-108 (quoted with these page references to the 1906 edition of Zavalishin's *Zapiski dekabrista* in: Strémooukhoff, 109).

287. Fallmerayer (as note 28), 373-375.

288. Although apparently already estranged from her husband, Countess Osterman-Tolstaya probably travelled with him to Germany in the summer of 1822. She is certainly known to have been living in Munich during the period 1824-1825 (see: I.I. Vorontsov-Dashkov to K.V. Nesselrode, Mu., 10/22 May 1825 [TPD], 183]). Osterman-Tolstoy himself went on to Italy, where he began (or had already begun) a long-term relationship with an Italian Countess, resulting in the birth of three children and eventually (after his wife's death in 1835) marriage in a Catholic ceremony which had no legal validity in Russia (*Tyutchevy*, 105 [an apparent misprint here gives the year of Countess Osterman-Tolstaya's death as 1853]).

289. F.I.T. to I.N. & Ye.L. Tyutchev, Mu., Oct. 1840. IV, 152.

290. Gregg, 54.

291. Ibid., 55. To the examples quoted by Gregg could be added, for instance, letters from T. to his second wife Ernestine in which separation from her is explicitly or implicitly likened to an amputation (Weimar, 6/18 June 1842; SPb., 20 June/ 2 July 1855. IV, 194; 211-212). There is also his reported remark on the death of a close friend, the Slavophile Aleksey Khomyakov: 'One feels what one would after losing a vital organ' (quoted from a letter written by Yu.F. Samarin in: K.V. Pigaryov, 'Iz otklikov sovremennikov na smert' F.I. Tyutcheva', *Izvestiya Akademii nauk SSSR. Seriya literatury i yazyka*, 1973, XXXII, No.6, 537).

292. Gregg, 55-56. The translation has been dated between 1820 (when Lamartine's poem first appeared in print) and March 1822 (*Lirika*, 333).

293. 'Odinochestvo (Iz Lamartina)', lines 19, 35 and 48. I, 33-34. Gregg (Gregg, 56) appears to have overlooked the instance in line 19, where the adjectival form '*siry*' ('orphaned') is used.

294. 'Gektor i Andromakha (Iz Shillera)'. I, 32.

295. [Anon.], 'Pis'mo redaktoru' (dated Moscow, 25 March), *Otechestvennye zapiski*, 1822, Part 10, No.25, 279. Snegiryov's authorship of this anonymous contribution was established by A.L. Ospovat (Ospovat [1986], 350).

296. Pogodin, 13 (diary, 27 May 1822). Pogodin meticulously preserved T.'s correspondence for the period 1820-1821 and again from 1850 onwards. The fact that no letters to him survive from T.'s years abroad strongly suggests that none were ever sent.

Chapter 2. A Golden Time

1. Custine, 586-587.

2. Ibid., 43.

3. Pfeffel-Z, 33.

4. Heinrich Heine, 'Briefe aus Berlin', Heine (1968), II, 25-29.

5. For details of T.'s itinerary see Dinesman (1999a), 282.

6. Golo Mann, *The History of Germany Since 1789*, Harmondsworth, 1974, 98-99.

7. Philipp Spitta, 'Carl Maria von Weber', *The New Grove Dictionary of Music and Musicians* (ed. Stanley Sadie), 20 vols., London, 1980. XX, 247.

8. Dinesman (as note 5).

9. 'Utro v gorakh', 'Snezhnye gory', 'Al'py'. I, 64, 65, 129. T.G. Dinesman dates the first two between 1825 and 1829 (as above, note 5).

10. In 1818 Munich had some 60,000 inhabitants (Polonsky [1998], 92); by 1830 this had risen to 77,500 (Jesse, 180). In 1835 the population of Moscow was 300,000 (*Baedeker's Leningrad*, Basingstoke, n.d., 12).

11. P.V. Kireyevsky to Ye.P. Yelagina, Mu., between 4/16 and 14/26 Sept. 1829. *RA*, 1905, No.5, 115.

12. Ibid., 116.

13. I.I. Vorontsov-Dashkov to K.V. Nesselrode, Mu., 13/25 July 1822. *Letopis'-1*, 57.

14. I.I. Vorontsov-Dashkov to K.V. Nesselrode, Mu., 10/22 May 1825. TPD, 183.

15. Pfeffel-Z, 33.

16. Lane (1994), 22.

17. Polonsky (1998), 93.

18. *Letopis'-1*, 59.

19. Binyon, 162.

20. Ibid., 162-163, 321-323.

21. They are both still listed as Attachés at the Embassy at the beginning of 1828, Rzewuski with the rank of Titular Councillor and T. one grade lower as Collegiate Secretary. Both are also said to hold the court rank of *Kammerjunker* (Gentleman of the Chamber). *HSH*, 1828, 76.

22. F.I.T. to Ern. T., Warsaw, 2/14 Sept. 1853. Lettres, XVIII, 50-51.

23. Hümmert, 7.

24. *Zhizn'*, 49.

25. I.S. Gagarin to A.N. Bakhmeteva, Paris, 16/28 Oct. 1874. TM, 42.

26. H. Heine to K.A. Varnhagen von Ense, Mu., 1 April 1828. Heine (1970), XX, 322. (Also in: Heine, *Briefe*, I, 353.)

27. Pogodin, 13 (diary, 20-25 June 1825 OS).

28. Polonsky (1998), 95.

29. I.S. Gagarin to A.N. Bakhmeteva, Paris, 23 Oct./ 4 Nov. 1874 (first draft of letter). TM, 61.

30. Pogodin (as note 27).

31. Aksakov, 261-262.

32. TM (as note 25), 43.

33. Pfeffel-Z, 33.

34. Turgenev (A.I.), 83 (diary, 15/27 April 1834); A.I. Turgenev to I.S. Arzhevitinov, Mu., 15/27 April 1834. Ibid., 93 (note 55).

35. Tyutchev (F.I. jr.), 192.

36. Aksakov, 18.

37. Ibid., 17.

38. Dolgopolova & Tarkhov (1989a), 604.

39. F.I.T. to N.I. Tyutchev, SPb., 13/25 April 1868. VI, 322.

40. 'Poslaniye k A.V. Sheremetevu'. I, 39.

41. *Letopis'-1*, 59.

42. K.Yu. Rogov, 'K istorii moskovskogo romantizma: kruzhok i obshchestvo S.Ye. Raicha', *Lotmanovsky sbornik. 2*, M., 1997, 523-576 (here: 536-537, 557, 562-564).

43. Dinesman (1999a), 277-278; Rogov, 100-101 (note 8).

44. 'Pesn' Radosti (Iz Shillera)'. I, 40-43.

45. 'Druz'yam pri posylke "Pesni Radosti" — iz Shillera'. I, 44. T.G. Dinesman's dating of this to 1823 is convincing (Dinesman [1999a], 277-279).

46. 'S chuzhoy storony'; 'Drug, otkroysya predo mnoyu...' (translations of 'Ein Fichtenbaum steht einsam...' and 'Liebste, sollst mir heute sagen...'). I, 47, 48

47. R. Lane, 'Pis'mo k P.B. Kozlovskomu', *LN1*, 549. (This is a revised and augmented version of Lane's earlier: 'An unpublished letter of F.I. Tyutchev to Prince P.B. Kozlovsky', *New Zealand Slavonic Review*, 1982, 17-23.)

48. Herzen, XVII, 69. Quoted in Lane, 'Pis'mo...' (as previous note), 550.

49. Custine, 47-54, 58-69.

50. F.I.T. to P.B. Kozlovsky, Mu., 16/28 Dec. 1824. IV, 15-16.
51. Ibid., 15.
52. Sverbeyev, II, 136, 142-143, 146.
53. Ibid., I, 249.
54. Ibid., II, 143.
55. I.S. Gagarin to A.N. Bakhmeteva, Paris, 15/27 Nov. 1874. TM, 54-55.
56. Dewey, 18.
57. I am grateful to Mr Magnus Linder of Helsinki, a descendant of Amélie, for details of Princess Therese's illegitimate children from the Fürst Thurn und Taxis Zentralarchiv, Regensburg.
58. Dewey, 17. See also: Oertzen, 34; *Genealogisches Handbuch des Adels*, LIX (*Freiherrliche Häuser A*, IX) (ed. Walter von Hueck), Limburg a. d. Lahn, 1975, 251. The statement in Oertzen, 34-35 (repeated in Polonsky [1998], 14) that the title granted in 1823 was Amalie von Lerchenfeld is contradicted by Hueck and other authoritative sources. The church record of Amélie's marriage two years later also gives her maiden name as von Sternfeld and describes her as the foster-daughter of the Countess von Lerchenfeld (LAELKB, Kirchenbücher: Pfarramt Regensburg [Obere Stadt], 6-12, Seite 70, No.12).
59. Polonsky (1998), 100.
60. F.I.T. to I.N. & Ye.L. Tyutchev, Tegernsee, 2/14 July 1840. IV, 142.
61. The church record of Amélie's marriage on 31 Aug. 1825 is unusual in not giving the date of her birth, stating merely that she was then 'seventeen and a half years old' (Dewey, 15). As Princess Therese is known to have given birth to another illegitimate child (see above, note 57) on 10 June 1807, it is unlikely that Amélie would have been born before March of the following year. Taken together, these facts suggest a birth date in the early spring of 1808.
62. SK. For a more detailed outline of Max's diaries and letters (nearly all to his mother) and other relevant documents of the von Lerchenfeld family held in this archive see Dewey, 17-18. The collection is at present unsorted and uncatalogued.
63. Dewey, 19.
64. Diary ('Schreibkalendar') of M. von Lerchenfeld, 1823. SK
65. Dewey, 19.
66. P.A. Vyazemsky to A.Ya. Bulgakov, 30 Aug./ 11 Sept. 1833. Ospovat (1994), 113-114.
67. Richard von Pfeil und Klein-Ellguth, *Das Ende Kaiser Alexanders II*, Berlin, 1903. Quoted (without page ref.) in Oertzen, 37.
68. Maximilian von Lerchenfeld to Maria Anna von Lerchenfeld, Köfering, 8 June 1826. SK.
69. Diary ('Schreibkalendar') of M. von Lerchenfeld, 1826. SK. The 'little one' is feminine, as the German original ('*kleine beynah traurig*') makes clear. In a letter to his mother of 12 Feb. 1825 Maximilian similarly refers to Amélie as '*notre bonne petite*'. SK.
70. Dewey, 20. The poem quoted is 'Slyozy' ('Lyublyu, druz'ya, laskat' ochami...'). I, 45. The indication 'Munich, 21 July 1823' printed beneath the poem on its first publication in *Severnaya lira* suggests a NS date.
71. 'Sey den', ya pomnyu, dlya menya...'. I, 131.
72. *Lirika*, I, 352; *Zhizn'*, 72.
73. See Appendix I (i).
74. As above, note 60. My italics.
75. 'K N.' ('To N.'). I, 46.
76. Lane (1983).
77. Aksakov, 17-18.
78. As described by T. (who later sent his own daughters there) in a letter to his parents from Mu. dated 18/30 Dec. 1842 (IV, 219). The name Max-Josef-Stift was established by A.E. Polonsky (see PTR, 54, note 4).
79. Dewey, 20.
80. Ibid., 28-30.
81. J. Fendl, *Die Burg Donaustauf*, Donaustauf, 1990, 26-28, 30.
82. For an illuminating analysis of this aspect of the poem see: Yury Lotman, 'Poetichesky mir Tyutcheva', *TS* (1990), 136-138.
83. 'Ya pomnyu vremya zolotoye...'. I, 162. That the young girl in the poem was Amélie was well known in T.'s family. His second wife Ernestine confirmed it in a letter to one of her stepdaughters dated 19 June/ 1 July 1888 (Dolgopolova, 60).
84. Dewey, 20-22.
85. O.N., 79.

86. 'K N.'. I,46.

87. Chulkov (1928),14; Kozhinov, 114-115; Chagin, 14.

88. *Tyutchevy*, 112.

89. I, 302. As the date is accompanied by no indication of place, readers in Russia will no doubt have taken it to be OS. However, even a NS date would allow for the possibility that T. made a proposal of marriage a few days before his formal coming of age.

90. Dewey, 23-25.

91. *Zhizn'*, 23-25. For a reproduction of Khlopov's icon (now in the Tyutchev Museum at Muranovo) see Dolgopolova & Tarkhov (1989a), 604-605.

92. *Letopis'-1*, 63.

93. Ibid., 63-64.

94. Ibid., 70.

95. Dewey, 25-26.

96. *Letopis'-1*, 63.

97. Maximilian von Lerchenfeld to Amalie von Sternfeld, Paris, 4 April 1825. Dewey, 26 (where through an oversight on my part the letter was incorrectly dated 4 March, prompting the unfounded assertion that Amélie was sent away to the country after the duel affair).

98. As above, note 14.

99. For a justification of this dating see Dinesman (1999a), 281.

100. S. Amfiteatrov [S. Ye. Raich], 'Rassuzhdeniye o didakticheskoy poezii (magisterskaya dissertatsiya)', *Vestnik Yevropy*, 1822, No.7, 205.

101. 'Problesk'. I, 52-53.

102. In his own copy of T.'s verse Tolstoy pencilled in the note 'T!!!!' (i.e., especially characteristic of T.) next to this poem and marked lines 23 and 24 ('To worthless dust it is not granted/ To breathe the sacred fire of gods'). (See I, 309-310.)

103. See A.A. Nikolayev's commentary on the poem in *PSS* (1987), 372.

104. *Letopis'-1*, 64.

105. Dewey, 15, 27.

106. F.I.T. to I.N. & Ye.L. Tyutchev, Mu., 31 Dec. 1836/ 12 Jan. 1837. IV, 59-60.

107. Diary of A.F. Tyutcheva, 2/14 July 1865. TPD, 375.

108. Diary of A.F. Tyutcheva, 22 Apr./ 4 May 1847. TPD, 220.

Chapter 3. A Time of Destiny

1. Khlopov's icon notes, reproduced in Dolgopolova & Tarkhov (1989a), 604. (To avoid any confusion, for the period of T.'s leave in Russia dates are given according to both calendars, i.e. OS/NS.)

2. Ibid.

3. *Letopis'-1*, 64.

4. Ibid.

5. Dolgopolova & Tarkhov (1989b), 614.

6. The icon bears an inscription dating it to 1825 (see the reproduction in Dolgopolova & Tarkhov [1989a], 605). To exploit light conditions at their best it was long customary in Russia to paint icons during the summer months.

7. Raich, 33.

8. Pogodin, 13 (diary, 20-25 June/ 2-7 July 1825).

9. G.V. Chagin, 'Tyutchev v sledstvennom dele D.I. Zavalishina', *LN-2*, 440.

10. Barsukov, I, 58-59.

11. Diary entry for 20-25 June/ 2-7 July 1825. *Zhizn'*, 67. (This passage is omitted in Pogodin, 13.)

12. As note 8.

13. Pogodin, 13 (diary, 17/29 Sept. 1825).

14. *Zhizn'*, 67.

15. Pogodin, 13 (diary, 17/29 July 1825), 24 ('Vospominaniye o F.I. Tyutcheve').

16. Kozhinov, 72.

17. M.P. Pogodin, 'Vospominaniye o Stepane Petroviche Shevyryove', SPb., 1869, 7 (quoted in A.A. Nikolayev, 'Sud'ba poeticheskogo naslediya Tyutcheva 1822-1836 godov i tekstologicheskiye problemy yego izucheniya', *Russkaya literatura*, 1979, No.1, 130). The other two poems were 'To Nisa' ('K Nise', I, 49) and a free translation of Herder's 'Morgengesang im Kriege' ('Pesn' skandinavskikh voinov', I, 50-51).

18. *Zhizn'*, 67.

19. D.I. Zavalishin, 'Vospominaniya o Griboyedeve', *Drevnyaya i novaya Rossiya. Illyustrirovanny istorichesky sbornik*, 1879, No.4, 314. Quoted in *Dok.*, 52-53.

20. Quoted in Chereysky, 197.

21. V.I. Sakharov, 'Dmitry Venevitinov i yego poeziya (1805-1827)', in: D. Venevitinov, *Stikhotvoreniya*, M., 1982, 8.

22. Ibid., 22.

23. 'Ty zrel yego v krugu bol'shogo sveta...'. I, 107.

24. *Lirika*, I, 345.

25. I.I. Gribushin, 'Zametki o Dmitrii Venevitinove', *Russkaya literatura*, 1968, No.1, 196-198.

26. Ibid., 197-198.

27. A.I. Odoyevsky, *Polnoye sobraniye stikhotvoreniy i pisem*, M. & L., 1934, 460 (quoted in Gribushin [as note 25], 197).

28. D.V. Venevitinov, *Sochineniya*, Part 1, M., 1829, iv-v (quoted in Gribushin [as note 25], 197).

29. Gribushin [as note 25], 197.

30. 'V tolpe lyudey, v neskromnom shume dnya...'. I, 108.

31. Koshelyov, 13.

32. *Tyutchevy*, 115-116.

33. *Zapiski, stat'i, pis'ma dekabrista I.D. Yakushkina* (ed. S.Ya. Shtraykh), M., 1951, 47-48. My italics.

34. As note 8.

35. Zavalishin, 175. Also quoted in *Dok.*, 53-54.

36. Mazour, 155.

37. Koshelyov, 14-15.

38. Zavalishin, 176. Also quoted in *Dok.*, 54. Although Zavalishin's memoirs tend to be regarded as unreliable by historians because of the way they exaggerate the author's role in the Decembrist movement, there seems no reason to suspect his more personal recollections in which this motivation is absent. Even if it is argued that Zavalishin invented Osterman-Tolstoy's attribution of political 'harmlessness' to T. in order to emphasise his own 'dangerousness', the anecdote is still of value as evidence that Zavalishin himself considered T. 'harmless'.

39. *Letopis'-1*, 67.

40. Zavalishin, 176-177.

41. I.S. Gagarin to A.N. Bakhmeteva, Paris, 28 Oct./ 9 Nov. 1874. TM, 48.

42. K. Pfeffel to Ern. T., Mu., 18/30 March 1833. TPD, 187. I am grateful to Dr R. Lane for supplying his transcript of the French original in the Muranovo archive.

43. F.I. T. to Ern. T., SPb., 19 June/ 1 July 1854. V, 172.

44. F.I. T. to A.F. Aksakova, Toeplitz, 31 July/ 12 Aug. 1870. VI, 387.

45. Dinesman (1999a), 286. D.D. Blagoy first suggested (in his *Tri veka: iz istorii russkoy poezii XVIII, XIX i XX vv.*, M., 1933, 207) that the poem was written as a reaction to the July Revolution of 1830, a supposition later taken up by Pigaryov (*Lirika*, I, 349) and other commentators. However, as the poem has since been firmly dated to no later than 1829, this can now be ruled out.

46. Pumpyansky, 27.

47. 'Tsitseron'. I, 122.

48. As note 1.

49. *Kommentariy*, 58.

50. *Letopis'-1*, 67.

51. V.I. Shteyngel' [Steingel], 'Zapiski', *MD*, 220.

52. Ibid., 221.

53. A.Ye. Rozen, *Zapiski dekabrista*, Irkutsk, 1984, 128.

54. Shteyngel' (as note 51), 222.

55. Ibid., 222-223.

56. Ibid., 224.

57. Mazour, 179.

58. Shteyngel' (as note 51), 224.

59. *MD*, 362-363.

60. Ibid.

61. From the papers of M.M. Popov, quoted in *MD*, 363. The account is corroborated by Steingel (ibid., 224).

62. Mazour, 178.
63. I.S. Gagarin, to A.N. Bakhmeteva, Paris, 15/27 Nov. 1874. TM, 54.
64. A.S. Pushkin to P.A. Vyazemsky, Mikhaylovskoye, August 1826. A.S. Pushkin, *Polnoye sobraniye sochineniy*, 17 vols. (incl. final vol. of corrections and indexes), Leningrad, 1937-1959. XIII, 291.
65. *Zapiski [...] Yakushkina* (as note 33), 56.
66. Ibid., 56-61.
67. *Tyutchevy*, 124-125.
68. Ibid., 124; Zavalishin, 220.
69. S.D. Sheremetev, *Zapisnaya knizhka*, Part 1, M., 1903, 20-21 (quoted in *Tyutchevy*, 44).
70. See *Letopis'-1*, 69, where T.'s reported statement is dated to the beginning of January (OS).
71. Chagin (as note 9), 440.
72. Ibid.
73. *Tyutchevy*, 115-116.
74. Chagin (as note 9), 440.
75. Dolgopolova & Tarkhov (1989b), 614. This cites N.I. Tyutchev's service record in the central military archive. *Letopis'-1*, 71, gives the date as 27 Feb./ 11 March on the basis of a separate document in the family archive at Muranovo.
76. N. Chulkov, 'Moskva i dekabristy', in: *Dekabristy i ikh vremya*, M., 1932. II, 295 (quoted in A.L. Ospovat, 'O stikhotvorenii "14-oye dekabrya 1825" (K probleme "Tyutchev i dekabrizm")', *TS* (1990), 237).
77. *Tyutchevy*, 71.
78. Shteyngel' (as note 51), 234.
79. *Tyutchevy*, 124; Chagin (as note 9), 440.
80. *Letopis'-1*, 73. Originally quoted (in a slightly variant version) in: Chagin (as note 9), 440.
81. F.I. T. to Ern. T., M., 2/14 July 1864. Lettres, XXI, 221.
82. Barsukov, I, 327-328; M.P. Pogodin, 'V pamyat' o Pavle Aleksandroviche Mukhanove', *Russkaya starina*, 1872, No.2, 337.
83. Barsukov, I, 327-329.
84. Pogodin, 'V pamyat'...' (as note 82), 337.
85. Barsukov, I, 329-334.
86. Zavalishin, 224.
87. Ibid., 146 (footnote).
88. A. Glasse & N.Ya. Eydel'man, 'Tyutchev o vosstanii dekabristov', *LN-2*, 436, 438.
89. Zavalishin, 223.
90. Ibid., 234.
91. Glasse & Eydel'man (as note 88), 436.
92. Ibid., 436-438.
93. Heine (1968), II, 379.
94. *Letopis'-1*, 74.
95. '14-oye dekabrya 1825'. I, 56.
96. Ospovat, 'O stikhotvorenii...' (as note 76), 233-237.
97. *RA*, 1881, No.2, 340.
98. G.I. Chulkov, 'Stikhotvoreniye Tyutcheva "14-oye dekabrya 1825 goda [*sic*]" ', *Uraniya*, 71-73.
99. Ibid., 76-78.

Chapter 4. Great Festival of Wondrous Youth

1. Maximilian von Lerchenfeld to Maria Anna von Lerchenfeld, Paris, 11/23 Jan. 1826. SK.
2. Oertzen, 37.
3. Polonsky (1998), 95, 98. The building housing the Embassy at 3 Karolinenplatz no longer stands.
4. *Letopis'-1*, 69
5. Maximilian von Lerchenfeld to Maria Anna von Lerchenfeld, Paris, 24 Jan./ 5 Feb. 1826. SK.
6. *Letopis'-1*, 70.
7. Ibid., 72, 76, 81.
8. Heine (1968), II, 320-325 (*Reisebilder*, Part 3, Chapter 3).
9. P.A. Vyazemsky to P.P. Vyazemsky, Mu., 27 Oct./ 8 Nov. 1834. Kauchtschischwili, 277-278; A.I. Turgenev to I.S. Arzhevitinov, Mu., 14/27 April 1834. Turgenev (A.I.), 63.

10. *Tyutchevy*, 132; *Letopis'-1*, 66.

11. Eleonore had four sons, not three as sometimes claimed. See *Letopis'-1*, 80.

12. Polonsky (1998), 94.

13. *Letopis'-1*, 66.

14. *HSH*, 1824, 138-139; 1833, 101.

15. K. von Nesselrode to A. Peterson, 1/13 May 1817. Dinesman (1999b), 301 *n*.7).

16. *Letopis'-1*, 103.

17. Ibid., 103-105, 324.

18. These and subsequent details of Karl von Bothmer's life are taken from his own autobiographical account (Bothmer).

19. German genealogical sources and Karl von Bothmer's own account (Bothmer, 10) agree on this date. Other dates from 1797 to 1801 given in Russian sources must be considered dubious. Some doubt remains as to Eleonore's birthplace. A. Polonsky (Polonsky [1998], 21) gives Kassel, whereas Karl von Bothmer's account, which is generally reliable, implies that his eldest daughter was born in Hanover (Bothmer, 9-11).

20. Polonsky (1998), 130-131.

21. Bothmer, 10.

22. Ibid., 43.

23. Polonsky (1998), 21; Bothmer, 34.

24. Bothmer, 35.

25. Ibid., 34.

26. *Letopis'-1*, 324.

27. According to Karl von Bothmer, Eleonore and Peterson were living in Nuremberg in April 1824 (Bothmer, 43). A. Polonsky quotes a document from the archives giving Nuremberg as the place of Peterson's death some eighteen months later (Polonsky [1998], 130 *n*.94).

28. Bothmer, 42, 47.

29. As note 5.

30. Aksakov, 24; *Zhizn'*, 54.

31. Heine, *Briefe*, I, 353; Ficquelmont, 137-138.

32. Gagarin, 118.

33. F.I. T. to I.N. & Ye.L. Tyutchev, Mu., 3/15 April 1837. IV, 63-64.

34. Diary of A.F. Tyutcheva, 4/16 May 1846. TPD, 216.

35. Gregg, 174.

36. Aksakov, 11.

37. El. T. to N.F. Tyutchev, Mu., 1/13 Jan. 1834; June-July 1833; 4/16 Feb. 1837. TPD, 193; 190; 196.

38. K.V. Pigaryov stated that T. and Eleonore were married on 5/17 March 1826, but gave no evidence for this (*Zhizn'*, 54). T.G. Dinesman reports a later conversation with Pigaryov in which he explained his reasoning. He apparently believed that the date on which Khlopov signed the dedication on his icon must refer to another significant date in T.'s life, which in 1826 could only be his marriage to Eleonore (Dinesman [1999b], 298). This appears to have been a long-standing assumption in the family, for in surviving rough notes for his biography of T. Aksakov too gives 5 April (evidently a slip for 5 March) as the date of the marriage (Dolgopolova, 62). However, it is now known that Khlopov remained in Moscow and could have learned of events in Munich only by letter, which would have taken about three weeks to arrive. Dinesman points out that in order for Khlopov to dedicate the icon on the same day as the wedding, T. would have had to write *within ten days* of his return to Munich on 5/17 February that he and Eleonore were planning to marry on 5/17 March (ibid., 298-299). This is so improbable as to render Pigaryov's hypothesis untenable.

39. Aksakov, 24; IV, 64, 113.

40. Dinesman (1999b), 300. The main document is quoted in *Letopis'-1*, 74 and (more fully) in *Tyutchevy*, 135-136. On the evidence of another diplomatic document written and dated in T.'s hand, he appears to have been still in Munich on or about 26 July (Lane [1994], 40). He returned at the end of August, as shown by a further document dated 30 August (*Letopis'-1*, 74: all dates quoted NS). Dinesman claims that the Lutheran church in Bavaria made demands unacceptable to Tyutchev as a Russian subject regarding the religious upbringing of children, forcing him and Eleonore to marry outside the country (Dinesman [1999b], 300]. This speculative interpretation is contradicted by the known facts. The 1803 edict on religious freedom, enshrined in later laws, allowed partners to mixed marriages in Bavaria to choose either a Catholic or Protestant ceremony (or both, if desired) for the union to be legally valid, and to determine the religious upbringing of their children themselves (Jesse, 77, 101, 123). Social and religious pressure on parents by the dominant Catholic Church, which was opposed to these laws, meant that in practice only a minority of the offspring of such marriages were brought up as Protestants (ibid., 124, 141). It is inconceivable that the Lutheran Church, depending as it did on the protection of these laws, would have demanded such an undertaking as a prerequisite for marrying Tyutchev and Eleonore. Dinesman further suggests on the basis of a speculative remark in one of Aksakov's letters that T. and Eleonore were married in Paris. This too must now almost certainly be discounted. Writing on 10 July 2001 in response to a query from me, Pastor Alain Joly of the Centre culturel luthérien in Paris stated that there is no record of such a marriage for 1826 and 1827 in the register of what was at the time the only Lutheran church in Paris. A letter from the Église Évangelique luthérienne de France (Synode régionale de Paris) dated 28 Sept. 2001 confirmed this, while pointing out that Lutheran weddings sometimes took place in the chapels of foreign embassies in Paris at that period. However, archival searches with reference to the two most likely Protestant states have also revealed no evidence for this. Despatches for 1826 and 1827 from Hanover's Ambassador in Paris were found to contain no indication of a marriage (Niedersächsisches Hauptstaatsarchiv, Magazin Pattensen, Dep. 103, VI, Nos. 3250, 3251), and in an email to me dated 10 June 2002 Dr Moegle-Hofacker of the Hauptstaatsarchiv Stuttgart confirmed that diplomatic documents of Württemberg's Embassy for the same period are similarly devoid of relevant information (Bestände E70a, E50/12).

41. Schmidt, 723-725; Jesse, 67-70, 180; Manfred Berger, 'C(K)aroline Friederike Wilhelmine, Königin von Bayern, Prinzessin von Baden und Hochberg, *Biographisch-Bibliographisches Kirchenlexikon*, Nordhausen, XXIII (2004), 199-207 (accessible online at: www.bautz.de/bbkl).
42. Jesse, 88.
43. Dinesman (1999b), 299.
44. LAELKB, Kirchenbücher: Pfarramt Burgfarrnbach.
45. Schmidt, 725. That the Protestant church registers for Würzburg from 1802 on were destroyed towards the end of the Second World War was confirmed to me by Dr Jürgen König of the LAELKB in an email dated 20 March 2009. The Tyutchevs' copy of the marriage certificate was presumably lost together with all their other family papers during the fire which destroyed the Baltic steamer *Nicholas I* in 1838 (see Chapter 10). It is interesting that in his autobiographical account (dated Karlsruhe, April 1827) Eleonore's father makes no mention of her having remarried, despite going into some detail about her first marriage to Peterson in 1817 (Bothmer, 34-35) and referring to his daughter Louise's marriage to Count Ludwig von Pückler Limpurg in May 1824 (ibid., 43). Similarly, Maximilian von Lerchenfeld's letters to his mother from Paris for 1826 and 1827 (SK) contain no allusion to a marriage, a matter which would surely have been commented on in their correspondence had either known about it. Clearly the secret was well kept, at least for the first year or so.
46. Polonsky (1998), 23.
47. Hippolyt, aged 14; Karl, 12; and Maximilian, 10 (ibid., 130-131).
48. Ibid., 105.
49. H. Heine to K.A. Varnhagen von Ense, Mu., 1 April 1828 (NS). Heine, *Briefe*, I, 353.
50. Despatch of A. Krüdener to Russian Foreign Ministry, Mu., 11/23 Aug. 1826. *Letopis'-1*, 74. Quoted more fully in *Tyutchevy*, 135-136. Vorontsov-Dashkov left Munich for St Petersburg on 27 April 1826 and returned from leave only on or just before 20 March 1827 (both dates NS). *Letopis'-1*, 72, 76. Whether he spent this whole period in Russia is not known.
51. In his letter to Varnhagen von Ense (see note 49).
52. Diary of G.N. Olenin, Mu., 3/15 Aug. 1828. TPD, 183.
53. *Letopis'-1*, 79.
54. Ibid., 80-81. The following account of the Orthodox marriage of T. and Eleonore and events leading up to it is based on Dinesman (1999b), 300-301, and *Letopis'-1*, 80-86.
55. F.I. T. to Ern. T., SPb., 26 Oct. 1853 (OS). Lettres, XVIII, 57 (here incorrectly dated 22 Oct.).
56. F.I. T. to I.N. & Ye.L. Tyutchev, Mu., 1/13 Sept. 1842. IV, 198.
57. *Letopis'-1*, 86-87. For the later history of this house see Polonsky (1998), 106 (footnote). Polonsky's implication (ibid., 96-97) that they lived at 1, Karolinenplatz from 1828 appears to result from a misinterpretation of one of Eleonore's letters. This is corrected in Polonsky (2003), 166-167.
58. *Letopis'-1*, 86-87.
59. Diary of A.F. Tyutcheva, entry for 4/16 May 1846. TPD, 216.

60. G. Chulkov (*Letopis'* [Ch.], 213) asserts that Nikolay 'participated in the Turkish campaign of 1827-1828'. (In fact the war lasted from April 1828 to Sept. 1829.) However, Nikolay's service record shows that he retired from the army on 27 Feb./ 11 March 1826 and returned to active service only on 23 Jan./ 4 Feb. 1831 (*Letopis'-1*, 71, 107; Ekshtut, 291-292).

61. *Letopis'-1*, 87.

62. Pfeffel-Z, 33. See also: A.N. Bakhmeteva to I.S. Gagarin, 2/14 Nov. 1874. TM, 44 *n*.8).

63. I.S. Gagarin to A.N. Bakhmeteva, Paris, 23 Oct./ 4 Nov. 1874. TM, 45-46.

64. IV, 17, 465. For a photograph of the card see *LN-2*, 51.

65. Zhukovsky (1999) XIII, 272.

66. See *Letopis'-1*, 75-77; Lane (1994), 40-41.

67. The present 21, rue d'Artois (on the corner of rue Frédéric Bastiat) is a modern building; only its immediate neighbour at 23 looks as if it could date back to the period of T.'s and Eleonore's visit.

68. Zhukovsky (1999), XIII, 258-272, passim. At the time of Tyutchev's stay in Paris Nikolay Turgenev was in London. See also the note on Countess Razumovskaya (ibid., 540-541).

69. In his diary Zhukovsky records going shopping with Aleksandr Turgenev on 9 July. Ibid., 272.

70. N.M. Rozhalin to A.P. Yelagina, Mu., 27 April/ 9 May 1830. *RA*, 1909, No.8, 596 (quoted in *Letopis'-1*, 100).

71. 'Letniy vecher'. I, 62.

72. Lirika, I, 340. The date of composition given in I, 321 (12 June 1829) is clearly wrong, as that was the (OS) date of the censor's approval for the poem's first publication in the journal *Galateya*. T. could have sent the poem for publication at any time up to the spring of 1829, but must have written it during one of the previous summers. In the 1886 edition of T.'s poems prepared by his second wife Ernestine the poem is actually dated 1827 (I, 321).

73. Nesta Roberts, *The Companion Guide to Normandy*, London, 1980, 29; Imbert de Saint-Amand, *The Duchess of Berry and the Court of Charles X*, London, 1892, 266-267 (accessible online, without pagination, at www.gutenberg.org: see Chapter XXVII, 'Dieppe').

74. *Journal d'Annonces Judiciaires, Affiches et Avis divers de l'Arrondissement de Dieppe*, XIII (1827), No.26 (23 June), 3.

75. Imbert de Saint-Amand (as note 73), 270-273.

76. Although the *Journal d'Annonces [...] de Dieppe* (see note 74) lists arrivals and departures of vessels at the port, neither it nor the *Journal de Rouen et du département de la Seine-Inférieure* for that period provides details of visitors to the resort.

77. As note 59.

78. A.N. Nadarzhinskaya to D.I. Tyutcheva, M., 30 Jan./ 11 Feb. 1830. *Letopis'-1*, 97.

79. D.I. Sushkova to N.N. Sheremeteva, M., 6/18 June 1845. TPD, 214.

80. 'Itak, opyat' uvidelsya ya s vami...'. I, 204.

81. Gregg, 49.

82. 'Vesennyaya groza'. I, 60.

83. 'Vecher'. I, 55.

84. 'Vesenniye vody'. I, 134.

85. 'Cache-cache'. I, 59.

86. Note by P.V. Bykov in: F.I. Tyutchev, *Polnoye sobraniye sochineniy* (ed. P.V. Bykov; 8th. edition), SPb., 1913, 618.

87. 'K N.N.'. I, 61.

88. In 1836 Pushkin selected 29 of T.'s poems for publication in his journal *Sovremennik* (one of which was subsequently vetoed by the censor). A.A. Nikolayev has identified a further 19 which were rejected by Pushkin (Nikolayev [1989], 506). Seven of these 19 are known to have been in Raich's possession earlier (ibid., 527-529), of which only 'K N.N.' and a translation from Goethe were not published by him.

89. It was first published in *RA*, 1879, No.5, 137.

90. Gregg, 59.

91. Ibid., 70.

92. Aksakov, 104.

93. Ibid., 16, 40, 23. My italics.

94. I.S. Aksakov to Ye.F. Tyutcheva, Turovo, Sept. 1873 (OS). TPD, 430.

95. F.I. T. to D.F. Tyutcheva, Geneva, 8/20 Sept. 1864. VI, 76.

96. Tyutchev (F.F.), 234.

97. Ibid., 235.

98. Georgievsky, 108.

99. A. Sokolova, 'Imperator Nikolay I i vasil'kovye durachestva', *Istorichesky vestnik*, 1910, No.1, 109-110.

100. Georgievsky, 109.

101. Pfeffel-Z, 33 (footnote).

102. I.S. Gagarin to A.I. Bakhmeteva, Paris, 15/27 Nov. 1874. TM, 54. Quoted in the original French in: Lane (1994), 33.

103. V.S. Solov'yov, 'Iz vospominaniy. Aksakovy', in: (idem.), *Literaturnaya kritika*, M., 1990, 367. (Accessible online at: http://lib.baikal.net.)

104. Georgievsky, 125.

105. Ibid., 108.

106. H. Heine to F.I. T., Florence, 1 Oct. 1828 (NS). Heine, *Briefe*, 377.

107. Diary entry, 4/16 Sept. 1833. Kauchtschischwili, 20 (footnote).

108. Turgenev (A.I.), 72 (note 28).

109. Ibid., 73.

110. V. Veresayev, *Pushkin v zhizni*, 2 vols. (6th. ed.), M., 1936. II, 157 (quoted in Binyon, 398).

111. F.I. T. to K. von Nesselreode, Mu., 22 Oct./ 3 Nov.1835. IV, 33.

112. '[dass] sich der Kaiser recht aufrichtig auf dich freut'. Max von Lerchenfeld to Amalie von Krüdener, 27 Nov. 1835 (NS). SK.

113. *Letopis'-1*, 157.

114. Amalie von Krüdener to Georg Köckenberger, SPb., 20 March 1852 (OS). Köckenberger.

115. Oertzen, 36; O.N., 79.

116. Smirnova-Rosset, 8-9.

117. O.N., 79.

118. Smirnova-Rosset, 9.

119. O.N., 78-79.

120. Smirnova-Rosset, 9.

121. O.N., 79.

122. Ibid.

123. Amalie von Krüdener to Georg Köckenberger, SPb., 23 Feb. and 20 March 1852 (OS). Köckenberger.

124. Ibid. (letter of 20 March).

125. Polonsky (1998), 19.

126. O.N., 80.

127. F.I. T. to I.N. & Ye.L. Tyutchev & D.I. Sushkova, Mu., 31 Dec. 1836/ 12 Jan. 1837. IV, 59-60.

128. F.I. T. to I.S. Gagarin, Mu., 7/19 July 1836. IV, 51.

129. I.S. Gagarin to I.S. Aksakov, Paris, 30 Nov./ 12 Dec. 1874. TM, 57.

130. Pigaryov (1935b), 408.

131. As note 128.

132. Ibid.

133. F.I. T. to I.S. Gagarin, Mu., 10/22 July 1836. IV, 55-56.

134. Mende, 66.

135. As note 49.

136. F. Bobertag (ed.), *Ch.D. Grabbe, M. Beer und E. von Schenk*, Berlin & Stuttgart, 1899, 358.

137. In a letter sent to T. after leaving Munich in the summer of 1828 Heine mentions both Schenk and Lindner as acquaintances of T. (as note 106, pp.376-377).

138. *Letopis'-1*, 78.

139. *Ludolf Wienbarg's Wanderungen durch den Tierkreis*, Hamburg, 1835, 147 (quoted in Tynyanov [1977], 358).

140. As note 49.

141. H. Heine to R. Christiani, 26 May 1825 (NS). Heine (1970), XX, 199.

142. This was confirmed to Ivan Aksakov by T.'s second wife, Ernestine (see note 94).

143. Heine (1970), IV, 249.

144. Tynyanov (1922), 30-31; Tynyanov (1977), 361-362. Hans Rothe has suggested on the other hand (Rothe, 334n46), that the 'witty foreigner' was Count A.G. Stroganov, who is said to have popularised a similar description of Goethe he had heard from Byron. This is unconvincing. To begin with, it is by no means certain that the source quoted by Rothe (*Goethes Gespräche, ohne die Gespräche mit Eckermann* [ed. Flodoard von Biedermann], Leipzig, 1949, 647-657 [no. 489]) can be identified as Stroganov, as an editorial note makes clear (ibid., 785). Nor does Rothe offer any evidence that Heine ever met Stroganov or even heard the alleged comment. In any case, Byron's reported aphorism mocking Goethe's hypocrisy ('he is an old fox who never leaves his den, and from there preaches most virtuously' [ibid., 656]) bears little resemblance to that quoted by Heine.

145. Polonsky (1998), 113-114. Heine moved there in the middle of January: see his letter to Wolfgang Menzel of 12 Jan. 1828 (Heine, *Briefe*, I, 344).

146. As note 106, p.376.

147. 'S chuzhoy storony'. I, 47.

148. Liedtke, 48.

149. 'Zakralas' v serdtse grust' — i smutno...'. I, 90.

150. In G. Chulkov's article 'Tyutchev i Geyne', *Iskusstvo*, 1923, No.1, 356.

151. E.g.: 'I grob opushchen uzh v mogilu...'; 'Ya lyuteran lyublyu bogosluzhen'ye...'; 'I chuvstva net v tvoikh glazakh...'. I, 138; 156; 172.

152. 'Mogila Napoleona'. I, 67. For the dating see Dinesman (as note 154).

153. See the note on Lindner in: Heine, *Briefe*, IV, 160.

154. Dinesman (1999a), 282-283. Dinesman points out that T. could have read Scott's work in its French translation, which was also published in 1827.

155. 'Dva demona yemu sluzhili...' (item II in the cycle 'Napoleon'). I, 219. In the original version submitted to *Sovremennik* in 1836 the poem consisted only of lines 1-8, with slightly different readings for lines 2 and 7 (*Lirika*, I, 385-386; I, 260). The echoes of the description of Napoleon in Heine's article 'Französische Zustände' were first noted by Yury Tynyanov in his *Arkhaisty i novatory*, M., 1929, 390. T.G. Dinesman has suggested that the original eight-liner was written at the beginning of Feb. 1832, immediately after the first publication of Heine's article (Dinesman [1999a], 287). At the end of the 1840s the poem, with eight lines added, was included in a cycle of three under the general heading 'Napoleon' (*Lirika*, I, 386).

156. I, 511.

157. I, 219 (lines 9-16).

158. *Letopis'-1*, 79.

159. Ibid.

160. 'Olegov shchit'. I, 71.

161. 'Imperatoru Nikolayu I'. I, 72-73. See also: I, 333.

162. H. Heine, *Reisebilder. Dritter Teil*, in: Heine (1968), II, 379.

163. Ibid., 380.

164. Ibid., 380-381.

165. Tynyanov (1922), 31; G. Chulkov (as note 150), 363-364; Pigaryov (1935a), 181; F. Hirth, in: Heine, *Briefe*, IV, 185-187; R. Lane, 'Russia and the Revolution in Tyutchev's Poetry: Some Poems of 1828-1830', *The Slavonic and East European Review*, LI, No.123, April 1973, 217. Lane also points out a passage on Russia in Heine's prose fragments containing 'thoughts similar to those of the later Tyutchev' (Lane [1994], 26 *n*.24, quoting Heine [1970], XII, 247-248).

166. Pigaryov (1935a), 181.

167. H. Heine, 'Einleitung zu: Kahldorf über den Adel'. Heine (1968), II, 665.

168. Mende, 79. For details of the extracts published in newspapers see: Heine (1968), II, 855.

169. Heine (as note 162), 381-382.

170. ' "Prekrasny budet den' " — skazal tovarishch...'. I, 93-94.

171. 'Ty zrel yego v krugu bol'shogo sveta...'; 'V tolpe lyudey, v neskromnom shume dnya...'. I, 107, 108. Pigaryov (*Lirika*, I, 345) dates both to immediately after the publication of *Reisebilder. Dritter Teil* (mistakenly given as Dec. 1829), Nikolayev (*PSS* [1987], 117) more cautiously to the beginning of the 1830s.

172. 'Poeziya'. II, 9.

173. 'Dusha moya, Elizium teney...'. I, 142.

174. Heine (as note 162), II, 325-326.

175. Tynyanov (1977), 363 (quoting Ernst Elster, editor of: H. Heine, *Sämtliche Werke*, 7 vols., Leipzig & Vienna, 1887-1890). According to Tynyanov, Elster identified ten poems addressed to Clotilde. More recent research puts the number of love poems thought to have been written in Munich in 1828 at eleven (see Klaus Briegleb's notes to *Neuer Frühling* in: Heine (1968), IV, 919-922).

176. She was born on 22 May 1809 (NS). See: Bothmer, 20; Polonsky (1998), 131.

177. I.S. Gagarin to A.I. Bakhmeteva, Paris, Oct. 1874 (first draft of letter). TM, 61.

178. 'Unterm weißen Baume sitzend...' (*Neuer Frühling*, I). Heine (1968), IV, 298-299.

179. 'Wenn du mir vorüberwandelst...' (*N.F.*, XIV). Ibid., 304-305.
180. 'Wieder ist das Herz bezwungen...' (*N.F.*, XIX). Ibid., 306-307.
181. 'Es haben unsre Herzen...' (*N.F.*, XXIV). Ibid., 309.
182. Adolph Stahr, *Zwei Monate in Paris*, 3 vols., Oldenburg, 1851. II, 338.
183. G. Karpeles, *Heinrich Heine. Aus seinem Leben und aus seiner Zeit*, Leipzig, 1899, 115. Here Karpeles identifies the original painting as one by Rotari and the young painter who copied it as Heine's fellow-lodger Theophil Gassen. Although Karpeles states that the copy was given to 'the two beautiful Bothmer sisters', Heine's own account clearly indicates a single recipient. Yu. Tynyanov is surely right in identifying her as Clotilde (Tynyanov [1977], 369).
184. Tynyanov (1977), 369. See also: Heine (1968), IV, 895.
185. A. von Platen to F. von Fugger, 12 March 1828 (NS). August von Platen, *Briefwechsel* (ed. Paul Bornstein), Munich, 1931. IV, 394.
186. Ignaz Döllinger, 'Die neuen politischen Annalen und einer ihrer Herausgeber', *Eos. Münchner Blätter für Poesie, Literatur und Kunst*, 1828, Nos. 135 & 136 (23 & 25 Aug.). Reprinted in full in: Heine (1968), IV, 873-876.
187. As note 106, p.376.
188. Ibid., 377
189. Mende, 77.
190. 'Schon wieder bin ich fortgerissen...' (*Neuer Frühling*, XXXIX). Heine (1968), IV, 316-317. Klaus Briegleb suggests in his commentary to the poem that it was written on Heine's departure for Italy in August 1828 (ibid., 921). However, it could equally mark his final departure from Munich in December.
191. *Letopis'-1*, 101.
192. There are no recorded instances of anti-Jewish remarks by Tyutchev, whether in his political articles, his published correspondence, or in private conversation as reported by contemporaries. The one small piece of evidence we have in this respect indicates that, on the contrary, he was later prepared to help the journal *Sion*, which represented the views of Russian Jewry, in its battles with the censorship (see: Georgievsky, 113).
193. H. Heine to K. Varnhagen von Ense, 21 June 1830 (NS). Heine, *Briefe*, I, 454.
194. Tynyanov (1977), 363 (footnote).
195. See: Heine (1968), IV, 931.
196. 'In welche soll' ich mich verlieben...'. Heine (1968), IV, 343.
197. 'V kotoruyu iz dvukh vlyubit'sya...'. I, 154. (For dating see: *Lirika*, II, 356).
198. M. Beer to H. Heine, 10 June 1831 (NS). Heine (1970), XXIV, 86.
199. H. Heine to F. Hiller, Paris, 24 Oct. 1832 (NS). Heine, *Briefe*, II, 24.
200. H. Heine to F. Lindner, Paris, 3 Nov. 1834 (NS). Heine (1970), XXI, 91.
201. 'Iz kraya v kray, iz grada v grad...'. I, 157.
202. 'Motiv Geyne'. II, 193.
203. F.I. T. to I.S. Gagarin, Mu., 7/19 July 1836. IV, 50-51.
204. Of the fifteen poems by Goethe known to have been translated by T., Pigaryov dates eleven within the period 1827-1830, and one ('Nochnye mysli', a translation of 'Nachtgedanken') to between the late 1820s and 1832 (*Lirika*, II, 343, 345-346, 350-351, 352-353). A.A. Nikolayev's subsequent textological researches have more or less confirmed these datings, while showing that 'Nochnye mysli' can have been written no later than 1829 (*PSS* [1987], 87; Nikolayev [1979], 134-135).
205. See, e.g.: N.A. Nekrasov, 'Russkiye vtorostepennye poety. G. F. T-v i yego stikhotvoreniya (1836-1840)', *Dok.*, 100 (reprint of Nekrasov's original article in *Sovremennik*, 1850, XIX, No.1 [Jan.], 56-74); Tynyanov (1979), 388-389; Strémooukhoff, 56-57.
206. 'K N.N.'. I, 61. The poem was written no later than 1829, and one of the two autographs is on a sheet watermarked '1827' (ibid., 319; *Lirika*, I, 342).

Chapter 5. Philosophical Intermezzo

1. G.L. Plitt (ed.), *Aus Schellings Leben. In Briefen*, 3 vols., Leipzig, 1869-1870. I, 242, 243.
2. P.V. Kireyevsky to I.V. Kireyevsky, Mu., 7/19 Oct. 1829. *RA*, 1905, No.5, 123.
3. Plitt (as note 1), III, 32.
4. Diary notes of A.I. Turgenev quoted in: Turgenev (A.I.), 71 (note 19).
5. F.I. T. to D.N. Bludov, SPb., [1860-1864]. VI, 66. The poem appears separately in: II, 100.
6. N.A. Melgunov to S.P. Shevyryov, Mu., 8/20 May 1839; S.P. Shevyryov, 'Khristianskaya filoso-

fiya. Besedy Baadera', *Moskvityanin*, 1841, No.6. Both quoted in: A.L. Ospovat, 'Tyutchev i stat'ya N.A. Mel'gunova o Shellinge', *LN-2*, 457 (note 13).

7. Hümmert, 41.

8. Ibid., 42.

9. For more on T.'s attitude to the *Altkatholiken*, see Chapter 15.

10. D. Cyzevskyj, 'Tjutcev und die deutsche Romantik', *Zeitschrift für slavische Philologie*, 1927, IV, No.3, 309-310, 312-318.

11. See e.g. his diary entries for 28 March & 29 April 1834 (NS), Turgenev (A.I.), 73, 84. For Turgenev's friendship with Schubert in 1832 see: ibid., 71 *n*.17).

12. P.V. Kireyevskyj to I.V. Kireyevsky, Mu., 9/17 Nov. 1829. TPD, 185; P.V Kireyevsky to A.P. & A.A. Yelagin, Mu., 5/17 Jan. 1830. *RA*, 1905, No.5, 130.

13. I.V. Kireyevsky to A.P. & A.A. Yelagin, Mu., 28 April/ 10 May 1830. *RA*, 1907, No.1, 81.

14. 'K N.'. I, 46. See the translation in Chapter 2.

15. The textual parallel is pointed out by A.A. Nikolayev in *PSS* (1987), 372. The corresponding passage in Schelling's work reads: 'that same light of life which shines in the depths of darkness in every single man grows in the sinner into a consuming fire' (Schelling, VII, 391).

16. *Letopis'-1*, 79.

17. I.S. Gagarin to A.N. Bakhmeteva, Paris, 23 Oct./ 4 Nov. 1874. TM, 45-46.

18. Pfeffel-Z, 33.

19. Victor Cousin, *Cours de philosophie. Introduction à l'histoire de la philosophie*, Paris, 1828.

20. Plitt (as note 1), III, 39.

21. P.V. Kireyevsky to A.P. & A.A. Yelagin, Mu., 5/17 Jan. 1830. *RA*, 1905, No.5, 130; P.V. Kireyevsky to A.P. Yelagina, Mu., 2/14 Feb. 1830. *RA*, 1894, No.10, 218.

22. P.V. Kireyevsky to I.V. Kireyevsky, Mu., 12/24 Sept. 1829. *RA*, 1905, No.5, 121.

23. P.V. Kireyevsky to I.V. Kireyevsky, Mu., 7/19 Oct. 1829. 'Otryvki iz chastnykh pisem', *Moskovsky vestnik*, 1830, Part 1, No.1, 115. The text of the same letter as published in *RA* (see next note) omits this phrase.

24. P.V. Kireyevsky to I.V. Kireyevsky, Mu., 7/19 Oct. 1829. *RA*, 1905, No.5, 124-125.

25. A.I. Turgenev, *Khronika russkogo. Dnevniki (1825-1826 gg.)*, M. & L., 1964, 293 (diary entry for 24 Aug. 1825 [NS]); Turgenev (A.I.), 70 (note 12).

26. See: Turgenev (A.I.), 64 (diary entry for 30 July 1832 quoted); P.Ya. Chaadayev to F.W.J. von Schelling, M., 1832. M. Gershenzon (ed.), *Sochineniya i pis'ma P.Ya. Chaadayeva*, 2 vols., M., 1913 (repr. Hildesheim & New York, 1972). I, 167-170. Dated 'Moscow, 1832', Chaadayev's letter was sent (via Turgenev) only on 20 April/ 2 May 1833 (ibid., 382).

27. *Letopis'-1*, 90.

28. As note 24, p.125.

29. I.V. Kireyevsky to A.P. & A.A. Yelagin, Mu., 21 May/ 2 June 1830. I.V. Kireyevsky, *Polnoye sobraniye sochineniy*, 2 vols., M., 1911. I, 43 (quoted in Toporov, 85).

30. Turgenev (A.I.) (as note 26).

31. Ibid., 72-73 (entries for 30 & 31 July 1832).

32. Chaadayev to Schelling (as note 26), 168. Later in the letter Chaadayev identifies his informant as Turgenev (ibid., 169).

33. Turgenev (A.I.), 76.

34. Ibid., 92 (note 43).

35. Victor Cousin, *Über die französische und deutsche Philosophie. Aus dem Französischen von Dr. Hubert Becker. Nebst beurteilender Vorrede des Herrn Geheimrats von Schelling*, Stuttgart & Tübingen, 1834. Schelling's earlier version of the Introduction appeared as a supplement to the journal *Bayerische Annalen*, 1833, No.35 (7 Nov.).

36. Diary, 11 Apr. 1834 (NS). Turgenev (A.I.), 78.

37. Pfeffel-Z, 33.

38. Pfeffel-Laurentie, 319.

39. Ibid.

40. N. Mel'gunov, 'Shelling. (Iz putevykh zapisok)', *Otechestvennye zapiski*, 1839, No.5, 120. Here Tyutchev is mentioned only as 'T.'. However, in a German translation of the article authorised by Melgunov and published later that year ('Besuch eines Russen bei Schelling', *Europa*, 1839, IV, 153) Tyutchev's name is given in full.

41. Ibid. (*Ot. zapiski*, 124; *Europa*, 156).

42. N.A. Melgunov to S.P. Shevyryov, Mu., 31 Aug./ 12 Sept. 1836. Quoted in: A.L. Ospovat, 'Tyutchev i stat'ya N.A. Mel'gunova o Shellinge', *LN-2*, 454.

43. As reported by the diplomat and scholar Karl von Bunsen, writing at the King's behest on 1 Aug. 1840 to offer Schelling the professorship. Quoted in: F.W.J. Schelling, *Philosophie der Offenbarung 1841/42* (unauthorised transcript of Schelling's lectures, ed. M. Frank), Frankfurt/Main, 1977, 408.
44. Jochen Kirchhoff, *Friedrich Wilhelm Joseph von Schelling*, Reinbek bei Hamburg, 1982, 56.
45. Pfeffel-Z, 34.
46. See, e.g.: K.M. Azadovsky & A.L. Ospovat (Introduction to:) Turgenev (A.I.), 65; Gregg, 25.
47. Diary entry for 6 July 1842 (NS). Quoted in: S. Jakobsohn, 'Ein unbekanntes Gedicht von Fedor Tjutcev', *Zeitschrift für slawische Philologie*, 1929, V, 409.
48. Kirchhoff (as note 44), 57.
49. Vladimir F. Odoyevsky, *Russkiye nochi*, M., 1913, 45. (Facsimile reprint in the series *Slavische Propyläen* as: Vladimir F. Odoevskij, *Russische Nächte* (Introduction by Alfred Rammelmeyer), Mu., 1967.
50. See Appendix I (iv).
51. 'Kolumb'. I, 194.
52. A. Schopenhauer, *Über die Grundlage der Moral*, in his: *Sämtliche Werke*, 12 vols., Stuttgart, n.d. [1894-1896]. VII, 291.
53. Heinrich Heine, *Zur Geschichte der Religion und Philosophie in Deutschland*, Stuttgart, 1997, 94-95.
54. 'La Russie et la Révolution'. III, 45.
55. Schelling, II, 56.
56. Ibid., 362.
57. A. Schopenhauer, *Parerga and Paralipomena* (tr. E.F.J. Payne), 2 vols., Oxford, 1974. I, 24.
58. Schelling, V, 321-322.
59. 'A.N.M.' ('Net very k vymyslam chudesnym...'). I, 31. The poem, addressed to his friend Andrey Muravyov, is dated 13 Dec. 1821 (OS) (ibid., 289-290).
60. A. Bely, 'Vostok ili Zapad', in the almanach *Epokha*, M., 1918, 187.
61. Diary, 3 Dec. 1911 (OS). A.A. Blok, *Dnevnik*, M., 1989, 361-362.
62. Kozyrev, 97-108.
63. Ibid., 98-99.
64. Ibid., 99-104. Apart from quoting many examples of water imagery, Kozyrev finds Anaximander's abstract concept of *apeiron* most clearly expressed in the poems 'O chom ty voyesh', vetr nochnoy?..'; 'Smotri, kak na rechnom prostore...'; and 'Ot zhizni toy, chto bushevala zdes'...' (see I, 133; II, 34, 234).
65. Ibid., 114. Some evidence that T. took an interest in the pre-Socratics comes in his report for the year 1865 as chairman of the Committee for Foreign Censorship, where he names Pythagoras and Thales as two of the earliest philosophers (Briskman, 574).
66. A.I. Neuslykhin, 'Tyutchev i Gyol'derlin', *LN-2*, 542-547.
67. Friedrich Hölderlin, *Hyperion, oder der Eremit in Griechenland*, Frankfurt am Main & Hamburg, 1962, 9. Compare e.g. T.'s poems 'Teni sizye smesilis'...'; 'Vesna' ('Kak ni gnetyot ruka sud'biny...') (I, 159, 183-184).
68. *Hyperion*, 40. Compare 'Kak okean ob"yemlet shar zemnoy...'; 'Son na more' (I, 110, 151).
69. *Hyperion*, 37.
70. Ibid., 10.
71. Ibid., 65.
72. In his *System des transzendentalen Idealismus* (*System of Transcendental Idealism*), published in 1800, Schelling gives what appears to be a somewhat ponderous paraphrase of Hölderlin's idea: 'If however it is art alone that can succesfully objectify with general validity that which the philosopher is able to represent only subjectively, then it is to be expected (to draw this conclusion too from the foregoing) that just as in the childhood of human knowledge philosophy — and with it all those branches of knowledge brought to perfection through it — was born from and nurtured by poetry, so too after its completion philosophy will flow back as the same number of separate streams into the general ocean of poetry.' (Schelling, III, 629.) The corresponding passage in Part I of *Hyperion* was published three years earlier, in 1797.
73. *Hyperion* (as note 67), 95. Compare 'Silentium!' (I, 123).
74. 'Al'py'. I, 129.
75. 'List'ya'. I, 127-128.
76. 'Osenniy vecher'. I, 126.
77. 'Letniy vecher'. I, 62.

78. 'Chto ty klonish' nad vodami...'. I, 136.

79. 'Ne to, chto mnite vy, priroda...'. I, 169-170.

80. Hans Rothe, ' "Nicht was ihr meint ist die Natur". Tjutcev und das Junge Deutschland', in: Hans-Bernd Harder & Hans Rothe (eds.), *Studien zu Literatur und Aufklärung in Osteuropa. Aus Anlaß des VIII. Internationalen Slavistenkongresses in Zagreb* (*Bausteine zur Geschichte der Literatur bei den Slawen*, 13), Giessen, 1978, 319-335. T. would most likely have read the suggested article as first published, one of a series by Heine under the general title 'État actuel de la littérature en Allemagne' which appeared (in French translation) in the Parisian journal *L'Europe littéraire* between March and May 1833. The original German text of Heine's articles was published in book form later that year (*Zur Geschichte der neueren schönen Literatur in Deutschland*, 2 vols., Paris & Leipzig, 1833). An alternative conjecture is offered by I. Shaytanov ('Zabyty spor', *Voprosy literatury*, 1980, No.2, 195-232), namely that 'Ne to, chto mnite vy, priroda...' was written during T.'s stay in Moscow in 1825 as a riposte to the view of nature expressed in Merzlyakov's poem 'Trud' ('Labour'). This is unlikely, given both the stylistic maturity of T.'s poem and the textual parallels (discussed below) with another piece composed on the death of Goethe in 1832. More persuasive is the suggestion of A. Nikolayev ('Khudozhnik-myslitel'-grazhdanin. (Chitaya Tyutcheva)', *Voprosy literatury*, 1979, No.1, 138) that it is directed against reactions by 'Right Hegelian' philosophers to Schelling's public attack on Hegel in his introduction to the work by Victor Cousin mentioned previously (see above, note 35). Unlike Rothe, however, Nikolayev is unable to point to any specific publication which might have sparked off T.'s poem.

81. 'Na dreve chelovechesta vysokom...'. I, 149.

82. In July 1800 Friedrich Schlegel wrote to his brother August Wilhelm after a conversation with Goethe that the latter 'always speaks with particular love of Schelling's *Naturphilosophie*'. A few months later Goethe himself wrote to Schelling that he felt a distinct affinity with his teaching, adding: 'I wish for a complete union, which I hope to achieve through a study of your writings, or even better through personal acquaintance with you'. (Both quoted in: Kuno Fischer, *Schellings Leben, Werke und Lehre* [4th. ed.], Heidelberg, 1923, 43.

83. Most notably, according to the Schelling scholar Jochen Kirchhoff, in the cycle of poems 'Gott und Welt' (Kirchhoff, 100).

84. D.D. Blagoy, *Literatura i deystvitel'nost'*. *Voprosy teorii istorii i literatury*, M., 1959, 446.

85. I.S. Gagarin to I.S. Aksakov, Paris, 29 Oct./10 Nov. 1874. TM, 50.

86. 'Bezumiye'. I, 120. A.A. Nikolayev dates this to no later than 1829 (*PSS* [1987], 86, 377).

87. 'A.A. Fetu' [2] ('Inym dostalsya ot prirody...'). II, 117.

88. F.I. Tyutchev, *Polnoye sobraniye stikhotvoreniy* (ed. K.V. Pigaryov), L., 1957, 343 (repeated in *Lirika*, I, 348).

89. Berkovsky, 37-38.

90. V.A. Mil'china, 'Tyutchev i frantsuzskaya literatura (zametki k teme)', *Izvestiya Akademii nauk SSSR, seriya literatury i yazyka*, XLV, No.5, 1986, 345-346. Mil'china's reference for the passage in question is: G. de Staël, *De l'Allemagne*, Paris, 1886, 191-192.

91. The title 'Rybak' ('The Fisherman') is included in a list made by Raich of poems sent to him by Tyutchev before 1830, although no poem of that title or fitting its description has survived (Nikolayev [1989], 514). A.A. Nikolayev, who first published Raich's list, surmises that this was a translation of Goethe's 'Der Fischer', and that the manuscript went missing during Ivan Gagarin's abortive preparations for an edition of T.'s verse in 1836 (ibid., 512, note 18).

92. Mil'china (as note 90), 346.

93. François Cornillot, 'Tiouttchev: poète-philosophe' (dissertation), University of Paris IV, 1973, 254-255. For T.'s translation of Theseus's speech ('Lyubovniki, bezumtsy i poety...') see I, 106.

94. Cornillot (as previous note), 256-259

95. Liberman, 175.

96. Gregg, 104-105.

97. Ibid., 25; Pumpyansky, 30.

98. Dudek.

99. Ibid., 496.

100. Ibid., 497.

101. 'Fontan'. I, 167.

102. *Faust, Zweiter Teil*, Act V (lines 12104-12105).

103. 'Kakoye dikoye ushchel'ye!..'. I, 160.

104. 'S polyany korshun podnyalsya...'. I, 161.

105. Cyzevskyj (as note 10), 305-318; Toporov, 47-54, 66, 76.
106. 'Kak sladko dremlet sad temnozelyony...'. I, 158.
107. Cyzevskyj (as note 10), 322.
108. Pratt, 73.
109. 'Den' i noch' '. I, 185.
110. Pratt.
111. Ibid., 74-75.
112. James Gutmann, (Introduction to:) F.W.J. Schelling, *Philosophical Inquiries into the Nature of Human Freedom* (tr. & ed. J. Gutman), Chicago, 1936, xlvii.
113. Pratt, 73.
114. Ibid., 74.
115. Ibid.
116. 'Svyataya noch' na nebosklon vzoshla...'. I, 215.
117. Pratt, 77.
118. Ibid.
119. Ibid. Pratt's reference for the passage quoted is: Schelling, IV, 258.
120. Pratt, 75.
121. Schelling, *Philosophical Inquiries...* (as note 112), 34.
122. Pratt, 78.
123. 'Smotri, kak na rechnom prostore...'. II, 34.
124. Pratt, 79.
125. Ibid., 80.
126. See, e.g.: Pumpyansky, 28-29; Gippius, 33-34; Wsewolod Setschkareff, *Schellings Einfluß in der russischen Literatur der 20er und 30er Jahre des XIX. Jahrhunderts*, Leipzig, 1939, 104-105; Nicolai von Bubnoff, 'Tjutcevs philosophische Dichtung', *Festschrift für Max Vasmer zum 70. Geburtstag*, Wiesbaden, 1956, 98-99; K.A. Afanas'yeva, '"Odizm" ili "tragizm"? Razmyshleniya na temu "Tyutchev i Derzhavin" ', *Tyutchev segodnya. Materialy IV Tyutchevskikh chteniy* (ed. Ye.N. Lebedev), M., 1995, 89-90.
127. Brian Magee, *The Philosophy of Schopenhauer*, Oxford, 1983, 379-380.
128. Ibid., 238.
129. Pratt, 83-86. She singles out in particular 'Lebed' ' and 'Kak okean ob"yemlet shar zemnoy...' (see I, 109, 110).
130. 'Teni sizye smesilis'...'. I, 159.
131. Gol'denveyzer, I, 24-25 (diary, 7 Dec. 1899). Quoted in *Dok.*, 249.
132. Gregg, 219-220, note 40. See *War and Peace*, Vol. IV, Part 2, Chapter XIV. (N.B. in the older English translation still in circulation, which numbers chapters differently, the passage in question will be found at Book XIII, Chapter III.)
133. 'O veshchaya dusha moya!..'. II, 75.
134. Schelling, III, 628.
135. '29-oye yanvarya 1837'. I, 175.
136. 'Na dreve chelovechestva vysokom...'. I, 149.
137. 'A.A. Fetu' [2] ('Inym dostalsya ot prirody...'). II, 117.
138. 'Ne ver', ne ver' poetu, deva...'. I, 186.
139. F.I. T. to I.S. Gagarin, Mu., 20-21 Apr./ 2-3 May and 7/19 July 1836. IV, 42, 50.
140. Fet (1983), 296.
141. Ibid., 383.
142. Ibid., 385.
143. 'Silentium!'. I, 123. Pigaryov (*Lirika*, I, 354) dates this no later than 1830, Nikolayev (Nikolayev [1979], 135) on further evidence no later than 1829. The maturity of its style suggests it is unlikely to have been written much before 1828.
144. See Brandt, Part 2, 173.
145. Gol'denveyzer, II, 303 (not quoted in *Dok.*).
146. V.F. Bulgakov, *Lev Tolstoy v posledniy god yego zhizni. Dnevnik sekretarya L.N. Tolstogo*, M., 1957, 410 (quoted in *Dok.*, 252).

Chapter 6. Anni Mirabilis

1. F.I. T. to A.F. Tyutcheva, Mu., 16/28 Apr. 1842. IV, 188-189.
2. F.I. T. to A.F. Aksakova, SPb., 19 Apr. 1867 (OS). VI, 218.

3. *Letopis'-1*, 86-87.
4. F.I. T. to Ern. T., SPb., 27 Sept. 1852 (OS). RGB. 308.1.20, *l.* 42-43*ob.*
5. F.I. T. to N.N. Sheremeteva, SPb., 26 Dec. 1845 (OS). IV, 328.
6. Diary of A.F. Tyutcheva, 3/15 May 1847. TPD, 221.
7. Ibid.
8. Darya Tyutcheva, as reported by her nephew Fyodor. Tyutchev (F.I. jr.), 186.
9. Although appointed Second Secretary on 17/29 Apr. 1828, T. had to wait until 6/18 Oct. for his first salary payment, made in arrears (*Letopis'-1*, 82).
10. See, e.g.: F.I. T. to I.N. & Ye.L. Tyutchev, Mu., 3/15 Apr. 1837. IV, 63.
11. F.I. T. to I.N. & Ye.L. Tyutchev, Tu., 13/25 Dec. 1837. IV, 89.
12. Despatch of I.A. Potyomkin to K.V. Nesselrode, Mu., 2/14 Feb. 1831. Dinesman (1999c), 147.
13. See: Lane (1984a), 228-231; Lane (1994), 41-42; Dinesman (1999c), 131, 145 (footnote).
14. Dinesman (1999c), 129-130.
15. Ibid., 140-141.
16. Heine, *Briefe*, 160-161. That Lindner was a Russian subject from the Baltic provinces was reported by Potyomkin in a despatch to Nesselrode dated 5/17 Feb. 1829 (Dinesman [1999c], 193 *n.*66).
17. Despatch of K.V. Nesselrode to I.A. Potyomkin, 24 Apr./ 6 May 1829. Dinesman (1999c), 141.
18. Despatch of I.A. Potyomkin to K.V. Nesselrode, 15/27 Oct. 1829. Ibid., 141-142.
19. P.V. Kireyevsky to I.V. Kireyevsky, Mu., 12/24 Sept. 1829. *RA*, 1905, No.5, 121-122 (Thiersch's reported comment on T.: 'a good intellect, a very educated man, and a diplomat', omitted here, is quoted in full in Ospovat [1986], 352).
20. F.I. T. to F. Thiersch, Mu., 20 Jan./ 1 Feb. 1830. IV, 21. See also: Lane (1984a), 227-230.
21. Despatch of I.A. Potyomkin to K.V. Nesselrode, 3/15 Feb. 1831. Lane (1984a), 231. See also: Dinesman (1999c), 145-146.
22. Raich, 34.
23. See: Nikolayev (1989), 513-516.
24. Raich's authorship (the article is signed '- i -') and the identification of T. as the 'friend abroad' were first established by K.V. Pigaryov in his article 'Poeticheskoye naslediye Tyutcheva', *Lirika*, I, 278-279.
25. Virgil, *Aeneid*, Book 6, lines 851-853.
26. - i - [S.Ye. Raich], 'Pis'mo drugu za granitsey', *Galateya*, Part I, 1829, No.1, 40-42. (Italics added to indicate T.'s words.)
27. *Letopis'-1*, 87.
28. Maria Fairweather, *Pilgrim Princess*, London, 2000, 215.
29. *Letopis'-1*, 87.
30. I.V. Kireyevsky, 'Obozreniye russkoy slovesnosti 1829 goda', in the almanach: *Dennitsa*, M., 1830, xvi. Reprinted in: I.V. Kireyevsky, *Kritika i estetika*, M., 1979, 65.
31. Rozhalin informed Pyotr Kireyevsky of his wish to move to Munich when they met in Dresden later that year. See: P.V. Kireyevsky to A.P. Yelagina, Mu., 14/26 Sept. 1829. *RA*, 1905, No.5, 117. In May Rozhalin stayed in Dresden and did not, as stated by Maria Fairweather (Fairweather [as note 28], 220) accompany Princess Volkonskaya to Italy as a second tutor to Aleksandr. See: N.M. Rozhalin to A.P. Yelagina, Dresden, 11/23 May 1829. *RA*, 1909, No.8, 583 (quoted in *Letopis'-1*, 87).
32. See Rozhalin's letter of 11/23 May (as previous note), 585.
33. Udolph, 20.
34. S.P. Shevyryov to M.P. Pogodin, Rome, 10/22 June 1829. TPD, 184. As shown by T.G. Dinesman (*Letopis'-1*, 88), Shevyryov is referring here to meetings with T. in Munich, as at the time of writing T. had not yet reached Rome.
35. Dinesman (1999b), 303.
36. Ibid.
37. H. Heine, 'Reise nach Italien', *Morgenblatt für gebildete Stände*, XXII, 1828, Nos. 288-293, 295, 297-298 (1-12 Dec.).
38. K. Pfeffel to Ern. T., 25 March/ 6 Apr. 1856. TPD, 283 *n.*3.
39. 'Vnov' tvoi ya vizhu ochi...'. I, 208.
40. Much of what is now known is thanks to an impressive piece of literary detective work by T.G. Dinesman, involving identification of the handwriting of various copies of poems by T. See: Dinesman (1999a), 284-286; Dinesman (1999b), 302-304.
41. Dinesman (1999b), 303.

42. Ibid., 302-303.
43. 'Rim noch'yu'. II, 11.
44. 'La question Romaine'. III, 55.
45. 'Tstitseron'. I, 122.
46. 'Mal'aria'. I, 130.
47. G.I. Chulkov, in *PSS* (1933), I, 344.
48. Udolph, 12.
49. Mme de Staël, *Corinne, ou l'Italie*, Paris, 1861, 110.
50. Gregg, 73-76.
51. Ibid., 75.
52. Ibid.
53. See Chapter 5.
54. Solovyov, 399.
55. Gregg, 76.
56. 'Priroda — sfinks. I tem ona verney...'. II, 208.
57. 'Ital'yanskaya villa'. I, 180.
58. 'O, kak ubiystvenno my lyubim...'. II, 35.
59. Dinesman (1999b), 304.
60. Dinesman (1999a), 284-285.
61. *The Tempest*, Act IV, lines 152-153. The parallel is pointed out by Ralph Matlaw in his 'The Polyphony of Tyutchev's "Son na more" ', *The Slavonic and East European Review*, XXXVI, 1957-1958, No.86, 200; also by N.Ya. Berkovsky (Berkovsky, 50). The combination of Naples, a stormy crossing and safe arrival on the island could have sparked off associations with *The Tempest* in T.'s mind. His interest in Shakespeare at the time is attested by his translations of two extracts from *A Midsummer Night's Dream* (I, 106), made according to A.A. Nikolayev no later than 1829 (*PSS* [1987], 93).
62. 'Son na more'. I, 151.
63. Gregg, 97.
64. Matlaw (as note 61), 198.
65. Ibid., 200-201; Pratt, 81-83.
66. Gregg, 98.
67. Ibid., 100.
68. Ibid., 99-100.
69. Ibid., 99.
70. In a comprehensive review of research on Tyutchev's sources published up to 1984 Ronald Lane also lists Victor Hugo's *Hernani*, Edward Young's *Night Thoughts* and Fyodor Glinka's poem 'Son' as influences on 'Son na more' suggested by various scholars (Lane [1984b], 44, 45, 67). Of these, the play *Hernani* can almost certainly be ruled out, as its first performance and publication did not take place until February-March 1830 (I, 365).
71. Ibid., 66-68. Here Lane summarises 54 claimed examples of influence by 29 separate writers on 41 of T.'s poems. For seven of the poems multiple influences (between two and four) are cited.
72. Ibid., 59.
73. 'Dusha moya, Elizium teney...'. I, 142.
74. Udolph, 77-85.
75. E.g., two dating from 1828: 'Stansy' ('Kogda bezmolvstvuyesh', priroda...'); 'Noch' ' ('Kak noch' prekrasna i tikha...'). S.P. Shevyryov, *Stikhotvoreniya* (ed. M. Aronson), L., 1939, 54, 54-55. Another, also entitled 'Noch' ' ('Nemaya noch', primi menya...') was written in June 1829, probably in Rome (ibid., 65-66).
76. A.S. Pushkin, 'Dennitsa. Al'manakh na 1830 god, izdanny M. Maksimovichem', *Literaturnaya gazeta*, I, 1830, No.8, (5/17 Feb.), 64.
77. Quoted in *Tyutchevy*, 235-236, with ref. to Brokgaus & Yefron's *Entsiklopedichesky slovar'*, XXXIX (Part 77), SPb., 1903, 363.
78. 'Poslaniye k A.S. Pushkinu' [Rome, 14 July 1830, NS]. Shevyryov (as note 75), 86-90.
79. Ibid., 149.
80. Even much later, after settling in Russia, T. found it quite natural to discuss Russian literature in French. A letter to Vyazemsky dated Jan. 1851 suggesting improvements to one of the latter's poems is (apart from quotations) written entirely in French (V, 26).
81. 'K neprigozhey materi' [16 July 1829, NS]. Shevyryov (as note 75), 68-70.
82. 'Petrograd' [9 Aug. 1829, NS]. Ibid., 70-72.

83. Dinesman (1999b), 303. These copies, in handwriting identified by Dinesman as that of Shevyryov and Volkonsky, are cited by her — together with the maritime theme of two of the poems and other circumstantial evidence — as proof of T.'s visit to Ischia while in Italy.

84. 'Silentium!', written at the end of the 1820s, also deviates from metrical norms in two of its lines. Later editors in T.'s lifetime — notably Ivan Turgenev — arbitrarily amended these and other poems without consulting the author in an attempt to iron out what they saw as inadmissible irregularities. For a detailed analysis by K.V. Pigaryov of T.'s experiments in mixed metre see: *Zhizn'*, 276-292.

85. 'Kon' morskoy'. I, 111.

86. Dudek, 514.

87. 'Dusha khotela b byt' zvezdoy...'. I, 115.

88. Ye. Maymin, 'Poety-lyubomudry i filosofskoye napravleniye v russkoy lirike 20-30-kh gg. 19-ogo veka', *Instituto Universitario di Napoli. Annali. Sezione Slava*, IX, 1966, 93-94.

89. Dinesman (1999b), 285-286.

90. This includes an estimated half a dozen averaged out from the number of poems datable no more accurately than to the periods 1825-1829 and 1830-1835 respectively. The actual total was almost certainly higher, as T. later claimed to have accidentally destroyed a large number of his manuscripts towards the end of 1833 (see Chapter 7).

91. Dinesman (1999b), 304.

92. The evidence for this is a road map of Germany and northern Italy, preserved in the Muranovo museum, with the inscription: 'Tutchef. 6 Septembre. MILAN. MDCCCVIIII.' The ever-practical Nikolay, in whose hand this appears to have been written, was evidently in charge of route planning (*Letopis'-1*, 89).

93. *Letopis'-1*, 90.

94. S.P. Shevyryov to M.P. Pogodin, Rome, 15/27 Oct. 1829. TPD, 184.

95. Ern T. to K. Pfeffel, SPb., 15/27 Dec. 1870. TPD, 414.

96. Aksakov, 11.

97. D.F. Tyutcheva to A.F. Tyutcheva, Ovstug, 2/14 Aug. [1855]. TPD, 272.

98. F.I. T. to I.N. & Ye.L. Tyutchev, Mu., 31 Dec. 1836/ 12 Jan. 1837. IV, 59.

99. El. T. to N.I. Tyutchev, Mu., 23 Nov./ 5 Dec. 1836. Muranovo: *f. 1, op. 1, yed. khr.* 723, *l.* 29-30. (Ru. tr.: *Letopis'-1*, 167.)

100. According to G.V. Chagin this was 'apparently as a result of some family drama' (*Kommentariy*, 55). If so, it may have had something to do with a certain Miss Zurikova whom T. mentions in an unpublished letter to his second wife Ernestine as 'our sister-in-law *manquée*' (F.I. T. to Ern. T., M., 21 June/ 3 July 1851. RGB. 308.1.19, *l.* 1-2ob.). As at that time Ernestine's only brother Karl Pfeffel had been married for over fifteen years (see Polonsky [1998], 134), the abortive marriage plans can only have involved Nikolay. In other letters T. hints at Nikolay's stubborn resistance to attempts by the family to interest him in marriage (see IV, 89; V, 9-10, 340n7).

101. 'K. B.'. II, 219. A.A. Nikolayev has shown that the poem is addressed to Clotilde Bothmer, as suggested by the title ('C' becoming 'K' in Cyrillic transliteration) (Nikolayev [1988]). Nikolayev's arguments are summarised in more detail in note 216 to Chapter 15.

102. 'Dvum syostram'. I, 116. In my translation I have in line 4 followed the variant '*svezhest'*' (for '*prelest'* ') used in two of the autograph manuscripts and adopted by A.A. Nikolayev in his edition of the poems (*PSS* [1987], 82).

103. Key to this identification is the question of the poem's dating. G.I. Chulkov originally gave 1828-1830 on the basis of textological evidence then available (*PSS* [1933], I, 342). K.V. Pigaryov subsequently narrowed this down to 1830 (*Lirika*, I, 347), but on grounds disputed by later scholars (Nikolayev [1979], 133; Gregg, 218 *n.*88). Pigaryov went on to speculate without firm evidence that the poem was written during T.'s stay in SPb. in the summer of 1830 and that the older of the two sisters was a hypothetical old flame from his youth whom he encountered again at that time (*Lirika*, I, 347, 352). G.V. Chagin has recently taken this idea further, arguing that the poem refers to Yelizaveta and Yekaterina, sisters of the Decembrist Vasily Ivashov, the younger of whom, Yekaterina (but not her sister) T. does appear to have met in SPb. that summer (*Tyutchevy*, 140-146). Unfortunately both for Pigaryov's theory and Chagin's ingenious elaboration of it, the most recent textological research indicates that as an item in the so-called 'Raich collection' the poem could have been written *no later than Feb. 1830*, i.e. at the very least three months before T. left Munich for SPb. (For the Raich collection and its relevance to dating see: Nikolayev [1979], 134-135; Ospovat [1986], 351-352; *PSS* [1987], 361-362; Nikolayev [1989],

504-507, 513-516; *Letopis'-1*, 96, 98-99). Now that Chulkov's original dating has been vindicated, Eleonore and Clotilde must be considered the only credible candidates for the two sisters, as argued independently by both R.A. Gregg and A.A. Nikolayev (Gregg, 59-60; Nikolayev [1979], 134; *PSS* [1987], 376).

104. Gregg, 60.

105. TM, 49 (note 5).

106. Diary of A.F. Tyutcheva, 4/16 May 1846. TPD, 216.

107. 'V dushnom vozdukha mol'chan'ye...'. I, 135. For dating (1833) see Appendix I (iii).

108. Gregg, 64. See also ibid., 63-67 for Gregg's discussion of this theme in other poems by T.

109. 'Chto ty klonish' nad vodami...'. I, 136. Written at much the same time as 'V dushnom vozdukha mol'chan'ye...' (see Appendix I [iii]). An intriguing further piece of indirect evidence for a relationship with Clotilde is found in a short collection of writings and aphorisms of Count Dmitry Bludov, published posthumously as a booklet by his daughter. This was circulated to Bludov's close friends, including T., whose poem on his death was appended to it (*Mysli i zamechaniya gr. D.N. Bludova*, SPb., 1866. See Liberman, 307-309). Bludov twice refers to a certain 'T.' (evidently Tyutchev), on one occasion quoting him as saying he had been 'passionately in love six times' (*Mysli...*, 9; quoted in Liberman, 308). By the time Bludov died in 1864, T. is known to have been 'passionately in love' with five women: Amélie, his first and second wives Eleonore and Ernestine, Hortense Lapp and Yelena Denisyeva. While the sixth could conceivably be a woman of whom we have no knowledge (including the purely hypothetical first love postulated by Pigaryov: see note 72 to Chapter 2; note 103 above), in view of the other evidence now available the most likely candidate is surely Clotilde.

110. Gregg, 66.

111. Letters of P.V. Kireyevsky to A.P. Yelagina (Mu., 14/26 Sept 1829) and to I.V. Kireyevsky (Mu., 10/22 Sept. 1829). *RA*, 1905, No.5, 116, 118-119.

112. A.P. Yelagina to V.A. Zhukovsky, M., June 1829 (OS). *LN*, LXXIX, 1968, 25.

113. See Aronson & Reyser, 158-161.

114. Toporov, 81-82 (footnote 97).

115. P.V. Kireyevsky to I.V. Kireyevsky, Mu., 7/19 Oct. 1829. *RA*, 1905, No.5, 123.

116. As note 19.

117. P.V. Kireyevsky to I.V. Kireyevsky, Mu., 7/19 Oct. 1829. *Moskovsky vestnik*, 1830, Part I, No.1, 115. The text of the letter published in *RA* (as note 115, p.125) omits Schelling's actual words.

118. His brother refers in a letter to an unspecified 'warning' about T. which Pyotr received before leaving Moscow (I.V. Kireyevsky to A.A. & A.P. Yelagin, Mu., 21 May/ 2 June 1830. *RA*, 1907, No.1, 83).

119. As suggested by Pigaryov in *Zhizn'*, 69.

120. Letter of I.V. Kireyevsky (as note 118).

121. P.V. Kireyevsky to A.A. & A.P. Yelagin, Mu., 5/17 Jan. 1830. *RA*, 1905, No.5, 130-131.

122. El. T. to N.I. Tyutchev, Mu., 20 May/ 1 June 1832. IV, 25. See also Polonsky (1998), 97.

123. Letter of P.V. Kireyevsky (as note 121), 130; P.V. Kireyevsky to A.P. Yelagina, Mu., 2/14 Feb. 1830. *RA*, 1894, No.10, 218.

124. Pyotr refers to these 'defects', of which he fears he will never be rid, in the letter to his mother and stepfather referred to in note 121 (p.131).

125. P.V. Kireyevsky to A.A. & A.P. Yelagin, Mu., 5/17 Jan. 1830. *RA*, 1905, No.5, 125. (Dated 'December 1829' in *RA*, in fact part of a letter written over several days. For the revised dating see *Letopis'-1*, 94, 95-96.)

126. P.V. Kireyevsky to A.P. Yelagina, Mu., 22 March/ 3 Apr. 1830. *RA*, 1894, No.10, 223.

127. *Letopis'-1*, 91.

128. *Tyutchevy*, 84.

129. N.V. Yakushkin, 'Nesostoyavshayasya poyezdka A.V. Yakushkinoy v Sibir' ', *Novy mir*, 1964, No.12, 154.

130. *MD*, 341 *n.*58).

131. F.I. T to N.N. Sheremeteva, Mu., 16/28 Dec. 1829. IV, 21.

132. Diary ('Schreibkalender') of Maximilian von Lerchenfeld, 6 Oct. 1829 (NS). SK.

133. As note 131, p.20.

134. Ibid.

135. Quoted without source in Kozhinov, 103.

136. I.V. Kireyevsky to A.A. & A.P. Yelagin, Mu., 5/17 Apr. 1830. *RA*, 1907, No.1, 77.

137. Ibid., 77-78.

138. Ibid., 78.

139. I.V. Kireyevsky to A.A. & A.P. Yelagin, Mu., 6/18 Apr. 1830. *RA*, 1907, No.1, 78-79.

140. N.M. Rozhalin to A.P. Yelagina, Mu., 27 Apr./ 9 May 1830. *RA*, 1909, No.8, 596.

141. N.M. Rozhalin, 'Al'manakhi na 1827-y god', *Moskovsky vestnik*, 1827, No.5 (21 Feb./ 8 March), 86.

142. *Zhizn'*, 69-70.

143. Quoted without source in Blagoy, 67.

144. Barsukov, IX, 118.

145. Chereysky, 184.

146. P.V. Kireyevsky to A.A. & A.P. Yelagin, Mu., (undated fragment). Ospovat (1986), 352. Ospovat dates the fragment 7/19 Oct. 1829 on questionable internal evidence. More recently T.G. Dinesman has shown this to be incorrect and has given persuasive reasons for considering the fragment to be more or less contemporaneous with a letter from P.V. Kireyevsky to S.P. Shevyryov dated 21 Feb./ 5 March 1830 (*Letopis'-1*, 98-99).

147. Nikolayev (1979), 134.

148. ('un journal passablement niais'): F.I. T. to I.S. Gagarin, Mu., 7/19 July 1836. IV, 51.

149. Kireyevsky (as note 30).

150. 'Na kamen' zhizni rokovoy...'. I, 38. First publ. in *Ateney*, 1829, No.1 (Jan.), 61-62.

151. Letter of I.V. Kireyevsky (as note 139).

152. *Letopis'-1*, 103-104.

153. Ibid., 101.

154. I.V. Kireyevsky to A.A. & A.P. Yelagin, Mu., 21 May/ 2 June 1830. *RA*, 1907, No.1, 83.

155. See: L.G. Frizman, 'Ivan Kireyevsky i yego zhurnal "Yevropeyets" ', *Yevropeyets. Zhurnal I.V. Kireyevskogo 1832* (ed. L.G. Frizman), M., 1989, 431-436.

156. Ibid., 457-458.

157. 'Devyatnadtsaty vek', in: I.V. Kireyevsky, *Kritika i estetika*, M., 1998, 92-93.

158. Ibid., 99.

159. Ibid., 95ff.

160. Potyomkin reported to Count Nesselrode that T. would be travelling to SPb. 'via Lübeck' (*Letopis'-1*, 101). That he and his family did so is clear from their visit to Heine near Hamburg. The only route to SPb. via Lübeck was by steamer.

161. Diary ('Schreibkalendar') of Maximilian von Lerchenfeld, 14 Sept. 1829 (NS). SK.

162. Custine, 77-78.

163. Ibid., 80.

164. Ibid., 83.

165. Ibid., 89.

166. There seem to have been no plans to go to Moscow. The hope expressed by Ivan Kireyevsky in a letter to his mother and stepfather in Moscow (Mu., 30 May/ 11 June 1830. *RA*, 1907, No.1, 84) that they might meet T. in Russia can be taken as no more than wishful thinking. His brother Pyotr's apparently more specific statement in a letter to them that the Tyutchevs would 'probably stay in St Petersburg until the winter' and then 'perhaps come to you in Moscow' (Mu., 2/14 June 1830. *RA*, 1909, No.8, 598) is evidently misinformed (T. had been granted leave only until the end of Sept.) and must be considered equally doubtful.

167. C. Maltitz to A.F. Tyutcheva, 9/21 Dec. 1846. *Letopis'-1*, 102.

168. F.I. T. to I.N. & Ye.L. Tyutchev, Mu., 29 Aug./ 10 Sept. 1837. IV, 74.

169. See M. von Lerchenfeld's letters of 26 July/ 7 Aug., 5/17 Sept. and 12/29 Sept. 1830, quoted below (notes 177, 203, 204).

170. General P.N. Ivashov (father of the Decembrist Vasily Ivashov), quoted in: O.K. Bulanova, *Roman dekabrista*, M., 1933, 101-102.

171. A.S. Pushkin, 'The Bronze Horseman' (tr. J. Dewey), *Translation and Literature*, VII, Part 1 (1998), 60-61.

172. F.I. T. to Ern. T., Warsaw, 2/14 Sept. 1853. Lettres, XVIII, 5.

173. Custine, 123.

174. Ibid., 105.

175. Ospovat (1986), 353.

176. Diary entry for 18/30 July 1830. Ficquelmont, 137-138.

177. 'Tutu est venu me voir hier — il est bien contrarié de ne pas trouver le C[om]te Ness[elrode] içi — et regarde pour ainsi dire son voyage comme entrepris sans but — et probablement sans résultat.' M. von Lerchenfeld to M.A. von Lerchenfeld, SPb., 26 July/ 7 Aug. 1830. SK.

178. Diary of P.D. Durnovo, entry for 12/24 June 1837. R.Ye. Terebenina, 'Zapisi o Pushkine, Gogole, Glinke, Lermontove i drugikh pisatelyakh v dnevnike P.D. Durnovo', in: *Pushkin. Issledovaniya i materialy*, VIII, L., 1978, 257 (quoted in *Letopis'-1*, 174).
179. Ospovat (1986), 353. Ospovat hoped the diaries of Helena Szymanowska might contain material relevant to T.'s biography (ibid., 354). These have since been published in full (Helena Szymanowska-Malewska, *Dziennik 1827-1857* [ed. Z. Sudolski], Warsaw, 1999), but unfortunately contain no references to T. or his family, apart from a few fleeting mentions of his daughters in the 1850s. References to others connected with him such as the Krüdeners and Lerchenfelds, or (much later) Yelena Denisyeva, are similarly absent.
180. P.A. Vyazemsky, 'O moskovskikh zhurnalakh', *Literaturnaya gazeta*, I, 1830, No.8 (5/17 Feb.), 60.
181. Ospovat (1986), 354.
182. Ibid.
183. V. Veresayev, *Pushkin v zhizni*, M., 1984, 220, 224-225.
184. In March 1836 Gagarin wrote to T. from SPb.: 'You and I have often spoken of the place occupied by Pushkin in the poetic world'. *LN-1*, 502.
185. A.S. Pushkin (as note 76).
186. Yury Tynyanov famously claimed this, Pushkin's only reference to T. in print, as evidence for his thesis that Pushkin, as an 'innovator' in Russian literature, was hostile to T. as a member of Raich's 'archaistic' school (see: Yu.N. Tynyanov, 'Pushkin i Tyutchev', in: *Poetika. Sbornik statey. Vremennik otdela slovesnykh iskusstv*, L., 1926, 107-126. Reprinted in: Yu.N. Tynyanov, *Pushkin i yego sovremenniki*, M., 1969, 166-191). While it is undeniable that T. made use of archaisms in his poetry, so did Khomyakov and especially Shevyryov (also protégés of Raich), whose 'genuine talent' Pushkin praises in the same breath. And when a few years later a number of T.'s poems were brought to Pushkin's attention, he was impressed and immediately agreed to publish a substantial selection in his journal *Sovremennik* (see Chapter 8). Later scholars have had little difficulty in demolishing the uncharacteristically eccentric thesis of an otherwise perceptive and astute critic (see, e.g.: G. Chulkov, 'Stikhotvoreniya, prislannye iz Germanii', *Zven'ya*, II, 1933, 255-266; Kozhinov, 159-177). Even so its ghost returns to haunt the literary scene from time to time, most memorably perhaps in fictional form in Andrey Bitov's novel of 1978 *Pushkinsky dom* (*Pushkin House*).
187. A.I. Del'vig, *Moi vospominaniya*, 4 vols., M., 1912-1913. I, 107.
188. H. Heine to F. Hiller, 24 Oct. 1832 (NS). Heine (1970), XXI, 40.
189. 'Lettre à M. le Docteur Gustave Kolb, rédacteur de la "Gazette Universelle" '. III, 23.
190. Pfeffel-Laurentie, 317-318.
191. 'I did not know him at all until 1830 and became closely acquainted only in 1833' (Pfeffel-Z, 33).
192. F. Lindner to H. Heine, Stuttgart, 10 Nov. 1834 (NS). Heine (1970), XXIV, 280.
193. I.S. Gagarin to A.N. Bakhmeteva, Paris, 15/27 Nov. 1874. TM, 54.
194. I.S. Gagarin to A.N. Bakhmeteva, Paris, 28 Oct./ 9 Nov. 1874. TM, 45-46.
195. I.S. Gagarin to I.S. Aksakov, Paris, 14/26 Nov. 1874. TM, 53.
196. F.I. T. to Ern. T., SPb., 17/29 Feb. 1854. Lettres, XIX, 108.
197. O.K. Bulanova-Trubnikova, *Tri pokoleniya*, M., 1928, 37.
198. Ibid., 36-38.
199. F.I. T. to Ern. T., Dresden, 15/27 Sept. 1841. IV, 179.
200. *Tyutchevy*, 145.
201. Bulanova-Trubnikova (as note 197), 50; *Letopis'-1*, 318.
202. *Letopis'-1*, 104.
203. 'Je cherche depuis quelques jours une pièce de Malachite que je voudrais envoyer à Amélie par les Tuttch[effs], ceux-ci n'attendant que le retour du C[om]te Ness[elrode] pour se mettre en route, et pour peu que le C[om]te tarde encore, ils seront forcés de quitter sans l'avoir vu. Car M[adam]e est de nouveau enceinte, et n'a plus que le tems nécessaire pour revenir à Munich. Je ne la voie presque jamais — parce qu'elle est souffrante, et ne dort pas, et qu'ils sont si modestement logés qu'ils n'ont jamais voulu me recevoir. Es mag eine schöne Casernen Wirtschaft seyn. Lui, vient presque tous les jours me voir et soupirer après le moment ou il reverra les clochers de notre Dame.' M. von Lerchenfeld to M.A. von Lerchenfeld, SPb., 5/17 Sept. 1830. SK.
204. 'Tutu ne tardera plus maintenant de partir parce que le C[om]te Nessel[rode] est arrivé — et c'est cela seul qu'il attendait'. ('Tutu will not delay his departure any longer now, because Count

Nesselrode has arrived — and that is all he was waiting for'.) M. von Lerchenfeld to M.A. von Lerchenfeld, SPb., 12/24 Sept. 1830. SK.

205. *Letopis'-1*, 103.

206. Ibid., 104.

207. 'Tutcheff part mercredi — il laisse içi les deux fils de Peterson'. ('Tyutchev is leaving on Wednesday — he is leaving Peterson's two sons here'.) M. von Lerchenfeld to M.A. von Lerchenfeld, SPb., 20 Sept./ 2 Oct. 1830. SK.

208. Clear evidence of this is a letter recently discovered by G.V. Chagin. Written by T.'s father, it is dated 'St Petersburg, 10 November 1830' (OS). See: *Tyutchevy*, 36.

209. Vyazemsky, 194.

210. El. T. to Ye.L. Tyutcheva, Mu., 4/16 Feb. 1837. TPD, 196.

211. For a discussion of transitional natural phenomena in T.'s poetry see: Liberman, 7.

212. Of the poem 'Brat, stol'ko let soputstvovavshy mne...' (II, 226) for instance, composed while travelling by train to SPb. after the funeral of his brother, T. wrote in a letter to his daughter Yekaterina that it 'came to me in a state of half-sleep, the night of my return from Moscow' (VI, 396).

213. 'Cherez livonskiye ya proyezzhal polya...'. I, 124.

214. See Appendix I (i).

215. 'Pesok sypuchy po koleni...'. I, 125.

216. See Dinesman (1999a), 282 for discussion of the overland travel options, in particular between Vienna and Munich.

217. 'Al'py'. I, 129.

218. N. Ammon, 'Neskol'ko mysley o poezii Tyutcheva', *Zhurnal Ministerstva narodnogo prosveshcheniya*, 1899, June, 463; Brandt, Part 2, 168-169 (both quoted in *Lirika*, I, 352-353). It is worth noting that on two occasions in his later political writings T. likened Russia to a great mountain (III, 12, 38). The symbolic representation of Russia as a massive granite cliff in the poem 'More i utyos' ('The Sea and the Cliff ') (I, 197-198) appears to belong to the same cluster of images.

219. 'List'ya'. I, 127-128.

220. 'Osenniy vecher'. I, 126.

221. Gregg, 80.

222. Ibid., 81.

223. *Letopis'-1*, 105.

224. Ibid.

225. P.V. Kireyevsky to A.P. Yelagina, Mu., [beginning of Nov.] 1830 (NS). *RA*, 1905, No.5, 144; N.M. Rozhalin to S.P. Shevyryov, Mu., 1/13 Nov. 1830. *RA*, 1906, No.2, 234.

226. N.M. Rozhalin to A.P. Yelagina, Mu., 21 Dec. 1830/ 2 Jan. 1831. *RA*, 1909, No.8, 600-601.

227. Ibid., 601.

228. Ye.I. Safonov to I.N. Tyutchev, 5 May 1836 (OS). Muranovo. I am indebted to Dr Ronald Lane for bringing this to my attention and allowing me to make use of his transcript.

Chapter 7. A Chaos of the Mind

1. See: Dinesman (1999c), 149.

2. *Letopis'-1*, 112.

3. Liedtke, 93.

4. Dinesman (1999c), 149, 152.

5. Ibid., 149.

6. Ibid., 150.

7. 'Lettre sur la censure en Russie'. III, 96-106.

8. Dinesman (1999c), 152-153.

9. F.I. T. to N.I. Tyutchev, Mu., 29 Oct./ 10 Nov. 1832. IV, 29-30.

10. See Chapter 4.

11. For the background to the publication of *Französische Zustände*, see: Liedtke, 92-94.

12. H. Heine, *Französische Zustände*, in: Heine (1968), III, 167.

13. Ibid., 209.

14. Ibid., 105.

15. 'Mogila Napoleona'. I, 67. (See Chapter 4.)

16. *Letopis'-1*, 111.

17. Aksakov, 116.
18. 'Kak doch' rodnuyu na zaklan'ye...'. I, 145-146.
19. See: El. T. to N.I. Tyutchev , Mu., 20 May/ 1 June 1832. IV, 25; Polonsky (2003), 167.
20. Polonsky (2003), 167-168.
21. Ibid. (a contemporary architectural plan of the building is reproduced on p.168).
22. El. T. to N.I. Tyutchev (as note 19).
23. Diary, 31 July 1832 (NS). Turgenev (A.I.), 73.
24. P.A. Vyazemsky to P.P. Vyazemsky, 27 Oct./ 8 Nov. 1834. Kauchtschischwili, 278.
25. Diary, 2 Aug. 1832 (NS). Turgenev (A.I.), 73.
26. Ibid., 74 (30 March 1834 [NS]).
27. El. T. to N.I. Tyutchev , Mu., 3/15 Apr. 1833. Dinesman (1999c), 164.
28. El. T. to N.I. Tyutchev , Mu., 1/13 Jan. 1834. Muranovo: *f.* 1, *op.* 1, *yed. khr.* 723, *l.* 15-17. (Ru. tr.: TPD, 193.)
29. Dinesman (1999c), 162.
30. Ibid., 147.
31. Despatch of I.A. Potyomkin to K.V. Nesselrode, 3/15 Sept. 1832. *Letopis'-1*, 118.
32. I.A. Potyomkin to K.V. Nesselrode (personal letter), 4/16 Sept. 1832. Dinesman (1999c), 165. (Ru. tr.: *Letopis'-1*, 118.)
33. El. T. to N.I. Tyutchev , Mu., 1/13 June 1833. Dinesman (1999c), 166. (Ru. tr.: TPD, 189.)
34. *Letopis'-1*, 113, 115.
35. Postcript by T. to: El. T. to N.I. Tyutchev, Mu., 20 May/ 1 June 1832. IV, 25.
36. Ibid., 24 (main section of letter, written by El. T.).
37. Ibid.
38. *Letopis'-1*, 107, 113; Ekshtut, 291 *n*.29).
39. As note 36.
40. Ibid.
41. *Letopis'-1*, 117.
42. El. T. to N.I. Tyutchev , Mu., 3/15 Apr. 1833. Dinesman (1999c), 164.
43. El. T. to N.I. Tyutchev , Mu., 29 Aug./ 10 Sept. 1833. Dinesman (1999c), 181.
44. K. Pfeffel to E. von Dörnberg, Mu., 23 Oct. 1833 (NS). *Letopis'-1*, 134.
45. As note 42.
46. El. T. to N.I. Tyutchev , Mu., 3/15 Apr. 1833. TPD, 187.
47. See: Dinesman (1999c), 163.
48. Ilyasova, 125.
49. El. T. to N.I. Tyutchev , Mu., 1/13 Jan. 1834. Muranovo, *f.* 1, *op.* 1, *yed. khr.* 723, *l.* 15-17. (Ru. tr.: TPD, 193.)
50. Ibid.
51. El. T. to N.I. Tyutchev , Mu., 1/13 June 1833. TPD, 188.
52. Ibid. For the original French text of the passage quoted see: Dinesman (1999c), 167.
53. El. T. to N.I. Tyutchev , Mu., 15 or 16 June 1833 (NS). *Letopis'-1*, 125. (For the dating of this letter see: Dolgopolova, 63.)
54. El. T. to N.I. Tyutchev, Mu., second half of June 1833 (NS). Muranovo, *f.* 1, *op.* 1, *yed. khr.* 723, *l.* 8-9ob. (Ru. tr.: TPD, 190.)
55. Ibid. (passage omitted in TPD; Ru. tr.: *Letopis'-1*, 125.)
56. *Letopis'-1*, 130.
57. First draft of letter from I.S. Gagarin to A.N. Bakhmeteva, Paris, [Oct.] 1874. TM, 61.
58. I.S. Gagarin to A.N. Bakhmeteva, Paris, 28 Oct./ 9 Nov. 1874 (final version of the draft referred to in the preceding note). TM, 48.
59. El. T. to N.I. Tyutchev, Mu., 29 Aug./ 10 Sept. 1833. Muranovo, *f.* 1, *op.* 1, *yed. khr.* 723, *l.* 10-12ob. (Ru. tr.: TPD, 191.)
60. Jamison (as note 61), 235.
61. See: K.R. Jamison, *Touched with Fire. Manic-Depressive Illness and the Artistic Temperament,* New York, 1994; A. Storr, *The Dynamics of Creation*, London, 1972. Eleonore's letters to her brother-in-law Nikolay testify not only to T.'s attacks of depression but also to those manic episodes of overexcited hyperactivity which characterise the other side of bipolar disorder. In one she writes of his 'cruelly overwrought excitement' (*'cruelle exaltation'*) and 'overheated imagination' (*'imagination délirante'*) which threaten to turn his whole life into 'an attack of high fever', and which she believes can be countered only by 'in everything you say, administer[ing] *tranquilliser*' (SPb., 15/27 Dec. 1837. Muranovo: Dr R. Lane's transcript). Elsewhere are refer-

ences to 'attacks of frenzied irritation, followed by listlessness, perpetual anxiety, depression' (Mu., 2/14 Apr. 1836. Muranovo: Lane transcript; Ru. tr.: *Letopis'-1*, 154) and to 'his insane irritability, his angry outbursts, his ideas which are almost absurd' (Mu., 14/26 Feb. 1837. Muranovo: Lane transcript; Ru. tr.: *Letopis'-1*, 171). Such *idées fixes* (delusional or paranoid thoughts), mentioned more than once by Eleonore in her letters, are recognised as being common to the manic experience (Jamison [as above], 13). In fact much in the behaviour of what Eleonore calls 'this extravagant nature' (*'cette tête extravagante'*) (Mu., 1/13 June 1833. Muranovo: Lane transcript; Ru. tr.: TPD, 188), many of 'the most extravagant eccentricities of character or mind' admitted to by Tyutchev himself (IV, 38), can be seen as part of the manic-depressive syndrome. His reckless pursuit of illicit romantic or sexual adventures is for instance recognizable as a common feature of mania or its milder manifestation, hypomania (Jamison, 13-14, 262-263), particularly as at least some of these liaisons appear to have begun as he emerged from a depressive phase. Much the same applies to the restlessness and nervous energy which frequently drove him to find diversion in social and intellectual activity. At such times, he once wrote, he led an existence 'of the most exhausting incoherence', which had 'no other aim, no other motive during eighteen hours out of twenty-four than to make me avoid at any price any serious encounter with myself ' (V, 68). Similarly, the renewed energy, heightened creativity and increased speed and fluency of thought and speech associated with benigner forms of hypomania (Jamison, 13-14) may have some bearing on Tyutchev's legendary reputation for brilliant impromptu eloquence. It also no doubt explains why he found the mechanical process of writing so tiresome and frustrating. Quite simply, it seems his pen was unable to to keep up with the torrent of ramifying ideas inside his head. The relevance of all this to T.'s poetic output is clear. Jamison cites various statistical studies which show the incidence of bipolar disorder among creative artists to be much higher than in the general population, with poets scoring highest of all (Jamison, 75-89). In an illustrative and by no means comprehensive list she includes over eighty English-speaking and European poets from Torquato Tasso to Dylan Thomas who appear to have suffered from bipolar disorder, cyclothymia (its milder temperamental variant), or major depression (267-270). A detailed case study of Byron (Chapter 5) contains much that is applicable to Tyutchev. Jamison writes for instance of the genetic factors in Byron's illness (155-159); the 'Proteus-like' or 'chameleon' nature of his personality, and his rapid changes of mood (151); his periods of deep depression (154-155); and the 'erratic financial behaviour [...], episodic promiscuity, violent rages, impetuousness, restlessness, risk taking, poor judgment, and extreme irritability', all of which constitute 'a classic presentation of manic behaviour' (153). For many creative artists a correlation has been observed between the cycle of depression and mania or hypomania on the one hand, and patterns of creative energy on the other (the classic example being Robert Schumann). Jamison suggests that periods of heightened productivity may coincide with 'mixed' states, common during transitions from depression to mania and vice versa, when manic energies and melancholic mood combine and interact (Jamison, 118-119, 132-133, 144-146). In Tyutchev's case certain periods (1829-1830, 1834, 1848-1851) are particularly fruitful in terms of poetic output, while others (notably 1839-1847) are relatively fallow. We might conclude that these correspond to periods of high manic-depressive disturbance on the one hand, and of 'normality' on the other (although other factors were doubtless at work too).

62. El. T. to N.I. Tyutchev, Mu., 11/23 Sept. 1833. Muranovo, *f.* 1, *op.* 1, *yed. khr.* 723, *l.* 14. (Ru. tr.: TPD, 192.)

63. 'Kak nad goryacheyu zoloy...'. I, 117. Among other poems written in the second half of the 1820s, 'Bessonnitsa' ('Insomnia'), 'Za nashim vekom my idyom...' ('We strive to keep up with our age...') and 'Bezumiye' ('Madness') (I, 75, 83, 120) could be singled out for their pessimistic or depressive tone. Conversely, something of the manic can be felt in the strange visions of 'Son na more' ('Dream at Sea'), with its line 'Like a god, on the heights of creation I strode', in the exultant fatalism of 'Tsitseron' ('Cicero'), and in the potent energy charging such poems as 'V dushnom vozdukha molchan'ye...' ('In the air's oppressive silence...'), 'Kon' morskoy' ('Sea Stallion') and 'List'ya' ('Leaves') (I, 151, 122, 135, 111, 127-128); while others such as 'Kak sladko dremlet sad temnozelyony...' ('How tranquilly the darkly verdant garden...') and 'Teni sizye smesilis'...' ('Shadows fall, dove-grey, and mingle...') (I, 158, 159) bear witness to what Jamison calls 'the mystical merging of identities and experiences so common to the manic experience' (Jamison, 28).

64. As note 59.

65. El. T. to N.I. Tyutchev, Mu., 2/14 Apr. 1836. Muranovo, *f.* 1, *op.* 1, *yed. khr.* 723, *l.* 24-270b. (Ru. tr.: *Letopis'-1*, 154.)

66. Both quoted in Jamison (as note 61), 122, 123.

67. 'Poeziya'. II, 9.

68. El. T. to N.I. Tyutchev, SPb., 15/27 Dec.. 1837. Muranovo, *f.* 1, *op.* 1, *yed. khr.* 721, *l.* 32-32*ob.* (Partial Ru. tr.: *Letopis'-1*, 181.)

69. F.I. T. to K.V. Nesselrode, Mu., 22 Oct./ 3 Nov. 1835. IV, 33.

70. See Dinesman (1999c), 161-162.

71. This account of Thiersch's proposals is summarised from the letters to Eynard and King Ludwig referred to in the following two notes.

72. F.W. Thiersch to Ludwig I, Mu., 10 Sept. 1829 (NS). In: F.W. Thiersch, *De l'état actuel de la Grèce et des moyens d'arriver à sa restauration*, 2 vols., Leipzig, 1833. I, 308-310.

73. F.W. Thiersch to J.G. Eynard, Mu., 10 Nov. 1829 (NS). Extracts from the French original are published in: Thiersch, *De l'état...* (as note 72), I, 311-313. It is published almost in full in German translation in: H.W.J. Thiersch, *Friedrich Thiersch's Leben*, Vol. I, Leipzig, 1866, 352-356. See Lane (1984a), 226, for a summary and extract; also Dinesman (1999c), 135-137.

74. F.W. Thiersch to Ludwig I, undated [after 11 Dec. 1829, NS]. Dinesman (1999c), 137-138. Quoted in Engl. tr. in: Lane (1984a), 225.

75. F.I. T. to F.W. Thiersch, Mu., (1) [second half of Nov.], (2) 11 Dec. 1829 (NS). IV, 18-19.

76. This is suggested by T.G. Dinesman in: Dinesman (1999c), 139.

77. F.W. Thiersch to Nicholas I, 21 Nov./ 3 Dec. 1829. Thiersch, *De l'état...* (as note 72), 314-315. See also: Lane (1984a), 225-226, 227.

78. Despatch of A.I. Potyomkin to K.V. Nesselrode, 21 July/ 2 Aug. 1832. *Letopis'-1*, 116.

79. Despatch of K.V. Nesselrode to G.I. Gagarin, SPb., 1/13 July 1833. Dinesman (1999c), 168-169.

80. Despatch of Baron Rouen (Fr. Ambassador in Nauplia), 19 Dec. 1833 (NS), which states that the French were working to persuade Otto to marry one of their royals. Lane (1988b), 268-269.

81. As note 79.

82. Despatch of G.I. Gagarin to K.V. Nesselrode, 15/27 July 1833. Lane (1988b), 268-269.

83. As note 74.

84. Despatch of Count Alfred de Vaudreuil to Duc de Broglie of 3 Aug. 1833 (NS). Lane (1988b), 266-267.

85. Despatch of Vaudreuil to Broglie, 25 Aug. 1833 (NS). Ibid., 267.

86. See: Lane (1988b), 268.

87. I.S. Gagarin to A.N. Bakhmeteva, Paris, 16/28 Oct. 1874. TM, 42.

88. See: King Ludwig I to King Otto, (1) 27 July, (2) 14 Nov. 1833 (NS). Lane (1988b), 277 *n.*25, *n.*29; Despatch of G.I. Gagarin to K.V. Nesselrode, 15/27 July 1833 (with attached letter from King Ludwig to Gagarin of same date). Ibid., 268-269; Despatch of K.V. Nesselrode to G.A. Katakazi, 5/17 Aug. 1833. *Letopis'-1*, 131.

89. As note 87.

90. El. T. to N.I. Tyutchev, Mu., 29 Aug./ 10 Sept. 1833. TPD, 191.

91. The day before T. left Munich the French Ambassador Vaudreuil reported that he 'speaks of travelling via Venice' (as note 84: Lane, 266). The Sardinian Ambassador confirmed this the following day, claiming that in Venice T. was to meet up with 'another Russian official, who will take [the despatches] to Greece; otherwise he will have to proceed to Napolie de Romanie [the French name for Nauplia] himself' (despatch of Count Bertou de Sambuy, 4 Aug. 1833 [NS]. Lane [1988b], 268). The reference to 'another Russian official' may be a garbled account of T.'s intention to meet Nikolay in Venice.

92. As note 90.

93. Ibid.

94. Despatch of Gasser (Bavarian Chargé d'Affaires at Nauplia), 7 Oct. 1833 (NS). Lane (1988b), 271; Glasse, 452 (note 12).

95. As note 90.

96. This is evident from a report by the French Consul in Trieste that T. stayed there for 'nearly three weeks'. See: Lane (1988b), 271.

97. Despatch of Gasser, 27 Aug. 1833 (NS). Glasse, 447. See also Gasser's despatch of 7 Oct. (as note 94).

98. As note 90.

99. By his own account he suffered seasickness 'for the first time in my life' on the Baltic in 1847. IV, 398.

100. The island, named 'Lusina' by Eleonore, is identified as Hvar by T.G. Dinesman and S.A.

Dolgopolova (*Letopis'-1*, 131). R. Lane suggests it could be present-day Lošinj (Lane [1988b], 278 n.37). However, this appears to be situated too far north of Dalmatia, and is only about 100 miles by sea from Trieste.

101. El. T. to N.I. Tyutchev, Mu., 11/23 Sept. 1833. Muranovo: *f.* 1, *op.* 1, *yed. khr.* 723, *l.* 14. (Ru. tr.: TPD, 192.)

102. Gasser's despatch (as note 94: Lane, 272-273).

103. Ibid., 272.

104. *AZ*, 8 Nov. 1833 (NS), No.312, Beilage, p.1248; despatch of G.A. Katakazi to G.I. Gagarin, 26 Sept./ 8 Oct. 1833. *Letopis'-1*, 132. The commander of the *Carolina* had told Gasser the journey from Trieste should take 'no more than fourteen days' (Gasser's despatch of 27 Aug.: as note 97).

105. Despatch of G.A. Katakazi to K.V. Nesselrode, 30 Sept./ 12 Oct. 1833. *Letopis'-1*, 132.

106. *AZ*, 12 Nov. 1833, No.316, Beilage, p.1264; Gasser's despatch of 7 Oct. (as note 94: Lane, 272).

107. Despatch of Vaudreuil, 21 Nov. 1833 (NS). Lane (1988b), 272. (As Lane points out, although sent from Munich, Vaudreuil's despatch undoubtedly relied on information supplied by Baron Rouen, the French Ambassador in Nauplia).

108. 'Iz pisem D.V. Polenova vo vremya poyezdki yego v Gretsiyu i sluzhby pri tamoshnem posol'stve. 1832-1835', *RA*, 1885, Part 3, 111-112. (The information that the letters are to Polenov's parents is given on p.99).

109. Tietz, II, 181-182.

110. Ibid., 208-209.

111. Ibid., 183.

112. Ibid., 183-184.

113. Ibid., 197-198.

114. Ibid., 200.

115. Roswitha Armansperg, *Josef Ludwig Graf Armansperg. Ein Beitrag zur Regierungsgeschichte Ludwigs I von Bayern*, Munich, 1976, 208 (quoted in Glasse, 448).

116. Polenov (as note 108), 111.

117. Despatch of Hohenlohe-Kirchberg, 27 March/ 8 April 1833. Glasse, 446 (in Ru. tr.).

118. Despatch of Gasser, 27 Oct. 1833 (NS). Glasse, 448.

119. Tietz, II, 198-199.

120. Polenov (as note 108), 122. (The letter in question is dated 15/27 Nov. 1833.)

121. Tietz, II, 190-191.

122. D.F. Tyutcheva to Ye.F. Tyutcheva, Ovstug, 28 July/ 9 Aug. 1855. TPD, 271.

123. *AZ*, 9 Nov. 1833 (NS), No.313, Beilage, p.1252; 12 Nov. 1833 (NS), No.316, Beilage, p.1264.

124. Despatch of G.A. Katakazi to K.V. Nesselrode, 30 Sept./ 12 Oct. 1833. *Letopis'-1*, 133 (in Ru. tr.). Original French partially quoted in: Dinesman (1999c), 176.

125. Despatch of G.A. Katakazi to G.I. Gagarin, 26 Sept./ 8 Oct. 1833. Dinesman (1999c), 175-176.

126. As note 124.

127. Gasser's despatch of 7 Oct. (as note 94: Lane, 272-273).

128. As note 125.

129. Dinesman (1999c), 176-177.

130. As note 124.

131. Dinesman (1999c), 177.

132. Tietz, II, 221.

133. Ibid., 281.

134. 'Tuttscheff hat vor Jahr und Tag eine Reise nach Griechenland gemacht, und ist begeistert von dem Anblick des Golfes von Lepanto'. F.L. Lindner to H. Heine, Stuttgart, 10 Nov. 1834 (NS). Heine (1970), XXIV, 280.

135. Byron, *Child Harold's Pilgrimage*, Canto I, verse 60.

136. Despatch of G.A. Katakazi to G.I. Gagarin, 31 Oct./12 Nov. 1833. *Letopis'-1*, 134.

137. As note 107.

138. Despatch of Vaudreuil, 22 Nov. 1833. Lane (1988b), 274. The letter from Armansperg has never been traced.

139. As note 136.

140. *AZ*, 9 Nov. 1833 (NS), No.313, Beilage, p.1252.

141. El. T. to N.I. Tyutchev, Mu., 1/13 Jan. 1834. Muranovo: *f.* 1, *op.* 1, *yed. khr.* 723, *l.* 15-17. (Ru. tr.: TPD, 193.)

142. *Letopis'-1*, 135.

143. Despatch of Gasser, 27 Oct. 1833. Lane (1988b), 274; Glasse, 450.

144. F.I. Tyutchev [grandson of the poet], 'Proyekt diplomaticheskoy depeshi po povodu grecheskikh del, sostavlenny F.I. Tyutchevym v 1833 godu', *Izvestiya otdeleniya russkogo yazyka i slovesnosti Akademii nauk SSSR*, I, (1928), Part 2, 529. (The French text of the draft despatch is on pp.529-532).

145. Ibid., 530.

146. Ibid., 531-532.

147. Ibid., 532.

148. As note 87.

149. G.I. Chulkov, 'Primechaniye k diplomaticheskoy depeshe', in: F.I. Tyutchev, *Stikhotvoreniya* (ed. G.I Chulkov), M., 1935, 359.

150. Kozhinov, 208.

151. K.V. Nesselrode to G.I. Gagarin, 1/13 July 1833. Barbara Jelavich, *Russia and Greece During the Regency of King Otton, 1832-1835. Russian Documents in the First Years of Greek Independence*, Thessaloniki, 1962, 74-75 (quoted in Glasse, 447).

152. Despatch of G.I. Gagarin (in T.'s hand) to K.V. Nesselrode, 14/26 Dec. 1833. *Letopis'-1*, 136.

153. Despatch of Rouen, 19 Dec. 1833 (NS). Lane (1988b), 267-268.

154. As note 136.

155. Tietz, II, 175-176.

156. Byron, *Childe Harold's Pilgrimage*, Canto II, verse 88.

157. Tietz, II, 279.

158. Ibid., 176.

159. As note 107 (Vaudreuil's despatch of 21 Nov.: Lane, 274).

160. As note 141 (French original quoted in: Lane [1988b], 274).

161. Ibid.

162. K.V. Pigaryov suggested that 'Son na more' ('Dream at Sea') might have been inspired by the storm during T.'s outward passage from Trieste to Patras (*Lirika*, I, 357). However, T.G. Dinesman has since shown conclusively that it was written during T.'s Italian journey in the summer of 1829 (Dinesman [1999a], 284-285). G.I. Chulkov's supposition (*PSS* [1933], I, 363) that the same storm inspired the poem 'Vsyo besheney burya, vsyo zleye i zley...' ('The storm grows more violent, its rage unappeased...') (I, 147) can also be discounted. In the style of a ballad, this clearly recounts imagined events rather than T.'s own experiences; its description of a storm appears in fact to be based on a literary antecedent, probably (as argued by R. Lane) A.A. Bestuzhev-Marlinsky's story 'Fregat "Nadezhda"' (Lane [1984b], 52-54).

163. F.I. T. to I.S. Gagarin, Mu., 7/19 July 1836. IV, 50-51.

164. Gregg, 30. For the relevant passage from T.'s letter to Gagarin of 20-21 April/ 2-3 May 1836 (referred to by Gregg on p.29) see: IV, 42.

165. Kozhinov, 214.

166. Pigaryov (1935b), 403.

167. 'Vostok belel. Lad'ya katilas'...'. I, 139.

168. 'Kak ptichka, ranneyu zarey...'. I, 140. See Appendix I (iii) for dating of this and the poem in the preceding note.

Chapter 8. Ernestine

1. Ernestine, 102.

2. Ibid., 100-103; Polonsky (1998), 57.

3. Ernestine, 102.

4. Turgenev (A.I.), 82 (diary, 27 Apr. 1834 [NS]); Polonsky (1998), 116.

5. He died on 20 Feb. (NS) (*Letopis'-1*, 121).

6. Ernestine, 103.

7. Karl Pfeffel to E. von Dörnberg, Mu., 18 March 1833 (NS). *Letopis'-1*, 122.

8. Karl Pfeffel to E. von Dörnberg, Mu., 24 March 1833 (NS). TPD, 187.

9. Pfeffel-Z, 33.

10. Eduard von Schenk, 'Biographie und Charakteristik Michael Beer's', in: Michael Beer, *Sämmtliche Werke* (ed. E. von Schenk), Leipzig, 1835, xxvi.

11. Ibid., xxix.

12. Ibid., xxvi.

13. Karl Pfeffel to E. von Dörnberg, Mu., 30 March 1833 (NS). *Letopis'-1*, 123.

14. See Appendix I (iii).

15. 'I grob opushchen uzh v mogilu...'. I, 138. For dating see Appendix I (iii).

16. S.A. Dolgopolova, 'Stikhi k Ernestine Dyornberg', *Letopis'-1*, 294.

17. Dolgopolova ('Ya pomnyu...'), 63.

18. El. T. to N.I. Tyutchev, Mu., 15 or 16 June 1833 (NS) Muranovo: *f.* 1, *op.* 1, *yed. khr.* 723, *l.* 23. (Ru. tr.: *Letopis'-1*, 125.) For the dating of this letter see Dolgopolova (as note 17).

19. As note 17. Dolgopolova's dating of 'Ya pomnyu vremya zolotoye...' is more convincing than my own earlier suggestion that it was written during a visit to Eglofsheim in July 1834 (Dewey, 30). K.V. Pigaryov had claimed the poem could have been written no earlier than 1834 on the grounds that the original manuscript version is on the same sheet as T.'s translation of a poem by Heine published that year in the collection *Neue Gedichte* (*Lirika*, I, 359; ibid., II, 356). However, Dolgopolova shows that in fact the Heine poem first appeared in print in 1829 and could therefore have been translated by T. before 1834. This, together with her publication of Ernestine's album entry for 17 June 1833, must be considered conclusive evidence for her dating.

20. 'Tam, gde gory, ubegaya...'. I, 163-164. (See also note 63, below.)

21. *Letopis'-1*, 125.

22. El. T. to N.I. Tyutchev, Mu., [second half of June 1833, NS: later than the letter referred to in note 18]. Muranovo: *f.* 1, *op.* 1, *yed. khr.* 723, *l.* 8-90b. (Ru. tr.: TPD, 190.)

23. ('... a paru se réjouir beaucoup de Vous revoir'). K. Pfeffel to E. von Dörnberg, 13 July 1833 (NS). Muranovo. An entry in Ernestine's herbarium shows that she was in Bad Kissingen on 29 July (S. Dolgopolova & A. Yungren, 'Al'bom-gerbariy Ernestiny Fyodorovny Tyutchevoy kak istochnik komentariya', *TS-II*, 115). It is just possible that she travelled there from Eglofsheim via Munich, although this would have involved a considerable detour. A more likely scenario is that Eleonore joined T. at Eglofsheim at the end of June or beginning of July and met Ernestine there.

24. K. Pfeffel to E. von Dörnberg, 11 Sept. 1833. Muranovo. I am grateful to Dr R. Lane for details of both this letter and that referred to in the previous note.

25. Polonsky (1998), 115.

26. At an audience on 20 Oct. King Ludwig asked Gagarin if he had any news of T.'s mission, adding that he himself knew no more than that T. had arrived in Nauplia more than a month previously (despatch of G.I. Gagarin to K.V. Nesselrode, 9/21 Oct. 1833. Lane [1988b], 270; *Letopis'-1*, 133). News of T.'s departure from Nauplia on 8 Oct. is unlikely to have reached Munich through diplomatic channels before the end of the month. It was first published, together with that of his arrival in Trieste on 3 Nov., in the *AZ* on 9 Nov. (No.313, Beilage, p.1252).

27. K. Pfeffel to E. von Dörnberg, Mu., 23 Oct. 1833 (NS). *Letopis'-1*, 134.

28. Despatch of G.I. Gagarin to K.V. Nesselrode, 25 Dec. 1833/ 7 Jan. 1834. *Letopis'-1*, 137.

29. El. T. to N.I. Tyutchev, Mu., 1/13 Jan. 1834. Muranovo: *f.* 1, *op.* 1, *yed. khr.* 723, *l.* 15-17. (Ru. tr.: TPD, 193.)

30. F.I. T. to Ern. T., SPb., 19/31 Dec. 1853. V, 151-152.

31. F.I. T. to I.N. & Ye.L. Tyutchev, Mu., 18/30 Dec. 1842. IV, 220.

32. Turgenev (A.I.), 73 (diary, 27 March 1834 [NS]), 88 (note 10).

33. On 25 April (NS, as all following refs. from the diary) Turgenev noted: 'Yesterday Schelling's wife told me that her husband loves me as a son' (ibid., 82).

34. Ibid., 76 (diary, 4 April).

35. Ibid., 79, 80-81 (diary, 17 and 21 April).

36. Ibid., 79 (diary, 18 April).

37. Ibid., 81 (diary, 22 April).

38. Ibid., 80 (diary, 20 April).

39. Ibid., 78 (diary, 12 April).

40. Ibid., 84 (diary, 28 April).

41. Ibid., 81 (diary, 23 April).

42. Ibid., 81 (diary, 24 April).

43. Ibid., 80 (diary, 21 April).

44. Ibid., 82 (diary, 24 April).

45. Ernestine, 102.

46. Turgenev (A.I.), 82-85 (diary, 25, 27, 29 & 30 April. Ernestine's presence is also recorded for all these gatherings except 27 April).

47. A.I. Turgenev to V.A. Zhukovsky & P.A. Vyazemsky, M., 24 June/ 6 July 1834. Ibid., 66.

48. A.I. Turgenev to N.I. Turgenev, Mu., 30 April 1834 (NS). Ibid., 66.

49. Ibid., 82 (diary, 25 April).

50. A.I. Turgenev to N.I. Turgenev, Mu., 26 April 1834 (NS). Ibid., 66.
51. Ibid., 84 (diary, 30 April).
52. Ibid., 79 (diary, 19 April).
53. Ibid., 85 (diary, 30 April).
54. Ibid., 85 (diary, 1 May).
55. *Zhizn'*, 365.
56. See Dolgopolova, 'Stikhi' (as note 16), 291-297.
57. Ibid., 293.
58. 'Yeshcho zemli pechalen vid...'. I, 171. For dating see Dolgopolova, 'Stikhi' (as note 16), 293.
59. 'I chuvstva net v tvoikh ochakh...'. I, 172. For dating see Dolgopolova, 'Stikhi' (as note 16), 293-294.
60. 'Abschied' ('Es treibt dich fort von Ort zu Ort...'). First published in Heine's collection of poems and articles *Der Salon*, Vol. I, Hamburg, 1834. S.A. Dolgopolova points out (with ref. to Mende) that this volume left the press at the beginning of December 1833, and that the first review of it appeared already on 19 December. She considers that T.'s version was written at about the time of Ernestine's departure from Munich (Dolgopolova, 'Stikhi' [as note 16], 294).
61. 'Iz kraya v kray, iz grada v grad...'. I, 157.
62. K. Pfeffel to E. von Dörnberg, Mu., 4 June 1834 (NS). TPD, 193.
63. 'Sizhu zadumchiv i odin...'. I, 165. According to Pigaryov, the manuscript (numbered 'V') is written on the same paper and in the same handwriting as 'Tam, gde gory, ubegaya...' (numbered 'VI'), indicating that they were composed within a relatively short time of each other (*Lirika*, I, 365). If we are correct in assuming that the second was written during T.'s visit to the Regensburg area in July 1834, 'Sizhu zadumchiv i odin...' most likely dates from earlier that year.
64. El. T. to N.I. Tyutchev, Mu., 23 Apr./ 5 May 1834. Muranovo: *f.* 1, *op.* 1, *yed. khr.* 723, *l.* 19-20. (Ru. tr.: *Letopis'-1*, 144.)
65. El. T. to N.I. Tyutchev, Tegernsee, 24 June/ 6 July 1834. Muranovo: *f.* 1, *op.* 1, *yed. khr.* 723, *l.* 21-22. (Ru. tr.: *Letopis'-1*, 144.)
66. Ibid.
67. All the letters written by T. to Ernestine before their marriage were later destroyed by her for reasons of discretion. There must have been 191 of them, for she had numbered his letters in chronological order, and those surviving begin at no.192. After his death she also destroyed all her letters to him. (*Zhizn'*, 365-366.)
68. F.I. T. to Ern. T., M., 14/26 Aug. 1846. IV, 353.
69. *Letopis'-1*, 144.
70. I.S. Gagarin to A.N. Bakhmeteva, Paris, 28 Oct./ 9 Nov. 1874. TM, 48.
71. K. Pfeffel to E. von Dörnberg, Eglofsheim, 21 July 1834 (NS). TPD, 194.
72. K. Pfeffel to E. von Dörnberg, Eglofsheim, 26-27 July 1834 (NS). Dinesman (1999c), 135. (Ru. tr.: TPD, 194.)
73. Gagarin, 93, 96.
74. *Letopis'-1*, 145.
75. F.I.T. to I.N. & Ye.L. Tyutchev, Oct. 1840. IV, 150; Schmidt, 726. For details of public Lutheran services held at Schloss Tegernsee (to begin with under Queen Karoline's patronage, then under that of her stepson Prince Karl, who inherited the castle on her death in 1841) see Jesse, 112, 182.
76. 'Ya lyuteran lyublyu bogosluzhen'ye...'. I, 156. The autograph manuscript has the inscription: 'Tegernsee. 16/28 October 1834' (I, 432).
77. I.S. Gagarin to A.N. Bakhmeteva, Paris, 23 Oct./ 4 Nov. 1874. TM, 45.
78. Gregg, 117.
79. Heine's original German text was first published (with cuts by the censor) in his collection *Der Salon*, Vol. II, Hamburg, 1835.
80. 'La question Romaine'. III, 56.
81. Vyazemsky, 223-224.
82. P.A. Vyazemsky to P.P Vyazemsky, Mu., 27 Oct./ 8 Nov. 1834. Kauchtschischwili, 277.
83. Ibid., 277-278.
84. Ibid., 278.
85. F.I. T. to Ern. T., SPb., 16/28 Oct. 1853.
86. Vyazemsky, 224 (entry dated 24-27 Oct./ 5-8 Nov. 1834).
87. Turgenev (A.I.), 76 (diary, 3 April 1834 [NS]).
88. For this and other entries in Ernestine's 'herbarium' (album of pressed flowers) see: Dolgopo-

lova & Yungren, 'Al'bom-gerbariy...' (as note 23), 115-120.
89. Polonsky (1998), 64.
90. Turgenev (A.I.), 85 (diary, 27 Feb. 1835 [NS]).
91. *Zhizn'*, 90.
92. The date of their marriage is from the anonymous and undated four-volume manuscript 'Geschichte der Familie von Lerchenfeld', IV, 213. SK.
93. *Letopis'-1*, 148.
94. M. von Lerchenfeld to A. von Krüdener, SPb., 20 Sept./ 2 Oct. 1835. SK. The reference could be to D.G. Bibikov, at that time Vyazemsky's chief at the Department of Foreign Trade.
95. F.I. T. to K.V. Nesselrode, Mu., 22 Oct./ 3 Nov. 1835. IV, 33.
96. *Letopis'-1*, 150; Dinesman (1999c), 199 (note 191).
97. Dinesman (1999c), 161.
98. Ibid., 180.
99. As note 95, 33-34.
100. (Draft of letter from) K.V. Nesselrode to F.I. T., SPb., 21 Jan./ 2 Feb. 1836. PTN, 150. (Ru. tr.: IV, 474.)
101. *Letopis'-1*, 152.
102. El. T. to N.I. Tyutchev, Mu., 3/15 Apr. 1833. Muranovo: *f.* 1, *op.* 1, *yed. khr.* 723, *l.* 3-4. (Ru. tr.: TPD, 188.)
103. F.I. T. to I.N. & Ye.L. Tyutchev, Mu., 31 Dec. 1836/ 12 Jan. 1837. IV, 59.
104. F.I. T. to I.S. Gagarin, Mu., 20-21 Apr./ 2-3 May 1836. IV, 42.
105. Kozhinov, 238; PTN, 147-148.
106. M. von Lerchenfeld to A. von Krüdener, SPb., 15/27 Nov. 1835. SK. Here Lerchenfeld writes of T.: 'Ich glaube kaum, daß euere* Demarchen für *ihn* etwas fruchten werden, u[nd] kann wirklich auch die Ansicht nicht theilen, daß er Ansprüche habe, da sind alle Botschaftsräthe, Staatsräthe die sich um die Stelle bewerben u[nd] sicher mehr Rechte haben. Man avancirt ja nicht in einer Legation, wie in einem Regiment.' ('I hardly think that your* démarches will achieve anything for *him*, and am also really unable to share the view that he has any claim: there are all these Legation Councillors and State Councillors applying for the post and who are certainly more entitled to it. One does not rise through the ranks in a legation the same way as in a regiment, after all.' [*Plural form, referring to both Amélie and Krüdener.])
107. I.S. Gagarin to A.N. Bakhmeteva, Paris, 9/21 Nov. 1874. TM, 52.
108. I.S. Gagarin to I.S. Aksakov, Paris, 29 Oct./ 10 Nov. 1874. TM, 50.
109. R. Tempest, 'Mezhdu Reynom i Senoy', in: Gagarin, 16, 26.
110. I.S. Gagarin to A.N. Bakhmeteva, Paris, Jan. 1875. TM, 59.
111. Ibid.
112. Ibid.
113. As note 104, 39.
114. Ibid., 42.
115. Tempest (as note 109), 34.
116. Gagarin, 131 (diary, 3/15 Nov. 1834).
117. As note 104, 38-39.
118. *Letopis'-1*, 148.
119. 'Reinhard, der hier ziemlich unbekannt ist, wurde ganz roth als ich ihm die Geburt des Hollenst[einschen] Sprößlings erzählte. Über die Tutcheffsche Niederkunft ist wohl sie allein roth geworden.' As note 106.
120. 'Lyublyu glaza tvoi, moy drug...'. I, 173.
121. *Lirika*, I, 371-372.
122. *Letopis'-1*, 149.
123. 'Vchera, v mechtakh obvorozhonnykh...'. I, 174.
124. Gregg, 72.
125. Ibid., 73.
126. 'en vers, comme sous le masque, on peut dire à peu près tout impunément'. F.I. T. to Ern. T., M., 13/25 Sept. 1846. RGB. 308.1.18, *l.* 28-29*ob.* (In Lettres, XVIII, 17, this passage is incorrectly transcribed as: 'en vers comme en musique tout, a peu près, peut se dire impunément'.)
127. Reproduced in *LN-1*, 39. See also *Zhizn'*, 90, where only the entry for 20 March is quoted.
128. As note 104, 39.
129. *Letopis'-1*, 153-154.
130. El. T. to N.I. Tyutchev, Mu., 2/14 Apr. 1836. Muranovo:*f.* 1, *op.* 1, *yed. khr.* 723, *l.* 24-27*ob.*

(Partial Ru. tr.: *Letopis'-1*, 152, 153, 154.)

131. Note by Dr R. Lane in his transcript of the letter.

132. El. T. to Ye.L. Tyutcheva, Mu., 4/16 Feb. 1837. Muranovo: *f.* 1, *op.* 1, *yed. khr.* 721, *l.* 9-13ob. (Ru. tr.: TPD, 197.)

133. As note 104, 39.

134. Ibid., 40-41.

135. Ibid., 41.

136. Franz von Baader to Julie Lasaulx, Mu., 12 May 1836 (NS). *Lettres inédites de Franz von Baader*, Paris, 1957, 276.

137. Despatch of G.I. Gagarin to K.V. Nesselrode, Mu., 21 Apr./ 3 May 1836. Dinesman (1999c), 187. (Ru. tr.: TPD, 194.)

138. TPD, 195 (note 3 to Gagarin's despatch of 21 Apr./ 3 May); *Letopis'-1*, 314; despatch of G.I. Gagarin to K.V. Nesselrode, Mu., 4/16 Jan. 1837 (ibid., 169-170).

139. *Letopis'-1*, 161, 164.

140. *Letopis'* (Ch.), 43. See also *Letopis'-1*, 162. The *chervonets* was a gold coin worth about three silver roubles.

141. Already on 3 May T. wrote to Ivan Gagarin: 'I wish for nothing more than to leave [Munich], but only at the price of a genuine promotion, otherwise...'. IV, 42.

142. I.N. Tyutchev to D.I. Sushkova, M., [May] & 12/24 May 1836. *Letopis'-1*, 156.

143. As note 104, 42.

144. Ibid., 40-41.

145. Turgenev (A.I.), 86 (diary, 17/29 Dec. 1836).

146. Ibid., 67 (Introduction by Azadovsky & Ospovat). It is not absolutely certain that the 'Prince Gagarin' referred to by Turgenev was Ivan, as the latter's cousin Grigory Grigoryevich Gagarin was also in SPb. at the time (see Yashin, 191 [footnote 6]). As son of the Ambassador in Munich, Grigory would of course have been an equally reliable source of information on events there.

147. El. T. to Ye.L. Tyutcheva, Farnbach [= Burgfarrnbach], 22 June/ 4 July 1836. Muranovo: *f.* 1, *op.* 1, *yed. khr.* 721, *l.* 1ob.-2ob. (Ru. tr.: TPD, 195.)

148. Ibid. (Ru. tr.: *Letopis'-1*, 158.)

149. *Letopis'-1*, 159.

150. Ibid., 162.

151. *Zhizn'*, 90.

152. See TPD, 195 (note 4 to passage no.20).

153. Yashin, 189.

154. I.S. Gagarin to F.I. T., SPb., March 1836. *LN-1*, 502 (Ru. tr., first published in 1899, of the French original, which has since been lost).

155. As note 104, 42.

156. I.S. Gagarin to F.I. T., SPb., 12/24 June 1836. L.A. Shur, 'Neosushchestvlyonnoye izdaniye stikhotvoreniy F.I. Tyutcheva 1836-1837 gg. (Po materialam arkhiva I.S. Gagarina)', *Oxford Slavonic Papers*, XIX, 1986, 103. (Reprinted from the original publication in *RA*, 1879, No.5, 120-121. Ru. tr.: *LN-1*, 509.)

157. Nikolayev (1989), 506.

158. As note 156.

159. Ibid.

160. [Anon.], 'Literaturnye izvestiya', *Literaturnye pribavleniya k 'Russkomu invalidu'*, No.48 (26 Nov./ 8 Dec. 1838), 957. It has been suggested that the author (or at least the source of the information) was the editor of the journal in question, Andrey Krayevsky, who had previously worked on Pushkin's *Sovremennik* (K.V. Pigaryov in *Zhizn'*, 88, footnote 125, with an acknowledgement to Ye.P. Kazanovich; see also *Letopis-1*, 319).

161. *Lirika*, I, 369-370.

162. As note 156.

163. F.I. T. to I.S. Gagarin, Mu., 7/19 July 1836. IV, 50-51.

164. Nikolayev (1989), 503, 505.

165. Ibid., 512 *n*.29.

166. L.A. Shur, 'K biografii I.S. Gagarina', *Simvol*, 1984, No.12, 303; Yashin, 194.

167. Ospovat (1989), 499-500.

168. F.I. T. to I.N. & Ye.L. Tyutchev, Mu., 31 Dec. 1836/ 12 Jan. 1837. IV, 60.

169. F.I. T. to I.S. Gagarin, Geneva, 30 March/ 11 Apr. 1838. IV, 96-98.

170. As note 163, 51; see also T.'s letter to Gagarin, Mu., 10/22 July 1836. IV, 56.

171. *Letopis'-1*, 158.
172. Quoted by T. in his letter to N.V. Sushkov, Mu., 21 June/ 3 July 1836. IV, 48.
173. Ye.L. Tyutcheva to D.I. Sushkova, Ovstug, 8/20 June 1836. *Letopis'-1*, 158-159.
174. As note 147.
175. *Letopis'-1*, 164.
176. Ibid., 165.
177. As note 168, 58.
178. El. T. to Ye.L. Tyutcheva, Mu., 17/29 Nov. 1836. Muranovo: *f.* 1, *op.* 1, *yed. khr.* 721, *l.* 3-4ob. (Ru tr.: TPD, 196.)
179. As note 168, 58.
180. El. T. to Ye.L. Tyutcheva, Mu., 10/22 Dec. 1836. Muranovo: *f.* 1, *op.* 1, *yed. khr.* 721, *l.* 5-6. (Ru tr.: *Letopis'-1*, 167.)
181. El. T. to Ye.L. Tyutcheva, Mu., 4/16 Feb. 1837. Muranovo:*f.* 1, *op.* 1, *yed. khr.* 721, *l.* 9-13ob.
182. El. T. to N.I. Tyutchev, Mu., 14/26 Feb. 1837. Muranovo:*f.* 1, *op.* 1, *yed. khr.* 723, *l.* 30-31ob. (Ru tr.: *Letopis'-1*, 171.)
183. As note 181. (Ru. tr.: *Letopis'-1*, 170.)
184. ('cette fatale ornière'). As note 182.
185. El. T. to Ye.L. Tyutcheva, Mu., 26 Dec. 1836/ 7 Jan. 1837. TPD, 196 (where the date is incorrectly given as 7/19 Jan. 1837: see *Letopis'-1*, 168).
186. F.I. T. to I.N. & Ye.L. Tyutchev, Mu., 3/15 Apr. 1837. IV, 63-64.
187. As note 168, 58.
188. *Letopis'-1*, 170.
189. Despatch of F.A. von Maltitz to K.V. Nesselrode, 12/24 Feb. 1837. *Letopis'-1*, 171.
190. As note 186, 63.
191. F.I. T. to I.N. & Ye.L. Tyutchev, Farnbach [= Burgfarrnbach], 9/21 May 1837. IV, 66.
192. El. T. to Ye.L. Tyutcheva, Farnbach [= Burgfarrnbach], 4/16 May 1837. *Letopis'-1*, 173.
193. As note 191, 65-66.

Chapter 9. Fair Prospects

1. Despatch of 29 Jan./ 10 Feb. 1837. Quoted in Vitale (as note 2), 1.
2. The following account of events leading up to Pushkin's fatal duel is based largely on the following sources: Robin Edmonds, *Pushkin. The Man and his Age*, London, 1994, 183-227; Serena Vitale, *Pushkin's Button*, London, 2000; Binyon, 541-636.
3. 'Smert' poeta'. M.Yu. Lermontov, *Sobraniye sochineniy*, 4 vols., M., 1964. I, 21.
4. Laurence Kelly, *Lermontov. Tragedy in the Caucasus*, London, 1983, 63-65.
5. '29-oye yanvarya 1837'. I, 175.
6. *PSS* (1933), I, 386. K.V. Pigaryov later stated (following an earlier suggestion by Ye.V. Petukhov) that T. is more likely to have written the poem in the summer of 1837 in SPb. 'under the immediate impression of gossip which disturbed him as to who was in the right, Pushkin or his killer' (he does not explain why T. should not have heard similar gossip in Munich) (*Zhizn'*, 92). This dating was adopted by Pigaryov in his standard edition of T.'s verse (*Lirika*, I, 372) and has been followed unquestioningly by subsequent editors and critics. For reasons given in the text, I consider Chulkov's dating more likely.
7. Kozhinov, 190ff., Yashin, 194.
8. They had left Travemünde on 22 May/ 3 June, and the voyage by steamer took 78 hours in fair conditions.
9. Yashin, 193, note 6.
10. F.I. T. to I.N. & Ye.L. Tyutchev, Tu., 1/13 Nov. 1837. IV, 81 (see also ibid., 487 *n*.5).
11. F.I. T. to P.A. Vyazemsky, SPb., 11/23 June 1837. IV, 67. The reference is to Chateaubriand's *Mémoires d'outre-tombe*.
12. *Zhizn'*, 93; Nikolayev (1989), 518, 522.
13. N.M. Smirnov, 'Iz pamyatnykh zapisok', *RA*, 1882, No.1, 235 (quoted in S. Vitale [as note 2], 155).
14. For a detailed analysis of the evidence see: P.Ye. Shchegolev, *Duel' i smert' Pushkina*, 2nd. ed., M., 1936 (and later editions). In more recent times there have been several tendentious and sometimes fanciful attempts by Soviet writers to resurrect the theory of Gagarin's guilt (usually on the basis that his Jesuit connections alone single him out as a prime suspect). The most substantial is Yashin (as detailed above under 'Sources'). Although this contains valuable new

archival material, Yashin's overall thesis of Gagarin's involvement in the 'diplomas' was convincingly refuted by A.S. Buturlin in 'Imel li I.S. Gagarin otnosheniye k paskvilyu na A.S. Puskhina?', *Izvestiya Akademii nauk SSSR. Seriya literatury i yazyka*, XXVIII, 1969, 277-285.

15. F.I. T. to I.S. Gagarin, Geneva, 30 March/ 11 Apr. 1838. IV, 96-98.

16. I.S. Gagarin to A.N. Bakhmeteva, Paris, 28 Oct./ 9 Nov. 1874. TM, 48 (Ru. tr. of Gagarin's French original). For T.'s actual words as quoted by Gagarin — a mixture of French, German and Russian — see *Tyutcheviana*, 21. '*Heimweh*' is German for 'homesickness'; '*Herausweh*' is T.'s own coinage, roughly translatable as 'get-out-of-here-sickness'.

17. Gagarin to Bakhmeteva (as note 16). According to Gagarin, the conversation took place in March, just after the sentence on d'Anthès had been announced. As this was demonstrably over two months before T. arrived in SPb., K.V. Pigaryov has thrown doubt on the whole story (*Zhizn'*, 93, note 138). Yet the witticism rings true. It seems likely that — recalling the conversation nearly forty years later — Gagarin merely placed it in the wrong context.

18. Turgenev (A.I.), 86 (diary, 16/28 June 1837).

19. As note 9.

20. Turgenev (A.I.), 86 (diary, 11/23, 14/26, 15/27 and 16/28 June 1837). Pushkin and Chaadayev were discussed on 15/27 June.

21. P.Ya. Chaadayev, *Sochineniya i pis'ma* (ed. M. Gershenzon), 2 vols., M., 1913-1914. I, 198.

22. *Novoye slovo*, 1894, No.2, 39.

23. Quoted in Yashin, 190.

24. El. T. to Ye.L. Tyutcheva, Mu., 4/16 Feb. 1837. TPD, 196.

25. F.I. T. to I.N. & Ye.L. Tyutchev, Farnbach [=Burgfarrnbach], 9/21 May 1837. IV, 65.

26. F.I. T. to I.N., Ye.L. Tyutchev & N.V. Sushkov, Lübeck, 15/27 Aug. 1837. IV, 71.

27. F.I. T. to N.V. Sushkov, Mu., 21 June/ 3 July 1836. IV, 48-49. Here T. thanks Sushkov for his 'friendly, fraternal letter'.

28. F.I. T. to Ern. T., M., 14/26 July 1843. IV, 242.

29. Ibid. Following his appointment as governor of Minsk in 1838 Sushkov had shown himself to be a man of principle, resigning three years later rather than carry out an official policy with which he disagreed. This effectively put paid to his career in public administration. See also: *Letopis'-1*, 327; F.I. T. to I.N. & Ye.L. Tyutchev, Mu., 1/13 March 1842. IV, 186.

30. See above, note 178 to Chapter 6; Turgenev (A.I.), 86 (diary, 15/27 June 1837).

31. A.L. Ospovat, 'Tyutchev letom 1837 goda', *Literaturny protsess i razvitiye russkoy kul'tury XVIII - XX vv. Tezisy nauchnoy konferentsii*, Tallin, 1985, 71.

32. *Zhizn'*, 92.

33. *Letopis'-1*, 176.

34. See: *Letopis'-1*, 104, 324; IV, 329, 486 *n.*6, 536-537, 550 *n.*2.

35. *Tyutchevy*, 175; see also *Letopis'-1*, 301 *n.*8.

36. F.I. T. to I.N., Ye.L. Tyutchev & D.I., N.V. Sushkov, SPb., 8/20 Aug. 1837. IV, 68-69; *Letopis'-1*, 176-177.

37. As note 26, 69. All dates given from here on in Chapter 9 are NS unless stated otherwise.

38. Ibid., 71-72.

39. F.I. T. to I.N. & Ye.L. Tyutchev, Mu., 29 Aug./ 10 Sept. 1837. IV, 72.

40. Chereysky, 281.

41. Ospovat (1994), 113.

42. As note 39, 73.

43. N.I. Grech, *Putevye pis'ma iz Anglii, Germanii i Frantsii*, Part 3, SPb., 1839, 97; see also Ospovat (1989), 499-500.

44. As note 39, 73.

45. In his letter to his parents T. writes that he is planning to leave Munich for Switzerland 'in a few days from now' (ibid.).

46. *Letopis'-1*, 178.

47. As note 39, 73.

48. Ibid., 73-74. A grant equal to half of T.'s annual salary to cover removal expenses and 'in recognition of zealous service' was approved on 26 March/ 7 April 1838 (*Letopis'-1*, 184).

49. Despatch of A.N. Obrezkov, 18/30 Sept. 1837. *Letopis'-1*, 179.

50. F.I. T. to K.V. Nesselrode, Tu., 25 July/ 6 Aug. 1838. IV, 106.

51. K.V. Nesselrode, 'Projet d'instruction pour Mr de Kokosckine', 12/24 May 1839. TPN, 175, 178.

52. F.I. T. to I.N. & Ye.L. Tyutchev, Turin, 1/13 Nov. 1837. IV, 78, 80.

53. *Tyutchevy*, 175-176.

54. F.I. T. to I.N. & Ye.L. Tyutchev, Tu., 13/25 Dec. 1837. IV, 89; as note 15, 97 (and see 489 *n*.1).
55. As note 52, 78.
56. See, e.g., IV, 80-81, 90.
57. As note 54 (letter to I.N. & Ye.L. Tyutchev). According to Obrezkov in a letter to Count Solaro dated 7 Dec. 1837, the Sardinian customs were then still holding five trunks of T.'s containing clothing and books (mainly in Russian) for his personal use. TAS: Materie Politiche: Lettere Ministri Esteri: Russia: Lettere dell'Inviato al Ministero Esteri Sardo: Mazzo 2: 36954 71. I am grateful to Dr R. Lane for details of this and other material from TAS referred to in subsequent notes.
58. F.I. T. to I.N. & Ye.L. Tyutchev, Tu., 13/25 Dec. 1837. IV, 86.
59. As note 52, 81.
60. See note 57; also IV, 78-79, 81; 100 (T.'s letters to his parents of 1/13 Nov. 1837 & 17/29 June 1838).
61. As note 52, 81.
62. Ibid., 78.
63. As note 58, 88-89.
64. Ibid., 87; F.I. T. to K.V. Nesselrode, Tu., 25 July/ 6 Aug. 1838. IV, 107.
65. As note 52, 78.
66. Ibid.
67. Ibid., 81.
68. As note 58, 87-88.
69. Ibid., 86-87.
70. Despatch of F.I. T. to K.V. Nesselrode, 7/19 Nov. 1838. *Letopis'-1*, 200.
71. *Letopis'-1*, 180.
72. 'Ital'yanskaya villa'. I, 180. A copy of the poem made by Ernestine is dated 'December 1837' (I, 463).
73. Gregg, 69; Fet (1859), 136.
74. Gregg, 69.
75. As note 58, 87-88.
76. '1-oye dekabrya 1837'. I, 176. In all other examples of T.'s poems with a date as title the date is unambiguously that of the event referred to, not of the poem's composition. Here it clearly refers to their parting, when either T. or Ernestine left Genoa. Soon afterwards he informed his parents that he had returned to Turin from Genoa 'in the first days' of December (as note 58, 87).
77. As it happened, '1st December 1837' appeared in print about a month before Eleonore left the city, but 'Italian Villa' only some six weeks afterwards (*Letopis'-1*, 184, 189).
78. El. T. to N.I. Tyutchev, Mu., 15/27 Dec. 1837. Muranovo: *f*. 1, *op*. 1, *yed. khr.* 723, *l.* 32-32ob. Brief extracts in Ru. tr.: *Letopis'-1*, 181; O. Pigaryova, 'Iz semeynoy zhizni F.I. Tyutcheva. 1832-1838 (Po neizdannym materialam)', *Zven'ya*, 1934, Parts 3 - 4, 284.
79. As note 58, 89-90.
80. Despatch no. 1556 of Solaro to Bertou de Sambuy, 9 Jan. 1838. TAS: Austria: Registri Lettere della Segreteria Estera: Mazzo 157. (Reference supplied by Dr R. Lane).
81. 'Davno l', davno l', o Yug blazhenny...'. I, 178-179. First published in *Sovremennik* in April 1838. K.V. Pigaryov considered it was written in Turin soon after T.'s return from Genoa, and dated it accordingly Dec. 1837 (*Lirika*, I, 374). However, T.G. Dinesman points out that the wintry mountainous scene depicted is inconsistent with the topographical and climatic features of the area around Turin (Dinesman [1999a], 288). Her conclusion — that the poem was written in Jan. 1838 during or just after T.'s journey across the Alps to Vienna — is altogether more convincing.
82. Despatch no. 122 of Marzano, 21 Jan. 1838. TAS: Lettere Ministri: Monaco: Serie 4: Mazzo 34.
83. Despatch no. 124 of Marzano, 4 Feb. 1838. (Ref. as preceding note; both supplied by Dr R. Lane).
84. The portrait is signed by the artist in the bottom left-hand corner: 'Fait d'après nature par Hippolite de Rechberg'. Beneath this has been added in pencil, in Ernestine's hand: '9 mars 1838' (Dolgopolova & Tarkhov [1989b], 615). It seems reasonable to conclude, as Dolgopolova and Tarkhov do, that Ernestine's dating refers to the completion of the portrait (ibid., 615-616); however, their supposition that it was painted in Geneva (ibid., 616) is doubtful, there being no evidence to place either T. or Hippolite von Rechberg there at that time. T.G. Dinesman and I.A. Korolyova suggest on the other hand that Ernestine's note refers to the date on which T. presented the portrait to her in Geneva, but again are unable to produce any evidence that T. was

there on 9 March (*Letopis'-1*, 182). Against this must be set the fact that one diplomatic document places T. in Munich on 23 March: on that date the Sardinian Ambassador Marzano reported that T. would be leaving on a courier mission to Turin in the following days (despatch no. 131; ref. as note 82). It seems unreasonable to suppose (as required by both versions of the portrait's genesis) that T. returned to Munich not long after his supposed arrival in Geneva, then set out for Geneva a second time at the beginning of April (each journey between the two cities taking perhaps four to five days). The only explanation to fit the known facts with any degree of credibility is that the portrait was painted in Munich on 9 March, and that T. presented it to Ernestine in Geneva after arriving there about a month later.

85. Polonsky (1998), 50.

86. Arkhipov, 314.

87. Heine (1968), IV, 968.

88. A. von Maltitz, *Vor dem Verstummen*, Weimar, 1858, 257-258, 268 (translations of 'Nedarom miloserdym Bogom...' and 'Vesennyaya groza').

89. 'Ne ver', ne ver' poetu, deva...'. I, 186. Yu. Tynyanov first suggested that the poem was addressed to Clotilde, although his supposition that the poet she is being warned against is Heine must be discounted on grounds of chronology (Tynyanov [1977], 365-366). It now seems certain that the poem was written in the late 1830s when Maltitz was wooing Clotilde, long after her association with Heine.

90. In a letter to Ivan Gagarin from Geneva on 11 April T. mentions both the diplomatic crisis and personnel changes at the Turin Embassy (IV, 97). This information presumably reached him in correspondence from Obrezkov.

91. On the evidence of Ernestine's flower album, she was in Cannes on 20 Feb. and in the Jura mountains en route for Geneva on 1 March; she then stayed in Geneva throughout March and until at least the middle of April (*Letopis'-1*, 182-184). From a letter to her from Karl Pfeffel it is clear that she was already in Geneva on 5 March (Dolgopolova & Tarkhov [1989b], 616).

92. Despatch no. 262 of Solaro to Marzano, 24 Apr. 1838. TAS: Lettere Ministri: Baviera: Registri di Copia Lettere Spedite da Turino all'Inviato Sardo a Monaco: Mazzo 50. (Ref. supplied by Dr R. Lane).

93. 'Der Schwan'. *Gedichte von A. von Maltitz*, 2 vols., Munich, 1838. I, 245-246.

94. 'Lebed' '. I, 109. See: Lane (1984b), 49-50; Dinesman (1999a), 289-290.

95. I, 182. The autograph has T.'s inscription: 'Lindau. 4 avril 1838' (I, 465). Translation: 'Weary from the journey, we two were able to sit down for a moment by the roadside — to feel the same shade hang loosely on our brows, and to gaze towards the distant horizon. // But time runs its course: its relentless downward slope soon separates that which it once united — and beneath the whip of an invisible power man founders, despondent and alone, in the infinity of space. // And what remains to us now, friend, of those hours passed, of that life together? A look, an inflexion, fragments of thoughts... Alas, did that which is no longer ever exist?'

96. For a discussion of Pascalian elements in this and other French poems by T. see Lane (1982), 321-322.

97. IV, 96.

98. *Letopis'-1*, 183.

99. F.I. T. to Ern. T., M., 8/20 Aug. 1846. IV, 350.

100. 'Vesna' ('Spring') ('Kak ni gnetyot ruka sud'biny...'). I, 183-184. T.G. Dinesman and I.A. Korolyova consider the poem was written in March - April 1838 (NS) while T. was still in Munich (*Letopis'-1*, 183). Although this is possible, a slightly later date would seem more likely, implying that it was written in Geneva or during T.'s onward journey to Turin.

101. *Letopis'-1*, 184.

102. Solaro's despatch to Marzano of 24 April (as note 92) reports T.'s arrival in Turin.

103. Lane (1990), 80; *Zhizn'*, 100-101.

104. Despatch of Heldewier, 7 Aug. 1838. Lane (1990), 80.

105. F.I. T. to K.V. Nesselrode, Tu., 25 July/ 6 Aug. 1838. IV, 106.

106. Despatch of Heldewier, 28 May 1838. Lane (1990), 80.

107. Despatch of K.V. Nesselrode to A.M. Obrezkov, 20 Apr./ 2 May 1838. *Letopis'-1*, 185.

108. He was officially accredited on 3 August (NS) (*Letopis'-1*, 190).

Chapter 10. The Hand of Fate

1. El. T. to N.I. Tyutchev, Mu., second half of June 1833. Muranovo: *f.* 1, *op.* 1, *yed. khr.* 723, *l.* 8-

90*b*. (For dating see *Letopis'-1*, 125-126.) Ru. tr.: TPD, 190.

2. According to one official document, T. was paid 2,252.87 roubles (paper) for the period May - Aug. 1838 (OS) (*Tyutchevy*, 177). Although he was appointed Chargé d'Affaires from 22 July (OS), pay rises on promotion seem to have taken effect from the following month. On this calculation the sum quoted breaks down as 1,550.50 roubles for the three months May - July (his annual salary as First Secretary was 6,222 roubles: see *Tyutchevy*, 175-176), plus 697.37 roubles for one month as Chargé. This implies an annual rate of 8,368.44 roubles (paper) as Chargé d'Affaires. At the exchange rate applied some months earlier for his salary as First Secretary (1 silver rouble = 4.148 paper roubles: see *Tyutchevy*, 176) this would equate to 2,017 silver roubles. Allowing for minor fluctuations in the exchange rate and/or bankers' fees, the actual figure was almost certainly 2,000.

3. Despatch of Carrega, SPb., 14/26 May 1838. Lane (1990), 81.

4. T. later wrote to his parents that the *Nicholas I* had left port on 14/26 May (IV, 100). This is incorrect: all other sources (see below, note 8) give 15/27 May.

5. They are listed as among the passengers in *Sankt-Peterburgskiye vedomosti*, No.90, 26 Apr. 1838 (OS), repeated in Nos. 92 & 94.

6. Indisputable evidence for this is found in two letters written to Turgenev by his mother in Dec. 1838 and May 1839 in response to correspondence from him which has not survived. They are quoted in: Avrahm Yarmolinsky, *Turgenev. The Man, his Art and his Age*, New York, 1959, 38; and in: *Turgenevsky sbornik I*, M. & L., 1964, 350.

7. Yarmolinsky (as note 6), 38; Gregg, 13, 211.

8. Details which follow of the fire on the *Nicholas I* and its aftermath are taken in part from Ivan Turgenev's two accounts of what happened. The better-known, 'Un incendie en mer', was dictated by him in French towards the end of his life, nearly half a century after the events in question (Turgenev *S*, XIV, 186-202). Lesser-known is a more immediate and factually more correct account taken down from Turgenev's own words just a month after the fire and shipwreck ('Turgenev v Geydel'berge letom 1838 g.: iz dnevnika Ye.V. Sukhovo-Kobylinoy', *LN*, LXXVI, 1967, 338-340). Other sources drawn on are: (1) Vyazemsky, 238 (brief diary notes made by Vyazemsky after the disaster); (2) 'O pozhare na parokhode': an anonymous eyewitness account later found in the archive of T.'s aunt Nadezhda Sheremeteva (quoted in full in IV, 489-491); (3) a report of the disaster in the SPb. newspaper *Severnaya pchela*, 1838, No.117, 27 May (OS); (4) despatches of the British Consul in Hamburg, Henry Canning, of 1 & 5 June (London: Public Record Office: Foreign Office: 33: 85; I am grateful to Dr R. Lane for details of these).

9. Turgenev, 'Un incendie...' (as note 8), 190-191.

10. Ibid., 193.

11. Ibid.

12. Before leaving she had told the Sardinian Ambassador in SPb. that she would be travelling via Paris. Despatch no. 713 of Carrega, 14/26 May 1838. TAS: Lettere Ministri: Russia: Serie IV: Mazzo 20 (details supplied by Dr R. Lane).

13. El. T. to D.I. Sushkova, Lübeck, 20 May/ 1 June 1838. Muranovo: *f.* 1, *op.* 1, *yed. khr.* 720. (Ru. tr.: *Zhizn'*, 97.)

14. This is mentioned by Carrega in his despatch no. 716 of 28 May/ 9 June 1838 (archival ref. as note 12).

15. Turgenev, 'Un incendie...' (as note 8), 189.

16. F.I. T. to I.N. & Ye.L. Tyutchev, Mu., 17/29 June 1838. IV, 100.

17. El. T. to I.N. Tyutchev, Mu., 16/28 June 1838. Muranovo:*f.* 1, *op.* 1, *yed. khr.* 722, *l.* 3. (Ru. tr.: *Letopis'-1*, 187.)

18. *Tyutchevy*, 175-176.

19. She was carrying Carrega's despatch no. 713 (see note 12). Carrega sent a further copy of this with his despatch no. 716 (see note 14), correctly assuming that it had been lost in the flames.

20. El. T. to I.N. Tyutchev, Hamburg, 25 May/ 6 June 1838. Muranovo: *f.* 1, *op.* 1, *yed. khr.* 722, *l.* 1-2. (Ru. tr.: *Letopis'-1*, 187.)

21. As note 17.

22. As note 20 (not included in Ru. tr.).

23. As note 17.

24. As note 16, 100-101.

25. Polonsky (1998), 105.

26. As note 17. (Ru. tr.: TPD, 198.)

27. Ibid. (not included in either of the Ru. translations).

28. As note 16.

29. As note 17. (Ru. tr.: TPD, 198.)

30. El. T. to Ye.L. Tyutcheva, Tu., 4/16 Aug. 1838. Muranovo: *f.* 1, *op.* 1, *yed. khr.* 721, *l.* 17-200*b*. (Ru. tr.: TPD, 198.)

31. As note 17. (Ru. tr.: TPD, 198.)

32. As note 25.

33. As note 30.

34. As note 25. Polonsky is however mistaken in asserting that the children stayed in Munich (see *Letopis'-1*, 189).

35. As note 30.

36. *Letopis'-1*, 190.

37. As note 17.

38. As note 30.

39. Ibid. (Ru. tr.: 199).

40. *Letopis'-1*, 190.

41. As note 30.

42. El. T. to S.N. Karamzina, Tu., 1/13 Aug. Muranovo: *f.* 1, *op.* 1, *yed. khr.* 719.

43. As note 30 (Ru. tr.: 199).

44. *Letopis'-1*, 191, 193.

45. Despatch no. 575 of Solaro to Carrega (Sardinian Ambassador in SPb.), 7/19 Sept. 1838. TAS: Lettere Ministri: Russia: Copia Lettere del Ministero Esteri all'Inviato: 1817-1846: Mazzo 25. (Ref. supplied by Dr R. Lane).

46. Polonsky (2003), 52 (footnote).

47. Despatch no. 65 of Rumigny (French Ambassador), Tu., 10 Sept. 1838. Paris: Archives du Ministère des Affaires Étrangères: Correspondance politique: Sardaigne: 313, p.46 (ref. supplied by Dr R. Lane). T. too wrote of Eleonore having died after 'the most atrocious suffering' (letter to K.V. Nesselrode, Tu., 6/18 Oct. 1838. IV, 114).

48. Tyutchev (F.F.), 236.

49. Diary of A.F. Tyutcheva, 4/16 May 1846. TPD, 216.

50. Polonsky (2003), 52 (footnote).

51. D.F. Tyutcheva to Ye.F. Tyutcheva, Tu., 10/22 Oct. 1871. TPD, 417.

52. As note 50.

53. Despatch of Olry, 7 May 1839. Lane (1987), 8.

54. F.I. T. to K.V. Nesselrode, Tu., 6/18 Oct. 1838. IV, 114.

55. *Letopis'-1*, 197; F.I. T. to V.A. Zhukovsky, Tu., 6/18 Oct. 1838. IV, 112-113.

56. Ibid., 113.

57. Zhukovsky (1903), 428 (diary, 13/25 Oct. 1838).

58. *Letopis'-1*, 199.

59. 'Pamyati V.A. Zhukovskogo' ('To the Memory of V.A. Zhukovsky'). II, 55-56.

60. Zhukovsky (1903), 429-430 (diary, 14/26 Oct. 1838).

61. 'Den' i noch' '. I, 185. This can be dated to no later than the beginning of 1839 (I, 468). I am indebted to Ronald Lane for suggesting to me that it can be seen as an immediate response to Eleonore's death, and that the thematically similar 'Svyataya noch' na nebosklon vzoshla...' (see note 77) marks the tenth anniversary of that event.

62. Liberman, 229-230.

63. Examples from T.'s letters are quoted in Lane (1982), 319-320. Other poems using the abyss image with these connotations are: 'Svyataya noch' na nebosklon vzoshla...'; 'Smotri, kak na rechnom prostore...'; 'Uvy, chto nashego neznan'ya...'; 'Ot zhizni toy, chto bushevala zdes' ' (I, 215; II, 34, 65, 234).

64. Leo Tolstoy, who presumably knew nothing of the poem's biographical context, appears to have grasped this instinctively. S.A. Stakhovich recalled him once pointing out that the word '*noch*' ' ('night') in the final line can appropriately be replaced with '*smert*' ' ('death'). (Quoted in *Dok.*, 249.)

65. V.A. Zhukovsky to P.A. Pletnyov, Venice, 4/16 Nov. 1838. K.Ya. Grot, *Neskol'ko dopolneniy k rukopisyam V.A. Zhukovskogo*, SPb., 1903, 3 (quoted in *Letopis'-1*, 200).

66. V.A. Zhukovsky to N.N. Sheremeteva, Vienna, first half of March 1839 (NS). V.A. Zhukovsky, *Sochineniya*, VI, SPb., 1878, 502 (quoted in *Letopis'-1*, 212).

67. Despatch no. 10 of F.I. T. to K.V. Nesselrode, 7/19 Nov. 1838. Gladkova & Lebedev, 'Razdalsya....' (as note 87), 136. See also Lane (1990), 82 (extract in Engl. tr.).

68. *Letopis'-1*, 199.

69. N.I. Tyutchev to I.N. & Ye.L. Tyutchev, Warsaw, 26 Oct./ 7 Nov. 1838. TPD, 200 *n*.2.

70. N.I. Tyutchev to I.N. & Ye.L. Tyutchev, Warsaw, 16/28 Sept. 1838. TPD, 199.

71. *Letopis'-1*, 199.

72. N.I. Tyutchev to I.N. & Ye.L. Tyutchev, Tu., 25 Dec. 1838/ 6 Jan. 1839. TPD, 200.

73. F.I. T. to I.N. & Ye.L. Tyutchev, Mu., 1/13 Dec. 1839. IV, 126.

74. Gregg, 14.

75. Blagoy, 73-75.

76. 'Yeshcho tomlyus' toskoy zhelaniy...'. I, 102. One of the two autograph manuscripts is dated '1848' in Ernestine's hand (*Lirika*, I, 379). For the suggestion that the poem was written to mark the tenth anniversary of Eleonore's death see Lane (1983), 127.

77. 'Svyataya noch' na nebosklon vzoshla...'. I, 215. Of the two surviving autograph manuscripts, K.V. Pigaryov dates the earlier to between 1848 and 1849 and the final version to no later than March 1850 (*Lirika*, I, 387-388). This is confirmed by A.A. Nikolayev (*PSS* [1987], 162).

78. As note 76.

79. Dolgopolova & Tarkhov (1989a), 609 *n*.49

80. N.I. Tyutchev to I.N. & Ye.L. Tyutchev, Warsaw, 26 Oct./ 7 Nov. 1838. *Letopis'-1*, 197.

81. F.I. T. to K.V. Nesselrode, Tu., 25 July/ 6 Aug. 1838. IV, 104-106.

82. Lane (1990), 83.

83. Despatch no. 10 of F.I. T. to K.V. Nesselrode, Milan, 13/25 Feb. 1839. Ibid.

84. Despatch of K.V. Nesselrode to F.I. T., SPb., 19/31 March 1839. Ibid., 84.

85. Zhukovsky (1903), 468 (diary, 7/19 Feb. 1839).

86. Ibid. (diary, 8/20 Feb. 1839); *Zhizn'*, 106; S. Pellico to unknown addressee, 22 Feb. 1839. N. Kauchtschischwili, *Silvio Pellico è la Russia. Un capitolo sui rapporti culturali russo-italiani*, Milan, 1963, 34-35 (quoted in *Letopis'-1*, 210).

87. T.'s despatches are listed, with brief synopses, in: R.C. Lane, 'An Index and Synopsis of Diplomatic Documents Relating to Tyutchev's Period in Turin (October 1837 - October 1839)', *New Zealand Slavonic Journal*, 1989-90, 73-95. Further details and extracts are to be found in *Letopis'-1*, 190-224 passim. These sources tally, with two exceptions: (1) Lane (p.77) counts T.'s private letter of 25 July/ 6 Aug. to K.V. Nesselrode, then in Toeplitz, as his despatch no. 2 for 1838. *Letopis'-1* (p.192) clarifies that despatch no. 2 was in fact addressed to P.G. Divov, Nesselrode's deputy in SPb., on 18/30 Aug. (this item is omitted by Lane). (2) *Letopis'-1* (p.223) also gives details of T.'s final despatch for 1839 (no. 28, dated 1/13 July), which is omitted by Lane. Ten of the despatches have been published in full (in Russian translation) in: L.V. Gladkova, Ye.N. Lebedev, ' "Razdalsya nash natsional'ny gimn na russkom yazyke". Pis'ma diplomata F.I. Tyut- cheva k K.V. Nessel'rode', *Moskva*, 1994, No.10, 132-146. A further three are published (in the original French, with Russian translations) in PTN, 162-174

88. Despatch no. 12 of F.I. T., Genoa, 23 Nov./ 5 Dec. 1838. AVPRI (K), 1838, No.212, *l*. 150-152. (Quoted in part in: *Zhizn'*, 105; *Letopis'-1*, 201.)

89. Despatch no. 22 of F.I. T., Genoa, 4/16 June 1839. AVPRI (K), 1839, No.207, *l*. 69-70ob. (Quoted in part in *Letopis'-1*, 222.)

90. Despatch no. 21 of F.I. T., Genoa, 4/16 June 1839. *Zhizn'*, 105.

91. For instance in his despatch no. 11, Genoa, 7/19 Nov. 1838. AVPRI (K), 1838, No.212, *l*. 147-148.

92. Despatch no. 12 of F.I. T., Tu., 4/16 Apr. 1839. Dinesman (2004), 120-121 (quoted in the original French); *Letopis'-1*, 215 (in Ru. tr.).

93. Binyon, 190 (footnote).

94. Dinesman (2004), 118. The foregoing account of Sardinia's internal politics is taken from T.'s despatches: no. 15, Genoa, 23 Nov./ 5 Dec. 1838; no. 9, Milan, 13/25 Feb. 1839; no. 13, Tu., 4/16 Apr. 1839. AVPRI (K), 1838, No.212, *l*. 159-159ob.; Gladkova, Lebedev, 'Razdalsya...' (as note 87), 144-145 (quoted in part in the original French in Dinesman [2004], 118); AVPRI (K), 1839, No.207, *l*. 49.

95. Despatch no. 4 of F.I. T., Tu., 5/17 Oct. 1838. Dinesman (2004), 102. Dinesman notes the similarity of this passage to the overall theme of T.'s article 'La question Romaine', written more than a decade later.

96. Despatch no. 14 of F.I. T., Tu., 4/16 Apr. 1839. AVPRI (K), 1839, No.207, *l*. 51-52.

97. Despatch no. 2 of F.I. T., Tu., 9/21 Jan. 1839. *Letopis'-1*, 205.

98. Florinsky, II, 778, 785-786.

99. Despatch no. 25 of F.I. T., Tu., 24 June/ 6 July 1839. *Letopis'-1*, 223.

100. *Letopis'-1*, 223.
101. F.I. T. to Ern. T., SPb., 28 Aug./ 9 Sept. 1843. IV, 267.
102. *Letopis'-1*, 200.
103. F.I. T. to Ern. T., M., 1/13 Sept. 1858. *Letopis'-2*, 299.
104. This is evident from his reply of 12 Dec. (her letter has not survived). *Letopis'-1*, 202.
105. F.I. T. to Ern. T., Weimar, 7/19 Sept. 1841. IV, 174.
106. 'S kakoyu negoyu, s kakoy toskoy vlyublyonnoy...'. I, 177. The poem was first published in *Sovremennik* in Oct. 1840 (*Letopis'-1*, 238). On the basis of internal evidence K.V. Pigaryov suggested it could have been written immediately after T. and Ernestine parted in December 1837 (*Lirika*, I, 374). In her article 'Stikhi k Ernestine Dyornberg (1834-1838)', *Letopis'-1*, 291-297 (here: 295), S.A. Dolgopolova posits an even earlier occasion: their parting in the summer of 1836, after Eleonore's suicide attempt. Neither suggestion explains why T. should have waited for up to three or even four years before submitting the poem for publication. All the other poems known to have been written between the spring of 1836 and the spring of 1838 that were published in *Sovremennik* appeared in that journal in 1838 and 1839 (the last — 'Lebed' ' — in July 1839 [*Letopis'-1*, 224]). More convincing for this reason alone is A.A. Nikolayev's dating of the poem to after Eleonore's death (*PSS* [1987], 145, 388).
107. Despatch no. 14 of F.I. T., 23 Nov./ 5 Dec. 1838. AVPRI (K), 1838, No.212, *l.* 154-1550b.
108. As note 72; see also *Letopis'-1*, 203.
109. *Letopis'-1*, 212. I am grateful to Dr R. Lane for the information that Karl Pfeffel's letters to Ernestine from Florence dated 2, 9, 16, 21 March and 1, 16 April (preserved in the Muranovo archive) are all addressed to her at Turin.
110. Polonsky (1998), 50; F.I. T. to K.V. Nesselrode, Tu., 1/13 March 1839. IV, 118.
111. Ibid. (IV, 118).
112. Lane (1987), 11; *Letopis'-1*, 224.
113. *Letopis'-1*, 216. T. reported Miklashevsky's departure in a letter to Ivan Gagarin from Geneva dated 30 March/ 11 Apr. 1838 (IV, 97).
114. *Letopis'-1*, 213, 216.
115. Despatch no. 16 of F.I. T., Tu., 19 Apr./ 1 May 1839. *Letopis'-1*, 216 (see also Lane [1990], 84); despatch of Solaro to Rossi, 19 Apr./ 1 May 1839. Lane (1990), 84.
116. Despatch of K.V. Nesselrode to F.I. T., SPb., 1/13 Apr. 1839. *Letopis'-1*, 214. This reached Turin on 27 or 28 April (T. informed Solaro of the appointment in a letter dated 28 Apr., while three letters which he sent Solaro the day before make no mention of it [ibid., 218]). Although the text of Nesselrode's despatch is not quoted in *Letopis'-1*, that it refers to Kokoshkin's arrival in the near future is clear from other sources, for instance Nesselrode's own later despatch of 15/27 April (ibid., 218) and, before that had even reached Turin, a report by the Bavarian Ambassador von Olry on 7 May (see note 117) that T. expected 'the arrival soon' ('*la prochaine arrivée*') of the new Ambassador. The source for Kokoshkin's previous post in Florence is Nesselrode's 'Projet d'instruction pour M. de Kokosckine', No.1718, of 12/24 May 1839 (PTN, 175).
117. Despatch no. 393 of Olry, Tu., 7 May 1839. Munich: Bayerisches Hauptstaatsarchiv: Ministerium des Äusseren: Sardinien, 2883. Quoted from 'if this diplomatic agent...' on in Lane (1987), 8. I am grateful to Dr Lane for making available a copy of the complete despatch.
118. Despatch no. 20 of F.I. T., Tu., 19 Apr./ 1 May 1839. *Letopis'-1*, 217. (Partially quoted in the original French in Dinesman [2004], 124.)
119. *Letopis'-1*, 217, 218.
120. Despatch no. 16 of F.I. T., Tu., 19 Apr./ 1 May 1839. *Letopis'-1*, 216, 217.
121. Despatch of Grouchy, Tu., 25 Apr. 1839. Lane (1990), 85.
122. Despatch no. 21 of F.I. T., Genoa, 4/16 June 1839. AVPRI (K), No.207, *l.* 66-67.
123. This is evident from Pfeffel's reply to her of 27 April. See *Letopis'-1*, 217.
124. Ernestine, 100.
125. *Letopis'-1*, 217.
126. Ibid., 220.
127. These were the excuses he gave Nesselrode for his protracted silence in his despatch no. 21 from Genoa of 4/16 June 1839. *Letopis'-1*, 222.
128. Ernestine, 100.
129. Entries in Ernestine's flower-album for 11, 21 and 29-30 May respectively. *Letopis'-1*, 220.
130. Writing to Ernestine from Florence on 23 April, Pfeffel refers to 'the hotel which I have chosen for you'. Ibid., 216.
131. K. Pfeffel to E. von Dörnberg, Florence, 12 June 1839. Ibid., 221.

132. In his letter to Ernestine of 12 June (ibid.) Pfeffel says he hopes T. will find letters with this information awaiting him *poste restante* in Lucca or Genoa.

133. See T.'s undated reply to Anna (Tu., early summer 1839). IV, 122.

134. These are T.'s plans as reported (presumably on the basis of correspondence with him) by Nikolay in a letter to their parents from Warsaw dated 21 July/ 2 Aug. 1839. TPD, 203.

135. *Letopis'-1*, 220.

136. Entries in Ernestine's flower-album for 8 and 9 June. Ibid., 221.

137. Ernestine, 100.

138. *Letopis'-1*, 221.

139. Despatches nos. 21 and 22 of F.I. T., Genoa, 4/16 June. AVPRI (K), No.207, *l*. 66-67, 69-700b. Quoted in part in *Letopis'-1*, 222.

140. *Letopis'-1*, 222.

141. Despatch of K.V. Nesselrode to F.I. T., SPb., 15/27 Apr. 1839. Lane (1987), 7.

142. Their daughter Maria was born in Munich on 6 March 1840. *Letopis'-1*, 234.

143. Despatch no. 24 of F.I. T., Tu., 20 June/ 2 July 1839. AVPRI (K), No.207, *l*. 73. Quoted in part in *Letopis'-1*, 223.

144. *Tyutchevy*, 184. The Foreign Ministry compiled a common dossier on the resignations of T. and Bogayevsky: 'Ob otozvanii sekretarey missii v Turine starshego, nadvornogo sovetnika Tyutcheva, i mladshego, kollezhskogo asessora Bogayevskogo ot sikh mest [...]'. Ibid.; see also *Letopis'-1*, 230, 308.

145. *Letopis'-1*, 224

146. Despatch no. 22 of Meysenbug, Tu., 15 July 1839. Vienna: Haus-, Hof- und Staatsarchiv: Staatenabteilung Sardinien: Karton 77, p.112. Referred to in Lane (1987), 11. I am grateful to Dr Lane for providing a copy of the complete despatch.

147. F.I. T. to I.N. & Ye.L. Tyutchev, Mu., 20-22 Jan./ 1-3 Feb. 1840. IV, 130.

148. Kazanovich, 132. K.V. Pigaryov suggested (*Zhizn'*, 107) that Kazanovich's informant was probably Sergey Petrovich Frolov (b. 1850), who as a young man knew and corresponded with T.

149. Despatch no. 18 of F.I. T., Tu., 19 Apr./ 1 May 1839 (but written before 16/28 Apr.). *Letopis'-1*, 217.

150. Despatch no. 28 of F.I. T., Tu., 1/13 July 1839 (written before 25 June/ 7 July). Ibid., 224.

151. Dinesman (2004), 128.

152. *Letopis'-1*, 224.

153. Ibid., 225.

154. C. Pfeffel to E. von Dörnberg, Florence, 6 Aug. 1839. Ibid.

155. Ibid. Here, as in some other sources, Paul Ludwig is confused with Amélie's husband Alexander. For details of Paul Ludwig's diplomatic career see Polonsky (2003), 152-160.

156. Lane (1987), 10; *Letopis'-1*, 227.

157. *Letopis'-1*, 225.

158. Lane (1987), 13.

159. Despatch of Chatry, Tu., 8 Aug. 1839. Ibid., 11.

160. *Letopis'-1*, 227.

161. There is some doubt as to the exact date of Kokoshkin's arrival in Turin in September. According to the British envoy it was on the 23rd, while the Austrian Ambassador reported it as being on the 27th. (Despatch no. 27 of the British envoy [Foster?], Tu., 23 Sept. 1839: London: Public Record Office: Foreign Office: 67: 108; despatch no. 32 of Schwarzenberg, Tu., 4 Oct. 1839: Vienna: Haus-, Hof- und Staatsarchiv: Staatenabteilung Sardinien: Karton 77. I am grateful to Dr R. Lane for these details.)

162. Although the Munich police register of aliens indicates that Ernestine arrived in the city on 6 September, it is not absolutely clear from the record whether T. was with her at the time. (The register entry for T. and his family, no. 38461, is reproduced in Polonsky [2003], 175.) A reference to T. in a letter from Maltitz to Shevyryov dated 26 September (NS) makes it clear that he was already settled in Munich by then (*Letopis'-1*, 228). Writing to his parents on 1/13 December, T. claimed that he *and Ernestine* had arrived in Munich 'at the end of September' — presumably OS, as he goes on to say that he had written his letter of resignation to Nesselrode, dated 6/18 October, 'on arriving here' (IV, 125). However, this date is clearly contradicted by the police aliens record in the case of Ernestine, and apparently so by Maltitz's letter as far as T. is concerned. The misinformation may have been deliberate. Knowing that the Third Section routinely opened letters to and from Russia, T. was no doubt anxious not to alert the authorities to his unauthorised premature abandonment of the Turin Embassy.

163. F.I. T. to K.V. Nesselrode, Mu., 6/18 Oct. 1839. IV, 123.
164. F.I. T. to I.N. & Ye.L. Tyutchev, Mu., 1/13 Dec. 1839. IV, 125.
165. *Tyutchevy*, 184-185; *Letopis'-1*, 230-231.

Chapter 11. In Search of a Role

1. Polonsky (1998), 105.
2. Ibid., 106.
3. F.I. T. to I.N. & Ye.L. Tyutchev, Mu., 1/13 Dec. 1839. IV, 125.
4. Ibid., 126; Polonsky (1998), 107 (this states that three of the Bothmer brothers lived in Munich, but gives the addresses of four).
5. As note 3, 126; F.I. T. to I.N. & Ye.L. Tyutchev, Mu., 3/15 Apr. 1837. IV, 63.
6. F.A. von Maltitz to S.P. Shevyryov, Mu., 26 Sept., 29 Sept. & 8 Oct. 1839. *Letopis'-1*, 228-229.
7. A.L. Ospovat, 'Tyutchev i stat'ya N.A. Mel'gunova o Shellinge', *LN-2*, 454-456 (Melgunov's letter from Hanau of 27 Oct. 1839 is quoted on p.456); *Letopis'-1*, 230.
8. F.A. von Maltitz to S.P. Shevyryov, Mu., 4 Oct. 1839. *Letopis'-1*, 229.
9. F.I. T. to I.N. & Ye.L. Tyutchev, Mu., 1/13 Dec. 1839 & 20-22 Jan./ 1-3 Feb. 1840. IV, 125, 130-131.
10. Polonsky (1998), 106.
11. *Letopis'-1*, 234.
12. F.I. T. to I.N. & Ye.L. Tyutchev, Mu., 14/26 Apr. 1840. IV, 136-137.
13. *Letopis'-1*, 231-232. The description of the service decoration is from: L.Ye. Shepelyov, *Chinovny mir Rossii: XVIII - nachalo XX v.*, SPb., 1999, 337-338 (quoted in Ekshtut, 100).
14. *Letopis'-1*, 233.
15. Ibid., 234-236.
16. F.I. T. to I.N. & Ye.L. Tyutchev, Mu., 8/20 July 1841. IV, 161.
17. Ibid., 161-162.
18. *Letopis'-1*, 241-242.
19. See the correspondence between K.V. Nesselrode, Minister of the Imperial Court Prince P.M. Volkonsky and *Oberhofmeister* Prince N.V. Dolgorukov, 3/15 - 6/18 July 1841, quoted in IV, 516-517. These documents also show that Aleksey Bogayevsky was punished together with T.: he too was dismissed from the service for 'protracted failure to return from leave' and deprived of his court rank (in his case, that of *Kammerjunker*).
20. *Letopis'-1*, 242.
21. Kozhinov, 237-238.
22. *Letopis'* (Ch.), 58.
23. Ekshtut, 98.
24. See: F.I. T. to Ern. T., M., 14/26 - 15/27 July 1843. IV, 248.
25. Pfeffel-Z, 34.
26. F.I. T. to I.N. & Ye.L. Tyutchev, Weimar, 10/22 Sept. 1841. IV, 164-165.
27. Darya and Kitty entered the Institute on 2 Oct. 1842 (*Letopis'-1*, 252). Anna, who had been living with the Maltitzes in Weimar, joined them the following spring at her own insistence (F.I. T. to I.N. & Ye.L. Tyutchev, Mu., 18/30 March 1843. IV, 223-224).
28. From 6 Ottostrasse they moved to 54 Karlstrasse on 15 Oct. 1840, and from there to 7 Ludwigstrasse (their final address in Munich) on 27 Oct. 1842 (Polonsky [1998], 108, 110).
29. F.I. T. to I.N. & Ye.L. Tyutchev, Mu., 6/18 Dec. 1840. IV, 156.
30. F.I. T. to I.N. & Ye.L. Tyutchev, Mu., 1/13 March 1842. IV, 185.
31. See, e.g.: as note 24, 246.
32. As note 30, 185-186.
33. Writing later to T.'s sister Darya of problems with her stepdaughters, Ernestine freely admitted: 'there is no-one less capable than I am of playing the part of mother to a family. You know how averse I am to lecturing or indeed to speaking at all, and you will understand the overwhelming compulsion I feel to *throw in my hand* ' (Ern. T. to D.I. Sushkova, SPb., 17/29 Sept. 1845. *Letopis'-2*, 29).
34. Tyutchev (F.I. jr.), 210-211.
35. From a letter from F.A. von Maltitz to Franz von Schober, quoted without indication of date in: Arkhipov, 319.
36. As note 26.
37. F.I. T. to Ern. T., Weimar, 19 Sept. 1841. IV, 175.

38. F.I. T. to Ern. T., Weimar, 18 June 1842. IV, 194.
39. As note 26, 165.
40. F.I. T. to Ern. T., Dresden, 27 Sept. 1841. IV, 178.
41. As note 26, 166.
42. As note 40, 179.
43. Letters to Ernestine of (in chronological order) 13, 27 Sept. 1841; 18 June, 7 Oct. 1842; 13, 11/23 June 1843. IV, 172, 178, 194, 205, 228-229, 236.
44. F.I. T. to Ern. T., Weimar, 11 June 1842. IV, 191.
45. I, 192. The poem appears to date from between 1840 and 1842, the autograph having been placed with a batch of T.'s letters to Ernestine covering that period (IV, 518). Translation: 'How unreal man is, how easily he is effaced! —/ So little when present, and nothing when far away!/ His presence is but a point, / And his absence — the whole of space.'
46. As note 26, 166.
47. F.I. T. to Vaclav Hanka, Mu., 28 Apr. 1843. IV, 227.
48. 'La Russie et la Révolution'. III, 51.
49. 'K Ganke'. I, 188-189.
50. T. argued the case for raising such forbidden topics in the Western press in a memorandum submitted to Tsar Nicholas in 1845 (understandably enough omitting to mention on this occasion the likely effects inside Russia). [Zapiska]. III, 39.
51. F.I. T. to Ern. T., Mu., 31 Aug., 3 Sept. 1840. IV, 146, 148; F.I. T. to N.I. & Ye.L. Tyutchev, Mu., c. 8/20 Oct. 1840. IV, 151 (with date 'Oct. 1840': for more precise dating see *Letopis'-1*, 239).
52. This is evident from a letter she wrote to P.A. Pletnyov, the editor of *Sovremennik*, on 20 Nov./ 2 Dec. 1840. See: Grot & Pletnyov, I, 183, 184 (quoted in *Letopis'-1*, 239).
53. 'Zhivym sochuvstviyem priveta...'. I, 187. Here it is printed immediately after 'Ne ver', ne ver' poetu, deva...' (186); comparison of these two poems on a similar theme is informative, revealing a marked decline in T.'s poetic powers since 1838.
54. F.I. T. to Ern. T., SPb., 3/15 Sept. 1852. *LN-1*, 521.
55. F.I. T. to N.I. & Ye.L. Tyutchev: Tegernsee, 2/14 July 1840; Mu., c. 8/20 Oct. 1840. IV, 142, 151 (see note 51).
56. Smirnova-Rosset, 9.
57. See: 'Iz zapisok barona (vposledstvii grafa) M.A. Korfa', *Russkaya starina*, 1899, No.12, 488-489 (quoted in Ospovat [1994], 135 *n.*22).
58. [Anon.], *Die europäische Pentarchie*, Leipzig, 1839.
59. P.S. Squire, 'The Metternich - Benkendorff Letters, 1835-1842', *The Slavonic and East European Review*, 1967, No.105, 383-386; Ospovat (1994), 117-118, 121. Ospovat (p.121) produces convincing evidence that Aleksandr Turgenev's informant for his account of this episode (as quoted from his letter to his brother of 7 July 1842) was T., who in turn was repeating what he had heard from Amélie during their meetings at Tegernsee and Munich in the summer of 1840.
60. 'Lettre à M. le docteur Gustave Kolb'. III, 21-22.
61. F.I. T. to A.I. Georgievsky, SPb., 30 March/ 11 Apr. 1866. VI, 132-133.
62. Ospovat (1994), 110-113; Ospovat (1999), 230.
63. A.I. Turgenev to N.I. Turgenev, Bad Kissingen, 25 June 1839. Ospovat (1994), 116.
64. Ospovat (1994), 123; Ospovat (1999), 229-230.
65. Ospovat (1994), 122; *Letopis'-1*, 267-269.
66. Contribution of Heine from Paris (dated 31 Jan. 1841) in *AZ*, quoted in Ospovat (1994), 119.
67. J.P. Fallmerayer, 'Die deutschen Publicisten und die europäische Pentarchie', Fallmerayer, II, 157-179 (here: 167-168). The article was originally published in *AZ*, then as a separate brochure (Augsburg, 1840).
68. N. Nadezhdin, 'Pis'mo iz Veny o serbskikh pesnyakh', *Moskvityanin*, 1841, Part 3, No.6, 515.
69. Thiersch published two related articles concerning Russia on consecutive days, 12 and 13 Dec. 1840 (*AZ*, No.347, Beilage, 2761-2763; No.348, Beilage, 2769-2770). See Lane (1984a), 231-233. In Dec. 1840 T. and Thiersch both lived in Karlstrasse, T. at No.54, Thiersch at No.11 (Polonsky [1998], 175).
70. Quoted in Lane (1984a), 232.
71. F.I. T. to F. Thiersch, Mu., 13 Dec. [1840]. IV, 218. (The dating of the letter here to 1842, following an earlier supposition of K.V. Pigaryov [*Pis'ma*, 73, 373], is rejected by other scholars. See: Lane [1984a], 231-233; Ospovat [1994], 118, 137 *n.*45; *Letopis'-1*, 239).
72. As note 70.
73. A.I. Turgenev to N.I. Turgenev, Bad Kissingen, 25 June 1842. Ospovat (1994), 121.

74. A.I. Turgenev to N.I. Turgenev, Bad Kissingen, 7 July 1842. Ibid., 122.

75. See the summary with extracts in Ospovat (1999), 229-230, of K.F. Schweizer's report of 31 May 1841 on his discussions with Cotta. As publisher, Cotta was more aware than the politically free-thinking journalists who worked for him of the need to placate the Holy Alliance powers. He knew that repressive measures against his newspaper could deprive it of commercially vital markets, particularly in Austria.

76. A.I. Turgenev to N.I. Turgenev, Bad Kissingen, 7 & 9 July 1842. Ospovat (1994), 122-123.

77. J.P. Fallmerayer, *Geschichte der Halbinsel Morea während des Mittelalters: ein historischer Versuch*, 2 vols., Stuttgart & Tübingen, 1830-1836 (accessible online at: www.literature.at).

78. For details of Fallmerayer's biography see: Kazanovich, 154-160; Ernst Molden, 'Jakob Philipp Fallmerayer. Eine Lebensskizze', in: J.P. Fallmerayer, *Schriften und Tagebücher* (ed. Hans Feigl & Ernst Molden), 2 vols., Munich & Leipzig, 1913. I, ix-xxxii; Herbert Seidler, *Jakob Philipp Fallmerayers geistige Entwicklung. Ein Beitrag zur deutschen Geistesgeschichte des 19. Jahrhunderts*, Munich, 1947.

79. As note 67 (further page references given in the text).

80. Details of these approaches are given by Varnhagen von Ense in his diaries for 1840-1841 (Varnhagen, I, 199, 210, 354).

81. S. Jakobsohn, 'Ein unbekanntes Gedicht von Fedor Tjutcev', *Zeitschrift für slavische Philologie*, 1929, V, 409.

82. 'Znamya i slovo'. I, 190.

83. *Letopis'-1*, 249-250.

84. Ibid., 246. According to his file in the Munich police register of aliens (Stadtarchiv München, Polizeikartenregister Nos. 48708 & 49753), Nikolay arrived in the city on 19 April, accompanied by his servant 'Johann' (Ivan?) Strelkov (no doubt related to Vasily Strelkov, the Tyutchevs' estate manager), and stayed at various addresses that spring and autumn, including T.'s old first-floor apartment at 1 Karolinenplatz (from 10 May). The file gives his religion as Catholic — presumably a misunderstanding on the part of the recording officer. (Information supplied by Dr R. Lane).

85. F.I. T. to I.N. & Ye.L. Tyutchev, Mu., 1/13 Sept. 1842. IV, 198.

86. Ibid.; Ern. T. to A.F. Tyutcheva, Ostend, 29 July 1842. *Letopis'-1*, 250.

87. As note 85, 197.

88. N.I. Tyutchev to I.N. & Ye.L. Tyutchev, London, 4/16 Aug. 1842. TPD, 204-206.

89. Ern. T. to A.F. Tyutcheva, Ostend, 20 Aug. 1842. TPD, 206.

90. As note 85, 197.

91. A.I. Turgenev to N.I. Turgenev, Bad Kissingen, 3 July 1842. Ospovat (1994), 122. As Ospovat points out (ibid., 121), the letter was written on a day when Turgenev's diary records him as having conversed with T. on a variety of topics (see Turgenev [A.I.], 86). The information in question is presented by Ospovat as part of the material 'undoubtedly deriving from Tyutchev' (ibid.).

92. Ibid., 124.

93. Kazanovich, 157-158.

94. Fallmerayer's diary entry for 9 Nov. 1842. Ibid., 145-146. The Tyutchevs had moved to 7 Ludwigstrasse on 27 Oct. (Polonsky [1998], 110).

95. Fallmerayer's diary entry for 12 March 1843. Kazanovich, 150-151. The newspaper article referred to — 'Das geographische Element im Welthandel mit besonderer Rücksicht auf die Donau' (Fallmerayer, II, 441-449) — was published in the *AZ* on 11 March 1843. In it Fallmerayer predicts Germany's re-emergence as an entrepôt for trade between Europe and Asia for the first time since Vasco da Gama's discovery of the Cape route. He expects this to be achieved in part through an expansion of railway communications in Russia, but more importantly through development of the Danube as a major waterway for steam traffic.

96. Kseniya Kostenich [= K. Koscienicz], '[Adamu Mitskevichu]', *LN-1*, 174-175.

97. 'Ot russkogo, po prochtenii otryvkov iz lektsiy g-na Mitskevicha'. I, 191.

98. *Letopis'-1*, 257.

99. F.I. T. to Ern. T., Vienna, 13 June 1843. IV, 228-229 (here misdated 13/25 June: T.'s date is NS).

100. F.I. T. to Ern. T., Warsaw, 11/23 - 12/24 June 1843. IV, 234-235 (here misdated 23 June/ 6 July - 24 June/ 7 July).

101. A. de Custine, *La Russie en 1839*, 4 vols., Paris, 1843; Turgenev (A.I.), 86 (diary, middle of June 1843).

102. As note 99, 230.

103. F.I. T. to Ern. T., M., 29 June/ 11 July, 2/14 July and 14/26 - 15/27 July 1843. IV, 239, 241 (misdated 14/26 July), 247; *Tyutchevy*, 195, 386; Ilyasova, 125.

104. F.I. T. to Ern. T., M., 14/26 - 15/27 July 1843. IV, 249.

105. F.I. T. to Ern. T., M., 2/14 July 1843. IV, 240-241 (here misdated: see note 103); *Tyutchevy*, 194.

106. *Letopis'-1*, 262.

107. A.P. Yelagina to M.P. Pogodin, M., undated [summer 1843]. Barsukov, VII, 134 (quoted in *Letopis'-1*, 262).

108. As note 104.

109. S.P. Shevyryov to M.P. Pogodin, Vyazema, 19/31 July 1843. Rogov, 80-81.

110. In the summer of 1844 Aleksandr Turgenev recorded a conversation in which T. told him of various meetings he had had in Russia the previous year: 'Tyutchev about Moscow, about Chaadayev: *il a de l'esprit, mais une vanité ridicule* [he has a sharp mind, but is ridiculously vain]. About Khomyakov, etc. About Petersburg: Benckendorff [...]'. TPD, 87 (diary, 4 June 1844 [NS]).

111. As note 109. Shevyryov left the Boarding School for the Nobility (*Moskovsky Blagorodny pansion*) to enter Moscow University only in 1822 (*Tyutchevy*, 94).

112. Rogov, 80-83.

113. F.I. T. to Ern. T., Berlin, 27 Sept. 1843. IV, 274.

114. Pogodin, 24-25.

115. Ibid., 28.

116. A.V. Koshelyov, 'Vospominaniya o Khomyakove', in: Khomyakov, VIII, 126.

117. As note 104, 248.

118. *Tyutchevy*, 211-212.

119. As note 105, 242. A deed dated 4/16 Aug. 1843 shows that Ivan Nikolayevich Tyutchev made over to his sons a total of 629 male serfs together with the lands on which they were settled in Bryansk district (IV, 523).

120. As note 104, 248.

121. F.I. T. to Ern. T., SPb., 14/26 Aug. 1843. IV, 258.

122. F.I. T. to K. Pfeffel, SPb., 25 Oct./ 6 Nov. 1870. Lettres, XXII, 291.

123. As note 121.

124. Kozyrev, 91-92.

125. As note 121; F.I. T. to I.N. & Ye.L. Tyutchev, 11/23 Aug. 1843. IV, 255; *Tyutchevy*, 197.

126. As note 121, 257-258, 260. In the text as printed here (p.257) Ernestine's letter is said to be 'une récompense' ('a reward') for the long and uncomfortable journey ahead. I have preferred the reading 'un réconfortatif ' ('a pick-me-up'), given in the letter transcripts made under the direction of K.V. Pigaryov. (The same source supplies the word given as indecipherable on p.257 as 'nommé'.)

127. *Letopis'-1*, 263.

128. As note 121, 258-259.

129. F.I. T. to I.N. & Ye.L. Tyutchev, Reval, 3/15 Sept. 1843. IV, 269-270.

130. IV, 530-531.

131. As: note 121, 257; note 129, 269.

132. F.I. T. to Ern. T., SPb., 28 Aug./ 9 Sept. 1843. IV, 265-266; as note 129, 268-269.

133. *Letopis'-1*, 265. Aksakov refers to a 'memorandum' by T. submitted to Tsar Nicholas via Benckendorff in 1843 (Aksakov, 28). However, there is no evidence for this in the surviving correspondence or other documents, and it may simply be that Aksakov confused the alleged memorandum with that submitted in 1845. This unfounded claim has been repeated by others, most recently A.L. Ospovat (Ospovat [1992], 89) and B.N. Tarasov (III, 288).

134. As: note 129, 268; note 113, 273-274. See also T.'s reported comment to A.I. Turgenev in Paris the following summer that Benckendorff had encouraged him to 'write about Russia abroad' (as note 110).

135. As note 113, 272-273; F.I. T. to I.N. & Ye.L. Tyutchev, Mu., 1/13 Oct. 1843. IV, 276. The date for T.'s arrival in Berlin given in *Letopis'-1*, 265 (28 Sept.) is based on a misdating of the first of these letters in Lettres, XVIII, 10.

136. Varnhagen, II, 216-217.

137. In his 'Lettre à M. le Docteur Gustave Kolb' of 1844 T. dismisses Custine's book as 'one more testimony to that shamelessness of spirit, that intellectual demoralisation [which are] the characteristic feature of our age' (III, 11-12), while in a private memorandum submitted to Nicholas I in 1845 he accuses its author of having viewed Russia through a distorting lens of 'hatred compounded by ignorance' (III, 34).

138. K.M. Azadovsky & A.L. Ospovat, 'Tyutchev i Varngagen fon Enze (K istorii otnosheniy', *LN*-2, 460-461. The authors note that Varnhagen's published diaries contain no references to further meetings with T. or indeed comments on his later political articles, although he will undoubtedly have read these. In explanation they offer a suggestion originally made in an unpublished article by Ye.P. Kazanovich: that such references probably are to be found in the original diaries, but were omitted by the editor of the published version as too unflattering or embarrassing to T., then still alive and fairly prominent in SPb. society.

139. F.I. T. to I.N. & Ye.L. Tyutchev, Mu., 1/13 Oct. 1843. IV, 276-277.
140. Ibid., 276.
141. Diary, 11 Oct. 1843. Kazanovich, 152.
142. Kazanovich, 153.
143. Diary, 14 Nov. 1843. Ibid.
144. Diary, 2 March 1845. Ibid., 166.
145. J.P. Fallmerayer, *Fragmente aus dem Orient*, 2 vols., Stuttgart & Tübingen, 1845. I, xiv. (Accessible online at: www.literature.at).
146. Ibid., xiii.
147. As note 74.
148. F.I. T. to I.N. & Ye.L. Tyutchev, Mu., 10/22 March 1844. IV, 280.
149. Ibid.; F.I. T. to I.N. & Ye.L. Tyutchev, SPb., 27 Oct./ 8 Nov. 1844. IV, 300.
150. As note 148.
151. Reporting in a despatch dated 9/21 March 1844 on T.'s first known publication in the *AZ*, the Russian Chargé d'Affaires in Munich L.G. Viollier stated that the author, 'prompted by zeal, [...] has already more than once published in the German press articles combining passion and sound views in equal measure' (*Letopis'-1*, 269). Ronald Lane also points to speculation by the French Ambassador in Munich in a despatch of 24 Dec. 1842 that *De la Russie. Par un Inconnu. Entretiens politiques et sociaux*, a book published anonymously in Paris earlier that year, could have been by T. Although Lane considers this unlikely, he finds it significant that T. should have been singled out as possible author. (Lane [1971], 206-207 [footnote].) Dr Lane has informed me that he subsequently searched German newspapers (mainly the *AZ*) as far back as 1839, but was unable to find any anonymous articles that could be attributed to T. with any degree of reliability.
152. [Anon.], 'Die russische Armee im Kaukasus', *AZ*, 1844, Nos. 76-78 (16-18 March), Beilage, 602-603, 609-611, 617-619.
153. Lane (1988a), 232.
154. ['Pis'mo russkogo']. III, 9-10. This is the German text of T.'s letter (translated from the French original, now lost) as it appeared in the *AZ*, 1844, No.81 (21 March), Beilage, 646-647.
155. Ibid., 646.
156. *AZ*, 1844, No.158 (6 June), 1260-1261. Quoted in Ru. translation in Lane (1988a), 232.
157. F.I. T. to A.F. Tyutcheva, Mu., 9 Oct. 1841. *Letopis'* (Ch.), 57-58.
158. The point is well made in Lane (1988a), 232.
159. Ibid., 232-233.
160. 'Lettre à M. le Docteur Gustave Kolb, rédacteur de la "Gazette Universelle" '. III, 11-28. Further page references are given in the text.
161. [Anon.], *Lettre à Monsieur le D-r Gustave Kolb, rédacteur de la Gazette Universelle*, Mu., 1841.
162. Lane (1988a), 233.
163. As note 149, 300-301.
164. *Letopis'-1*, 270, 273-274. Ernestine's plan to consult specialists in Paris is already mentioned by T. in a letter to her from SPb. of 14/26 Aug. 1843 (IV, 261).
165. Heine (1968), II, 601.
166. Heine was in Paris throughout May, June and the first half of July; he departed for Hamburg on 19 July (Mende, 221-223). T. arrived in Paris on 15 May and left apparently a few days after Heine, joining Ernestine at Vichy on or about 25 July (*Letopis'-1*, 270, 274).
167. For details of Heine's close friendship with Marx during the latter's time in Paris (Oct. 1843 to Feb. 1845) see Liedtke, 122-123.
168. Turgenev (A.I.), 87 (diary entries, 20 May - 9 June 1844).
169. A.I. Turgenev to P.A. Vyazemsky: Paris, 28 May/ 9 June 1844; Bad Kissingen, 24 June/ 6 July 1844. *OA*, 286, 290.

170. Turgenev (A.I.), 87 (diary, 4 June 1844).

171. A.I. Turgenev to P.A. Vyazemsky: Bad Kissingen, 24 June/ 6 July 1844; Champrosay, 16/28 Oct. 1844. *OA*, 290, 301.

172. Ern. T. to K. Pfeffel, Paris, 2 June 1844. TPD, 207.

173. As note 148, 281.

174. As note 172.

175. TPD, 207-208. Some two years later Ernestine outlined her ongoing financial concerns in a letter to her brother Karl from SPb. dated 14/26 Aug. 1846 (ibid., 218).

176. Ern. T. to K. Pfeffel, Paris, 2 June 1844. *Letopis'-1*, 271-272.

177. As note 148, 281.

178. F.I. T. to A.F. Tyutcheva, Paris, July 1844. IV, 285-286.

179. Ern. T. to K. Pfeffel, Vichy, 4 Aug. 1844. TPD, 209.

180. *Letopis'-1*, 274-275.

181. See Chapter 14.

182. Ern. T. to K. Pfeffel, SPb., 26 Sept./ 8 Oct. 1844. TPD, 209-210; Ospovat (1994), 130-131.

Chapter 12. The Return

1. F.I. T. to I.N. & Ye.L. Tyutchev, SPb., between 12 and 16 Oct. 1844 (OS). IV, 295-296. (All dates henceforth are OS unless otherwise indicated).

2. F.I. T. to I.N. & Ye.L. Tyutchev, SPb., 10 Oct. 1844. IV, 292.

3. F.I. T. to I.N. & Ye.L. Tyutchev, SPb., 27 Oct. 1844. IV, 300.

4. Ern. T. to K. Pfeffel, SPb., 14/26 Nov. 1844. TPD, 211.

5. F.I. T. to I.N. & Ye.L. Tyutchev, SPb., 7 Dec. 1844. IV, 308.

6. Ern. T. to K. Pfeffel, SPb., 14/26 Oct. 1844. TPD, 211.

7. As note 4.

8. Ibid.; F.I. T. to I.N. & Ye.L. Tyutchev, SPb., 2 March 1845. IV, 316; Ern. T. to K. Pfeffel, SPb., 21 May/ 2 June 1845. TPD, 213.

9. F.I. T. to I.N. & Ye.L. Tyutchev, SPb., 29 Dec. 1844. IV, 311. For T.'s meetings with Grand Duchess Maria Nikolayevna at Tegernsee and Munich in the autumn and winter of 1841 see *Letopis'-1*, 238-241.

10. F.I. T. to I.N. & Ye.L. Tyutchev, SPb., 2 March 1845. IV, 316; Ern. T. to K. Pfeffel, SPb., 21 May/ 2 June 1845. TPD, 213.

11. P.A. Vyazemsky to A.I. Turgenev, SPb., 2 Oct. 1844. *OA*, 298.

12. P.A. Vyazemsky to A.I. Turgenev, SPb., 29 Jan. 1845. *OA*, 309.

13. V.A. Sollogub, *Vospominaniya*, SPb., 1887, 215-216 (quoted in *Dok.*, 83).

14. F.I. T. to P.A. Vyazemsky, SPb., Nov.-Dec. 1844. IV, 305-306.

15. Grot & Pletnyov, II, 327.

16. 'Glyadel ya, stoya nad Nevoy...'. I, 193.

17. 'Ty znayesh' kray, gde mirt i lavr rastyot...'. II, 45. This appears to date from 1851 (II, 382).

18. F.I. T. to I.N. & Ye.L. Tyutchev, SPb., 7 Dec. 1844. IV, 308-309.

19. F.I. T. to I.N. & Ye.L. Tyutchev, SPb., 2 March 1845. IV, 317.

20. 'Kolumb'. I, 194. (See also Appendix I [iv]).

21. '[Zapiska]'. III, 29-41. Further page references are given in the text.

22. See: Ospovat (1992), 115, note 5; III, 310.

23. *Letopis'-2*, 20-22.

24. Ern. T. to K. Pfeffel: M., 27 July/ 8 Aug. 1845; SPb., 8/20 Apr. 1846. TPD, 214, 215.

25. *Letopis'-2*, 23-24.

26. Ern. T. to K. Pfeffel, M., 27 July/ 8 Aug. 1845. Separate extracts are quoted in TPD, 214, and *Letopis'-2*, 24.

27. Pogodin, 14 (diary, 15 June 1845).

28. P. Ya. Chaadayev to P.A. Vyazemsky, M., 26 Apr. 1846. *Letopis'-2*, 38.

29. A.I. Turgenev to P.A. Vyazemsky, M., 8 Oct. 1845. *OA*, 326.

30. A.I. Turgenev to N.I. Turgenev, M., 17/29 Sept. 1845. Ospovat (1992), 90.

31. Quoted by A.I. Turgenev in a letter to P.A. Vyazemsky, 14 Nov. 1845. *OA*, 333.

32. A.I. Turgenev to P.A. Vyazemsky, M., 6 Oct. 1845. *OA*, 324.

33. F.I. T. to N.N. Sheremeteva, SPb., 26 Dec. 1845. IV, 329.

34. *Letopis'-2*, 28.

35. Ern. T. to D.I. Sushkova, SPb., 16 Sept. 1845. IV, 548-549.

36. F.I. T. to: A.F. Tyutcheva, SPb., July-Aug. 1845; I.N. & Ye.L. Tyutchev, SPb., 25 Nov. 1845. IV, 321-322; 325.

37. *Pri dvore-1*, 61.

38. *Letopis'-2*, 36.

39. F.I. T. to I.N. & Ye.L. Tyutchev, SPb., 11 Apr. 1845. IV, 319.

40. Ern. T. to K. Pfeffel, SPb., 14/26 May 1846. TPD, 217.

41. Ern. T. to K. Pfeffel: SPb., 8/20 Apr. 1846; SPb., 14/26 May 1846. TPD, 215, 217.

42. Ern. T. to K. Pfeffel, SPb., 14/26 Aug. 1846. TPD, 218. The Tyutchevs stayed in the apartment (now 3, Marsovo pole) until the summer of 1847 (ibid. *n*.3).

43. F.I. T. to Ye.L. Tyutcheva, SPb., beginning of May 1846. IV, 337.

44. F.I. T. to P.V. Muravyova, SPb., May 1846. IV, 334.

45. As note 43.

46. Diary of A.F. Tyutcheva, 4 May 1846. TPD, 216.

47. As: note 43, 338; note 44, 335.

48. *Letopis'-2*, 41.

49. Ibid., 44; F.I. T. to Ye.L. Tyutcheva, SPb., 26 June 1846. IV, 347.

50. *Letopis'-2*, 43; F.I. T. to Ern. T., M., 8 Aug., 14 Aug. 1846. IV, 350, 355.

51. F.I. T. to Ern. T., M., 20 Aug. 1846. IV, 358-359. In subsequent letters to his mother (31 Aug.) and daughter Anna (14 Sept.) he corrected the figure of 27 years to 26 (ibid., 362, 374).

52. F.I. T. to Ern. T., Ovstug, 31 Aug. 1846. IV, 364-365.

53. Ibid.; F.I. T. to A.F. Tyutcheva, M., 14 Sept. 1846. IV, 373.

54. F.I. T. to Ern. T., M., 13 Sept. 1846. IV, 368-369, 370.

55. The deed regulating the division of the estate between T. and Nikolay, confirmed by court order on 26 Feb. 1847, is quoted in full in IV, 555-557. Already the previous summer T. had written of Nikolay's insistence that 'in view of my family' he (T.) accept land with more than a hundred serfs in excess of the inheritance due to him (F.I. T. to Ern. T., M., 20 Aug. 1846. IV, 358-359). A comparison of this with the figures in the deed suggests that T. was legally entitled to only one third of the residual estate.

56. IV, 552 (note 1 to letter 120); PTR, 57 *n*.2. Revealing in this context is a note concerning Vasily Strelkov addressed by T. to his sister Darya soon after their father's death: 'I should also [...] like you to tell our good Vasily from me that I know very well and feel most deeply what Papa was for him and what he was for Papa... [...] he can of course be in no doubt that one who loved our late father with filial affection as he did will meet with the most kindred of friendship from myself and my brother'. (F.I. T. to Ye.L. Tyutcheva and D.I. Sushkova, SPb., 30 May 1846. IV, 345.)

57. Ern. T. to P.A. Vyazemsky, Hapsal, 5 Aug. 1847. IV, 569.

58. As note 40.

59. F.I. T. to Ern. T., M., 14 Aug. 1846. IV, 354.

60. Ern. T. to K. Pfeffel, SPb., c. 25 March/ 6 Apr. 1847. TPD, 219.

61. F.I. T. to Ern. T., SPb., 19 June 1847. IV, 389-390 (and see ibid., 563, note 1 to letter 135).

62. F.I. T. to Ern. T., Frankfurt am Main, 17/29 Aug. 1847. IV, 428.

63. As note 57, 567-568.

64. Ern. T. to K. Pfeffel, Hapsal, 25 June/ 7 July 1847. TPD, 222.

65. F.I. T. to K. Pfeffel, Baden-Baden, 8/20 July 1847. IV, 400-401.

66. F.I. T. to Ern. T., SPb., 21 June 1847. IV, 394-396; Ern. T. to P.A. Vyazemsky, Hapsal, 14 July 1847. IV, 564; *Letopis'-2*, 59, 60-61. Details of T.'s itinerary in the subsequent account have been taken from his letters at the time (IV, 394-435), supplemented by published extracts from Anna Tyutcheva's diaries (TPD, 222-224; *Letopis'-2*, 70) and entries detailing arrivals and departures of spa visitors in the official published registers for Baden-Baden and Bad Ems (*Badeblatt für die großherzogliche Stadt Baden*, No.106, 19 July 1847 [NS]; *Emser Kurliste der anwesenden und durchreisenden Fremden*, No.13, 14 Aug. 1847 [NS]).

67. F.I. T. to Ern. T., Berlin, 25 June/ 7 July 1847. IV, 399.

68. Arkhipov, 317.

69. F.I. T. to Ern. T., Baden-Baden, 10/22 July 1847. IV, 404.

70. Ibid., 406.

71. F.I. T. to Ern. T., Karlsruhe, 17/19 July 1847. IV, 412.

72. F.I. T. to Ern. T., Frankfurt am Main, 29 July/ 10 Aug. 1847. IV, 419-420.

73. F.I. T. to Ern. T., Frankfurt am Main, 17/29 Aug. 1847. IV, 428.

74. Ibid., 427.

75. Ibid., 429.

76. F.I. T. to Ern. T., Weimar, 4/16 Sept. 1847. IV, 434.

77. Diary of A.F. Tyutcheva, 20 Sept./ 2 Oct. 1847. *Letopis'-2*, 70.

78. As note 69.

79. Ibid., 403.

80. Ibid., 406.

81. As note 72, 420.

82. Ibid., 421.

83. As note 69.

84. Ibid., 403.

85. As note 71, 413.

86. Ibid.

87. F.I. T. to P.A. Vyazemsky, Frankfurt am Main, 28 July/ 9 Aug. 1847. IV, 417.

88. As note 69.

89. As note 87.

90. F.I. T. to K. Pfeffel, Baden-Baden, 8/20 July 1847. IV, 401.

91. J.H. Lapp to L.N. Tolstoy, Vienna, 4/17 Oct. 1900. Moscow: Muzey L.N. Tolstogo: Otdel rukopisey (Tolstoy Museum: Dept. of Manuscripts): T.S./225/45. Details of the letter and some extracts in Russian translation were published in Chulkov (1928), 30-34. Subsequent scholars and biographers have largely ignored this publication, presumably on the grounds that (as conceded by Chulkov) Hortense was clearly mentally disturbed at the time of writing to Tolstoy (she makes for instance the bizarre accusation that Tyutchev's widow was using hired agents to persecute her — bizarre if for no other reason than that Ernestine was already six years dead). Yet her central claim cannot be dismissed so easily. To do so one would have to explain how she knew, more than half a century after the event, that Tyutchev had been in Germany in 1847. What is more, Chulkov is able to produce independent evidence in corroboration of her claim. He himself concludes (p.33) that an affair definitely took place.

92. Strasbourg: Archives Départementales du Bas-Rhin: AD67: 5Mi482/294 (birth certificate of Joséphine Hortense Romer). (In Chulkov [1928], 30 her maiden name is incorrectly given as 'Romes'.)

93. Ibid.: AD67: 5Mi482/363 (marriage certificate of Laurent Lapp and Joséphine Hortense Romer).

94. Ibid.: AD67: 5Mi482/310 (birth certificate of Jules Lapp).

95. Archival searches for evidence of Hortense's presence in those German towns where T. stayed for any length of time in 1847 all proved negative or inconclusive. She is not listed among the spa visitors to Baden-Baden and Bad Ems; records for Bad Wildbad, Frankfurt am Main and Weimar were either destroyed in the Second World War or have otherwise gone missing.

96. Chulkov (1928), 33.

97. F.I. T. to Ern. T., Mu., 28 Sept./ 10 Oct. 1842. IV, 210.

98. Chulkov (1928), 32-33.

99. Ibid., 33. The letter from Darya Tyutcheva to Yekaterina Tyutcheva, dated Tsarskoye Selo, 10 Aug. 1873 (OS), is preserved in the Muranovo archive.

100. Note made by Darya in her album of verse. *Letopis'-2*, 70-71.

101. 'Un rêve'. I, 195-196. Translation of the verses quoted: 'And consulting with your beloved hand many a sweet and cherished page of your flower album, you reawaken in its fragrant bed a whole Past of love which had been slumbering...// A whole Past of youth and life, a whole Past which cannot be forgotten... and whose ashes when gathered up gleam once more in this faithful album...// [...] When a flower — that frail, sweet splendour — loses its colour, wilts and fades, one has only to hold its stem to the glowing fire for the poor flower to bloom again instantly...// And so it is that on that fateful day dreams and destinies are always fulfilled... When memories fade within our hearts, Death makes them blossom once again in his hands...'

102. Of the biographies published since Chulkov's monograph, *Zhizn'*, Kozhinov, Chagin and *Tyutchevy* make no mention of Hortense Lapp. Richard Gregg in his biographical chapter and Semyon Ekshtut in his recent account of T.'s life limit themselves to a brief summary of Chulkov's findings, adding nothing new (Gregg, 17; Ekshtut, 148-150).

103. *Letopis'-2*, 71.

104. Ibid., 85.

105. Ern. T. to K. Pfeffel, Ovstug, 25 Aug./ 6 Sept. 1857. TPD, 292.

106. P.S. Usov, 'Iz moikh vospominaniy', *Istorichesky vestnik*, VII, 1882, Jan., 126.

107. See: *Zhizn'*, 158-160.

108. Ern. T. to K. Pfeffel, SPb., 15/27 March 1848. IV, 438.
109. Ibid.
110. P.A. Vyazemsky to D.P. Severin, SPb., 1848. *Russkaya starina*, LXXXVI, 1896, No.1, 91.
111. F.I. T. to K. Pfeffel, SPb., 15/27 March 1848. IV, 439.
112. F.I. T. to P.A. Vyazemsky, SPb., March 1848. IV, 443. (The phrase printed here as 'le plus grand silence' is clearly a misreading for 'le plus grand service', as indicated both by the context and the Russian translation on p.445.)
113. 'La Russie et la Révolution'. III, 42-54. Further page references are given in the text.
114. Quoted in: III, 319.
115. 'More i utyos'. I, 197-198. The final stanza was printed in the army newspaper *Russky invalid* in Sept. 1848, but the poem was published in full only three years later (I, 484). Various critics have detected thematic and lexical borrowings from Zhukovsky, Benediktov and Boratynsky (see, respectively: D.D. Blagoy, *Tri veka*, M., 1933, 217-220; Gregg, 150, 228; Lane [1984b], 54-56). A further possible influence which appears to have gone unnoticed is Pushkin's depiction of the St Petersburg flood of 1824 in his narrative poem 'Medny vsadnik' ('The Bronze Horseman').
116. Ern. T. to K. Pfeffel, SPb., 18/30 May 1848. TPD, 225. Here Ernestine also claims that Nicholas I 'greatly approved' the memorandum. Shevyryov too wrote to Pogodin on 22 July that the Tsar 'wanted it [the memorandum] to be published' (Barsukov, IX, 273). On the other hand Vyazemsky claimed to have heard reports that the Tsar was 'very displeased' by it (as note 110, p.90). No doubt Nicholas did have reservations, but decided nevertheless that publication would be in Russia's interest. Support for this interpretation is provided by Ernestine's comment later that year regarding the memorandum: 'The Emperor is prepared to accept his [T.'s] point of view in theory, but certainly not in practice' (Ern. T. to K. Pfeffel, SPb., 19 Sept./ 1 Oct. 1848. TPD, 229). In any case it seems unlikely that T. would have attempted to have the document published abroad without authorisation at the highest level.
117. Ern. T. to K. Pfeffel, SPb., 18/30 May 1848. TPD, 225.
118. K. Pfeffel to Ern. T., Tegernsee, 30 Aug./ 11 Sept. 1848. TPD, 228.
119. P.Ya. Chaadayev to F.I. T., M., July (?) 1848. NPTT, 589.
120. S.P. Shevyryov to M.P. Pogodin, M., 22 July 1848. Barsukov, IX, 273.
121. P. de Bourgoing, *Politique et Moyens d'Action de la Russie*, Paris, 1849. See also the following note.
122. K. Pfeffel to Ern. T., Mu., 16/28 May 1849. TPD, 231-232.
123. As note 121, iv, v.
124. Ibid., i, vii, xvi.
125. E. Forcade, 'Chronique de la Quinzaine', *Revue des Deux Mondes*, 1849, 2/14 June, 1053-1056.
126. 'Denkschrift, dem Kaiser von Rußland nach der Februar-Revolution übergeben von einem höheren Beamten im Ministerium der auswärtigen Angelegenheiten', *AZ*, 1849, No.175 (12/24 June), 2707-2709.
127. As note 125, 1053.
128. K. Pfeffel to Ern. T., Mu., 15/27 June 1849. TPD, 232.
129. Ern. T. to K. Pfeffel, Ovstug, 13/25 - 16/28 July 1849. TPD, 233. For a comprehensive survey of Western reaction to T.'s political publications, including this memorandum, see: Lane (1971); Lane (1988a).
130. Kazanovich, 159-160.
131. F.I. T. to K. Pfeffel, SPb., 22 Jan./ 3 Feb. 1851. Lettres, XXII, 283.
132. Quoted in: K.V. Pigaryov, 'F.I. Tyutchev o frantsuzskikh politicheskikh sobytiyakh 1870-1873 gg.', *LN*, XXXI-XXXII, 1937, 758.
133. The surviving materials comprise: 'La Russie et l'Occident'. III, 75-94; '[Otryvok]' (a further note referring to the work). III, 95; 'La question Romaine' (Chapter 2 of the planned work, published separately). III, 55-74. Further page references are given in the text. For an earlier publication of some of this material with commentary see also: K.V. Pigaryov, V.V. Kozhinov, L.R. Lanskoy, 'Nezavershonny traktat "Rossiya i Yevropa" ', *LN-1*, 183-230. Two of the three surviving plans of chapter headings have 'La Russie et la Révolution' as Chapter 8 (the other, apparently earlier, draft omits it). This would evidently have been the revised and updated version of T.'s 1848 memorandum eventually published in Russia under that title in 1873 (*RA*, 1873, No.5, 895-912 [French original], 912-931 [Russian translation]. Reprinted: III, 42-54).
134. See: as note 118.
135. F.I. T. to L.V. Tengoborsky, SPb., 3 Dec. 1849. IV, 447.

136. III, 19.
137. Aksakov, 215; Kozhinov, 286; B.N. Tarasov's commentary in: III, 481.
138. A.V. Meshchersky, 'Iz moyey stariny. Vospominaniya', *RA*, 1901, No.2, 473 (quoted in Ospovat [1999], 242).
139. Smirnova-Rosset, 5.
140. See Chapter 14.
141. It has been pointed out by B.N. Tarasov in his commentary to 'La Russie et l'Occident' (III, 460) that T. cannot have been aware at this time of the doctrine of 'Moscow the Third Rome' as formulated most fully by the monk Filofey in epistles written at the beginning of the sixteenth century, as these documents were published only in the 1860s. However, later versions of the doctrine from the reign of Ivan IV and in the act instituting the patriarchate of Moscow in 1589 were certainly in the public domain by then. They are discussed for instance in a work well-known to T.: N.M. Karamzin's *Istoriya Rossiyskogo gosudarstva* (*History of the Russian State*), published 1816-1818 (VIII, Chapter 3; X, Chapter 2).
142. F.I. T. to P.A. Vyazemsky, SPb., end of March 1850. V, 13.
143. 'Russkaya geografiya'. I, 200.
144. 'Prorochestvo'. II, 14.
145. Ern. T. to K. Pfeffel, SPb., 9/21 Oct. 1849. TPD, 235.
146. Ern. T. to K. Pfeffel, SPb., 1/13 Jan. 1850. TPD, 240-241.
147. Lane (1988a), 236.
148. Ibid., 238.
149. Ibid., 236.
150. Ern. T. to K. Pfeffel, SPb., 19/31 Jan. 1850. TPD, 242.
151. For a detailed survey of the critical response to T.'s article see Lane (1988a), 236-247.
152. F. Buloz to K. Pfeffel, [Paris?], 22 Dec. 1849/ 3 Jan. 1850. *Zhizn'*, 129.
153. K. Pfeffel to Ern. T., Mu., 15/27 June 1849. TPD, 232.
154. As note 146, 242.
155. As note 150.
156. F.I. T. to L.V. Tengoborsky, SPb., 3 Dec. 1849. IV, 446-447.
157. As note 146, 240.
158. Vadim Kozhinov has argued (in his Introduction to 'Nezavershonny traktat...': as note 133, 185-187) that T. hoped his planned book *La Russie et l'Occident* would initiate a 'peaceful dialogue' with the West, and that he abandoned it because the first critical responses to the sections published abroad convinced him that such a dialogue was no longer possible. Yet Western responses to Bourgoing's publication of his memorandum (which in revised form would undoubtedly have formed the basis of the chapter 'La Russie et la Révolution') were already known to him when he embarked on the book in the autumn of 1849, and nothing had been added to these by the time he abandoned work on it at the end of the year (the first Western reviews of 'La question Romaine' reached SPb. only after the middle of Jan. 1850 [OS]: see: Ern. T. to K. Pfeffel, as note 150; Lane [1988a], 237-239). Nor does the polemical tone of his work suggest a desire for 'peaceful dialogue'. It is curious that Kozhinov, who elsewhere (Kozhinov, 202-213, 272-273, 332-333, 338-341) develops something approaching a conspiracy theory from the differences over foreign policy between Nesselrode and T., should have overlooked such differences as a likely factor in this instance.
159. As note 150.
160. 'Net, karlik moy! trus besprimerny!..'. II, 16. The poem was written in May 1850 (ibid., 349).
161. See: 'La question Romaine'. III, 68; 'La Russie et l'Occident'. III, 83, 85-86.
162. *Zhizn'*, 130.
163. Solovyov, 408; idem, *O khristianskom yedinstve*, Brussels, 1967, 320; G. Florovsky, 'The Historical Premonitions of Tyutchev, *Slavonic Review*, III, 1924, No.8, 347; D.S. Merezhkovsky, *V tikhom omute. Stat'i i issledovaniya raznykh let*, M., 1991, 469.
164. 'La Russie et la Révolution'. III, 42.
165. Lane (1971), 230. (See also Lane [1988a], 249.)

Chapter 13. Poetic Rebirth, Last Love

1. See Chapter 5.
2. *Lirika*, I, 387-388.
3. Gregg, 102-104, 106.

4. Ern. T. to K. Pfeffel: SPb., 5/17 Jan. 1849; SPb., 23 March/ 4 Apr. 1849. TPD, 230.
5. *Letopis'-2*, 87-89.
6. 'Neokhotno i nesmelo...'. I, 203. Autograph versions bear the note 'Groza dorogoy' ('Thunder-storm on the journey') and the date '6 June 1849' (ibid., 489-490). T. and his family arrived in Ovstug the following day (*Letopis'-2*, 89).
7. 'Itak, opyat' uvidelsya ya s vami...'. I, 204. Dated '13 June 1849' in the autograph (ibid., 491).
8. The reference to Eleonore appears to have been first pointed out by K.V. Pigaryov (*Lirika*, I, 381).
9. Ern. T. to K. Pfeffel, Ovstug, 13-16/ 25-28 July 1849; A.Ya. Bulgakov to P.A. Vyazemsky, M., 23 Aug. 1849. TPD, 233, 235.
10. Ern. T. to P.A. Vyazemsky, Ovstug, 5/17 July 1852. TPD, 251-252.
11. 'Tikhoy noch'yu, pozdnim letom...'. I, 205. The autograph is dated '23 July 1849' (ibid., 494).
12. See Chapter 4.
13. As notes 9 and 11; *Letopis'-2*, 91.
14. Ern. T. to P.A. Vyazemsky, SPb., 19/31 Oct. 1849. TPD, 236.
15. D.V. Grigorovich, *Literaturnye vospominaniya*, M., 1961, 113 (quoted in *Dok.*, 89). Grigorovich's testimony appears to relate to a year or so previously, for according to him Wielhorski (1788-1856) was then 'getting on for sixty'.
16. As note 14.
17. Ibid.
18. G.V. Chagin, 'Zapiski literaturoveda. "Vnov' tvoi ya vizhu ochi..." ', *Russkaya slovesnost'*, 1997, No.5, 31, 58. Chagin's suggestion that T. may have heard Grisi perform on a previous occasion in western Europe can almost certainly be discounted in view of the known facts of her singing career. This in no way invalidates his basic hypothesis, however. It is clear from Ernestine's testimony of 19 Oct. (see note 14) that T. had by then already attended more than one of Grisi's performances in SPb. that autumn. This (together with likely meetings in a social setting) would adequately account for the previous encounter or encounters implied by the poem.
19. I, 497.
20. 'Vnov' tvoi ya vizhu ochi...', I, 208.
21. Kozyrev, 94.
22. Aksakov, 84.
23. 'Slyozy lyudskiye, o slyozy lyudskiye...'. I, 211. The English translation, by Peter Tempest, is from: *Russian 19th-Century Verse. Selected Poems by Pushkin, Baratynsky, Tyutchev, Koltsov, Lermontov, Tolstoy, Fet, Nekrasov* (ed. Irina Zheleznova), Moscow, 1983, 199. It is reproduced here by kind permission of Raduga Publishers, Moscow.
24. 'Russkoy zhenshchine'. I, 209.
25. The poem appeared with this title ('Moyey zemlyachke') on its first publication in the journal *Kievlyanin*, 1850, No.3, 191 (see: I, 499).
26. 'Dva golosa'. II, 25.
27. The borrowing seems first to have been noted by N.V. Aleksandrovskaya in: 'Dva golosa (Tyutchev i Gyote)', *Possev. Odessa-Povolzh'yu: Liter.-kritich. i nauchno-khud. al'manakh*, Odessa, 1921, 96.
28. A.I. Neuslykhin, 'Tyutchev i Gyol'derlin', *LN-2*, 542-547.
29. Kozyrev, 92-93.
30. E.g.: 'Svyataya noch' na nebosklon vzoshla...'; 'Ne rassuzhday, ne khlopochi...'; 'Smotri, kak na rechnom prostore...'. I, 215; II, 18, 34.
31. 'Vesna' ('Spring') ('Kak ni gnetyot ruka sud'biny...'). I, 183-184.
32. F.I. T. to Ern. T., Weimar, 30 May/ 11 June 1842. IV, 191.
33. N. N[ekrasov], 'Russkiye vtorostepennye poety. 1', *Sovremennik*, 1850, XIX, No.1 (Jan.), section 6, 56-74. Reprinted in *Dok.*, 90-109 (page references from which are given in the text).
34. Pigaryov (1965), 292.
35. A.S. Khomyakov to A.N. Popov, M., Jan. 1850. Khomyakov, VIII, 200.
36. F.I. T. to M.P. Pogodin, SPb., March 1850. V, 12.
37. *Letopis'-2*, 110, 112-113, 121, 133, 137.
38. *Moskvityanin*, 1850, Part 2, No.7 (Apr.), 162.
39. *Zhizn'*, 136.
40. P.A. Pletnyov to V.A. Zhukovsky: 3 Jan., 4 March 1850. P.A. Pletnyov, *Sochineniya i perepiska*, 3 vols., SPb., 1885. III, 621, 640.
41. F.I. T. to A.I. Georgievsky, Nice, 3/15 Feb. 1865. VI, 96.

42. Georgievsky, 107, 159 *n*.9. Although Georgievsky became a close friend of T. and Yelena only a decade after the events in question through his marriage to her half-sister Marie, his memoir (first published in 1989) provides a well-informed and balanced account of the affair. This is fortunate, as apart from T.'s poems and letters it remains practically our only source of information on the matter.

43. Ibid., 107, 125.

44. Ibid., 107.

45. F.I. T. to I.N. & Ye.L. Tyutchev, SPb., 25 Nov. 1845. IV, 325.

46. The first known reference to Yelena in the Tyutchev family correspondence occurs in a letter from Ernestine to Anna dated 14 Nov. 1846 stating that Yelena and her aunt would be coming to dinner the following day (*Letopis'-2*, 51). Returning from abroad in 1847, Anna wrote in her diary that she was looking forward to seeing again 'the elegant Lyolya', Anna Dmitrievna and another of her aunts (entry for 20 Sept./ 2 Oct. 1847. Ibid., 70).

47. Georgievsky, 107, 112. There is a reproduction of Yelena's portrait in water colours (c. 1850) in II, after p.224; the three surviving photographs of her (all from the late 1850s and early 1860s) are reproduced in: V, after p.352; VI, after p.384; *Lirika*, I, opp. p.145.

48. Georgievsky, 107-108.

49. 'Bliznetsy'. II, 13. K.V. Pigaryov was able to date this no more precisely than to before the beginning of 1852 (*Lirika*, I, 400). More recent examination has found autographs of 'Bliznetsy' and 'Poeziya' to be written on matching halves of a single sheet of torn paper. As 'Poeziya' was submitted for publication in *Moskvityanin* before the end of March 1850, the likely date of composition for 'Bliznetsy' can be moved back to 1849 or the earlier part of 1850 (see: II, 345).

50. Kozyrev, 107; Gregg, 180 (and footnote).

51. 'Poshli, Gospod', svoyu otradu...'. II, 19.

52. 'Nash vek', II, 40.

53. ' "Ne day nam dukhu prazdnoslov'ya!"...'; 'I grob opushchen uzh v mogilu...'; 'Ya lyuteran lyublyu bogosluzheniye...'; 'I chuvstva net v tvoikh ochakh...'. I, 35, 138, 156, 172.

54. See, from the earlier period: 'Olegov shchit' and 'Ot russkogo po prochtenii otryvkov iz lektsiy g-na Mitskevicha' (I, 71, 191). Examples from more recent times (1848-1850) are: 'Russkaya geografiya'; 'Rassvet'; 'Prorochestvo'; 'Uzh tretiy god besnuyutsya yazyki...' (I, 200, 218; II, 14, 15).

55. Apart from the previously mentioned 'Nash vek' (note 52), some of the more striking examples from the 1850s are: 'Pamyati V.A. Zhukovskogo'; 'Eti bednye selen'ya...'; 'O veshchaya dusha moya!..'; 'Vsyo, chto berech' mne udalos'...'; 'Nad etoy tyomnoyu tolpoy...' (II, 55-56, 71, 75, 78, 83).

56. Kozyrev, 95-97.

57. See: 'K N.', lines 15-16; 'V dushnom vozdukha molchan'ye...', lines 9-12; 'Ital'yanskaya villa', lines 27-28; 'O, kak ubiystvenno my lyubim...', lines 9-12 (I, 46, 135, 180; II, 35). To these images can be added the conflagration depicted in 'Plamya rdeyet, plamya pyshet...' (II, 69), which threatens the sense of serene fulfilment enjoyed by the poet and his lover with intimations of loss and deprivation.

58. Ern. T. to P.A. Vyazemsky, SPb., 7/19 May 1850. TPD, 245.

59. Ern. T. to K. Pfeffel, SPb., 29 June/ 11 July 1850. TPD, 245-246 (note 1 to passage 93).

60. Ern. T. to P.A. Vyazemsky, SPb., 2/14 July 1850. TPD, 245.

61. Georgievsky, 108.

62. As note 60.

63. '15 iyulya 1865 g.'. II, 147.

64. 'Kak ni dyshit polden' znoyny...'. II, 21.

65. Petrova, 58; Pigaryov (1965), 298; D.S. Merezhkovsky, *Dve tayny russkoy poezii. Nekrasov i Tyutchev*, Petrograd, 1915, 110.

66. Georgievsky, 111.

67. Ibid.

68. 'O, kak ubiystvenno my lyubim...'. II, 35.

69. Georgievsky, 108.

70. Ibid., 125.

71. 'Na Neve'. II, 20.

72. A.F. Tyutcheva to D.I. Sushkova, SPb., 10 Aug. 1850. TPD, 246-247.

73. 'Pod dykhan'yem nepogody...'. II, 22.

74. Georgievsky, 110, 125.

75. 'Chemu molilas' ty s lyubov'yu...'. II, 53.

76. Georgievsky, 110.

77. Ibid.

78. 'Ya ochi znal, — o, eti ochi!..'. II, 51.

79. Although no autograph manuscript survives, the existence of a copy in the 'Sushkov notebook' dates it reliably to before the beginning of 1852. According to Chulkov, 'It must be assumed that the poem refers to Ye. Denisyeva; however, the past tense introduced by the poet in the first lines of the piece and maintained until the end gives some cause for doubt' (Chulkov [1928], 98). Chulkov's remarks are quoted and endorsed by the compilers of all subsequent major editions: *Lirika*, I, 399; *PSS* (1987), 396; II, 388-389.

80. Tyutchev (F.F.), 237.

81. *Zhizn'*, 148.

82. Georgievsky, 125.

83. As note 68, 35-36.

84. Chulkov (1928), 37.

85. Georgievsky, 111-112.

86. 'Ne raz ty slyshala priznan'ye...'. II, 39.

87. Chulkov (1923), 15.

88. 'Des premiers ans de votre vie...'. II, 28.

89. *Lirika*, I, 394-395; *Zhizn'*, 149-150.

90. 'Ne znayu ya, kosnyotsya l' blagodat'...'. II, 37.

91. *Letopis'-2*, 121.

92. F.I. T. to Ern. T., M., 18 June 1851. RGB.308.1.19, *l.* 3-4. (Here he also writes of being treated for haemorrhoids.)

93. F.I. T. to Ern. T., M., 2 July 1851. V, 33-34.

94. Tyutchev (F.F.), 227.

95. F.I. T. to Ern. T., SPb., 16/28 Nov. 1853. V, 146-147.

96. F.I. T. to Ern. T., M., 6 July 1851. V, 36-37.

97. *Letopis'-2*, 125. Foreign Ministry records show that on 5 June T. had been granted 28 days' leave (ibid., 121).

98. Georgievsky, 112, 126.

99. 'Predopredeleniye' ('Predestination'). II, 50.

100. 'O, ne trevozh' menya ukoroy spravedlivoy...'. II, 42.

101. F.I. T. to D.F. Tyutcheva, Geneva, 8/20 Sept. 1864. VI, 75.

102. 'Ne govori, menya on, kak i prezhde, lyubit...'. II, 52.

103. F.I. T. to Ern. T., M.: 29 June; 25 June 1851. V, 28, 29; RGB.308.1.19 (page ref. unavailable).

104. F.I. T. to Ern. T., SPb., 31 July 1851. V, 60.

105. F.I. T. to Ern. T., SPb., 3 Aug. 1851. V, 67.

106. 'V razluke yest' vysokoye znachen'ye...'. II, 44.

107. F.I. T. to Ern. T., SPb., 6 Aug. 1851. V, 74.

108. *Letopis'-2*, 136.

109. 'Den' vechereyet, noch' blizka...'. II, 46. No autograph manuscript has survived, but a copy in Ernestine's album bears the date '1851'. The first publication (in *Sovremennik*, 1854, XLV, No.5, 13-14) is dated more precisely '1 November 1851'. (See: II, 382; *Lirika*, I, 397.)

110. This is particularly apparent in the Russian texts of the poems. 'Ya pomnyu vremya zolotoye...' has: '*den' vecherel*' ('day was turning to evening'); '*kray neba dymno gas*' ('the edge of the sky grew hazily dark'); '*nad nami proletala ten''* ('above us the shadow flew by') (I, 162, lines 3, 18, 24). Compare in 'Den' vechereyet, noch' blizka...': '*den' vechereyet*' ('day is turning to evening'); '*na nebe gasnut oblaka*' ('in the sky the clouds grow dark'); '*dlinney s gory lozhitsya ten''* ('the shadow from the mountain grows [lit. "falls"] longer') (II, 46, lines 1, 3, 2).

111. A.P. Auer, notes to the poem in: II, 383.

112. F.I. T. to Ern. T., SPb., 28 Aug. 1851. V, 94.

113. A.A. Blok, *Sobraniye sochineniy*, 8 vols., M. & L., 1962. VII, 32.

114. Ern. T. to P.A. Vyazemsky, SPb., 19/31 May 1852. TPD, 250; *Letopis'-2*, 125, 141.

115. A.F. Tyutcheva, *Pri dvore dvukh imperatorov. Vospominaniya i dnevniki*, M., 2004 [not to be confused with *Pri dvore-1, -2*], 88-89 (diary, 16 Aug. 1852).

116. Ern. T. to P.A. Vyazemsky, Ovstug, 5/17 July 1852. TPD, 251-252.

117. Ern. T. to K. Pfeffel, SPb., 7/19 Sept. 1850. TPD, 247 (and see 248 *n.*1); *Letopis'-2*, 141-143. The new railway link had been opened for public use on 1 Nov. 1851 (*Letopis'-2*, 133).

118. F.I. T. to Ern. T., SPb.: 2 July; 9 July 1852. RGB.308.1.20, *l.* 3-4; Lettres, XVIII, 34.

119. 'Siyayet solntse, vody bleshchut...'. II, 57 (and see ibid., 394).

120. Kozyrev, 94.

121. 'Ty, volna moya morskaya...'. II, 54.

122. Kozyrev, 112-114.

123. 'Poslednyaya lyubov''. II, 59 (for dating see ibid., 396).

124. 'K N.'; 'Sey den', ya pomnyu, dlya menya...'. I, 46, 131.

125. F.I. T. to Ern. T., SPb.: 27 Sept.; 1 Nov. 1852. Lettres, XVIII, 41; RGB.308.1.20, *l.* 58-59*ob.*

126. F.I. T. to Ern. T., SPb., 31 July 1851. V, 60.

127. F.I. T. to Ern. T., Kamenny Ostrov, 9 July 1852. RGB.308.1.20, *l.* 5-6*ob.*; A.F. Tyutcheva (as note 115).

128. F.I. T. to A.F. Tyutcheva, Kamenny Ostrov, 2 Aug. 1852. V, 113.

129. F.I. T. to Ern. T., SPb., 17 Dec. 1852. V, 128.

130. F.I. T. to Grand Duchess Maria Nikolayevna, SPb., 31 Aug. 1852. V, 116-117; F.I. T. to Ern. T., SPb., 27 Sept. 1852. RGB.308.1.20, *l.* 42-43*ob.* (summarised in *Letopis'-2*, 152).

131. Writing to Ernestine on 26 Nov. 1852, T. gives a 'timetable' of his typical round of engagements, including invitations to soirées (often two at a time) for every day of the week. 'To this accumulation of soirées' (he continues) 'add invitations to dinner, and then the Italian opera, the French theatre, morning concerts' (*Letopis'-2*, 158).

132. N.I. Tyutchev to Ern. T., M., 3 Dec. 1852. Ibid., 159.

133. K. Pfeffel to Ern. T., Paris, 10/22 Sept. 1852. Ibid., 151.

134. F.I. T. to Ern. T., SPb., 27 Sept. 1852. Ibid., 152.

135. F.I. T. to Ern. T., SPb., 26 Dec. 1852. Lettres, XVIII, 44-45.

136. 'Charodeykoyu zimoyu...'. II, 58. The autograph is dated '31 December 1852' (ibid., 395).

137. Diary of A.F. Tyutcheva, 1 & 2 Jan. 1853. TPD, 252-253.

138. Ibid., 253 (diary, 2 Jan.); letters to A.F. Tyutcheva from Ovstug of Ye.F. Tyutcheva (5 Jan.), D.F. Tyutcheva (5 Jan.) and Ern. T. (7 Jan.) 1853. TPD, 253.

139. Ye.F. Tyutcheva to A.F. Tyutcheva, Ovstug, 11 Jan. 1853. *Letopis'-2*, 164.

140. F.I. T. to Ern. T., Roslavl, 22 Jan. 1853. RGB.308.1.21, *l.* 1-2.

141. F.I. T. to Ern. T., SPb., 25 Feb. 1853. V, 133.

142. F.I. T. to Ern. T., SPb., 14 Feb. 1853. RGB.308.1.21, *l.* 9-10*ob.*

143. Ibid.; F.I. T. to Ern. T., SPb., 18 Feb. 1853. *Letopis'-2*, 168.

144. F.I. T. to Ern. T., SPb., 22 March 1853. V, 138; Ern. T. to K. Pfeffel, SPb., 11/23 May 1853. *Letopis'-2*, 172.

145. *Pri dvore-1*, 116-117, 118.

146. Details of the Tyutchevs' travels abroad up to this point have been taken from Anna's and Ernestine's letters from 15/27 June to 5/17 July in: TPD, 256; *Letopis'-2*, 174.

147. See the eyewitness accounts quoted in Liedtke, 135-136.

148. Varnhagen von Ense's diary for 26 Oct. 1853 (NS) records the receipt of a letter from Maltitz in Weimar containing 'greetings via Tyutchev from Heine in Paris [...] Tyutchev found Heine still full of life' (Varnhagen, X, 323).

149. R. Leyn [= R. Lane], 'Zagranichnaya poyezdka Tyutcheva v 1853 g.', *LN-2*, 468-469.

150. Heine (1970), XXIII, 291-292. For a list of the books sent with the letter see Lane (as note 149), 470 *n.*42.

151. *Letopis'-2*, 176.

152. F.I. T. to Ern. T., Weimar, 27 Aug./ 8 Sept. 1853. RGB.308.1.21, *l.* 21-22.

153. F.I. T. to Ern. T., SPb., 14/26 Sept. 1853. Ibid., *l.* 27-30*ob.*

154. Ibid. In the transcripts made under the direction of K.V. Pigaryov the place-name is given as 'Soldau', evidently a misreading for 'Goldau'. The same letter also mentions the Rigi and Lake Lucerne (incorrectly given as 'Lake Léman' in the extract published in Lettres, XVIII, 52).

155. F.I. T. to Ern. T., SPb., 27 July 1854. V, 182. See also his recollection of having ascended the Rigi-Kulm (the highest peak of the massif) in a letter to Ernestine of 18 Aug. 1855 (V, 190).

156. Ern. T. to A.F. Tyutcheva, Lindau, 21 Aug./ 2 Sept. 1853. *Letopis'-2*, 177; F.I. T. to Ern. T.: Weimar, 27 Aug./ 8 Sept.; Warsaw, 2/14 Sept. 1853. RGB.308.1.21, *l.* 21-22, 25-26 (published with omissions in: Lettres, XVIII, 49-51).

157. Ern. T. to A.F. Tyutcheva, Lindau, 6/18 Sept. 1853. *Letopis'-2*, 178.

158. F.I. T. to Ern. T., SPb., 18/30 Sept. 1853. RGB.308.1.21, *l.* 31-32*ob.*

159. F.I. T. to Ern. T., SPb., 14/26 Sept. 1853. Lettres, XVIII, 51.

160. 'Neman'. II, 60-61. For an account of the poem's composition and publication history see ibid., 397-399. A translated extract from the poem is quoted in Chapter 1.

161. F.I. T. to Ern. T., Warsaw, 2/14 Sept. 1853. Lettres, XVIII, 51.
162. As note 153 (and see note 154 re the misreading of 'Lake Lucerne' in Lettres).
163. As note 153. (The text as printed in Lettres [XVIII, 52] does not make it clear that the reference is to *silver* roubles)
164. As note 153 (this section is omitted in Lettres).
165. F.I. T. to Ern. T., SPb., undated, 1853. Quoted (in Russian translation) with the date 29 Sept./ 11 Oct. in Kozhinov, 382. The same letter is quoted in a different translation in *Letopis'-2*, 183, where it is dated 14/26 Oct. on the basis of its supposed context among other letters. Kozhinov's dating is more convincing. In the archive the letter is preserved (presumably in the order in which Ernestine received it — and she is known to have been careful about such matters) between two others dated 27 Sept./ 9 Oct. and 3/15 Oct. respectively (see the archival references in *Letopis'-2*, 181, 182, 183). In the letter dated 27 Sept./ 9 Oct. T. writes of the 'feeling of incredible pity' which he had experienced on reading her 'long awaited letter': 'You tell me that our present separation is more important for us than that of last year... Who are you telling? Do you think I see it any differently?' (ibid., 181). The undated letter would appear to be a second response to the same letter from Ernestine after its impact had had time to sink in. It is marked 'Wednesday' (ibid., 183), allowing us to date it 30 Sept./ 12 Oct. 1853 (Kozhinov's dating of it a day earlier must be assumed to reflect an error in calculation).
166. Kozhinov, 377-378.
167. F.I. T. to Ern. T., SPb., 27 Sept./ 9 Oct. 1853. *Letopis'-2*, 181.
168. 'When you tell me that I have plenty of strings to my bow, etc., etc., it all has an air of mockery,' he writes to Ernestine on 16/28 Oct. in response to one of her letters (V, 143).
169. F.I. T. to Ern. T., SPb., 10/22 Oct. 1853. RGB.308.1.21, *l.* 41.
170. F.I. T. to Ern. T., SPb., 26 Oct./ 7 Nov. 1853. Ibid., *l.* 44-45ob.
171. A.F. Tyutcheva to Ye.F. Tyutcheva, Tsarskoye Selo: 26 Oct.; beginning of Nov. 1853. *Letopis'-2*, 184; TPD, 258.
172. See: Ern. T. to A.F. & D.F. Tyutcheva, Mu., 18/30 Nov. 1853; Ern. T. to A.F. Tyutcheva, Mu., 9/21 Jan. 1854. TPD, 258, 259-260.
173. As note 172 (letter of 9/21 Jan.).
174. F.I. T. to Ern. T., SPb.: 23 July; 27 July 1854. V, 177, 182.
175. Ern. T. to D.F. Tyutcheva, Mu., 17/29 Apr. 1854. TPD, 262. The French and British declarations of war against Russia came into effect on 15 and 30 April (NS) respectively (Florinsky, II, 868-869).
176. F.I. T. to Ern. T., M., 9 June 1854. V, 163; A.F. Tyutcheva to Ye.F. Tyutcheva, SPb., May (after the 11th) 1854. TPD, 263.
177. A.F. Tyutcheva to Ye.F. Tyutcheva, SPb., (between 3 and 10) May 1854. TPD, 262 (see also note 2 to the letter).
178. *Pri dvore-1*, 138 (diary, 26 May 1854); F.I. T. to Ern. T., M., 9 June 1854. V, 163.
179. *Letopis'* (Ch.), 104, states on the basis of one of T.'s unpublished letters that Ernestine left Ovstug on 5 October. *Letopis'-2*, 220, suggests a later date, pointing out that according to Anna's diary (*Pri dvore-1*, 165) Darya was still 'in the country' on 8 November. It may simply be that Darya stayed on at Ovstug after Ernestine left with the younger children.
180. F.I. T. to Ern. T., SPb., 23 July 1854. V, 175-176.
181. F.I. T. to Ern. T., SPb., 27 July 1854. V, 181.
182. 'Pominki (Iz Shillera)'. II, 29-33.
183. *Raut na 1852 god* (ed. N.V. Sushkov), M., 1852, 201. The poems were: 'Grafine Ye.P. Rostopchinoy (v otvet na yeyo pis'mo)'; 'Pervy list'; 'Volna i duma'; 'Ne ostyvshaya ot znoyu...'; 'Ty znayesh' kray, gde mirt i lavr rastyot...' (a translation of Goethe's 'Kennst du das Land, wo die Zitronen blühn...'). II, 26-27, 38, 41, 43, 45.
184. *Zhizn'*, 138.
185. Pigaryov (1935b), 377-379; K.V. Pigaryov, 'Stikhotvoreniya Tyutcheva v "Biblioteke Poeta" ', in: *Izdaniye klassicheskoy literatury. Iz opyta 'Biblioteki Poeta'*, M., 1963, 179.
186. A.F. Tyutcheva to D.F. Tyutcheva, SPb., 11 March 1853. TPD, 254.
187. N.V. Sushkov, 'Oboz k potomstvu s knigami i rukopisyami', *Dok.*, 111 (first publ. in *Raut*, III [ed. N.V. Sushkov], M., 1854, 350-351).
188. See his review of *Raut na 1852 god* in: *Sovremennik*, 1852, XXXII, No.4 (April), section 4, 77-78 (reprinted in: N.A. Nekrasov, *Polnoye sobraniye sochineniy i pisem*, 12 vols., M., 1948-1953. IX, 664-665).
189. F.I. T. to Ern. T., SPb., 10 Dec. 1852. V, 124.

190. Ibid.; Ern T. to P.A. Vyazemsky, Ovstug, 10/22 Dec. 1852. TPD, 252.

191. A.F. Tyutcheva to Ye.F. Tyutcheva, SPb., 28 Dec. 1853. TPD, 259 (see also note 2 to the letter). Already in Jan. 1853 Turgenev had written that the poetry of T. and Fet would 'find an echo in the heart' of their readers (I. T[urgenev], 'Zapiski ruzheynogo okhotnika Orenburgskoy gubernii S. A[ksakov]-a, M., 1852', *Sovremennik*, 1853, XXXVII, No.1 [Jan.], section 3, 43. Reprinted in: Turgenev *S*, V, 420).

192. I.S. Turgenev to S.A. Aksakov, SPb., 10 Feb. 1854. Turgenev *P*, II, 216-217. The earliest documented reference to plans by the *Sovremennik* editors to publish T.'s poetry is a diary entry by the literary historian and bibliophile G.N. Gennadi dated 5 Jan. 1854 (Ospovat [1989], 500). It is not clear from this whether T. had by then agreed to the proposal.

193. A.A. Fet, *Moi vospominaniya*, M., 1890, Part 1, 134-135.

194. P.A. Pletnyov to P.A. Vyazemsky, SPb., [Feb.] 1854. Ospovat (1980), 42.

195. Pigaryov (1935b), 377-378.

196. 'Stikhotvoreniya F. Tyutcheva', *Sovremennik*, 1854, XXXXIV, No.3 (March), and XXXXV, No.4 (Apr.); *Stikhotvoreniya F. Tyutcheva*, SPb., 1854 (censor's approval dated 30 May).

197. I. T[urgenev], 'Neskol'ko slov o stikhotvoreniyakh F.I. Tyutcheva', *Sovremennik*, 1854, XXXXV, No.4 (April), section 3, 23-26. Reprinted in *Dok.*, 112-115, page references for which are given in the text.

198. At the beginning of Sept. 1848 T., Vyazemsky and Pletnyov met to read and discuss a manuscript copy of Zhukovsky's poem 'K russkomu velikanu' ('To the Russian Giant'), in which Russia is compared to a granite cliff standing firm against the tempestuous waves of revolution. While admiring the poem as a whole, they found the ending somewhat weak. The following day T. showed the other two his suggested rewriting of the final lines, together with a short poem of his own on the same theme (subsequently reworked and expanded as 'More i utyos' ['The Sea and the Cliff ']). They all agreed that Zhukovsky's poem should be published in T.'s amended version, and a few days later it appeared (together with T.'s own poem) in the newspaper *Russky invalid*. When Zhukovsky (then abroad) learned of this, he expressed his displeasure at such unauthorised meddling with his verse. See: V.A. Zhukovsky to A.Ya. Bulgakov, Frankfurt, 27 Sept./ 9 Oct. 1848. Zhukovsky (1999), II, 733-734; P.A. Vyazemsky to V.A. Zhukovsky, SPb., 18/30 Oct. 1848. *Perepiska P.A. Vyazemskogo i V.A. Zhukovskogo (1842-1852)* (ed. M.I. Gippel'son), L., 1980, 61. (Both letters are also quoted in *Letopis'-2*, 80-81, 82.)

199. Quoted in: G.I. Chulkov, 'Ob izdanii stikhotvoreiy Tyutcheva', *PSS* (1933), I, 71-72.

200. See Ivan Aksakov's first-hand account of his experiences as editor of the 1868 edition of T.'s verse (Aksakov, 323-324), also T.'s own comments on the latter publication after it had appeared (F.I. T. to Ye.F. Tyutcheva, SPb., 26 March 1868. VI, 316-317; 'Mikhailu Petrovichu Pogodinu'. II, 191).

201. G.S. Gagarin to P.V. Bykov, Bordighera, 14 Nov. 1912 (NS?). A.A. Nikolayev, 'Ob izdanii "Polnogo sobraniya sochineniy" Tyutcheva (1912)', *LN-2*, 537. T. first met Kovalevsky at the very end of the 1850s (ibid., 540 *n*.29).

202. A.A. Fet, *Vecherniye ogni*, M., 1888, Part 3, 242.

203. For a full review of this evidence see: Pigaryov (1935b), 380-383.

204. Ibid., 383.

205. For a survey of the reviews in 1854 see: Ospovat (1980), 50-56; *Zhizn'*, 140-143.

206. Ospovat (1980), 64-65.

207. *Vsemirnaya illyustratsiya*, 1873, No.244, 155 (quoted in: Ospovat [1980], 73).

208. Fet (1859), 121.

209. Ospovat (1980), 59.

210. Ibid., 58.

211. 'Na knizhke stikhotvoreniy Tyutcheva'. A.A. Fet, *Stikhotvoreniya i poemy*, L., 1986, 331.

Chapter 14. New Beginnings

1. F.I. T. to Ern. T., SPb., 16/28 Nov. 1853. V, 148.

2. *Pri dvore-1*, 128 (diary, 14 Nov. 1853).

3. F.I. T. to Ern. T., SPb., 3 July 1855. Lettres, XIX, 141. The reference is to Mozart's *Don Giovanni*.

4. F.I. T. to Ern. T., SPb., 2/14 Feb. 1854. Ibid., 104, 105.

5. F.I. T. to Ern. T., SPb., 10/22 Feb. 1854. Ibid., 106.

6. See: Pogodin, 14 (diary entries for June and Nov. 1854, Aug. 1855); D.I. Sushkova to N.V. Sushkov, M., 5 Aug. 1855. TPD, 272.

7. *Pri dvore-1*, 132-133.

8. See: Pogodin, 14 (entries for 1854 and 1855, passim). Writing to Pogodin after the war (on 13 Oct. 1857), T. made it clear that he fully endorsed Pogodin's articles and advised him to have them printed abroad (V, 265-266). Pogodin eventually followed this advice; the letters and articles appeared as: Pis'ma i stat'i M. Pogodina o politike Rossii v otnoshenii slavyanskikh narodov i zapadnoy Yevropy, published in the series: *Russky zagranichny sbornik*, IV, Nos. 2-4, Leipzig, 1860-1861. (The letters addressed to T. are numbered 18 and 23.)

9. *Pri dvore-2*, 52.

10. In a document dated 18 Jan. 1854 the Executive Director of the Third Section, L.V. Dubelt, wrote of the Slavophiles: 'Expressing themselves in a declamatory and ambiguous fashion, they have not infrequently given cause for doubt as to whether behind their protestations of patriotism are not concealed aims inimical to our government' (quoted in: M.K. Lemke, *Nikolayevskiye zhandarmy i literatura 1826-1855 gg. Po podlinnym delam Tret'yego otdeleniya sobst. ye. i. velichestva kantselyarii*, SPb., 1908, 217). For testimony of Slavophiles to harassment and surveillance by the government, including the interception of mail, see for instance: Koshelyov, 87; Yury Samarin, *Sochineniya* (ed. D. Samarin), 12 vols., M., 1877-1911. XII, 151, 281.

11. Yury Samarin and Ivan Aksakov, for instance. See: V.N. Kasatkina, 'I.S. Aksakov — biograf Tyutcheva', *Kommentariy*, 10.

12. K. Pfeffel to Ern. T., Mu., 13/25 March 1855. TPD, 269.

13. F.I. T. to Ern. T., SPb., 26 Oct./ 8 Nov. 1853. Lettres, XVIII, 57 (here incorrectly dated 22 Oct.: see *Letopis'-2*, 184).

14. F.I. T. to Ern. T., SPb., 17 Feb./ 1 March 1854. Lettres, XIX, 107.

15. F.I. T. to Ern. T., SPb., 23 Nov./ 5 Dec. 1853. Lettres, XVIII, 60.

16. As note 13.

17. F.I. T. to Ern. T., SPb., 11/23 Dec. 1853. Lettres, XVIII, 62.

18. Florinsky, II, 870.

19. As note 14, 108.

20. F.I. T. to Ern. T., SPb., 8/20 Apr. 1854. Lettres, XIX, 113.

21. F.I. T. to Ern. T., SPb., 19 June 1854. V, 172.

22. Lane (1971), 224; Lane (1988a), 243.

23. F.I. T. to Ern. T., SPb.: 21 Apr./ 3 May; 5 Aug. 1854. Lettres, XIX, 114; *Letopis'-2*, 216. For further comments by T. on the publications see his letters to Ernestine of 29 June and 25 Aug. 1854 (Lettres, XIX, 122-123; V, 195).

24. See: K. Pfeffel to Ern. T., Baden, 16/28 Oct. 1855. TPD, 278.

25. Lane (1971), 224-226; Lane (1988a), 243.

26. Quoted in Lane (1971), 224, 225.

27. Quoted in: ibid., 226. Although Lane suggests here that the article in question could be by Forcade, in a subsequent publication (Lane [1988a], 243) he is positive in identifying the author as Mazade.

28. E. Forcade, 'L'Autriche et la politique du cabinet de Vienne dans la Question de l'Orient', *Revue des Deux Mondes*, 1854, VI, 1 June, 870-893.

29. Lane (1971), 225; Lane (1988a), 243. See also : Lettres, XIX, 104-105, 112.

30. See: K. Pfeffel to Ern. T., Mu., 28 May/ 9 June 1854. TPD, 263.

31. Ibid.

32. See T.'s letters to Ernestine of 29 June and 5 Aug. 1854 (Lettres, XIX, 123, 127).

33. F.I. T. to Ern. T., M., 9 June 1854. V, 165.

34. F.I. T. to Ern. T., SPb., 23 July 1854. V, 177.

35. F.I. T. to Ern. T., SPb., 10/22 March 1854. V, 161.

36. As note 20, 112.

37. F.I. T. to Ern. T., SPb., 27 July 1854. V, 182.

38. F.I. T. to Ern. T., SPb., 19 June 1854. V, 172.

39. F.I. T. to Ern. T., SPb., 13 June 1854. Lettres, XIX, 118.

40. See *Pri dvore-1*, 174-184 (diary, 19 Feb. 1855) for Anna's detailed account from inside the palace of Nicholas's last days and death. The facts as laid out here contradict later rumours that the Emperor committed suicide.

41. Ibid., 185. (See also *Tyutcheviana*, 26, where T.'s comment is quoted in the original French.)

42. F.I. T. to K. Pfeffel, SPb., 20 Feb./ 4 March 1855. V, 203.

43. *Pri dvore-1*, 197 (diary, 27 Feb. 1855).

44. 'Po sluchayu priyezda avstriyskogo ertsgertsoga na pokhorony imperatora Nikolaya'. II, 68.

45. Copies were even circulating in Moscow within a few days, as is clear from diary entries by Pogodin on 6 March (Pogodin, 14) and Vera Aksakova on 8 March (V.S. Aksakova, *Dnevnik. 1854-1855*, SPb., 1903, 81).

46. As note 42, 203-204.

47. Florinsky, II, 871.

48. *Pri dvore-2*, 16 (diary, 15 March 1855).

49. F.I. T. to Ern. T., SPb., 21 May 1855. V, 207.

50. F.I. T. to Ern. T., SPb., 20 June 1855. V, 213.

51. 'Vot ot morya i do morya...' ('From one sea unto the other...'). II, 72.

52. F.I. T. to Ern. T., M., 9 Sept. 1855. V, 219.

53. *Pri dvore-2*, 49-50 (diary, 3 Sept. 1855).

54. F.I. T. to Ern. T., SPb., 17 Sept. 1855. V, 225.

55. As note 24.

56. 'Ne Bogu ty sluzhil i ne Rossii...'. II, 73. K.V. Pigaryov considers the poem to have been written soon after the fall of Sevastopol (*Lirika*, I, 408).

57. F.I. T. to M.P. Pogodin, SPb., 11 Oct. 1855. V, 231.

58. Florinsky, II, 871.

59. Ern. T. to K. Pfeffel, SPb., 10/22 Jan. 1856. TPD, 282 (here the letter is said to have been sent from Munich: clearly an error).

60. Fisher, II, 1034.

61. G.M. Trevelyan, *English Social History*, London, 1942, 548.

62. For evidence that the term originated with T., see: I.S. Aksakov to S.T. Aksakov, M., 8 Apr. 1855. *I.S. Aksakov v yego pis'makh*, 4 vols., M., 1888-1896. III, 115; Aksakova (as note 45), 102 (diary, 10 Apr. 1855).

63. See: F.I. T. to Ern. T., SPb., 5 June 1858. V, 267-268.

64. Ern. T. to K. Pfeffel, SPb., 13/25 Nov. 1861. TPD, 326.

65. F.I. T. to A.D. Bludova, SPb., 28 Sept. 1857. *Pis'ma*, 250-252.

66. See D.F. Tyutcheva's account in letters from Ovstug in Aug. 1858 to A.I. Kozlova (15 Aug.) and A.F. Tyutcheva (17 Aug.). TPD, 273-274.

67. Most notably in *The Brothers Karamazov* (in the chapter 'The Grand Inquisitor'); he also quoted it in his 1880 speech on Pushkin.

68. 'Eti bednye selen'ya...'. II, 71.

69. 'Nad etoy tyomnoyu tolpoy...'. II, 83.

70. Aksakov, 275-276.

71. 'Aleksandru Vtoromu' ('To Alexander II'). II, 108.

72. Empress Maria Aleksandrovna to D.F. Tyutcheva, SPb., end of March (after the 25th) 1861. TPD, 323.

73. Ye.M. Feoktistov, *Vospominaniya. Za kulisami politiki i literatury. 1846-1896*, L., 1929, 188.

74. Tyutchev (F.F.), 230.

75. D.F. Tyutcheva to Ye.F. Tyutcheva, SPb., 27 Feb. and 6 March 1861. TPD, 322.

76. F.I. T. to Ern. T., SPb., 23 July 1854. V, 177. (The text as printed in Lettres, XIX, 124 appears on this occasion to be more accurate. It includes immediately after '*dans le moment donné* ' the phrase '*une vive jouissance*', omitted in V, 177 yet clearly required by the sense.)

77. *Tyutchevy*, 305.

78. Ern. T. to K. Pfeffel, SPb., 18/30 Apr. 1856. TPD, 283. T.'s letter to Ernestine of 19 June 1854 (V, 172) implies that he was then already well acquainted with Gorchakov. It is quite possible that they met in the 1830s when Gorchakov was serving on the staff of the Russian Embassy in Vienna.

79. F.I. T. to Ern. T., SPb., 25 May 1857. Lettres, XIX, 163.

80. Kozhinov, 210-211.

81. T. was widely credited in SPb. circles with describing Gorchakov as 'le Narcisse de l'écritoire' ('The Narcissus of the inkwell') (quoted from the unpublished notebook of B.A. Kozlov in: *Tyutcheviana* [2nd. ed., revised and augmented by G.V. Chagin], M., 1999, 23). However, in a letter to Ernestine dated 31 Aug. 1867 T. denied authorship of the aphorism (VI, 262; see also ibid., 513-514, *n*.1).

82. As note 79, 163-164.

83. *Letopis'-2*, 262.

84. F.I. T. to Ern. T., SPb., 25 May 1857. Ibid., 266. For details of T.'s salary that year see: Ern. T. to K. Pfeffel (as note 85).

85. Ern. T. to K. Pfeffel, Ovstug, 25 Aug./ 6 Sept. 1857. TPD, 292.

86. Aksakov, 266-267.

87. 'Lettre sur la censure en Russie'. III, 96-106. Further page references are given in the text. See also: D.F. Tyutcheva to Ye.F. Tyutcheva, SPb., 27 Oct. 1857; N.I. Tyutchev to Ern. T., M., 6 Dec. 1857; D.I. Sushkova to S.D. Poltoratsky, M., 16 Jan. 1858. TPD, 293.

88. Timashov's memo, dated 8 Nov. 1857, is quoted in: I.V. Porokh (ed.), *Iz istorii obshchest-vennoy mysli i obshchestvennogo dvizheniya v Rossii*, Saratov, 1964, 128.

89. *Letopis'-2*, 284-285; Aksakov, 274.

90. A.Ye. Yegorov, 'Stranitsy iz moyey zhizni', *Dok.*, 243 (reprinted from: *Istorichesky vestnik*, 1912, CXXVII, No.1 [Jan.], 59-66).

91. Ern. T. to K. Pfeffel: Ovstug, 19/31 May 1862; Nice, 29 Jan./ 10 Feb. 1865. TPD, 329, 369.

92. F.I. T. to P.K. Shchebalsky, SPb., [1861-1863?]. NPTT, 584.

93. *Letopis'-2*, 284, 360.

94. Ibid., 306.

95. D.I. Sushkova to Ye.F. Tyutcheva, M., 28 Apr. 1858; Ern. T. to K. Pfeffel, SPb., 20 Oct./ 1 Nov. 1858. TPD, 295, 297.

96. M.L. Zlatkovsky, *Apollon Nikolayevich Maykov. 1821-1897. Biograficesky ocherk* (2nd., revised ed.), SPb., 1898, 61.

97. Ibid., 85.

98. For details of the Committee of Foreign Censorship's working methods and organisation see: Zlatkovsky (as note 96); Yegorov (as note 90), 241-243. (Yegorov began work at the Committee's head office only in the autumn of 1872: ibid., 241, 466-467 [note].)

99. F.I. T. to Ern. T., SPb.: 16 June 1860; 18 Aug. 1862. Lettres, XXI, 175, 176.

100. 'O nekotorykh izmeneniyakh v poryadke tsenzurnogo rassmotreniya inostrannykh knig' (unsigned memorandum, drawn up under T.'s direction and submitted to Minister of Education A.V. Golovnin in 1862). Printed in full in *Tyutchevy*, 316-318 (here: 316-317).

101. *Zhizn'*, 165.

102. Briskman, 567; 'O nekotorykh...' (as note 100), 318.

103. Nikitenko, II, 37 (diary, 5 Oct. 1858).

104. F.I. T. to Ern. T., SPb., 17 Sept. 1858. Lettres, XIX, 189.

105. Nikitenko, II, 12-13, 16-20, 24-27, 36-37, 50, 59-60, 65, 75; F.I. T. to Ern. T., SPb., 14 Sept. 1858. *Letopis'-2*, 302.

106. P.V. Dolgorukov to N.V. Putyata, 21 Dec. 1858. *Muranovsky sbornik*, Muranovo, 1928, 112-114.

107. Briskman, 568.

108. Ibid., 571.

109. *Zhizn'*, 162-164.

110. 'O nekotorykh...' (as note 100), 317.

111. 'Velen'yu vysshemu pokorny...'. II, 222.

112. F.I. T. to Ern. T., SPb., 1 June 1857. Lettres, XIX, 165.

113. F.I. T. to Ye.P. Kovalevsky, Wiesbaden, 25 July/ 6 Aug. 1860. VI, 9-10.

114. F.I. T. to Ern. T.: Berlin, 1/13 June; Mu., 15/27 June 1859. Lettres, XXI, 157, 159; F.I. T. to A.F. Tyutcheva, Bad Reichenhall, 3/15 June 1859. V, 294.

115. Diary of A.F. Tyutcheva, 4 Jan. 1860. TPD, 309. The image is biblical in origin: see Proverbs, XXVI, 11; Second Epistle of Peter, II, 22.

116. F.I. T. to A.M. Gorchakov, SPb., 21 Apr. 1859. V, 284-286. For evidence of T.'s frequent meetings with Gorchakov at this time see TPD, 300 (note 1 to passage 220).

117. *Pri dvore-2*, 193 (diary, 16 Apr. 1859). Here Anna states that the pro-Austrian party at court included several government ministers (Sukhozanet, Chevkin, Panin) and the Head of the Third Section,Vasily Dolgorukov.

118. F.I. T. to Ern. T., M., 5 Sept. 1858. Lettres, XIX, 185.

119. T. acknowleged Khomyakov as his intellectual equal (V, 38) and described his theological writings as 'the most intelligent glorification of the Orthodox Church and doctrine' (VI, 360); of Samarin he asserted that none could match his intellect (TPD, 287 [passage 186]); while the political writings of Ivan Aksakov displayed in his opinion a 'superiority to everything without exception written and printed in our country' (VI, 13).

120. F.I. T. to Ern. T., SPb., 6 June 1858. V, 276.

121. F.I. T. to Ern. T., M., 27 Apr. 1859. V, 289.

122. F.I. T. to I.S. Aksakov, SPb., 23 Oct. 1861. VI, 13 (my italics). For later references to 'your teaching' and 'your belief' in letters to Aksakov see: VI, 197, 364; *LN-1*, 355.

123. Aksakov, 61.

124. F.I. T. to Ern. T., M., 1 Aug. 1863. Lettres, XXI, 207.

125. F.I. T. to Ern. T., Tsarskoye Selo, 8 June 1863. Ibid., 202.

126. R. Lane, 'Tjutcev's Role as Mediator Between the Government and M.N. Katkov (1863-1866)', *Russian Literature*, XVII, 1985, 116-117; V.A. Tvardovskaya, 'Tyutchev v obshchestvennoy bor'be poreformennoy Rossii', *LN-1*, 143, 146-147; Florinsky, II, 915-916.

127. F.I. T. to Ern. T., SPb., 19 May 1863. Lettres, XXI, 198-199.

128. F.I. T. to Ye. F. Tyutcheva, SPb., 18 May 1863. Summarised in *Letopis'* (Ch.), 151-152; F.I. T. to Ern. T., SPb., 1 June 1863. Lettres, XXI, 200.

129. 'Uzhasny son otyagotel nad nami...'. II, 121.

130. See diary entries by Maria Tyutcheva for 17 March 1863 (TPD, 335) and A.V. Nikitenko for 21 May 1863 (Nikitenko, II, 333).

131. TPD, 339 (note 10 to passage 310,).

132. Ye.F. Tyutcheva to D.F. Tyutcheva, Novoye, 16 June 1863. TPD, 337.

133. F.I. T. to Ern. T., M., 1 Aug. 1863. Lettres, XXI, 207-208.

134. F.I. T. to A.F. Tyutcheva, M., 25 June 1863. Pigaryov (1935a), 222.

135. A.M. Gorchakov to F.I. T., SPb., 25 July 1863. Unpublished, but summarised with brief quotations in Tvardovskaya (as note 126), 143, and VI, 438 *n.1*.

136. Georgievsky, 116. Georgievsky recalls Gorchakov praising him later that year for some of his editorials on the Polish question in *Moskovskiye vedomosti* (ibid., 118). He also states that while working as a journalist for another newspaper in 1863-1864 he received from T. 'information and pointers' relating to foreign affairs and found these 'of great use' (ibid., 117). Of a somewhat later period Georgievsky writes that Tyutchev 'was not averse to sharing his views with the wider public through the medium of myself and *Moskovskiye vedomosti*; sometimes he was expressly authorised to do this by Prince Gorchakov and even Valuyev — the latter on matters concerning the press. As far as I could, I made use in my articles of his reports and even some of his particularly felicitous expressions' (ibid., 146).

137. Tvardovskaya (as note 126), 143-144, 168 *n.56*; VI, 438-439, *n.3*.

138. As note 134.

139. F.I. T. to A.M. Gorchakov, M., 11 July 1863. VI, 24-25; see also 430-431, *n.1*

140. F.I. T. to Ern. T., SPb., 6 Nov. 1863. Lettres, XXI, 214.

141. F.I. T. to Ern. T., SPb., 13 Nov. 1863. Ibid., 215. See also II, 483.

142. 'Yego svetlosti knyazyu A.A. Suvorovu' ('To His Grace Prince A.A. Suvorov'). II, 122.

143. Ye.A. Denisyeva to A.I. Georgievsky, SPb., Oct. 1863. Chulkov (1928), 115.

144. *Kolokol*, 1 Jan. 1864 (NS), 1452. Herzen's editorial comments on the poem are quoted in II, 483.

145. F.I. T. to Ya.P. Polonsky, Nice, 8/20 Dec. 1864. VI, 84.

146. Georgievsky, 138.

147. *Pri dvore-2*, 85 (diary, 24 Nov. 1855).

148. A.F. Tyutcheva to Ye.F. Tyutcheva, SPb., 23 Apr. 1855. TPD, 269.

149. From 1 June 1863, for instance, they rented a dacha in the Chornaya Rechka district, to the north of the Islands. See: Ye.A. Denisyeva to M.A. Georgievskaya, SPb., 29 May 1863. Chulkov (1928), 118.

150. 'Plamya rdeyet, plamya pyshet...'. II, 69.

151. Gippius, 40; Kozyrev, 122-123.

152. Gregg, 159.

153. *Lirika*, I, 405.

154. 'Tak, v zhizni yest' mgnoven'ya...'. II, 70.

155. Kozyrev, 120; *Faust I*, 'Studierzimmer II', line 1700.

156. 'O veshchaya dusha moya...'. II, 75.

157. *Faust I*, 'Vor dem Tor', line 1112; *Hamlet*, Act I, scene 5, line 40.

158. F.I. T. to Ern. T., SPb., 13 May 1857. V, 254.

159. D.F. Tyutcheva to A.F. Tyutcheva, Ovstug, 19 Aug. 1855. TPD, 275.

160. D.F. Tyutcheva to Ye.F. Tyutcheva, Ovstug, 20 Aug. 1855. TPD, 276-277.

161. D.F. Tyutcheva to Ye.F. Tyutcheva, M., 24 Aug. 1857. TPD, 290.

162. II, 436-437. (Here, as earlier in *Lirika*, I, 411, T.'s travelling companion is incorrectly stated to have been his daughter Marie.)

163. 'Yest' v oseni pervonachal'noy...'. II, 84. For my translation I have followed not the autograph variant for line 3 printed here ('*Prozrachny vozdukh, den' khrustal'ny*'), but that preferred by the editors of all previous major editions (Chulkov, Pigaryov and Nikolayev): '*Ves' den' stoit kak by khrustal'ny*'.

164. Gol'denveyzer, I, 315 (diary, 1 Sept. 1909) (quoted in *Dok.*, 249).

165. *L.N. Tolstoy v vospominaniyakh sovremennikov*, 2 vols., M., 1955. I, 413 (quoted in *Zhizn'*, 140).

166. V.F. Lazursky, *Vospominaniya o L.N. Tolstom*, M., 1911, 46 (quoted in *Dok.*, 250).

167. Gol'denveyzer, I, 182-183 (diary, 24 Aug. 1906) (quoted in *Dok.*, 248-249).

168. *Tyutchevy*, 222-225.

169. F.I. T. to Ern. T., M., 29 Aug. 1858. Lettres, XIX, 184-185.

170. A.F. Tyutcheva to Ye.F. Tyutcheva, Tsarskoye Selo, 19 May 1860. TPD, 317.

171. F.I. T. to Ern. T., SPb., 11 Sept. 1858. Lettres, XIX, 186-187.

172. 'V chasy, kogda byvayet...'. II, 88. We have it on Kitty's authority that the poem was addressed to her mother (ibid., 441).

173. Kozhinov, 119.

174. For a detailed discussion of the arguments for and against the various putative addressees see Appendix I (v).

175. R.C. Lane, 'The Life and Work of F.I. Tyutchev' (unpublished dissertation), University of Cambridge, 1970, 280-282.

176. 'Ona sidela na polu...'. II, 89.

177. *Pri dvore-2*, 150, 163 (diary, 10 Aug., 10 Sept. 1858).

178. Feoktistov (as note 73), 348.

179. F.I. T. to Ern. T., SPb., 3 July 1855. Lettres, XIX, 141-142.

180. Aksakov, 40-41, 261-262; Tyutchev (F.F.), 227.

181. A.F. Tyutcheva to D.F. Tyutcheva, Peterhof, 11 July 1856. TPD, 284.

182. Tyutchev (F.F.), 228-229.

183. F.I. T. to Ern. T., M., 13 May 1857. V, 254-255.

184. Tyutchev (F.F.), 228.

185. A.F. Tyutcheva to Ye.F. Tyutcheva, Tsarskoye Selo, 4 Sept. 1862. TPD, 331.

186. F.I. T. to Ern. T., SPb., 5 June 1858. V, 270-271.

187. He left SPb. on 9/21 May and returned on 2/14 Nov. (*Letopis'-2*, 322, 340). The following account of T.'s travels abroad in 1859 is based on his letters of the time (V, 292-329; Lettres, XXI, 156-173), and on documents quoted in TPD, 302-308, and *Letopis'-2*, 322-340. For details of the Hotel *Vier Jahreszeiten* in Munich see Polonsky (1998), 116-117.

188. F.I. T. to Ern. T., Vevey, 8/20 Sept. 1859. Lettres, XXI, 168, 169.

189. F.I. T. to Ern. T., Vevey, 27 Sept./ 9 Oct. 1859. Ibid., 170.

190. F.I. T. to Ern. T., Berlin, 24 Oct./ 5 Nov. 1859. Ibid., 172.

191. 'Na vozvratnom puti'. II, 92-93.

192. T. left SPb. on 20 June/ 2 July (*Letopis'-2*, 364) and returned on 4/16 Dec. (Ern. T. to K. Pfeffel, SPb., 13/25 Dec. 1860. TPD, 321).

193. *Letopis'-2*, 364-377.

194. F.I. T. to Ern. T., Wiesbaden, 7/19 July 1860. *Letopis'-2*, 354 (and in the original French, with omissions, in Lettres, XXI, 178).

195. Georgievsky, 111.

196. F.I. T. to A.I. Georgievsky, Nice, 13/25 Dec. 1864. VI, 88-89.

197. F.I. T. to A.F. Tyutcheva, Geneva, 19 Sept./ 1 Oct. 1860. *Letopis'-2*, 372.

198. F.I. T. to A.I. Georgievsky, Geneva, 6/18 Oct. 1864. VI, 81. See also: *LN-1*, 384 n.3 (according to this Petrov was attached to the Russian Embassy 'at Geneva'; in fact it was situated in the Swiss capital, Berne).

199. F.I. T. to D.I. Sushkova, Geneva, 8/20 Oct. 1860. *Letopis'-2*, 374.

200. *Zhizn'*, 147 (footnote).

201. Georgievsky, 106-107, 111.

202. *Letopis'* (Ch.), 147-148; K. Pfeffel to Ern. T., Mu., 29 June/ 11 July 1862. TPD, 331; F.I. T. to D.F. Tyutcheva, [Lake Geneva, mid-July (OS)/ end July (NS) 1862]. VI, 18. The notes to T.'s letter to Darya in VI (428) repeat word for word the claim made in notes to the first publication (*LN-1*, 448-449) that the letter was written from Geneva, where T. is said to have returned on 25 July (presumably, NS) from his tour of the Bernese Oberland as described therein. This is puzzling, as the source quoted for the information (*Letopis'* [Ch.], 147-148) makes no reference to his having been in Geneva on that date or indeed at any other time in 1862. Moreover, in his letter T. gives no indication of date and states quite clearly that he has returned, not to Geneva itself, but to 'the shores of *Lake* Geneva' (VI, 18; my italics). The dating suggested for the letter in *LN-1* and VI ('end of July - beginning of August') fits the known facts on the assumption that it is NS (i.e., mid-July OS). On 23 June/ 5 July T. had still not left Vernex (see below, note 204), and he was away on his tour for two weeks (VI, 16-17), so he cannot have returned earlier than about 8/20 July. The letter appears to have been written soon afterwards.

203. F.I. T. to D.F. Tyutcheva (as note 202).

204. T. is known to have left Wiesbaden immediately after 17/29 June (TPD, 331 *nn*.2, 3). On 19 June/ 1 July he wrote to his daughter Darya from Montreux (*Letopis'* [Ch.], 148) and on 23 June/ 5 July to Ernestine from Vernex (see note 206).

205. F.I. T. to D.F. Tyutcheva (as note 202), 19.

206. F.I. T. to Ern. T., Vernex, 23 June/ 5 July. Lettres, XXI, 195.

207. F.I. T. to D.F. Tyutcheva (as note 202), 16-17.

208. 'Khot' ya i svil gnezdo v doline...'. II, 103.

209. F.I. T. to D.F. Tyutcheva (as note 202), 17-18.

210. As note 206, 195-196.

211. F.I. T. to Ern. T., SPb., 12 May 1862. Lettres, XXI, 189; Ern. T. to K. Pfeffel, Ovstug, 19/31 May 1862. TPD, 329.

212. F.I. T. to Ern. T., SPb., 18 Aug. 1862. Lettres, XXI, 196. T.'s own testimony here is presumably more reliable than that of his daughter Marie (then at Ovstug) that he returned on 11/23 Aug. (quoted in *Letopis'* [Ch.], 148). T. had been granted three months' leave on 20 May/ 1 June and had left SPb. five days later (ibid., 146, 147).

213. Kozhinov, 371.

214. Georgievsky, 104, 106-107, 112-114.

215. Indirect evidence of Yelena's presence is Ivan Snegiryov's statement in his diary that on 19 Oct. he met T. and 'a female relative' of his in the Kremlin (*RA*, 1903, No.2, 303). Anna's guarded reply from Tsarskoye Selo at the end of Oct. to comments made to her about their father by Kitty in a letter (now lost) from Moscow may also be indicative: 'I well understand everything you say to me about him. There is nothing of comfort in any of our family relationships' (TPD, 332).

216. Georgievsky, 114-115.

217. A.F. Tyutcheva to Ye.F. Tyutcheva, Tsarskoye Selo, 6 May 1863. TPD, 337; Ye.A. Denisyeva to M.A. Georgievskaya, SPb.: 8, 29 May 1863. Chulkov (1928), 116-117, 117-118.

218. As note 132.

219. F.I. T. to A.M. Gorchakov, M., 11 June 1863. VI, 25; *MAT*, 155.

220. Georgievsky, 117; Ye.A. Denisyeva to M.A. Georgievskaya, SPb., 29 May 1863. Chulkov (1928), 118.

221. Georgievsky, 115-116.

222. F.I. T. to A.I. Georgievsky, Nice, 10/22 - 11/23 Dec. 1864. VI, 87.

223. As note 221.

224. F.I. T. to M.A. Georgievskaya, M., 14 July 1863. *DN*, 220. This undated note in pencil is quoted by Georgievsky in his account of T.'s two visits to Moscow in 1865 (Georgievsky, 142). However, it must be assumed that G.V. Chagin's precise dating in *DN* is based on sound evidence.

225. F.I. T. to M.A. Georgievskaya, M., 14 July 1865. VI, 105. See also Georgievsky, 162 *n*.84.

226. D.I. Sushkova to Ye.F. Tyutcheva, M., 1 July 1863. TPD, 338. (Darya states that T. was due to leave for the monastery the following day, but does not say if anyone would be accompanying him.)

227. See his sister Darya's letters to Kitty during this period (TPD, 337-341).

228. D.I. Sushkova to Ye.F. Tyutcheva, M.: 20 June, 15, 28 July 1863. TPD, 337, 340, 341.

229. Ibid. (letter of 28 July).

230. F.I. T. to Ern. T., SPb., 16 Aug. 1863. Lettres, XXI, 208.

231. Georgievsky, 117.

232. Earlier in the year Ernestine had indicated her intention to return 'not before November' (Ern. T. to D.F. Tyutcheva, Ovstug, 10 Aug. 1863. TPD, 341). T.'s last known letter to her that year is dated 13 Nov. (see: *Letopis'* [Ch.], 156-157; VI, 59-61), suggesting that she returned towards the end of the month.

233. Georgievsky, 118. Even before this Yelena had regularly read and discussed Georgievsky's newspaper articles with T. and corresponded with Georgievsky on T.'s behalf. See letters from her to the Georgievskys in: Chulkov (1928), 113-114, 115, 116, 117.

234. Georgievsky, 112.

235. Chulkov (1928), 37.
236. Diary of M.F. Tyutcheva, 10/22 May 1864. TPD, 349.
237. F.I. T. to Ern. T.: SPb., 1/13 June; M., 22 June/ 4 July 1864. Lettres, XXI, 218, 219.
238. Ye.A. Denisyeva to M.A. Georgievskaya, SPb., 5 June 1864. Chulkov (1928), 124-125.
239. Ye.A. Denisyeva to M.A. Georgievskaya, SPb.: 31 May; 1 June 1864. Ibid., 122, 123.
240. F.I. T. to Ern. T.: SPb., 25 May/ 6 June 1864. Lettres, XXI, 217.
241. Ye.A. Denisyeva to M.A. Georgievskaya, SPb., 31 May 1864. Chulkov (1928), 123. See also ibid., 39, for the relevant passage quoted in the original French.
242. As note 238, 125.
243. As note 241, 122.
244. Ye.A. Denisyeva to M.A. Georgievskaya, SPb., 1 June 1864. Chulkov (1928), 124.
245. F.I. T. to M.A. Georgievskaya, SPb., 12 June 1865. *DN*, 208; Ya.P. Polonsky to Ye.A. Shtakenshneyder, SPb., 30 May 1865. TPD, 373.
246. F.I. T. to M.A. Georgievskaya, SPb., 29 June 1865. *DN*, 208. Documented addresses of Yelena and her aunt Anna for the period 1862-1864 are, in chronological order: (i) 1862: Kirochnaya ul. (now 14, ul. Saltykova-Shchedrina) (Georgievsky, 112; Kozhinov, 371); (ii) from late 1862: unknown address, opposite (iv), below (Chulkov [1928], 120); (iii) from 1 June 1863: dacha in the Chornaya Rechka district (*DN*, 118); (iv) from Oct.(?) 1863: flat 19, Matushevich's house, corner of Ivanovskaya and Kabinetskaya (Kabinetnaya?) ul. (now 12, ul. Pravdy) (Chulkov [1928], 120; Chagin, 136 [photograph]); (v) from 29 June 1864: new, unknown address (*DN*, 208).
247. F.I. T. to Ern. T., M., 2 July 1864. Lettres, XXI, 221.
248. Ye.F. Tyutcheva to D.I. Sushkova, Königsberg, 20 July/ 1 Aug. 1864. TPD, 350.
249. Chulkov (1923), 17; *Zhizn'*, 169. The first sanatorium for the then still experimental treatment of tuberculosis with a regime of fresh air and healthy diet had been established by Hermann Brehmer at Gorbersdorf (Silesia) only ten years previously.
250. F.I. T. to D.F. Tyutcheva, Geneva, 15/27 Sept. 1864. VI, 78.
251. 'Ves' den' ona lezhala v zabyt'i...'. II, 129.
252. As note 250; F.I. T. to A.I. Georgievsky, SPb., 8 Aug. 1864. VI, 73; Chulkov (1928), 35 (footnote).

Chapter 15. The Final Years

1. Georgievsky, 122. As late as 4 Aug. Darya Sushkova reported the Georgievskys to be 'calm and unperturbed' about Yelena's health (D.I. Sushkova to Ye.F. Tyutcheva, M., 4/16 Aug. 1864. TPD, 350).
2. F.I. T. to A.I. Georgievsky, SPb., 8 Aug. 1864. VI, 73-74.
3. Georgievsky, 124; Ye.F. Tyutcheva to D.I. Sushkova, Arcachon, 19/31 Aug. 1864. TPD, 350-351, 351 *nn*.2, 4.
4. F.I. T. to Ya.P. Polonsky, Nice, 8/20 Dec. 1864. VI, 83; Fet (1983), 384-385.
5. Fet (1983), 385. On p.383 Fet incorrectly remembers this visit as having taken place in Jan. 1864; on p.384 he makes it clear that it was in fact after T.'s 'fateful loss'.
6. F.I. T. to A.I. Georgievsky, SPb., 13 Aug. 1864. VI, 74.
7. Georgievsky, 124-126; diary of M.F. Tyutcheva, 14/26 Aug. 1864. TPD, 350; Ye.F. Tyutcheva (as note 3), 351.
8. Ern. T. to D.F. Tyutcheva, 25 Nov./ 7 Dec. 1874. *Zhizn'*, 170.
9. D.I. Sushkova to Ye.F. Tyutcheva, M., 23-24 Aug./ 4-5 Sept. 1864. TPD, 351.
10. Ye.F. Tyutcheva to D.I. Sushkova, Arcachon: 19/31 Aug.; 2/14 Sept. 1864. TPD, 351, 354.
11. Ye.F. Tyutcheva (as note 3), 350-351; D.I. Sushkova (as note 9), 351-352; A.F. Tyutcheva to Ye.F. & D.F. Tyutcheva (as note 15), 354.
12. On 6/18 Oct. T. wrote to Marie Georgievskaya from Geneva that he had recently met Grand Duchess Yelena Pavlovna, 'who even promised me her support [*appui*] for my little *Loele* [i.e. Lyolya], whom she will see at Mad[emoiselle] Trouba's on her return to Petersb[urg]' (VI, 82).
13. On 15 Aug. T. wrote to Polonsky that he intended to go abroad 'almost a week' from then, and suggested that Polonsky might like to accompany him (VI, 75). The invitation not taken up.
14. Ye.F. Tyutcheva (as note 3), 351.
15. A.F. Tyutcheva to Ye.F. & D.F. Tyutcheva, [Jugenheim, end Aug. (OS) 1863] (quoted in: Ye.F. Tyutcheva to D.I. Sushkova, Arcachon, 2/14 Sept. 1864). TPD, 353-354; diary of A.F. Tyutcheva, quoted (without date) in: Chulkov (1928), 63.

16. Diary of M.F. Tyutcheva, 4/16 and 5/17 Sept. 1864. TPD, 355.
17. Ye.F. Tyutcheva to D.I. Sushkova (quoting a letter from A.D. Bludova), Arcachon, 8/20 Sept. 1864. TPD, 355.
18. Diary of M.F. Tyutcheva, 8/20 Sept., 22 Sept./ 4 Oct., 26 Sept./ 8 Oct., 27 Sept./ 9 Oct. 1864. TPD, 355, 357; Ye.F. Tyutcheva to D.I. Sushkova, Geneva, 2/14 Oct. 1864. TPD, 358.
19. Diary of M.F. Tyutcheva, 13/25 Sept., 6/18 and 8/20 Oct. 1864. TPD, 357-359; F.I. T. to A.I. Georgievsky, Geneva, 6/18 Oct. 1864. VI, 81.
20. F.I. T. (as note 19), 80-81.
21. Diary of M.F. Tyutcheva, 7/19 and 15/27 Sept. 1864. TPD, 355, 357; A.F. Tyutcheva to Ye.F. & D.F. Tyutcheva (as note 15), 354.
22. F.I. T. to D.F. Tyutcheva, Geneva, 15/27 Sept. 1864. VI, 78.
23. Diary of M.F. Tyutcheva, 12/24 Oct. 1864. TPD, 360.
24. 'Utikhla biza... Legche dyshit...' (The wind has dropped... Now breathes more freely...'). II, 128. See also diary of M.F. Tyutcheva, 11/23 Oct. 1864. TPD, 359.
25. Diary of M.F. Tyutcheva, 7/19 Oct., 24 Oct./ 5 Nov. 1864. TPD, 358, 360.
26. Diary of A.F. Tyutcheva (as note 15), 63-64.
27. Ye.F. Tyutcheva to D.I. Sushkova, Geneva, 28 Sept./ 10 Oct., 2/14 Oct. 1864. TPD, 358.
28. F.I. T. (as note 4), 84.
29. F.I. T. to A.I. Georgievsky, Nice, 13/25 Dec. 1864. VI, 88.
30. F.I. T. to A.I. Georgievsky, Nice, 10/22 - 11/23 Dec. 1864. VI, 87.
31. F.I. T. to A.I. Georgievsky, Nice, 3/15 Feb. 1865. VI, 95-96.
32. Quoted by his and Yelena's son Fyodor from an otherwise unpublished letter in: Tyutchev (F.F.), 237. As the letter is said to have been in French, it was most likely addressed to Marie Georgievskaya.
33. As note 30, 86.
34. F.I. T. (as note 4), 84.
35. Ern. T. to K. Pfeffel, Nice, 11/23 Dec. 1864. TPD, 363.
36. As note 30, 86.
37. F.I. T. to A.F. Tyutcheva, Paris, 17/29 March 1865. VI, 97.
38. 'O, etot yug, o, eta Nitstsa...'. II, 131.
39. As note 29, 88-89. A misreading first occurring in *Pis'ma*, 275 is repeated here. Lines 16-17 on p.89 should in fact read: 'pochemu *zhe* eti bednye, nichtozhnye virshi, *i* moyo polnoye imya pod nimi' (my italics). This is the version given in the first publication of the letter (Chulkov [1923], 26), which comparison with the autograph has since shown to be correct (see: Georgievsky, 161, *n.57*).
40. F.I. T. to the editors of *Russky vestnik*, Nice, 1/13 Feb. 1865. VI, 94.
41. 'Kak khorosho ty, o more nochnoye...' ('How you enchant me, O sea, in the darkness'). II, 135.
42. As note 29, 88-89.
43. As note 31, 96-97. See also Georgievsky, 128-131, for the background to the poems' publication.
44. I.S. Aksakov to A.F. Tyutcheva, M., 2 Oct. 1865. Chulkov (1923), 27. Already on 22 Jan. Aksakov had published in *Den'* an earlier, incomplete draft of 'Kak khorosho ty, o more nochnoye...', sent to him by Darya without T.'s knowledge and incorrectly copied. It was T.'s anger at this 'mutilated' version that prompted him to send the completed poem to Katkov to add to the other three (see note 40). Georgievsky comments that Aksakov found the whole episode 'highly embarrassing' (Georgievsky, 130).
45. A.F. Tyutcheva to Ye.F. Tyutcheva, Nice, 20 Jan./ 1 Feb. 1865. TPD, 367.
46. A.F. Tyutcheva to Ye.F. Tyutcheva, Nice, 27 Nov./ 9 Dec. 1864. TPD, 363.
47. F.I. T. to A.F. Aksakova, SPb., 11/23 July 1872. VI, 412.
48. A.D. Bludova to unidentified recipient, Nice, 12/24 Jan. 1865. TPD, 366.
49. A.F. Tyutcheva to Ye.F. Tyutcheva, Nice, 10/22 Jan. 1865. TPD, 364.
50. Ya.P. Polonsky to Ye.A. Shtakenshneyder, SPb., 30 May 1865. TPD, 372-373; diary of M.F. Tyutcheva, 19 Apr./ 1 May 1864. TPD, 349.
51. F.I. T. to Ern. T., M., 12/24 Jan. 1866. Lettres, XXI, 223.
52. TPD, 366 *n.3*.
53. Ern. T. to K. Pfeffel, Nice, 29 Jan./ 10 Feb. 1865. TPD, 369-370 (and notes). For the date of the Tyutchevs' departure see TPD, 371 (note 1 to passage 369).
54. As note 30, 86-87.
55. F.I. T. to A.F. Tyutcheva, Paris, 17/29 March 1865. VI, 98.

56. Turgenev's account of the meeting is quoted in: Fet (1983), 385.
57. A.I. Herzen to N.P. Ogaryov, Paris, 9/21 & 11/23 March 1865. Herzen, XXVIII, 48, 50.
58. Herzen, XI (*Byloye i dumy*), 494-495, 645.
59. *Letopis'* (Ch.), 167; I.D. Delyanov to M.N. Katkov, SPb., 22 Apr. 1865. TPD, 372.
60. Georgievsky, 137-138; A.F. Tyutcheva to Ye.F. Tyutcheva, Nice, 24 Feb./ 8 March 1865. TPD, 370-371.
61. Chulkov (1928), 37-38.
62. Georgievsky, 137.
63. Ya.P. Polonsky (as note 50), 372-374.
64. F.I. T. to M.A. Georgievskaya, SPb., 29 June 1865. *DN*, 208.
65. F.I. T. to M.A. Georgievskaya, SPb., 2 June 1865. *DN*, 207. T.'s welcoming of painful memories as an antidote to his numbness of spirit is expressed in one stanza of the poem 'There are in my stagnation of the spirit...', written just after his return from abroad in March 1865: 'Lord, let me feel the pain of desolation;/ Dispel this deadness of the heart in me — / *Her* Thou hast taken: leave as consolation/ The living torment of her memory.' ('Yest' i v moyom stradal'cheskom zastoye...'. II, 137.)
66. '15 iyulya 1865'. II, 147.
67. *Letopis'* (Ch.), 107.
68. D.I. Sushkova to Ye.F. Tyutcheva, M., 12 July 1865. TPD, 375; diary of M.F. Birilyova, 22 June 1865. TPD, 374.
69. V.P. Alekseyev, *Tyutchevsky Ovstug. Ocherk-putevoditel'*, Bryansk, 2000, 140-141, 151-155.
70. F.I. T. to M.A. Georgievskaya, Ovstug, 16 Aug. 1865. VI, 106; Georgievsky, 141-142; *Letopis'* (Ch.), 170-173.
71. The date can be inferred from the fact that they arrived at Ovstug on the evening of 6 Aug. (diary of M.F. Tyutcheva, TPD, 376).
72. Kozhinov, 425. I have used Kozhinov's convincing reconstruction of the poem's genesis (ibid., 424-425) as the basis of my own account.
73. 'Nakanune godovshchiny 4 avgusta 1864 g.'. II, 149.
74. Florinsky, II, 1055-1056; VI, 461 *n*.2.
75. *Letopis'* (Ch.), 172.
76. F.I. T. to M.N. Katkov, SPb., 13 Oct. 1865. VI, 110-111; V.P. Bezobrazov to M.N. Katkov, SPb., Oct. (after the 13th) 1865. TPD, 379; F.I. T. to A.I. Georgievsky, SPb., 25 Oct. 1865. VI, 112.
77. A.V. Nikitenko, *Zapiski i dnevniki (1804-1877)*, 2 vols., SPb., 1905. II, 265-266 (diary, 19 & 23 Dec. 1865) (quoted in NPTT, 595 *n*.1); F.I. T. to I.S. Aksakov, SPb., 8 Dec. 1865. VI, 118.
78. F.I. T. to A.I. Georgievsky, SPb., 4 Apr. 1866. VI, 134-136, 470-471 (*n*.1).
79. F.I. T. to A.I. Georgievsky, SPb., 8 May 1866. VI, 150; Ye.M. Feoktistov to M.N. Katkov, SPb., 8 May 1866. TPD, 381; V.P. Meshchersky, *Moi vospominaniya*, 2 vols., SPb., 1897-1898. II, 48-49; Nikitenko, III, 35.
80. F.I. T. to A.M. Gorchakov, SPb., 24 Apr. 1866. Pigaryov (1935a), 228.
81. Nikitenko, III, 29.
82. *Dnevnik P.A. Valuyeva, ministra vnutrennikh del, 1861-1876 gg.*, 2 vols., M., 1961. II, 133-134.
83. F.I. T. to Ern. T., SPb., 2 July 1866. Lettres, XXI, 225.
84. For remarks critical of Katkov and his newspaper in T.'s letters, see: VI, 144, 394; Pigaryov (1935a), 241, 242. In April 1866 Nikitenko reported T. as 'displeased' with Katkov's refusal to print the official caution in *Moskovskiye vedomosti* (Nikitenko [1905 edition: as note 77], II, 283). And in 1870 Marie Birilyova wrote of her father that 'Katkov's articles annoy him more and more' (letter to A.F. Aksakova, SPb., 20 Nov. 1870. TPD, 413).
85. Diary of A.F. Tyutcheva, 2 July 1865. TPD, 375; I.S. Aksakov to A.F. Tyutcheva, M., 3 Sept. 1865. TPD, 378.
86. Nikitenko, II, 540; F.I. T. to A.F. Aksakova, SPb., 25 Feb. 1866. VI, 129.
87. N.I. Tsimbayev, *I.S. Aksakov v obshchestvennoy zhizni poreformennoy Rossii*, M., 1978, 128-134.
88. F.I. T. to I.S. Aksakov, SPb., 4 Jan.1868. VI, 303-304. Enclosed with the letter was a copy of a report from a Russian secret agent in Paris. This gave details of the French government's attitude to the Eastern question as outlined in private conversation by the Foreign Minister Léonel de Moustier (ibid., 525-526).
89. For evidence see, e.g.: F.I. T. to A.F. Aksakova, SPb., 13 Feb. 1867. VI, 206; B.M. Markevich to M.N. Katkov, SPb., 17 Oct. 1867. TPD, 385.

90. Tsimbayev (as note 87), 140.
91. B.M. Markevich to M.N. Katkov, SPb., 3 Oct. 1867. TPD, 391.
92. F.I. T. to A.F. Aksakova, SPb., 22 Jan. 1867. VI, 200.
93. VI, 490 (note 1 to letter 102).
94. F.I. T. to Ern. T., SPb., 24 Aug. 1867. VI, 259.
95. In Dec. 1865 for instance T. encouraged Aksakov to express solidarity in *Den'* with the left-wing journal *Sovremennik*, which had just received an official caution for attacking Aksakov's newspaper and Slavophile doctrine in general. Aksakov followed this advice. See: G. Chulkov, 'Tyutchev i Aksakov v bor'be s tsenzuroyu', *Muranovsky sbornik*, Muranovo, 1928, 10-12; I.S. Aksakov to A.F. Tyutcheva, M., 3 Dec. 1865. *Letopis'* (Ch.), 174; F.I. T. to I.S. Aksakov, SPb., 8 Dec. 1865. VI, 117-118.
96. F.I. T. to A.F. Aksakova, SPb., 3 Apr. 1870. VI, 381.
97. F.I. T. to A.I. Georgievsky, Nice, 2/14 Jan. 1865. VI, 91.
98. F.I. T. to Ye.F. Trubetskaya, SPb., 15/27 July 1872. Aksakov, 163 (Aksakov does not name the recipient; this information is given in a later publication of the letter: Pigaryov [1937], 765-768).
99. As note 31, 94-95; F.I. T. to I.S. Aksakov, SPb., 16 Apr. 1866. VI, 146.
100. F.I. T. to A.F. Aksakova, SPb., 1 Dec. 1870. Pigaryov (1935a), 246.
101. F.I. T. to A.F. Aksakova, SPb., 4 Jan. 1872. *Pis'ma*, 357.
102. F.I. T. to A.I. Georgievsky, SPb., 16 Apr. 1866. VI, 145.
103. F.I. T. to Ern. T., SPb.: 8, 13 & 20 July 1871. Lettres, XXII, 272-273.
104. F.I. T. to A.F. Aksakova, SPb., 17 July 1871. VI, 400-401, 555 (note 3 to letter). See also: as note 103 (letter of 8 July), 272.
105. F.I. T. to M.F. Birilyova, SPb., mid-Aug. 1867. VI, 254-255. (The well-known line, attributed by T. to Hamlet, is spoken by Marcellus in Act I, scene 4.)
106. F.I. T. to A.F. Aksakova, SPb., 5 Dec. 1870. *LN-1*, 474.
107. Aksakov, 76.
108. 'Umom — Rossiyu ne ponyat'...'. II, 165.
109. Ern. T. to K. Pfeffel, SPb., 6/18 Feb. 1867. TPD, 387.
110. F.I. T. to A.I. Georgievsky, SPb., 30 March 1866. VI, 132-133; F.I. T. to Ern. T., SPb., 28 July 1866. Lettres, XXI, 229.
111. F.I. T. to Alexander II, July (?) 1866. Pigaryov (1935a), 206.
112. F.I. T. to Ern. T., SPb., 21 July 1866. VI, 163. At this time, as on previous occasions (see note 136 to Chapter 14), T. used his contacts with the press to publicise his views on the European situation. Already in April his analysis of the Austro-Prussian conflict in a letter to Georgievsky was used by the latter as the basis for an article in *Moskovskiye vedomosti* (VI, 469: note 4 to letter 68). On 2 July T. wrote to Ernestine that articles on foreign affairs currently appearing in Katkov's '*journal*' had been 'inspired' by himself (Lettres, XXI, 225). The French term could refer either to the newly reinstated daily *Moskovskiye vedomosti* or the monthly *Russky vestnik*, both edited by Katkov. Ronald Lane has identified articles in the July-August issue of *Russky vestnik* which closely echo T.'s views (Lane [1985], 118-120), while in his memoirs Georgievsky refers to an article reflecting those views published in *Moskovskiye vedomosti* on 12 July (Georgievsky, 151).
113. F.I. T. to A.I. Georgievsky, SPb., 3 July 1866. VI, 158.
114. F.I. T. to A.F. Aksakova, SPb., 16 Aug. 1866. VI, 176-177.
115. F.I. T. to I.S. Aksakov, SPb., 5 Jan. 1867. VI, 195. In the text as printed here T. puzzlingly describes Solovyov's article as 'satisfactory' (ibid., 194-195). The editor of the letter's first publication (*LN-1*, 281) points out that in the manuscript a gap has been left before that word and that the sense clearly requires this to be filled with 'not'.
116. F.I. T. to A.I. Georgievsky, SPb., 15 Feb. 1866. VI, 126.
117. Most of the details of the Slavonic Congress in the subsequent account are taken from: N.K. Zhakova, *Tyutchev i slavyane*, SPb., 2001, 13-25.
118. Fisher, II, 1130.
119. F.I. T. to V.I. Lamansky, SPb., 7 May 1867. VI, 225.
120. F.I. T. to I.S. Aksakov, SPb., 10 May 1867. VI, 227; Zhakova (as note 117), 16.
121. Ibid., 20-21.
122. 'Slavyanam' ('Privet vam zadushevny, brat'ya...'). II, 176-178.
123. *Sankt-Peterburgskiye vedomosti*, 12 May 1867 (quoted in Zhakova [as note 117], 18).
124. F.I. T. to I.S. Aksakov, SPb., 16 May 1867. VI, 230. Here T. is referring to his second poem 'To the Slavs' (see note 131).

125. Aksakov, 116.
126. F.I. T. to A.F. Aksakova, SPb., 6 Oct. 1871. *LN-1*, 370-371.
127. F.I. T. to Ya.F. Golovatsky, SPb., 12 May 1867. VI, 229.
128. VI, 505-506.
129. F.I. T. to Yu.F. Samarin, SPb., 15 May 1867. *Pis'ma*, 300 (first publ. in: Pigaryov [1935a], 236).
130. F.I. T. to I.S. Aksakov, SPb., 10 May 1867. VI, 228.
131. 'Slavyanam' ('Oni krichat, oni grozyatsya...'). II, 179-180.
132. Zhakova (as note 117), 23.
133. K. Pfeffel to Ern. T., Wildbad, 9/21 July 1867. TPD, 389.
134. F.I. T. to Yu.F. Samarin, SPb., 24 Nov. 1867. VI, 295.
135. N.Ya. Danilevsky, *Rossiya i Yevropa*, SPb., 1871.
136. F.I. T. to V.I. Lamansky, [SPb., 1869]. *Pis'ma*, 341. V.V. Kozhinov has speculated that T. came to disagree with Danilevsky's book as further chapters appeared in *Zarya* because of its over-emphasising of ethnic or racial ('*plemenny*') factors. In evidence Kozhinov cites the lack of any further documented links between T. and Danilevsky (Kozhinov, 463). The following objections can be made to his thesis: (i) As T.'s letter to Lamansky praising Danilevsky is undated, it is impossible to say at what stage of his acquaintance with *Russia and Europe* it was written. (ii) As evidence for T.'s alleged antipathy to 'ethnic/racial' factors Kozhinov points to the inclusion of non-Slavs such as the Hungarians in his proposed Graeco-Slavonic empire (ibid., 282-283). However, this is also true of Danilevsky's scheme, the role envisaged for the Hungarians by both men being in any case unambiguously that of a subject people. (iii) Other 'national' or Slavophile figures for whom evidence of links with T. after 1869 is similarly lacking include Samarin and Lamansky. Even for such an old friend as Pogodin only one piece of evidence has survived (*LN-1*, 425). To conclude from this that there was a cooling of relations between T. and any or all of these representatives of the 'national' movement would clearly be misguided. The same must be true for Danilevsky.
137. Georgievsky, 152, 153, 155-157, 161 *n*.47; *Tyutchevy*, 325.
138. Georgievsky, 158. See also letters from T. to Marie Georgievskaya for the period 1866-1871: *DN*, 220-221 (nos. 23, 24, 28, 29; the year 1861 given for the last of these is evidently a mistake for 1871).
139. Tyutchev (F.F.), 231-232.
140. Ye.F. Tyutcheva to D.F. Tyutcheva, M., 4 Sept. 1868. TPD, 399.
141. F.I. T. to A.F. Aksakova, SPb., 19 Oct. 1870. VI, 391.
142. Tyutchev (F.F.), 230-231.
143. 'Iyun' 1868 g.' ('Opyat' stoyu ya nad Nevoy...'). II, 188. This is the last poem to refer directly to Yelena. Despite this Irina Petrova names 'Dve sily yest' — dve rokovye sily...' ('There are two forces — two momentous forces...'), written the following year, as the last in the 'Denisyeva cycle' (Petrova, 59). In the poem T. identifies two forces that rule our destinies 'from birth unto the grave', namely 'the Judgement of the World, and Death'. Of these Death is the more honest: 'He cuts down all with sword unswerving, zealous/ To reap both the rebellious and the meek', whereas the World, 'selective in its scything', 'culls but the best ears, torn out at the root'. Beauty in particular 'must surely come to woe' when she ventures forth against the Judgement of the World, and, 'Scorning the guise of insincere excuses,/ Her head held high, with fearless dignity,/ Shakes from her youthful locks, like dust, the curses,/ The threats, and the inflamed contumely... // Yes, woe to her — and harsher the detraction/ The less she has of falsehood and pretence.../ Such is the world: inhuman in exaction/ Where manifestly human the offence.' (II, 198-199). Although the poem is couched in general terms and makes no specific reference to Yelena, it seems fairly obvious that T. must have had society's treatment of her in mind. It would certainly be reasonable to include it as a general epilogue to the cycle (rather in the same way as 'Poshli, Gospod', svoyu otradu...' ['Lord, grant to him Thy consolation...'] can be seen as a prologue).
144. F.I. T. to Ern. T., M., 12 Jan. 1866. VI, 122.
145. F.I. T. to A.F. Aksakova, SPb., 25 Feb. 1866. VI, 128-129.
146. F.I. T. to Ern. T., Tsarskoye Selo, 31 July 1866. VI, 172.
147. Meshchersky (as note 79), I, 441-442 (also in: *Dok.*, 145).
148. F.I. T. to Ye.F. Tyutcheva, SPb., 3 Jan. 1869. *Pis'ma*, 332; S.D. Sheremetev, 'Knyaz' P.A. Vyazemsky', *RA*, 1891, No.4, 499 (quoted in *Letopis'* [Ch.], 199).
149. See Dostoyevsky's letters to Kh.D. Alchevskaya (9 Apr. 1876) and S.Ye. Lur'ye (17 Apr. 1877) in: F.M. Dostoyevsky, *Pis'ma*, 4 vols., M., 1928-1959. IV, 206, 264.

150. V.P. Botkin, I.S. Turgenev, *1851-1869. Neizdannaya perepiska*, M. & L.,1930, 264.

151. 'Dym' ('Smoke'). II, 174-175.

152. K.P. Pobedonostsev to Ye.F. Tyutcheva, SPb., 2 March 1871. TPD, 415.

153. Aksakov, 324.

154. *Stikhotvoreniya F. Tyutcheva*, M., 1868. The print-run figure of 1,800 is quoted from a contemporary source in: Ospovat (1989), 501. For comparison, in recent times editions of 100,000 have not been unusual (e.g., K.V. Pigaryov's popular 1984 two-volume *Sochineniya*, comprising poems and letters, or the volume *Izbrannoye*, edited by A.N. Petrov and published in Moscow in 1985). Even Pigaryov's scholarly *Lirika* edition was printed in 40,000 copies.

155. I.A. Korolyova, A.A. Nikolayev, K.V. Pigaryov, *F.I. Tyutchev. Bibliografichesky ukazatel' proizvedeniy i literatury o zhizni i deyatel'nosti. 1818-1973*, M., 1978, 7.

156. Aksakov, 324.

157. M.F. Birilyova to A.F. Aksakova, SPb., 25 March 1868. TPD, 392.

158. F.I. T. to Ye.F. Tyutcheva, SPb., 26 March 1868. VI, 316-317.

159. VI, 530 *n*.3.

160. 'Mikhailu Petrovichu Pogodinu' ('Stikhov moikh vot spisok bezobrazny...'). II, 191.

161. Publication details of the two reviews are given in Korolyova et al. (as note 155), 8; for an extract from the longer of these illustrating the reviewer's crude attempt to make T.'s poetry fit the utilitarian aesthetic criteria of the 1860s see Ospovat (1980), 71-72. Details of book sales are from Pigaryov (1935b), 385.

162. Quoted in *Lirika*, II, 396.

163. Gregg, 185-186, 203-207.

164. 'Motiv Geyne'; 'Radost' i gore v zhivom upoyen'ye...'. II, 193, 215. Translations (the first fairly free) of Heine's 'Der Tod, das ist die kühle Nacht...' and of the song 'Freudvoll und leidvoll...', sung by Klara in Goethe's play *Egmont*.

165. Ern. T. to D.F. Tyutcheva, SPb., 3/15 June 1865. TPD, 374.

166. *TPBF*, 9-11.

167. Ibid., 8-9.

168. Ibid., 18-34 (eighteen letters to her, written between 1866 and 1870).

169. Ibid., 33 (no.17), 26 (no.11).

170. Ibid., 22 (no.7).

171. Ibid., 20 (no.3), 29 (no.15).

172. F.I. T. to Ern. T., SPb.: 30 Aug.; 5 Sept. 1868. Lettres, XXII, 250-251; VI, 342-343.

173. See the letters in *TPBF*, 2-40 passim (in particular nos. 3, 5, 11-15).

174. Ibid., 18 (no.1), 21 (nos. 5,6), 24 (no.9), 26 (no.11), 29 (no.15), 35 (no.19), 38 (no.22).

175. Ibid., 27 (no.12).

176. Eight of T.'s letters to this son, Sergey Frolov, are published in: ibid., 35-40 (nos. 19-26).

177. 'Kak nas ni ugnetay razluka...' ('Though separation may torment us...'). II, 209.

178. 'Khotel by ya, chtoby v svoyey mogile...' ('I wish that I might lie once in my coffin...'). II, 245.

179. F.I. T. to N.I. Tyutchev, SPb., 8 June 1867. VI, 233.

180. Ern. T. to D.F. Tyutcheva, SPb., 11 May 1868. TPD, 395.

181. F.I. T. to S.P. Frolov, Staraya Russa, 23 June 1868. *TPBF*, 36-37.

182. F.I. T. to A.F. Aksakova, Staraya Russa, 27 June 1868. VI, 334.

183. Ibid.; F.I. T. to Ern. T., Staraya Russa, 26 June 1868. Lettres, XXII, 246-247.

184. As note 181: 36, 74 (note to letter no.21).

185. F.I. T. to A.F. Aksakova, SPb., 7 June 1869. *LN-1*, 356.

186. Ern. T. to A.F. Aksakova, Ovstug, 18 Aug. 1869. TPD, 404 (note 1 to passage 433).

187. F.I. T. to Ern. T., Kiev, 4 Aug. 1869. Lettres, XXII, 257.

188. F.I. T. to A.N. Maykov, Ovstug, 12 Aug. 1869. VI, 374-375.

189. Ern. T. to K. Pfeffel, Ovstug, 1/13 Sept. 1869. TPD, 405.

190. 'Andreyu Nikolayevichu Murav'yovu'. II, 203 (and note, 565-566).

191. F.I. T. to A.F. Aksakova, SPb., 21 June 1869. VI, 238.

192. F.I. T. to A.F. Aksakova, SPb., 2 Sept. 1871. *LN-1*, 367.

193. 'Osenney pozdneyu poroy...'. II, 91.

194. F.I. T. to Ern. T., SPb., 22 May 1869. Lettres, XXII, 254.

195. F.I. T. to Ern. T., SPb., 8 Oct. 1867. VI, 280.

196. Ern. T. to D.F. Tyutcheva, SPb., 9/21 Apr. 1868. TPD, 394; Fet (1983), 424-425, 489-490 (*n*. 167).

197. F.I. T. to A.D. Bludova, Ovstug, 17 July 1869. *Pis'ma*, 334. The lines quoted by T. are from

'I grob opushchen uzh v mogilu...' ('And now the coffin has been lowered...') (I, 138).
198. 'Priroda — Sfinks. I tem ona verney...'. II, 208.
199. *Letopis'* (Ch.), 220.
200. 'Ot zhizni toy, chto bushevala zdes'...'. II, 234.
201. F.I. T. to Ern. T., M., 22 Aug. 1871. *Letopis'* (Ch.), 220.
202. L.N. Tolstoy to N.N. Strakhov, 13 Sept. 1871. Tolstoy, XVII, 347; L.N. Tolstoy to A.A. Fet, 24-26 Aug. 1871. L.N. Tolstoy, *Perepiska s russkimi pisatelyami* (ed. S.A. Rozanova), 2 vols., M., 1978 (2nd. ed.). I, 414. (Both letters are also quoted in *Dok.*, 246.)
203. T. predicted that Napoleon III's policies would lead to armed conflict between France and the German states in a letter to Marie Georgievskaya from SPb. on 13 July 1866 (VI, 161).
204. Ern. T. to A.F. Aksakova, Ovstug, 8/20 July 1870. TPD, 408-409 (and notes).
205. F.I. T. to Ern. T., Warsaw, 6/18 July 1870. Lettres, XXII, 259-260.
206. A.F. Aksakova to Ye.F. Tyutcheva, SPb., 7/19 July 1870. TPD, 408.
207. F.I. T. to A.V. Pletnyova, Berlin, 7/19 July 1870. VI, 384. A.A. Nikolayev (Nikolayev [1988], 196) states without citing further evidence that although police records show T.'s date of arrival in Karlsbad as 10/22 July, he actually got there a day earlier.
208. The content of T.'s unpublished letter to Ernestine is summarised in: M.F. Birilyova to I.F. Tyutchev, Ovstug, after 27 July/ 8 Aug. 1870. Nikolayev (1988), 196.
209. F.I. T. to D.F. Tyutcheva, Toeplitz, 1/13 Aug. 1870. *Pis'ma*, 346.
210. F.I. T. to Ern. T., Karlsbad, 21 July/ 2 Aug. 1870. Lettres, XXII, 260-261.
211. Writing to Yelena Bogdanova from Toeplitz on 27 July/ 8 Aug., T. states quite explicitly that he had spent twelve days at Karlsbad (*TPBF*, 30). As he is known to have arrived at that resort on 9/21 or 10/22 July, he must have left it either on 21 July/ 2 Aug. or the following day.
212. The poem 'K.B.' (see note 216) is dated '26 July, Karlsbad' (II, 580). This is evidently OS (on 14/26 July T. would almost certainly have been too distressed to write the poem, having only the previous day learnt of the death of his son Dmitry). On 30 July/ 11 Aug. he wrote to Ernestine from Toeplitz that he had been there for four days (VI, 385). This is confirmed by police registration documents showing his date of arrival as 27 July/ 8 Aug. (Nikolayev [1988], 196).
213. Nikolayev (1988), 196.
214. Ibid.; N.M. Mikhaylova, 'Rodovoy arkhiv Tyutchevykh v Muranove', *LN-2*, 655.
215. As note 206.
216. 'K.B.' ('Ya vstretil vas — i vsyo byloye...'). II, 219. It was A.A. Nikolayev who deciphered the initials 'K.B' as 'Clotilde Bothmer' ('C' becoming 'K' in Cyrillic transliteration) (Nikolayev [1988], 193). Despite her married name, this is how T. would have remembered her from the 'golden time' of his youth. Nikolayev comprehensively demolishes a claim advanced in 1912 by Pyotr Bykov that the poem was addressed to Amélie von Krüdener (or Adlerberg, as she then was). Other critics before Bykov had noted the echo of the earlier 'Ya pomnyu vremya zolotoye' (lit.: 'I remember a golden time'), dedicated to Amélie, in this poem's 'Ya vspomnil vremya zolotoye' (line 3; lit.: 'I remembered a golden time'), and had wondered whether this might possibly be a clue to the addressee rather than just a general evocation of lost youth and lost love. On its own, however, such a stylistic parallel was clearly insufficient proof. Bykov's 'contribution' was an evidently contrived explanation of the initials 'K.B.' as standing for 'Baroness Krüdener' reversed (*Polnoye sobraniye sochineniy F.I. Tyutcheva* [ed. P.V. Bykov], SPb., 1913 [8th. ed.], 638). In answer to this Nikolayev shows that nowhere else in T.'s writings is such an example of cryptic reversal to be found; that elsewhere T. consistently abbreviates 'baron' and 'baroness' as 'bar.', never as 'B.'; and that whenever he uses two initials they invariably stand for a first name and surname (Nikolayev [1988], 192-193). Nikolayev also cites evidence that in the summer of 1870 Amélie was nowhere near Karlsbad, but stayed in Russia (ibid., 191), and points out that whereas it is clear from the poem that T. and the woman in question had met for the first time in many years, he and Amélie had had frequent occasion to do so in SPb. (ibid., 192). On the other hand his last meeting with Clotilde had been in 1859 (see V, 326) (not in fact 1847 as claimed by Nikolayev [p.195], although this in no way negates his thesis). To lend added weight to his claim that the poem was addressed to Amélie, Bykov alleged that he had been assured of this by T.'s close friend Yakov Polonsky (*Polnoye...*, 638). Unfortunately (or conveniently), Polonsky had died fourteen years previously, making Bykov's claim impossible to verify. Bykov has so often been exposed as an unreliable and even untrustworthy informant on other matters relating to T. (most notably by K.V. Pigaryov in his 'Tyutchev v memuarakh, dnevnikakh i pis'makh sovremennikov', *Dok.*, 9-10; see also commentaries by G.V. Chagin in *Dok.*, 459-460, and A.A. Nikolayev in *PSS* [1987], 423), that there is no compelling reason to believe him in this instance.

217. F.I. T. to Ye.K. Bogdanova, Toeplitz, 3/15 Aug. 1870. *TPBF*, 32.
218. F.I. T. to Ern. T., Toeplitz, 30 July/ 11 Aug. 1870. VI, 385-386.
219. F.I. T. to Ern. T., Toeplitz, 14/26 Aug. 1870. Lettres, XXII, 263; *Letopis'* (Ch.), 209-210.
220. F.I. T. to A.F. Aksakova, Toeplitz, 31 July/ 12 Aug. 1870. VI, 387.
221. As note 217, 32-33.
222. F.I. T. to K. Pfeffel, Toeplitz, 10/22 Aug. 1870. Lettres, XXII, 288-289.
223. As note 220, 389.
224. F.I. T. to A.F. Aksakova, Karlsbad, 19/31 July 1870 (unpublished: see the summary given by Anna in her letter to Kitty of 30 July/ 11 Aug. 1870. TPD, 409).
225. F.I. T. to Ern. T., SPb., 15 Oct. 1870. Lettres, XXII, 267-268.
226. T.'s characterisation of the Prussians as 'des Huns qui ont fait leurs classes' was noted by A.A. Kireyev in his diary for 4 Oct. 1870 (TPD, 410). The other quotations are from: F.I. T. to K. Pfeffel, SPb., Feb. 1873. Lettres, XXII, 392.
227. 'Dva yedinstva' ('Two Unities'). II, 221.
228. F.I. T. to A.M. Gorchakov, SPb., 3 Nov. 1870. VI, 393; 'Da, vy sderzhali vashe slovo...' ('Yes, you have kept your sacred promise...'). II, 224.
229. *Pri dvore-2*, 205, 206-207 (diary, 5 & 10 Nov. 1870).
230. Florinsky, II, 967-970.
231. *Pri dvore-2*, 207-219; Pigaryov (1935a), 213-214.
232. Pigaryov (1935a), 214-215; F.I. T. to A.F. Aksakova, SPb., 1 Dec. 1870. Ibid., 245-246; *Pri dvore-2*, 213 (footnote).
233. F.I. T. to Ye.F. Tyutcheva, SPb., 5 Dec. 1870. *LN-1*, 474.
234. 'La question Romaine'. III, 59-60.
235. 'Encyclica'; 'Vatikanskaya godovshchina' ('Vatican Anniversary'). II, 132, 232-233.
236. F.I. T. to Ern. T., SPb., 14 Sept. 1871. Lettres, XXII, 276; F.I. T. to I.S. Aksakov, SPb., 2 Oct. 1871. *LN-1*, 369-370; [I.S. Aksakov], *Brief an Döllinger von einem Laien der russischen orthodoxen Kirche aus Moskau*, Berlin, 1872.
237. F.I. T. to I.S. Aksakov, SPb.: 13 March 1870; 16 Oct. 1871. Aksakov, 185-186; VI, 408.
238. This was reported to have been the general verdict of several figures sympathetic to the Slavophile cause (they included Aleksandr Gilferding, Aleksandr Kireyev, Apollon Maykov and Georgievsky) who had gathered in SPb. on 16 Oct. 1871 to hear Aksakov's article read out. (Diary of A.A. Kireyev. TPD, 418-419.)
239. F.I. T. to A.F. Aksakova, SPb., 4 Jan. 1872. *LN-1*, 373; Aksakov, 186.
240. F.I. T. to N.I. Tyutchev, SPb., 13 Apr. 1868. VI, 322.
241. TPD, 406 (note 2).
242. F.I. T. (as note 239), 373, 374-375 (*n*.4).
243. F.I. T. to Ern. T., Spasskoye, 10 June 1871. Lettres, XXII, 270.
244. Aksakov, 50; Tyutchev (F.F.), 230; Ya.P. Polonsky, 'F.I. Tyutchev. Nekrolog', in: *Dok.*, 273 (reprinted from: *Vsemirnaya illyustratsiya*, 1873, X, No.244, 155); A.P. Pletnyov, 'F.I. Tyutchev', in: *Sovremenniki o F.I. Tyutcheve*, Tula, 1984, 89 (reprinted from: A. Pletnyov, *Sobraniye sochineniy*, III, Odessa, 1913, 13-16).
245. Pogodin, 24.
246. Aksakov, 49-50.
247. F.I. T. to Ern. T., SPb., 14 Sept. 1871. Lettres, XXII, 275.
248. F.I. T. to A.F. Aksakova, SPb.: 28 Feb. 1870; 17 July 1871. *Letopis'* (Ch.), 206; VI, 399-400; F.I. T. to Ern. T., SPb., 8 July 1871. Lettres, XXII, 271-272.
249. A.F. Aksakova to D.F. Tyutcheva, Abramtsevo, 18 May 1866. TPD, 382.
250. F.I. T. to Ye.E. Trubetskaya, SPb., 3 May 1867. VI, 222, 503 *n*.1; F.I. T. to Ern. T., SPb., 22 Oct. 1867. VI, 286.
251. As note 179.
252. Ern. T. to K. Pfeffel, SPb., 15/27 Dec. 1870. TPD, 414-415.
253. 'Brat, stol'ko let soputstvovavshy mne...'. II, 226. He later told Kitty that the poem 'came to me in a state of half-sleep, the night of my return to Moscow' (F.I. T. to Ye.F. Tyutcheva, SPb., 31 Dec. 1870. VI, 396).
254. Ibid., 395.
255. D.F. Tyutcheva to Ye.F. Tyutcheva, SPb., 12 Apr. 1872. TPD, 419; I.S. Aksakov to Ye.F. Tyutcheva, Turovo, 18 June 1872. Ibid.; Aksakov, 308; *Letopis'* (Ch.), 223.
256. F.I. T. to A.V. Pletnyova, SPb., 10 Feb. 1872. VI, 410.
257. F.I. T. to A.F. Aksakova, SPb., 20 May 1872. *Letopis'* (Ch.), 223.

258. Ern. T. to K. Pfeffel, SPb., 11/23 Dec. 1872. TPD, 420; D.F. Tyutcheva to Ye.F. Tyutcheva, SPb., 18/30 Dec. 1872. *Letopis'* (Ch.), 225.

259. 'Napoleon III'. II, 243-244.

260. Ern. T. to K. Pfeffel, SPb., 6/18 Jan. 1873. TPD, 421-422; Meshchersky (as note 79), II, 194-195 (also in *Dok.*, 146); I.S. Aksakov to Ye.F. Tyutcheva, SPb., 3 Jan. 1873. *Letopis'* (Ch.), 226-227.

261. Ern. T. to A.F. Aksakova, SPb., 16 Feb. 1873. TPD, 424.

262. I.S. Aksakov to Ye.F. Tyutcheva, SPb., 6 Jan. 1873. TPD, 423.

263. 'Vsyo otnyal u menya kaznyashchy Bog...'. II, 251.

264. A.V. Pletnyova to K.K. Grot, SPb., 27 Jan. 1873. *LN-1*, 564.

265. F.I. T. to A.F. Aksakova, SPb., 7 Feb. 1873. VI, 415.

266. A.V. Pletnyova to K.K. Grot, SPb., 31 March 1873. *LN-1*, 565.

267. As recalled by T.'s daughter Darya (*Tyutcheviana*, 39-40). One is unavoidably reminded of the dying Disraeli's reluctance to be visited by Queen Victoria: 'She would only ask me to take a message to Albert' (Robert Blake, *Disraeli*, London, 1969, 747).

268. F.I. T. to A.F. Aksakova, SPb., Feb.-March 1873. Aksakov, 312.

269. F.I. T. to K. Pfeffel, SPb., Feb. 1873. Lettres, XXII, 292-293.

270. D.F. Tyutcheva to Ye.F. Tyutcheva, SPb., 28 Apr. 1873. Chulkov (1928), 68.

271. F.I. T. to A.F. Aksakova, April 1873. Aksakov, 313. Similar sentiments are expressed in another letter to Anna from this period (ibid., 311).

272. F.I. T. to D.F. Tyutcheva, SPb., 1 Apr. 1873. VI, 416.

273. Aksakov, 301.

274. F.I. T. to Ern. T., SPb., 14 Sept. 1871. Lettres, XXII, 275-276.

275. 'O tsenzure v Rossii. Pis'mo F.I. Tyutcheva odnomu iz chlenov gosudarstvennogo soveta', *RA*, 1873, No.4, 607-632.

276. F.I. T. to Ye.F. Tyutcheva, SPb., Apr. 1873. *LN-1*, 479-480; F.I. T. to A.F. Aksakova, SPb., Apr. 1873. *Pis'ma*, 359-360 (extracts in the French original: Aksakov, 313).

277. D.F. Tyutcheva to Ye.F. Tyutcheva, SPb., 28 Apr. 1873. *Letopis'* (Ch.), 230; Diary of Ern. T., 19 May 1873. TPD, 425.

278. Diary of Ern. T., 26 & 28 May 1873. *Letopis'* (Ch.), 231; Ern. T. to D.F. Tyutcheva, Tsarskoye Selo, 3/15 June 1873.TPD, 425.

279. D.F. Tyutcheva to Ye.F. Tyutcheva, Bad Kissingen, 9/21 June 1873. Chulkov (1928), 69.

280. A.V. Nikitenko to Ye.K. Bogdanova, Pavlovsk, 31 May/ 12 June 1873. *TPBF*, 7 (also, without the final sentence quoted: TPD, 425).

281. I.S. Aksakov to Yu.F. Samarin, Tsarskoye Selo, 18 July 1873. Ospovat (1980), 84 (reprinted in *Dok.*, 257). Aksakov's dating here of the first of the two strokes to 13 June — later changed to 11 June in his biography of T. (Aksakov, 315) — is confirmed by Ernestine's diary (TPD, 426).

282. Aksakov to Samarin (as note 281), 79 (*Dok.*, 253).

283. Aksakov, 316.

284. Aksakov to Samarin (as note 281), 79 (*Dok.*, 253).

285. L.N. Tolstoy to A.A. Tolstaya, end Jan. — beg. Feb. 1873. Tolstoy, XVII, 363.

286. Tolstoy's description of T. as his 'favourite poet' was recorded by Anna Chertkova, the wife of Tolstoy's friend and disciple V.G. Chertkov (A.K. Chertkova, 'Iz vospominaniy o L.N. Tolstom', in: *Tolstoy i o Tolstom. Novye materialy*, II, M., 1926, 97-98). For a survey of Tolstoy's attitude to T.'s poetry see: D. Blagoy, 'Chitatel' Tyutcheva — Lev Tolstoy', *Uraniya*, 224-256.

287. 'Nekrolog', *Grazhdanin*, 1873, No.30 (23 July), 842. (Quoted in full in: Bel'chikov [as note 293], *Dok.*, 420).

288. F.M. Dostoyevsky to S.Ye. Lur'ye, 17 Apr. 1877. Dostoyevsky (as note 149), III, 264.

289. I.S. Turgenev to A.A. Fet, Bougival, 21 Aug. 1873. Turgenev *P*, X, 143.

290. Fet (1983), 383.

291. Nikitenko, III, 287, 289 (diary, 17 & 18 July 1873).

292. Aksakov to Samarin (as note 281), 80-82 (*Dok.*, 254-255). The poem remembered by Aksakov at the graveside is 'I grob opushchen uzh v mogilu...' ('And now the coffin has been lowered...') (I, 138).

293. V.P. Meshchersky, 'Svezhey pamyati F.I. Tyutcheva', *Dok.*, 279. This first appeared in *Grazhdanin*, 1873, No.31 (30 July), 846-848. Meshchersky was the publisher and editor of *Grazhdanin*, and his article is known to have been fairly heavily amended by his co-editor, Dostoyevsky. In his article 'Dostoyevsky o Tyutcheve' (*Byloye*, 1925, No.5, 155-162; reprinted in *Dok.*, 420-425) N.F. Bel'chikov attempted to show that whole sections of the article (including that containing the phrase 'the mirror of his soul': ibid., 161/424) had been completely rewritten by Dostoyevsky. More recently Richard Gregg attributed the same phrase to Dostoyevsky, citing Bel'chikov's arguments in support (Gregg, 31). Since then, however, those arguments have been disputed by A.V. Arkhipova. While conceding that certain phrasings may be Dostoyevsky's, she concludes that in general his corrections do not appear to have far exceeded customary editorial practice, and that Meshchersky's authorship must therefore be considered beyond dispute. (A.V. Arkhipova, 'Dostoyevsky o Tyutcheve (K attributsii odnoy stat'ye v "Grazhdanine")', *Russkaya literatura*, 1975, No.1, 172-176.) On balance it would seem more likely that the formulation in question was Meshchersky's.

294. Gregg, 29-30.
295. F.I. T. to Ern. T., SPb., 3 Aug. 1851. V, 68.
296. Fet (1859), 125.

Appendix I

1. Nikolayev (1989), 526; I, 385-395.
2. *Zhizn'*, 72; *Lirika*, I, 352; ibid., II, 439.
3. A manuscript version is included in the so-called 'Raich collection' of poems sent by Tyutchev to S.Ye. Raich at various times before the beginning of March 1830 (NS) (see below, note 6).
4. See above, pp.64-65.
5. Dinesman (1999a), 287.
6. For the Raich collection as a tool for dating certain poems, see: Nikolayev (1979), 134-135; Ospovat (1986), 351-352; *PSS* (1987), 361-362; Nikolayev (1989), 504-507, 513-516; *Letopis'-1*, 96, 98-99.
7. *Lirika*, I, 346; ibid., II, 439.
8. *PSS* (1987), 377
9. I, 401; *Lirika*, I, 361.
10. *Lirika*, I, 361.
11. Despatch of K.V. Nesselrode to G.I. Gagarin, SPb., 27 June/ 9 July 1833. *Letopis'-1*, 127.
12. F.I. T. to A.F. Tyutcheva, M., July-Aug. 1845 (OS). IV, 322.
13. I am grateful to Herr Oelschläger of the LAELKB for this information.
14. As for example at the Protestant funeral in Munich some years previously of the Ambassador of the Grand Duchy of Hessen, despite an appeal by the Papal Nuncio Serra Cassano to Catholic diplomats not to attend (Jesse, 102).
15. LAELKB, PfA München, Beerdigungen 1832-1843, Sign. 024-41, S. 53. I am grateful to Dr Jürgen König of LAELKB for supplying details of this record.
16. *Letopis'-1*, 124.
17. Schmidt, 725. A case in point is the dedication ceremony on 25 August 1833 for the first Lutheran church in Munich, the Matthäuskirche. A contemporary account describes the Dean of Munich, Friedrich Boeckh (see next note) taking the leading role, assisted by other named pastors and curates. Although Queen Karoline attended the ceremony, Schmidt is not mentioned as having taken any active part (Jesse, 106).
18. Jesse, 132-133; Friedrich Wilhelm Bautz, 'Boeckh, Friedrich von', in: *Biographisch-Bibliographisches Kirchenlexikon*, Nordhausen, I (1990), 656 (accessible online at: www.bautz.de/bbkl).
19. *PSS* (1933), I, 401.
20. S.S. Dudyshkin first remarked on the poem's general similarity to Schiller's 'Kolumbus' in an article published anonymously in the journal *Otechestvennye zapiski* in 1854 (quoted in: I, 483). The more specific parallel was pointed out by R.F. Brandt in 1911 (Brandt, Part 3, 45-46).
21. Gregg, 121.
22. III, 17.
23. Gregg, 122.
24. III, 17-18.
25. III, 17.
26. Ospovat (1999), 238; B.N. Tarasov, 'Kommentarii', in: III, 270-271.
27. Ye.Yu. Khin, 'V.F. Odoyevsky', in: V.F. Odoyevsky, *Povesti i rasskazy*, M., 1959, 22.
28. *Tyutchevy*, 95.
29. Vladimir F. Odoyevsky, *Russkiye nochi*, M., 1913, 416-423 (reprinted with same pagination as: Vladimir F. Odoevskij, *Russische Nächte*, Munich, 1967 [in the series *Slavische Propyläen*, XXIV]).
30. Ibid., 45-46.

31. See: 'Kak okean ob"yemlet shar zemnoy...'; 'Son na more'; 'Vesna' ('Kak ni gnetyot ruka sud'biny...'); 'Smotri, kak na rechnom prostore...'; 'Volna i duma' (I, 110, 151, 183-184; II, 34, 41).

32. See: 'Kak okean ob"yemlet shar zemnoy...'; 'O chom ty voyesh', vetr nochnoy...'; 'I grob opushchen uzh v mogilu...'; 'Son na more' (I, 110, 133, 138, 151). The words in question are used in other poems, but without any recognisably metaphysical connotation.

33. II, 440, 442.

34. *Lirika*, I, 413.

35. *Zhizn'*, 365.

36. Ibid., 366.

37. Ibid., 90.

38. The case for Yelena seems first to have been advanced by G.A. Gukovsky (in his article 'Nekrasov i Tyutchev', *Nauchny byulleten' Leningradskogo Gosudarstvennogo ordena Lenina Universiteta*, Nos. 16-17 [1947], 59), followed by R.A. Gregg (Gregg, 171-172) and N.Ya. Berkovsky (Berkovsky, 73).

39. Tyutchev (F.F.), 226-227.

40. R.C. Lane, 'The Life and Work of F.I. Tyutchev' (unpublished dissertation), Cambridge University, 1970, 281-282.

41. *Zhizn'*, 365. For T.'s note to Eleonore (appended to a letter to his parents from Turin dated 13/25 Dec. 1837. IV, 89-90) see above, pp.238-239.

42. N.M. Mikhaylova, 'Rodovoy arkhiv Tyutchevykh v Muranove', *LN-2*, 653.

43. *Zhizn'*, 365.

44. See: Lane (1983).

45. II, 441.

46. II, 90.

47. Lane(1983), 127-129.

48. The image of a tapestry or carpet is borrowed from Yury Lotman's illuminating analysis of the time-scales in 'Ya pomnyu vremya zolotoye...' (Yu.M. Lotman, 'Poetichesky mir Tyutcheva', *TS* [1990], 136-138).

INDEX OF NAMES

Abrantès, Laure, Duchess d' (1784-1838);
lady-in-waiting; writer 58
Addison, Joseph (1672-1719); poet, essayist
and critic, 41
Adlerberg, Amalie: see Krüdener, A. von
Adlerberg, Nikolay Vladimirovich, Count
(1819-92); Governor-General of Finland,
1866-81; from 1855 second husband of
A. von Krüdener, 108-9
Aksakov, Ivan Sergeyevich (1823-86);
writer and journalist; Slavophile; son-
in-law of Tyutchev, 16, 22-3, 25-6,30,
32-3, 36, 49, 51-2, 58, 95-6, 104-6, 109,
158, 178, 358, 364-6, 387, 393-9, 401-3,
411-17, 424, 492*n*133, 505*n*11, 507*n*119,
512*n*44, 514*n*95, 519*n*281
Aksakov, Konstantin Sergeyevich (1817-
60); writer and critic; Slavophile, 364
Aksakov, Sergey Timofeyevich (1791-1859);
writer; father of I.S. and K.S. Aksakov,
347
Aksakova, Anna Fyodorovna, née
Tyutcheva (1829-89); daughter of F.I.
and El. Tyutchev; Maid of Honour
from 1852; governess to Alexander II's
daughter Maria Aleksandrovna, 1858-
66; from 1866 wife of I.S. Aksakov,
73-74, 95, 99, 102, 106, 147, 158-9, 165,
167, 181, 210, 246-50, 252, 261-2, 265,
267-8, 288-9, 293-7, 300, 322, 325, 327,
336, 339-43, 345-7, 350-1, 354-5, 363,
367, 369-71, 373, 379, 383-9, 393, 398,
401-2, 405, 408-9, 412-17, 421, 489*n*27,
505*n*40, 510*n*215
Alcaeus (active c.600 BC); Greek poet, 44-5
Aleksandrovskaya, N.V.; literary scholar,
499*n*27
Alembert, Pierre Ron d' (1717-83);
philosopher and mathematician, co-
editor of the *Encyclopédie*, 43
Alexander I (1775-1825); Emperor of Russia
1801-25, 37, 80, 87, 108, 213, 228, 251-
2, 254, 256, 259-61, 293, 297, 340, 351,
354, 356, 358-64, 367, 373-5, 378, 388-
9, 392, 394, 396-8, 406, 411, 415
Alexandra Fyodorovna, née Princess
Charlotte of Prussia (1798-1860);
Empress of Russia (consort of Alexander
I), 36-7, 63, 108, 168, 288-9, 327, 375
Alexis (Aleksey Mikhaylovich, 1629-76);
Tsar 1645-76, 29
Alexis (Aleksey Petrovich, 1690- 1718);
Tsarevich; son of Peter I, 308

Amélie: see A. von Krüdener
Amfiteatrov, Semyon Yegorovich: see S.Ye.
Raich
Anaximander (611-c.546 BC); Greek
philosopher, 130, 461*n*64
Ancelot, Jacques-François (1794-1854);
dramatist, poet and novelist, 90
Andrassy, Gyula (Julius), Count (1823-90);
Prime Minister of Hungary 1867-71;
Foreign Minister of Austria-Hungary
1871-79, 397
Anne (1693-1740); Empress of Russia,
1730-40, 23
Anthès, Georges Charles d', Baron (from
1836 de Heeckeren, 1812-95); French
royalist émigré; officer in Russian
Imperial Horse Guards, 225-9
Anthès, Yekaterina Nikolayevna d', née
Goncharova (1809-43); from 1837 wife
of G.C. d'Anthès, 226
Apraksin, Fyodor Matveyevich, Count
(1661-1728); Admiral and statesman, 29
Apukhtin, Aleksey Nikolayevich (1840-93);
poet, writer and critic, 404
Arakcheyev, Aleksey Andreyevich, Count
(1769-1834); General and statesman
with extensive responsibility for military
affairs under Alexander I, 51, 89
Arco-Valley, Anna d', Countess (1813-
1885[?]); wife of Bavarian Court
Chamberlain Count Maximilian d'Arco-
Valley, 203-4
Argenteau, Charles Mercy d', Count,
Archbishop (1787-1879); Papal Nuncio
in Munich, 1827-38, 180, 205
Arina Rodionovna: see A.R. Yakovleva
Arkhipova, A.V.; literary scholar, 519*n*293
Armansperg, Josef Ludwig von, Count
(1787-1853); Minister of Interior (1826-
31) and Foreign Minister (1828-31) of
Bavaria; President of Regency in Greece,
1832-35, 186-7, 189-93
Armansperg, Countess von; wife of J.L. von
Armansperg, 190-1, 195
Azadovsky, Konstantin Markovich (1941-);
literary scholar, 125, 493*n*138

Baader, Franz Xaver von (1765-1841);
philosopher, 121-2, 218, 423
Bakunin, Mikhail Andreyevich (1841-76);
anarchist thinker and revolutionary, 126
Balfe, Michael William (1808-70); Irish
operatic tenor; composer, 101

Fet, Afanasy Afanasyevich (1820-92); poet,
15, 135, 143-5, 237, 347-9, 371, 383, 408,
416-18, 504*n*191, 511*n*5
Fichte, Johann Gottlieb (1762-1814);
philosopher, 48, 128-9
Ficquelmont, Darya (Dorothea, Dolly)
Fyodorovna, Countess. née Countess
Thiesenhausen (1804-63); wife of K.L.
von Ficquelmont, 95, 107, 167-8, 171
Ficquelmont, Karl Ludwig von, Count
(1777-1857); Austrian Ambassador in St
Petersburg, 1829-39, 107, 167
Filofey (Philotheos, active after 1500);
Russian monk who first formulated the
doctrine of 'Moscow the Third Rome',
440*n*5, 498*n*141
Fischer, Karl von (1782-1820); architect,
180
Fomina, Vera Mikhaylovna; landowner in
the vicinity of Ovstug, 407
Fonvizin, Denis Ivanovich (1745-92);
playwright, 50-1
Forcade, Eugène (1820-69); French
journalist, 305, 310, 353, 505*n*27
Franz Joseph I (1830-1916); Emperor of
Austria, 1848-1916, 352
Friedrich, Caspar David (1774-1840);
painter, 139
Friedrich Wilhelm III (1770-1840); King of
Prussia, 1797-1840, 57, 211
Friedrich Wilhelm IV (1795-1861); King of
Prussia, 1840-61, 126, 352
Frolov, Sergey Petrovich (1850- ?[after
1926]); son of Ye.K. Bogdanova, 404-5,
488*n*148, 516*n*176

Gagarin, Grigory Grigoryevich, Prince
(1810-93); son of G.I. Gagarin; artist,
479*n*146
Gagarin, Grigory Ivanovich, Prince (1782-
1837); Russian Ambassador in Munich,
1833-37, 57, 107, 182-3, 185, 187-8, 191,
193-6, 201, 209, 212, 218, 223-4, 255,
476*n*26
Gagarin, Ivan Sergeyevich, Prince (1754-
1810); leading mason and promoter of
Enlightenment ideals, 27
Gagarin, Ivan Sergeyevich, Prince (1814-
82); nephew of G.I. Gagarin; diplomat;
Attaché at the Russian Embassy in
Munich, 1833-35; from 1844 Jesuit priest
and publicist; custodian and promoter of
Tyutchev's poetic manuscripts, 57-8, 62,
81, 84, 95, 99, 106, 109-10, 116, 123, 132,
134, 168-70, 183, 187-8, 195, 197, 209-10,
213-22, 228-30, 292, 310, 348, 462*n*91,
469*n*184, 479*n*146, 480*n*14, 481*n*17
Gagarin, Yevgeny Grigoryevich, Prince
(1811-66); son of G.I. Gagarin; diplomat,
218
Gassen, Theophil (Gottlieb) (1805-78);

artist; associate of Heine in Munich,
459*n*183
Gasser; Bavarian Chargé d'Affaires in
Nauplia from 1833, 188-9, 191, 194, 420,
474*n*104
Gennadi, Grigory Nikolayevich (1826-80);
bibliophile and literary historian,
504*n*192
Georgievskaya, Maria Aleksandrovna, née
Denisyeva (1831-1916); half-sister of
Ye.A. Denisyeva; wife of A.I. Georgievsky,
322, 327-8, 379-81, 383-4, 386,
390, 401-2, 500*n*42, 511*n*1, 512*n*32
Georgievsky, Aleksandr Ivanovich (1830-
1911); educationalist and journalist;
brother-in-law of Ye.A. Denisyeva,
105-6, 322, 325-6, 328-9, 334, 337-8,
366, 377, 379-81, 383-7, 389-90, 392,
396, 401-2, 500*n*42, 508*n*136,
510*nn*224/233, 511*n*1, 512*n*32, 514*n*112,
518*n*238
Giech, Counts von; Bavarian aristocratic
family; 58
Gilferding, Aleksandr Fyodorovich (1831-
72); historian, folklorist, publicist,
518*n*2238
Gilliardi, Domenico (1785-1845); Swiss
architect, 38
Gippius, Vasily Vasilyevich (1890-1942);
literary scholar, 368
Glinka, Fyodor Nikolayevich (1786-1880);
poet and writer; Decembrist, 50-1,
465*n*70
Goethe, Johann Wolfgang von (1749-1832);
poet, playwright and novelist, 15, 41-2,
112, 117, 121, 130, 132-6, 138, 144, 151,
155, 242, 268, 291, 296-7, 319, 336, 369,
441*n*63, 457*n*144, 462*nn*80/82/91,
503*n*183, 516*n*164;
translated by Tyutchev: 120, 136, 197,
291, 404, 459*n*204
Gogol, Nikolay Vasilyevich (1809-52);
novelist, playwright and short story
writer, 21, 34, 290
Goldmann, K.-E. von; German in Russian
service; presumed author of *Die
europäische Pentarchie* (1839), 272
Golitsyn, Aleksandr Mikhaylovich, Prince;
son of M.N. Golitsyn; Decembrist, 48-50
Golitsyn, Aleksandr Nikolayevich, Prince
(1773-1844); Minister of Religious Affairs
and Education, 1817-24, 48-50, 447*n*256
Golitsyn, Dmitry Vladimirovich, Prince
(1771-1844); Governor-General of
Moscow, 1820-43, 79, 81
Golitsyn, Leonid Mikhaylovich, Prince
(1806-60); son of M.N. Golitsyn, 48-50
Golitsyn, Mikhail Nikolayevich, Prince
(1756-1827); brother of A.N. Golitsyn, 48
Golitsyn, Valerian Mikhaylovich, Prince
(1802/3-1859); son of M.N. Golitsyn;

Ivan III (the Great, 1440-1505); Grand Duke of Moscow, 1462-1505, 29

Ivan IV (the Terrible, 1530-84); Grand Duke of Moscow, 1533-47; Tsar of All Russia, 1547-84, 498n141

Ivashov, Pyotr Nikanorovich (? –1837); General, 170, 268, 468n170

Ivashov, Vasily Petrovich (1794-1839); son of P.N. and V.A. Ivashov; Decembrist, 85, 170, 268, 466n103

Ivashova, Camille, née le Dantu (? –1839); wife of V.P. Ivashov, 170, 268

Ivashova, Vera Aleksandrovna, née Tolstaya (? –1837); wife of P.N. Ivashov; cousin of Tyutchev's mother, 170, 268

Ivashova, Yekaterina Petrovna (1811 or 1812 - ?); daughter of P.N. and V.A. Ivashov, 170, 466n103

Ivashova, Yelizaveta Petrovna (daughter of P.N. and V.A. Ivashov); see Ye.P. Yazykova

Jamison, Kay Redfield; academic psychiatrist and writer, 471n61, 472n63

Jardin, Katharina (1814 or 1815 - ?); the Tyutchevs' Swiss governess (mid-1830s), 246, 252

Joseph (? – 1833); Tyutchev's manservant, 188, 193

Kachenovsky, Mikhail Trofimovich (1775-1842); historian; Professor at Moscow University, 39, 46, 48

Kakhovsky, Pyotr Grigoryevich (1797-1826); Decembrist, 83

Kalaganis, Gregorios; priest at the Greek church in Munich in 1829, 98

Kant, Immanuel (1724-1804); philosopher, 48, 128-9, 161, 275

Kapodistrias, Ioannis, Count (1776-1831); Greek freedom fighter; joint (with Nesselrode) Foreign Minister of Russia, 1815-22; first President of independent Greece, 1827-31, 52-3, 186, 190-2

Karakozov, Dmitry Vladimirovich (1840-66); student revolutionary; hanged for attempted assassination of Alexander II, 392-3, 395

Karamzin, Nikolay Mikhaylovich (1766-1826); writer and historian, 28-9, 39, 42, 87-8, 254, 441n63

Karl Friedrich (1783-1853); Grand Duke of Sachsen-Weimar-Eisenach, 1828-53, 268

Karl Theodor, Prince (1795-1875); brother of King Ludwig I of Bavaria, 477n75

Karoline (Caroline) Friederike Wilhelmine, (1776-1841); Queen consort of Maximilian I of Bavaria, 57-8, 96-7, 125, 179, 210, 232, 421, 477n75, 520n17

Katakazi, Gavriil Antonovich (1794-1867);

Russian Ambassador in Nauplia, 1833-34, 187-9, 191-6

Katkov, Mikhail Nikiforovich (1818-87); journalist and publicist, 365-6, 379, 381, 387, 392-3, 401, 512n44, 513n84, 514n112

Kazakov, Matvey Fyodorovich (1738-1812); architect, 27, 29, 38

Kazanovich, Yevlaliya Pavlovna (1886-1942); literary scholar, 262-3, 284, 479n160, 488n148, 493n138

Keats, John (1795-1821); poet, 15

Khlopov, Nikolay Afanasyevich (1770-1826); Tyutchev's peasant *dyad'ka*, later manservant, 19-20, 26, 49, 59, 62, 66, 70-1, 75, 82, 443n126, 454n38

Khomyakov, Aleksey Stepanovich (1804-60); Slavophile philosopher, theologian and poet, 150-1, 157, 164, 168, 280, 321, 364, 411, 448n291, 469n186, 492n110, 507n119

Khvostov, Dmitry Ivanovich, Count (1757-1835); minor poet, 87

Kierkegaard, Søren (1813-55); philosopher; 126

Kirchmayer, Joseph Heinrich (1773-1845); sculptor, 162, 180

Kireyev, Aleksandr Alekseyevich (1833-1900 or 1838-1910); publicist close to the Slavophiles, 518nn226/238

Kireyevsky, Ivan Vasilyevich (1806-56); Slavophile philosopher, critic and journalist, 21, 47, 76, 78, 121-2, 124, 161, 163-5, 168, 175, 446n243, 467n118, 468n166

Kireyevsky, Pyotr Vasilyevich (1808-56); Slavophile writer and folklorist; brother of I.V. Kireyevsky, 21, 47, 56, 76-7, 121-3, 161-5, 175, 446n243, 464n31, 467nn118/124, 468n166

Kiselyov, Pavel Dmitrievich, Count (1788-1872); Minister of State Domains, 1837-55; Russian Ambassador in Paris, 1855-62, 256, 342

Kitty: see Ye.F. Tyutcheva

Klenze, Leo von (1784-1864); architect, 92

Klopstock, Friedrich Gottlieb (1724-1803); poet, 40

Köckenberger, Georg; steward of Alexander and Amalie von Krüdener, 108

Köckenberger, Karl; great-grandson of G. Köckenberger, 11, 432

Kokoshkin, Nikolay Aleksandrovich (1792-1873); Russian Ambassador in Turin, 1839-48, 233, 259-61, 263, 266, 487n116, 488n161

Kolb, Gustav (1798-1856); journalist; friend of Heine, 273, 286

Kollar, Jan (1793-1852); poet; active in the Czech national revival movement, 269

Koloshin, Pavel Ivanovich (1799-1854);

529

Mathilde, Princess (1812-62); daughter of King Ludwig I of Bavaria, 202

Matlaw, Ralph (1926 or 1927 – 1990); literary scholar, 155, 465n61

Matveyev, Artamon Sergeyevich (1625-82); Boyar; minister at the court of Tsar Alexis, 29

Maximilian I Joseph (1756-1825); Elector of Bavaria, 1799-1806; King, 1806-25, 57-9, 92, 94-6, 179, 421

Maykov, Apollon Nikolayevich (1821-97); poet; censor, 371, 518n238

Mazade, Charles de (1820-93); French historian and journalist, 353, 505n27

Melgunov, Nikolay Aleksandrovich (1804-67); writer, translator and critic, 126, 265, 446n243, 460n40

Menshikov, Aleksandr Sergeyevich, Prince (1787-1869); military commander and statesman; special envoy to Constantinople, 1853; C.-in-C. of Russian forces during the Crimean War, 256

Merzlyakov, Aleksey Fyodorovich (1778-1830); poet and literary scholar; Professor at Moscow University, 35-6, 39-40, 45-6, 48-9, 76, 462n80

Meshcherskaya, Nastasya Borisovna, Princess (1796-1841); Tyutchev's cousin; engaged to Count A.I. Kutaysov (fell at Borodino, 1812); subsequently married S.N. Ozerov, 31

Meshcherskaya, Sofya Ivanovna, Princess (? – 1881); friend and patroness of I.S. Turgenev, 347

Meshchersky, A.V.; memoirist, 308

Meshchersky, Vladimir Petrovich, Prince (1839-1914); journalist and writer, 414, 416, 519n293

Metternich, Klemens Wenzel von, Prince (1773-1859); Austrian Foreign Minister, 1809-48, 48, 53, 57, 149, 176, 178, 272, 276, 302

Meyendorff, Peter von, Baron (1796- 1863); Russian Ambassador in Berlin, 1839-50, 272-3, 283, 296

Meyerbeer, Giacomo (pseudonym of Jakob Beer, 1791-1864); composer; brother of Michael Beer, 111

Meysenbug; Austrian Ambassador in Turin in 1839, 262

Michael (Mikhail Pavlovich), Grand Duke (1798-1849); brother of Alexander I and Nicholas I, 82, 84, 324

Michelet, Jules (1798-1874); French historian, 310

Mickiewicz, Adam (1798-1855); Polish poet, 76-7, 151, 278

Miklashevsky; Second Secretary at the Russian Embassy in Turin until 1838, 234, 258

Milchina, Vera Arkadyevna (1953-);

literary critic, 135-6

Miloradovich, Mikhail Andreyevich, Count (1771-1825); Governor-General of St Petersburg in 1825, 83

Milton, John (1608-74); poet, 40

Molé, Louis, Count (1781-1855); Prime Minister of France, 1836-39, 305

Montgelas, Maximilian von, Count (1759-1838); First Minister of Bavaria, 1799-1817, 58-9, 96, 180, 267

Moustier, Léonel de, Marquis (1817-69); French Foreign Minister, 1866-68, 513n88

Mukhanov, Pyotr Aleksandrovich (1799-1854); army officer; Decembrist, 87

Müller, Johann (1752-1809); German historian, 41

Muravyov, Aleksandr Nikolayevich (1792-1861); son of N.N. Muravyov; army officer; Decembrist, 43

Muravyov, Andrey Nikolayevich (1806-74); son of N.N. Muravyov; poet and Church historian, 37, 46, 406, 461n59

Muravyov, Mikhail Nikolayevich, Count (1796-1866); son of N.N. Muravyov; early member of Decembrist societies (inactive after 1820); subsequently prominent government official, 37, 43, 85, 282, 365-7, 374-5, 392

Muravyov, Nikita Mikhaylovich (1795-1843); Decembrist, 80

Muravyov, Nikolay Nikolayevich (1768-1840); General; founder in 1815 of a Military Academy (*uchilishche kolonnovozhatykh*) in Moscow, 34, 37, 43, 47, 50, 86-7

Muravyov-Apostol, Sergey Ivanovich (1796-1826); Decembrist, 86

Muravyova, Pelageya Vasilyevna, née Sheremeteva (1802-71); Tyutchev's cousin; from 1818 wife of M.N. Muravyov, 34, 37, 282, 365, 374-5

Muravyova, Sofya Nikolayevna (1804 – before 1826); daughter of N.N. Muravyov, 37

Musin-Pushkin, Aleksey Ivanovich (1744-1817); bibliophile and collector of antiquities, 28

Nadezhdin, Nikolay Ivanovich (1804-56); journalist and critic; Professor of Literature at Moscow University, 230, 273

Napoleon I Bonaparte (1769-1821); Emperor of France, 1804-14, 29-33, 55, 59, 113, 149, 178, 260, 275, 285, 306, 343, 347, 458n155

Napoleon III (Louis Napoleon Bonaparte, 1808-73); nephew of Napoleon I; President of France, 1848-52; Emperor of France, 1852-70, 305-6, 362-3, 375,

bibliophile; son of P.A. Rumyantsev, 28

Rumyantsev, Pyotr Aleksandrovich, Count (1725-96); Field-Marshal, 28-9

Ryleyev, Kondraty Fyodorovich (1795-1826); poet; Decembrist, 50, 78, 80, 86-7

Rzewuska, Ewa: see E. Hanska

Rzewuska, Karolina: see K. Sobanska

Rzewuski, Adam, Count; father of H. Rzewuski, 57

Rzewuski, Henryk, Count (1791-1866); writer; honorary Attaché at the Russian Embassy in Munich, 1823-27, 57, 449n21

Safarik, Pavel Josef (1795-1837); Slavist and social anthropologist; active in the Czech national revival movement, 269, 278

Safonov, Yevtikh Ivanovich; distant relative of Tyutchev, 175 (and see 470n228), 294, 342, 344

Salm-Salm, Florentin zu, Prince (1786-1846); society acquaintance of Tyutchev in Munich, 205

Saltykova, Aleksandra Grigoryevna, Countess (1805-71); married P.I. Koloshin in 1824, 85

Saltykova, Darya Nikolayevna, née Ivanova, (1730-1801); the notorious 'Saltychikha', sentenced in 1768 for sadistic cruelty to her serfs to life imprisonment and confiscation of her estate, 21-2

Samarin, Yury Fyodorovich (1819-76); Slavophile philosopher, publicist and politician; 351, 364, 399, 411, 505nn10/11, 507n119, 515n136

Sambuy: see Bertou de Sambuy

Schelling, Friedrich Wilhelm Joseph von (1775-1854); philosopher, 47-8, 58-9, 73, 80, 93, 121-36, 138-46, 148, 155-6, 161-2, 203-4, 213, 230, 252, 267, 291, 422-4, 446nn241/246, 460nn15/35, 461n72, 462nn80/82, 476n33

Schenk, Eduard von (1788-1841); poet and dramatist; Bavarian Minister of the Interior, 1828-32, 111, 117-18, 176, 200, 457n137

Schiller, Friedrich von (1759-1805); dramatist, poet and historian, 40-2, 121, 129, 133, 242, 268, 422-3, 445n189, 446n246, 520n20;
translated by Tyutchev: 53, 60, 346

Schlegel, August Wilhelm (1767-1845); literary theorist, critic and translator, 41, 121, 462n82

Schlegel, Friedrich (1772-1829); literary theorist, critic and novelist; brother of A.W. Schlegel, 121, 462n82

Schlözer, August Ludwig (1735-1809); historian, 38, 41, 44

Schlözer, Christian August (1774-1831); lawyer and political economist; Professor at Moscow University, 1804-26; son of A.L. Schlözer, 38-9

Schmidt, Ludwig Friedrich von (1764-1857); Lutheran pastor and Church administrator; chaplain to Queen Karoline of Bavaria, 96-7, 210, 421, 520n17

Schopenhauer, Arthur (1788-1860); philosopher, 128-9, 143, 153, 407

Schubert, Gotthilf Heinrich von (1780-1860); natural scientist and philosopher, disciple of Schelling, 122, 139

Schweizer, Karl von, Baron; head of Russian propaganda operations in Germany in the late 1830s, 272-3, 491n7

Scott, Sir Walter (1771-1832); Scottish novelist and poet, 113, 458n154

Sercey, Félix Édouard de, Count (1802-81); French Ambassador in Munich in 1832; Secretary at the French Embassy in St Petersburg in 1838, 239-40

Serra Cassano, Francesco (1783-1850); Papal Nuncio in Munich, 1818-26, 520n14

Shakespeare, William (1564-1616); dramatist and poet, 136, 154-5, 369, 395, 465n61;
translated by Tyutchev: 136

Shakhovskoy, Valentin Mikhaylovich, Prince (1800-50); instructor at N.N. Muravyov's Military Academy, 47

Shaytanov, Igor (1947-); literary scholar, 462n80

Shchepin-Rostovsky, Dmitry Aleksandrovich, Prince (1798-1858); Decembrist, 83

Shelley, Percy Bysshe (1792-1822); poet, 157, 363

Sheremetev, Aleksey Vasilyevich (1800-57); son of N.N. Sheremeteva; Tyutchev's cousin, 34, 37, 45, 50, 52, 59-60, 76, 78-9, 85-7, 102, 162-3, 447n284

Sheremeteva, Anastasiya Vasilyevna: see A.V. Yakushkina

Sheremeteva, Nadezhda Nikolayevna, née Tyutcheva (1775-1850); Tyutchev's aunt, 32-4, 37, 43, 85, 162-3, 252, 277, 293, 365, 484n8

Sheremeteva, Pelageya Vasilyevna: see P.V. Muravyova

Shevyryov, Stepan Petrovich (1806-64); poet and critic; from 1837 Professor of Literature at Moscow University; Slavophile, 47, 76, 119-52, 155-8, 164, 168, 221, 265, 280, 305, 446n243, 464n34, 465n75, 466n83, 469n186, 492n111, 497n116

Shuvalov, Pyotr Andreyevich, Count (1827-

538

INDEX OF TYUTCHEV'S POEMS

Quotations of complete poems are indicated in **bold type**, partial quotations in *italics*.

RUSSIAN TITLES/FIRST LINES, WITH THEIR ENGLISH EQUIVALENTS

References in brackets are to the six-volume 'Klassika' edition of Tyutchev's works (Moscow,
2002-2005)

'Priroda — Sfinks. I tem ona verney...'
(II, 208): 'Nature, just like the Sphinx,
contrives to set...'
Problesk (I, 52-3): A Gleam
Prorochestvo (II, 14): Prophecy

Rim noch'yu (II, 11): Rome at Night
Russkaya geografiya (I, 200): Russian
Geography
Russkoy zhenshchine (I, 209): To a
Russian Woman

'S kakoyu negoyu, s kakoy toskoy
vlyublyonnoy...' (I, 177): 'With what
sweet tenderness, what lovesick
melancholy...'
'S polyany korshun podnyalsya...' (I, 161):
'Here where the forest thins, a kite...'
'Sey den', ya pomnyu, dlya menya...'
(I, 131): 'That day remains in memory...'
Silentium! (I, 123): Silentium!
'Siyayet solntse, vody bleshchut...' (II, 57):
'The sun gleams brightly, waters
sparkle...'
'Sizhu zadumchiv i odin...' (I, 165): 'I sit
alone and contemplate...'
Slavyanam [1] (II, 176-8): To the Slavs [1]
Slavyanam [2] (II, 179-80): To the Slavs
[2]
Slyozy (I, 45): Tears
'Slozy lyudskiye, o slozy lyudskiye...'
(I, 211): 'Tears of humanity, tears of
humanity...'
'Smotri, kak na rechnom prostore...'
(II, 34): 'See on the trackless river,
riding...'
Son na more (I, 151): Dream at Sea
'Svyataya noch' na nebosklon vzoshla...'
(I, 215): 'Now holy night has claimed the
heavenly sphere...'

'Tak, v zhizni yest' mgnoven'ya...' (II, 70):
'How rarely we encounter them...'
'Tam, gde gory, ubegaya...' (I, 163-4):
'Where the mountains, as if fleeing...'
'Teni sizye smesilis'...' (I, 159): 'Shadows
fall, dove-grey, and mingle...'
'Tikhoy noch'yu, pozdnim letom...' (I, 205):
'On a still night, late in summer...'
Tsitseron (I, 122): Cicero
'Ty, volna moya morskaya...' (II, 54): 'You,
my wave upon the ocean...'
'Ty zrel yego v krugu bol'shogo sveta...'
(I, 107): 'At glittering soirées you saw
him mainly...'

'Umom — Rossiyu ne ponyat'...' (II, 165):
'Who would grasp Russia with the
mind?..'
Uraniya (I, 20-25): Urania
'Utikhla biza... Legche dyshit...' (II, 128):

'The wind has dropped... Now breathes
more freely...'
'Uzhasny son otyagotel nad nami...'
(II, 121): 'A fearful, gruesome nightmare
weighs upon us...'

'V chasy, kogda byvayet...' (II, 88):
'At those times when the bosom...'
'V dushnom vozdukha mol'chan'ye...'
(I, 135): 'In the air's oppressive silence...'
'V razluke yest' vysokoye znachen'ye...'
(II, 44): 'There is a higher truth in
separation...'
'V tolpe lyudey, v neskromnom shume
dnya...' (I, 108): 'Amidst the throng, in
uncouth din of day...'
Vatikanskaya godovshchina (II, 232-3):
Vatican Anniversary
'Vchera, v mechtakh obvorozhonnykh...'
(I, 174): 'Last night, in reverie
enchanted...'
Vecher (I, 55): Evening
'Vecher mglisty i nenastny...' (I, 137): 'Such
a wet and gloomy evening...'
'Velen'yu vysshemu pokorny...' (II, 222):
'Commanded at the highest level...'
'Ves' den' ona lezhala v zabyt'i...' (II, 129):
'All through the day unconscious she had
lain...'
Vesenniye vody (I, 134): Spring Waters
Vesennyaya groza (I, 60): Thunderstorm in
Spring
Vesna (I, 183-4): Spring
'Vnov' tvoi ya vizhu ochi...' (I, 208): 'Once
again my eyes encounter...'
'Vostok belel... Lad'ya katilas'...' (I, 139):
'Pale showed the east... Our craft sped
gently...'
'Vot ot morya I do morya...' (II, 72): 'From
one sea unto the the the other...'
'Vsyo besheney burya, vsyo zleye i zleye...'
(I, 147): 'The storm grows more violent,
its rage unappeased...'
'Vsyo otnyal u menya kaznyashchy Bog...'
(II, 251): 'Of so much — sleep, health,
will-power, even air...'

'Ya lyuteran lyublyu bogosluzhen'ye...'
(I, 156): 'I love the Lutheran service,
with its simple...'
'Ya ochi znal, — o, et ochi!..' (II, 51): 'Those
eyes... I loved them to distraction...'
'Ya pomnyu vremya zolotoye...' (I, 162):
'A golden time still haunts my senses...'
Yego svetlosti knyazyu A.A. Suvorovu
(II, 122): To His Grace Prince A.A.
Suvorov
'Yeshcho tomlyus' toskoy zhelaniy...'
(I, 201): 'Still love torments me with a
vengeance...'
'Yeshcho zemli pechalen vid...' (I, 171):

'The earth still wears a sombre air...'
'Yest' i v moyom stradal'cheskom zastoye...'
(II, 137): 'There are in my stagnation of
the spirit...'
'Yest' v oseni pervonachal'nom...' (II, 84):
'There comes with autumn's first
appearance...'

'Za nashim vekom my idyom...' (I, 83): 'We
strive to keep up with our age...'
'Zhivym sochuvstviyem priveta...' (I, 187):

'With gracious, heartfelt recognition...'
Znamya i slovo (I, 190): The Banner and
The Word

1-oye dekabrya 1837 (I, 176): 1st December
1837
14-oye dekabrya 1825 (I, 56): 14th
December 1825
15 iyunya 1865 g. (II, 147): 15 June 1865
29-oye yanvarya 1837 (I, 175): 29th
January 1837

547